LATER WRITINGS

OF

BISHOP HOOPER.

The Parker Society.

Instituted A.D. M.DCCC.XL.

For the Publication of the Works of the Fathers and Early Writers of the Reformed English Church.

LATER WRITINGS

OF

BISHOP HOOPER,

TOGETHER WITH

HIS LETTERS AND OTHER PIECES.

EDITED FOR

The Parker Society,

BY THE

REV. CHARLES NEVINSON, M.A.

WARDEN OF BROWNE'S HOSPITAL, STAMFORD, LATE FELLOW OF WADHAM COLLEGE, OXFORD.

WIPF & STOCK · Eugene, Oregon

Wipf and Stock Publishers
199 W 8th Ave, Suite 3
Eugene, OR 97401

Later Writings of Bishop Hooper
Together with His Letters and Other Pieces
By Hooper, John
ISBN 13: 978-1-60608-748-0
Publication date 6/30/2009
Previously published by Cambridge University Press, 1852

ADVERTISEMENT.

The Editor on the completion of his labours desires to record his obligations to the most noble the Marquis of Exeter, and to the Dean and Chapter of Peterborough, who kindly allowed him access to their libraries: to the Rev. J. F. Russell, of Enfield Highway, for the loan of several originals; and to the Rev. Robert Scott and other friends for much valuable assistance. To these must be added the Rev. Samuel Carr, Editor of the Early Writings of Bishop Hooper, who offered to overlook the work during its progress through the press.

In the preparation of the work for the press the text of the original editions has been in almost all cases rigidly adhered to: the marginal notes and references are original, with the exception of the bracketed portions, which have been supplied by the Editor; and the references to the fathers and other writings have been, as far as practicable, carefully verified.

The Editor regrets that, owing to a severe illness which attacked him while the sheets were passing through the press, some confusion has arisen in the headings of sheets 8, 9, and 10. The heading on the left hand pages from 118 to 156 inclusive should have been "Visitation Book;" and on the opposite pages "Articles, Injunctions, Interrogatories, &c." according to the subjects.

The *Epistola ad Episcopos* &c., and the *Appellatio ad Parlamentum*, ought, perhaps, to be considered as introductory epistles to the Treatise which follows them: but the Editor felt that the position which they occupy in Foxe's work did not quite justify the adoption of this arrangement.

CONTENTS.

		PAGE
I.	A Lesson of the Incarnation of Christ	1
II.	A brief and clear Confession of the Christian Faith	19
III.	A godly Confession and Protestation of the Christian Faith	64
IV.	Annotations on Romans XIII	93
V.	Copy of Visitation Book	117
VI.	Homily to be read in the time of Pestilence	157
VII.	Expositions of Psalms XXIII., LXII., LXXIII., and LXXVII	176
VIII.	A brief Treatise respecting Judge Hales	374
IX.	Epistola ad Episcopos, Decanos &c.	381
X.	Appellatio ad Parlamentum	388
XI.	Hyperaspismus de vera Doctrina et Usu Cœnæ Domini	399
XII.	De falsa Religione dignoscenda et fugienda (Dedicatory Epistle to)	542
XIII.	Apology against a slanderous Report	549
XIV.	Letters	568

BIOGRAPHICAL NOTICE

OF

BISHOP HOOPER.

It has been stated in the brief notice of Bishop Hooper given in the volume of his Early Writings, that he was born in Somersetshire, towards the close of the fifteenth century. He was only son and heir to his father, who seems to have been possessed of considerable wealth. Having graduated at Oxford, where, according to Foxe, he made great progress in his studies, he subsequently embraced the monastic life, becoming a member of the Cistercian order at Gloucester[1]: but at what time or under what circumstances he abandoned his profession, is not recorded[2].

While residing probably in London, and "living," as he expresses it, "too much of a court life in the palace of the king[3]," his attention was first seriously drawn to the subject of religion by the perusal of some of the writings of Zuinglius and Bullinger's Commentaries upon the Epistles of St Paul: and so deep was the impression which these works produced upon him, that he studied them night and day with unwearied attention. Under the influence of the feelings thus called forth he appears to have returned to Oxford, where he applied himself with great diligence to the study of the holy scriptures; "in the reading and searching whereof," says Foxe, "as there

---

[1] In the sentence pronounced upon him by Gardiner he is described as "olim monachum domus sive monasterii de Cliva, ordinis Cisterciensis." The sentence is preserved amongst the Harleian MSS. in the British Museum: also in Strype's Eccles. Mem. Vol. III. Part II. No. XXVIII.

[2] Strype says, "About the year 1535 or 1536, I meet with one John Howper, a black friar of Gloucester, whether our John Hoper or no I cannot affirm; who, with six monks more of the same house, desired licence from Cromwell, then lord privy seal and the king's vicar spiritual, to change their habit."—Eccles. Mem. Vol. III. Part I. p. 282. Oxford, 1822.

[3] Zurich Letters, I. xxi. p. 33.

lacked in him no diligence joined with earnest prayer, so neither wanted unto him the grace of the Holy Ghost to satisfy his desire, and to open unto him the light of true divinity."

His zealous support of the principles of the Reformation soon attracted the notice, and drew upon him the displeasure, of some of the authorities, and especially of Dr Smith, professor of Divinity; and, the Act of the Six Articles being in force, he was compelled to retire from the university. He was received into the house of Sir Thomas Arundel, and became his steward: but at length his master, "having intelligence of his opinions and religion, which he in no case did favour, and yet exceedingly favouring the person and conditions of the man, found the means to send him in a message to the bishop of Winchester, writing his letter privily to the bishop, by conference of learning to do some good upon him; but in any case requiring him to send home his servant to him again. Winchester, after long conference with master Hooper four or five days together, when he at length perceived that neither he could do that good which he thought to him, nor that he would take any good at his hands, according to master Arundel's request he sent home his servant again, right well commending his learning and wit, but yet bearing in his breast a grudging stomach against master Hooper still[1]."

Hooper was not suffered to remain long unmolested: an intimation of impending danger was conveyed to him, and he was warned to provide for his safety. He escaped to the sea-side, and, crossing over to France, proceeded to Paris. Shortly afterwards, however, he returned to England, and resided for a time in the house of a Mr Sentlow: but finding that plots were again laid for his destruction, he once more sought safety in flight; and "was compelled (says Foxe), under pretence of being captain of a ship going to Ireland, to take the seas; and so escaped he, although not without extreme peril of drowning, through France to the higher parts of Germany."

While sojourning at Strasburgh, as we learn from one of his letters to Bullinger dated from that city, he met with a lady of the name of Anna, whom he describes as of noble family[2];

---

[1] Foxe, Acts and Monuments, p. 1502. Lond. 1583.
[2] Bullinger also in his Diary speaks of Hooper's wife as *nobilis*.

and from the language which he employs respecting her, it is probable that this was the Ann de Tserclas, who shortly afterwards became his wife: her parents resided not far from Antwerp. Before his marriage, which took place probably at Basle towards the latter part of 1546, Hooper, having resolved to settle at Zurich, returned once more to England in the hope of obtaining pecuniary assistance from his father. He appears to have succeeded in his object: but, owing to the tempestuousness of the weather and the malice of his enemies, his journey was attended with much danger to himself and heavy loss of his fortune.

He arrived at Zurich in March 1547; and during his sojourn there of two years' duration he enjoyed the intimacy of Bullinger, and other leading members of that community. For Bullinger he entertained the highest regard, and was a diligent attendant at his lectures: and his letters in after years abound with expressions of gratitude for past instruction, and with requests for copies of his sermon-notes and other writings. We find him at this period corresponding with Bucer on the subject of the sacraments: John a-Lasco also was amongst the number of his associates; and the friendship which was commenced between them here was continued subsequently in England[3].

Prompted at length by a sense of duty to offer his aid in the religious work which was going on in his native country, Hooper resolved to return. Foxe gives an interesting account of his parting interview with his friends at Zurich. Bullinger, on taking leave of him, expressed his fears that the wealth and honours which awaited him in England might make him

[3] Strype relates that in 1550, when the German church was first constituted in Austin Friars, Hooper spent a whole day in friendly converse with a-Lasco and some members of his church. The following is Hooper's answer to a-Lasco's invitation, conveyed through Utenhovius:

S. P. Per me non stabit quin, Deo volente, cras adero: et, si valetudo uxoris meæ non obstet, votis D. nostri a-Lasco annuet. Hodie multa capitis gravedine fuit multata. Scio, et si corpore absit, mente nos comitabitur: quod perpetuo erga vos faciet Deus suo Spiritu. Interim ematur aliquid quod cum gratiarum actione una accipiamus: ego aliquod, si Deo visum fuerit, sumptus faciam. Dominus vos, &c.

T. T.   Jo. HOPERUS.

—Eccles. Mem. Vol. II. Part I. p. 400.

forgetful of his former friends, and begged that he would sometimes write to them. Hooper, in answer, assured him that he should always retain a grateful recollection of the kindness which he had experienced; and, after promising to write to them from time to time, added these memorable and prophetic words: "But the last news of all I shall not be able to write; for there (said he, taking master Bullinger by the hand) where I shall take most pains, there shall you hear of me to be burnt to ashes: and that shall be the last news, which I shall not be able to write unto you; but you shall hear it of me[1]."

Leaving Zurich in March 1549, Hooper with his wife and an infant daughter arrived in London towards the end of May, and was shortly afterwards appointed chaplain to the duke of Somerset. He at once devoted himself to the work of teaching, lecturing generally twice every day; and so great was his success, that the churches could not contain the crowds that flocked to hear him. The strongest testimony to the influence which he acquired is borne even by his maligner Dr Smith, who, in the dedicatory epistle to his book on the celibacy of priests, is forced to confess that "he was so admired by the people, that they held him for a prophet; nay, they looked upon him as some deity." Foxe relates that "in his sermons, according to his accustomed manner, he corrected sin, and sharply inveighed against the iniquity of the world, and corrupt abuses of the church... In his doctrine he was earnest, in tongue eloquent, in the scriptures perfect, in pains indefatigable." The same writer describes him as "of body strong, his health whole and sound, his wit very pregnant, his invincible patience able to sustain whatsoever sinister fortune and adversity could do." He complains however of the excessive severity and gravity of his countenance and manners, relating the following anecdote in support of his remarks: "There was an honest citizen, and to me not unknown, which, having in himself a certain conflict of conscience, came to his door for counsel, but being abashed at his austere behaviour durst not come in, but departed seeking remedy of his troubled mind at

---

[1] Foxe also relates what he calls "another like prophetical demonstration, foreshewing before the manner of his martyrdom, wherewith he should glorify God."—See Acts and Monuments, p. 1503.

other men's hands; which he afterwards by the help of Almighty God did find and obtain."

Immediately upon his return Hooper became involved in controversy. His views upon divorce, as set forth in his "Declaration of the Ten Commandments," which was printed abroad the year before, had been made the subject of much misrepresentation, and he was called upon to defend them; which he appears to have done with great success. This led to a new edition of the above-named work, in which was inserted additional matter in support of his opinions. He engaged in a warm and protracted dispute with Traheron respecting predestination; and he also drew upon himself the displeasure of Bonner by controverting his teaching from the pulpit at Paul's Cross. The ill-will which he thus incurred was shortly afterwards greatly aggravated by his joining with Latimer in presenting to the council a bill of complaint against the bishop, charging him with neglect of their orders in a sermon which he had been desired by them to preach. Bonner in the subsequent proceedings, which ended in his deprivation and imprisonment, used the most violent and insulting language towards his accusers; and so bitter was the hostility which he displayed, that Hooper, alluding to the circumstance in one of his letters, observes, "Should he be again restored to his office and episcopal function, I shall, I doubt not, be restored to my country and my Father which is in heaven[2]." Gardiner also challenged him to a public disputation; but, finding that he was fully prepared to meet him, again withdrew from the contest. Hooper speaks in his letters of the "great odium and not less danger" which he incurred by his lectures on the sixth chapter of the gospel by St John: and we learn from Strype that he was also assailed with satire and "railing libels cast into pulpits." These attacks were answered by Edward Underhill, who hence acquired the title of "Hooper's champion:" for Underhill, who was a very witty man, set up a bill upon St Paul's door in defence of Hooper, and another at St Magnus' church, where especially such ignominious lampoons had been divulged against that reverend man[3]." By the king however Hooper was held in great esteem: it was by his majesty's command that he remained

[2] Zurich Letters, I. xxxv. p. 70.
[3] Strype, Eccles. Mem. Vol. II. Part I. p. 181.

in London to aid the cause of the Reformation; and on one occasion he was sent by him into the counties of Kent and Essex to oppose the errors of the Anabaptists.

On the fifth of February, 1550, he received through Cranmer the orders of the king and council to preach before the court once a week during the ensuing Lent. He chose for his subject the prophet Jonas[1]: and in the course of his sermons he took occasion to attack the Book of Ordination, which had been set forth by authority in the preceding year. He directed his censures principally against the oath of supremacy, which he denounced as downright blasphemy, as requiring a man to swear by saints, that is, by creatures, and not by God alone. He also objected to the vestments appointed to be worn during divine service, describing them as Aaronical, superstitious, and antichristian. These censures excited the hostility of the archbishop, who accused him before the council, and on his appearance spoke against him with great asperity: but, though a long and sharp discussion ensued, no further proceedings appear to have been taken against him at the time.

The dispute however was soon afterwards renewed, and attended by more serious results. Hooper having, in consequence of his objections to the oath and vestments, refused the bishoprick of Gloucester, which had been offered to him on the termination of the Lent sermons, was summoned before the council to give a reason for his conduct. His arguments against the oath appear to have been conclusive; for the king with his own hand erased the obnoxious clause: and the council shewed themselves inclined to yield to his scruples respecting the vestments; the earl of Warwick writing a letter to the archbishop by the hands of Hooper, desiring his grace that at his request, which had been prompted by the king, he would yield to the bearer's scruples; and "especially that he would not charge him with an oath burdenous to his conscience[2]." The king also issued a dispensation to the archbishop, freeing him from any pains and penalties which he might incur by a departure from the usual forms of consecration. As Cranmer and the other bishops hesitated to comply, attempts were made to satisfy Hooper's scruples; and Ridley was desired to discuss the matter with him. Long

[1] See "Early Writings," p. 435.
[2] Foxe, Acts and Monuments, p. 1504.

and angry disputes ensued between them; Hooper asserting with much warmth that the vestments were plainly impious, and opposed to scripture; while Ridley, on the other hand, as firmly maintained that they were in themselves indifferent; but that, having been enjoined by law for order's sake, they were not to be lightly set aside to meet the prejudices of an individual. Ridley offered however that, if Hooper would "revoke his errors, and agree and subscribe to the doctrine, and not to condemn that for sin that God never forbade, ungodly adding unto God's word, he would not, for any necessity that he put in these vestments, let to lay his hands upon him, and to admit him bishop, although he came, as he used to ride, in a merchant's cloak; having the king's dispensation for the act, and my lord archbishop's commission orderly to do the thing[3]." These conditions Hooper rejected, and continued, both in the pulpit and elsewhere, to declaim against the vestments, and to brand with impiety those who used them. By this conduct, together with the arguments of Ridley, the minds of the councillors were at length alienated from him: and, being called before them, he was ordered to lay aside his scruples, and to submit to consecration in the appointed form. Finding he could no longer obtain a hearing, he begged permission to state his objections in writing; and, leave having been granted, his arguments were placed in the hands of Ridley, who, by the direction of the council, drew up an answer to them. Cranmer, in the meantime, acting with his usual caution, wrote to Bucer, soliciting his advice, and submitting more especially the following questions: "Whether, without offending of God, the ministers of the church of England may use those garments which are now used, and prescribed to be used by the magistrates?" and, "Whether he that affirms it unlawful or refuseth to use these garments sinneth against God, because he saith that is unclean which God hath sanctified; and against the magistrate, who commandeth a political order[4]?" To both these questions Bucer replied in the affirmative, supporting the archbishop's views: yet he expressed a wish that an early opportunity might be taken to lay aside the vestments, which had proved

---

[3] Extract from MS. containing Ridley's answer to Hooper's objections.

[4] Strype's Cranmer, Vol. I. ch. XVII. p. 303.

a source of so much superstition and dispute. Hooper also addressed both to Bucer and Peter Martyr the following letter[1], accompanied by a statement of his views:

> Causam ob quam lis mihi intenditur, vir præstantissime, ab isto internuncio accipies. Rogo ut digneris semel tua lectione eam agnoscere; et si quid erroris deprehenderis, id mihi per literas tuas significes precor. Quod obscurius vel paucioribus verbis quam res postulat fuerit dictum, tua quæso perspicuitate et aptioribus verbis in margine illustres. Si causam videas justam, ac pio ministro dignam æstimes, ei subscribas in fine, vehementer oro. Mitto etiam quæ ante tres annos scripserim in Decalogum, ut sciat tua præstantia quid de divortio senserim. Ea præterea tua lectione digneris, ut si humanitus hac in parte erraverim, per tuam eruditionem et paternam admonitionem admonitus corrigam. Quam multis et falsis calumniis hoc nomine traducar, jam non est scribendum. Rogo igitur tuam paternitatem, nec dubito quin facile exorem, ut decertantem ecclesiam donis Dei magnis proculdubio et præclarissimis in te collatis adjuves. Idem peto a domino Doctore Martyre, ad quem (sententia ac judicio tuæ prudentiæ cognitis) iter facturus est quem tu hic habes nuncium. Dominus Jesus tuam præstantiam diu servet.
>
> Voto et oratione tuus totus,
> Londini, 17° Octob. 1550.   Jo. HOPPERUS.
>
> *Domino Martino Bucero, theologo absolutissimo, domino ac præceptori suo reverendissimo.*

The answers of these two learned men were nearly to the same effect as that of the former to the archbishop. While they deprecated disputes amongst professors of the gospel, and expressed a desire for perfect simplicity in the outward forms of religious worship; they yet maintained the vestments to be things indifferent, and therefore lawful to be used, if so required: urging moreover, that no abuse of them in popish times could invest them in themselves with a character of impiety, or bar the use of them to Christians, who were taught in scripture that "to the pure all things are pure." Martyr also took occasion to caution Hooper against his unseasonable and too bitter sermons, by which he was in danger of becoming a hindrance to himself. By a-Lasco and Micronius he was encouraged in his opposition.

[1] From a collection of MSS. in the possession of the Rev. J. F. Russell, of Enfield. A translation is given by Strype, Eccles. Mem. Vol. II. Part II. p. 455.

As he still resolutely refused to be consecrated according to the form prescribed by law, and besides continued his public denunciations of that form, he was at length forbidden by the council to preach or lecture without further licence; and was "commanded to keep his house, unless it were to go to the archbishop of Canterbury, or the bishops of Ely, London, or Lincoln, for counsel and satisfaction of his conscience[2]." Notwithstanding this order he went about complaining of the council, and "printed (says Strype) *A Confession of his Faith*, written in such a manner that it gave more distaste, and wherein was contained matter he should not have written." Provoked by his obstinacy and disobedience, the council, on the 13th of the following January, consigned him to the custody of the archbishop, to be reformed by him, or further punished as the case required: but, the archbishop reporting that he could make no impression on him, he was on the 27th of the month committed to the Fleet. Overcome at length by the arguments which had been urged upon him, he wrote to the council, signifying his willingness to comply with their demands: but his intention being misunderstood, he shortly afterwards addressed the following more explicit letter to the archbishop[3].

Domino Archiepiscopo Cantuariensi.

Valde mihi doluit quod non satisfecerim meo scripto voluntati Dominorum Consiliariorum. Atqui sperabam hoc meo scripto ita satisfecisse, ut nihil ultra possent a me exigere. Quid enim poteram amplius quam, mea conscientia liberata ab omni scrupulo quo ante fuit sollicitata, judicium hujus quæstionis vestræ clementiæ deferre, et polliceri me facturum quicquid statuissetis? Ego scripto illo nolui contendere; sed hoc solum, ut me purgarem omni crimine inobedientiæ et contemptus auctoritatis regis ac vestræ clementiæ; atque in hunc finem pauca induxi argumenta quæ me hactenus movissent. Id etiam volebam intelligeretis me nunc agnoscere libertatem filiorum Dei in rebus externis omnibus: quas nec per se impias, nec usum earum quemlibet per se impium, assero aut sentio; abusum solum, qui omnibus esse potest vitio, utentium superstitiose, aut alioqui male, reprehendo cum D^{no} Bucero, D. Martyre, et omnibus piis ac doctis viris. Ceterum, quod ad me attinet in hac causa usus ves-

[2] Strype's Cranmer, I. xvii. p. 307.
[3] From a collection of MSS. in the possession of the Rev. J. F. Russell, of Enfield. See also Durell's Vindiciæ Ecclesiæ Anglicanæ, cap. xvi. p. 140. Lond. 1669.

tium ac rituum inaugurationis episcopalis, si adhuc dubitarem aut hærerem in aliquo, attamen abunde putarem me satisfacturum omni officio reverentiæ vel obedientiæ, si, volens meum sensum ac judicium ceteris omnibus præferre, ipse vestræ clementiæ judicio subjicerer, quicquid judicaturi fueritis ex animo facturus: id quod meo scripto volebam; et nunc idem facio et polliceor. Etenim in hac causa cœpi meum judicium sensumque meum ita habere suspecta, ut vestræ clementiæ judicio, vel eorum quoscunque nominaveritis pios ac doctos in lege Dei, stare ac niti quam meo unius existimem consultius et christiana humilitate dignius. Id non puto in me esse mutatum. Ago gratias reverendæ tuæ clementiæ, quod tam multas molestias ac labores meo nomine subire dignatus sis. Rogo etiam supplex sic agas cum reliquis dominis, ut contenti esse velint in nomine Christi; neque ita sentiant de me, quasi aliquid faciam simulate, ullo metu, aut ulla alia causa nisi ecclesiæ: Dominus Jesus testis est, qui abdita cordium novit. Idem reverendam tuam clementiam suo Spiritu semper augeat, atque omnibus bonis beet. In carcere, 15 Feb. 1551.

Reverendæ tuæ clementiæ observantissimus,

Jo. HOPPERUS.

On his submission Hooper was set at liberty, and was consecrated on the 8th of March; the conditions imposed upon him being, that he should wear the prescribed vestments at his consecration, and when he preached before the king, or in his cathedral, or on any public occasion: at other times he was left to the exercise of his own discretion. And thus, to the great joy of the friends of the Reformation, ended a dispute which for many months had seriously disturbed the peace of the church, and threatened to deprive it of the services of one of its most zealous and useful ministers. Ridley and Hooper appear to have been estranged from one another for some time after: but it is satisfactory to find that, when both were imprisoned in the Marian persecution, all feelings of bitterness were laid aside, and that they were from the heart united as brethren in that truth for which they were shortly afterwards to shed their blood[1]. By the archbishop Hooper was treated with his accustomed friendliness; and on one occasion, when summoned to London by the meeting of parliament, he was received as a guest at Lambeth palace.

Immediately after his consecration he prepared to enter upon his new duties. He addressed a letter of admonition to his clergy, and apprised them of his speedy coming; and on visiting his diocese commenced a course of preaching with

[1] See Ridley's Letter to Hooper. Acts and Mon. p. 1504.

so much diligence as to cause apprehensions for the failure of his health. His wife, in a letter to Bullinger, dated April 3rd, 1551, says, " I entreat you to recommend master Hooper to be more moderate in his labour : for he preaches four, or at least three, times every day; and I am afraid lest these over-abundant exertions should cause a premature decay[2]." Knowing that many of his clergy were extremely ignorant, and moreover hostile to the Reformation, he drew up a body of fifty articles[3], to which he required them to subscribe. He also laid before them a number of injunctions, together with interrogatories relating to the conduct both of the clergy and laity: and finally he proceeded to an examination of the several ministers as to their knowledge of the Ten Commandments, the Apostles' Creed, and the Lord's Prayer, subjects upon which a considerable portion of them were lamentably ignorant. At this visitation he constituted certain of the clergy to be superintendents, whose duty it was to maintain a watchfulness over the inferior ministers.

In the course of the summer the lives of himself and several members of his household were placed in jeopardy by the sweating sickness, a malady which proved very destructive throughout the kingdom: he makes a touching allusion to the circumstance in one of his letters[4].

About this time he was nominated one of a body of thirty-two commissioners who were to undertake the revision of the ecclesiastical laws; and early in the following year, as a further proof of the confidence reposed in him, he was appointed to the bishoprick of Worcester (then vacant by the deprivation of bishop Heath), which he was to hold *in commendam* with that of Gloucester. This in many respects inconvenient arrangement was continued till the end of the year, when the two sees were thrown into one, and he became bishop of the united diocese of Worcester and Gloucester.

In July 1552 he commenced a visitation of his new diocese; but was shortly afterwards compelled to return to Gloucester, in consequence of the misconduct of the clergy of that see, who had taken advantage of his absence to fall back into their old superstitious practices. While engaged in the correction of

[2] See Zurich Letters, I. xlix. p. 108.
[3] See "Copy of Visitation Book," p. 118 of this volume.
[4] Zurich Letters, I. xl. p. 94.

these disorders, he wrote the following letter to Sir William Cecil[1].

To the Right Honourable my singular friend SIR WILLIAM CECIL, KT., *one of the king's majesty's chiefest secretaries.*

The grace of God be with you. Amen. Since my coming down I have been at Worcester, gentle Mr Secretary, and thought not to have departed thence till I had set things in a good order as near as I could. But the negligence and ungodly behaviour of the ministers in Gloucestershire compelled me to return, except I should leave them behind as far out of order as I should find the other to whom I am going unto. I have spoken with the greatest part of the ministers; and I trust within these six days to end for this time with them all.

For the love of God, cause the Articles that the king's majesty spake of when we took our oaths to be set forth by his authority. I doubt not but they shall do much good: for I will cause every minister to confess them openly before their parishioners. For subscribing privately in the paper I perceive little availeth; for, notwithstanding that, they speak as evil of good faith as ever they did before they subscribed. I left not the ministers of Gloucestershire so far forward when I went to London but I found the greatest part of them as far backward at my coming home. I have a great hope of the people. God send good justices and faithful ministers in the church, and all will be well.

For lack of heed corn so passeth from hence by water, that I fear much we shall have great scarcity this year. Doubtless men that be put in trust do not their duties. The statute of Regrators[2] is so used that in many quarters of these parts it will do little good: and in some parts, where as licence by the justices will not be granted, the people are much offended that they should not as well as other bag as they were wont to do.

God be praised, yet all things be quiet, and, I trust, so will continue. Thus desiring God to continue you long in health to his pleasure, fare ye well: and for God's sake do one year as ye may be able to do another. Your health is not the surest: favour it as ye may, and charge it not too far. Ye be wise and comfortable for others; be so for yourself also. I pray you let God be the end whereunto ye mark in all your doings; and if they for lack of knowledge then happen otherwise than ye would, the thing ye sought shall partly excuse your ignorance, that may hap to miss men in weighty affairs. If ye see the means good, and yet evil follow of them, content your-

---

[1] From the Lansdowne Collection of MSS. in the British Museum.

[2] An Act against Regrators, Forestallers, and Ingrossers. Anno quinto et sexto Edvardi VI^{ti} cap. 14.—Statutes at large.

self with patience. For the second cause, when God will, be it never so like to bring forth the effect, misseth her purpose: as ye know by wise men's counsels that ruled in commonwealths before you. God give his grace to look always upon him; and then with mercy let him do his holy will. Glouc. 6 Julii, 1552.

Yours with my daily prayer,
JOHN HOPER, Bishop of Worcester.

Having completed his labours in Gloucestershire, Hooper returned once more to Worcester, taking with him the same articles that he had used in his visitation of the preceding year. This brought him into a controversy with two of the canons of the cathedral, named Henry Joliffe and Robert Johnson, who objected to the articles as opposed to the catholic faith, and refused to subscribe them. The bishop held a public disputation with them, and afterwards sent up an account of the controversy to the council; who gave orders to Mr Cheke and Mr Harley to inquire into and report upon the matter, that further order might be taken therein. With his report to the council the bishop sent another letter to Sir William Cecil[3]:

The grace of God be with you for ever. Amen. I have wroten herewith long letters to the council; yet not so long as the matter contained in them doth require. I trust it will be your chance to read them, that the matter may be the better understand. Ye know I am but an evil secretary. Do the best ye can they may be well taken. It is truth that I write, and God's cause: let God do as his blessed pleasure is with it. I have sent the matters that these two canons, Johnson and Joliffe, dislike in writing: whereby ye may understand what is said of both parts. The disputation Mr Harley can make true relation of, and how unreverently and proudly Joliffe used both him and me.

Forasmuch as my jurisdiction ceaseth until the letters-patent be past for both churches, these shall be to pray you to obtain the king's majesty's letters for my warrant in the mean time. For in case I do not at this time take account of the clergy in Worcester and Gloucestershire, how they have profited since my last examining of them, it will not be well. Also such as I have made superintendents in Gloucestershire, if I commend not myself presently their well-doings, and see what is evil done, I shall not see the good I look for. Ah, Mr Secretary, that there were good men in the cathedral churches! God then should have much more honour than he hath, the king's majesty more obedience, and the poor people more knowledge. But

---

[3] From the Lansdowne Collection of MSS. in the British Museum.

the realm wanteth light in such churches where as of right it ought most to be.

I suppose ye had heard that there should be a great spoil made of this church here; for what can be so well done, that men of light conscience cannot make by suggestion to appear evil? Doubtless the things done be no more than the express words of the king's majesty's injunctions commanded to be done. And I dare say there is not for a church to preach God's word in, and to minister his holy sacraments, more goodly within this realm. But, Mr Secretary, I see much mischief in men's hearts by many tokens; and such as speak very fair meaneth craftily, and nothing less than they speak: I have too good experience of it.

Thus God give us wisdom and strength wisely and strongly to serve in our vocations. There is none that eateth their bread in the sweat of their face but such as serve in public vocation. Yours is wonderful, but mine passeth. Now I perceive private labours be but plays, nor private troubles but ease and quietness. God be our help. Amen. I pray you send me my jurisdiction as soon as may be. Worcester, 25 Octobris, 1552.

Yours, and so will be whiles I live, with my prayer,

JOHN HOPER, Bishop of Worcester.

Postscript.—When that I perceived my request for jurisdiction made before unto you, upon further deliberation I thought it good to unrequest that again, praying you to make no mention of it; and thereupon wrote the letters to the council anew. The cause is, I send for a precedent, to see the jurisdiction how it is given in the like state as I am; which pleaseth me not. Therefore, good Mr Secretary, let it pass till I write to you again[1].

On the conclusion of his visitation the bishop again went over both his dioceses, to ascertain what improvement had taken place amongst his clergy since his last examination, and to observe how his superintendents had fulfilled the duties entrusted to them.

These labours over, he devoted himself with no less assiduity to the other duties of his exalted office. His character cannot be better described than in the admirable summary

[1] An account of the above-mentioned controversy was published by Joliffe at Antwerp in 1564, under the following title: "Responsio venerabilium sacerdotum, Henrici Joliffe et Roberti Johnson, sub protestatione facta, ad illos articulos Joannis Hoperi, episcopi Vigorniæ nomen gerentis, in quibus a catholica fide dissentiebat: una cum confutationibus ejusdem Hoperi, et replicationibus reverendissimi in Christo patris bonæ memoriæ Stephani Gardineri, episcopi Vintoniensis, tunc temporis pro confessione fidei in carcere detenti."

given by Foxe: "He employed his time (says that writer) which the Lord lent him under king Edward's reign with such diligence as may be a spectacle to all bishops...So careful was he in his cure, that he left neither pains untaken nor ways unsought, how to train up the flock of Christ in the true word of salvation, continually labouring in the same. No father in his household, no gardener in his garden, nor husbandman in his vineyard, was more or better occupied than he in his diocese amongst his flock, going about his towns and villages, in teaching and preaching to the people there. That time that he had to spare from preaching he bestowed either in hearing public causes, or else in private study, prayer, and visiting of schools. To which his continual doctrine he adjoined due and discreet correction, not so much severe to any as to them which for abundance of riches and wealthy state thought they might do what they listed. And, doubtless, he spared no kind of people, but was indifferent to all men, as well rich as poor." Of his firm and impartial conduct an instance is given by John ab Ulmis, who relates that Sir Anthony Kingston, a man of rank in Gloucestershire, was cited by the bishop on a charge of immorality, and, on his appearance, rebuked by him with his wonted severity. He replied with abusive language, and even blows; but the case being reported to the council by the bishop, he was severely punished for his contumacy[2]. By some however even amongst his friends the bishop's strictness appears to have been considered extreme: for Micronius, in a letter to Bullinger, dated November the 7th, 1551, writes, "Let him be exhorted to unite prudence and christian lenity to the severity of discipline."

But to return to Foxe: we learn that, "although he bestowed and converted the most part of his care upon the public flock and congregation of Christ," his children and other members of his household were not forgotten or neglected. His palace in all its arrangements presented abundant evidence of his piety and wisdom. His liberality too was no less conspicuous, his surplus revenue being expended in the exercise of the most enlarged hospitality. It was his daily custom to provide a table for a certain number of the poor of Worcester,

---

[2] Zurich Letters, II. ccviii. p. 441.

who, after being examined as to their knowledge of the Lord's Prayer, the Articles of their Faith, and the Ten Commandments, were regaled with an ample and wholesome repast.

On the death of king Edward, Hooper, true to the principles which he had always professed, supported the claims of Mary to the throne, and exerted his influence in her behalf. This conduct however was of no avail to screen him from the fury of the papists. Being warned by some friends to flee from the dangers which were impending over him, he nobly answered, "Once I did flee, and took me to my feet: but now, because I am called to this place and vocation, I am throughly persuaded to tarry, and to live and die with my sheep." He was one of the first who were summoned before the council. He appeared before them at Richmond, where they were then assembled, on the 29th of August, and was received by Gardiner with taunts and insults on account of his religion: but, as the laws of persecution were not yet revived, he was detained on a false pretence of his being indebted to the queen, and sent on the 1st of September to the Fleet. He has left in one of his letters an interesting account of the cruel treatment which he experienced in that prison[1].

His wife at an early stage of these troubles escaped with her two children to the continent, and took up her abode at Frankfort, where she hoped she might be able to maintain a correspondence with her husband.

In the following March he was brought before Gardiner and other commissioners; and, on the ground of his being married, and refusing to forsake his wife, and also his denial of the corporal presence in the eucharist, he was adjudged to be deprived of his bishoprick. The papists proceeded in this examination with their usual violence, drowning Hooper's voice with furious outcries, and assailing him with the most opprobrious epithets. Not long after this occurrence he received intelligence, that it was in contemplation to send him, with Ferrar, Taylor, Bradford, and Philpot, to Cambridge, under the pretence of a disputation similar to that which had been held at Oxford a short time before. He therefore wrote to his fellow-sufferers to warn them of the design, proposing that they should come to some agreement amongst themselves as to the course which should be pursued. In accordance with

---

[1] See Letter XLVIII. p. 619 of this volume.

his suggestion a declaration of their willingness to dispute in writing, or before the queen and council, or before the houses of parliament, and not otherwise, together with a confession of their faith, was drawn up and subscribed[2].

The sufferings of a long and rigorous imprisonment had no power to damp the good bishop's ardour in the cause to which he was devoted; and though unable to aid it by his personal exertions, he was by no means inactive. Notwithstanding the strictness with which he was watched, he contrived to write numerous letters of exhortation to his friends, together with several important treatises and other works, of which the greater part will be found in the following pages.

At length, on the 22nd of January, 1555, he was again brought before Gardiner at his house in Southwark, when he was earnestly exhorted to return to the bosom of the Roman church, and to acknowledge the pope's supremacy; being assured that by compliance he would secure the clemency of the queen, together with the papal blessing. To these offers he undauntedly replied, that he could not acknowledge even as a member, much less as the head, of Christ's holy church one whose teaching was contrary to that of Christ: nor could he allow the papal to be the true catholic church. As to the queen, if he had unwittingly committed any offence against her, he was ready to implore her mercy, provided it might be done without violence to his conscience. He was informed in reply, that the queen would extend no mercy to the enemies of the pope, and recommitted to the Fleet. Six days afterwards he was again summoned before the commissioners in the church of St Mary Overy, to answer the charge of heresy. The offer of mercy on his recantation was again renewed, but again as firmly rejected. The following charges were then severally brought against him: first, that "being a priest, and of a religious order, he had himself married, and openly maintained and taught the lawfulness of the marriage of the clergy;" secondly, that "he had maintained and taught that married persons, in case of adultery, may by the word of God and his authority, and by the ministry of the magistrates, be wholly separated from the bond of matrimony, and divorced from one another." Hooper, in his reply, confessed the truth of both these charges, and offered to defend his views against

[2] Foxe, Acts and Monuments, p. 1469.

all opponents. Thirdly, it was charged against him, that he had asserted, held, and taught, that "in the eucharist, or sacrament of the altar, is not truly the true and natural body of Christ and his true and natural blood under the species of bread and wine; and that there is there material bread and material wine only, without the truth and presence of the body and blood of Christ." To this he answered, that "the very natural body of Christ is not really and substantially in the sacrament of the altar; and that the mass is the iniquity of the devil, and the mass an idol."

Finding that Hooper remained immoveable, Gardiner committed him to the Counter in Southwark till the following morning, in order that he might have time to reflect, and retract his opinions: but as on his re-appearance he remained unchanged, he was at length condemned as an obstinate heretic and excommunicated, and delivered over to the secular power. He was then conveyed by the sheriffs of London to the Clink, a prison not far from Gardiner's residence, where he was detained till night: and thence under cover of the darkness, as though it was feared that the people might make an attempt at rescue, he was led to Newgate. During his detention here Bonner and others made repeated efforts to shake his constancy, but without success. The frequency of their visits however gave rise to a rumour of his recantation, which caused him much annoyance, and was the occasion of his writing the letter of denial which will be found in the collection [1].

On Monday, the 4th of February, he was, with Rogers, formally degraded by bishop Bonner in the chapel of the prison; and at night he received an intimation from his keeper that he was to be sent to Gloucester for execution. This intelligence he received with the liveliest satisfaction, praising God that he was to be sent amongst his own people, to confirm before them by his death the truth which he had taught them during life. He immediately made his preparations with great alacrity; and at four o'clock on the following morning, after being strictly searched, he was led out of Newgate, and delivered to six of the queen's guards, who were appointed to convey him to Gloucester. He commenced his journey at day-break, precautions being taken to prevent

[1] Letter XLIX. p. 621.

recognition, and conducted himself throughout with such cheerfulness and docility as to win the good-will and favour of his escort. On the afternoon of Thursday he arrived at Gloucester, amidst the tears and lamentations of a crowd of people, and was conducted to the house of one Robert Ingram, where he remained till the time of his execution. The greater part of this short interval he spent in prayer: but one or two interesting incidents which have been preserved by Foxe deserve attention.

Sir Anthony Kingston came to see him, and with many assurances of gratitude and affection entreated him to consult his safety, urging that life was sweet, and death was bitter, and that life hereafter might do good. "I thank you (said Hooper in reply) for your friendly counsel, although it be not so friendly as I could have wished it. True it is, M. Kingston, that death is bitter, and life is sweet: but alas! consider that the death to come is more bitter, and the life to come is more sweet. Therefore for the desire and love I have to the one, and the terror and fear of the other, I do not so much regard this death, nor esteem this life; but have settled myself, through the strength of God's Holy Spirit, patiently to pass through the torments and extremities of the fire now prepared for me, rather than to deny the truth of his word; desiring you and others in the mean time to commend me to God's mercy in your prayers."

Not long after a blind boy, who had suffered imprisonment at Gloucester for his attachment to the truth, obtained admission to him; when the bishop, having questioned him as to his belief, and the cause of his imprisonment, said with tears in his eyes, "Ah! poor boy, God hath taken from thee thy outward sight, for what consideration he best knoweth: but he hath given thee another sight much more precious; for he hath endued thy soul with the eye of knowledge and faith. God give thee grace continually to pray unto him, that thou lose not that sight; for then shouldest thou be blind both in body and soul." To a papist who intruded upon him with hypocritical expressions of sorrow for his troubles he administered a stern rebuke: "Be sorry for thyself, man, (said M. Hooper,) and lament thine own wickedness: for I am well, I thank God, and death to me for Christ's sake is welcome."

The guard, having now accomplished their commission,

delivered him into the custody of the sheriffs, who with the mayor and aldermen repaired to his lodging, and at the first meeting saluted him, and took him by the hand. Hooper upon this addressed them in the following terms: "M. mayor, I give most hearty thanks to you, and to the rest of your brethren, that you have vouchsafed to take me a prisoner and a condemned man by the hand; whereby, to my rejoicing, it is some deal apparent that your old love and friendship towards me is not altogether extinguished: and I trust also that all the things I have taught you in times past are not utterly forgotten, when I was here, by the godly king that dead is, appointed to be your bishop and pastor. For the which most true and sincere doctrine, because I will not now account it falsehood and heresy, as many other men do, I am sent hither (as I am sure you know) by the queen's commandment to die; and am come where I taught it, to confirm it with my blood. And now, M. sheriffs, I understand by these good men and my very friends (meaning the guard), at whose hands I have found so much favour and gentleness by the way hitherward as a prisoner could reasonably require, for the which also I most heartily thank them, that I am committed to your custody, as unto them that must see me brought to-morrow to the place of execution. My request therefore to you shall be only, that there may be a quick fire, shortly to make an end; and in the mean time I will be as obedient unto you as yourselves would wish. If you think I do amiss in any thing, hold up your finger, and I have done. For I come not hither as one enforced or compelled to die (for it is well known I might have had my life with worldly gain), but as one willing to offer and give my life for the truth, rather than to consent to the wicked papistical religion of the bishop of Rome, received and set forth by the magistrates in England, to God's high displeasure and dishonour: and I trust by God's grace to-morrow to die a faithful servant of God, and a true obedient subject to the queen."

The order for Hooper's execution, addressed to lord Chandos, Sir Anthony Kingston, Sir Edmund Bridges, and other commissioners, is expressed as follows: "Whereas John Hooper, who of late was called bishop of Worcester and Gloucester, is by due order of the laws ecclesiastic condemned and judged for a most obstinate, false, detestable heretic, and committed to our secular power to be burned, according to the wholesome and good laws of our realm in that case provided; forasmuch as in those cities and diocese thereof he hath in times past preached and taught most pestilent heresies and doctrine to our subjects there; we have therefore given order that the said Hooper, who yet persisteth obstinate, and hath refused mercy when it was graciously offered, shall be put to execution in the said city of Gloucester, for the example and terror of others such as he hath there seduced and mistaught, and because he hath done most harm there: and will that you, calling unto you some of reputation dwelling in the shire, such as you think best, shall repair unto our said city, and be at the said execution assisting our mayor and sheriffs of the same city in this behalf. And, forasmuch also as the said Hooper is, as heretics be, a vain-glorious person, and delighteth in his tongue, and having liberty, may use his said tongue to persuade such as he hath seduced to persist in the miserable opinion that he hath sown amongst them; our pleasure is therefore, and we require you to take order, that the said Hooper be, neither at the time of his execution, nor in going to the place thereof, suffered to speak at large, but thither to be led quietly and in silence, for eschewing of further infection and such inconveniency as may otherwise ensue in this part. Whereof fail you not, as ye tender our pleasure[1]."

Early on the morning of the ninth of February the commissioners arrived at Hooper's lodging, and he was desired to prepare himself for execution. On being led forth by the sheriffs, and perceiving the crowd of armed attendants by whom they were surrounded, he exclaimed: "Master sheriffs, I am no traitor, neither needed you to have made such a business to bring me to the place where I must suffer: for if ye had willed me, I would have gone alone to the stake, and have troubled none of you all." When he beheld the multitudes of people who had come together to witness his demeanour, he remarked to those around him, "Alas! why be these people assembled and come together? Peradventure they think to hear something of me now, as they have in times past; but alas! speech is prohibited me. Notwithstanding, the cause of my death is well known unto them. When I was appointed

[1] From the Cottonian MSS. in the British Museum, Cleopatra, E. V. 81.

here to be their pastor, I preached unto them true and sincere doctrine, and that out of the word of God. Because I will not now account the same to be heresy and untruth, this kind of death is prepared for me." He walked cheerfully to the fatal spot, and surveyed the preparations with a smiling countenance: and then, beckoning to him several of his acquaintance, that they might hear his words, he knelt down and prayed; "the which prayer he made (says Foxe) upon the whole creed." Whilst he was thus engaged, a box, said to contain his pardon on condition of his recantation, was placed before him: but as soon as he saw it, he cried, "If you love my soul, away with it; if you love my soul, away with it." He was heard by those who were listening to him to say these words: "Lord, I am hell, but thou art heaven: I am swill and a sink of sin, but thou art a gracious God and a merciful Redeemer. Have mercy therefore upon me, most miserable and wretched offender, after thy great mercy, and according to thine inestimable goodness. Thou that art ascended into heaven, receive me hell to be partaker of thy joys, where thou sittest in equal glory with thy Father. For well knowest thou, Lord, wherefore I am come hither to suffer, and why the wicked do persecute this thy poor servant: not for my sins and transgressions committed against thee, but because I will not allow their wicked doings, to the contaminating of thy blood, and to the denial of the knowledge of thy truth, wherewith it did please thee by thy holy Spirit to instruct me: the which, with as much diligence as a poor wretch might (being thereto called), I have set forth to thy glory. And well seest thou, my Lord and God, what terrible pains and cruel torments be prepared for thy creature, such, Lord, as without thy strength none is able to bear, or patiently to pass. But all things that are impossible with man are possible with thee. Therefore strengthen me of thy goodness, that in the fire I break not the rules of patience; or else assuage the terror of the pains, as shall seem most to thy glory[1]."

His prayer being ended, and other preparations com-

[1] Foxe, in the "Rerum in Ecclesia gestarum," &c. p. 295, expresses a hope that the remainder of Hooper's prayer may be published by those who heard it; and accordingly the following fragment was preserved. It is extracted from a small volume of miscellaneous pieces

pleted, he was bound to the stake with an iron hoop, and
the fire applied. His sufferings were very protracted and
severe: for owing to the greenness and insufficiency of the
materials used, together with the violence of the wind, the
fire at first had but little effect; and it was necessary to renew
it on two several occasions before it reached a vital part.
During the whole of this trying interval, which was extended
to three quarters of an hour, the martyr's fortitude remained
unshaken: he evinced but little sense of suffering; and, as long
as he retained the power of speech, he employed it in prayer

preserved in the Bodleian Library. Two editions of it appear to have
been printed in the same year, viz. 1559.

The wordes of Maister Hooper at his death.

O Lord Jesus, that for whose love I leave wyllynglye this lyfe, and
desyre the bitter death of the crosse wyth the losse of all my worldlye
thinges, then eyther to abyde the blasphemye of thy moste holye
name, or to obey unto menne in breakynge of thy commaundementes;
thou seest, Lord, that where I myght lyve in wealth to worship a false
god, and to honor thyne ennemy, I choose rather the tormentes of
my bodye, and the losse of thys my lyfe, and I have counted all
thynges but vile dust and doonge, that I might wyn thee; whych
death is more deare unto mee then thousandes of gold and sylver:
such love, Lorde, hast thou layd up in my brest, that I hunger for
thee as the deere that is wounded desireth the soyle: so send thy
holye Comforter to ayde, comfort, and strengthen this weake peece of
yearthe, whiche is of itselfe empty of al strength: thou remembrest
that I am but vyle duste and doonge, and of myselfe able to doo
nothinge; therfore, O Lorde, as thou of thine accustomed love hast
bydden me to thys banket, and counted me worthy to drinke of this
thy cuppe amongest thine elect, geve me strength against this thy
ellement, that as to my syghte it is moste yrkesom and untollerable,
so to my mynd it may at thy commaundement go as an obedient servant, be swete and pleasaunt, and through the strength of thy holy
Spirite I maye passe through the furie of this fyre into thy bosom,
according to thy promise, and for this mortall lyfe receyve an immor-
talitie, and for this corruptible receyve an incorruptible. Accept thys
burnt sacrifice, O heavenly Father, not for the sacrifice' sake, but for
thy deare Sonne's sake my Saviour; for whose testimonie I offer this
my free-wyll offeryng with all my harte, with all my strength, with all
my soule. O heavenly Father, forgeve me my synnes, as I forgeve all
the worlde. O swete Sonne of God my Saviour, spreade thy wynges
over me. O God the Holye Ghost, comforte, strengthen, and stablish
me: and as through thy mightye power thou hast brought me hyther
to dye, so conduct me into everlastyng blysse. O Lorde, into thy

to him whose battle he was fighting. The last words that he was heard to utter were, "Lord Jesu, have mercy upon me; Lord Jesu, have mercy upon me; Lord Jesus, receive my spirit."

Several years ago some workmen, in levelling the ground in St Mary de Lode's square, in Gloucester, discovered buried in the earth the butt-end of the stake at which the martyr suffered: and the spot is marked by a simple monument erected by the pious munificence of a stranger.

handes I commende my spirite; thou haste redeemed me, O God of truthe. Lorde, have mercye upon me; Christ, have mercy upon me; Lord, have mercy upon me. Amen.

To this may be added the following lines, which form part of a volume containing "The Complaynt of Veritie, made by John Bradford," and other pieces, and printed A.D. 1559.

These are the wordes that Maister John Houper wrote on the wall with a cole, in the newe Inn in Gloceter, the night before he suffered:

<blockquote>
Content thyself with patience
  With Christ to bear the cross of pain,
Who can or will recompense
  A thousand-fold with joys again.
Let nothing cause thy heart to fail;
Launch out thy boat, hoise up thy sail,
  Put from the shore;
And be thou sure thou shalt attain
Unto the port that shall remain
  For evermore.

Fear not death, pass not for bands,
  Only in God put thy whole trust;
For he will require thy blood at their hands;
  And thou dost know that once die thou must:
Only for that thy life if thou give,
Death is no death, but amens for to live.
  Do not despair:
Of no worldly tyrant see thou dread;
Thy compass, which is God's word, shall thee lead,
  And the wind is fair.
</blockquote>

THE Editor of the "Early Writings of Bishop Hooper" has supplied for insertion here the following list of

CORRIGENDA.

p. 65. note 4, for *Valentine* read *Valentinus*.

p. 122. note 5, and in the Index, for *Henry VI.* read *Henry VII.*

p. 160. note 1, for *Tertullian and Origen* read *Theodoret and Augustine*.

p. 174. line 18, for *to save him. He wax not mange his horse, &c.* read, *to save him, he wax not mangy. His horse, &c.*

p. 276. note 1. The reference should have been to the "Falsa Donatio Constantini." The Editor hesitated to believe that Bishop Hooper had affirmed "the Bishop of Rome and *all his adherents* gave evidence and faith" to a Charter which so many eminent Romish divines had then acknowledged to be apocryphal.

A LESSON

OF THE

INCARNATION OF CHRIST.

A Lesson

of the Incarnation of Christe, that he toke his humanite in and of the Blessyd Virgine: made the twentithe daye of June by John Hoper.

1549.

Roma ix.

❡ Christe is of the fathers concernynge the fleshe.

[This treatise was written against the anabaptists, whose opinions occasioned much trouble at the time. Hooper was frequently engaged in opposing them. See Epist. XIII. and XIX.]

⁋ A DAILY PRAYER TO BE SAID BEFORE THE LESSON.

O eternal and most merciful God, whose word is the light unto our steps, and the lantern unto our feet, we most humbly beseech thee to illuminate our minds, that we may understand the mysteries contained in thy holy law; and into the same self thing that we godly understand, we may be virtuously transformed, so that of no part we offend thy high majesty, through our Saviour Jesus Christ. So be it.

⁋ A PREFACE.

SEEING we be even so appointed by the ordinance of God to live and take the experience and danger of the last time, in the which (as the scripture saith) iniquity shall abound, and the true knowledge of God so obscured, that scarce the Son of man, when he cometh, shall find any faith upon the earth; it is the office of all Christians, and especially of such as teach the word of God, not only to remove and take away false and pernicious doctrine, and then to plant the truth; but also in time to crop and cut off the springing and towardly evils, before they be full ripe, lest they should oppress and keep under the doctrine of truth.

Among all other pernicious doctrine contrary unto the truth, there is one most pestilent and dangerous, which denieth Jesus of Nazareth, our Saviour, to have received his humanity and manhood of the blessed and holy Virgin Mary; and supposeth, either he brought his humanity with him from heaven, or else took it of some other than of her. Forasmuch, therefore, as this ungodly opinion crept not only into the church immediately after the apostles, but also the same (being buried and condemned by the scripture) in our miserable and most perilous time is gotten into the hearts of many, for whom Christ in his humanity shed his precious blood, and some it holdeth in trouble and perplexity of conscience; to confirm and help the well-persuaded in the christian and catholic faith, and also to call again (if God will) such as be gone, I purpose to entreat and reason this matter of Christ's incarnation at large, that the truth may, as right is in this case, take here place.

Nothing else in this preface I demand but that the christian reader tarry with the truth, and not to be offended, though in this time many errors (upon the beginning of the reformation of true religion in this realm) daily be brought in; seeing it was so in the apostles' time by the craft of the devil, that men by the diversity of opinions troubled the truth of the gospel; which was and is done to prove the faithful. Now therefore to the matter, in the which I will observe this order: first, I will shew out of the old testament and the new, that Christ took his humanity of the blessed Virgin: afterwards, I will answer to the objections of the contraries.

✛

A LESSON

OF THE

INCARNATION OF CHRIST.

REASONS OUT OF THE OLD TESTAMENT.

THE first is the promise of God unto Adam and Eve, Gen. iii., that the seed of a woman should break the serpent's head. This promise was spoken of Christ; for he solely and only brake the serpent's head, that is to say, destroyed the works of the devil, satisfied for sin, and overcame it, and also the world, hell, and the devil, and set God and man at one, removing the occasion of enmity and the enmity itself in his precious blood; breaking the writings of our condemnation upon the cross, Ephes. ii.; and this our Saviour and peacemaker is called the seed of a woman. The which word alone were sufficient to confound the contrary part, that saith Christ took not the substance of his humanity of the blessed Virgin. Wheresoever ye find this word, "the seed of a woman," in the holy scripture, ye shall see always it is taken for the child and birth that hath of the substance of his mother, and not for anything that passeth through the mother, as the water passeth through a pipe; but that part of the mother's substance doth concur, and necessarily is required to the procreation of the child, as all physic holdeth.

And this way wrought God Almighty the humanity of his only Son, our Saviour, Jesus of Nazareth, without the knowledge of man, using the blessed Virgin by the operation of the Holy Ghost to conceive and bring forth this blessed seed, which was made of her, and took the original of his humanity of and in her, by the operation of the Holy Ghost; and neither nourished in her womb, neither brought forth she the humanity of Christ, as a thing that God had given Christ from heaven, or else from some other where; but nourished in her, and brought forth the blessed seed that God had made by his holy power of her own substance: other[1] else were this

[1 Other: either.]

promise false, The seed of a woman shall break the serpent's head. It is no seed of a woman, nor hath any thing to do to be called the seed of a woman, that never taketh ought of a woman. But God doth warrant that he, that shall break the serpent's head, shall be the seed of a woman. If it be true (as it cannot be false), that the serpent's head is broken, who can deny but that it is broken by the seed of a woman, that is, by him that took his humanity of the woman's substance? Men must beware they be not deceived in this case with allegories and wrong interpretation of the word; but plainly make answer, Christ is the seed of a woman, and not a thing that passed through her, nor was partitaker[1] of her nature. For then should she not have brought forth her son, but such a son as she knew neither father neither mother of.

Other promises made God unto Abraham and unto Jacob of the same seed. To Abraham, Gen. xxii., "In thy seed shall they say all the nations of the earth to be blessed." Unto Jacob, Gen. xxvi.[2], God saith thus, "In thy seed shall all the people of the world be blessed." Here again see we Christ called "the seed;" for none other purpose doubtless, but only to take away all suspicion and doubt that the world might have of his humanity; and lest the world might have said, as now-a-day (the more pity) many doth say, we believe that Christ is of the seed of the fathers, but he brought that seed with him from heaven, or else wrought the same seed, and made it not out of the sinful nature of the fathers, but some other ways unknown unto man. The scripture in these promises, and in other that shall follow, putteth expressly this pronoun, *thine*, saying, "thy seed." In *thy* seed, not in the seed that Christ shall bring from heaven, shall be the blessing of all people. How can that be Abraham's or Jacob's seed, that never took any of their substance, but came from heaven, and was made of another kind of nature than Abraham and Jacob was of? Who is able by good authority of the scripture to warrant Christ's humanity, in case it be unknown of whom he should take it; as these men knoweth not, that denieth Christ to take the nature of man of the blessed Virgin? Unto David God made the like promise of

[[1] Partitaker: partaker.]
[[2] In chapter xxvi. the promise is made to Isaac. It is renewed to Jacob in chap. xxviii.]

Christ to be born of his seed: 2 Samuel vii., "When thy days be past, and thou sleepest with thy fathers, I will suscitate thy seed after thee, that shall come out of thy belly." The same have ye 1 Paral. xvii, and also Psalm cxxxii., "The Lord swore a truth unto David, and will not go from it; I will set upon thy seat (one) of the fruit of thy belly." Nothing is more clear than these words. No man doubteth but all these places appertain unto Christ, the son of the holy Virgin, who is called here the seed of David: also that it should come out of his own belly, concerning his posterity. Then is Christ called the fruit of David ['s] belly. God did swear he would this do: except he be forsworn, he hath done it; and in that (God be praised) we be agreed. Therefore we will not tarry long in the proof thereof, seeing it needeth no probation. One thing I desire the christian reader of, that he mark well every word of the promise, whereas he calleth him that is promised, now, the seed of David, then, the fruit of his womb: if he so do, it shall be easy to comprehend how far these men be from the verity, that Christ should be a man of the fathers' nature, according to the scriptures, and yet never received his human nature of none of them all. Look in the scripture, and see what the fruit of the belly is; and thou shalt find in every where it is taken for the child that taketh the beginning of his humanity not only in his mother, but also of his mother and parent; and calleth not that the fruit of the belly, that passeth the belly without the commixtion and participation of the mother's substance; as the water runneth and passeth through the pipe, that mingleth itself nothing with substance of the lead. For a more ample declaration and defence of the truth concerning the humanity of Christ and the original thereof, Esay the prophet hath more open prophecies, not only assuring of what family and tribe Christ should be born, but also nameth the condition of his mother, saying, "Behold, a virgin shall conceive, and bear a child," the vii. chap. St Matthew saith, not only that she had conceived, but also that the blessed fruit grew in her, so that she was great, chap. i.

Esay in the eleventh chapter saith, "There shall come forth of the race of Jesse a branch and a flower of his root," and so forth: read the place. Now, note the words of the Holy Ghost, "conceive," "being great," and, "to bring forth child;" whether ever ye did read in the holy scriptures, or in any other book, that these properties were found, or may be found in any, saving in her of whose nature and substance the child is formed and made. Therefore the virgin, which Esay here saith shall conceive and bring forth, must minister the part of her substance to her fruit: otherwise, how shall it be called her son? The text amplifieth this matter so itself, that it needeth no help of any rhetorical amplification. First, with this word, " behold:" for this word declareth that it should be wonderful and above reason, that the nature of a virgin should minister matter and substance to any child, never being known of man. Had she done no more than waxed great with nothing of herself, and brought forth the thing that was made without her, it had not been a thing to be wondered at at all, so much as the prophet speaketh. But it is a greater miracle, a virgin of her own nature to be mother unto a child (by God's operation), and never touched by man, than to bring forth the burden that she taketh from another, made without her assistance and help.

Then goeth forth the prophet and discusseth the doubt farther by a similitude and metaphor taken from a tree, after this sort; "There shall," saith Esay, "come forth of the stock of Jesse a branch," that is to say, the blessed Virgin Mary, (note the process of the text,) and from the root of this branch shall spring a flower, to say, Christ our Saviour. This is the order of the text and the meaning thereof: I make the christian reader judge. Out of the which text note those things: first, that Jesus of Nazareth our Saviour, concerning his humanity, hath not his beginning from heaven nor elsewhere, but from the substance of the root of Jesse. Mark the words of the prophet. He saith not that Christ shall be a flower graft or feigned to be annexed to the root; but he shall be born of the same root. Consider the similitude and the words of the scripture. Christ is called the flower of the branch. It is not unknown unto all men but that the flower is of the nature and substance of the tree that beareth the flower. How can they then prove (tarry in the text of Esay), seeing our Saviour Christ is the flower of that sacrate Virgin Mary, should not be of her substance and nature? Shew us any flower, that is either of apple-tree, nut, or other, that is not of the same nature and substance that the tree is, of whom it springeth. If ye grant the flower to be of the nature and substance of the stock that beareth the flower, be no more injurious and cruel against Christ, the flower and fruit (by God's ordinances) of the sacrate Virgin, than unto the stock and root of every flower of the field. Shew us the flower of an orange to spring of an oak; and then we will grant the humanity of Christ nor to take his original of man, but from heaven, or else from some other beginning, as you do feign, ye know not what. And then it must be granted, even as of the nature of no orange can come no orange, so of none of Abraham's nature and stock can come Abraham's natural kinsman, our Saviour Christ Jesus, according to the flesh. But ye will not, contrary to reason, grant to us the first: no more can we, contrary both to reason and to the holy scripture, grant you the second. These places and promises of the old testament considered, we will bring forth the authority of the new testament, that shall confirm the same.

¶ Testimonies of the New Testament.

Out of the old testament we have heard that Christ should be born according to the holy scriptures. Now let us hear how the effect answereth to the former prophecies. In case the new testament should not in effect perform as much as the old testament figured by shadows, and saw before by prophecy, they both might be justly suspected; and no force though both of them were denied. And for a probation, let us take the experience of it in this matter concerning the humanity of Christ, and that it took his beginning in and of the holy Virgin by the operation of the Holy Ghost. The angel said unto the blessed Virgin, Luke the first, "Behold, thou shalt conceive in thy womb, and bear a son:" the which things St Matthew expresseth thus: "Thou shalt be great, and bear a son." Mark the whole state of the scripture, and the words here rehearsed, "to conceive and bear a child;" and ye shall always find it is none other thing but that the mother shall be a very true and natural parent with participation of her own substance with her child. Therefore St Matthew, in the first chapter, to help this doubt, among other things touching the genealogy and stock of Christ saith thus, speaking of the blessed Virgin Mary, "Of whom is born Christ;" and doth not say, by whom, or through whom Christ passed. The same word, "of," useth St Paul twice to the Romans, and once to the Galatians; the which word he would not have used so many times, in case Christ hath taken no substance of his mother, but passed through her without participation of her nature, as the water through a conduit. To the Romans, in the first chapter, he saith thus, "Which was born of the seed of David as touching the flesh;" and in the ninth chapter, "Christ after the flesh is of the fathers;" and in the fourth to the Galatians he saith, "When the time was fulfilled, God sent his Son born of a woman." What can be more plainly said to prove our Saviour Jesus Christ to have taken of the Virgin the substance of human nature; namely because the new testament and the authorities thereof doth so godly correspond and answer to the prophecies of the old law? Gen. xxii. "In thy seed," saith Moses, and not in another seed, or in a heavenly seed. The same doth St Paul repeat, saying, "Christ is of the fathers as concerning to the flesh." Mark the word, "of," and it shall destroy that fond opinion of them that say, "True it is, we grant that Christ is of the seed of David; yet it followeth not he should take of the nature and substance of the sacrate Virgin." Note well the words, and they shall satisfy thee. Unto this objection and other I will answer unto hereafter in the end of the oration. Now to the proof of our proposition: read the first of St Luke, and mark the greeting of Elizabeth unto the holy Virgin being great: "Blessed," said she, "is the fruit of thy womb." This holy woman calleth Christ the fruit: but whereof, and from whence had she this fruit? Of heaven, or other where? No, truly: but it was the fruit of her own belly; then of her own substance; or else it were a manifest lie to call Christ the fruit of her belly. Neither, I think, there is no man that would call a thing the fruit of a tree, that never had the nature of a tree. What man was ever so found[1] to say that a pear were the fruit of a cherry-tree? Or who is he that can say that Jesus of Nazareth, taking his humanity from heaven,

[[1] Probably a mistake for *fond*, i. e. foolish.]

or of some other thing beside his mother, can truly call him the fruit of his mother's womb? The scripture saith Christ is her son, and she is his mother, not a feigned mother, but a true and very natural mother.

So saith St Matthew, in the first chapter, "She brought forth her son." And so the Virgin called him, Luke the second, "Son, why hast thou done thus unto us?" Believe the scriptures, and ponder accordingly the words and sentences thereof. Matth. i. Luke iii. Joh. ii. xix.

One place more there is in St Paul, written in the second to the Hebrews, which is this: "Forasmuch then as the children were partakers of flesh and blood, he also himself likewise took part with them." And in the same place he saith, "He took the seed of Abraham, and not of the angels; so that he must be like unto his brothers in all things." This place appertaining to the nativity of Christ, let us consider diligently the words of St Paul's oration, how he proveth Christ to have our nature, which he took of his mother. If it be so, saith St Paul, that the children, that is to say, men, be partakers of flesh and blood, Christ, because he might destroy him that hath the dominion of death by the death in his own body, was made partaker of the same, to wit, of flesh and blood. Here he useth three words, "likewise," "partaker," "of the same." Read the text, and note the words.

First, it is out of doubt that our flesh is of the nature and substance of a woman. Now, saith St Paul, Christ likewise, that is to say, after the same manner, took flesh as his brothers. I say not, like unto us; for we receive our nature with sin, and in sin, and by natural conjunction. Christ received his humanity of his mother without sin, by the operation of the Holy Ghost. But to St Paul's words: like as man taketh his nature of his parents, so likewise took Christ his human nature of the blessed Virgin; or else St Paul's simile proved nothing.

The second word of St Paul saith that he was made participant, or partaker. Now there is no participation, nor can be, except it be of such things as is common between them that be partakers of one thing. It cannot be, therefore, that Christ hath taken other flesh than his brothers had, which was of the seed of man. Farther, he addeth, "Christ took the seed of Abraham, and not of angels;" that is as much to say, Abraham's flesh, verily human, and not any body of flesh celestial, or made of the air. In this place St Paul sheweth plainly, from whence and of whom Christ took his humanity. In the same chapter St Paul saith, "Christ is made like unto his brothers in all things." How can this, I pray you, be true, in case he never took his human nature of any of his brothers' substance? The which thing if ye take from Christ, there is nothing can be more unlike than Christ and us, that be his brothers.

In the last reason, St Paul saith that "Christ was tempted, that he might succour such as were tempted." Now there is no flesh can be tempted but man's flesh. And there is no man's flesh but hath taken his beginning of the substance of man, except it were Adam, the first man, that was made of the earth, Gen. i. Farther, how can he help us, as St Paul saith, being in another flesh from us? If he have another flesh than we have (I except sin, and now, mortality), how or wherein is the justice of God satisfied for sin? How can he be a faithful mediator between God and man, that never took his humanity of the substance or nature of any man?

These places and authorities, I trust, sufficeth every christian heart for the stablishment of this article of our belief, where we confess that Christ was conceived by the Holy Ghost, and born of the Virgin Mary. By the which word, "of," we believe that he took his humanity of her substance, and had none other beginning, as touching his humanity, than in her, and of her, by the operation of the Holy Ghost. There now resteth no more to be said of me in this part, but to answer unto such objections as the contrary part resisteth this truth withal.

The first Objection.

⁋ If Christ took his flesh of a woman, then were he a sinner, and partaker of the sin that naturally dwelleth in every of Adam's posterity. Romans v. xi.

We answer.

⁋ In case Christ had been in all things conceived and born as we be, their objection were true. But the angel, in the first of St Luke, declareth the diversity between the conception and birth of Christ and ours: "The Holy Ghost," saith he unto the holy Virgin, "shall come upon thee, and the might of the Highest shall shadow thee." And in case the Almighty had not sanctified and hallowed the seed of David in the sacrate Virgin, which Christ took in her womb, it might have ministered some suspicion that Christ, being man of sinful nature, should also [have] been a sinner himself. But the scripture declareth not only Christ to be the seed and fruit of the Virgin, but also a seed and fruit without sin, saying, "The thing that shall be born of thee is holy, and shall be called the Son of God." This testimony of the will of God in the scripture should suffice the people of God. Why seek we a knot in a rush, and put doubt in a manifest verity? or to fear of the thing that God's word plainly putteth out of fear, and saith, It shall be no sinful fruit, nor vitiated seed, that the blessed Virgin shall bring forth; but it shall be an holy fruit? Luke i. And in the same place Elizabeth saith, "Blessed is the fruit of thy belly." The holy woman will admit no curse or malediction of sin in this fruit. The prophet Hier. xxiii. saith, that God promised to suscitate unto David a righteous branch.

¶ In this prophet there is contained two verities of Christ: the first is, that he shall be of the seed of David, as the branch of a tree is of the tree itself. Now it is known that the tree and the branch thereof is participant of one and of the same nature, of the same sap and condition. So is Christ, touching his humanity, of the same nature that his mother was of, that is to say, of the seed of David. And this proveth the article of our faith, "He was born of the Virgin Mary."

¶ The second part of the prophecy proveth the confutation of such as would infer and make to follow, if Christ be of the substance and nature of his mother, then is he a sinner. Mark the text, and it will answer the contrary. The text saith it shall not only be a branch, but a just branch, that is to say, innocent and without sin before the face and judgment of God: as though the prophet had said, This branch shall take his being and original of David's posterity, and yet want sin.

¶ So doth the prophet Esay say, chap. liii., speaking of this blessed and innocent seed, "Who did no sin, neither fraud was found in his mouth." The same writeth St Peter, 1 Pet. ii., and St John, 1 John iii., "He appeared to take away our sin, and no sin was found in him." Of these places we humbly beseech all christian men to judge, whether the word of God proveth not as well Christ to take of the substance of his mother, as to prove the same branch and fruit of her belly to be void of all sin, the Holy Ghost working the same, as it is written, Luke i.

The second Objection.

⁋ St Matthew in his first chapter saith, "That which is born of her is of the Holy Ghost:" then it is not of the nature and substance of the Virgin.

We answer.

⁋ If the circumstance of the place be marked, they shall know they do injuries to the text here, as in other places. For when the Virgin heard there should be a child born of her, and she yet in the grace and perfection of her virginity, as of a thing impossible by nature to be done, wondereth at the tidings, and requireth the angel of the means how it may be done. Whereunto the angel maketh answer, to satisfy the admiration of the troubled Virgin, thus: "The Holy Ghost shall come upon thee, and he shall work this wonderful work in thee, although above the consent of thy reason, yet not without the assistance of thy nature, which shall be shadowed by the Holy Ghost." This interpretation of St Luke admitteth St Matthew in the first chapter; where as Joseph was no less troubled to see his affianced and promised wife to be with child, thought it had been by some sinister and forbidden means, as well as the poor Virgin with reason thought it could never be without the knowledge of man. As from heaven her reason was confounded, and made to give place unto faith and the power of God; so was Joseph by night admonished of his over-hasty judgment and light suspicion, that l promised wife was not great by any man, but by the Holy Ghost. Thus mindeth the Evangelist to take out of Joseph the suspicion that he had of the godly Virgin for her being with child, and not to prove that the child within her was not of her own substance and nature. Read the place, and mark the state and argument thereof; then shall the text interpretate itself. If it be so (as God forbid it should), any would wrest and constrain this word, "of the Holy Ghost," against the circumstance and meaning of the Evangelist, we wish and require it to be admitted of all men for the scriptures' sake, that[1] all the prophecies saith Messias should be born of a woman, and not by a woman, or passing through a woman. If they will not thus be contented[2], but force the letter that saith, "of the Holy Ghost," that is to say, Christ was born of the substance of the Holy Ghost; then should they prove either Christ to have no flesh, because the Holy Ghost hath none, nor never had; or else the God to be turned into the nature of man; and so, whereas God before was and is ever immortal, should by their reason be made mortal, which were a blasphemy to grant.

The third Objection.

⁋ Christ, the Son of God, took not our nature; but by a certain change and commutation the Word, that before was God, to be made flesh, according to the scriptures, "And the Word is made flesh."

We answer.

⁋ This wrong interpretation of the scriptures cometh by the equivocation, or diverse signification of this word, "made," which hath in the scriptures two significations. The first, it signifieth a change of one nature into another, as John ii., "The water was made wine:" and also Gen. xix. "The wife of Lot was made into a stone of salt."

This word, "made," in the scripture in many other places signifieth as much as to say, received; as St Paul writeth, Galat. iii., "Christ is made for us the curse," or execration; that is to say, received in him the curse and malediction of God for our sins. And again, 2 Cor. v., "He that knew no sin made sin for us;" that is to say, was the sacrifice for our sin. Good christian reader, remember to take the meaning of the scripture according to the circumstance thereof; and then thou shalt perceive, for the immutability of God's nature, that where St John saith, "and the Word was made flesh," is even as much to say as the Son of God

[1 "All the prophecies that," 1549.]
[2 Contendyd, 1549.]

received flesh. And no other sense nor meaning can it have than this; except ye would the Word, that was God before and immortal, is now changed into man, and become mortal; which sentence repugneth every book of the scripture. Farther, it should follow, that he that was before God, as St John saith, now leaveth to be God, and is made man; as the water that was turned into wine, Joh. ii., left to be[1] water, and became wine; and as the corn of salt was no more the wife of Lot, but a corn of salt.

¶ Beside all this, if God be turned into man, how standeth their first interpretation, that his flesh and true humanity is of the Holy Ghost?

¶ No manner of way, doubtless; for no substance of flesh is of the substance of the Holy Ghost, nor no substance of the Holy Ghost can or may be the substance of the flesh. Thus, therefore, with the scriptures we conclude the Word, remaining still the Word, annexed unto it the nature of man, which he took of the blessed Virgin, and truly is called the fruit of her belly.

The fourth Objection.

¶ Whatsoever is born of a woman, hath a carnal body; but St Paul attributeth unto Christ a spiritual body, 1 Cor. xv.; therefore, he was not conceived nor born of the woman's nature.

We answer.

¶ St Paul in that place speaketh not of the incarnation of Christ, whether it be of the Virgin, or from heaven; as it is easily to be seen by the matter he entreateth of: but he writeth of the state and condition of the body after the resurrection, and answereth there to the objection of them that demanded in what body the dead should rise. In the same, saith he, that they lived, but no more rtal, nor subject unto the pain of mortality, as Adam's boc was after he sinned, but spiritual, as Christ's body was after his resurrection: spiritual, I say, not that it losteth[2] his humanity, or is turned into the nature of a spirit; but because it shall lack all mortal qualities. Thus proveth St Paul, when he saith, "It is sown a natural body; it shall rise a spiritual body."

[1 Left to be wine and become water, 1549.]
[2 Losteth: loseth.]

Here St Paul speaketh of the body of Christ after the resurrection, and not of his incarnation. Wherefore their reason concludeth nothing; for they infer a wrong conclusion of an evil-understood principle.

The fifth Objection.

¶ If Christ should receive his humanity of the nature of man, it should be to the ignominy and contempt of his person, whose holiness will not admit any conjunction with the unperfection of man.

We answer.

¶ It is no ignominy or contempt at all, but rather a certain argument of God's mercy (which passeth all his works), that he would not abhor to be partaker of our infirm nature.

¶ Other common Objections.

St Paul, Col. i., Eph. iii., Heb. i., Jo. iii., 1 Cor. xv., Jo. vi., Heb. xiii., Eph. iv. In these places it is plain that Christ is called the first-begotten of creatures: that he came from heaven: that he is the bread given from heaven: he is to day, and was yesterday also: he ascended, that first descended. These places, say they, prove he took not his original of his mother.

We answer.

¶ Christ, as he is very God, so is he very man, and according to his Godhead he hath been, is, and ever shall be without beginning: and of this his divine nature speaketh the places afore-rehearsed, and not of his humanity. Farther, it is the manner of the scripture, because of the union and conjunction of these two natures in one person, many times to ascribe and put that unto the one nature, which properly is due unto the other.

The Conclusion.

¶ Seeing the scripture hath in this point as well stablished the truth that Christ our Saviour took his humanity of the blessed Virgin, as also answered all the objections that can be brought against the truth, it shall be the duty and office of as many as love the Lord in Christ, with humbleness rather to consent unto the truth, than, of affection, to stand at the defence of a lie. The living God grant us his Holy Spirit, that once we may all know one thing in Christ Jesu to our salvation. So be it.

⁌ Imprented at London by
Edwarde Whitechurch.
1549.
Cum Privilegio ad Im-
-primendum Solum.

A BRIEF AND CLEAR CONFESSION

OF THE

CHRISTIAN FAITH.

2—2

A briefe and clear confession of the *Christian faith*[1], *conteining an* hūdreth articles, according to 𝔱𝔥𝔢 𝔬𝔯𝔡𝔢𝔯 𝔬𝔣 𝔱𝔥𝔢 𝔒𝔯𝔢𝔢𝔡𝔢 of the Apostles: 𝔴𝔯𝔦𝔱𝔱𝔢𝔫 𝔟𝔶 𝔱𝔥𝔞𝔱 𝔩𝔢𝔞𝔯- ned and godly Martyr, I. 𝔥𝔬𝔬𝔭𝔢𝔯, 𝔰𝔬𝔪𝔢𝔱𝔦𝔪𝔢 𝔅𝔶- shop *of Glocester in his* 𝔩𝔦𝔣𝔢 𝔱𝔦𝔪𝔢.

Imprinted at London
by Christopher Barker, Printer
to the Queene's most excellent
Maiestie.

[1 Ed. 1584, 'fayth.']

[It appears from Bishop Tanner's list of Hooper's works that the first edition of the 'Brief and clear Confession' was published in 1550. The editor however has not been able to meet with a copy of this edition; but has compared the editions of 1581 and 1584 (both printed by Christopher Barker), which differ in nothing but spelling.]

THE DIVISION OF THE CREED.

This Creed following, being made by the reverend father John Hooper, is divided into five principal parts. The first whereof entreateth of God the Father: the second of God the Son: the third of God the Holy Ghost: the fourth of the Catholic Church: the fifth and last part entreateth of the benefits or fruits which we receive by the same faith, which he maketh in number three; the first is the forgiveness of sins; the second is the resurrection of the flesh; the third and last fruit is life everlasting. Of these five parts he hath made an hundred several articles: the first part containeth 14: the second, 27: the third, 5: the fourth, 41: the fifth and last part containeth thirteen articles; the contents of which articles are handled as followeth.

(∴)

A brief and clear confession of the Christian faith, containing an hundred articles, according to the order of the Creed of the Apostles.

---

1. *I believe in God, the Father Almighty, Maker of heaven and earth.*

THE FIRST ARTICLE.

I BELIEVE in one God only, one in essence and substance, three in person; the Father, the Son, and the Holy Ghost. I believe in the Father, as the original and beginning of all things, as well visible as invisible: of whom also they depend, as well in their being, as also in their conservation: and he dependeth upon none but on himself, being eternal and everlasting, without end or beginning.

I believe in the Son, as the divine word and wisdom of the Father, which is eternally and before all worlds engendered of the Father, of his proper substance and nature; because in him shineth his shape and proper image, which otherwise is invisible unto mortal man.

I believe in the Holy Ghost, as a virtue and eternal power, which neither is made, nor created, neither engendered, but proceeding of the Father and of the Son eternally, even as a love proceeding from both persons.

THE SECOND ARTICLE.

I believe that these three Persons are of one and the selfsame essence and substance, nature, authority, power, will, goodness, wisdom, and eternity: and that these three are but one spiritual substance, eternal, without end or beginning, true, good, just, merciful, of a sovereign power and wisdom, having and containing in itself all goodness, not needing anything.

The Third Article.

I believe that this God, which is one in essence and three in person, ought only to be served, honoured, feared, loved, worshipped, and to be called upon in all our necessities, as he that only can and will provide therefore, and none other. And therefore I say and confess that I believe in one God only, that is to say, that I knowledge and receive him for one only Lord, Master, and Saviour: of whom proceedeth all that is good in me; by whom I can do all things; and without whom I can do nothing. In him only do I set mine affiance and set mine heart, hoping that he, assisting me with his Holy Spirit, shall be with me against all men, and that he will deliver me from all perils and dangers, through his grace and mercy, without any merits of mine own; and that he shall minister to me all things necessary, as well for my soul as body, even like a good Father, as he hath promised by his holy word.

The Fourth Article.

I believe that the same God Almighty hath of nothing created from the beginning both heaven and earth, and all things in them contained; that is to say, all things as well heavenly as earthly, visible as invisible, reasonable as unreasonable, sensible as insensible: the which he doth entertain, lead, guide, and govern by his divine wisdom; without whose providence nothing cometh to pass either in this world or in the other.

The Fifth Article.

I believe that the same God, the Father, the Son, and Holy Ghost, after that he had created all things, did create and shape man to his own image and likeness; that is to say, immortal, good, just, true, wise, merciful, and perfect in all things; making him partaker of the goodness, justice, and other perfections of God, having a will that could agree in all things unto the will of his Lord: but all that through grace, without any kind of merit.

The Sixth Article.

I believe also that, as the Lord hath created all things heavenly and earthly for the service of man, and to the end that by his creatures he might come to the knowledge of the Creator; even so also hath he formed and made man for himself, that of him and by him he might be known, loved, feared, served, and honoured, which is the greatest good thing that is or can be in man; and that in him might shine the image of divine virtues and perfections through good works, the which God hath ordained, because we should walk in them unto his honour and praise, and to the confusion of the adversary; and that by this mean the fall of the angels might be repaired, and that man might possess the everlasting kingdom made and prepared for him before the foundations of the world were laid.

The Seventh Article.

I believe that the same man was ordained of the Lord God a master and ruler over all his creatures: the which thing he hath lost through his sin, as well for his own part, as also for all his posterity: the which rule and lordship, I believe, doth chiefly appertain unto Jesus Christ, verily God and man, and to those unto whom he will communicate the same, as unto his own faithful, and not unto the infidels and damned.

The Eighth Article.

I believe that the first man, through the craft and subtlety of Satan, did slide and fall from the excellency wherein the Lord had created him; consenting, through his own free will (which at that time he had), unto the subtle suggestion of the serpent, whereby he lost the graces that the Lord had given him; in such sort, that of wise he became foolish, of just unjust, of true a liar, of perfect altogether unperfect: having from thenceforth a will wholly corrupted, which neither could nor would agree with the will of God, but altogether with the will of the devil, the world, the 1 1, and sin; which could do nothing of himself but evil, seeing that he is altogether carnal, bond, captive, and sold under sin. This is the free, yea, to say more truly, the bond-will that man hath in this present life.

The Ninth Article.

I believe that this disorder and corruption of nature was not only in Adam, because of his sin, but is also in all men generally, which come of him (Jesus Christ only excepted); and that in such sort, that all men after their own nature are corrupt, unjust, liars, ignorant, unkind, and imperfect in all things, and have no power of their own nature to do, think, speak, or will anything that may please God, until that they be regenerate and renewed by the Spirit of the Lord.

The Tenth Article.

I believe that this corruption of nature, otherwise called original sin, is the fountain and root of all other sins: for the which all the miseries and adversities that we endure in this present life, as well in body as soul, do come unto us; yea, and in the end double death, that is to say, both of body and soul. These be the fruits and rewards of sin. But although the same be due and common to all men generally, nevertheless the Lord through his mercy hath reserved to himself a certain number (which are only known to himself), the which he hath drawn from this corrupt heap, and hath sanctified and cleansed the same in the blood of his Son Jesus Christ, and by means thereof hath made them vessels of election and honour, apt unto all good works.

The Eleventh Article.

I believe that the Father in Jesu Christ his Son through the Holy Ghost hath elected and chosen those that are his own, according to his good will, before the foundations of the world were laid, whom he hath predestinate unto eternal life; that thereby they might be his children adoptives, over whom he hath without comparison a much greater care, than the best father can have over the best child in the world: for he suffereth not that any thing shall come to pass, either on high in heaven, or beneath on earth, which shall not be for their good and great profit.

The Twelfth Article.

I believe that the Father, through his Son, with the Holy Ghost, hath always from the beginning intended to restore man: unto whom, after he had sinned, he shewed himself, promising unto him that blessed Seed, by whom the head of the serpent should be trodden down, and by whom the faithful should receive blessing. By this promise (which hath since been oftentimes ratified and confirmed to the holy fathers) man (which otherwise had despaired in sin) is relieved, holpen, comforted, and clothed with hope, even unto the full performing thereof.

The Thirteenth Article.

I believe also that after this promise the Lord hath prescribed and given the law of the commandments to man, promising life to the observers thereof, and death to the transgressors of the same. And he gave them, not to the end that man should seek justification, salvation, or life therein; but for the policy, peace, and tranquillity of his people, for the defence of the good, for the chastening and punishing of the wicked, and to preserve each one in his office: but especially[1] that thereby man might the better know himself, his disease, his poverty, and imperfection; and by mean thereof to take an occasion to humble himself before this lawgiver, and to seek remedy, salvation, and life in some other, that is to say, in the holy promised Seed, which is Jesus Christ. For this cause the law is called a schoolmaster to come to Christ, the which also serveth us for a glass to know our sins by, and to increase the same knowledge in us. Likewise it serveth us for an accuser, to accuse us before the Lord, and for a severe and cruel judge, to declare the wrath and judgment of God over us, and his condemnation unto eternal death; and by this mean to make us afraid, and to bring us unto despair, until we be comforted by the gospel through faith in Jesus Christ, whereby we are delivered from all these causes. These are the offices of the law, the which are turned into our good through faith in the gospel, the which hath other offices, and clean contrary. For the rest, I confess that the law of the Lord is good, just, holy, and perfect: and where the same doth not bring us unto perfection, it is not long of[2] itself, but of us, which are altogether imperfect, and can in no wise accomplish the same, no, not to touch it with our little finger.

The Fourteenth Article.

I believe and confess Jesus Christ to be the fulness, the end, and accomplishment of the law, to the justification of all

[1 Specially, 1584.]
[2 Long of: along of, by the fault of.]

that believe, through whom and by whom only all the promises of the Father be accomplished, yea, even to the uttermost; the which also alone hath perfectly satisfied the law in that which no other amongst men could perform; forsomuch as the law doth command things impossible, the which nevertheless man must accomplish, not by working, but through believing: for so is the law accomplished, through faith, and not through works; and by this means shall man find the righteousness of faith to be available before the Lord, and not the righteousness of works, the which leadeth nothing unto perfection.

As concerning the first point of my faith, this is that which I believe of the Father, and the things that are made by him, and consequently of the Holy Trinity, and also of the soul of man. Now let us come to the second point, which is of the Son of God, and of the things done by him, especially of the restoring and repairing again of man.

2. *And in Jesus Christ, his only Son, our Lord; which was conceived by the Holy Ghost, born of the Virgin Mary; suffered under Pontius Pilate, was crucified, dead, and buried; he descended into hell; the third day he rose again from the dead; he ascended into heaven, and sitteth on the right hand of God the Father Almighty: from thence he shall come to judge the quick and the dead.*

The Fifteenth Article.

I believe that Jesus Christ is verily God and verily man, having two natures comprehended in one person: a nature divine, after the which he is the only natural Son of God, equal with the Father in all things; and a nature human, after the which he is very man, in all things like unto us, sin excepted.

The Sixteenth Article.

I believe that Jesus Christ, the Son of God, in the fulness of the time appointed of the Father from the beginning, was sent into the world by the Father, and was made perfect man, and was conceived in the womb of a woman being a pure virgin, called Mary, of her proper substance, and of her proper blood; so that he was found a perfect man, descending of the seed of Adam, Noe, Abraham, Isaac, Jacob, David, and other fathers, unto whom the promise was made.

THE SEVENTEENTH ARTICLE.

I believe also that all this was done by the working of the Holy Ghost, without the work of man, to the end that all that was wrought therein might be holy and without spot, pure and clean; and that thereby our conception might be made clean and holy, which of itself is altogether spotted and defiled with sin.

THE EIGHTEENTH ARTICLE.

I believe that Jesus Christ was born of the Virgin Mary without any manner of sin, and without breach of her virginity; so that by his pure and holy nativity he hath purified and made holy ours, which of itself is altogether unclean and defiled with sin. In this nativity of Christ I see and consider the first estate and condition of man, with his fall, which was the cause of Christ his coming into the world. Likewise in this I see and consider the favour and inestimable love of God the Father, which hath presented and given his only Son to serve us. I see also and consider in this nativity the charity of the Son, which hath abased and humbled himself to lift us up, became poor to make us rich, became bond to make us free, and became the Son of man to make us the children of God, and heirs of eternal life: by whose coming the nature of man is repaired and made noble, and man, that was lost and destroyed, was thereby relieved and set in his perfection, and hath recovered all that he hath lost through sin, yea, and more. By the same mean also all the treasures, graces, and blessings of the Lord, are given and communicated unto man; but all this through grace, without any merits.

THE NINETEENTH ARTICLE.

We must conceive Christ spiritually, and so bring him forth in our mouths and actions as occasion shall serve.

I believe also and confess by the holy scriptures another conception and birth of Jesus Christ, which is spiritual; the which, I say, is of no less dignity than the first: the which is, that every one that is faithful ought to conceive into his heart and spirit Jesus Christ, through a true and lively faith, and to bring him forth by open confessing of him with his mouth as often and whensoever it shall be needful. I do esteem this conception and nativity to be so necessary to salvation, that if the Virgin Mary had not more blessedly borne Jesus Christ in her heart and spirit than in her belly, her carnal motherhood would have profited her little. By and for this cause are we called mothers, brethren, and sisters of Jesus Christ.

The Twentieth Article.

I believe that the same Jesus Christ is verily Christ, that is to say, the Messias, anointed by the Holy Ghost, because he was the very King, the Prophet, and great Sacrificer, that should sacrifice for all that believe; the which also is promised in the law, and is the same of whom all the prophets have spoken. This anointing of Christ is not corporal, of a material and visible oil, as was that of the kings, priests, and prophets in times past; but it is spiritual, of an invisible oil, which is the grace and gifts of the Holy Ghost, wherewith he is replenished above all others. So that this anointing is descended even unto us, which have felt and proved the sweetness thereof: and by it also we bear the name of Christians, that is to say, anointed.

The Twenty-first Article.

I believe that this sacrificing of Jesus Christ was not Levitical or carnal, to immolate, offer up, and to sacrifice beasts, kine, and other sensible things, as did Aaron and his successors; but spiritual, to offer and sacrifice himself, that is to say, his body and blood, for the remission of the sins of the whole world. Even as likewise his kingdom is not of this world, carnal, but spiritual; which consisteth in the guiding and governing of his own by his Holy Spirit, over whom he reigneth by his word, and that to the destruction of all his adversaries, which are sin, death, hell, Satan, and all infidels, wicked, and reprobate.

The Twenty-second Article.

I believe that Jesus Christ hath verily exercised these three offices, that is to say, of a prophet, of a king, of a sacrificer, not only in this world, being a mortal man as we are; but also that he exerciseth yet daily the same in heaven before the face of the Father, where he sitteth and appeareth continually for us, and from thence by his Holy Spirit doth teach, help, maintain, and defend his own: and therefore is he called a prophet, a king, and a great sacrificator, after the order of Melchizedek, that is to say, eternal, and not after the order of Aaron, which had his end with the law.

THE TWENTY-THIRD ARTICLE.

Our Saviour Jesus Christ preached here in this life in Judea about the space of three years or thereabout.

I believe that the same Jesus Christ (after that he had preached the gospel in the country of Judæa and Galilee, by the space of three years or thereabout, and declared himself to be the natural Son of God, as well by his marvellous works, as by his words, and the writings of the prophets) was unjustly and falsely accused by the priests; whom when they had taken, and in their council unjustly had condemned him to death, they brought him bound to Pilate, the provost then at Hierusalem; who, at the instance of the said priests, did unjustly, wrongfully, and without cause, condemn him to death, and that the most horrible and slanderous death that could be imagined or devised, that is to say, to be put on the cross, crucified between two thieves, as if he had been their prince and captain; the which thing he suffered and endured willingly and innocently, without deserving the same. For otherwise could he not have satisfied for us, neither could his cross have profited us.

THE TWENTY-FOURTH ARTICLE.

What is meant by Christ's descending into hell.

I believe also that while he was upon the said cross, dying and giving up his spirit unto God his Father, he descended into hell; that is to say, he did verily taste and feel the great distress and heaviness of death, and likewise the pains and torments of hell, that is to say, the great wrath and severe judgment of God upon him, even as if God had utterly forsaken him, yea, as though God had been his extreme enemy; so that he was constrained with loud voice to cry, "My God, my God, why hast thou forsaken me?" This is simply my understanding of Christ his descending into hell. And besides, I know well that this article hath not from the beginning been in the Creed, and that many others have otherwise both understood and interpreted it; which esteem that Christ verily and in deed descended into hell, to the place of the damned, alleging the text of St Peter; the which I confess is yet covered and hid from me. The Lord vouchsafe to open the gate unto us, and to give us an entrance into such mysteries!

[1 Pet. iii. 19, 20.]

The Twenty-fifth Article.

I believe that all this was done, not for himself, which never committed sin, in whose mouth was never found deceit nor lie; but for the love of us poor and miserable sinners, whose place he occupied upon the cross, as a pledge, or one that represented the person of all the sinners that ever were, be now, or shall be unto the world's end. And because they through their sins have deserved to feel and taste of the extreme pains of death, to be forsaken of God and of all creatures, to feel the wrath and severe judgment of God upon them; Christ, which was their pledge, satisfying for them upon the cross, hath felt and endured all the same, and that altogether to make us free, to deliver us from all these pains, from the wrath and judgment of God, from condemnation and eternal death. And I do clearly reject and esteem as fables all the limbos of the fathers, and of young children, purgatory, and such other like, to be follies, mockeries, and abuses, which are invented and found out by man, without the word of the Lord. For I neither believe nor receive more than two places in the world to come; that is to say, heaven for the faithful and elect, with the angels; and hell for the infidels and reprobate, with the devils.

The Twenty-sixth Article.

I believe and consider this death and passion, even as I do all other mysteries of Jesus Christ, not only as touching the history, as a pattern and example to follow, as was that of the holy men and women which are dead for the Lord's quarrel; but also principally as touching the cause, fruits, and uses thereof, thereby to know the greatness of my sins, the grace and mercy of the Father, and the charity of the Son, by whom we are reconciled unto God, delivered from the tyranny of the devil, and restored to the liberty of the Spirit. This is the glass without spot, to teach us to know our filthiness, the laver or clear fountain to wash and cleanse us, the infinite treasure to satisfy all our creditors: of whom and by whom only the divine justice is fully satisfied for all the sins of all that have been, be now, or shall be unto the end of the world. And therefore I do believe and confess that Christ his condemnation is mine absolution; that his crucifying is my deliverance; his descending into hell is mine ascending into heaven; his death is my life; his blood is my cleansing and purging, by whom only I am washed, purified, and cleansed from all my sins: so that I neither receive neither believe any other purgatory, either in this world or in the other, whereby I may be purged, but only the blood of Jesus Christ, by the which all are purged and made clean for ever.

The Twenty-seventh Article.

I believe that Jesus Christ by the sacrifice of his body, which he offered upon the tree of the cross, hath defaced and destroyed sin, death, and the devil, with all his kingdom; and hath wholly performed the work of our salvation, and hath abolished and made an end of all other sacrifices; so that from thenceforth there is none other propitiatory sacrifice, either for the living or the dead, to be looked for or sought for, than the same: for by this one only oblation hath he consecrated for ever all those that are sanctified.

The Twenty-eighth Article.

I believe that the holy Supper of the Lord is not a sacrifice, but only a remembrance and commemoration of this holy sacrifice of Jesus Christ. Therefore it ought not to be worshipped as God, neither as Christ therein contained; who must be worshipped in faith only, without all corruptible elements. Likewise I believe and confess that the popish mass is the invention and ordinance of man, a sacrifice of Antichrist, and a forsaking of the sacrifice of Jesus Christ, that is to say, of his death and passion; and that it is a stinking and infected sepulchre, which hideth and covereth the merit of the blood of Christ; and therefore ought the mass to be abolished, and the holy Supper of the Lord to be restored and set in his perfection again.

The Twenty-ninth Article.

I believe also that, as the prophet Jonas was in the whale's belly (which is a place of corruption) three days and three nights without being corrupted, and the third day came out of him alive without any manner of hurt; even so Jesus Christ, after he was dead, was laid and put in a new sepulchre (which is a place of corruption), in the which he was three days and three nights, not touched with any kind of infection of filthiness, or corruption; but continued in his perfection, to declare the virtue of his blood, to accomplish the writings of the holy prophets, and to verify the truth, as well of his body, as of his death: with whom I believe that the law was buried, abrogated, and abolished, as touching the faithful; not as the acquitting of an obligation, whereby they should be no more bound to live and walk therein, but only as concerning condemnation; that is to say, that the transgression of the law condemneth them not before the judgment-seat of God, because of their faith which they have in Jesus Christ. And therefore within one sepulchre I do comprehend three things to be buried; that is to say, Christ, the law, and all the faithful, which ought to be crucified and buried with Christ through the mortification of their flesh.

THE THIRTIETH ARTICLE.

I believe that, as Jesus Christ was put to death for our sins, so also he rose again the third day for our justification unto everlasting life; wherein he hath openly declared himself both God and man, obtaining the victory over all his adversaries, and hath confounded and beaten down all his enemies, that is to say, the world, sin, death, hell, and Satan, not for himself, but for us that believe in him, knowing that his victory is ours, and that in him and by him we overcome the self-same enemies, obtaining the victory over them, unto the honour of the Lord and our great profit.

THE THIRTY-FIRST ARTICLE.

I believe and consider this resurrection of Jesus Christ not only as an history, as was that of Lazarus and other such like, which miraculously were raised up by the virtue of the Lord; but also as the example and cause efficient of my rising again, and as the earnest and first-fruits of the general resurrection of all that believe: that, as Jesus Christ was raised up the third day after his death unto eternal life through his divine virtue, even so by the same virtue I hope one day to be raised up in body and soul unto eternal life, after that I have here in this world been raised up in spirit through lively and true faith in newness of life, mortifying and crucifying the flesh with the affections and concupiscences of the world, the which ought to be dead and crucified to us, and we to it. For we are buried with Christ in his death through baptism; to the end that, as he is risen from death by the glory of the Father without dying any more, even so we should walk in newness of life without serving of sin any more, searching always principally for the things that are on high, heavenly and eternal, and forsaking the earthly and transitory things of the world, knowing that we have not here an abiding city, but that we must seek for that which is to come.

The Thirty-second Article.

I believe and confess that Jesus Christ the fortieth day after his resurrection visibly and before all his apostles did ascend into heaven, that is to say, in the majesty of his Father in glory and eternal felicity, in the which he was before he came into this miserable world to become man, yea, even before the foundation of the world was laid, that is to say, from everlasting.

The Thirty-third Article.

I believe that he is ascended into heaven to accomplish and to finish all things, and to open heaven for us, that we might ascend after him, and follow him as our head, to be eternally knit with him in glory, the which thing here we begin through faith. In like manner he hath done the same for the benefit of his church, that he might send unto his apostles that Comforter that he promised them, by the which they were comforted, instructed, and guided in all truth; and thereby is his church supported, maintained, and defended against all the blasts of Satan and all the gates of hell.

The Thirty-fourth Article.

I believe also that he is ascended into heaven to be our patron, intercessor, mediator, and advocate; and that he now appeareth for us before the face of the Father, obtaining for us grace and abundance of all good things; in such sort, that I neither knowledge nor receive any other mediator betwixt God and man, neither any other advocate or intercessor before God the Father, than his only Son Jesus Christ our Lord. To him do I resort; with him do I hold myself contented, and none other do I search for, neither will

I; fearing to blaspheme the name of God by giving that unto the creature that appertaineth only to the Creator, and to the servant that which only appertaineth unto[1] the master.

The Thirty-fifth Article.

I believe that all they which demand, seek for, or receive any other mediator, intercessor, or advocate towards God the Father, than Jesus Christ his Son, the same blasphemeth against God, and doeth dishonour unto Jesus Christ, and unto the saints by whom he prayeth. For as God the Father will be known, served, loved, feared, and honoured in his Son, and by his only Son Jesus Christ, and not by any other means, even so will he be prayed unto and called upon in his and by his only Son Jesus Christ, and none otherwise. In this I will neither dispraise, nor think or speak evil of the blessed saints, which are in heaven with the Lord; but I will have them in honour, and reverence them as the faithful saints of the Lord, as the temple of the Holy Ghost, and as the true members of Christ; and have them as glasses and patterns before mine eyes, to follow them, as well in their honest life and good conversation, as also in their faithful and holy doctrine. And as concerning them or by them I do understand none other thing, knowing that all my good, my help, and succour, proceedeth of God only, by the mean of Jesus Christ alone, which hath made the saints worthy of his glory by his only grace; by the which also I believe he will make me worthy with them to be their companion in glory, that we altogether should give unto him only all honour, praise, and glory for evermore.

The Thirty-sixth Article.

I believe that the same Jesus Christ is set on the right hand of God the Father Almighty; that is to say, that he reigneth in one and the same majesty and equal power with God his Father, by the which he so governeth his own unto the world's end, that the power of none adversary can annoy them without his permission and will. I believe also that the Father hath made him Lord and ruler over all creatures, as well heavenly as earthly, giving unto him all power over heaven and earth; and that he hath lift him up

[1 To, 1584.]

above all rule, power, and lordship, and above every name that is named, not only in this world, but also in the world to come; and hath made all things subject under his feet, and hath appointed him over all things to be the head of his church, which is his body, Eph. i.; and therefore I neither receive neither acknowledge any other head of the church, but only Jesus Christ, which hath given his blood to wash away the filthiness and to heal the wounds thereof, and the same to preserve, nourish, defend, and govern by his Holy Spirit. The same is the only head and foundation of the church, whereon every one ought to build according to his vocation.

The Thirty-seventh Article.

I believe that Jesus Christ is ascended into heaven, and that he is there corporally, that is to say, in flesh, in body, and in soul, after such sort, that he neither is nor can, after the same mean and fashion, be here beneath on earth with us: forasmuch as his body, although it be glorious, cannot be in divers and many places at one time, but be so in one place, after the nature of a glorified body, that it cannot be in another; otherwise it should not be a true and natural body, but fantastical, that is to say, a thing apparent and not in deed, which is false and wholly against our faith. And therefore do I say and confess that the true and natural body of Christ is in heaven, and that from thence he shall not come, until he hath made all his enemies his footstool, and then shall he come to judge the quick and dead.

The Thirty-eighth Article.

I believe that when the number of the elect children of God shall be accomplished, the Lord Jesus, in the self-same body in the which he suffered and was crucified, with the which he rose and ascended into heaven, in the self-same shall he come with great power and majesty visibly in a cloud, even as he ascended, and that to judge both the quick and the dead, and shall render unto every one according to justice; unto the good that he shall find amongst them according to their goodness, and unto the evil according to their wickedness. This judgment shall be general; that is to say, all shall be called and personally summoned thereunto by the voice of an angel; at the which all shall appear, as well the good as the evil, the elect as the reproved[1]; to the end that every one may render an account and reckoning before the judgment-seat of Christ of all that hath been done by them in this world, whether it be good or evil, yea, even of their idle words, the which they esteem no sin. Then shall be saved all those that are found written in the book of life.

The Thirty-ninth Article.

I believe that then shall be made the total and last separation of the good from the evil, of the elect from the reprobate; the which now are all mingled together, as the good and the evil fish in one net, the chaff and the corn, and the cockle with the wheat: but when the harvest cometh, he which hath the fan in his hand shall make a separation, and shall gather the corn into his garner, but the chaff and cockle he shall cast into the fire, to burn eternally. Then shall perfectly be declared and known the justice and mercy of the Lord, and likewise the fruit of the cross and blood of Jesus Christ, the which thing now we know only but in part: but then the good and elect shall know the Father, upon whom they have builded their hope, and shall not be confounded; and in like manner the wicked shall know the Father, against whom they have stumbled, and whom they have refused, contemned, and despised, and shall be confounded. Then shall the Lord make an end of his office and ministry: for his mystical body shall then be wholly finished and accomplished with all his members, and he shall render up his kingdom and his espouse, which is the church, unto God his Father, altogether glorious, irreprehensible, and acceptable, without spot or wrinkle. Then shall perfectly be overcome, destroyed, and confounded Satan and hell, sin and death, and all other adversaries of Christ, the which presently do yet exercise tyranny upon all his members, and hold them under their claws, chains, and bonds. But then we, as people ravished with joy, shall say this word which is written, "O death, where is thy victory? Thanks be unto God, which hath given us victory, through Jesus Christ our Lord."

The Fortieth Article.

I believe that this marvellous, terrible, and fearful judg-

[1 reproved: reprobate.]

ment unto the evil, wicked, and reprobate, is very much desired, and of great consolation unto the good, the faithful, and the elect; because that then their whole redemption, that is to say, of the body, shall be made an end of, and they shall receive the fruit of their labours. Then their innocency shall openly be declared and known to all the world, and they shall see the vengeance and condemnation of the wicked, which have used them tyrannously, afflicted and tormented them in this world; whose iniquity shall be manifested by the Lord, and shall be clearly known of all, to their great confusion, and to the honour and glory of the righteous children of God, the which shall be in peace and perfect tranquillity, and shall have full rejoicing and fruition of all that he hath promised and prepared for all those that love him, the which no eye hath seen, no ear hath heard, neither can be comprehended by the heart of man. Therefore do I abide this great day of retribution with a great desire, as the same which shall bring and shew unto me the self-same good thing.

The Forty-first Article.

I believe that we shall not all die, but that we shall be changed in a moment: that is to say, that in this last day and judgment general some shall be found alive, the which died not, neither shall they die, as concerning the separation of the body from the soul, but shall continue alive eternally; to the end that Christ may be known to be Lord and Judge of the living and dead, and that his grace and merits may be found greater than the sin of Adam. For "as sin hath reigned unto death, so likewise must grace reign through Jesus Christ unto eternal life." The same nevertheless shall be changed and transformed from corruption unto incorruption, from mortality unto immortality, from contempt and ignominy unto glory, after such sort, that they shall be made partakers of all the gifts, graces, and benefits, the which the Lord shall give unto those that before were dead in him: the which shall not be before the others, but all together shall be taken up in the clouds and in the air, and shall all together be with the Lord.

This is the second point of my faith, touching Jesus Christ, the second person in Trinity, and of his restoring and repairing of man. Let us now come to the third point, which is of the Holy Ghost, by whom man (being restored) is maintained and preserved in his integrity and perfection.

3. *I believe in the Holy Ghost, the holy Catholic Church, the communion of Saints, the forgiveness of sins, the resurrection of the body, and the life everlasting. Amen.*

The Forty-second Article.

I believe that the Holy Ghost is a divine person, distinct from the Father and the Son, proceeding from them both, in and through all things equal and co-eternal with them; by the which Holy Ghost the church hath always been, is now, and shall be ruled, guided, directed, and governed unto the end of the world: by whom also the saints, patriarchs, prophets, and apostles of our Lord Jesus Christ have spoken. And therefore I do neither believe nor receive any other vicar or lieutenant to Christ upon earth within his church, than this Holy Ghost, which cannot be received of the wicked.

The Forty-third Article.

I believe that the Holy Ghost is the pledge and earnest of our heavenly heritage, by the which we be assured, ascertained, and certainly persuaded in our consciences that we be the children of God, and brethren adoptives to Jesus Christ, and consequently coheirs of eternal life. The same Holy Ghost also is the finger of God, the which imprinteth in our hearts and spirits the faith of these things aforesaid. It sealeth and confirmeth the promises of the Lord within our hearts through his goodness and grace, because we should in no wise doubt.

The Forty-fourth Article.

I believe that this Holy Spirit dwelling in us through his grace and virtue doth regenerate us into a newness and change of living, mortifying in us all that is of us and of the old man, of the flesh and of the world, and quickening all that is his in us: so that we live not thenceforth after our own lusts, but according to the will of God. Which Holy Ghost also worketh in us all good works, and doth reprove, rebuke, and condemn the world of sin, of righteousness, and judgment.

The Forty-fifth Article.

I believe that the Holy Ghost is the teacher of the ignorant, which teacheth, guideth, and leadeth us unto the knowledge of the truth; and by it only are we brought and delivered out of darkness, and set in the perfect light. Likewise I believe that it is the comforter of the poor, afflicted, and persecuted; and in all their troubles, vexations, and adversities doth so help, strengthen, comfort, and assist all such, that it will not suffer them to despair, as do the wicked and reprobate, but maketh them to taste and feel the sweetness, goodness, and mercy of God the Father, which by persecution and divers tribulations leadeth his own unto eternal glory.

The Forty-sixth Article.

I believe that this Holy Ghost is the Spirit of life, which quickeneth all other spirits, as well heavenly as earthly, and that the same only of itself is holy, and that all others by it are made holy: so that, if any spirits be holy (as there be) either in heaven or in earth, they are none otherwise holy but by the holiness of the same Holy Ghost: and that is the cause why I believe in him; that is to say, for that cause I put my whole faith, hope, trust, and affiance in him, even as I have said before of the Father and the Son.

This is the third point of my faith, which is concerning the Holy Ghost, the third person in the Holy Trinity; by the which Holy Ghost, after that we are made by the Father, and repaired and restored by the Son, we are maintained and governed unto the end. There remaineth now to entreat of the fourth point of my faith, which is concerning the church, and of the things that concern the same.

4. *I believe the holy Catholic Church, the communion of Saints.*

The Forty-seventh Article.

I believe and confess one only catholic and universal church, which is an holy congregation and assembly of all faithful believers, which are chosen and predestinate unto everlasting life, before the foundations of the world were laid: of whose number I count myself, and believe that I am, through the only grace and mercy of the Father, and by the merits of my good Lord and Master Jesus Christ, and not by means of my good works and merits, which indeed are none.

The Forty-eighth Article.

I believe that this church is invisible to the eye of man, and is only to God known; and that the same church is not set, compassed, and limited within a certain place or bounds, but is scattered and spread abroad throughout all the world; but yet coupled together in heart, will, and spirit by the bond of faith and charity, having and altogether knowledging one only God, one only head and mediator Jesus Christ, one faith, one law, one baptism, one spiritual table, wherein one meat and one spiritual drink is ministered to them unto the end of the world. This church containeth in it all the righteous and chosen people, from the first righteous man unto the last that shall be found righteous in the end of the world: and therefore do I call it universal. For as touching the visible church, which is the congregation of the good and of the wicked, of the chosen and of the reprobate, and generally of all those which say they believe in Christ, I do not believe that to be the church, because that church is seen of the eye, and the faith thereof is in visible things.

The Forty-ninth Article.

I believe that this invisible church is the field of the Lord God, wherein is neither darnel nor cockle. It is the house and dwelling-place of the Holy Ghost, and within that church is neither Cain, Judas, neither the wicked rich glutton. That church also is the fold of Christ, wherein is no stinking and infected beasts, but all clean and undefiled sheep and lambs, which bring forth their fruits in due time and season. The same church is the body of Christ, wherein there is never a rotten, corrupt, or infected member. It is the spouse of Christ, which is pure and clean, without wrinkle and without spot. It is holy and without blame, cleansed and sanctified in the blood and by the word of her Head and well-beloved Spouse, Jesus Christ: and for that cause they can in no wise perish, which by lively faith are grafted therein.

The Fiftieth Article.

I believe that the gifts and graces of the Holy Ghost are scattered and given unto every member of the same church, not so much for their particular profit and commodity, as for the general profit and commodity of the whole congregation and church, and that through grace wholly, without any merit, according to the good pleasure and providence of God, to some more, to some less; and that to the end we should know that one hath need of another, and that we should be ready to help one another in all necessities, as well bodily as spiritually, even as it becometh members of one body.

THE FIFTY-FIRST ARTICLE.

I believe the communion of Saints: that is to say, I believe that all whatsoever our Lord God giveth in this world, whether it be benefits and blessings that concern the body or the spirit, he giveth the same singularly to the profit and commodity of the whole church, and therefore ought the same to be distributed and communicated to all that are faithful, but chiefly to those that are in necessity; that, like as we do communicate and are knit in one God, one faith, one law, one baptism, and be partakers of one spiritual table; even so we may communicate and be partakers together of and in those things which do proceed and come unto us by means of the aforesaid things. For otherwise we cannot be Christians or faithful stewards of Christ. Here utterly I renounce and abhor the Anabaptists' manner of making common goods, wives, and such other like things, and only do I allow the apostles' making of things common, which, having and possessing any goods privately, used to distribute thereof to every one, according as the same had need, and as necessity required.

THE FIFTY-SECOND ARTICLE.

I believe that this church is like unto the ark of Noah, within the which is safety and life, and without the same is but death, decay, and destruction. For as Christ is and doth reign in his church, even so Satan is and doth reign in and through all that are out of that church: the which true church is maintained and upholden by the Spirit of Christ, is ruled and governed by his holy word, and is nourished and fed with his holy sacraments. That church shall always have enemies, and shall still be tormented in the sea of this world with the thunderings of Antichrist, and by the wounds[1]

[[1] So in ed. 1581 and 1584; probably a mistake for *winds*.]

and tempests of Satan: for all the gates of hell do arm and set out themselves against this church. But in these waves she shall not be drowned, but shall abide for ever, because she hath a good defence and foundation, which is Jesus Christ the righteous. And for this cause I call her the church militant, which waiteth for the triumph of those that be blessed, which are where as is nothing but peace, joy, and everlasting consolation.

The Fifty-third Article.

I believe that the Lord God hath given us three principal signs and marks by the which we may know this his church, that is to say, the word, the sacraments, and discipline. I call that only the word, which was revealed by the Holy Ghost unto the holy patriarchs, prophets, and apostles of Jesus Christ; the which word is contained within the canonical books of the old and new testament; by the which word we are made clean, and thereby do receive the self-same thing and as much as we do by the sacraments; that is to say, Jesus Christ by his word, which is the word of faith, giveth and communicateth himself unto us, as well as by the sacraments, albeit it be by another manner and fashion.

The Fifty-fourth Article.

I believe that the same word of God is of a far greater authority than the church; the which word only doth sufficiently shew and teach us all those things that in any wise concern our salvation, both what we ought to do, and what to leave undone. The same word of God is the true pattern and perfect rule, after the which all faithful people ought to govern and order their lives, without turning either to the right hand or to the left hand, without changing anything thereof, without putting to it or taking from it, knowing that all the works of God are perfect, but most chiefly his word.

The Fifty-fifth Article.

I believe that, as only Jesus Christ amongst all men is holy and true, and that all others are sinners and liars; even so likewise the only doctrine of the same Jesus Christ is holy and true, and all other doctrines are unpure and false. This doctrine of Jesus Christ is a well, a fountain of life, a lamp or pillar of fire to guide us, the bread of the soul, and the power of God unto salvation to all that believe. And therefore whatsoever happeneth, the same ought only to be advanced, preached, heard, understood, and received of all the world, to the comfort and salvation of those that believe, and to the greater damnation of the unbelievers, the wicked, and reprobate, that believe not. For, as the manna in the desert was to some sour, and to other some a good and pleasant meat; and as Christ is to some a stumbling-stone to be offended at, and is appointed for the fall of the wicked, and the rising up of the godly; even so the word of the gospel to some is a savour of death unto death, and to other some a savour of life unto life. The which word of the gospel I receive and take only to be my guide, and according to the same to die and to live.

The Fifty-sixth Article.

I believe that the reading of the same word and gospel ought not, neither can it be prohibited and forbidden from any manner of person, of what estate, sort, or condition soever the same be of; but it ought to be common unto all the world, as well to men as women; yea, and that in a vulgar or common language, which all do understand, because it is ordained and appointed for all. And likewise the promises of God, which are therein contained, do appertain unto all. And therefore Antichrist and his members do exercise great and cruel tyranny upon the faithful children of God, as well in that they take from them and utterly do forbid them to read the same word, and instead thereof set before them dreams, lies, canons, and damnable traditions; as also because, upon pain of deadly sin and eternal damnation, they both forbid and command things that indeed are but indifferent: which manner of theirs is the only note and mark to know Antichrist by.

The Fifty-seventh Article.

I believe that this holy doctrine of the gospel in the very time by God appointed was confirmed and approved by heavenly miracles, as well by Jesus Christ himself, the prophets, and apostles, as also by other good and faithful ministers of the same gospel; and that after such a sort, that for the confirming thereof there is now no more need of new miracles; but rather we must content ourselves with that is done, and simply and plainly believe only the holy scriptures, without seeking any further to be taught; watching and still taking heed to ourselves, that we be not beguiled and deceived with the false miracles of Antichrist, wherewith the world at this day is stuffed; which miracles are wrought by the working of Satan, to confirm all kind of idolatry, errors, abuses, and iniquities, and thereby to blind the poor and ignorant: the which thing the Lord God suffereth justly to be done, because they would not receive the Spirit of truth to be saved. Yea, God suffereth them to receive the spirit of lying, which hath power to deceive, to the end they should be damned, because they have allowed lying and iniquity, and have refused righteousness and truth. The true miracles then are wrought by the only power of God for the confirming of his doctrine, and are wrought for the infidels' sakes, and not for the faithful. But the preaching and true receiving of the holy word of God is only given and ministered to the faithful, and to those that believe.

The Fifty-eighth Article.

I believe also the holy sacraments (which are the second mark or badge of the true church) to be the signs of the reconciliation and great atonement made between God and us through Jesus Christ. They are seals of the Lord's promises, and are outward and visible pledges and gages of the inward faith, and are in number only twain, that is to say, baptism and the holy supper of the Lord. The which two are not void and empty signs, but full; that is to say, they are not only signs, whereby something is signified, but also they are such signs as do exhibit and give the thing that they signify indeed, as by God's help we will declare hereafter. But, as touching all the other five sacraments, which with great abuse and superstition are received and used in the papistical church, that is to say, confirmation, confession, marriage, absolution, otherwise called the sacrament of the priesthood, and extreme unction or annealing; I say that all these were ecclesiastical ceremonies, the which the holy fathers in their time used holily without any superstition, even as by their example the same may be used this day, so that it be done without any error, abuse, and superstition, and that in no wise it be hurtful to the christian liberty of the gospel, the which doth deliver our consciences from all outward beggarly ceremonies by man ordained and devised without the word of God.

The Fifty-ninth Article.

I believe that baptism is the sign of the new league and friendship between God and us, made by Jesus Christ; and it is the mark of the Christians now in the time of the gospel, as in time past circumcision was a mark unto the Jews, which were under the law. Yea, baptism is an outward washing done with water, thereby signifying an inward washing of the Holy Ghost, wrought through the blood of Christ: the which baptism ought as well to be given and communicated to little children as to those that be great, according to Jesus Christ his ordinance, once for all, without any re-baptizing. This baptism is the Red Sea, wherein Pharao, that is to say, the devil, with his army of sins are altogether drowned, and the Israelites pass through it safely; and afterward, walking through the desert of this world in great sorrows, vexations, and troubles, do use daily for their comfort the heavenly manna, which is the holy word of God, until through death they may enter into the heavenly land of promise.

The Sixtieth Article.

I believe also that baptism is the entry of the church, a washing into a new birth, and a renewing of the Holy Ghost, whereby we do forsake ourselves, the devil, the flesh, sin, and the world. For being once rid of the old man with all his concupiscences, we are clothed with the new man, which is Jesus Christ, in righteousness and holiness, and with him we die, and are buried in his death, to the end that with Christ we may rise from death to the glory of the Father. And even likewise being thus new born, we should walk in newness of life, always mortifying in us that which is of us, that thereby the body of sin may be utterly destroyed, and plucked up by the root.

The Sixty-first Article.

I believe that this baptism ought to be ministered, not with oil, salt, spittle, and such-like baggage, but only in clean and fair water; and that in the name of the Father, the Son, and the Holy Ghost, according to the institution and ordinance of God, without changing any thing therein, putting any thing thereunto, or taking any thing therefrom; and the same also to be used in a vulgar and common language, that all the people may understand. For whatsoever is done or said in the church of Christ, ought to be understanded and known of all that be faithful. By this baptism we are changed and altered from children of wrath, of sin, of the devil, and of destruction into the children of God, of grace, and salvation; thereby to be made the Lord's, heirs and coheirs with Christ of eternal life. And for that cause the same ought to be given and communicated only to reasonable creatures, which are apt and meet to receive such things; and not unto bells and such-like, which neither can receive nor use the thing signified by baptism.

The Sixty-second Article.

I believe that this baptism with water is not so necessary to salvation, that one may not be saved without it in case of necessity. And likewise I doubt not in the salvation of little children which die without baptism, but that the same are saved in the faith of their parents, as well as if they were baptized; even as in time past under the law the little children dying without circumcision were saved in the faith of their parents. But this only do I understand of the children of the faithful, unto whom the promises of God do appertain, and not of the infidels and reprobate.

The Sixty-third Article.

I believe that the holy sacrament of the supper is an holy and outward ceremony, instituted by Jesus Christ in the gospel a day before his death, in the nature and substance of bread and wine, in remembrance and for a memorial of his death and passion, having and containing in it a promise of the remission of sins. By this sacrament we are indeed made partakers of the body and blood of Jesus Christ, and be therewith nourished and fed in the house of the Lord, which is his church, after that into the same we are entered through baptism. The same ought to be given and ministered to all under both the kinds, according to the ordinance and commandments of Christ, for the altering whereof none ought to be so hardy as to attempt any thing.

THE SIXTY-FOURTH ARTICLE.

I believe that in this holy sacrament these signs or badges are not changed in any point, but the same do remain wholly in their nature: that is to say, the bread is not changed and transubstantiated (as the fond papists and false doctors do teach, deceiving the poor people) into the body of Jesus Christ, neither is the wine transubstantiated into his blood; but the bread remaineth still bread, and the wine remaineth still wine, every one in his proper and first nature. For the words that Christ spake to his disciples in giving them the bread, saying, "This is my body," I understand and believe to be spoken by a figurative manner of speech, called *metonomia*, which is a manner of speaking very common in the scriptures; as the same was understood[1] and also declared by the writings of the holy fathers and doctors of the church, Irenæus, Cyprian, Tertullian, Ambrose, Augustine, Chrysostom, and other like, which lived before the council of Lateran, where it was concluded that the bread was transubstantiated into the body of Christ, and the wine into his blood; and then was it given forth for an article of our faith, to the great dishonour of God, and to the great slander of all the church. And it was done in the year of our Lord[2] 1050, by pope Leo the Ninth: in the which time the devil was unbound, as it was prophesied of in the Apocalypse, and troubled the church of Christ more than ever he did before.

Transubstantiation never heard of before the Council of Lateran, where it was most blasphemously concluded.

THE SIXTY-FIFTH ARTICLE.

I believe that all this sacrament consisteth in the use thereof; so that without the right use the bread and wine in

[1 Edd. 1581 and 1584, understand.]

[2 The Second Roman Council assembled by Leo the Ninth in the year 1050 condemned as heretical the opinions of Berengarius, who denied the conversion of the bread and wine in the eucharist into the actual body and blood of Christ. In the year 1215 Innocentius III. in the Fourth Lateran Council authoritatively decreed the doctrine of transubstantiation as an article of faith.—See Binii Concil. Tom. VII. p. 263. col. 1. Lutet. Paris. 1636. Also Hooper's Answer to the Bishop of Winchester's book, "Early Writings," p. 118, and his Treatise on the Sacrament, infra.]

nothing differ from other common bread and wine that is commonly used; and therefore I do not believe that the body of Christ can be contained, hid, or inclosed in the bread, under the bread, or with the bread; neither the blood in the wine, under the wine, or with the wine. But I believe and confess the very body of Christ to be in heaven on the right hand of the Father (as before we have said); and that always and as often as we use this bread and wine according to the ordinance and institution of Christ, we do verily and indeed receive his body and blood.

The Sixty-sixth Article.

I believe that this receiving is not done carnally or bodily, but spiritually, through a true and lively faith; that is to say, the body and blood of Christ are not given to the mouth and belly for the nourishing of the body, but unto our faith for the nourishing of the spirit and inward man unto eternal life. And for that cause we have no need that Christ should come from heaven to us, but that we should ascend unto him, lifting up our hearts through a lively faith on high unto the right hand of the Father, where Christ sitteth, from whence we wait for our redemption; and we must not seek for Christ in these bodily elements.

The Sixty-seventh Article.

I believe that this holy supper is a sacrament of faith unto the faithful only, and not for the infidels; wherein a man findeth and receiveth no more than he bringeth with him, saving peradventure the increase of faith, grace, and virtue. And therefore they only find and receive Jesus Christ unto salvation, which through true and lively faith bring the same with them: but the others find and receive only the outward and visible signs, and that to their condemnation, as Judas and other such-like wicked and reprobate.

The Sixty-eighth Article.

I believe that this sacrament containeth two things: the one is earthly, carnal, and visible; and the other is heavenly, spiritual, and invisible. And I confess that, as our body and outward man receiveth the thing that is earthly and visible, which is the bread and the wine, whereby the body is nourished and fed; even so verily our spirit and inward man receiveth the thing that is heavenly and spiritual, which is signified by the bread and wine, that is to say, the body and blood of Christ, after such sort, that thereby we are become one with him, bone of his bones, and flesh of his flesh, and made partakers with him of all righteousness and other virtues, gifts, and graces, the which the eternal Father hath bestowed on him.

The Sixty-ninth Article.

I believe that the holy fathers, patriarchs, prophets, and all other faithful and good people that are gone before us, and have died in the faith, through the word and faith saw him beforehand which was to come, and received as much and the same thing that we receive by the sacraments. For they were of the self-same church, faith, and law that we be of. They were as well Christians as we, and used the same sacraments in figure that we use in truth.

The Seventieth Article.

I believe that to this holy table only those that are faithful, and are truly contrite and penitent, ought to be admitted; and that all such as are unworthy should be refused, for fear of defiling and contaminating the holy meats, the which the Lord giveth not but unto the faithful and to those of his own household. I call those unworthy which are infidels, idolaters, blasphemers, despisers of God, heretics, and all other that make sects to divide themselves from the people, thereby to break the unity of the church; all that are perjured; all that resist and are disobedient to father, mother, and their superiors; all seditious persons, murderers, quarrellers, sowers of discord, whoremongers, thieves, covetous persons, drunkards, gluttons, and, generally, all those that lead a wicked and a slanderous life. For such manner of people have no part nor portion of the kingdom of God; and for that cause such ought to be cast and thrust out of the church. For with such it is not lawful to keep any company, to eat, drink, or to have any friendship, except it be for the winning of them and bringing of them to repentance.

The Seventy-first Article.

I believe that the popish mass is not, neither can be, the

holy supper of the Lord, but the mere invention of men, which were both liars and wicked: yea, it is as contrary to the holy supper as the night is unto the day, and Belial to Christ; as it may appear to all people more clear than the noon-day, by conferring and comparing the institution of the holy supper (as the same is recited and written by the evangelist and, especially, by the apostle St Paul) unto the celebration of the mass. And therefore the mass can be no remembrance of true sacrifice, that is to say, of the death and passion of Christ, as the holy supper is: but the mass is an utter forsaking of the same, because it doth attribute and ascribe to itself that which doth appertain only to the blood of Christ shed upon the cross, that is to say, satisfaction, purgation, and remission of sins, with the increase of grace; and because men are compelled to do godly honour unto the creature instead of the Creator, to a morsel of bread in the stead of Jesus Christ our only Lord, Saviour, and Redeemer.

The Seventy-second Article.

I believe that the third mark or cognisance of the church, which is ecclesiastical discipline, is very commodious and profitable, yea, and very necessary to the catholic church for the comfort of the good, and for the punishment of the evil; the which also I do receive, and to the same do submit myself, because I know that it is the ordinance of Christ in his church, and in like manner the same was practised by the apostles in the primitive church, and that because all should be done honestly and in good order; which is a thing honest and necessary for every congregation.

The Seventy-third Article.

I believe that the power to bind and loose, to excommunicate and to absolve, that is commonly called the keys of the church, is given of God not to one or two, or to some particular person, but to the whole church, that is to say, to all the faithful and believers in Christ, not for to destroy, undo, or cast away, but to edify and to advance all. And therefore I say and confess that excommunication and absolution ought not, neither can it be given at the lust and pleasure of some particularly, but by the consent of all the church, or, at the least, by the greater or most sound part of the same, when they be congregated and assembled together in the name of Christ, and the same to be done with prayer.

THE SEVENTY-FOURTH ARTICLE.

I believe that this excommunication, exercised and executed rightly, according as Jesus Christ hath declared and commanded the same in the gospel, is of so great authority, strength, and power, that it may shut up heaven from men in such wise, that all those that are worthily excommunicated are cast out of the church militant, and also shall be cast out of the church triumphant, which is heaven, except they repent. It is the sword that is so sharp to cut off the rotten members of Christ's mystical body, which is his church. It is the key to shut up the heavens from the wicked. It is a rod to chasten them, which nevertheless is not used to confound them, but as a spiritual medicine to amend them, to receive them, to make them whole, and bring them again to the same estate from the which they are fallen.

THE SEVENTY-FIFTH ARTICLE.

I believe that this excommunication, which is the last rod of the church, ought not, neither can it be exercised toward any manner of person which first hath not received and professed the faith and religion of Christ. And even likewise the same cannot be pronounced for small matters, as for money, debts, and such-like; neither ought it to be executed toward all sinners, but only against open, rebellious, and obstinate sinners, when brotherly correction commanded by Christ in the gospel doth take no place. And therefore all they do generally abuse this rod, which do excommunicate the Christians for small trifles, without using first brotherly correction; and likewise do they also that excommunicate the Jews, Turks, the heathen and other infidels, yea, and brute beasts, meaning thereby to thrust and cast out of the christian church those that never were in it.

THE SEVENTY-SIXTH ARTICLE.

I believe herewith that the unity of the Spirit, peace, concord, and charity, that is to say, true amity and brotherly love, the sweet and friendly helping and supporting one of another, is also one of the works and signs of the true catholic church and of the faithful children of God, by the which they are known to be of the school and of the number of Jesus Christ his disciples. And we must not glory in ourselves in the title of Christianity, or of the faith, saying, "I believe, I believe," if we have not this charity, peace, love, and true unity of heart together, agreeing one with another in all good works. For the true faith never goeth without these things, by the which also it declareth and manifesteth itself to all. These are the signs and marks of the true christian church, unto the which it is linked and bound, and not unto any certain place, time, or personages. And there is the church perfect, where these marks are found and used; and on the other part, if any one of the same be lacking, then is not the same perfect. And albeit that this whole perfection for the estate of this present world cannot be found in the church militant, nevertheless the fault thereof must be acknowledged before the Lord, and the remedy and ordering thereof be committed to him.

The Seventy-seventh Article.

I believe and receive in this church two swords, that is to say, two powers: the one is ecclesiastical and spiritual, the which lieth and consisteth in the only administration of the word and of the sacraments; the which beareth neither rod nor staff, other than the tongue, neither doth use any other knife than the sword of the Spirit, which is the word of God. Likewise I confess that all those that have this sword in their hands, ought to be without blame as well in their living as in their doctrine; otherwise, they ought to be deposed, and others to be placed in their rooms, and to put and ordain others that are better in their places. The other power is temporal, that is to say, the magistrate; which hath authority over extern and civil things, to render according to right to every man that which of right to him appertaineth.

The Seventy-eighth Article.

I believe that the magistrate is an ordinance of God set in his church for the defence of the good and godly, and to chasten and punish the wicked: and also to the magistrate must be given tribute, honour, and reverence and obedience in all things that be not in any wise contrary to God's word. And I do understand this not only of the faithful magistrate, but also of the infidel and wicked tyrant, unto whom we must obey as unto the Lord in all things, so that he command nothing contrary to the word of God: for then we ought rather to obey God than man, after the example of the apostles Peter and John.

THE SEVENTY-NINTH ARTICLE.

I believe that to the magistrate it doth appertain, not only to have regard unto the commonwealth, but also unto ecclesiastical matters, to take away and to overthrow all idolatry and false serving of God, to destroy the kingdom of Antichrist and all false doctrine, to promote the glory of God, and to advance the kingdom of Christ, to cause the word of the gospel everywhere to be preached, and the same to maintain unto death; to chasten also and to punish the false prophets, which lead the poor people after idols and strange gods, and instead of the gospel preach and teach the fables and traditions of men, to the dishonour of God and Christ his Son, and to the great decay of the whole church. To such a magistrate every person, of what estate, degree, or condition soever he be, ought to be subject, and him in all honest and reasonable things to obey, because he representeth the person of a great Lord, before whom every knee ought to bow. And the same must not be forgotten in our prayers, to the end that the Lord may vouchsafe to guide and direct all his ways, and that under him we may live in godly peace and tranquillity.

THE EIGHTIETH ARTICLE.

I believe that the magistrate, as also the use of oaths and such-like, is the ordinance of the Lord, for to lead the imperfection of man in his corrupt nature after his fall: the which the faithful, after that he hath assayed all other means, may holily and justly use in matters of controversy which may chance between him and his neighbour, to set an order, and to make peace in all things. And therefore he that in necessity will not use this way ought rather to be judged an Anabaptist than a Christian.

THE EIGHTY-FIRST ARTICLE.

I believe that the magistrate holily may minister an

oath unto the faithful in judgment for the knowledge of the truth, and to make an end of all controversies and matters in variance between man and man; the which oath ought to be taken in the only name of the living God, because it is the third commandment of the first table. And albeit the perfection required to be in a Christian ought simply to use yea yea, and nay nay, without any swearing; nevertheless the faithful may holily use an oath in place and time with discretion, and in the fear of the Lord, for things honest, just, and true, for the verifying of the truth, when the honour of God or the saving of a man's neighbour dependeth upon it, or else not: for the man that accustometh to swear shall be filled with iniquity, and his house shall not be without the plague. And I confess also that, as every oath, vow, and promise made according to God's word, be it to God or to men, doth bind, and ought to be kept and observed without breaking; even so those that are made without and contrary to God's word and commandment, as are the religious vows and such-like, which promise things impossible and contrary to the word of God, do not bind a man in any wise, but with a good conscience may be violated and broken. For in wicked promises and in foolish and undiscreet vows the faithful, wise, and sage may change their purpose.

The Eighty-second Article.

I believe and confess that marriage is an honourable estate amongst all men, and the bed undefiled is holy and ought not to be broken. It is instituted and ordained of God for the bringing forth of children, and to eschew fornication; from the which estate of marriage none ought, nor can be restrained, if there be no just and lawful let by the word of God; but the same ought to be free to everybody, of what estate, sort, or condition soever the same be of: for it is much better to marry than to burn; and for that cause all, whatsoever they be, men or women, which have not the gift to live unmarried, ought to marry, to the intent the temple of the Holy Ghost, that is to say, our bodies, may not be polluted and defiled.

The Eighty-third Article.

I believe also that the forbidding of marriage for certain persons, likewise the forbidding of certain meats, the difference of days, garments, and such-like, is the devilish doctrine of Antichrist, and wholly against the christian liberty of the gospel taught by Jesus Christ, the which delivereth us from all outward ceremonies of the law, and setteth us at liberty to use all things with giving God thanks, so that it be not done to the hurt of our neighbour. For all things are made holy by the word of God and prayer to him that knoweth and receiveth the truth. Therefore to compel the Christians to these things is but to take from them and to rob them of their christian liberty, and by tyranny to set them under the curse of the law, from the which Christ by his death and passion hath delivered them: and it is one true mark and note to know Antichrist by.

The Eighty-fourth Article.

I believe that the pure and true service of God doth not consist in these ceremonies and outward things, neither in babbling much and mumbling of long prayers, neither in crying and braying in the church like asses, or the priests of Baal; but in spiritual things, as lively and true faith in God and his word taught by Jesus Christ his only Son, which is of power, and worketh through charity toward our neighbour, true and perfect calling upon God's name, with due obedience to his commandments in humbleness of spirit, according to his word. For as God is a spirit, so will he be worshipped and served in spirit and truth.

The Eighty-fifth Article.

I believe that all God's services without God's word and contrary to his commandment is idolatry and iniquity. I call idolatry, after the fashion of the prophets, not only that which is done unto the honour of an idol or strange gods, but also that which is done to the honouring of the living God contrary to his word and commandment. And therefore they are not only idolaters, which worship and serve idols and strange gods, as the ethnics and such-like; but also all those which worship and serve the true God of heaven after their own fantasy, or after the traditions of men, without faith, without the word of God, and otherwise than God hath commanded them. And they only are Christians, which do confess and serve one only God, which is in heaven, according to his word and commandment; all whose works, as well outward as inward, corporal as spiritual, be the true service of the Lord, because the same are done in the faith of the Son of God, and according to the calling of the Lord, after the which every faithful body ought to walk.

The Eighty-sixth Article.

I believe and confess, that it is not lawful for a Christian to be present, either in spirit either in body, at the idolatrous sacrifices, neither to enter into their temples while they are in doing of their idolatries and sacrifices, if it be not of purpose to rebuke and utter their impiety, and to teach the truth, as the holy prophets and apostles did, and not to dissemble, as the hypocrites do. For if the body be the creature of God (as it is indeed), as well as the soul, and be the temple of the Holy Ghost, and a member of the mystical body of Christ; and if it shall one day rise and possess eternal life with the soul; it must then follow of necessity, that it ought to be wholly dedicated unto the right service of God in this world together with the soul and the spirit: or else they cannot at the general resurrection be coupled together, but must be separated asunder, the one to be with God in heaven, whom it loved, and the other to be in hell with the devil, whom it served; the which thing is impossible: and for that cause I say that all such dissimulation is a plain forsaking of Christ and of his gospel. Likewise I believe and confess, that all manner of such dissemblings, by the which the truth of the gospel is hid, the word of the Lord despised, infidelity and ignorance confirmed, and the weak are offended, the same cannot be of God, but of the devil, and altogether against the truth of God's word. And therefore there must be no halting on both sides, but we must go and walk forthright and straightly before this great Lord, which seeth, beholdeth, and knoweth all things, yea, even before they are begun.

The Eighty-seventh Article.

I believe also that the beginning of all idolatry was the finding out and invention of images, which also were made to the great offence of the souls of men, and are as snares and traps for the feet of the ignorant to make them to fall. Therefore they ought not to be honoured, served, worshipped, neither to be suffered in the temples or churches, neither in any other places where christian people do meet together to hear and understand the word of God; but rather the same ought utterly to be taken away and thrown down, according to the effect of the second commandment of God; and that ought to be done by the common authority of the magistrate, and not by the private authority of any particular man. For the wood of the gallows whereby justice is done is blessed of God; but the image made by man's hand is accursed of the Lord, and so is he that made it. And therefore we ought to beware of images above all things.

This is that I believe of the catholic faith and of the things that concern the same, and is for the fourth point of my faith. Now resteth to speak of the fruits that proceed out of the same, and what I receive by the same faith; which fruits are in number three, whereof the first is,

5. *The Forgiveness of Sins.*

THE EIGHTY-EIGHTH ARTICLE.

I believe that all those that are come and shall come of the race and line of Adam generally are conceived and born in iniquity and corruption (except Jesus Christ only), and that they are all sinners, transgressors, and breakers of the law and will of the Lord; and according to their nature they are corrupt, the children of wrath, worthy of God's judgment, of condemnation and eternal death, all needing the grace and mercy of God and of Christ's blood-shedding. For God hath wrapped all under sin, to the intent he would have mercy upon all through Jesus Christ our Lord.

THE EIGHTY-NINTH ARTICLE.

I believe that the knowledge of sin proceedeth of the law, but the remission and forgiveness of sin cometh of the gospel, and is given us by the only grace and mercy of God in the blood of Jesus Christ through the faith we have therein; whereby we are counted righteous before God, not through our good works or deservings, neither by the merits of any other creature either in heaven or in earth. For I know not, neither do I allow, any other merits but the merits of my good Lord, Master, and only Saviour Jesus Christ, who hath merited and sufficiently satisfied for us, and hath paid for his own their debt in wiping out the hand-writing and obligation which was against us, and in taking the same from us hath fastened it unto the cross.

The Ninetieth Article.

I believe that this justifying faith is a mere and singular gift of God, the which is commonly given by the hearing of God's word, whereupon only it is built, and not upon the doctrines and traditions of men. I call a justifying faith a certain assurance and earnest persuasion of the good-will, love, grace, bounteousness, and mercy of God toward us, whereby we are assured and verily persuaded in our hearts of the mercy, favour, and good-will of God the Father; that he is on our side and for us against all that are against us, and that he will be a merciful Father unto us, pardoning our sins, and will give us his grace, make us his children by adoption, and admit us for heirs unto eternal life; and all this freely in his Son, and by his only Son Jesus Christ our Lord, and not for our merits or good works. This faith can do all things, and to it nothing is impossible: the which faith is never perfect nor great enough in us, and therefore ought we always to pray with the apostles, saying, "Lord, increase our faith, help our unbelief." For that faith only doth comfort us, maketh us holy, maketh us righteous and acceptable before the Lord; it declareth us to be the children of God and heirs of eternal life: the which faith also is the mother, the spring, and root of all good works, like as infidelity is the fountain and root of all wickedness.

The Ninety-first Article.

I believe also that good works are not superfluous, vain, and unprofitable, but necessary to salvation. I call good works, not those which are done after the fantasy or commandment of men, but only those that God by his word hath commanded to be done: the which ought to be done, not to deserve or merit anything thereby at God's hand, or by the same to escape eternal condemnation; but only because God hath commanded them, and that they might testify the love that we have unto our Lord, and our obedience to his holy word and commandment; and to the intent that in us and by us he might be glorified, and that our neighbours, as well the infidels and unbelievers as the faithful, might thereby be edified; and in like manner to shew and to manifest the faith that we have in God and in his word, as the good tree sheweth itself and is known by his fruit; yea, and to make sure and certain unto us our calling, election, and predestination. To these ends serve all the good works commanded by God; and whosoever doeth them to any other end, doth misuse them, sinneth, and doeth injury to the blood of Christ, and dishonoureth God and his word; for in so doing he declareth Christ died in vain.

The Ninety-second Article.

I believe that there is none, either in this world or in the other world, either in heaven or in earth, which can forgive me and pardon my sins, but only God, which hath given power and authority to the ministers of his word to declare to all faithful believers, which are of a contrite heart and be truly penitent, that all their sins through the free mercy of God are forgiven them through the blood of Jesus Christ, which was shed for them; yea, to declare unto them that they are pardoned of their sins: and that the same is done by the ministry of the word of the holy church, in the which this remission is exhibited and given, and not otherwise. But on our part is required perfect repentance, the which hath two parts: the first is contrition, that is to say, the knowledging, hating, and abhorring of sin; the which thing is administered by the law, and bringeth us to despair, if with the contrary we be not holpen with a lively faith and the mercy of God the Father through the blood of Jesus Christ, which proceedeth out of the gospel. This faith comforteth us, maketh us stedfast, and causeth us to find favour before the judgment-seat of God.

The Ninety-third Article.

I believe that sin dwelleth still in man, yea, in the very saints and children of God after their new birth through baptism and the Holy Ghost: the which sin nevertheless shall not be laid to their charge, because of the faith they have in Jesus Christ. For as all the sins of the infidels and reprobate be damnable, and shall not be pardoned, because of their infidelity; even so all the sins of the faithful and chosen be venial sins and forgiveable because of their faith. And therefore I believe that there is one only sin that is mortal and irremissible, which is unbelief or infidelity, that is to say, not to believe in the Son of God. For where true faith in Christ is found, there all sins are hid, covered, and pardoned.

I believe the resurrection of the flesh, which is the second fruit of my faith.

The Ninety-fourth Article.

I believe that there shall be one resurrection, which shall be general to all the world, as well of the good as of the bad, which shall be in the end of the world by the power of Christ and through the ministry of the angels, the which with a great voice of a trumpet shall call together all the world before the Lord, and shall gather together the elect and chosen from the four winds, even from the highest of the heavens unto the ends of the earth, and divide the evil from the good; and the wicked shall they cast into the fiery furnace, where is weeping and gnashing of teeth: and then shall the righteous shine as the sun in the kingdom of their Father, and shall be together and be companions with the angels of God. This is the second resurrection, and blessed is he that shall have part or portion therein; for the same shall not be touched with the second death.

The Ninety-fifth Article.

I believe that this resurrection shall be of the flesh, and not of the spirit; that is to say, that the spirit or soul of man shall not rise, because it is immortal and dieth not: but the body, which before, as well by the reason of nature, as also because of sin, was subject unto death and corruption, to rot and to be brought to ashes, shall be raised up, and shall be coupled with his own proper soul and spirit, and shall be set in a more perfect estate than that wherein the first man was before he sinned, and shall be clearly exempted from all manner of corruption of sin, and so, consequently, from all manner of imperfections, and shall be fashioned like unto the glorious body of Christ.

The Ninety-sixth Article.

I believe that I shall rise, not in any other man's flesh and body, but in mine own that I brought out of my mother's womb, even with the self-same body and bones that I have at this present, but the same altered and changed, made of mortal immortal, of corruptible incorruptible, of vile and contemptible glorious. And therefore I do wait for the coming of my Saviour Jesus Christ; the which through his power will change my vile body, which was but a cast-away, to make it like unto his own glorious body, according to the power whereby he is able to subject all things to himself.

I believe eternal life, which is the third and last fruit of my faith.

The Ninety-seventh Article.

I believe that I shall rise (as I have said) with all the faithful and elect, not to die any more, as did they that miraculously were raised up from death as well by Christ, the prophets, the apostles, and such other, but unto a life that is immortal, everlasting, and shall endure for ever, to reign eternally with God both in body and soul. And thereof I am sure, and doubt nothing at all, knowing that whosoever doubteth of his salvation by Christ, the same shall not be saved. Wherefore as I am sure and certain that Christ is dead and risen again for me, and therein do not doubt; even so am I sure and certain of my salvation wrought by him, and that without fail I shall be saved, and by him shall enter into eternal life.

The Ninety-eighth Article.

I believe that then I shall see him face to face, whom now I see as through the glass of faith, and then shall know him perfectly, whom now I know but in part: who, after that he hath destroyed and confounded all his adversaries, and hath made them his footstool, shall make all things new for the glory of those that are his. Then shall he be an whole God in all and over all things. Then shall none teach his brother, saying, "Know the Lord;" for then all shall know him from the greatest unto the least.

The Ninety-ninth Article.

I believe also that, as the spirits of the infidels, wicked, and reprobate, after they are departed from their bodies, incontinently do go to hell unto everlasting fire, their bodies nevertheless abiding in the earth corrupting and rotting; even so likewise the souls and spirits of the faithful and chosen children of God, incontinently after they do depart from their bodies, without any tarrying are on high in heaven, to be in glory with the Lord, and there do still wait with an earnest desire for the coming and whole redemption of their bodies, the which they have left rotting and corrupting in the earth; the which thing they shall obtain at the last day, and not before. Wherefore I refuse the fond opinion of the sleepers, which affirm that the spirits of the saints are not yet in heaven, but do sleep in a certain place unknown to us, until they shall receive their bodies at the last day; at which day the mystical body of Christ wholly, perfectly, and fully, must enter into eternal glory.

The Hundredth Article.

I believe, for a conclusion, that, as the saints and the blessed, when the judgment is ended, shall go with Christ triumphantly through the air in body and soul, to dwell everlastingly in glory with him and his angels; even so the wretched, wicked, and miserable damned shall go to hell in body and soul with the devil and his angels, eternally to dwell and to be tormented with him in the fire of hell, which never shall be quenched, where as shall be continual weeping, wailing, and gnashing of teeth, stung to the quick with the worm that never shall die. From the which the Lord God, of his great mercy and grace, vouchsafe to preserve and keep us. Amen.

Imprinted at London, by Christopher Barker, Printer *to the Queene's most ex-* cellent Maiestie. Anno 1581.

A GODLY CONFESSION AND PROTESTATION

OF THE

CHRISTIAN FAITH.

A godly Confession and protestacion

of the christian faith, made and set furth by Jhon Hooper, wherin is declared what a christiā manne is bound to beleue of God, hys King, his neibour, and hymselfe.

The herte belebeth to justice, confession by the mouth is to salbation. Roma X.

Imprinted at London
by John Day dwellyng ouer Aldersgate.

Cum privilegio ad imprimendum solum. Per septenium.

[Two editions of the Godly Confession appeared in 1550, both printed by John Day, the earlier small quarto, the later of a smaller size. In this reprint the text of the latter has been chiefly followed, the variations being given in the notes, in which the two editions are distinguished as A and B.]

[THE EPISTLE.]

⁋ To the most virtuous and mighty Prince Edward the Sixth, our most redoubted Sovereign Lord, King of England, France, and Ireland, defender of the faith, and in earth, next and immediately under God, the supreme head of the churches of England and Ireland: and also unto the most wise, godly, and honourable Lords of his Highness' Privy Council, and unto the rest of the most wise, godly, and learned assembled of all the Honourables and other appointed to be of his Majesty's most high and godly court of Parliament; John Hooper, his most humble, loving, and obedient subject, wisheth all grace and peace from God, with long, godly, and most prosperous reign over us in all godly knowledge, honour, health, and perpetual felicity.

Offici. Lib. 1. THE wise man Cicero, most gracious and mighty prince, saith that he[1] doth not only wrong, that by violence oppresseth wrongfully another man; but also he that defendeth[2] not (if it lie in his power) the wrongs offered, and is no less faulty[3] than though he had forsaken parents, friends, or[4] country. The same doctrine practised he in defence[5] and propulsing the injuries and wrongs attempted wrongfully against Milo by the friends of Clodius; as it appeareth by his eloquent and facundious oration made for that purpose in the senate of Rome. The same kind of injuries other godly

[[1] Injustitiæ genera duo sunt; unum eorum qui inferunt; alterum eorum qui ab iis quibus infertur, si possunt, non propulsant injuriam.—Qui autem non defendit, nec obsistit, si potest, injuriæ, tam est in vitio, quam si parentes aut amicos aut patriam deserat.—Cic. de Offic. Lib. I. c. vii. s. 7, 8.]
[[2] Defendeth: forbiddeth, preventeth.]
[[3] 'In no less faultless' in A.]   [[4] 'And' in A.]
[[5] 'The defence' in A.]

men in the scriptures of God have always, according to the law, eschewed: for it is written, "If a man see his neighbour's ass fall under his[6] burden, or his ox to go astray, his neighbour is bound to help them both[7], the ass from burden[8], and the ox from his straying." The same practised Abraham, when he perceived his nephew Loth oppressed with the wars of the infidels, propulsed and revenged the injuries, and set his nephew at large and liberty. Even so be there two sorts of people, that two sundry ways do injuries and wrongs unto the soul and conscience of men. The one of them by force or subtlety defraudeth them from the truth and perfection of God's words, as heretical and superstitious ministers: the other, at such time as they should with prayer, diligence, and preaching defend the people of God from such injuries and wrongs, are negligent or dumb. The which kind of injury doubtless the Lord God Almighty will at length grievously revenge. Therefore against this kind of injury he spake unto the prophet Ezekiel: "If I purpose to send a plague upon the people, and thou give them not warning thereof, I will require their blood at thy hand." The same said he unto St Peter: "Feed my lambs," "feed my sheep." And unto all the apostles he said, "Make ye all Gentiles my disciples." And St Paul, fearing to fall in the danger of the second kind of doing wrong, in saving[9] the wrongs of false religion from the church of Christ, said, "Wo be unto me, if I preach not."

Exod. xxiii.
Gen. xiv.
Ezek. iii. xxxiii.
John xxi.
Mark xvi.
1 Cor. ix. Rom. xv. (see also ch. i. 14.)

Upon the consideration of the[10] premises, seeing all things be written for our doctrine, I have thought it good to write and set forth this confession and protestation of my faith, submitting myself and my faith also most humbly to be judged by your majesty, your most honourable council, with the godly assemblance of your majesty's most high court of parliament, according to the word of God; that by this means I may avoid the pain and danger due unto all them that neglect or omit the injuries and wrongs that may happen and chance by sinister report and false slander of God's word to the conscience of any of your majesty's subjects. For I am credibly informed that many false and erroneous opinions

[6 'Her' in A.]   [7 'In both' in A.]   [8 'His burden' in A.]
[9 Saving: withholding.]   [10 'These' in A.]

is entered into their heads of me[1] (God forgive them that hath been the occasion thereof). If any way these injuries and dangerous slanders may be holpen, I think this to be the way, to offer most humbly myself and my faith to be known and judged by your majesty after the word of God. I protest before God and your majesty, I write not this confession for any apology or defence, to contend or strive with any man in any matter, nor for any private affection or displeasure I bear unto any man living, or for any inordinate or partial love unto myself, but for the cause and to the same end before rehearsed.

Likewise for three other great causes that shall follow. The one toucheth God, the other your majesty, the third your loving subjects. As concerning God, seeing both his majesty, mine own conscience, and my auditory know that I have neither in doctrine, neither in manners, taught no other thing than I received of the patriarchs, prophets, and the apostles, it were not only sin, but also the very part of a miscreant, to deny or betray the innocency of that doctrine, or to be ashamed to stand to the defence thereof, seeing all godly men have esteemed more the true word of God than their own mortal lives.

<small>Matt. x.
Mark viii.
Luke xii.</small>

The second cause, that toucheth your majesty and your most honourable council, is, because upon credit and good opinion, and partly by experience that your majesty had both of my true faith and godly zeal, appointed me (among other of your preachers), though most unworthy, to teach your subjects their duty to God and man. What true subject can hear and understand such untrue bruits of those that a king's majesty shall appoint to preach, and would not be glad, both for God's sake and his king's, to remove such ungodly bruits, if he can, for the peace and quietness of their subjects?

<small>Matt. v.</small>

As for the cause that toucheth the people, it is no less worthy than eternal[2] damnation. In case he be worthy of judgment, and in danger of hell-fire, that is angry with his brother, and calleth him fool, how much more if he call his brother heretic and a denier of God! If the first be worthy hell-fire, much more the last. Therefore lest my brother should die, and then receive condign reward due for

[[1] 'Of me' not in A.]   [[2] 'Eternal' not in A.]

a slanderer, what it lieth in me, I do by this protestation of my faith call him to repentance. And in case any man stand ^{Gal. vi.} ^{James v.} in doubt of mine opinion and meaning in religion, let him not damn me beforetime, but use the means with me that the ten tribes of Israel used with the tribe of Reuben, Gad, and half ^{Josh. xxii} the tribe of Manasses, that built, at their return to their possessions, an altar upon the borders of Jordan, the which fact was like to have engendered great wars. But it was stayed by the means of consultation and communication had with those that builded it: and, their minds known, the dissension was ended and appeased. Even so I would desire my christian countrymen to use me (for I have built no altars of idolatry), if they be in doubt of me in any thing, and not to kill by hearsay, neither before they have heard me speak.

Thus I pray God, both they and I may search always
to live in his fear, to obey our king, and to be
profitable and true members of this realm
of England. So be it. The 20th
day of December, in the year
of our Lord God, A. M. D.
and fifty
(.!.)

The Confession and Protestation of John Hooper's faith.

<small>Matt. iii. xxviii. Zech. iii. Gen. i.</small>

I. I BELIEVE, according to the holy scripture, to be things without time and before time; also to be things with time and made in time. The thing without and before time is God only and solely: three in diversity of persons, and one in essence and equality of the Godhead, the Father, the Son, and Holy Ghost: not three Gods, but one God. Things with time and in time be all things that ever was, now is, or ever shall be created in heaven or in earth, until the day of the last general judgment, when as both body and soul shall begin together (for the soul ever liveth) immortality and joys without time, of such as be ordained by God to eternal salvation; and of such as be appointed, and have deserved it, to eternal damnation, to begin eternal pains, and so to endure without time.

<small>Matt. xxv. John ix.</small>

<small>Jude. 2 Chron. ii. Luke xvi. Matt. xxv. Gen. i.</small>

II. I believe the spirits, both good and bad, and likewise the souls of men and women created by God, to be immortal, and from their creation to live for ever, and never to die. I believe all things created by God, as concerning their creation, to be perfect and good; without hatred, displeasure, grudge, contumacy, rebellion, disobedience, or pride, against their Maker.

<small>Col. i.</small>

III. I believe that things created by God, part of them, by grace and God's favour, hath and ever shall persevere and continue in the perfection and excellency of their creation; as the spirits or angels that never fell, nor hereafter shall fall, through the means of Christ.

<small>Luke xvi.</small>
<small>Rom. viii.</small>
<small>Matt. vii.</small>
<small>John vii.[2]</small>

IV. I believe that part of these creatures, which God made in their perfection, now to be subject, part of them to immortal pains, part to mortal pains, part unto both: as the devil and man, that fell into this ruin and perdition of themselves, although divers ways: the devil[1] by pride and arrogancy, while he would be like unto God; man by ignorance,

[1 'To say, the devil,' &c. A.]
[2 Perhaps intended for John viii. 44.]

and by craft of the devil deceived, and not by any imperfection of God's part in their creation, nor by any force, compulsion, or violence of God's part, that compelled them to evil.

For I believe God to be the author of life and salvation, and the will of the devil and of man to be the occasion of both their loss. *Zech. i. John iii. ix. Rom. xv. James i.*

V. I believe all the people of the world to be either the people of God, either the people of the devil. The people of God be those that with heart and mind know, worship, honour, praise, and laud God after the doctrine of the prophets and apostles. The people of the devil be those that think they worship, honour, reverence, fear, laud, or praise God, any other ways besides or contrary to the doctrine of the prophets and apostles. *John viii. x. Eph. ii. Rom. i.*

VI. I believe that this people of God, which be the very true church of God, to have a certain doctrine, [that] never was, is, or hereafter shall be, violated by time or any man's authority. This doctrine only and solely is comprehended in the sacred and holy bible. *Matt. xvi. Eph. ii. Ps. xix. Ps. cxix. Ps. cxlix.*

VII. And I believe this doctrine of the patriarchs and prophets to be sufficient and absolutely perfect to instruct me and all the holy church of our duties toward God and toward our neighbours. Of God it teacheth that he is but one, almighty, maker of all things, merciful, just, and all things that good is. And seeing we know nothing of God, nor can judge nothing of God, as touching our salvation, but after his word, we must judge of him as we be taught therein, as well of his divine nature, as of the division of the persons in the divine essence. So that we be compelled by the authority of God's word to confess the plurality of persons, the Father, the Son, and the Holy Ghost, in the unity of one divine Godhead and essence. *John v. 1 Tim. iii. Ps. xix. Deut. vi. Exod. xx. John v. 1 Cor. ii. Deut. xxxii. Isai. xiv. 1 Cor. ix. (see 1 Cor. viii.) Eph. iv. Matt. iii. xxviii.*

VIII. I believe, as touching the Father of heaven, as much as holy scripture teacheth us to believe, and is set forth by parts in the three creeds, the creed commonly called the Apostles' creed, where as we say,

IX. I believe in God the Father Almighty, Maker of heaven and of earth, and so forth; with all such things as the creed of Nice believeth, and after the faith and creed of Athanasius in this behalf.

X. I believe the second person in Trinity to be one God with the Father in Godhead, and divers in person. I believe him to be the very substance, image, and figure of God, without beginning or ending, with all other properties and conditions that the holy scripture of God, or the decree or doctrine of any of the three former creeds, affirm.

XI. I believe that the mercy of the Father, the Son, and the Holy Ghost, pitied and had compassion upon Adam the lost man, and was provoked[1] to ordain the Son of God, second person in Trinity, to debase and humble himself unto the nature of man, and also to become man, to redeem and save the lost man. For even as he was by external[2] malice and craft of the devil brought to confusion, to sin, and so to death both of body and soul, nothing having in himself, as touching his first creation, that provoked, stirred, enticed, or allured him to evil; even so after his fall was there nothing in him, or ever after could be in his posterity, that might or may allure or[3] provoke him or any of his posterity to the means or help of his or their salvation. But even as he was lost by malice and deceit of the devil, so is he, and so shall all his posterity be, saved by the mercy and merits of Christ. The devil and Adam's will wrought sin and death: God's mercy and Christ his merits wrought grace and life. The will of Eve and Adam straying and wandering abroad upon the fruit, an object and matter forbidden of God that they should not eat of, brought them into death: Jesus Christ, the seed of the woman, applying both body and soul to the obedience of God, deserved life; as it is in the scriptures, and in the second part of the common creed.

XII. I believe in Jesus Christ, his only Son, our Lord, which was conceived by the Holy Ghost, born of the Virgin Mary, suffered under Poncius Pilate; he was crucified, dead, and buried; he descended into hell, and the third day he arose again from death unto life, and ascended into heaven, and there sitteth on the right hand of God, the Father Almighty. And from thence he shall come to judge both the quick and the dead.

I believe that by this means, and no other, the sins of believers to be forgiven without the merits and deservings of

[1 Provoked: moved, excited.]   [2 'Eternal' in B.]
[3 'To' in B.]

Adam's posterity. By Adam sin came into the world, and by sin death: even so, without all merits, respects, and worthiness of Adam, either of any of his posterity, by Jesus Christ came remission of sin and life everlasting. And even as I believe stedfastly sin and death by this means to be overcome and destroyed, and everlasting life to follow it, so believe I the Son of God to be perfect God and man, according to the scriptures; and do condemn the heresies of Arian[5] and Marcion[6], with their complices and adherents, that wickedly believed the contrary. And as I confess and believe the means of our salvation to be only Christ, so I condemn the Pelagian[7] and all such other as believed and taught that they could by their own powers, strength, and will, work their own salvation; which false opinion conculcateth, frustrateth, slandereth, condemneth, and blasphemeth all the deservings of Christ. Therefore the Pelagian is called worthily "the enemy of grace."

John vi. xii.4
Rom. xv.
Eph. i. ii.
Heb. ii. ix.
Col. i. ii.

XIII. Farther, I believe that the grace of God, deserved by the passion of Christ, doth not only freely and without all merits of man begin, teach, and provoke man to believe the promises of God, and so to begin to work the will of God: but[8] I believe also all the works, merits, deservings, doings, and obedience of man towards God, although they be done by the Spirit of God, in the grace of God, yet being thus done, be of no validity, worthiness, nor merit before God, except God by mercy and grace account them worthy, for the worthiness and merits of Jesus Christ, that died under Poncius Pilatus. So that I believe grace not only to be the beginner of all good works, but that all good works done by man in their greatest perfection have need and wanteth grace to pardon their imperfection.

Luke xvi. [xvii.]
Rom. xiv.

XIV. I believe in the Holy Ghost, equally[9] God with the Father and the Son, and proceeding from them both: by

---

[4 Perhaps intended for xx. 31.]

[5 See Socrat. Scholast. Hist. Eccles. Lib. I. cap. 5 et seqq. Also Theodoret. Hist. Eccl. Lib. I. cap. 2 et seqq. Also Epiphan. adv. Hæres. LXVIII. LXIX.]

[6 See Euseb. Hist. Eccles. Lib. IV. cap. 11. Also Epiphan. adv. Hæres. XLII. Also Tertull. and Iren.]

[7 See August. Lib. de Hæres. Op. Tom. VI. col. 32. Basil, 1569.]

[8 'And' in A.]   [9 'Equal' in A.]

*Matt. iii.
xviii.
Acts ii.
1 Cor. xii.
Eph. ii. iii.
John xiv.
Gal. iii.
Joel ii.*

whose virtue, strength, and operation the catholic church is[1] preserved from all errors and false doctrines, and teacheth the communion of saints in all truth and verity: the which Holy Spirit shall never forsake the holy church, which is Christ his mystical body.

XV. I believe that this Holy Spirit worketh the remission of sin, resurrection[2] of the flesh, and everlasting life, according to the holy scripture[3].

XVI. This is my faith and doctrine concerning the Godhead and diversity of persons in the Holy Trinity, and also of the two natures in Christ, his Godhead and manhead; abhorring and detesting the heresies of Samosatenes[4], Arian, Nestor[5], Eutyches[6], who were condemned by godly councils, Nice, Constantinople, Ephesin, Chalchedon and other. I detest and abhor the Marcion and Maniche[7], that feigneth to be two gods, and both eternal, one good and the other evil, always at debate among themselves. I detest and abhor the monstrous doctrine of the Valentines[8], and so generally of all those that have denied to be any God, or would have many gods. Also all those I detest that have erred and maintained[9] their error in any thing concerning the essence of God, or denied the plurality of persons, as of the Father, the Son, and the Holy Ghost.

This is the faith of God's Spirit in my conscience, which I have learned in his word, and have[10] faithfully and religiously preached and taught the same[11] in all my sermons, as I will be judged by mine auditory. Also[12] the same doctrine I have furthered and set forth in all my books and writings, though some calumniators and slanderers would gladly make the poor people believe the contrary. But I do decline and appeal from such uncharitable spirits unto the charitable reader, and

[1 'To be' in A.]   [2 'The resurrection' in A.]
[3 'Scriptures' in A.]
[4 See Euseb. Hist. Eccles. Lib. VII. cap. 27 et seqq. Also Socrat. Schol. Hist. Eccl. Lib. II. cap. 19.]
[5 See Socrat. Schol. Hist. Eccl. Lib. VII. cap. 32. Also Evag. Schol. Lib. I. cap. 2 et seqq.]
[6 See Evag. Schol. Lib. I. cap. 9.]
[7 See Euseb. Hist. Eccl. Lib. VII. c. 31. Also Soc. Schol. Lib. I. c. 22.]
[8 See Euseb. Hist. Eccl. Lib. IV. c. 11. Also Epiphan. adv. Hæres. XXXI.]
[9 'Maintain' in B.]   [10 'Which I have' in A.]
[11 'The same' not in A.]   [12 'And' in A.]

loving heart of all them that be endued with God's holy Spirit; for they will not constrain nor force letter, syllable, word, or sentence contrary to the mind of the speaker and writer; but will judge, and search for judgment in the processes and circumstances of the writer, and content themselves [13] with the writer's mind, rather than to bring their [14] affection and corrupt minds [15] to make their [14] own imaginations and fantasies [16] another man's doctrine, as the Arian, Pelagian, Anabaptist, papist, and other do, and have done, bringing corrupt minds to the lesson and reading of Christ's testament, and would that their false heresies and untrue imaginations should be Christ his doctrine. Seeing both God's laws and man's laws suffereth and giveth liberty to every man in a cause of religion to be interpretater of his own words, it were contrary to justice to put any man from it. For, if the author may not be interpreter of his own mind, what would not malice, envy, spite, and disdain gather of works most truly and faithfully meant and written? And seeing charity and the laws of this realm, as it appeareth in an act [17] of parliament made in the first year of the reign of our sovereign lord king Edward the Sixth, giveth liberty and licence to him that shall be accused for a matter of religion upon malice, evil will, hatred, disdain, or by made and suborned records, to repel and convict all such false records and their accusers by other faithful and indifferent records; the which act of parliament God forbid should be denied to any of the king's majesty's preachers; for if the testimony of their audiences [18] shall not quit them from despite [19] and calumniation of malicious and uncharitable men, they shall not long preach the truth. For either the papists will accuse them, because they wish the pope and all monuments of papistry to be taken out of the way; either the carnal gospeller, that cannot abide to hear his faults and carnal life rebuked. And I think if the king's majesty and his most honourable council prepare not the sooner a bridle and correction for sin, the true preacher of God hereafter shall be more persecuted for reprehending of sin and ungodly life, than ever yet hitherunto he hath been persecuted by the papists.

[13 'Himself' in A.]   [14 'His' in A.]
[15 'Mind' in A.]   [16 'Imagination and fantasy' in A.]
[17 See Burnet's Hist. of Reform. Vol. II. Book I. p. 40. Lond. 1683.]
[18 Audientes, in the originals.]   [19 'The spite' in A.]

Thus I have declared my faith and belief towards God, according to the scriptures, in the which I trust to continue until death end this miserable and wretched life.

Now I will declare also the same towards the church of Christ, what I believe of the magistrates, the ministers of the word, and the people I dwell withal. And of these things I will speak according to the doctrine of the prophets and apostles. For many times, as well heretofore as in our days, have been superstitious hypocrites and fantastical spirits, that have neglected and condemned the office of magistrates, judgments, laws, punishments of evil, lawful dominion, rule, lawful wars, and such-like, without which a commonwealth may not endure. They have condemned also the ministry and ministers of Christ's church; and as for christian society and charitable love, they confound. They use the ministry of the church so that it is out of all estimation, supposing themselves to be of such perfection, that they need neither the ministry of the word, neither use[1] of Christ his holy sacraments, baptism and the supper of the Lord. And the other they use with such devilish[2] disorder, that they would by a law make theirs their neighbours', and their neighbours' theirs, confounding all propriety[3] and dominion of goods. Before our time the fury and damnable heresy of Marcion and the Maniches against the magistrates troubled many a year dangerously both Asia and Africa; and not yet four hundred years sith agone a sort of people, called Flagelliferi[4], did the same.

And now in our time, to the great trouble and unquietness of many commonwealths in Europe, the Anabaptists hath resuscitated and revived the same errors: which is an argument and token of the devil's great indignation against civil policy and order. For he knoweth, where such errors and false doctrines of political orders be planted, two great evils necessarily must needs follow: the one is sedition, that bringeth murders, blood-shedding, and dissipations of realms; the other is blasphemy against Christ's precious blood: for these[5] sects think they be able to save themselves of and by themselves.

[1 'The use' in A.]   [2 'Devilish' not in A.]
[3 Propriety: property.]
[4 See Mosheim's Eccl. Hist. Vol. III. p. 218. Lond. 1826; and Boileau's Historia Flagellantium, Paris. 1700.]
[5 'Those' in A.]

Farther, where as the magistrates be cumbered with those dangerous sort of people, the devil knoweth they shall have no leisure at will to take some order by God's word to oppress such false doctrine. But thus[6] we be taught out of the scripture, that even as man is ordained to the order, change, and alteration of time; as the order of the year appointeth now to be subject unto summer, now unto winter, now to the spring, and now to the fall; so hath God ordained and commanded man to be obedient to policies and orders, wheresoever he be, so they be not repugnant nor contrary to the word of God: as Joseph in his heart bore abroad wheresoever he went the true knowledge and invocation of God, also of Christ to come; yet outwardly in courts, judgments, contracts, and in possession of goods, he used the law of the Egyptians: even so did Daniel in Babylon. There is no more to be taken heed of in laws and civil policies, but to see the law repugn not the law of God, and that the lawmakers, and those to whom the execution of the law is commended unto, have a special and singular eye unto the effect and the meaning of the law, wherefore it was made a law: the which St Paul wonderfully exhorteth people to understand, saying of the law and magistrates, "Let them be a fear and terror to the evil-doers, and a praise and commendation to the well-doers." Neither forceth it, though the form and manner of laws, of judgments, of pain[8], and punishments be not like in all places, as the laws of feuderies[9] be not like in Italy, England, France, Spain, nor Germany; yet should every nation be subject unto the laws of his own realm and civil policy: and in this doing[10] he shall offend God no more than the Englishmen, that have longer days in the summer, shorter days in the winter[11], than those that dwell near to the south; or St Paul, that had longer days at the solstitium and pitch of the sun in Macedon than Christ had at Jerusalem. But even as we be content with our measure and length of day and night, and others be contented with theirs, so must both they and we submit ourselves, and be contented with the measure and order of our own laws.

margin: Dan. iii. 7 ; Rom. xii. [xiii.] Exod. xxii.

[6 'This' in A.]
[7 Dan. ii. 48. vi. 2.]
[8 'Pains' in A.]
[9 Tenures of property.]
[10 'His so doing' in A.]
[11 'And shorter days in winter' in A.]

I do therefore bewail and lament that the preachers in the church, and schoolmasters in their schools, the householder in his household, do know no better what the dignity and honour of a civil policy is, by whom it is ordained, and by whom it is preserved; how dangerous and damnable a thing it is before God and man to trouble and disquiet it by any furor and madness of opinion; as the Marcion, Maniches, and Anabaptists do. I see and know by experience much trouble and danger to arise[1] among the unlearned and ungodly people by ignorance[2]: for when they see such deformities and confusions rise and chance, as we see many times to happen in kingdoms, courts, judicials, laws, governors that more fancy private profit and singularity than the profit of the whole commonwealth, and indifferency of all men and all causes indifferently; they suppose verily (for lack of knowledge in God's word) that all orders, policies, kingdoms, and dominions be no other thing than cruel tyranny and oppression of the poor; and also to have their beginning and original either of the devil, or of pride and covetousness of men. This same evil upon the same occasion of ignorance[2] caused natural wise men much to be troubled and vexed about the considerations of kingdoms, policies, rules, and dominions; because they perceived all kingdoms to be subject unto troubles and alterations; and not only that, but they perceived right well no kingdom to be perpetual, nor for ever. And indeed whoso beholdeth the beginning, the continuance, and end of the empire of Rome, shall see right well their imaginations to be no vain things.

Rom. xiii.

How much of her own blood and of strangers' blood did Rome shed before she came to the regiment and rule of all the world! When she was aspired thereunto, and was a fear to all the world, how much blood of her own shed she by civil wars and contentions, the gests and writings that mentioneth of Sylla, Marius, Cinna, Cæsar, Pompeius, Brutus, Antonius, August, and other, declareth. Thus when the Lord God would take from Rome for her sins the dominion of the world, he sent the Goths, Vandals, Huns, Arabies, and Turks, that wasted not only Italy, but also Egypt, Africa, and Asia, and so brought the empire of Rome to nought. As many times as I read and mark this history

[1 'Rise' in A.]   [2 'Ignorancy' in A.]

and other like, it causeth me to look upon many evil Englishmen as Scipio[3] looked upon the great city of Carthage, whiles it was a-burning, saying with a lamentable voice, "The inconstancy of fortune in human things is to be lamented:" which voice sprang upon this occasion, that Carthage, being a city of great renown and dominion, was now become a prey unto the fire, and devolted[4], as wisdom always doth, the consideration of present evils unto other yet flourishing in hault[5] and prosperous felicity; and declared, as a man seeing before the ruin and fall of things that stood destinated, the fall of Rome to come, that should perish by like plague.

Even so, when I behold the evil, pestiferous, affected minds of Englishmen, and perpend and weigh the fruits of such corrupt minds, contempt, hatred, grudge, and malice against their king, magistrates, laws, orders, and policies; doubtless I cannot other think but these men, as much as is in them, conspire and work the destruction of this realm. For it can no otherwise be, but as contempt of godly laws and sedition among the people and subjects, of what degree soever they be, have wrought the destruction of other realms; so must it, and can no otherwise do unto this realm. But what realm or kingdom soever will avoid these evils, let them provide the word of God to be truly and diligently preached and taught unto the subjects and members thereof. The lack of it is the chief cause of sedition and trouble, as Salomon saith: "Where prophecy wanteth, the people are dissipated." [Prov. xxix.] Wherefore I cannot a little wonder at the opinion and doctrine of such as say a sermon once in a week, in a month, or in a quarter of a year, is sufficient for the people. Truly it is injuriously and evil spoken against the glory of God and salvation of the people. But seeing they will not be in the whole as good unto God as before they have been unto the devil, neither so glad to remove false doctrine from the people, and to continue them in the true; whereas they did before occupy the most part of the forenoon, the most part of the afternoon, yea, and a great part of

The chief remedy against sedition.

[3 See Polybii Histor. Lib. xxxix. cap. 2. Tom. iv. p. 703. Lipsiæ. 1790. Also Appian. Rom. Hist. Lib. viii. c. 132. Tom. i. p. 307. Lips. 1829. Oros. Lib. iv. c. 23. p. 307. Colon. 1582.]

[4 Devolted: turned.]   [5 Hault: high.]

the night, to keep the estimation and continuance of dangerous and vain superstitions; were it much now to occupy one hour in the morning, and another hour towards night, to occupy the people with true and earnest prayer unto God in Christ's blood, and in preaching the true doctrine of Christ, that they might know and continue in the true religion and faithful confidence of Christ Jesu?

Exercise and diligence bringeth credit unto religion, whether it be true or false. For it never taketh place nor root in the people without diligence, as it is to be perceived by the acts and gests done in the time of Jeroboam and Roboam, the kings of Israel and Judah. What brought the mass and all other idolatry into estimation but daily preaching and saying thereof, with such laud and praise as every old wife knew what a mass was worth?

Fifteen masses in a church daily were not too many for the priests of Baal; and should one sermon every day be too much for a godly bishop and evangelical preacher? I wonder how it[1] may be too much opened and declared unto the people. If any man say, labour is left, and men's business lieth undone by that means, surely it is ungodly spoken; for those that bear the people in hand of such things[2], knoweth right well that there was neither labours, cares, needs, necessity, nor any things else, that heretofore could keep them from hearing of mass, though it had been said at four a clock in the morning. Therefore, as far as I see, people were contented to lose more labour, and spent more time then to go to the devil, than now to come to God: but my faith is, that both master and servant shall find vantage and gain[3] thereby at the year's end, though they hear morning sermon and morning prayers every day of the week. Now by this means they should learn not only to know God, but also their magistrates, and to put difference between the office and the person that is in office, and between the office and the troubles necessarily annexed unto the office: which bringeth not only knowledge of office and officer, but also honour and reverence unto them both; as St Paul, that loved the policy, laws, order, and wisdom of the Romans, yet disliked very much the vice and naughtiness of Nero, unto whom he submitted, and will-

[1 It, i. e. the gospel.]   [2 'Such a thing' in A.]
[3 'Vauntage the gain' in B.]

ingly brought into servitude both his body and goods[4], and rebelled not, though Nero was a naughty emperor, for his office sake, which was the ordinance of God. So did Elias love the state, honour, and dignity of the kings of Israel, yet detested[5] and fell foul out with the faults of Hachab.

The same doctrine teacheth St Peter unto all servants, commanding them to obey their masters, though they be evil, having a respect to the place they be in, which is the order of God, and not unto the vice and abuse of the person in God's order. Truly, be the ruler himself never so evil, yet the laws, judgments, punishments, and statutes, made for the punishment of evil and the defence of the good, be the very work of God; for the magistrates be the keepers of discipline and peace. Therefore as the motion of the heavens, the fertility of the earth, be the works of God, and preserved by him, even so be the governors and rulers of the earth, as David saith, "He giveth health to princes;" as it was shewed in himself, Salomon, Josophat, and others. The regiment and policy of king David was troublous and full of miseries; the reign of king Salomon his son peaceable and quiet; the reign of Josua victorious and prosperous; the reign of the Judges that followed so troublous and unquiet, as a more rent and torn commonwealth I have not read of: yet was the order of God all one, as well in the one as in the other, and required as much love, assistance, and obedience of the people to their king and magistrates in their trouble, as in their quietness and peace. So doth Daniel the prophet most godly and wisely teach by his image that he saw made of four sundry metals; but he concludeth, whether the regiment and regent were[6] gold, silver, copper, or iron, the people always obeyed. The same teacheth also the doctrine and example of John Baptist, Christ, St Stephen, and St James, John's brother. For although the regiment were neither so godly nor so quiet in Herod's time[7] and Poncius Pilatus', as it was in Salomon's time, yet gave they always like reverence, honour, and obedience unto them for their order's sake, as though they had been the virtuousest princes of the world; as their doctrine, tribute, and blood recordeth. For they gave unto Cæsar the things due unto Cæsar, as their bodies and

Deut. xvii.

Psal. cxliv.

Dan. ii.

[4 'His goods' in A.]   [5 'Tested' in B.]
[6 'Be' in A.]   [7 'Times' in A.]

their goods; but their souls they owed to none but unto God: and when diversity of religion and doctrine should be discussed and determined by their laws, they declined from their judgment, and appealed unto the word of God, to have all controversies ended thereby. When that took place, they gave thanks to God; when it did not, they were content patiently to bear whatsoever God's hand[1] would permit the magistrates to lay upon them.

Were these examples known and kept before men's eyes, people would not, for a fault or two that should happen in the regiment, irritate and provoke the regents and princes with contumacy and rebellion, as it is seen commonly at this day; but rather follow the example of the Jews[2], that, when they heard of the facts and doings of Ptolome Lathure, that killed twenty thousand of their countrymen, and caused those that he took captive to eat the flesh of their own dead fathers and brothers, yet rebelled they not, but knew it was for their sin, and therefore exhorted one the other to penance and amendment of life. The same self doctrine teacheth our Saviour Christ in his holy evangelist Luke.

[Luke iii. in A.]

This[3] I thought good to put in my creed for the declaration of my faith towards civil magistrates, orders, and laws; and to open the difference between the orders, the person, and such troubles as be annexed unto the order; lest any man should, for trouble and confusion's sake, damn order and regiment itself, or else by the means thereof to detract, and forsake to take pains in such vocation, as the Epicures did: whereas indeed rule and regiment themselves be the great benefits of God; and therefore now, in the later time, more to be preached and taught to the people, for divers considerations, than ever heretofore; specially because contempt of honesty and laws, labours, and godly exercises, reign more than ever they did. For at the beginning men so obeyed reason, and were ruled thereby, that they brought themselves into order and policy; and for the maintenance thereof

[1 'Hands' in A.]

[2 See Joseph. Antiq. Lib. XIII. cap. 21. Op. p. 458 C. Colon. 1601. Josephus does not state that the *Jews* were compelled to partake of the flesh of their countrymen. His account differs in other respects also from that given in the text.]

[3 'Thus' in A.]

sought out crafts and arts necessary for the preservation of policy and order, and so were glad rather to be ruled by reason than by force and violence. This time being expired, and reason corrupt aspiring farther than reason by nature would, partly for too much love of their[4] self, partly to tame and keep in subjection such as disordered all good order and rule, descended from the regiment of reason unto the force of war and martial laws; the same seeming good unto Almighty God, to tame and reclaim man by force that would not be ruled by reason.

But now are we fallen into the last time and end of the world, wherein for reason ruleth lust, and for just battle ruleth immoderate concupiscence; for scarce is there one of a hundred that love to seek for wisdom and knowledge of reason and of arts that other men found out and left unto us. And as for the pains and travails of war, let every man judge and consider himself, whether our weak nature can suffer as much as David, Achilles, Cyrus, Alexander, Hanibal, Marcellus, Scipio, C. Cæsar, and other did. Then shall we perceive that nature now in man[5] consumed, effeminated, and worn out, is a thing most unable to do that fore-age hath done. Therefore have these latter days more need of much teaching in civil causes than the old age before us, which better and more modestly governed themselves by only reason, than now we do by God's word and reason. And this is not known only by the holy scriptures, but also by profane writers, that declare with the age of the world to increase iniquity. And our experience may be a commentary in this behalf to God's laws and man's laws. For whereas St Paul declareth the civil magistrates not only to be ordained, but also preserved by God, and that all men should accept and account him to be the true magistrate that God had appointed, and not such a one as the people and subjects appoint themselves[6]; and even as wise Cicero[7] perceived at the beginning of the mortal dissension and debate between Pompeius and Julius Cæsar, [and] gave counsel according to the will of God (declared unto him by the suffrages and voices of the Romans), that Cæsar should

[4 'Her' in A.]
[5 'Manner' in A.]   [6 'Theirselves' in A.]
[7 See Cic. Epist. ad Attic. Lib. VII. 5, 6: but the precise sentiment contained in the text has not been found.]

have been chief ruler of the people; now, for lack and contempt of knowledge, both St Paul and Cicero be neglected. For either the people will have no magistrate at all, or else such a one as it pleaseth themselves, and not him that God hath appointed. If this adventure take no place, they will change (if they can) the state of the commonwealth, that where as one reigneth a monarch or king, they would change it into the regiment of many; and where as many reign (as men never contented with the state that God hath appointed), turn the regiment of many into the governance of few: whose nature Horace well declareth, *Libro Epist*.

Optat ephippia bos piger, optat arare caballus[1].

<small>Rom. xiii.</small> Against whose preposterous judgment and fickle minds St Paul vehemently writeth: "The powers," saith he, "that be, are ordained of God," and not the powers that subjects shall choose and make at their pleasures. For no man, of what degree, state, or authority soever he be, being a private man (as all men be in a monarchy, where as one ruleth, in respect of the king that ruleth), should meddle with the state of a realm. For it is God that ordained it, and he <small>Dan. ii. Psal. cxxvi. and cxliii. Prov. xvi. 2 Chron. ii. Isai. i. Psal. viii.</small> that dissolveth it. Neither should this fond opinion take any place in a christian man's head, that any offices appointed by God should cause the officers to be evil before God. For the Lord giveth them titles and names of great honour and love; <small>Psal. lxxii. Isai. xlix. Gen. ix.</small> as gods, and such as serve and please him: also the nurses of the church; as the examples of Adam, Henoch, Noe, with other, who were in those days very godly rulers to maintain virtue and punish vice. This saw not only the patriarchs and godly men of the scripture, but also natural wise men, that saw and reverenced order and policy, as Plato writeth, <small>De Legibus.</small> saying: "As the ox is not ruled by the ox, nor the goat by the goat, but by a more pure nature, to say, by man; so the nature of man is more infirm than can rule itself[2]." Therefore God appointed not only men to rule, but also such men as excelled in wit and wisdom, adjoined with the special and

[1 Horat. Epist. Lib. I. Epist. XIV. l. 43. 'The lazy ox longs for horse-trappings, the horse longs to plough.']

[2 Plato de Legib. Lib. IV. Οὐ βοῦς βοῶν, οὐδὲ αἶγας αἰγῶν ἄρχοντας ποιοῦμεν αὐτοῖς τινὰς, ἀλλ' ἡμεῖς αὐτῶν δεσπόζομεν ἄμεινον ἐκείνων γένος.—Oper. Tom. II. p. 713 D. Paris, 1578.]

singular grace of God: and so saith Plato *De Legibus, Ubi non Deus sed mortalis aliquis dominatur, ibi malorum vel ærumnarum nullum esse effugium*[3]: "Where as any mortal man beareth dominion, and not God, there can be none escape of calamities and miseries." Of the same opinion is Homer[4] the poet, who saith that the gods appointeth their shields to defend princes, as Pallas defended Achilles. That doth Josophat the king in the place afore rehearsed wonderfully declare. And whosoever will consider the execution and due pains towards evil doers, shall right well perceive that God himself is in the magistrate: for Christ saith, "He that striketh with sword shall perish with the sword." And of the oppressors it is spoken, "Wo be unto thee that spoilest, for thou shalt be spoiled." So that we see God to defend civil justice upon earth[5]. Matt. xxvi.
Isai. xxxiii.
Job xi.
Eccles. viii.
Gen. i⁶.
Jer. xxix.
1 Tim. ii.

Abraham, Jeremy, and St Paul declareth that the civil policy is the ordinance of God by such prayer as they commanded the people to pray for it; and this prayer for the magistrates declareth what diversity is between a magistrate christened and a heathen; wherein Cicero differeth from Esay, and[7] king David from Julius Cæsar. Cicero gave counsel after reason and experience to rule the commonwealth; but many times it took not good effect for lack of the wisdom of God. Esay and the rest of the prophets gave counsel not of themselves, but from God; and what prince soever obeyed their counsel, he prospered always, and had good success. The same[8] may you see in the fashions and manner of their wars. Alexander thought himself strong enough by natural strength to conquer his enemies: king David added to his sling-stones the prayer and help of God's name. Therefore if heathen magistrates should be obeyed, much more christian magistrates.

And in case the king's majesty of England may find no less obedience in his subjects than Scipio, Alexander, and other found among theirs, England shall be too strong with

---

[3 Plato de Legib. Lib. IV. E. Ὅσων ἂν πολέων μὴ θεὸς ἀλλά τις ἄρχῃ θνητός, οὐκ ἔστι κακῶν αὐτοῖς οὐδὲ πόνων ἀνάφυξις.]

[4 Hom. Il. Lib. XVIII. 203. Ἀμφὶ δ' Ἀθήνη Ὤμοις ἰφθίμοισι βάλ' αἰγίδα θυσσανόεσσαν.]

[5 'The earth' in A.]   [6 See Gen. xx. 17.]
[7 'And' not in A.]   [8 'And the same' in A.]

God's help for all the world. But Englishmen, I speak it with sorrow and grief of heart, have learned of Cleon[1], a man that Aristophanes writeth of, that had one foot in the senate, and the other in the field; so have Englishmen one hand at the plough, and the other against the magistrates; the ministers of the church, persons, and vicars, one hand upon the portesse[2], and the other to strike at the king's crown. They do follow the ape that Hermogenes' fable speaketh of, that would have had other apes to have builded houses, towns, and cities, to have defended themselves from the dominion of their lord and ruler, man; and thought it not meet to live in the state that God had appointed them. Even so subjects now-a-days (God amend it) would make themselves defences, cities, castles, towns, tents, pavilions, to defend them against their king, lord, and magistrate, and will not be content to live in the state that God appointed them unto. But it shall happen unto them as it did unto the apes; their counsel and conspiracy shall never take place.

[Rom. xiii. in A.] Let us therefore remember St Paul, that saith the powers that be be of God, and not such as we would make; and let us be contented with them, and obey them for conscience sake: for such as disobey and rebel against superior powers, rebel against God, and so God punisheth it with eternal damnation. This is enough to keep every good man and true subject in obedience to their higher powers. If the reader of the scripture of God note the first and the second chapter of Genesis, he should perceive rule and policy, or ever man wist what sin meant: for the Lord gave the superiority and dominion to Adam over all beasts; of whom now we may right well learn obedience, if we were not worse than beasts.

Now a word or two of the magistrates' duty. Aristotle[3] calleth the magistrate φύλαξ νόμου, a keeper of the law. Let him use it therefore indifferently without respect of per-

[[1] See Aristoph. Equit. 75. Ἔχει γὰρ τὸ σκέλος Τὸ μὲν ἐν Πύλῳ τὸ δ' ἕτερον ἐν τῇ 'κκλησίᾳ.]

[[2] Portesse, or portoise, Lat. Portiforium, Breviary, which was sometimes divided into four parts, so as to be more portable. Palmer's Orig. Liturg. Vol. I. p. 208. Oxf. 1836.]

[[3] Ἔστι δ' ὁ ἄρχων φύλαξ τοῦ δικαίου.—Aristot. Ethic. Lib. v. cap. 8. p. 193. Oxf. 1836.]

sons, in punishing such as trouble by inordinate means the commonwealth; and also such as blaspheme the living God, as godly kings and rulers have done, David, Josias, Nabuchodonosor, Constantine, and other. For although a civil law and punishment cannot change the heresies of the mind, neither the desire that men have to do evil; yet when they break forth against the honour of God, and trouble the commonwealth, they should be punished. For the magistrate is as one that hath the two testaments tied at his neck, and should defend them as his own life: and therefore St Paul calleth him not only the revenger of evil, but the maintainer of good; and Esay the prophet saith the same. Rom. xii.4

XVII. Now I will declare my faith concerning the external and visible church of Christ, and of the ministers thereof. I call this visible church a visible congregation of men and women, that hear the gospel of Christ, and use his sacraments as he hath instituted them: in the which congregation the Spirit of God worketh the salvation of all believers, as St Paul saith, "The gospel is the power of God to the salvation of the believer." As though he had said, [By] the gospel of Christ, where it is heard and believed, the mind is changed by the virtue of the Holy Ghost from the love of sin unto the love of virtue: the will is wrought to consent; and the consent so assisted by the Holy Ghost, that faith obtaineth the remission of sin, and the beginning of everlasting life. And these two marks, the true preaching of God's word and right use of the sacraments, declare what and where the true church is. Rom. i.

Unto the which church I would all christian men should associate themselves, although there may happen to be some things desired in manners and discipline. For no church, as touching this part, can be absolutely perfect. But where as the doctrine is sound, and no idolatry defended, that church is of God, as far as mortal man can judge. And where as this doctrine and right use of sacraments be not, there is no church of Christ, though it seem never so holy. For in the blessed Virgin's time the Pharisees and bishops were accounted to be the true church; yet by reason their doctrine was corrupt, the true church rested not in them, but in Simeon, Zachary, Elisabeth, the shepherds, and other. The Luke i. ii.

[4 Rom. xiii. 4.]

same doth St Paul teach us, that whosoever[1] he be that preacheth other doctrine than the word of God, is not to be credited, though he were an angel of heaven. Neither will such as know God hearken unto them, but will hear Christ, the prophets, and apostles, and no other.

<small>Gal. i.
John x.
John iii.
1 Cor. i.
Rom. x.
Eph. ii. iv.
Isai. viii.
xlix.</small>

The other mark is the right use of sacraments, whereof were two in number with the fathers in the ministry of the church, and so many yet be with us in the ministry of the church, and have annexed unto them the promise of eternal salvation, and also of eternal damnation, if they be contemned, and may be lawfully had. In the law of Moses was circumcision and the paschal lamb: and in their places we have baptism and the supper of the Lord, diverse in external elements and ceremonies, but one in effect, mystery, and thing itself; saving that their sacraments shewed the graces of God to be given unto men in Christ to come, and ours declare the graces of God to be given in Christ that is already come: so that the sacraments be not changed, but rather the elements of the sacraments. And every one[2] of these sacraments have their peculiar and proper promises, unto the which they hang annexed, as a seal unto the writing[3]; and therefore be called, after St Paul, the confirmations or seals of God's promises. They have peculiar elements, by the which they signify the heavenly mysteries that sacramentally they contain, and be the thing indeed. They are called sacraments, that is to say, visible signs of invisible grace; they have their proper ceremonies, that testify unto us the obsignation and confirmation of God's heavenly gifts. They have also their proper commandment, because we should not change, add, nor take from them anything at our pleasures. Thus in general I think of all God's sacraments in the ministry of the church.

<small>Gen. xvii.
Exod. xii.
Matt. iii.
xxvi. xxviii.
Mark xiv.
Luke xxii.
1 Cor. xi.</small>

<small>Rom. iv.</small>

XVIII. And of baptism, because it is a mark of our christian church, this I judge, after the doctrine of St Paul, that it is a seal and confirmation of justice, either of our acception into the grace of God. For Christ his[4] innocency and justice by faith is ours, and our sins and injustice by his obedience are his; whereof baptism is the sign, seal, and confirmation. For although freely by the grace of God our

<small>Rom. iv.</small>

[1 'Whatsoever' in A.]   [2 'One' not in A.]
[3 'Writings' in A.]   [4 'For his innocency' in A.]

sins be forgiven, yet the same is declared by the gospel, received by faith, and sealed by the sacraments, which be the seals of God's promises, as it is to be seen by the faith of faithful[5] Abraham. Baptism hath his promises, as is aforesaid; his element the water; his proper commandment and his proper ceremonies, washing in the water. As for other men's opinions, that say circumcision was the seal not only of Abraham's acceptation freely into the grace of God by faith, but also of his obedience and proper justice, I believe it not to be true; for St Paul confuteth it in the same place as an error, saying, "Abraham had nothing whereof he might glory before God." If he had nothing, God confirmed that he gave him, and not that he found in him; for St Paul saith that circumcision was the seal of the justice that came by faith, and not by works. They be out of the way, that have the like opinion of baptism; for St Paul disputeth not in that place, whether works please God, but sheweth that our salvation cometh by grace, and not by works. There be other that think sacraments to be the confirmations not only of our free acceptation into God's favour by faith, but also of our obedience towards God hereafter. And because infants and young babes cannot profess obedience, nor put off the old man, nor put on the new, they would exempt and defraud the young children of baptism. St Paul confuteth also this opinion in the same place: "Abraham," saith he, "believed God, and it was accounted unto him for justice;" and saith not, Abraham professed obedience. Therefore God confirmed his own infallible truth and promises to Abraham by circumcision, and not Abraham's obedience: for if he had, he had confirmed the weak and uncertain infirmity of man, and not his own infallible truth. For Abraham with all his obedience was infirm and imperfect without Christ, yet was bound to work in a godly life. As for those that say circumcision and baptism be like, and yet attribute the remission of original sin to baptism, which was never given unto circumcision, they not[6] only destroy the similitude and equality that should be between them, but also take from Christ remission of sin, and translate it unto[7] the water and element of baptism.

Rom. iv.

Gen. xvii.
[xv. 6.]

[5 'The faithful' in A.]
[6 'Only destroy not' in the originals.]   [7 'Into' in A.]

XIX. As for the supper of the Lord, which is the other sacrament whereby the church of Christ is known, I believe it is a remembrance of Christ's death, a seal and confirmation of his precious body given unto death, wherewith we are redeemed. It is a visible word, that preacheth peace between God and man, exhorteth to mutual love and godly life, teacheth to contemn the world for the hope of the life to come, when as Christ shall appear, and come down in[1] the clouds, which now is in heaven, as concerning his humanity, and nowhere else, nor never shall be, till the time of the general resurrection.

<small>Matt. xxvi.
Mark xiv.
Luke xxii.
1 Cor. xi.</small>

I believe that this holy sacrament hath his proper promises, proper elements, proper commandment, and proper ceremonies.

XX. As concerning the ministers of the church, I believe that the church is bound to no sort of people, or any ordinary succession of bishops, cardinals, or such like, but unto the only word of God; and none of them should be believed <small>Eph. iv.</small> but when they speak the word of God. Although there be diversity of gifts and knowledge among men, some know more, and some know less: and if he that knoweth[2] least, teach Christ after the holy scriptures, he is to be accepted; <small>Gal. i.</small> and he that knoweth most, and teacheth Christ contrary, or any other[3] ways than the holy scriptures teach, is to be refused. I am sorry therefore with all my heart to see the church of Christ degenerated into a civil policy: for even as kings of the world naturally by descent from their parents must follow in civil regiment, rule, and law, as by right they ought; even so must such as succeed in the place of bishops and priests that die, possess all gifts and learning of the Holy Ghost, to rule the church of Christ, as his godly predecessor had; so that the Holy Ghost must be captive and bondman to bishops' sees and palaces. And because the Holy Ghost was in St Peter at Rome, and in many other godly men that have occupied bishopricks and dioceses; therefore the same gifts, they say, must needs follow in their successors, although indeed they be no more like of zeal nor diligence than Peter and Judas, Balaam and Jeremy, Annas and Caiaphas to John and James. But thus I conclude of the ministers, of what degree or dignity soever they be, they be no better than

[1 'Into' in A.]   [2 'Know' in A.]   [3 'Another ways' in A.]

records and testimonies, ministers and servants of God's word and God's sacraments; unto the which they should neither add, diminish, nor change anything. And for their true service and diligence in this part they should not be only reverenced of the people, but also honoured by the magistrates, as the servants of God. And I believe that as many souls as perish by their negligence or contempt of God's word, shall be required at their hands. Matt. xxviii.
1 Cor. iv.
Acts i.

Ezek. ii.
xxiii[4].

XXI. Of the people thus I believe, that they owe their duty and obedience to God, to their king and magistrates, unto their neighbours, and unto themselves. Unto God they owe both body and soul, to laud and praise him, according to God's book, to call upon him in the days of their trouble, and upon none else, to conform both their doctrine and their lives to promote and set forth the glory of God. 1 Cor. vii. x.

Their duty to the king's majesty is their obedience to him, his laws, and the realm, for conscience sake, and rather to lose both body and goods than to offend his highness or his laws. And whensoever any subject be called to serve with body or goods, at home or from home, willingly they must obey without question or farther inquisition to search whether the king's cause be right or wrong. For, whether it be or be not, it maketh the death of him that serveth in this respect neither better nor worse. For I believe such as obeyed king Josias, and were slain in the battle against the Egyptians, were acceptable unto God in Christ, though king Josias had not the best quarrel. In this case the subject oweth his body and goods unto this lawful magistrate, and may deny him of none of them both. Unto their neighbours they owe goodwill and charity, help, and preservation of their bodies, souls, goods, and fame, that none of all those perish, if they may preserve them. They owe unto themselves the study and labour to read and hear the scripture of God, until such time as they have laid a true foundation of faith in Christ. When that is done, they be bound to themselves to build upon that foundation all charitable works, as well to God as to man, with innocency of life. After that, they owe to themselves study and diligence to make defences for their true religion against the devil, the flesh, the world, sin, the wisdom of man, and Rom. xiii.
1 Tim ii.
1 Pet. ii.

2 Chron.
xxxv.
Matt. v.
Luke vi.
John xv.
Rom xiii.
Gal v.
John ii. iii.
Exod. xiii.
Deut. vi.
Eph. vi.
Col. i.

Psal. cxix.
1 Cor. iii.

[4 The references here intended are probably Ezek. iii. 18, and xxxiii. 8.]

superstitious hypocrites, which cease not to pervert and destroy in man the image and work of God.

Away! away! I pray you, with this opinion, that thinketh a man to owe no more unto himself for religion than to learn by rote the creed, ten commandments, and pater-noster. St Paul rebuketh that opinion, as it is to be seen in his epistle.

Psal. cxix. We owe unto ourselves due labours in praying unto God daily for the necessities of both body and soul, and likewise to give him thanks for all the goodness that[1] he hath given unto us. Also we owe unto ourselves the eschewing and avoiding of idleness and ocivity[2], and the labours of our own hands, with the industry and gift of reason, learning, and wit, to eat our

Gen. iii. own bread with the sweat and pain of our own bodies, according to the commandment of God.

Thus I conclude my faith; the which, being examined by the word of God, is catholic and godly; who send us of his grace to fear him, honour the king, and to love one
the other, as Christ loveth us
all. So be it.
The twentieth of December
anno MDL[3].
Lord bless thy church,
and save our king.

[1 'That' not in A.]   [2 Ocivity: indolence.]
[3 'And fifty' in A.]

The Colophon in A is,

𝕴𝖒𝖕𝖗𝖎𝖓𝖙𝖊𝖉 𝖆𝖙 𝕷𝖔𝖓𝖉𝖔𝖓
𝖇𝖞 𝕴𝖍𝖔𝖓 𝕯𝖆𝖞𝖊 𝖉𝖜𝖊𝖑𝖑𝖞𝖓𝖌 𝖔𝖇𝖊𝖗
𝕬𝖑𝖉𝖊𝖗𝖘𝖌𝖆𝖙𝖊 𝖇𝖊𝖓𝖊𝖙𝖍 𝕾𝖆𝖞𝖓𝖙
𝕸𝖆𝖗𝖙𝖞𝖓𝖘, 𝖆𝖓𝖉 𝖆𝖗𝖊 𝖙𝖔
𝖇𝖊 𝖘𝖔𝖑𝖉 𝖆𝖙 𝖍𝖎𝖘 𝖘𝖍𝖔𝖕
𝖇𝖞 𝖙𝖍𝖊 𝖑𝖎𝖙𝖑𝖊 𝖈𝖔𝖚𝖓=
𝖉𝖚𝖎𝖙 𝖎𝖓 𝕮𝖍𝖊𝖕𝖊=
𝖘𝖞𝖉𝖊.

Cum privilegio ad imprimendum solum per septennium.

ANNOTATIONS ON ROMANS XIII.

¶ Godly and most

necessary Annotations in yͤ xiii Chapyter too the Romaynes:

Set furth by the

right vigilant Pastor, Jhō Hoper, by gods calling, Busshop of Gloucestre.

Anno Do. 1551.
Mense Maii.
Cum privilegio ad imprimendum solum.

The following is the colophon at the end of the "Annotations:"

Imprynted
the xiii. day of
May.
Anno. Do. 1551.
At Worceter
by Thō Oswen, Printer appoynted by yͤ
kings Maiestie, for
yͤ Principalitie of
Wales, and Marches of yͤ same.

Cum privilegio ad imprimendum solum.

To my very loving, and dear-beloved fellow-labourers in the word of God, and brethren in Christ, William Jenins, dean of the cathedral church in Gloucester, John Williams, doctor of the law and chancellor, and to the rest of all the church appointed there to serve the living God, with all other, archdeacons, officials, deans, parsons, vicars, and curates, within this the king's majesty's diocese of Gloucester, grace and mercy from the Lord ever-living, in the blood of Jesus Christ, our only Saviour.

IF the dangers and perils of St Paul's time, dear-beloved, ministered and gave occasion unto him for to fear of the loss of such people as then were converted unto the knowledge and understanding of God's holy word, lest by negligence or corrupt doctrine of the bishops and pastors they might be seduced and brought into error; doubtless the dangers of this our time, that be not only to be feared, lest such as know the truth be by error seduced and brought from the truth, or else, by continuance in ungodly life, continue in the truth in vain, but also that the most part of people be yet ignorant and not converted unto the truth, should minister and give occasion unto us a great deal more to be vigilant and circumspect, not only to keep those in truth to whom God hath revealed it, but also to win and convert with all prayer, diligence, preaching, and other instruction, such as yet be ignorant and out of the way, unto the truth and knowledge of God's word: and so much the rather, because we see by experience, and also feel it in ourselves, that the just God is offended and angry with our sins, and will not be contented with these troubles, miseries, and crosses, that already he layeth upon us, but doth doubtless prepare and make ready many more and more grievous. Our office therefore is to be diligent and circumspect for the people of God; and now, the hand of God being stretched forth, to admonish the flock committed unto our charges in time, lest they die, and their blood required at our hands. Certain I am that our sins be the only cause wherefore this most just God is offended; and certain we be that the only way and means to please and quiet him again, is to leave and wash away our sins.

What the sins of the people be wherewithal God is thus offended, you that have the oversight of them know, or ye ought to know. I mean not to descend particularly to any sin, lest peradventure I might seem to be temerous[1] and over-hardy, to judge more than I perfectly know; or else, in naming such sins as many good, simple people have not heard of, might rather learn to augment the evil they know, than to learn the good they know not. It is the duty of every good pastor and curate diligently to search and know what virtue is most meet to be commended, and what vice most to be reprehended, in the church that he serveth. I will leave therefore the unknown evils unto me to the shepherd of every parish, requiring him to mark the sins of the people after and by the estimation of God's word, and thereby to ponder the condition of his people, lest that he cause them, and do the same himself, swallow a camel, and be choked with a flea; leap over a block, and stumble at a straw. Before all things, see that the people know their commandments, and the works thereof, appertaining unto God in the first table, that they honour no wrong nor false God, nor yet the true God a wrong way, but as he hath commanded himself in the old testament and the new: and also that they avoid all such sins, faults, and disobedience, as be contrary to the commandments of God in the second table. And for a help unto you, and also to the people, in this behalf, I have set forth here the thirteenth chapter of St Paul to the Romans, which entreateth of all the second table, and duty of a christian man, how he should use himself with and towards all sorts of people: most heartily praying you, and also in God's name and the king's majesty's name command you, that as many as serveth any cure within this diocese, that cannot, for lack of learning or exercise, teach nor preach himself to the people the like doctrine, that they do, every Saturday and Sunday, read unto the people this thirteenth chapter, as I have here set it forth; that the people may learn to know, love, and fear the better the king's majesty, and other such magistrates as be by him appointed over the people. And all such as God hath given grace of preaching unto, in their sermons shall oftentimes inculcate and persuade this argument and rule of obedience unto the people. And the cause why I have written in this chapter more than another, and think it very expedient to be

[[1] Temerous: rash, hasty.]

now taught unto the people, is the great and dangerous offences and sins of the richer sort of people, and also of the poor, both in this shire, and other the king's majesty's in this realm. And certain I am that both of them shall die eternally, if they amend not.

Wherefore, to deliver my soul, I give such as be commended by God and the king's majesty unto my charge, warning of the judgment and damnation to come before. The rich man so encroacheth, gathereth together, and obtaineth so much into his own hands, that he alone possesseth the earth, liveth thereby, and his poor neighbour ready to die for lack; so that he is brought into Tantalus' pain, meat and drink, cattle and corn enough of every side of him, yet shall rather die for lack, than that unsatiable and never contented covetous persons will price their goods so as poor men, their wives, and their children may be able to buy reasonable penny-worths of God's abundant plenty and riches that he bringeth out of the earth. These men, except they repent, cannot be saved, nor be partakers of the merits of Christ's passion. For God would the rich to give unto the poor: but our men, that care neither for God nor the king's laws, will neither give nor sell whatsoever necessity do require. If they would not care for God's word, yet should they have respect to nature and to their country. Though the poor man be not a rich man, yet is he a Christian, and thy countryman, of whom nature and countryship requireth thee to have compassion. The poor man, partly provoked by necessity and need, and partly of unchristian hatred and disdain he hath at his neighbour's wealth and prosperity, conspireth, worketh, provoketh, and desireth by all means to oppress and rob his richer neighbour; and will by force, strength, treason, sedition, commotion, assemblance, and gathering together of such as he is himself, against God's laws, God's ordinances, magistrates and superior powers, take away and usurp every man's goods, he careth not how; not remembering the judgment and terrible damnation of God for his so doing, and that it is his bounden duty to suffer and bear such needs and necessities as God layeth upon us for our sins; and that, upon pain of hell-fire, no man should revenge his own wrongs, but commend himself to God, who can and will hear the prayers of the poor in their troubles and needs: and that they should offer their

[HOOPER, II.]

supplications to the king's majesty, and to such other as be appointed for the redress of such oppression and wrongs; and not to take weapons, armour, and force against God and his ordinances. In case the king's majesty, and the rest appointed to see poor men's causes redressed, will not hearken to their clamour, doubtless the ire and vengeance of God will punish them, and so much the rather, if the people quietly and obediently commend their causes unto him; the which if they do not, they perish eternally. For there is no traitor nor seditious man can be saved; but obedient and quiet men shall inherit the kingdom of heaven, and such as suffer wrong, and not such as do wrong, or intend to revenge by strength their own wrongs. Therefore to keep the people of this diocese from the displeasure of God and their king, and myself from everlasting damnation, I require you most diligently to teach them this chapter every week, one part of it the Saturday at even-song, the other the Sunday at the morning prayer, and the third part the Sunday at even-song. Thus fare ye all well, and God give us grace all well to discharge our offices commended unto us.

Yours with all my heart,
Brother and fellow-preacher,
John Gloucester.

Annotations in the thirteenth chapter to the Romans.

⁋ THE PROLOGUE.

THE office and duty of a christian man is contained in two parts: the first, that he use himself aright and reverently with God; the second, that he use him comely and honestly with man. In the epistle to the Romans, from the beginning, St Paul hath fully and sufficiently declared the duty and office of man towards God: towards the end he declareth how we may honestly do our duties towards men. Both these offices must diligently be known and exercised. And because a civil and outward life, seem it never so honest, is mere and very hypocrisy, and cannot please God, except the mind and soul inwardly be well affected towards him, I think it convenient briefly to declare wherein St Paul in this epistle doth put the religion of the heart of man towards God; and then we shall the better descend unto such duties and offices as appertaineth to all manner of persons, as well public as private.

First, St Paul perceiveth that the grace and promises of God cannot be known of man, until such time as he be brought to acknowledge and displeasure of his sins. The physician and physic be unprofitable unto such as know not that they be sick, as Christ said, "I came not to call the just, but sinners to repentance." Therefore we must know the wound of our souls and the sickness of sin, before we can get any profit by the grace of God. We must confess that all men and women, except Christ, are born the children of ire and of God's displeasure; and that we bear about in us sin, that always repugneth the Spirit, whereby we are ascertained that we be always subject unto sin; as St Paul saith, "He concluded all men under sin, because he might have mercy upon all." Seeing we be all sinners, and "the reward of sin is death," St Paul's conclusion, where he saith "We are born all the children of God's displeasure," is true. How then may we be delivered from this great ire and displeasure? By the mercy of God the Father towards us, that first loved us, ere we loved him, whiles we were yet his enemies. But what is that, wherewithal we may be annexed and reconciled unto God by his

^{Matt. ix.}
^{Rom. xi.}
^{Rom. vi.}
^{Ephes. ii.}
^{1 John iv. Rom. v.}

mercy, when there is no good thing in us, but all filthy and sinful? It is Jesus Christ, the Son of God, most dear-beloved, in whom the Father is contented, and by whom he is reconciled unto all sinners that repent, and believe his promises, for the merits and shedding of Christ's blood, his dear-beloved Son. After that we see and perceive so great a mercy and pity of our heavenly Father, that would not favour nor spare his only Son to die for our redemption, but gave him to the most cruel and vile death of the cross for us; how should not we trust to so merciful a Father in all our troubles and adversities, whether they be of body or soul? Why should we not call only upon so merciful a God? If we do thus amend our lives, believe his promises, and study a better life, we shall not only be saved by his mercy, but also glad to serve him, and walk before him in innocency and pureness of life, and also obediently and quietly in the world; give reverence and love to all persons accordingly; to whom honour, honour; to whom love, love; to whom justice, justice; to whom mercy, mercy. Unto this christian quietness, reverence, love, and fear doth all the scripture exhort us, and chiefly this present thirteenth chapter to the Romans: for the understanding whereof the better, I note at the beginning a certain diversity and difference of persons. There be, and ever hath been, some public persons and some private persons. Public persons be those that bear any office, rule, regiment, or dominion, in a commonwealth: as a king with all his justices, mayors, sheriffs, bailiffs, constables, and other. Private persons be such as be subjects, and under these officers. These two persons must be diversely used, and the duty that is due unto the one is not due unto the other in civil respects. And seeing we must live with both these persons and states appointed to be in the world by Almighty God, St Paul in this chapter is very diligent to teach and instruct us how we should live accordingly in truth and honesty towards them both.

⁋ *The division of the Chapter.*

Parts
1. Why the superior powers should be obeyed.
2. How we be debtors of love to the public person and magistrate, and to the private person that is a subject, indifferently.
3. Containeth an exhortation to innocency and honesty of life, that, the truth being once known and received, every man should abstain and keep himself from filthiness and unclean life.

The first part, concerning the obedience of the Magistrates.

Let every soul submit himself unto the authority of the higher powers. The text.

St Paul pronounceth generally that every soul, that is to say, every man, should be obedient unto the higher power: in a kingdom and monarchy, where one is appointed to rule, all the subjects of the same realm are bound to obey the one king appointed by God, of what condition, state, or degree soever they be; as the king himself is bound to be obedient unto the law, and unto God, where as the laws be not contrary to the law of God and the law of nature. And here is no exception to be made. No man in a kingdom is or ought to be privileged or exempt from the obedience of the king, which is the higher power. And the ecclesiastical laws, that do exempt and privilege any spiritual (as they be called) or temporal person from this general rule, "Every man be obedient to the higher power," is damnable and heretical, manifestly condemned by the word of God. For Christ and his apostles paid tribute and other duties unto the higher powers of the earth. Matt. xvii.

And the powers that here St Paul speaketh of, be not only kings and emperors, but all such as be appointed to any public office and common regiment, either for a king, where as is a kingdom, or in the place of a king, where as the state of the commonwealth is no monarchy, but a rule and dominion commended to many. To all these St Paul commandeth obedience, honour, reverence, and love to be borne. And this is specially to be noted in St Paul, that he saith simple and plainly, we should obey "the higher powers," to Rom. xiii.

confute, argue, and reprehend those that cloke and excuse their disobedience, either for the age of the rulers, or else for conditions and manners of the rulers. And that age dischargeth no man for inobedience, the word of God declareth how that he was present to help young kings, and to defend them in their under age; as it is to be seen by king Josias. Also God punisheth young kings as often as they walk not after his word; as it is to be seen by Jehoiakim[1], that was crowned in the eighth year of his age, and within three months and ten days, for the sins he committed before God, he was taken prisoner by Nebuchadnezzar. Even so was Manasseh, being of twelve years of age. Neither doth the manners and condition of the magistrates excuse our inobedience, though they be naught. For Paul biddeth us look upon the power and authority of the higher powers, and not upon their manners. And St Peter commandeth the servants to obey their masters, though they be evil. So Joseph obeyed Pharaoh; and Christ, our Saviour, Pilate; St Paul the emperors of Rome, Caligula and Nero. And when St Paul commandeth us to be obedient, he meaneth not only we should speak reverently and honourably of the higher power, or make courtesy unto him, but to obey the laws set forth by the powers, except they command things against God's laws: then must we obey more God than men; and yet not to strive and fight with the magistrates, but suffer patiently death rather than to offend God: or else our obedience is nothing but hypocrisy and dissimulation. Who would accept his own child's making of courtesy, when all his facts be contrary to his commandments? What master would be content, or think his servant did his duty in putting off his cap, and in his doing contemneth all his master's laws and commandments? The laws of a magistrate be of two conditions and sorts: either they concern God, or man. If they concern or appertain to God, either they be according to the word of God, or contrary to the

margin notes: 2 Chron. xxi. [xxxiv.]; 2 Chron. xxxvi.; Pet. ii.; Acts v.

[[1] This is related of Jehoiachin, who, when eight years of age, was associated with himself in the kingdom by his father Jehoiakim. Upon the death of the latter ten years later, Jehoiachin became sole king, and after reigning *by himself* for a period of three months and ten days was taken prisoner by Nebuchadnezzar.—Compare 2 Kings xxiv. 8, and 2 Chron. xxxvi. 9. See also Patrick's Comment. in loc.]

word of God. If they be according to the word of God, of necessity and bondage, upon pain of damnation they must be obeyed. If they be repugnant to the word of God, they should not be obeyed. Yet rather should a man suffer death than to defend himself by force and violent resisting of the superior powers, as Christ, his apostles, and the prophets did. If the laws concern and appertain unto man, and unto things civil, they must simply, without exception, be obeyed, except they repugn and be contrary to the law of nature: as Pharaoh's laws and commandment was to the midwives, Exod. i. that they should have killed all the men-children that the women of Israelites brought forth.

Seeing St Paul commandeth us to give obedience unto the higher powers, how much be these men worthy hell-fire, that resist them both with hand, heart, and tongue? In the book of Exodus the people is commanded not to speak Exod. xxii. evil of the higher powers: read the place, and learn to detest and abhor those runagates that in every tavern and tap-house spue out their blasphemous and traitorous talks against magistrates, when they should rather look upon their own faults, and study to amend them. And also pray God to do the same in the magistrates, that it might please him, of his great mercy, to amend and redress all things that be amiss.

After that St Paul hath generally commanded all men to be obedient to the higher powers, he sheweth the causes wherefore they should be obeyed.

> For there is no power (saith he) but of God. The The text. powers that be are ordained of God. Whosoever therefore resisteth power, resisteth the ordinances of God.

Because that naturally there is in every man a certain desire of liberty, and to live without subjection and all manner of laws, except such as please himself, St Paul is not content generally to exhort and command all men to obedience of the higher powers, but giveth many great and weighty causes wherefore men should be obedient and in subjection unto them.

The first is, because the office of a magistrate is the ordinance of God: and seeing all the ordinances and powers of

God are to be obeyed, necessarily it followeth that without all tergiversation, hypocrisy, and collusion that the magistrate must be obeyed, except we will say, in some respects God is not to be obeyed. Of this reason of St Paul we must note, first, the dignity and honour of a public person, that his office and place is the ordinance and appointment of God. And therefore the magistrates be called gods in the holy scripture. For no man can come to the office of a magistrate but by the permission and sufferance of God. Many times some persons come unto the place of a ruler by false and preposterous means; as those do that for a private lucre, or private hatred to other, put up themselves, and pull down those that God hath appointed. But such ungodly coming to honour God suffereth, and appointeth for the sins of the people such evil and dissembling hypocrites to reign. But let the king and magistrate be as wicked as can be devised and thought, yet is his office and place the ordinance and appointment of God, and therefore to be obeyed. And as it is the subjects' duty to obey them, so is it their duty to watch and be circumspect that they trouble nor unquiet any thing in their offices contrary to the word of God, whose officers they be. In case they do, although the subjects may not, nor, upon pain of eternal damnation, ought not, by force nor violence to resist the officer in his high power; yet he should, and is bound to think himself, that God can and will as well revenge the abuse of his office in him, as punish the subject for the disobedience of his ordinances towards the higher power.

<small>Exod. xxii.
Psal. lxxxii.</small>

If it be true, that St Paul saith, the higher power to be the ordinance of God, it is very damnable iniquity, that for any private affection, or other injust oppressions, for any man to depose the magistrates from their places and honour appointed by God; or else privily or openly, craftily or violently, to go about to change or alter the state and ordinance of God: and therewithal God is sore offended; as it doth appear by the grudging and murmuring of the people against Moses in the desert, the which thoughts and conspiracies of the people against their magistrate and governor the Lord punished with death, and killed them all before they came to the land of Canaan. For even as kings and magistrates be appointed and ordained of God, even so be they also defended

<small>1 Sam. viii.

Numb. xiv.</small>

by him, as it appeared by David, Jehoshaphat, and other. And the sedition and treason redounded always to the destruction of the people at length; as it is to be seen in Absalom, Ahithophel, Catiline, Brutus, Cassius, and other, that destroyed not only themselves, but also the people, by such treason and disobedience against the ordinance and appointment of God: as ye may see here by the text of St Paul that followeth, which is his second cause why the higher powers should be obeyed. And as he said first, they should be obeyed, because their place and authority is the ordinance of God, so now in his second cause he sheweth what great danger and peril it is to resist and disobey God's ordinances. 2 Sam. xvii. xviii.

And they that resist shall receive to themselves damnation. The text.

As though he had said, Lest ye should think it a light thing, and but a trifling matter to withstand and disobey the magistrates, understand ye that in your so doing ye withstand and fight against God; and therefore ye provoke judgment and vengeance against yourselves, and be culpable and guilty of God's everlasting displeasure, if ye repent not, and give over your obstinate and disobedient rebellion. Here St Paul hath set forth the end and success of sedition, treason, conspiracy, and rebellion, to say, destruction both of body and soul. Who is able to contend and fight with God, and overcome him? Is not he only Almighty, and only strength?

Absalom, with a thousand traitors against one true subject, prevailed not against his father David; but died the death of a traitor. Even so did those whom before I named. And as St Paul speaketh here, so speaketh Christ to Peter, "He that striketh with the sword shall perish by the sword." If God's word be true (as it cannot be false), all such as do by thought, word, or deed, intend to trouble, unquiet, change, alter, move, or resist the ordinance of God, which is the magistrates and higher powers, must needs of necessity perish, as well in this world, as in the world to come, except they repent, and cease from doing of evil. Now goeth St Paul forth with the text. Matt. xxvi.

The text. **For rulers be not to be feared of such as do well, but of such as do evil.**

By these words St Paul declareth two things. First, he warneth the magistrate of his office, lest, when he shall perceive it to be the ordinance of God, and that no man should more resist and contrary it than to resist and contrary God, should wax arrogant and proud, and begin to favour and flatter himself too much under the title and pretence of God's power. But God forbid (saith St Paul) that the magistrate should think any such thing: he should remember rather that he is appointed to his place to defend, help, and preserve such as be good, and punish such as be naught and evil. This commandment did God command to the higher powers in the commonwealth of the Israelites, and that they should not lift up their hearts above their brothers, but to use indifference and justice with all indifferently without exception of persons; as ye may read in the holy scripture.

<small>Exod. xviii. Numb. xxvii. Deut. i. xvi. xvii. 2 Chron. xxxix.[1]</small>

The second part of St Paul's words commendeth the magistrates for their utility and commodity in the commonwealth, because that by their authority evil-doers among the people are punished and corrected, that honest and true men may live in rest and quietness. And for this commodity and necessary use we be bound to obey them. For through their diligence, labour, and pains, under God, we eat, hear the word of God, labour, bring up youth, households be in quietness, the goods thereof, with cities, towns, and villages of the realm. These commodities be great and worthy of thanks, specially to God, and then to the higher power.

<small>Psal. lxxii. lxxxii. ci.</small>

St Paul followeth his purpose with these words:

The text. **Wilt thou be without fear of the higher power? Do well then, and so shalt thou be praised of them.**

Whereas before he said the high power was a fear to evil-doers, in these words he sheweth how men may be without fear of the magistrates, to say, if men do well: for well-doing pleaseth God's order; and God's order being pleased feareth not[2], nor punisheth the well-doer. And whereas St Paul speaketh of fear to the higher power, we must understand

[1 So in the original: probably a misprint for 2 Chron. xix. 6.]
[2 Feareth not: maketh not afraid.]

that fear is of two sorts. One is of love and good-will annexed and knit with reverence and love; and this fear is only in godly and virtuous men, that delight to be ordered and ruled after the order and appointment of God.

The other fear is annexed with spite, hatred, envy, and disdain, that wisheth there were no order, law, nor magistrates, and those that be, to destroy them, or to bring them out of credit and estimation among the people. This fear is wicked and damnable, and a testimony of an evil and cursed conscience, and forbidden here in this place by St Paul. St Paul continueth in the commendation of the magistrates, saying:

For he is the minister of God for thy wealth. *The text.*

Here St Paul addeth another commendation of the higher power, the which consisteth in two members, wherefore he should be obeyed. The first is, because he is "the minister of God:" the second, because he was instituted and appointed by God for the wealth and commodity of the subject. In this, that St Paul calleth him the minister of God, he putteth the subject in mind again, that whosoever contemn or disobey the higher power, contemneth and disobeyeth God. And so saith Christ, "Whoso contemneth such as I appoint and send *Luke x.* contemneth me." And the same said God unto Moses[3], "They have not cast off thee, but me." Also the magistrate there is warned to take heed he do nothing but as the minister of God, to rule and govern after his word. For this God *Deut. xvii.* requireth of him, that he be a faithful minister. And whensoever he begin to wax lofty, haughty, arrogant, and proud, let him remember St Paul's words, that he is but a minister. *1 Cor. iv.*

And whereas St Paul saith the magistrate is ordained for the wealth of the people, he must take heed of the end whereunto he is appointed, and be indeed, as God would him to be, a wealth and salvation of the people, to defend just causes, and to condemn such as be unjust; to remove false and superstitious religion, and to plant true and godly religion; to maintain such as profit the church and flock of Christ, and to remove such as hinder and deceive them. St Paul now pro-

[3 See Exod. xvi. 8. These words, however, were addressed not to Moses, but to Samuel.—See 1 Sam. viii. 7.]

secuteth his matter, and sheweth who should fear the higher powers, with these words:

The text. If thou do evil, then fear; for he beareth not a sword for nought: but he is the minister of God, to take punishment of them that do evil.

Even as St Paul saith here, that the cause of fear to an evil man is that the magistrate beareth a sword, even so doth he declare that it is not enough for the magistrate to bear a sword, but to use and execute the sword, as the sins of the people require, to punish and kill them, if the law so find them guilty: and for fear of the use of the sword, which is not in vain, they should keep evil-doers in obedience and fear; and so much the more, because he is the minister of God, and his punishment is the very hand and will of God, when he punisheth evil-doers. And it is not he that killeth, but God, whose place he occupieth, being a magistrate and higher power: for God commandeth him to punish, and not to favour such evil and naughty persons.

Exod. xxiii. xxii.
Lev. xix. xx.
Deut. xix.

It is very devilishness to accuse the magistrates of evil doings, when they punish or put to death evil-doers; seeing in their this doing they be none other but God's ministers. And whereas the scripture forbiddeth punishment and revenging, it meaneth that no private man should revenge his own cause, nor fight at his pleasure, but rather suffer wrongs, if the law will not redress it. And if the judge and magistrate, in a cause of the law, for lucre, fear, love, friendship, or any other respect, kill any man that is not worthy by the law to die, the judge and magistrate is a very murderer. And so he is, if he save any man that the law condemneth. For he is, as St Paul saith, a minister of God, who never saveth one and condemneth the other in like causes. St Paul, when he hath sufficiently declared the dignity and honour of the higher power, gathereth by two necessary causes more that the magistrate is to be obeyed, with these words:

The text. Wherefore ye must needs obey, not for fear of vengeance only, but also because of conscience.

The one cause wherefore we must obey, is the fear of pain and punishment, the which the magistrate must minister by the commandment of God unto all such as disobey and contemn the ordinance of God.

The other is conscience: for although the magistrate do not see nor know how thou dost disobey and break the order of God; or else if thou couldest, by power and strength, overcome the magistrates, yet thy conscience is bound to obey, and that for many causes: first, because the magistrate is the ordinance of God; then, because disobedience and breaking of God's laws troubleth the public and common peace, and giveth other stomach and encouraging to disobey. All these evils followeth disobedience, the which, of conscience, we are bound to eschew and avoid.

There be some so indurate and past grace, that think themselves not bound to obey this order and higher power, appointed and commanded of God: but doubtless those shall perish with their captains, as Ahithophel did with his Absalom.

If the higher power command anything contrary unto God's word, they should not be obeyed. Notwithstanding, there should be such modesty and soberness used as should be without all violence, force, and rebellion: as Peter and John used, saying, "God is more to be obeyed than man." And so in saying of truth they continued in the truth without moving of sedition, and suffered death for the truth; as Fabian and Cyprian[1], holy martyrs and records of God, suffered in Africa under Decius, the emperor of Rome. How we are bound in conscience to obey them, St Paul declareth further, saying:

And even for this cause pay ye tribute; for they are God's ministers appointed to the same purpose. *The text.*

If we were not bound in conscience to obey them, we should not need to pay tribute unto them; but, seeing we ought to pay tribute, taxes, and subsidies, we know they do defend us against all force, violence, and wrongs of our enemies. Therefore tribute is a note and knowledge of our obedience, which we must pay willingly and gladly, of duty, as Christ saith, "Give unto God that which is God's, and to the emperor that which is the emperor's."

[[1] Fabian suffered martyrdom at Rome under Decius, about A.D. 250, Euseb. Hist. Eccl. Lib. VI. c. 39; Cyprian in Africa under Valerian, A.D. 258. See Hieron. Catal. Scriptor. Ecclesiast. 77, Op. Tom. I. fol. 102 G, Paris. 1534.]

St Paul sheweth the cause why tribute ought to be paid unto the higher powers, because, saith he, they be ordained of God, to preserve and defend the commonwealth in peace and quietness; to punish the evil, and to defend the good. And without the magistrate's help this cannot be done; as ye may read in the book of the Judges, how the people fell into all mischief, when they wanted a lawful magistrate and superior power, and every man did as it seemed best in his own eyes. And in the prophet Esay the Lord threateneth the wicked Jerusalem, because there was none in it worthy to bear rule. Even as subjects be bound to obey this higher power, so must the higher power alway take heed that virtue and good men be commended, and evil men with sin and disobedience punished. Now followeth the second part of the chapter.

<small>Isai. iii.</small>

<small>The second part of the chapter.</small>

<small>The text.</small>

Give to every man therefore his duty; tribute to whom tribute belongeth; custom to whom custom is due; fear to whom fear belongeth; honour to whom honour pertaineth.

When St Paul hath sufficiently told us our duties to the higher power, he descendeth from that particularity and one sort of persons to a generality, how we should do our duties to all manner of persons. First, generally he saith, we should give every man his due. Then numbereth he certain kinds and particulars of duties. "Tribute" we owe to kings and magistrates: that must we faithfully pay, or else the withholders commit theft; and therefore Christ paid tribute. "Custom" is the revenues or profits that cometh by land, or trade of merchandise; and, in this point, faith must be kept to all men, according to the laws appointed by the higher power. "Fear" is due unto God, the king, to parents, and to all other of whom we be holpen in body or soul; and so is "honour" due likewise. Therefore saith the law, "Fear God, honour the king," "Honour father and mother," &c. "Arise to a hoary head." St Paul breaketh his disputation of duties, and will tarry no longer in the enumeration and numbering of the parts and particulars of duties, but referreth all together to charity in this wise:

<small>1 Pet. ii. Exod. xx.</small>

Owe nothing to any man but to love one the other. _{The text.}

As though he had said, What needeth it to write much of duties, contracts, of buying, lendings, and such other like things? Let charity be the rule of all these things; unto the which if the subject submit himself, he will use his higher power none otherwise than he would be used himself, if he were an higher power; the higher power the subject none otherwise than though he were a subject himself. Whatsoever thing agreeth with charity is good; whatsoever agreeth not with charity is evil. But many men cannot tell what charity is; and therefore it is no marvel though all their doings be against charity.

Charity is a fervent desire and earnest study to do well unto all men, yea, even with the hurt of him that doth it, if necessity so requireth, as St Paul teacheth. And St John _{Phil. ii.
1 John iii.} saith, "Christ gave his life for us, and we ought to give ours for our brothers." The effects, properties, and conditions of this charity St Paul sheweth, and saith, "Charity suffereth, will not do evil for evil, looketh not her own profit, charity will not conspire nor work traitorously, but pray for them that persecute her," &c. Thus St Paul declareth that we be debtors to keep peace and quietness among our neighbours, and to do all men good as long as we live. Faith maketh us free before God in Christ Jesu: charity maketh us servants to our neighbours for the love of Christ. St Paul proveth by examples that charity should be the rule of all our doings, with these words that follow:

> **For he that loveth another fulfilleth the law. For these** _{The text.} **commandments, Thou shalt not commit adultery, Thou shalt not kill, Thou shalt not steal, Thou shalt not bear false witness, Thou shalt not desire, and so forth (if there be any other commandment), they are all comprehended in this saying, Love thy neighbour as thyself.**

A wonderful commendation of charity, that whoso observeth her fulfilleth the whole law; meaning the law that appertaineth for the duty and offices to be done between man and man; and not that any man can satisfy the law before God, saving only Christ: no, nor all parts towards man; for no man loveth his neighbour so fervently as the law of God requireth. Yet St Paul saith we fulfil the law, when we give ourselves earnestly and wholly, as much as lieth in us, to work the law: and then our lack and imperfection shall be perfected and accounted full and sufficient for Christ's sake. He addeth yet another commendation of charity:

The text.

Love hurteth not his neighbour.

That is to say, he that hath a christian love cannot hurt his neighbour. By this rule men may know whether they have charity, or not: for in case we diminish the goods of our neighbours, whether they be of his body or his soul, or else of his possessions, honour, place, or dignity; or if we increase not these goods towards all men, if we may, there is no charity in us. Or else, if we diminish not their evils and troubles, as we may; either if we do the evils in any sort by ourselves, or by other, we have no charity in us. By this rule we may now know whether we love our brothers or not: and duly examining ourselves, we shall see how far we be from charity, and that it is an easy thing to speak and talk of charity, and a very hard matter to practise and lead our lives according to charity. For if we had as much charity as we profess to have, we should satisfy all the law, as St Paul saith.

The text.

Therefore is love the fulfilling of the law.

Meaning by the law the second table of the ten commandments, in the which is contained the duty and office of every man to all manner of persons, of what condition soever they be: as for the law of the first table, which containeth the religion of God, fear, faith, love, prayer, obedience, patience, right use of sacraments, with such other as appertaineth only unto God, and be the fountain and original of all good works. For here his argument and state is to tell what men should do to men; and in the first table is declared what man should do to God, fully and sufficiently. These two former parts sufficiently declared by St Paul, he followeth with the third part of the chapter, which containeth an exhortation unto innocency and honesty of life.

The third part of the chapter.

Because we know the season, how that it is time we should awake now out of sleep. *The text.*

Hitherto St Paul hath taught how christian men should behave themselves, not only towards the public person, the king and magistrate, whom they be bound to honour and obey, but also towards private persons that bear no office, whom they be bound to love. And that the same obedience to the higher power, and love towards all men may the better preserve and continue, he addeth now an exhortation to honest living and godly conversation, which he taketh metaphorically, or by similitude of the time; saying, it is meet we should live honestly now, for it is time; meaning by the time the season and time wherein the grace of God in Christ Jesu is preached and opened to the world; the which should not give us occasion of wickedness and sin; but rather wake us out of our sleep, and to rear us out of sin.

Here mark what the apostle calleth "sleep," and what to rise and "wake out of sleep." Sleep is a stupor and deadness of the mind that resteth and is asleep in evil and mischief, and careth not for the law nor will of God; but will follow religion of will, fantasies, idolatry, superstition, ignorance, and all ungodly conversation, without all fear, feeling, or remorse of God's displeasure. In this sleep resteth all idolaters, obstinate, drunken, covetous, envious, seditious, traitorous, adulterous, slanderous, proud, and negligent persons, that feel not, nor repent not, though they be sunk down even to the bottom and very dregs of these evils. From this sleep the gospel of Christ provoketh, excitateth, and stirreth, if obstinacy have not indured and made hard our hearts; and would have us to correct and amend ourself and idolatrical judgment in religion, form[1] our wills to honesty and obedience, and to a new life, that we might be new creatures in the Lord, and to be ready to all service and obedience both of God and his word; that we might have a true, old and patriarchal, prophetical, and apostolical faith, like fear, like love, like obedience of the magistrates, and like charity towards all men. For all they that walk not in these virtues, sleep yet in their sins, and never felt yet the light of the gospel, whose marvellous nature and condition St Paul sheweth in the words that follow:

[[1] MS. *from.*]

The text. **For now is our salvation nearer than when we believed.**

As though he had said, Of congruence and decentness it is meet that we should now live honestly and godly in all love and obedience; for our salvation is now nearer unto us by the preaching of the gospel, which saveth us by Christ, than it was beforetime by preaching of the law or philosophy, when we thought to be saved by the ceremonies and works of them. Of this text of St Paul we see what is the nature and condition of all men, that then they must trust and hope *Rom. x.* whiles they be in a false religion: so did the Jews seek to be saved, and required justice of the law: so did the Pharisees, and exalt themselves above Christ and his apostles. Therefore St Paul saith here, "than when we believed;" to say, by the works of the law and the doctrine of men we should be saved. But this faith was an error and lie; for we know our salvation to be by the preaching of the gospel.

The second we learn of these words is, that only the gospel sheweth and openeth unto us our salvation, and doth *Luke xxiv.* not deceive us, and therefore it is called "the power of God to *Rom. i.* all that believe." Let us therefore embrace and receive this only gospel obediently and thankfully, which the Lord willed his apostles to teach unto all the world, and willed that their successors should do the same; as they do never almost, the more pity. St Paul tarrieth and goeth forth with his metaphor and figure, saying:

The text. **The night is passed, and the day is come nigh.**

The night is called the time of false doctrine and ignorance, in which men live naughtily unpunished. Whereas the true light, Christ and his word, is not preached, there the greatest virtue is accounted vice, and vice accounted for virtue, and sins rebuked are excused and extenuated. So is all true judgment taken from the world; for in the night no man can judge colours. In papistry ye see matrimony judged to be incest; the use of God's creatures, flesh and such like, to be heresy: again, manifest idolatry taken for the honouring of God; monkery for perfect life; whoredom for mockery, and not worth a halfpenny pardon, &c. The day that St Paul speaketh here of, is the time wherein the gospel of Christ is opened to the world, the which bringeth not only true doctrine, but also life everlasting. For Christ is the light of the world: if then Christ, the very Son and brightness of God, hath illuminated us, we must, saith St Paul, diligently walk in him, and live an honest and virtuous life, as he exhorteth earnestly in the words that follow.

Let us therefore cast away the deeds of darkness, and let us put on the armour of light, as men walking honestly in the day-light: not in eating and drinking, neither in chambering and wantonness, neither in strife and envying. *The text.*

This exhortation of St Paul consisteth in two parts: in the one he sheweth what we should not do; in the other, what we should do.

The first, what we should not, exhorting us to "cast off the works of darkness." These works be the sins we would be ashamed to do openly, and in the sight of the world; and so they be called the sins of darkness, because they love darkness: therefore Christ saith, "This is the condemnation, that light is come into the world, and men loveth darkness better than light: their works were evil: every man that doeth evil hateth the light, and cometh not to the light, lest his works should be rebuked." Such works, pleasant unto darkness, St Paul here willeth us to cast away. And the thing that we cast away we have not. As many therefore as tarry in these sins, as long as he tarrieth, he is no christian man.

The first thing that he exhorteth us to do, is to "put on the armour of light;" that is to say, to work good works, of the which we should not be ashamed, neither before God neither man, but boldly and honestly to walk in them. St Paul calleth the first works of a christian man armour, by the name of war, because a christian man's life is a perpetual and a continual fight and battle against the devil, the world, the flesh and sin. The crafts of the devil be marvellous subtle and dangerous, in case our hearts be not well fenced with fruits in Christ Jesu, and with fear we should be overcome. And if he so do, no remedy, except we repent; we shall be the everlasting enemies of God. If in Christ we resist and overcome, we shall have in him all the glory and honour that he hath won in heaven for us.

St Paul annexeth three capital and dangerous evils, that

8—2

we must eschew. The first, that we be ware of inordinate eating and drinking. Here is the abuse of meats and drinks forbidden, and not the meat and drink itself. From the which vices Christ himself exhorteth us, and Esay the prophet, and Salomon in his Proverbs. The other capital evil is incontinent and unchaste living; by the which words he condemneth all scortation, adultery, and whoredom, and so all uncleanliness: and in removing of these incontinencies he commendeth chaste and pure matrimony between man and wife. The third capital evil that we must avoid is strife and contention, against the which writeth St James; the which riseth many times of the bitter zeal of him that is admonished for his faults against him that admonisheth. How much this vice is contrary unto charity, St Paul sheweth when he saith, "If that one of you bite the other, take heed one consume not the other." Where such contentions and strifes be, there is no charity. St Paul, after these evils, returneth again to that we should do, saying:

Luke xxii. [xxi. 34.] Isai. v. xxviii. Prov. xxiii.

1 Cor. vi. Ephes. v.

Chap. iii.

The text.

But put ye on the Lord Jesus Christ.

To put on a thing, figuratively taken, is exactly and studiously to follow and to pursue a thing. So he doth[1] on Hercules's person, that expresseth and sheweth forth the facts of Hercules. So to put on Christ, is to accommodate and apply our faith and works to the example of his life and doctrine; as he biddeth us to believe, so to believe; as he biddeth us to work, even so to work; and not to follow our own imagination. St Paul concludeth the chapter with a lesson, which we should avoid and eschew:

The text.

And do not the cares of the flesh, to fulfil them.

That is to say, do not the thing that the flesh suadeth and would have thee to do; neither live not after the affection of the flesh. This is the sum and conclusion of a christian life, that we follow not the lusts and desires of our corrupt nature. The necessities of our flesh we must help, that it may serve us, and not we it: as the Lord give us grace to do.
Amen.

[¹ Perhaps *doth on* for *donneth:* or supply *put.*]

COPY OF BISHOP HOOPER'S VISITATION BOOK.

[The following Letter, Articles, Injunctions, and Interrogatories, are extracted from a volume of manuscripts in Dr Williams's Library, Redcross Street, London. The reference to Strype's Work, which is apparently in the same handwriting as the rest of the MS. shews that the "Copy" is not older than the time of that writer.

It will be seen that several of the Articles are similar to those which were set forth by the king's authority in the following year.]

A true Coppey of Bishop Hooper's Visitation
Booke made by him in Anno Dom. 1551, 1552.

[This letter to his Clergy printed in Append. to Strype's Cranmer, p. 135. (Num. XLVII.) MS. note.]

To the glory of God the Father, the Son, and the Holy Ghost. Forasmuch as of all charges and vocations the charge of such as be appointed to the ministry and function of the church is the greatest, it is to be provided and foreseen that such as be called and appointed to such vocation and office be such as can satisfy the said office; which may be done, as St Paul[1] saith, two manner of ways: the one, if they be of sound doctrine, apt to teach, and to exhort after knowledge, and able to withstand and confute the evil-sayers: the other, if their life and manners be unculpable, and cannot justly be blamed; which consisteth in this: if the minister be sober, modest, keeping hospitality, honest, religious, chaste, not dissolute, angry, nor given to much wine, no fighter, no covetous man, such as governeth well his own house, and giveth an example of virtue and honesty unto others. For as the godly life and conversation of the parson or doctor doth no less avail in the reformation of other than the doctrine itself, so likewise they which hath no respect nor regard what evil, mischievous, and devilish example of life outwardly appeareth to be in them, cannot have in them any just authority to reform or correct the faults of other. For by what just means canst thou reprehend and blame any other in that fault wherein thou thyself art to be blamed? Or by what occasion canst thou praise charity, or desire to have the same in another man, when as thou thyself, despising both God and holy matrimony, dost other[2] nourish and keep a whore or concubine at home in thy house, or else dost defile other men's beds? Neither is he anything less to be ashamed, that will persuade other to live in sobriety, he himself being drunk. Wherefore what authority shall he obtain or get unto himself and his ministry, which is daily seen and marked of his to be a common haunter of alehouses and taverns, of whores, cards, dice, and such like? Hereby

[1 See 1 Tim. iii. and Tit. i.]   [2 Other: either.]

shall you perceive and know how that the old priests and pastors of Christ's church did by their truth and gravity subjugate and bring under the hard-necked and stiff stubborn ethnicks, and caused them to have the same in fear; insomuch that the wicked emperor[3] Julian caused the priests of the pagans to order their lives according to the example of the other. But look, what authority and reverence that old severity and graveness of the pastors and priests did bring unto them at that time, even as much shame and contempt (or else a great deal more, as I fear,) doth the lechery, covetousness, ambition, simony, and such other corrupt means, bring unto the priests, pastors, and ministers that be now in our days, of all men. Wherefore I (being not forgetful of my office and duty towards God, my prince, and you) do desire and beseech all you, for Christ's sake, who commanded that your light should so shine before men that they, seeing and perceiving the same, might glorify the Father which is in heaven, give your diligence together with me, well-beloved brethren, so that the dignity and majesty of the order of priests and pastors, being fallen in decay, may not only be restored again, but that, first and principally, the true and pure worship of God may be restored; and that so many souls, being committed to my faith and yours, may, by our wholesome doctrine and cleanness of conversation, be moved unto the true study of perfect charity, and called back from all error and ignorance, and finally to be reduced and brought unto the high Bishop and Pastor of souls, Jesus Christ. And to the intent ye may the more easily perform the same, I have (according to the talent and gift given me of the Lord) collected and gathered out of God's holy word a few articles, which I trust shall much profit and do ye good. And if that anything shall be now wanting or lacking, I trust (by the help of your prayers and good counsel) they shall be shortly hereafter performed. Let every one of you, therefore, take good heed to approve yourselves faithful and wise ministers of Christ; so that when I shall come to visit the parishioners committed to my cure and faith from God and the king's majesty, ye be able not only to make answer unto me in that behalf, but also unto our Lord

[3 See Julian. Imp. Fragm. Op. pp. 529, 530, 549, 556, 557.—Paris. 1630.]

Jesus Christ, judge both of the quick and the dead, and a very strait revenger of his church. Thus fare you well unto the day of my coming unto you.

ARTICLES CONCERNING CHRISTIAN RELIGION, given by the reverend father in Christ, John Hooper, Bishop of Gloucester, unto all and singular deans, parsons, prebends, vicars, curates, and other ecclesiastical ministers within the diocese of Gloucester, to be had and retained of them for the unity and agreement, as well for the doctrine of God's word, as also for the conformity of the ceremonies agreeing with God's word.

I. First, that none of the abovenamed do teach or preach any manner of thing to be necessary for the salvation of man other than that which is contained in the book of God's holy word, called the old and new testament; and that they beware to establish and confirm any manner of doctrine concerning the old superstitious and papistical doctrine, which cannot be duly and justly approved by the authority of God's holy word.

II. Item, that they and every of them do faithfully and diligently teach and instruct the people committed unto their charge, that there is but one God, everlasting, incorporate, almighty, wise, and good, maker and conserver of heaven and earth, and of all things contained therein, the Father of our Lord Jesus Christ, our only Redeemer, by whom only he will be called upon by us, and will also hear us for his sake. And albeit there be but one God in essence and unity of the Godhead, nevertheless in the same unity there be three distinct persons, co-equal, everlasting, and one in dignity and essence, the Father, the Son, and the Holy Ghost.

III. Item, that they and every of them do diligently teach and preach, as is aforesaid, all the doctrine contained in the creed or articles of our faith, commonly called and known by the name and names of the creed of the apostles, Nicen, and Athanasius; for that as those creeds are in such wise taken out of the word of God, that [they] do contain in them the sum of all christian doctrine.

IV. Item, that they and every of them do diligently teach and preach that the church of God is the congregation of the faithful, wherein the word of God is truly preached, and the sacraments justly ministered according to the institution of Christ, and his doctrine taught unto us by his holy word: and that the church of God is not by God's word taken for the multitude or company of men, as of bishops, priests, and such other, but that it is the company of all men hearing God's word, and obeying unto the same; lest that any man should be seduced, believing himself to be bound unto any ordinary succession of bishops and priests, but only unto the word of God, and to the right use of his sacraments.

V. Item, albeit that the true church of Christ cannot err from the faith, for that it is the only pillar of verity; yet nevertheless, forasmuch as no man is free from sin and lies, there is nor can be any church known and apparent unto us (be it never so perfect or holy) but it may err.

VI. Item, that the doctrine of the Anabaptists, denying the christening of infants, and affirming the rebaptizing and christening again of those which were before baptized in their infancy, as also affirming all manner of goods and chattel to be in common (saving such as are contained in the law of charity), and that all authority of magistrates should be removed from the church of God, and such other like doctrines, and their sects, are very pernicious and damnable.

VII. Item, that they and every of them do diligently teach and preach the justification of man to come only by the faith of Jesus Christ, and not by the merit of any man's good works; albeit that good works do necessarily follow justification, the which before justification are of no value or estimation before God.

VIII. Item, albeit that good works do not justify, as before is said, but only by faith by Jesus Christ, yet good works do please Almighty God by the faith in Christ, and for Christ's sake; and therefore are required to be had and done of every christian man; and that all works which do repugn or be against the works of the law of God are utterly to be forsaken and kept under.

IX. Item, that the doctrine of the schoolmen of purgatory, pardons, prayers for them that are departed out of this world, the veneration, invocation, and worshipping of saints or images, is contrary and injurious to the honour of Christ our only Mediator and Redeemer, and also against the doctrine of the first and second commandment of God, contained in the first table.

X. Item, that in the sacrament of the body and blood of the Lord there is no transubstantiation of the bread and wine into the body and blood of Christ, or any manner of corporal or local presence of Christ in, under, or with the bread and wine, but spiritually by faith, believing the Son of God Jesus Christ to be made man, and that by his death he might satisfy for the sins of the world. So we receive the confirmation and augmentation of all the merits and deservings of Christ, that merited for us the promises of everlasting life in his[1] pains and passion, that now sitteth at the right hand of God the Father.

XI. Item, that they which unworthily do come to baptism, or unto the supper of the Lord, do not receive the virtue and true effect of the same sacraments, although they receive the external signs and elements of the sacraments.

XII. Item, that the sacraments are so necessary to our salvation, that whosoever receiveth them with faith, according to the institution of Christ, by the secret working of the Holy Ghost receiveth also necessarily the things that be promised, signified, and represented by the sacraments: yet be not the sacraments to be judged so necessary, that whosoever use them any other way than God hath appointed, receiveth his salvation; or that God cannot save the children, or such elder persons as believe his word, without them, when they be omitted in any case of necessity, as death or the like, and not of any contempt of the sacraments.

XIII. Item, that no man, although he be regenerated, but sin doth remain in him as long as he liveth; albeit in some sin doth not reign or bear any rule. Wherefore if he sin, being admonished by the Spirit of God, by his word, or some other way, he repenteth his sins, and so by faith shall obtain the remission thereof: and whereas we speak of a man, we intend not to make any difference of ages; for a child is also a man, which being conceived and born in sin, by reason thereof he is subject to the wrath of God and everlasting damnation, if his sins be not forgiven.

XIV. Item, that, according to the doctrine of St Paul, it is not lawful for any man to sing or say in the church in any

[1 MS. *this*.]

kind of tongue other than such as the people shall be able to understand; and that it is not sufficient to speak or read in the English, or mother-tongue, but that there be due and distinct pronunciation, whereby all the people may have true knowledge.

XV. Item, that the oblation of Christ once made on the cross is a full satisfaction for all manner of sins, be they original, actual, present, past, or to come, to all men believing in the same sacrifice; and that there is not other means, propitiation, redemption, satisfaction, or sacrifice for sin.

XVI. Item, that it is not necessary that the ceremonies of the church should be one everywhere, and at all times used and frequented; but that they may be lawfully changed and altered, according to the diversity of time and manner of countries, so that there be nothing done or made contrary to the word of God; and that all those which willingly or openly with slanders do violate and break any ceremonies made and approved by the king's majesty's authority, are to be esteemed and taken as persons that do offend against the common order of the church and the magistrates, wounding the conscience of their weak and sick brethren, so that other thereby may have occasion of tumult and sedition; and therefore worthy of rebuke and punishment: not that we think or put any religion, or honour of God in them; but as far as they serve to a political order or edification, we judge and acknowledge them profitable.

XVII. Item, that it is not lawful for any manner of person, of his own private authority, to take upon him to preach the word of God, or to minister his sacraments openly, unless the same be lawfully called or sent; and those do we think only lawfully called or sent, which are called and sent of God, whose calling and sending ought to be known either by manifest signs and tokens out of heaven, or else by such men unto whom appertaineth (by office) to appoint and send forth ministers into the Lord's vineyard and church. Also we do condemn all manner of simony in all kinds of ministers and orders of the ecclesiastical ministry. We understand by the ministry and know it not by the name alone, but by the work and administration in it, to the edifying of the church and body of Christ by the faithful administration of God's word and his sacraments, according unto the commandment of Christ; from the which if any minister cease, he leaveth to be a minister, and should not be taken for such one.

XVIII. Item, even as all vain and unadvised oaths are of Christ and his apostle St James forbidden unto all christian men, even so it is lawful for all men, at the command of the magistrate or otherwise, in the cause of faith and charity to swear, so that (according to the mind of the prophet) it be done in judgment, justice and verity.

XIX. Item, that we ourselves cannot anything will or work, without the grace of God do prevent us, and work together with us.

XX. Item, Christ in the substance of our nature took flesh of the substance of the Virgin Mary without the seed of any man, like unto us in all things, except in sin, from the which he was clear and void, as well in his body as in his soul: for he came to be a Lamb without sin, that with his own immolation and sacrifice he might take away the sins of the world; for, as St John saith, "There was no sin in him;" and on the other side, "If any of us shall say that we have no sin in us, we shall seduce ourselves."

XXI. Item, even as our Lord Jesus Christ would have his people of the old testament, so would he have them of the new, not only by doctrine to be brought unto a knowledge of him, but also all his gifts and promises to be sealed in them with certain sacraments, and with the same to be annexed into the society of one godly people, so that they do receive them with faith. And further also, whereas he hath testified and witnessed his yoke to be light, so hath he in like manner instituted a small number of sacraments, which are as easy to be kept as they are most worthy in signification, and (as St Augustin[1] saith) most august and excellent; which we do see in baptism by the most sacred and holy name of the Trinity, and the communion of the body and blood of Christ.

XXII. Item, that the sacraments are instituted of Christ to be used, and not to be gazed upon; and that all they which shall worthily use the same with faith shall thereby receive the increase and confirmation of all the fruits of health and salvation.

XXIII. Item, that the said sacraments are not only

[1 Unde sacramentis numero paucissimis, observatione facillimis, significatione præstantissimis societatem novi populi colligavit, &c.— August. Op. Epist CXVIII. Tom. II. col. 556, B. Basil. 1569.]

signs and notes of the profession of christian men, but also certain impressions or prints of the grace and good-will of God towards us; which thing is made perfect in us, when inwardly the Holy Ghost worketh that our faith may apprehend the thing that is signified by the word and the sacraments.

XXIV. Item, that the sacraments are not of any force by virtue or strength of any outward work of the same (which of superstition is called *opus operatum*), but only by the virtue and means of the Holy Ghost working in the hearts of the doers and receivers by faith, lest that any man should trust or have confidence in the outward works.

XXV. Item, that the church of God is not to be contemned for certain evil parsons annexed unto it, so that the things afore noted be observed, that is to say, true preaching and right use of the sacraments, with correction and discipline. For the malice of the minister cannot derogate nor hurt the doctrine, verity, and majesty of God's word and his sacraments: although when their malice and ignorance is known, they should be put from their office; for they ought to be found blameless in all their lives and conversation, having good report and testimony of all men; and therefore to beware of all such things as may cause them to be had in contempt; as of riotous eating and drinking, of whoredom, adultery, unlawful games, dice, cards, and all other like; nor the time which they should of their bounden duty bestow in reading and studying of the holy scriptures, should be misspent in hunting, hawking, and such other vain pastimes, if they will be approved or allowed faithful ministers of Christ and his church.

XXVI. Item, that which is spoken of the sacraments, that they were not instituted for a spectacle or wondering-stock, doth evidently prove that they ought not to be kept nor worshipped, or any other ways to be used than as Christ did institute them, who, speaking simply and plainly of baptism by these words, "Do ye baptize," said also of the bread and wine, "Take, eat, and drink you all;" of the which words we learn that as many as be present ought to communicate, or to depart in the time of the administration.

XXVII. Item, no man ought to receive the communion of the body and blood of our Lord for another, neither yet one for many, but every man for himself; for no more doth the communion prevail, being taken of one for another, than doth baptism. Wherefore the communion ought not to be kept or celebrated within the church, unless that the whole congregation (or at least a good part of the same) do receive it.

XXVIII. Item, that such doctrines doth plainly approve that the popish mass is a mere enemy against God's word and Christ's institution; and albeit it doth retain in it certain lessons of the holy scriptures, yet it is nothing better to be esteemed than the verses of the sorcerer or enchanter, that be nothing more to be esteemed [than] for certain holy words murmured and spoken in secret.

XXIX. Item, seeing that St Paul doth plainly say that the forbidding of marriage is the doctrine of devils, therefore it is not to be judged that the marriage of priests, bishops, or any other ministers of the church, should be unlawful, but that the same is both holy, and agreeable with God's word.

XXX. Item, that the supper of the Lord ought not to be celebrated or kept in any one church but once in the day, and that in one place only.

XXXI. Item, that the catechism be read and taught unto the children every Sunday and festival-day in the year, at one or two of the clock after dinner, and that they may be thereof duly examined one after another by order; and that all other elder people be commanded to be present at the same.

XXXII. Item, that, albeit that the consents of parties being free, and not under the power of their parents, doth make matrimony, yet nevertheless it is both meet and necessary that no man shall presume to confirm or solemnizate the same, before that he doth well and perfectly know the liberty of the parties, or else the parents' consents; and that there be had thereof lawful testimony and witness, confirmed by the knowledge of the magistrates, at all such time as the parties so contracted together shall be unknown; or, at the least, that the banns of matrimony be three times openly proclaimed by three Sundays in the parish-church, before that they be so married and coupled together.

XXXIII. Item, that a christian and brotherly admonition, correction, and punishment is lawful to be had by the word of God, and also excommunication against rebels and obstinate persons, which are not to be admitted unto any communion of the sacraments or prayers, before that they have openly reconciled themselves unto the church with public and open penance.

XXXIV. Item, that the king's majesty of England is to be taken and known as the only and supreme magistrate and power of the church of England and Ireland, of all manner of persons, of what estate, dignity, or degree soever they be.

XXXV. Item, that the bishop of Rome hath not (nor by God's word or of right ought to have) any manner of authority, power, or jurisdiction within this realm of England and Ireland, or any part of the same.

XXXVI. Item, that every man ought to give place and obedience unto the civil magistrates (being lawfully authorised) in all things, so that they do command nothing that is contrary unto God and his law.

XXXVII. Item, that it is lawful amongst christian men to exercise and use punishments and pains of death in certain offences; and also to bear weapon, and armies to go unto the wars withal, for the tuition and defence of his country, so that the same be done by the commandment of the king's majesty, or by his lawful authority.

XXXVIII. Item, for that as the cure and charge of the poor are chiefly commended unto us by Christ, it is therefore very necessary that collections and gatherings should be had and made in every parish-church, whereby the poor of the same parish and other strangers may be relieved.

XXXIX. Item, forasmuch as our Lord Jesus Christ, very God and man, hath commanded and instituted but only two sacraments in number, that is to say, baptism and the communion of his supper, by the communicating whereof he would give himself unto us, no man therefore ought to be so bold as once to invent or make any more. And albeit that the imposition of hands be tokens of the approbation of the ministers of the church, according to the example of the apostles, yet it may not therefore be called a sacrament by like reason as the other two sacraments are.

XL. Item, that you do not read any such injunctions as extolleth and setteth forth the popish mass, candles, images, chantries, and such like.

XLI. Item, that none of you do counterfeit the popish

mass in blessing the Lord's board, washing your hands or fingers after the gospel, or receipt of the holy communion, shifting the book from one place unto another, laying down and licking of the chalice after the communion, blessing his eyes with the sudary[1] thereof, or paten, or crossing his hands with the same, holding up his forefingers and thumbs joined together towards the temples of his head after the receiving of the sacrament, breathing on the bread or chalice, saying the "Agnus" before the communion, shewing the sacrament openly before the distribution of the same, or making any elevation thereof, ringing of the sacring-bell, or setting any light upon the Lord's board.

XLII. Item, that you make no market of the holy communion by buying or selling the receipt thereof for money, as the popish mass in times past was wont to do.

XLIII. Item, whereas in divers places some use the Lord's board after the form of a table, and some of an altar, whereby dissension is perceived to arise among the unlearned; therefore, wishing a godly unity to be observed in all our diocese, and for that the form of a table may more move and turn the simple from the old superstitious opinions of the popish mass, and to the right use of the Lord's supper, we exhort you to erect and set up the Lord's board after the form of an honest table, decently covered, in such place as shall be thought most meet; so that the ministers and communicants may be seen, heard, and understood of all the people there being present; and that ye do take down and abolish all the altars or tables. Further, that the minister in the use of the communion and prayers thereof turn his face towards the people.

XLIV. Item, that the homilies be read orderly (according unto the king's majesty's injunctions[2]) every Sunday and holy-day, without omission of any part thereof, so that no sermon be made upon any of those days.

XLV. Item, that common prayer be had and used in

[1 Sudary: Gr. σουδάριον, vestis sacerdotalis, quæ alias mappula. Glossar. Man. Tom. VI. p. 408. Halæ, 1773. See also Rer. Liturg. Lib. I. c. XXV. "De sudariolo seu purificatorio, quo nunc utimur ad tergendum calicem." p. 251. Romæ, 1671.]

[2 See Burnet's Hist. of the Reformation, Vol. II. Lib. I. p. 28. London, 1683.]

every church upon Wednesdays and Fridays, according to the king's grace's ordinances, and that all such as conveniently may shall diligently resort unto the same.

XLVI. Item, that none of you maintain the Six Articles[3], bead-rolls, images, relics, rubrics, primers, holy bread, palms, ashes, candles, sepulch, paschal, creeping to the cross, hallowing of the fire or altar, and other such like abuses and superstitions taken away by the king's grace's most godly proceedings.

XLVII. Item, that you do move the people committed unto your charge to the often and worthy receiving of the holy communion, and not to talk or walk in the time of the sermon, communion, or common prayers, but rather to behave themselves godly and devoutly at the same; and to admonish the churchwardens to be diligent overseers in that behalf.

XLVIII. Item, that the churchwardens do not permit any buying, selling, gaming, outrageous noises, tumult, or any other idle occupying of youth, in the church, church-porch, or church-yard, during the time of common prayer, sermon, or reading of the homily.

XLIX. Item, that every one of you (having licence and authority) shall preach every Sunday and festival-day; and that all those which have no licence or authority shall diligently procure some of their neighbours (which are authorised) to preach in their cures four times every quarter in the year at the least.

L. Item, that you be diligent in reading and studying of the holy scriptures, according unto the king's grace's injunctions heretofore given you; so that the people committed unto your charge may thereby have consolation and comfort at your hands, and to be truly instructed of the doctrine contained in God's holy word.

And as we have heretofore admonished you, even so we now eftsoons exhort and require you, and every of you, faithfully and diligently to observe and keep all and singular injunctions and ordinances which shall be commanded unto you by the king's majesty, or his highness' authority.

FINIS.

GOD SAVE THE KING.

[3 For an account of the Six Articles, see Burnet's Hist. of the Reform. Vol. I. Lib. III. p. 259. Lond. 1683.]

INJUNCTIONS given by John Hooper, bishop of Gloucester, in his visitation in the year of our Lord God a thousand five hundred and fifty-one, and in the fifth year of the reign of our sovereign lord king Edward the Sixth, to be observed and kept of all parsons, vicars, curates, and ministers within the diocese of Gloucester.

I. First, that they nor none of them teach, upon the pains of God's displeasure and the king's, any other doctrine, faith, prayer, or religion unto the people necessary for salvation than such as they can duly, justly, and manifestly prove out of the word of God.

II. Item, that no man teach privately or openly the destruction, loss, and confusion of any of the two natures in Christ, but that they attribute with reverence and religion to each and every of them their due, proper, just qualities and conditions; and not to confound, mix, mingle, or attribute the qualities, conditions, and properties due unto the Godhead of Christ unto his humanity, nor the properties, nature, condition, or proportions of his humanity unto his divinity; but reverendly and religiously to keep and hold, as a faith most catholic and godly, to be two divers natures, conditions, and properties in one Christ, which is both God and man; one in person, and divers in qualities, conditions, and nature; the humanity to be in one place always at one time, his Godhead to be in all places in every time.

III. Item, that every of them read and use the common prayers, lessons, homilies, and such other service as is appointed for the people in the king's majesty's book, plainly, distinctly, openly, treatably, solemnly, honourably, and devoutly, and in such sort, and such place of the church, as the people may best understand, hear, and learn, bear away, and follow the godly knowledge, learning, and prayers there appointed. And also that the reverend and modest gesture, sober manner and fashion of the minister may provoke the people to a reverend honour and comely majesty to the word of God, so that they may with knowledge be brought to a love of the English form of prayer and honouring of God, as both God and the king's majesty require and demand.

IV. Item, that they do exhort by word, and provoke by example of their doings, the people to believe that God is better served in the congregation in the English tongue, amongst English men, than ever he was or may be in Latin, whereas the people understandeth not what is said.

V. Item, that, forasmuch as both God and the king commandeth[1] that the word of God, that teacheth knowledge, the law, the gospel, faith, charity, love, hope, fear, obedience, heaven, hell, salvation, damnation, sin, virtue, and all other duties of a christian man, as well how to behave himself towards God as towards man; and the same is very godly, richly, virtuously, and compendiously appointed and set forth in the king's majesty's book of common prayer; and both God and the king would all men to be partakers thereof; and that the scripture of God should heal, help, succour, and comfort as well the poorest as the richest, the unlearned as the learned, him that sitteth next the church-door, or nearest the belfry, as him that sitteth in the chancel, or nearest the chancel-door; I do therefore, in both their names, God's and the king's majesty's, straitly charge all and every curate, parson, and vicar within this diocese, to distribute, give, shew, set forth, minister, and declare the most holy treasure of God's word set forth by the king's majesty to all the people. And in case the chancel stand far from the people, or else by reason of rood-lofts, belfries, or any such inclosure, the psalms spoken by the minister cannot be heard into the lowest part of the church, or else if the curate or minister have so small and soft a breast or voice that he cannot be heard into the lowest part of the church, that then every of them come into the body of the church, and there reverendly, plainly, as is afore-spoken, see that all things be read in such sort, that all the people may understand the treasures and inspeakable riches of God's laws and promises. And then if they or any of them of the parish will be ignorant, their blood and damnation be upon their own heads, and the loss of their own souls be laid unto their own wickedness. I and you shall this way deliver our own souls, and discharge ourselves according to the trust and confidence that both God and the king's majesty hath appointed us unto.

VI. Item, that, whereas the people of God cannot be instructed in the truth of his word, except the parsons and

[1 The sense here is incomplete, owing either to a change of construction by the author, or, what is perhaps more probable, the omission by the copyist of some words such as "be taught," or the like.]

curates, that have the oversight of them, be learned and exercised in the testaments of God, the new and the old, I do command, in the king's majesty's name, that every parson, vicar, and curate within this diocese, from this day forth, accounting from the day of this visitation unto the end of the year next following the date hereof, that they study every quarter of the year such books as I here in these injunctions appoint to be studied and learned; so without the book that every quarter unto me, or to mine assigns, they make rehearsal of the contents of every book in Latin or English: that is to say, the first quarter the epistle of St Paul to the Romans; the second quarter the book of Moses called Deuteronomy; the third quarter the evangelist or gospel of St Matthew; the fourth quarter the first book of Moses called Genesis.

VII. Item, that every parson, vicar, or curate, or other that serve cures within this diocese, four times in the year appear personally in their deanery before me, or my deputies, in such synods, councils, and assemblies as I will appoint, for the determination of such questions and doubtful matters in religion as may happen to stand and be in controversy between men learned and them; and there to speak modestly, soberly, and learnedly what they will: so that I in the mean time command them not to dispute nor reason before the unlearned of any matters in religion but such as may be manifestly proved out of the word of God.

VIII. Item, that every parson, vicar, curate, and minister within this diocese, without all excuses, make as many sermons themselves, or by their assigns, in their parishes as is enjoined unto them by the king's majesty and my last articles, as they will answer for the loss of the people; and in the same sermons to preach nor teach any doctrine or learning but such as may be plainly, truly, openly, and manifestly proved out of the word of God

IX. Item, that every curate, parson, and vicar cause all such persons, men or women, that shall come to the communion, before the receiving of it, to make a rehearsal of the ten commandments, of the articles of our faith, and then to make the general confession of sins set forth in the king's majesty's book of common prayer; and, that confession of sin made, to pray the Lord's prayer in English called the paternoster. And if it happen there be so many communicants that all cannot one after another make rehearsal of the commandments, the articles of our faith, and the pater-noster, then the curate or minister to read out of the twentieth chapter of Exodus the said commandments, word for word, as they be written there, treatably, plainly, distinctly, openly, and reverendly, and so point and mark the sentences that the people may say them after him, and likewise the creed, the pater-noster, and the general confession, that is set forth in the king's majesty's book; so that the people may receive the holy communion and sacrament of Christ's death and passion with profit, gain, and commodity of grace and favour from God; which cannot be where the receivers lack the true knowledge of God, hatred of their sinful self, and the purpose and intent never to sin again.

X. Item, that every parson, curate, and minister teach the ten commandments of God out of the twentieth chapter of Exodus, as they stand there, and no otherwise, not taking one word, letter, or syllable from them, but in all things to follow in this case the book of God.

XI. Item, where as knowledge of the ten commandments, the creed, and the pater-noster lacketh in such as be of discretion, there lacketh also God's grace and favour, as well in the parson, vicar, and curate, as in the parish and people: for eschewing and avoiding whereof, every curate, parson, and vicar (as they will answer unto God and the king's majesty) shall upon every Christmas-day, Easter-day, Whitsunday, and the first Sunday in September, cause half his parish before noon, and the other half in the afternoon, to make open confession of the ten commandments, the articles of the faith, and the pater-noster in English: so that by this means (if curates be diligent) the people may come to the knowledge of God in Christ; of which if they be ignorant of negligence or contempt, they cannot be saved.

XII. Item, that the parsons, vicars, and curates shall diligently exhort the multitude of their parishioners to use the communion and sacrament of Christ's precious body and blood, and not to permit in any wise one neighbour to receive for another, as it is commonly used in this diocese; for when he that should receive it himself, by the order of the king's law, is not disposed to receive, he desireth his neighbour to receive for him, which is contrary to God's word.

XIII. Item, that every parson, vicar, curate, or minister exhort and charge the churchwardens of every parish to take diligent heed to the talk and behaviour of the people, that nothing be spoken to the hinderance and slander of God's word, to the disobedience of the king's majesty, or any of his officers; and that no unchaste or ungodly life be used; and that the churchwardens every quarter present such faults as shall happen to be found and known in any of the said causes, unto their curate or minister, to present them unto me, or to mine officers, four times every year, as duly as they would do at the bishop's visitation; that such faults and evils by reason of long continuance and use fall not into custom, whereby the punishment thereof must needs be the more grievous to the offender, the pains of the judge more troublesome, and the ire and vengeance of God more kindled against the people among whom these offenders live unpunished; as the word of God plainly sheweth us it doth and will do, until the evil be removed.

XIV. Item, that every parson, vicar, curate, and minister, without all excuses, at the beginning of the quarter, exhort such men as be already sworn before me in my visitation, with the churchwardens, to take heed diligently of the manners and conditions of the parson, vicar, and curate of the parish, and of the manners and conditions of the parishioners; and so by writing deliver, or cause to be delivered, every quarter unto me, or to mine officers, all such faults and transgressions as shall be committed by any of them, that shall be done contrary unto God's laws and the king's, in any unhonest life or false religion: that I may in time take such order, as God may have his honour, the king's majesty his reverence, and the people of God their quietness; which cannot be where sin doth reign unpunished.

XV. Item, that ye be diligent and careful yourselves, and also exhort the church-proctors and wardens, with all other that be appointed for the continuance and preservation of true religion and godly conversation in your parishes among the people, that no man nor woman maintain openly or privately, by talking, reading, preaching, disputation, argument, or other reasoning, the defence of transubstantiation of the bread and wine in the sacrament of Christ's precious body and blood, any corporal, fleshly, bodily, or real presence of Christ's body in the sacrament, any use or necessity of masses, prayers unto saints, purgatory, pardons, indulgence, beads, images, or such other superstition as is most justly condemned by God's word and the king's majesty's authority.

XVI. Item, that you exhort your parishioners and such as be under your cure and charge for the ministry of the church, that they take down and remove out of their churches and chapels all places, tabernacles, tombs, sepulchres, tables, footstools, rood-lofts, and other monuments, signs, tokens, relics, leavings, and remembrances, where such superstition, idols, images, or other provocation of idolatry have been used. And also that ye take away all the greis[1], ascenses, and upgoings that heretofore went to any altar within your churches or chapels: and to take down all the chapels, closets, partitions, and separations within your churches, whereat any mass hath been said, or any idol, image, or relic used to be honoured: and so to make the church and house appointed to serve God in without all closures[2], imparting, and separations between the ministers and the people, to avoid all mosaical and Jewish imperfection, and such typical separation as shewed Christ yet to come, and not already now come and past, as touching the imperfection of the law. Provided notwithstanding, that in case any honest man, of what estate soever he be, that hath a seat within the church for his quietness, for himself and his to hear the common prayer, that it stand, and no man meddle with it, except it were before a secret and appointed place to do idolatry in: then if any man will use it as a seage[3] or seat, to take down from the higher place, and also round about it, as many things as heretofore have served and been as a help unto idolatry.

XVII. Item, that ye ne[4] suffer nor permit any Latin primers, beads, images, relics, or any other monuments of superstition in your parishes, as well to avoid them in the church as in private houses. And in case ye know any man or woman, being the king's subject, within this shire,

[1 Greis, or grise, a flight of steps: Lat. gressus. Gloss. Man. "gresium, collis, agger editus."]

[2 Closures: inclosures, partitions.]

[3 From the French siége, seat.]   [4 Ne: neither.]

that doth use, maintain, or keep secretly or openly any such images, beads, Latin primers, relics, or others, that charitably ye admonish them to put them away, and to destroy them: if you cannot cause them so to do, to advertise me of their obstinacy and contempt of God's laws and the king's majesty's, by the which they are condemned and abolished most justly.

XVIII. Item, that the curate or minister, with the advice and consent of the whole parish, shall agree upon one certain hour as well for saying of the morning prayers upon the Sundays and other holy-days, as also the evening prayers, appointed and set forth in the king's majesty's book of common prayer: and so the most convenient hour agreed upon to be observed and kept, that all the parish may come thereunto, except they have just occasion and causes to the contrary; so that from henceforth none of the parishioners break, violate, contemn, and neglect the common prayer upon the Sundays and other holy-days, as hitherunto they have done.

XIX. Item, that from henceforth in no parish in the diocese shall the bells be rung to noon upon the Saturdays or other holy-days' even, nor at evening to curfaye (as it was called), nor yet in the time of service in the church, for the oppressing of the sound of the minister that readeth the word of God; but before service, as well in the morning as at even, to warn the people by as many peals or ringings as they think good: and in case there be any pause between the morning prayer and the communion, then, to advertise and signify unto the people of the ministration of the holy sacrament, to toll one bell, such as the parish shall think most meet and convenient.

XX. Item, that there be no noise, bruit, walking, talking, or jangling, or any other unquiet behaviour in the church in the time of service, nor none to remain in the church-yard or at home in their houses, to be absent from such prayers and holy use of the sacraments as there shall be used upon such days as be appointed to serve God, both by his word and the king's majesty's commandment.

XXI. Item, that there be no markets kept nor used upon the sabbath-days in the time of service within the church, church-yard, or parish. But in case the need and necessity of the people so require to have such things as upon the Sunday are to be sold, that they buy and sell for their needs upon the same day before, after, or between the hours appointed to serve God in upon the same day: so that in the time of service the churchwardens shall cause all men, both buyers and sellers, to cease and give over their business in buying and selling, and to charge them to hear God's word and service for that time and hour.

XXII. Item, that all parishioners do duly and truly content and pay their clerks their wages, as heretofore have been accustomed, as well for his pains in keeping clean the church, ringing the bells, and serving the minister in this godly order now appointed by God, and set forth by the king's majesty, as they did before in the time of papistry and superstition.

XXIII. Item, that from henceforth there be no knells or forth-fares rung for the death of any man; but in case they that be sick and in danger, or any of their friends, will demand to have the bell toll whiles the sick is in extremes, to admonish the people of their danger, and by that means to solicitate the hearers of the same to pray for the sick person, they may use it. And then, if the person die for whom the bell tolled, and to give warning of his death, to ring out with one bell it may be sufficient.

XXIV. Item, that there be no man within the parish that use to keep open any tavern, alehouse, tap-houses, or any such banqueting places upon the Sundays and holy-days at the time of service before noon, or after noon, but for such as travel by the way, and must for the necessities of their journeys be relieved. But such as be of the town, village, or country near about, to be kept from such drinking and abuse of the sabbath-day, according to the law of God and the king's majesty's.

XXV. Item, that every minister within this diocese do diligently exhort and teach the parishioners that all privy and secret contracts be forbidden by God's laws, and not to be used among christian people, not only because it dishonoureth the means and entrance into marriage, offendeth the parents and such as of duty have the tuteal[1] and govern-

[1 So in the MS. for tutelage, guardianship.]

ance of the parties so contracted; but also for the most part causeth much unhonest and unchaste life, with such difficulties and pains to bring the parties (privily contracted) together in matrimony, as not only the judge shall suffer great troubles, but also sundry times many that privily have given faith of marriage, openly deny the same, to their great danger and hurt of conscience; and such as be by honest exhortation at the first content to marry wax weary of their doings, and repent it within few days. Therefore it is the duty of all godly men to dissuade, as much as in them lieth, all men and women from such privy and secret contracts.

XXVI. Item, that all curates and ministers exhort and provoke their parishioners, and especially the rich men, four times every year at the least, to make and have in a readiness their last wills and testaments, whiles they be in health and of perfect memory; that when sickness cometh, they may be occupied only about such things as appertaineth to them that must or be like to depart out of this world. And in their so doing they shall not only have quietness of mind, but also advisedly bestow and bequeath their lands and goods to whom they lust, and be an occasion of great quietness and peace between such as many times fall at strife and contention about the goods of the dead, for lack of a good and perfect made will whiles the owner of the same lived.

XXVII. Item, that when any persons be contracted and faithed[1] together in matrimony, either by two or three records[2] out of the congregation, or else openly proclaimed in the church by banns, after the godly laws of the realm, that the same persons be compelled with all convenient speed to marry openly in the face of the church, and the persons contracted cohabitate nor dwell together before the matrimony be solemnized.

XXVIII. Item, that when any glass windows within any of the churches shall from henceforth be repaired, or new made, that you do not permit to be painted or purtured[3] therein the image or picture of any saint: but if they will have anything painted, that it be either branches, flowers, or posies[4] taken out of the holy scripture. And that ye cause to be defaced all such images as yet do remain painted upon

[1 Faithed: betrothed, pledged.]   [2 Records: witnesses.]
[3 Probably for pourtrayed.]   [4 Posies: mottoes.]

any of the walls of your churches, and that from henceforth there be no more such.

XXIX. Item, that ye make certificate and advertisement unto me truly and faithfully, how many times in the quarter ye leave the king's majesty's act of parliament that I delivered unto you, for the keeping of the people in peace, quietness, and obedience, unread upon the Sundays; and what be the causes ye so leave them unreaden, contrary unto the king's majesty's commandment.

XXX. Item, that there be provided in every church within this diocese a bible of the largest volume in English, the paraphrases of Erasmus upon the new testament in English, a box or a chest for the poor, and a chest to keep the book wherein is to be written the names of such as die, be christened, and married, according to the king's majesty's commandment heretofore given unto [you] in this behalf, as ye will avoid the danger of his majesty's laws.

XXXI. Item, that whereas the Almighty God, for the sins and wickedness of the people, the neglecting of God and his word, the contemning of the king's majesty and his laws, hath now in those days extended his wrath against us, and poured his strange plagues[5] of sudden death almost upon the whole realm, the like thereof hath not been heretofore seen, the appeasing whereof cannot other ways be had than only by amendment of life, with fervent and earnest prayer unto God from the bottom of our hearts; wherefore I will, and, in both their names, God's and the king's majesty's, straitly charge and command you, that every curate or minister within this diocese do exhort, and in like wise straitly charge and command, in the king's majesty's name, that of every house within your parish one at the least do resort unto the temple or church every Monday, Wednesday, and Friday; and there all the congregation being assembled, godly, religiously, and devoutly to pray together from the bottom of their hearts the common prayer set forth in the king's majesty's book, with also diligent study of the amendment of their lives, that by this means (if it be possible) we may provoke God the sooner to withdraw his wrathful ire and displeasure from us, and to accept and take us into his fatherly and gracious favour again; and that ye fail not hereof, as ye

[5 The sweating sickness. See Epist. xx.]

will not only avoid the indignation and judgment of Almighty God, but also the contempt of the king's majesty's most godly will and pleasure, according unto his gracious letters directed unto me and others in this behalf.

FINIS.

INTERROGATORIES and DEMANDS of the people or parishioners and their conversation to be required and known by the parsons, vicars, and curates.

I. First, whether they be diligent, willing, and glad to hear and learn the commandments of God, the articles of the christian faith, and the Lord's prayer called the pater-noster.

II. Item, whether they be glad to know and learn to come to the right knowledge of the sacraments of Christ, the supper of the Lord and baptism, and use the same religiously, and at such time as the laws of the realm appoint them to be used.

III. Item, whether they come to the church upon the Sundays and other days appointed to hear the word of God, to learn their duties to God and their king, and to obey them both.

IV. Item, whether they talk, walk, molest, unquiet, or grieve the minister, whiles he is at the divine service, within the church or church-yard with any noise, brute cries, clamours, plays, games, sports, dancing, or such like.

V. Item, whether they can say their commandments, creed, and pater-noster in English, and whether they presume to receive the communion before they can say it, or whether any of them neglect or disdain to learn them.

VI. Item, whether any of the parish do refrain, absent, and keep himself from such service in the church, and such sermons as is made there, without lawful cause.

VII. Item, whether there be any that doth disdain, being thereunto required by the minister, to make a confession of his faith, or will not himself, nor suffer his or their servants and children to learn upon the holy-days their catechism and faith, according to God's laws and the king's.

VIII. Item, whether any of them that were diligent

hearers and comers to the mass and matins in time of papistry and superstition, that now be slow comers to the holy communion and common prayer set forth by the word of God and the king's majesty's authority.

IX. Item, whether any of them elevate[1] and oppress, hinder or slander, extenuate or diminish the service and honouring of God now used and commanded; exalt, praise, and prefer, alloweth, and defendeth the service that was used before.

X. Item, whether any of them refuse their own parish, and frequent and haunt other, where as the communion is more like a mass than in his own: or whether he take the communion where as he knoweth his faith shall not be examined; or marry where as he knoweth no man shall be to forbid it, as it should have been perchance, if he had not married out of his own parish.

XI. Item, whether the midwives at the labour and birth of any child do use any prayers or invocations unto any saint, saving to God in Christ, for the deliverance of the woman; and whether they do use any salt, herbs, water, wax, cloths, girdles, or relics, or any such other like thing or superstitious means, contrary to the word of God and the laws of the realm.

XII. Item, whether any midwife refuse to come to any woman labouring of child for religion's sake, or because she is wife unto a minister of the church, that hath married and doth marry both by God's laws and the king's.

XIII. Item, whether there be any man that raileth, speaketh uncharitably, or calleth any minister's wife whore, or detest and abhor their companies; and so when as they should come to the church to leave sin and augment charity, for lack of grace and knowledge they increase in sin, and decay all love.

XIV. Item, whether there be any common drunkards, swearers, adulterers, lecherous men, peace-breakers, tale-tellers, slanderers of the higher powers, and seditious to the king and his proceedings, and murderers of the neighbour's good names.

XV. Item, whether any man do occupy any such primers or books of prayers in Latin as be forbidden by the

[[1] Elevate: speak slightingly of, or disparage.]

laws of the realm, or any beads, knots, relics, or any such other superstition: or whether any man pray in the church his private and own prayer, whiles the common prayer is a-saying, to the trouble or hinderance of the understanding thereof.

XVI. Item, whether any of them for malice, hatred, or for religion detract or withhold any part of their duties, tithes, and offerings commanded by God's laws and the king's to be paid for the finding and sustentation of the minister.

XVII. Item, whether any of them occupy to his own use any of the church-stock, plate, vestments, bells, or any other, or do alienate the same, contrary to the laws of the realm.

XVIII. Item, whether the churchwardens make truly every year their account, according to the receipt of their gain and the trust that the parish putteth in them.

XIX. Item, whether any man withholdeth any legacies or bequests from any man, contrary to the will of the dead man and his testament.

XX. Item, whether the parish honestly repair and keep the church and church-yard, so that in the one the people may quietly, easily, and without storms hear the word of God, and in the other the dead bodies may reverently be buried, and so kept under the ground.

XXI. Item, whether upon the holy-days there be kept in the church or church-yard any market, buying or selling, with such doings as becometh neither the day nor the place.

XXII. Item, whether the people come in due time upon the holy-days and sabbath-days to hear their service appointed by the word of God and the king's majesty's laws of this realm.

XXIII. Item, whether the table for the communion be decked and apparelled behind and before, as the altars were wont to be decked; and whether the table stand in such a place as the people may most conveniently hear the godly psalms and prayers said by the minister at the time of service and the communion.

XXIV. Item, whether any man speak unreverently of God the Father, the Son, and the Holy Ghost, or mock or scorn at the word, laws, and promises of God.

XXV. Item, whether there be in the church a bible

of the largest volume and the paraphrases upon the new testament in English; and whether they be placed in some convenient place of the church, so that every body may come to the same at time convenient.

XXVI. Item, how many priests within this deanery have subscribed unto the articles that I did put forth unto them.

XXVII. Item, that every one of you, being a parson, vicar, or curate, do present how long you have been so; who is the patron of your benefice; and how many you have that doth receive the communion; and what is the value thereof.

Item, that every one of you do make payment of your tenths and subsidies due unto the king's majesty either to the lord bishop, or unto such as he shall appoint.

FINIS.

INTERROGATORIES and EXAMINATIONS of the ministers and of their conversation to be required and known by the parishioners.

I. First, whether your minister be parson, vicar, or curate, and how long he hath been so.

II. Item, if he be a parson or vicar, whether he be resident or not; and if he be not resident, what is the cause he is not resident, and whether he have left for him in his absence a sufficient and lawful minister to discharge his cure.

III. Item, whether all such images as heretofore hath been in the temple be burned and destroyed.

IV. Item, whether all relics and pieces of relics as before were kept[1], and yet remain in any parish or parishioner or not; or whether all imagery be clean taken out of the church.

V. Item, whether the communion be used in such place, and after such sort, as most varieth and is distant from the popish mass.

VI. Item, whether the curates do plainly, distinctly, and

[1 The sense is imperfect here, owing probably to the substitution by the copyist of 'and' for 'as.']

religiously speak and pronounce aloud, that every man may hear, what is contained in the king's majesty's book of communion.

VII. Item, whether the curates do weekly teach and hear the youth of the parish their catechism.

VIII. Item, whether any of them have sung or said any mass since the time it was justly abrogated by the king's majesty.

IX. Item, whether any of them have or do preach any doctrine to vouch and maintain purgatory, pardons, auricular confessions, praying unto saints, the false and usurped power of the bishop of Rome, holy water, holy bread, palm ashes, beads, or such other like as justly by God's holy word are condemned, and taken away from the people by the king's majesty's authority.

X. Item, whether any parson, vicar, or curate do teach, privily[1] with secret persons, or openly with many, any doctrine, reasons, or persuasions that should cause the people to trust in any thing, saving in God's mercy, for the remission of sin and everlasting life, but in the merits of Christ.

XI. Item, whether any of them have or do teach anything, privily or openly, by word, writing, or signs, that should be against the king's majesty's supremacy, and in the maintenance of the bishop of Rome, or any other bishop, within this realm or without this realm: or whether they allure and provoke the people to the love of any other person or persons within this realm or without, to this intent that the people should favour them, and to withdraw in any part their love, fear, honour, and obedience from their and our only and sole king Edward the sixth.

XII. Item, whether they do diligently and often stir and provoke the people to the knowledge after God in Christ, after God's word, and also to obedience unto their king, in their sermons and homilies every holy-day.

XIII. Item, whether they use study and diligence at their books to obtain knowledge after the word of God; and whether their lives be chaste, sober, modest, temperate, and an example to their parishioners.

XIV. Item, whether they use alehouses and taverns, dice or cards, hunting or hawking, bowls, tennis-play, or any

[1 Prevaile in MS.]

such other unlawful games as be forbid by the law of this realm, and also by the word of God, when they be a hindrance to virtue, prayer, modesty, and study.

XV. Item, whether they hold up their fingers, wash their fingers, kiss their vestments, book, chalice, corporas [2], or any thing about the table, as they did in their mass.

XVI. Item, whether they be meek, gentle, loving, tractable, peace-makers, living after knowledge of charity among their neighbours.

XVII. Item, whether they say one part of their service softly and with a small voice, and the other part with a loud voice, as they were wont in the time of their Latin service to say the pater-noster at the beginning with a small and still voice, and the psalms with a loud voice.

XVIII. Item, whether they sit at one part of their service, kneel at another, and stand at another, as they were wont to sit when they said or sang the psalms, kneel at Kyrie-eleyson, and stand up at Magnificat, Te Deum laudamus, and Benedictus; the which alterance of their gesture caused the people to think that the hearing of the service were sufficient.

XIX. Item, whether they hold forth, offer, or shew any sign unto the people upon the offering-days, that they should kiss their vestments, chalice, paten, or any other thing.

XX. Item, whether they break the bread in the holy communion into any more pieces than two, as they were wont in their masses to break it in three pieces; or whether he break it before he give it to the people or not.

XXI. Item, whether any of them teach, talk, reason, or defend any prophecies and lies of men besides God's holy word, or use themselves, or suffer any other to use, witchcraft, palmistry, and such other forbidden arts: or whether any of them put their trust in such forbidden and damnable crafts.

XXII. Item, whether any of them use the communion as

[2 Corporas, (*corporale*): the cloth which was used for covering the sacrifice on the altar. The term was also applied to the napkin which was placed folded on the cup.—See Glossar. Man. in verb. and Innocentius de Mysteriis Missæ, Lib. II. cap. 56, quoted in Rer. Liturg. Lib. I. cap. xxv. p. 250. Romæ, 1671.]

they used trentals[1] of masses, that is to say, whether two receive at one time, three or four at another time, at the burial and funeral of any dead body: or whether any men be hired to receive the communion one for another: and whether in any church at any burial be any more than one communion, or any more do minister at the burial more than one minister, or any more times than once for one corpse.

XXIII. Item, whether they keep and use any month-ends[2], anniversaries, exequies, funerals, or offices for the dead after the corpse is buried, which is the maintenance of the purgatory and false belief of the state and condition of the dead.

XXIV. Item, whether they teach or bear the people in hand, that the psalms appointed for the burial in the king's majesty's book for thanksgiving unto God for the deliverance of the dead out of this miserable world, be appointed or placed instead of the dirge, wherein they prayed for the dead.

XXV. Item, whether they use any corporas cloth besides the communion cloth upon the table in the time of the communion.

XXVI. Item, whether they ring or knoll the bells at the time of the communion, or between the morning prayers, which is commonly called matins, and the communion, as they were wont to ring out of matins to mass before this order was brought in.

XXVII. Item, whether they suffer or cause the people to sit at the epistle, and to stand at the gospel, and so use them both now as superstitiously as they did in the time of their massing.

XXVIII. Item, whether they require and demand of such as come to the communion, first to make their auricular confession unto the curate, as they did in the time of papistry.

XXIX. Item, whether they say, pronounce, and sound openly, clearly, plainly, and audibly the general confession of sin set forth in the king's majesty's book, so that the people may understand and perceive every word and sentence thereof.

[1 Trental, Fr. *trentel:* a service of thirty masses. The term also signifies the fee paid to the priest for performing the service.—See Glossar. Man.]

[2 Month-ends or month-minds: commemorative-services repeated at the end of the month.]

XXX. Item, whether they go in sober, modest, and comely apparel, without any cuts, jaggs, or such like external[3] and undecentness not to be used in our ministers of the church.

XXXI. Item, whether they preach themselves, or cause some other to preach for them, as many times in the year as the king's majesty's commandment bindeth them, and as many times as I command them in the quarter in my articles at my first coming into the diocese.

XXXII. Item, whether at the visitation of the sick they bear the sacrament with covering their head with the surplice, or at their breasts before them, to cause the people to honour it, or with any light, lanthorn, torch, taper, or other; or, when they come into the house, they suffer the people to kneel and honour it.

XXXIII. Item, when the sick man desire to be anointed before his death, whether the curate do give himself, or cause any other to give, any reverence to the oil, or else persuade and teach any man to put any trust in the oil, or use it as they did before time under the pope.

XXXIV. Item, whether any of your curates, or any other also that serveth the ministry of the church, do teach or persuade, suffer or permit any cross, wax, or wood, or any other thing to be sewed or put secretly upon or about the dead body; or else whether any pardons, cloths, relics, or such other to be buried with the dead body.

XXXV. Item, whether the parson, vicar, or curate observe All Souls' day (as it was called), and use to say dirige, openly or secretly, for the dead, and permit ringing of bells upon the same day, or night before, as it was used after the popish and superstitious order.

XXXVI. Item, whether any of your curates or such as appoint your curates, do secretly hinder or bring out of estimation any manner of ways any such doctrine, learning, and setting forth of God's word, as the king's majesty, after the word of God, would have openly to be known of the people.

XXXVII. Item, whether they secretly or openly exhort the people to keep any vigils or fasting-days abrogated by

[3 So MS. Either some word must have been omitted, or perhaps *external* may be used here as a substantive.]

the king's majesty, and for the which days there is no service appointed in the king's majesty's book of common prayers.

XXXVIII. Item, whether they do dispute or reason among the unlearned people of any such doctrine as is not agreeable with God's word, nor approved by the king's majesty's authority.

XXXIX. Item, whether parsons, vicars, and other keep up accordingly their houses, maintain hospitality, and give the fourth part of his or their benefice to the poor, according to the word of God and the laws of this realm.

XL. Item, whether such as have as much as the laws of this realm assigneth, that is to say, one hundred pounds by the year, or above, do for every hundred pounds keep one scholar to the schools.

XLI. Item, whether any of them keep any suspect woman or man to maintain vicious and corrupt life, contrary unto the word of God and the laws of this realm.

XLII. Item, whether any of them do use and keep any land, ground, or pasture, and leases otherwise than for the maintenance of his or their house or houses, contrary unto the laws and statutes of this realm.

XLIII. Item, whether there be any man that hath a benefice of his own, and yet, leaving his own benefice, serveth another man's cure.

XLIV. Item, whether any parson, vicar, or curate have entered and do enjoy any benefice, coming to the same by simony, buying, or selling, contrary unto the laws of God; and through any other unlawful covenants departing with part of the tithes, glebe-land, or any other commodity belonging to the same.

XLV. Item, whether there be any curate or parson that doth make the will of any dead man, or do add or diminish, convey or suppress the will of the dead man, or take upon him the craft, subtlety, or fraud to alter any part thereof.

XLVI. Item, whether any of them make or write any man's testament with this style, "I commend my soul unto God, to our blessed lady, and the saints of heaven;" which is injurious to God, and perilous as well for the salvation of the dead, as dangerous unto the maker.

XLVII. Item, whether the parsons, vicars, and curates that serve, that be not weekly occupied with preaching, teach and bring up the youth and children of theirs or their parishioners in the catechism and rudiments or principles of their faith.

XLVIII. Item, whether the curates and such as serve the people, four times in the year declare and teach unto the people that all privy and secret contracts for matrimony be condemned by God's laws; and that no man ought to assure himself unto any woman, nor any woman unto any man, if any of them both be under law and dominion of their fathers, or other tutors, without their fathers' or tutors' consent.

XLIX. Item, whether any curate, or he that serveth in the ministry of the church, marry or couple any persons together without lawful and solemn proclamations of the banns, according to the laws of this realm.

L. Item, whether any curate marry any such persons, and adjoin them in matrimony, whose conjunction, for consanguinity, kindred, or affinity, the law of God forbiddeth.

LI. Item, whether any man serve in the ministry of the church not being appointed thereunto upon knowledge of such as first should examine their faith and conversation.

LII. Item, whether the curates have testaments and paraphrases in Latin and in English, according to the king's majesty's injunctions, and how they have profited in the same.

LIII. Item, whether the church be maintained sufficiently in all things as it ought to be, or not.

LIV. Item, whether they have in the church a chest or box for the poor, and whether they do exhort the parishioners to offer liberally unto the same, and whether the thing offered be godly distributed, or not.

LV. Item, whether the curates write diligently into the book appointed the names of all that die, be christened, and married; and whether they have in the chest any such book, or not.

LVI. Item, whether any man speak unreverently of God the Father, the Son, and the Holy Ghost, or mock or scorn at the word, laws, and promises of God.

LVII. Item, how many priests in the deanery have subscribed unto the articles that I put forth unto them.

LVIII. Item, whether there be any person or persons within your parishes which do live in evil conversation, either in fornication, adultery, incest, or after any other sort of evil conversation: and of all manner of persons that doth receive, maintain, or uphold any vicious livers; and of all such that be married, and do not cohabit together.

LIX. Item, that ye do not only inquire of the faults of your minister, but also of all other kind of evils that be in any of the parishioners, as well against the laws of God, as also the king's majesty's laws.

LX. Item, whether the parson, vicar, or curate have commanded to keep any holy-days other than be set forth in the king's majesty's book of common prayer.

LXI. Item, that you and every of you do diligently inquire, and truly present of all and singular your parsons, vicars, and curates, whether that they or any of them be men qualified and learned to preach and declare unto your parishioners God's word, according unto the king's majesty's injunctions heretofore given them in that behalf: and whether that they and every of them have preached according to their bounden duties, or not.

ΤΕΛΟΣ.

EXAMINATIO decani et prebendariorum ac aliorum ministrorum ministrantium infra ecclesiam cathedralem Gloucestriæ, necnon omnium et singulorum prebendariorum, rectorum, vicariorum, ac ceterorum ministrorum ministrantium infra totam diocesim Gloucestrensem aut aliquam ejus partem, habita et facta per reverendum in Christo patrem Johannem Hoperum, ejusdem diocesis (auctoritate regia) Gloucestrensis episcopum, ordinaria sua visitatione inchoata quarto die mensis Maii, anno Domini 1551, ac regni illustrissimi in Christo principis et domini nostri Edwardi Sexti, Dei gratia Angliæ, Franciæ, et Hiberniæ regis, fidei defensoris, et in terris ecclesiæ Anglicanæ et Hiberniæ sub Christo capitis supremi, anno quinto.

Articuli supra quibus ministri omnes examinati sunt, videlicet de præceptis traditis a Deo Moisi 20mo Exodi, de articulis fidei, et de petitionibus christianæ orationis.

De Decem Præceptis.

Partes
1. Primo, quot sunt Dei mandata.
2. Secundo, ubinam sunt scripta.
3. Tertio, an memoriter recitare valeant.

De Fide Christiana.

Partes
1. Primo, qui sunt articuli fidei christianæ.
2. Secundo, an memoriter recensere possint.
3. Tertio, an scripturarum auctoritate corroborare queant.

De Oratione Dominica.

Partes
1. Primo, an memoriter petitiones orationis christianæ recitare valeant.
2. Secundo, quomodo sciunt esse Domini orationem.
3. Tertio, ubi scriptam esse.

[Here follow the examinations of three hundred and eleven of the Clergy, one hundred and sixty-eight of whom were unable to repeat the ten commandments, thirty-one of that number being further unable to state in what part of the Scriptures they were to be found. There were forty who could not tell where the Lord's prayer was written, and thirty-one of this number ignorant who was its author.]

ARTICLES[1] whereunto William Phelps, pastor and curate of Cirencester, upon good advisement and deliberation, after better knowledge given by God's grace and goodness to him, hath subscribed, consented, and agreed willingly, without force, compulsion, and all manner of impulsion, and is willing and desirous to set forth the same unto his parishioners, for the better edifying of them, and declaration of his new agreement unto God's verity and holy word, ministered unto him by John Hooper, bishop of Gloucester, the twenty-ninth day of April, in the fifth year of the reign of king Edward the Sixth, 1551.

FIRST, that the holy word of God doth acknowledge, confess, maintain, avouch, hold, and defend, that in the holy sacrament and communion of Christ's precious body and blood the very substance, matter, nature, and condition of bread and wine to remain after the words (as they be called) of consecration, as verily and truly as they were in substance and matter bread and wine before, although that the use of bread and wine in the sacrament be changed; for whereas before it was common bread and common wine, now by the virtue of God's word it is made the sacrament of Christ's precious body and blood, and a seal, confirmation, and augmentation of God's mercy and gracious promise to all men that receiveth it in the faith of Christ Jesus, with hatred of sin, and instant purpose and mind to lead always a virtuous life. And that is the very transubstantiation and change that God delighteth in [in] the use of the sacrament most, that we should earnestly and from the bottom of our hearts be converted into Christ and Christ's holy commandments, to live a christian life, and die from sin, as he gave us example both by his life and his doctrine; and meaneth not that the bread and wine should in substance be

[[1] This printed in the collections at the end of Strype's Cranmer, p. 156, (MS. note.)]

turned or converted into the substance of his body and blood, or else that the substance of bread should be taken away, and in the place thereof to be the substance, matter, and corporal presence of Christ's holy human and natural body.

Item, that the same holy word of God doth confess, hold, defend, acknowledge, and maintain, that the very natural, substantial, real, and corporal body of Christ, concerning his humanity, is only and solely in heaven, and not in the sacrament and communion of his precious body and blood. But whosoever worthily with true repentance and lively faith in the promises of God receiveth that holy sacrament, receiveth sacramentally by faith all the mercies, riches, merits, and deservings that Christ hath deserved and paid for in his holy blood and passion. And that is to eat Christ and to drink Christ in the holy sacrament, to confirm and seal sacramentally in our souls God's promises of eternal salvation, that Christ deserved for us, not in nor by his body eaten, but by and for his body slain and killed upon the cross for our sins.

As for the eating of his flesh and drinking of his blood really, corporally, materially, or substantially, it is but a carnal and gross opinion of men, besides and contrary to the word of God and the articles of our faith and christian religion, that affirmeth his corporal departure from the earth, and placeth it in heaven above at the right hand of God the Father Almighty, and keepeth, retaineth, holdeth, and preserveth the same corporal body of Christ there until the general day of judgment; and the word declareth from thence he shall come to judge the quick and the dead.

And that heretofore I have been in the contrary opinion, and believed myself, and also taught other to believe the same, that there remain no substance of bread and wine in the sacrament, but the very same self body and blood of Christ Jesus that was born of the holy virgin Mary, and hanged upon the cross, I am with all my heart sorry for mine error and false opinion, detesting and abhorring the same from the bottom of my heart, and desire God most heartily, in and for the merits of his dear Son's passion, to forgive me and all them that have erred in the same self opinion by and through my means; praying them in the tender compassion and great mercies of God now to follow me in the truth, verity, and singleness of God's most true word, as they were contented to follow me in error, superstition, and blindness, and to be no more ashamed to return to the truth than they were ready to be corrupt by falsehood. If the holy apostle St Paul, and the great clerk St Augustine, with many more noble and virtuous members of Christ's church, were not ashamed to return, acknowledge, and confess their error and evil opinions; what am I, most miserable creature of the world, inferior unto them both in holiness and in learning, that should be ashamed to do the same? Nay, I do in this part thank, and rejoice from the bottom of my heart, that God hath revealed unto me the truth of his word, and given me life to live so long to acknowledge my fault and error; and do here before you protest that from henceforth I will with all diligence, study, and labour set forth mine amended knowledge and reconciled truth as long as I live, by the help of God in the Holy Ghost, through the merits of Jesus Christ, our only Mediator and Advocate, to whom be all honour for ever and ever. Amen.

FINIS.

An Assertion and defence of the true knowledge and use of the sacrament of Christ's precious body and blood, made by John Wynter, Master of Arts, Parson of Stawnton, and professed by him in the cathedral church of Gloucester, 8 November, Anno Domini, 1551.

Forasmuch as there is nothing more acceptable nor like unto God than verity and truth, and that of all things chiefly truth is required to be in man, and specially in religion and faith, which be the instruments and means that he useth to apply his mercies and grace to every of his elected children, and that nothing is or may be more injurious unto God, nor hurtful unto man, as false religion and corrupt faith; for the assertion and defence of the one, and denial and subversion of the other, I do with all my heart, being throughly persuaded upon good knowledge, long and advised deliberation, without compulsion, fear, and dread, for the truth's sake and contentation of mine own conscience, protest, hold, maintain, and defend, that in the holy sacrament of Christ's precious body and blood there is no alteration of the substance of bread and wine, but they both to remain in substance very bread and very wine, as well after the words (as they be called) of consecration, as verily as they were bread and wine in substance before: and that in the same sacrament by no manner of means, reasons, or ways the body and blood of Christ is carnally, bodily, really, or substantially present, but only spiritually to the soul and eye of faith; that is to say, as verily as corporal bread and wine is present to the senses of the outward man being upon the earth, even so is the body of Christ present to the mind and faith of man, which is then erected up into heaven. And, even as the bread and wine with the word of God and Christ's institution is broken, and entereth into the outward man presently, even so is the body of Christ rent and torn for the remission of sin to the consideration of faith presently: as Christ doth say, "This is my body which is given for you:" for even as the bread is a sacrament of his body, and the wine of his blood, so is the breaking of it a sacrament of the death of his body, and the wine received according unto Christ's institution a sacrament of his precious blood shedden; yet not two sacraments, but one sacrament, as his body and the pains thereof was not two bodies, but one body. And as in the breaking of the bread in the sacrament, after the words of Christ, which be these, "That is given for you," there is no sensible feeling or painful passion, nor killing again of Christ's precious body, no more is there in the bread, or under the bread of the sacrament, after the words, which be these, "This is my body," any natural, corporal, or substantial presence of the body that died, or of the blood that was shed; but that the bread and wine remaining in their substance be sacraments of Christ's body and blood, which be present unto the eyes spiritually of faith, which is in the receiver, and not substantially nor corporally in the elements of bread and wine. And whosoever be of the contrary opinion, and would defend transubstantiation or corporal presence, I do condemn his faith as an error and opinion contrary to the express word of God, and will, with all my learning, wit, diligence, and study, daily improve[1], confute, speak against, and utterly subvert unto the uttermost of my power, as God help me in the blood of Christ; to whom with the Holy Ghost be laud and praise, world without end : so be it.

God save the King.

FINIS.

[1 Improve: disprove.]

HOMILY TO BE READ IN THE TIME

OF

PESTILENCE.

An Homelye

to be read in the tyme
of pestylence and
a moste pre-
sente
remedye for the
same.

Fear God Honour the Kynge.
1. Pet. 2.

To all pastors and curates within the king's majesty's diocese of Worcester and Gloucester.

EVEN as we be blind and unthankful for God's favourable mercies, wherewithal he followeth us in health, wealth, and prosperity; so be we blind and unsensible for his most just plagues, wherewithal he persecuteth and punisheth us in sickness, scarcity, and troubles: and now, amongst other tokens of his displeasure and wrath, hath sent us, in divers places, Ezek. xiv. one of the extremest plagues that ever he devised to punish man withal in this life—the plague of pestilence[1]: forasmuch as he meaneth thereby not only to kill and destroy the bodies of such as by this plague he purposeth to take out of this mortal life; but also, without repentance and turning to his mercy in Christ before death, the soul of such as depart from hence must needs perish by God's just judgment. And not only this to be the end of such as it pleaseth God to strike to death by this his servant and messenger, the plague of pestilence; but also, the like danger of his displeasure remaineth to me, and to all other that have the cure and charge of the people's souls in this the king's majesty's most noble realm, over whom God and he hath made us watchmen and overseers, to admonish and Ezek. xviii. warn the people of all dangers and plagues that God shall [xxxiii.] send for their punishment. In case we admonish not in time the people committed unto our charge of such plagues as for sin he purposeth to punish us withal, their loss and damnation shall be required at our hands.

For the discharge of myself, and also for the better instruction of such as have cures within this diocese of Worcester and Gloucester, and yet not best able to discharge them; and furthermore for the profit and salvation of the people, among whom it may please God to send his fearful

[[1] The sweating sickness, which two years before this Homily was written had proved very fatal, especially in London. Hooper and several members of his household were attacked by it at that time, as appears by one of his letters to Bullinger.—See Epist. xx.]

plague of pestilence, I have thought it my bounden duty, seeing at all times I cannot comfort the sick myself, to collect or gather into some short sermon or homily a medicine and most present help for all men against the plague of pestilence°; and in the same also to provide some present remedy for such as shall be infected with that disease. And for the better understanding of the medicine, I will use this order, that all physicians learned do use in their practice of physic: first, I will shew the chiefest cause of the pestilence; and then, what remedy is best to be used against it, and to heal it when it hath infected any man.

And although I will speak herein somewhat as other physicians have done; yet because they have spoken already more than I can in the matter, though it be a great deal less than the matter of the disease requireth (for none of them have shewed any ascertained remedy, be their reason never so good); I will briefly, as by the way, somewhat speak of this disease, as they do: but as a preacher of God's word, and as a physician for the soul rather than for the body, entreat of the sickness and the remedy thereof after the advice and counsel of God's word; who supplieth all things omitted and not spoken of, concerning this most dangerous plague, by such as have written, besides the scripture of God, their mind touching the same. For indeed the chiefest causes of all plagues and sickness is sin, which, remaining within all men, worketh destruction not only of the body, but also of the soul, if remedy be not found.

<small>Lib. 1. de diffe. feb. cap. 5.</small>

And whereas Galen saith that "Omnis pestilentia fit a putredine aëris[1];" that is to say, "All pestilence cometh by the corruption of the air, that both beast and man, drawing their breaths in the air corrupt, draweth the corruption thereof into themselves," he saith well, yet not enough. He saith also, very naturally, that[2] "When the air is altered from his natural equality and temperature to too much and intempe-

---

[1 Galen. De Differ. Febr. Lib. I. cap. 6. Κατὰ δὲ τὰς λοιμώδεις καταστάσεις ἡ εἰσπνοὴ μάλιστα αἰτία, κ.τ.λ. Ὡς τὰ πολλὰ δὲ ἐκ τῆς ἀναπνοῆς ἄρχεται τοῦ πέριξ ἀέρος ὑπὸ σηπεδονώδους ἀναθυμιάσεως μιανθέντος.— P. 112, B. C. Op. Tom. VII. Lutet. Paris. 1679.]

[2 Οὕτω δὲ κἀπειδὰν ἡ κατὰ τὸν ἀέρα κρᾶσις ἀμέτρως ἐκτραπῇ τοῦ κατὰ φύσιν ἐς ὑγρότητά τε καὶ θερμότητα, λοιμώδη μὲν ἀνάγκη γενέσθαι νοσήματα. —Ib. p. 113, A.]

rate heat and moisture, pestilence is like then to reign. For as he saith in the same place that "Heat and moisture distemperated be most dangerous for the creatures of the world[3]," yet that is not enough. As Ezekiel saith, where as God sendeth all these distemperances, and yet if Noah, Daniel, and Job were in the midst of them, they shall be safe; even so saith David also: "Though they die at the right hand ten thousand fold, and die at the left a thousand fold, the plague shall not touch him that sitteth under the protection of the Highest." *(margin: Lib. i. de temp. cap. 4. Cap. xiv. Psal. xci.)*

And whereas reason hath many good and probable arguments in this matter touching the cause of pestilence[4]; that it should come sometime by reason of such humours as be in the body disposed and apt to corrupt, then is the man quickly (by drawing and breathing as well the corruption of himself as the infection of the air) infected; and that such humours as be gross and inclined to corruption riseth of evil and immoderate diet; and the infection taketh his original and beginning from such beasts, carrion, and other loathsome bodies that rot upon the face of the earth not buried, or else from moorish, standing, and dampish waters, sinks, or other such unwholesome moistures; so that, towards the fall of the leaf, both the air that man liveth in, as also man's body itself, be more apt and disposed to putrefaction more in that time than in any other time, for divers natural causes: these causes are to be considered as natural and consonant to reason; yet there be reasons and causes of pestilence of more weight, and more worthy of deep and advised considerations and advertisements than these be: and the more, because they lie within man, and be marked but of very few, and hide themselves secretly, till they have poisoned the whole man, both body and soul. For indeed physicians that write, meddle with no causes that hurt man, but such as come unto man from without: as the humours, they say, take their infection from unwholesome meat and evil diet, or else from the corruption of the air, with such

[3 Galen. De Temper. Lib. I. c. 4. Ὥστε πᾶν τοὐναντίον ἀποφαίνομαι χειρίστην εἶναι κατάστασιν κράσεως τοῦ περιέχοντος ἀέρος τὴν θερμὴν καὶ ὑγράν.—Tom. III. p. 38, E.]

[4 See Gal. De diff. Febr. Lib. I. cap. 4. p. 110, D; p. 111, A; cap. 6. p. 112, c. Tom. VII.]

[HOOPER, II.]

<small>Matt. xv.</small> like: but our Saviour Christ sheweth that our corruption and sickness riseth from within us, as I will declare hereafter in the causes that the scripture teacheth of pestilence and all other diseases; requiring you diligently to look upon the same, and to read it in your churches: that the people may understand both the cause of this God's plague of pestilence, and how to use themselves in the time of this sickness, or any other that shall happen unto them by God's appointment; as God may be glorified in them, and you and I discharged of our bounden duties; and they themselves that shall happen to be infected with the plague of pestilence, and by the same be brought to death, may be assured, through true and godly doctrine, to die in the Lord, and so be eternally blessed straightway after
<small>Rev. xiv.</small> their death, as St John saith: and in case God reserve
<small>Rom. xiv.</small> them to longer life, they may live in truth and verity unto him, with detestation and hatred of sin, the original cause of man's misery and wretchedness, and with the love
of mercy and grace, the original and only workers
of man's quietness and everlasting salvation,
given unto us from God the Father Almighty, through Jesus Christ, his only
Son, our Lord; to whom, with the
Holy Ghost, be all honour
and praise, world
without end.
So be
it.

AN HOMILY

TO BE READ

IN THE TIME OF PESTILENCE,

CONTAINING THE TRUE CAUSE OF THE SAME; AND LIKEWISE A MOST PRESENT REMEDY FOR AS MANY AS BE ALREADY, OR HEREAFTER SHALL BE INFECTED WITH DISEASE.

GATHERED OUT OF THE HOLY SCRIPTURE

BY JOHN HOPER,
BISHOP OF WORCESTER AND GLOUCESTER.

Anno Domini 1553.

Repent, and believe the gospel. Mark i. 15.

It is the desire of all sick men to know what medicine and remedy hath been known most to prevail, best to remove, and soonest to cure and make whole the person diseased; and the greater and more dangerous the sickness is, the more circumspect and wise the sick man must be in knowledge and choice of the medicine, lest haply he seek a remedy inferior and too weak for the greatness and strength of his disease.

The nature and condition therefore of pestilence being so dangerous (as it is indeed), that whosoever be infected or attainted therewithal, hath need to be well instructed and thoroughly persuaded of a sufficient remedy, stronger than the sickness itself; or else the disease shall more hurt the sick patient than the medicine can do him good; then must needs follow the death and the destruction of the diseased person; it behoveth therefore all men, that be mortal, to know the most general and most dangerous diseases that mortality shall be troubled withal; and then, as he seeth his great and necessary adversaries and sickness, to know also the greatest and most necessary remedy and help against his diseases. And because sin hath so prevailed in us, that truth, persuaded unto us by the examples of others, sooner instructeth and longer tarrieth than any thing taught us by doctrine or testimony; I shall, before I enter into the causes of the pestilence, shew the strength and nature of sickness from the examples of such godly persons as in the word of God are mentioned of for our instruction.

King David, amongst other diseases, fell into the pestilence; the greatness and danger whereof passed all human and worldly helps, as it appeareth by his lamentable cry and complaint unto the Lord: "My soul (saith he) is sore troubled: but how long, Lord, wilt thou defer thy help?" And the same cry and complaint he made unto the Lord, when the plague of pestilence had infected his whole realm from Dan to Beersheba, and saw the remedy thereof to be only in God, praying him to command his angel to strike the people no more.

Ps. vi. xlii.

2 Sam. xxiv.

Isai. xxxviii.

Ezekias the king saw that, besides God, all medicines and remedies were too weak and inferior for the strength and power of the pestilence and sickness: wherefore he turned himself to the wall, and prayed God to do that for him that no physic nor medicine was able to do.

1 Cor. xv.

And St Paul, in his wonderful oration that he maketh concerning the resurrection of the dead, weigheth most deeply the nature and condition of man's miserable estate in this life, burdening him with such strong adversaries, sickness, and diseases, both of body and soul, that every man may see how impossible it is for man to find deliverance from the tyranny and strength of sickness, except only the mercy of God in Christ Jesus; numbering there six adversaries so strong, as the least of them, except Christ help, is able to destroy both body and soul.

The first is corruption; the second, mortality; the third, sin; the fourth, the law condemning sin; the fifth, death; the sixth, hell; necessary and indivisible plagues and sickness of man in this life: against the which he findeth no remedy, neither by Galen nor Hippocrates, neither yet by the earth of Para, that men say cureth all wounds; but with great faith and confidence marketh and weigheth the strength of diseases, though they be never so strong, to be yet inferior to the medicine and remedy that God hath provided for us only in Christ: therefore compareth the inferior strength of all those sicknesses unto the sufficient remedy of God through

Plin. lib. xxiv. c. 96¹.

[¹ This should be Lib. II. c. 96. In Taurorum peninsula in civitate Parasino terra est qua sanantur omnia vulnera.—C. Plin. Sec. Hist. Nat. p. 40. Francof. 1599.]

Christ, saying after this manner: "Thanks be unto God, which hath given us victory through our Lord Jesus Christ." Whereby it is evident and plain that God is the only remedy for all plagues and diseases. Howbeit, now I shall more specially open the causes of the plague, and the nature of the same; that our sickness and the causes thereof may be more known, and the better avoided.

The principal cause of pestilence is opened by St Paul by these words: "By sin (saith he) came death into the world:" Rom. v. and for the cause of sin God sendeth the plague of pestilence and all other diseases that punisheth towards death; as king David saith, "Thou dost punish the children of men for sin." Psal. xlii. [xxxix.] Moses also plainly sheweth that the principal and chief cause Deut. xxviii. of pestilence is not in the corruption of the air, nor in the superfluous humours within man; but that sin and the transgression of God's law is the very cause and chief occasion of pestilence and of all other diseases. And the experience thereof was tried in the pestilence that reigned in king David's time 2 Sam. xxiv. for his sins, and the sins of the people. So that all the scripture of God manifestly declareth, that the contempt and breach of God's laws is the chief and principal cause of pestilence, and of all other plagues that he sendeth for our punishment. And from this cause proceedeth those causes that physicians speak of, the corruption of the air, which is never corrupted, nor can corrupt man or beast, except man, for whose sake and comfort both air and all other beasts were made, be first corrupted by sin and transgression of God's laws. Neither could man take any surfeit by meats, nor any evil humours could be engendered of any meats, were not the man that useth them corrupt and first infected with sin. But when the Lord doth see that the people forget or contemn his blessed commandments, and that such as be appointed to rebuke and punish such transgressors of God's laws, suffer without punishment the glory of God and his holy commandments to be oppressed and set at nought, as we see daily they be indeed; —from these causes, our sin and abomination, the Lord taketh occasion to turn his good creatures, made for our life, to be a means of our death; which never would be, were not[2] our heinous dishonouring and contempt of God.

For the Lord's creatures be perfectly good, and made all Gen. i.

[2 Probably for "were it not for."]

to comfort and rejoice; wholesome, clean, and pure without all infection. But seeing that the contempt of God and the filthiness of sin is neither by the clergy declared, opened, ne detected, neither by the heads of the country and officers appointed under God and the king punished; except, therefore, there should nothing else live in this world than sin, abomination, and contempt of God, God is forced, for the taking away and destruction of filthy life and filthy livers, to appoint an extraordinary magistrate to reform and punish the mother of all mischief, sin and contempt of God's holy word: and so altereth, not by chance, nor by the influence of stars, the wholesomeness of the air into pestilent and contagious infection, and the meat and drink with their nutriment and food into poison and venom; that by their mean sin and sinners might be slain and taken out of this world, and no longer to blaspheme God.

Thus doth the word of God declare the effectuous and principal cause of pestilence to be the contempt of God's word, that should keep men in order both to God and man: the breaking whereof hath always brought these plagues into realms, as profane writers also manifestly declare. Orosius[1] *Lib. vii. cap. 1.* saith that the great dearth and famine that came amongst the Romans in the time of Cæsar Augustus, was because Caius, his nephew, contemned to honour the living God, as he was taught at Jerusalem, when he passed into Syria. Wherefore it is expedient, and before all things necessary, forasmuch as the plague is come into sundry places about us, for every one to try himself, what just causes of this pestilence each man hath within himself. Every christian man and woman must search whether their religion and christianity be such as God by his word doth maintain to be good: for there is no greater occasion of pestilence than superstition and false religion.

The bishop, parson, vicar, and curate, must examine themselves, what knowledge of God's word is in them, and

[[1] Caium nepotem suum Cæsar Augustus ad ordinandas Ægypti Syriæque provincias misit; qui præteriens ab Ægypto fines Palæstinæ, apud Hierosolymam in templo Dei tunc sancto et celebri adorare contempsit, sicut Suetonius Tranquillus refert. Quod Augustus ubi per eum comperit, pravo usus judicio, prudenter fecisse laudavit. Itaque anno imperii Cæsaris quadragesimo octavo adeo dira Romanos fames consecuta est ut, &c.—Oros. Hist. Lib. vii. c. 3. p. 575. Colon. 1582.]

what diligence they have taken to bring the people to a right knowledge and perfect honour of God: for there is no greater danger of pestilence than where as the clergy is either ignorant of God's word, or negligent in teaching thereof.

The justices and gentlemen must look how they keep themselves and the king's majesty's people in the true knowledge and obedience of God's laws and the king's: for nothing provoketh the pestilence more dangerously than where as such as sit and be appointed to do justice, do their own affections with contempt and injuries both to God and man; and the plague of God will revenge it.

All we, therefore, that be subjects, and live under one God and one king, must (now that God hath sent us this pestilence) see that we have true, loving, faithful, trusty, and obedient hearts; with one whole mind altogether to obey, reverence, love, help, succour, defend, and uphold with all our wits, goods, riches, and strength, this our only king, the magistrates and counsellors that be appointed under his highness. For, as St Paul saith, "He that disobeyeth and resisteth the higher powers appointed by God, resist[eth] God," provoke[th] the pestilence and vengeance of God against us. And we must take heed also that we hate not one another: if we do, the plague will not cease, and the places that yet be not infected God shall infect, whatsoever defence man maketh against it. And although Galen, of all remedies, saith, "To fly the air that is infected is best;" yet I know that Moses by the word of God saith: "Flee whither thou wilt, in case thou take with thee the contempt of God and breach of his commandment, God shall find thee out." Yea, and although many medicines be devised, and assureth the infected to be made whole; yet, notwithstanding, I know God's word saith the contrary, that he will send unto unsensible, careless, and wilful sinners such a plague and incurable a pestilence, that he shall not be delivered, but die and perish by it. *Rom. xiii.* *1 John iii.* *Deut. xxviii.*

Therefore, forasmuch as sin is the occasion chiefly of pestilence, let every man eschew and avoid it both speedily and penitently; and then shall ye be preserved from the plague sufficiently, as ye shall perceive in the remedy of this dangerous plague that beginneth to reign amongst us. For doubtless, although we could fly to Locris or Crotone, where as Pliny[1] saith the pestilence was never, yet God saith, in case we fear not him, we shall surely be infected.

<small>Lib. i. cap. 96.
Deut. xviii.</small>

THE REMEDY AGAINST THE PESTILENCE.

Like as the scripture of God only sheweth the very cause of pestilence, so doth it the very true and only remedy against it. I do not dislike the remedies that natural physic hath prescribed; yet I do not hable[2] them as sufficient remedies, for their imperfection's sake. I would also they were used, and the remedies prescribed in God's book not omitted; for I see all the remedies that ever was devised by man is not able to remove assuredly the pestilence from him that is infected therewithal, although they be never so excellent and good. And I find the same concerning the preservation from the pestilence devised by man, also insufficient for man's preservation, yet not to be contemned; for the reason of their chiefest preservation is very good and allowable, and yet not sufficient, which is of all things chiefly to be used against the pestilence, fleeing and departure from the place where as the air is corrupt. Wherefore, for such as may, nothing is better than to flee; and except he do, he offereth himself to a present danger of death: but yet the word of God saith plainly that, "flee whither we will, if we forsake not sin, and serve the living God, the plague shall overtake us."

And this cannot be a sufficient remedy; for there be certain persons that cannot flee, although they would; as the poorer sort of people, that have no friends nor place to flee unto, more than the poor house they dwell in. Likewise, there be such offices of trust as men for no cause may flee from it; as the bishop, parson, vicar, and curate, who hath the charge of those that God pleaseth to infect with the pestilence; and if they forsake their people in this plague-time, they be hirelings and no pastors; and they flee from God's people into God's high indignation. Such also as have places and offices of trust for the commonwealth; as the captains of soldiers in the time of war, judges and justices in the time of peace; in case they should flee their countries, or leave their

<small>John x.</small>

[1 Locris et Crotonæ pestilentiam nunquam fuisse annotatum est.—Plin. Hist. Nat. Lib. ii. c. 96.]

[2 Hable: hold.]

wars for the plague of pestilence, they shall never be good soldiers nor good justices for the commonwealth; and they shall be accountable to Almighty God for all the hurt and detriment that hath happened unto the people in their absence.

Wherefore, seeing there is no certain remedy devised by man, neither for such as cannot flee, nor for them that may flee, we must seek another medicine and help at God's hand, who can and will preserve those that be whole, and make them whole that be sick, if it be expedient for man, and most for his own honour. The best preservative, therefore, to keep men from the pestilence is this that Moses speaketh of: "Let us do sacrifice unto the Lord, lest we be stricken with pestilence or sword." And Joshua and Caleb told the people that a faithful trust in the Lord was the best remedy for them: which if they contemned, they should find that God there threatened, speaking to Moses, "How long will this people be unfaithful? I will strike them with pestilence, and consume them." Also, David knew that the only remedy to keep Jerusalem from the plague was, that God should turn his wrath from the city for his sins and the sins of the people. *Exod. v.* *Numb. xiv.* *2 Sam. xxiv.*

But now, to bring the remedy the better to the understanding of the people, I will shew it by this place of St Mark, "Repent ye, and believe the gospel:" in the which words is contained the only medicine against the pestilence, and also all other diseases, if the text be well and advisedly considered, wherein Christ useth a very natural order to heal all diseases; for as the remedy naturally of all diseases be taken from contrary conditions and qualities [to] that [which] worketh and maintaineth the sickness, so doth Christ in these words declare that the preservation and help of sin and wickedness, the cause of pestilence, proceedeth from virtues and conditions contrary to the qualities and nature of such things as preserve and keep this wicked sin and sickness in man. As when a man is fallen into sickness by reason of too much cold and moisture, the remedy must be gathered naturally from the contrary, heat and drought; for this is a common and true principle, "Contraries be holpen by their contraries[3]." If nature wax too cold, it must be holpen with *Chap. i.* *Galen. de temp.*

[3 Gal. De Temper. Lib. I. c. 3. Τὸ μὲν θερμότερον τοῦ δέοντος σῶμα κελεύοντες ἐμψύχειν, τὸ δ' αὖ ψυχρότερον θερμαίνειν, ὡσαύτως τὸ

heat: if it be too hot, it must be cooled: if it be too moist, it must be dried: if it be too dry, it must be moisted: if it be too cold and moist, it must be heated and dried: if it be cold and dry, it must be heated and moisted: if it be too hot and moist, it must be cooled and dried: if it be hot and dry, it must be cooled and moisted. These be very natural remedies, if they be well used with true proportion and convenient use after physic.

And as these be good and natural for the body wherein the pestilence dwelleth, even so is Christ's medicine in the first of St Mark a more present and certain remedy for the soul, that keepeth the body in life, to remove or to remedy the sin of man, which is the cause of all plagues and pestilence; in case to remove sin, the cause of sickness, this medicine of Christ be used, as the other is used to remove the effect of sin, which is sickness: as the body that is fallen into sickness by too much cold or moisture, either by nature, that originally was corrupted by Adam, either by our own accustomed[1] doing of sin, it must be made whole by the heat of repentance and true faith in the merits of Christ Jesus, who died for the sins of the world.

For this is a true and most certain principle of all religion, "One contrary must remedy the other." Seeing Adam by his fault began our death by sin, it must be cured by Christ, that is without sin. And whereas our own works be sin and filthiness, wherewithal God is displeased, we must desire the works of Christ, to work the good will and favour of our heavenly Father again. And whereas by our own wits, wisdoms, religion, and learning we have committed idolatry and superstition, we must now by God's wisdom, God's word, and his most true religion amend our faults, and turn to true and godly honouring of him. Further, whereas our own inventions hath brought us from the knowledge of God, the remedy is, that God's word must bring us to him again; for against all untruths brought in by man the word of God is the only remedy.

Ps. xix. cxix.
2 Tim. iii.

The experience thereof we may have plainly in the

μὲν ὑγρότερον ξηραίνειν, τὸ δὲ ξηρότερον ὑγραίνειν, κ. τ. λ.—Opp. Tom. III. p. 35, D. Lutet. Paris. 1679. See also De diff. Febr. Lib. I. c. 6. Tom. VII. p. 113, C. D.]

[1 "Accustomed and doing" &c. 1553.]

scripture. Whereas, for the salvation of the world, God appointed Christ his only Son to be born, and also to be opened unto the world, that by him it might be healed of all sickness and sin, as it appeareth by St Matthew, and other of the evangelists; yet was the world so blind and so corrupted with sin, that Christ was born and opened unto them, and they of the world nothing the better, as it appeareth in St Matthew, where as St John the Baptist in few words, which be these, "Repent ye, for the kingdom of God is at hand," sheweth the remedy of all sins and sickness, and the means how to receive and take the same remedy. The remedy was only Christ, as he saith in St John, and also in St Matthew; and the means to come by the remedy was to repent, as ye shall know further hereafter, when ye know what repentance is. Matt. i. ii.
Luke ii.
John i.

Chap. iii.

John i. iii.
Matt. iii.

The same may you also see in St John, in the dialogue between Christ and Nicodemus, a man, after the judgment of the world, that knew life and death, sickness and health, the cause of the one, and also of the other, as well as any learned man among all the congregation and church of the Jews; yet, indeed, as ignorant of his own sickness, and also so far from the true knowledge how to come to health, as an ignorant man might be. And the cause was, that he understood not the nature of sin, as it is esteemed by the word of God, neither the remedy thereof that God hath prescribed and appointed. Wherefore Christ told him by plain words, except he were holpen and cured of his disease and sickness by contrary remedies, he could never understand nor come by his health: and no marvel; for he knew the sickness of sin no otherwise than his forefathers and the worldly men knew sin, that is to say, knew such sins as were known to reason, and done by the body and outward action of men; and the same knowledge had he, and no more, of the remedy against the sickness of sin. And as his fathers and the world thought, so did he, that the merits of their sacrifices and the welldoing of themselves was a sufficient remedy to heal them both in body and in soul. Whereupon Christ most mercifully pitieth the poor man, and with contrary knowledge both of sickness and the remedy thereof sheweth, that the disease man is infected with goeth further than reason and the outer action of the body, and occupieth the soul of man with concupiscence, rebellion, frowardness, and contumacy against God: Chap. iii.

wherefore he calleth all that man hath of himself but flesh; and sheweth that the remedy against this sickness cometh not of the worthiness of any sacrifice or merits of his, or any sinful man's works; but that the remedy thereof dependeth only upon the merits of his blood and passion, and sheweth the same by the comparison of the brasen serpent appointed by Moses; and argueth this way: as the people that were stung with the serpents in the wilderness were not made whole by their own works, or for the dignity or service of any sacrifice that they offered, but by the sight of the serpent, that represented Christ to come; even so Nicodemus, nor any other that is stung with the serpents of sin, be made whole by their own works, or any sacrifice they can offer, but only by the merits of Christ. And even as the people could not come to the knowledge of this remedy by the serpent through their fathers' or their own wisdom, no more can Nicodemus, or any man living, come to the knowledge of the remedy for sickness and sin in our Saviour Christ, except he learn it by the word of God through the instruction of the Holy Ghost.

The same remedy also useth Christ in his words before rehearsed: "Repent ye, and believe the gospel." In the which words our Saviour Christ sheweth all things to be considered in sin, and in the remedy thereof. For in the first part of his words he declareth how that men should know the causes of sickness; and in the second part the remedy and help for the same. The cause of sickness, as it appeareth by this word "Repent," is, that men have by their own folly turned themselves from the truth of God to the error and fond opinion of man; from true faith to uncertain fables; from virtuous and godly works to uncleanliness and corruption of life. Christ, therefore, seeing the world how it is in danger, by reason it hath forsaken the wisdom and rule of God's word, calleth it home again to a better way, bidding it repent: as though he had said, "Turn to a better mind, and leave the ways accustomed, and learn to be wise, and walk in the ways and wisdom appointed by God."

Here appeareth also, that the causes of all the dangers that Christ willed his audience to repent for, was their sin and iniquity. The cause of sin was infidelity and accustomed doing of evil. The cause of infidelity and accustomed doing of evil was ignorance or misunderstanding of God's word. The cause of ignorance or misunderstanding of God's word was Satan, God's and man's enemy, and man's willing consent to the devilish sophistry and false construing of God's word. And from these causes springeth all diseases and sickness, death, and everlasting damnation; from the which Christ was sent, of God's inestimable love towards us, to redeem and save us. Notwithstanding, these effects of pestilence, sickness, death, and everlasting damnation cannot be removed, except first the causes of them be eschewed. John iii.

Wherefore learn ye, and teach other to know the causes above-mentioned, and also, how they may be removed; for as long as they work their proper nature in man, so long will they bring forth their natural effects, sickness, troubles, death, and damnation. The original cause of all evil was Satan, and the ungodly consent of our forefather Adam in paradise, in crediting more the devil's sophistry and gloss than the plain and manifest word of God. And the remedy of this cause is God, that, of love against Satan's hatred, promised in the seed of a woman help again for man; and that every man that believeth the devil in evil must repent and believe God and his word in good. *Gen. iii.* *John i. iii. v.*

Ignorance and mistaking of God's word is the second cause of evil; the remedy whereof is knowledge and right understanding of God's word. *John i. iii.*

Infidelity and accustomed doing of evil be the third cause of evil; true faith and accustomed doing of good remedieth them. *John xvi.*

Sin and iniquity be the causes of sickness, death, and damnation; virtue and godliness healeth and removeth, that they shall not bring man to everlasting death. Although sin and sickness be not clean taken from man, yet doth God in Christ take away the damnation of sin, and suffereth death to destroy by sickness none other thing than the body of the sinner, so that he use this remedy, "Repent, and believe the gospel;" and shall at length call the body, dead by death, out of the earth, and place it alive with the soul in heaven.

But now, to use this help and remedy against the pestilence, which Christ calleth "Repent, and believe the gospel:" the sick man must remember what the first word, "Repent," meaneth, and how he may come by it. Repentance, that God requireth, is the return of the sinner from sin into a new life in Christ; which return is an innovation and renovation of the mind of man by God's Spirit in Christ, with denial of the former life, to begin a new and better life. And this repentance springeth from the knowledge of sin by the law of God: from the knowledge of sin cometh the hatred of sin: from the hatred of sin proceedeth the leaving and departure from sin: from the departure from sin cometh, by faith through Christ's blood, remission of sin: from remission of sin cometh our acceptation into God's favour: from our acceptation into God's favour cometh the gifts of the Holy Ghost to do and work by virtuous life the will of God: from the doing in Christ the will of God cometh God's defence and favour, that taketh from us all plagues and pestilence: from the deliverance of plagues and pestilence cometh everlasting life, as Christ saith, and as this medicine, called, "Repent ye, and believe the gospel," declareth.

<small>John iii. v. vi.</small>

There be, also, many that be sick and in great danger and peril by reason of sin, and yet feel not the sore and grief thereof. Therefore, they pass not whether they seek for any remedy or not; and, for lack of taking heed, they fall daily to more wickedness than other. Wherefore it is every minister's office of the church diligently (and especially in the time of pestilence and plagues) to call upon the people for amendment of life, and to shew them truly, diligently, and plainly, this medicine of repentance, which consisteth of these parts: first, in knowledge of sin; then, in hatred of sin; thirdly, in forsaking of sin; fourthly, in believing the forgiveness of sins for Christ's sake; and fifthly, to live in virtuous and godly life, to honour God, and to shew his obedience to God's law, that by sin is transgressed.

And these parts of penance, which be the very true and only medicines against sickness and sin, be known only by God's laws; for by the law of God sin is known, detested, and forsaken. If it be heard or read by men that pray unto God, they may understand it. Faith also, that believeth remission of sin, is shewed, opened, and offered by the gospel, wherein be contained God's merciful promises towards sinners; and those promises sinners receive by faith, that believeth whatsoever God hath promised in Christ he will perform it. Faith doth credit and receive forgiveness of sins by the operation of God's Holy Spirit in the poor sinner. The sinner studieth and liveth a virtuous life, being led by the Holy Ghost, and worketh to serve God with such works as God's holy commandment commandeth every true christian man to work and do. And for the better assurance and further stablishing of repentance and acceptation into the favour of God by believing the gospel, the poor sinner useth and receiveth the holy sacrament of Christ's precious body and blood, in remembrance that Christ died to be his medicine against sin, and the effect thereof.

Wherefore, now that it pleaseth God for our offences to shew by plagues and sickness how he is offended, let us all, that be ministers of the church, and the watchmen of the people, call upon them diligently to "repent, and believe the gospel," and to live a godly and virtuous life; that for Christ's sake he will turn mercifully his plagues from us, and give us his most gracious favour to preserve his universal church, our most godly sovereign lord and king, king Edward the Sixth, his majesty's most honourable council, and the whole realm. So be it.

18 *Maii.* 1553.

Imprinted at Worceter
by Jhon Oswen, prynter appointed by the Kinge's Majestie for the principalitie of Wales and Marches of the same.

Cum privilegio ad imprimendum solum.

EXPOSITIONS UPON PSALMS
XXIII, LXII, LXXIII, AND LXXVII.

CERTEINE
comfortable Expositions
of the constant Martyr of Christ, M. John Hooper,
Bishop of Glocester and Worcester,
written in the time of his tribulation and
*imprisonment, upon the XXIII, LXII,
LXXIII, and LXXVII psalmes
of the prophet Dauid.*

Newly recognized, and neuer
before published.

MATTH. xxiv. 13.
¶ Whoso continueth to the end
shall be saued.

AT LONDON,
Printed by Henrie Middleton.
ANNO, 1580.

[Title page of the edition of 1580.]

An Exposition

on upon the 23. psalme of Dauid full of frutefull and comfortable doctrin, written to the Citye of London by John Hooper, bushop of Gloceter and Worceter, and holy Martyr of God for the testimonye of hys truth.

ℂ Whereunto is annexed an Apology of his, agaynst such as reported that he cursed Quene Mary, with certaine Godlye and comfortable letters in the ende.

Prouer. ii.

ℂ By the blessinge of the righteous the cytye prospereth: But when the ungodly haue the rule it decayeth.

Anno. 1562.

[Title page of the edition of 1562.]

[The edition of 1562, duodecimo, contains an Exposition of only one Psalm, the twenty-third, with other matter, as indicated in the title page. The Edition of 1580, small quarto, contains the Expositions of the four Psalms, without any addition. In this reprint the text of 1580 is followed, and the variations of ed. 1562 are noted. The Apology and Letters included in ed. 1562 will be found in a subsequent part of this volume.]

[Colophon at the end of the edition of 1562.]

❡ Imprynted
at London, by Jhon
Tisdale, and Thomas
Hacket, and are to be solde
at their shoppes in
Lombarde
strete.

Anno. 1562.

[Address to the Reader, prefixed to the Expositions, M.D.LXXX.]

To all the faithful flock of Christ, grace and peace from God the Creator, Christ the Redeemer, and the Holy Ghost the Comforter.

MANY are the monuments, beloved in the bowels of Christ Jesus, and volumes of the faithful left as legacies to the church of Christ; which, as they are the true riches (for they are spiritual), so ought they to be reverenced, not only with outward service of body, but also with inward submission of soul. Among which monuments, being the treasure of the church, and such jewels indeed as the price of them is invaluable, this excellent work (though wanting bigness, yet full of brightness) of that most learned, godly, faithful, zealous, constant, and in all points praiseworthy protestant, Master John Hooper, bishop of Gloucester and Worcester, challengeth no small title of dignity. For, if the words of our Saviour be true (which to improve what incestuous mouth, without horrible blasphemy, a trespass unpardonable, dare presume, seeing he is the very substance of truth itself?), that he is a true disciple of Christ, which continueth to the end; then is it the duty of us all, except we hide our profession under the hive of hypocrisy, not only by looking at the life of such a loadesman[1] to reform our deformities; but also, by tracing over and through the testimonies of the truth (such godly books I mean, as are left in writing to the world as undoubted assurances of an unspotted conscience), to thank God for so singular an instrument of his gospel; and to beseech him to work in us the like love to his law, that we may be partakers of such glory as (no doubt) this notable martyr of God doth immortally enjoy. Of whom briefly to insert and say somewhat (because the brightness of such a glittering star cannot be overcast with the clouds of obscurity and darkness) shall

Constancy and continuance required in the professors of the truth.

[1 Loadesman: leader, pilot.]

be a means to make the work more commendable, although in very deed precious things have their proper price, and therefore consequently will have their deserved praise. And, first, to touch his blessed beginning, blessed (I say) even from above with the dew of God's grace, his education in Oxford, his prosperous proceeding in the knowledge of divinity, his forsaking not only of the university, but also his common country, his flight into Germany, his return into England, his painfulness in preaching, his fame and credit among the people, his obtained favour with the king's majesty, his advancement to more than a bishop-like dignity, his dispensation for his ceremonious consecration, his secret enemies the supporters of papistry, his supplantation by their privy conspiracies, his faithful continuance notwithstanding in sowing sincere doctrine, his painfulness in hearing public controversies, his visiting of schools and fountains of learning, his maintaining of godly discipline, his want of partiality in judgment betwixt person and person, his bishop-like behaviour abroad in his diocese, his fatherly affection at home towards his house and family, &c. do warrant him the name of a saint upon earth; and surely God hath registered him in the kalendar of his chosen servants in heaven. Again, the falling away of his favourers when religion languished, the malicious practices of his adversaries threatening his destruction, the blood-thirsty broaching of his persecution, his appearing before the queen and her council, the tyrannical contumelies of his arch-enemy, his spiteful accusation, his mild purgation, his undeserved deprivation, his cruel imprisonment, his hard entertainment, his lamentable lodging, his succourless sickness, his pitiful complaints, his restless tribulations, his strait examinations, his apologetical avouchments, the committing of him to the Fleet, the tossing of him from the Fleet to the Counter in Southwark, from the Counter in Southwark to the Clinke, from the Clinke to Newgate, his unjust degradation, his cruel condemnation, and his lamentable execution, &c., all these pageants considered, as they were done, would make a flinty heart to melt, and stony eyes to sweat not only water, but also blood; and, to be short, the whole body, though all the limbs thereof were as strong as steel, even for pity's sake to tremble. This coming within the compass of my poor consideration, I remembered that Christ Jesus, the only-begotten

An abridgement of Bishop Hooper's life and death truly gathered in circumstances.

Bishop Hooper in estimation with king Edward the Sixth.

Stephen Gardiner, Bishop of Winchester, Bishop Hooper's professed enemy.

If Christ the head have

been perse-cuted even to the death, the members must needs be subject to affliction.

Son of the almighty and eternal God, had passed the like, yea, and worse perils, as by the history of his death and passion may appear; that the proto-martyr, St Stephen, had his tormentors, St Paul the apostle his persecutors, and other of Christ's disciples their afflicters: then thought I that these sanctified vessels made their vocation honourable even by their deaths, which were opprobrious; and therefore how can it be but that this our martyr, worthy bishop Hooper, offering up his body a burnt sacrifice, lively, reasonable, and acceptable unto God, should give good credit to his doctrine, assure his profession, affirm his vocation, and live in everlasting memory by the dispersion of his books, though his favour be forgotten, and his body consumed? Of such a soldier, so valiantly fighting under the ensign of his captain, I cannot

2 Cor. v.

say sufficient. Of this I am resolved, that although his earthly tabernacle be destroyed, yet hath he a building given him of God, even an house not made with hands, but eternal in the heavens; where God grant us all to reign as joint heirs with Christ his anointed!

The laying down of his life for the gospel's sake deserveth belief and reverence.

To proceed and approach nearer to our purpose (for the premises are effectual enough to breed belief and to kindle reverence in the heart of any true Christian towards this our excellent martyr, replenished with the abundance of God's Holy Spirit), I commend unto thy mind, good reader, a good work of this so good a man, namely, "Certain Expositions upon the twenty-third, sixty-second, seventy-second, and seventy-seventh psalms of the prophet David," of the which the three last (being gathered together by a godly professor of the truth, Mr Henry Bull[1]) were never before printed. Their beginnings are usually read in this manner: 23. "The Lord feedeth me, and I shall lack nothing." 62. "My soul truly waiteth upon God." 72. "Truly God is loving unto Israel, even unto such as are of a clean heart." 77. "I will cry unto God with my voice, even to God will I cry with my voice, and he shall hearken unto me." The expositions of which psalms to be pithy and profitable this may be a substantial proof, because they were written in the time of his trouble, when (no doubt) he was talking in spirit with God; and being so occupied, his exercises could not but be heavenly, and therefore effectual, fruitful, and comfortable.

[1 He edited the Exposition upon Psalm xxiii., Apology, &c.]

Come therefore, thou sorrowing soul, which groanest for relief, to this spring: come hither, and hear what a good man wrote, *ex carcere et vinculis*, "out of bonds and imprisonment," for thy consolation. Hear him once, hear him twice, hear him often; for thou canst not hear him enough. He giveth thee a pleasant pomander; vouchsafe it the smelling: he soundeth sweet music; it deserveth good dancing: he bids thee to a sumptuous banquet; be not dainty in feeding: he presenteth unto thee a precious diamond; it is worth the taking. O give God thanks for all, and glorify the Lord's name, whom it hath pleased to plant in his vineyard so fruitful a vine, which beareth grapes, God's plenty; of whose juice, O Christ, vouchsafe us to taste, that, our vessels being seasoned with true sanctification, they may be made sweet to receive and preserve the water of the river of life, flowing from the lively rock Christ Jesus: to whom, with the Father and the Holy Ghost, one Trinity in Unity, be all laud and praise everlasting. Amen.

Thine in Christ,
A. F.

[Preface to Psalm XXIII. 1562[1].]

¶ To the faithful and
lively members of our Saviour
Jesus Christ inhabiting the city of
London, grace and peace from the
Heavenly Father through
our Lord Jesus Christ.

YOUR faith and firm hope of eternal life, dearly beloved, which of long time ye have learned and thoroughly persuaded yourselves in by the truth and infallible verity of the heavenly word, sealed with Christ's most precious blood, is very sore and dangerously assaulted, and by all means possible attempted to be taken from you; that ye should have no longer credit to God's truth, but believe man's lies, no more to have salvation[2] by Christ, that once died and offered himself once for all[3] for sin, but that ye must[4] believe now your salvation in Christ many times[5] offered by wicked men every day in the abominable mass, to the utter conculcation and oppressing[6] of Christ's death, as the wicked pope and his adherents would persuade you, and not as Christ your Saviour hath taught you. But this sudden and miserable change from the truth unto falsehood, and from God and Christ to the devil and antichrist, doubtless cometh of God for our manifold sins towards the heavenly Father our Shepherd, that taught us a long time with his blessed word, and we were neither thankful for it, nor yet put our trust in him, as in one that only could save and defend his own word: but we thought in our foolishness

[[1] This Preface was not reprinted in ed. 1580: but it occurs amongst Coverdale's Letters of the Martyrs, ed. 1564. The texts of the two editions, 1562 and 1564, have been carefully collated, and the variations of the latter, distinguished by the initial C. are appended in the notes.]

[[2] C. nor have your salvation.]   [[3] C. for sin once for all.]
[[4] C. should.]   [[5] C. to be many times.]   [[6] C. defacing.]

that the world was so much and so many ways with the
word of God, that even by man's strength it might have
been defended; whereas the truth of God's word is permanent and never faileth, saying, "Cursed be they that make Jer. xvii.
flesh their defence and shield." For as king David, when
God had brought him to possess his kingdom peaceably,
said, like a fool as he was, "I shall never be more unquieted," Psalm xxx.
but yet the Lord turned his face from him, and he found
straightway such an alteration as he never found before,
with increase of new dangers more troublous than ever he
had before; even likewise, when God had given us a blessed
and holy king, and such magistrates (although they were
sinners) as wished the glory of God only to be preferred
by true doctrine, we, like carnal men, thought ourselves so
sure and so stablished, that it had not been possible to have
seen such a piteous and miserable change, and the truth of
God's word oppressed[7], as we see at this present day. But
we be most worthily punished, and even the same ways
that we offended[8]. We put[9] our trust in flesh, and whereas
God's Spirit in flesh dwelled, as in our holy and blessed
king departed[10], Edward the Sixth (who is dead[11] in the flesh,
and his holy soul resteth with the heavenly Father in joys
for ever), he[12] is taken from us now, and cannot help us;
and such as in his time seemed much to favour the glory
of God are become God's enemies, and can both hear other
to proceed against the glory of God, and also set forth the
same themselves as much as they may: so that such spiritual
and godly persons as sought in the flesh God's glory are
taken from us, or else in such place as they can do[13] no
good; and such flesh as followed and loved God in the
sight of the world, and had great vantage by his word, are
become his very enemies, and not only his, but also enemies
to his members. But yet, as king David knew his foolish
folly, and with repentance repented and found grace; so it
may please God to give us of his grace and holy Spirit to
amend our faults in the like offences, and help us, as he did
him. But doubtless great is our iniquity. For there was
never so great abomination read of, and so quickly to pre-

[7 C. so oppressed.] [8 C. have offended.] [9 C. did put.]
[10 Not in C.] [11 C. he is now dead.]
[12 C. he is now (I say).] [13 C. do us.]

vail, as this abomination of the wicked mass hath prevailed in England. And all christian men know that the Turks and heathen neither have, nor yet had ever, any so sensibly known and manifest an idol.

<small>Upon this Psalm (as upon divers other) he wrote a godly and most comfortable treatise, whereunto he annexed this letter as a preface.</small> Wherefore, that Almighty God of his mercy may preserve his people in this noble city of London, I have written upon this[1] 23rd Psalm of king David, to advertise men how they shall beware of heresies and false doctrine, and so to live to his honour and glory. And[2] I know, dearly beloved, that[3] these godly people which seek God's honour, and all other that wish them well, be accompted the queen's enemies, although we daily pray for her grace, and never think her harm. But we must be content to suffer slander[4], and give God thanks for them. Nevertheless, this is out of doubt, that the queen's highness hath no authority to compel any man to believe anything contrary to God's word, neither may the subject give her grace that obedience: in case he do, his soul is lost for ever. Our bodies, goods, and lives be at her highness' commandment, and she shall have them as of true subjects; but the soul of man for religion is bound to none but unto God and his holy word.
(∴)

[1 C. the.]   [2 C. Albeit.]
[3 C. all those which seek God's honour and the furtherance of his gospel.]
[4 C. and patiently to bear all such injuries.]

¶ The argument or matter
which the prophet chiefly entreateth
of in this Psalm.

IT should seem by the marvellous and wonderful description and setting forth of Almighty God by the prophet and king David in this Psalm, that he was inflamed with the Holy Ghost, being delivered from all his enemies, to declare unto all the world how faithful and mighty a defender and keeper God is of as many as put their trust in him. He was in great danger, and specially in the wars that he made against the Ammonites, the event and success whereof, it seemeth by the twentieth Psalm, his subjects greatly feared: wherefore they commended their king (as true subjects always use) with earnest prayer unto God. And that battle and many other dangers more ended (wherein the godly king found always the protection and defence of the heavenly Father ready and at hand), now being at rest, he would have this merciful defence of God known to all others, that as he in all his adversities put his trust in the Lord, and had the over-hand of all his enemies; even so, by his example, all other men should learn to do the same, and assure themselves to find (as he found) the Lord of heaven to be the succour and defence of the troubled, and their keeper from all evil.

And because the hearers and readers of this his most divine and godly hymn should the better understand the same, and the sooner take credit thereof in the heart, he calleth the heavenly Father, the God of all consolation, in this Psalm a shepherd or herdman feeding his flock; and the people, with himself, he calleth sheep, pastured and fed by the shepherd. And by these two means, as by a most convenient allegory or translation meet for the purpose, from the office of a shepherd and the nature of sheep he setteth out marvellously the safeguard of man by God's providence and good-will towards man. And in the same allegory or translation he occupieth the four first verses in this Psalm. In the first verse, and so to the end of the Psalm, he declareth still one matter and argument of God's defence towards man, and how man is preserved. But yet it seemeth that he expresseth the same by other words and by another translation, shewing the nature of God Almighty in feeding and nourishing of man under the name of a lord or king, that hath prepared a table and plenty of meats to feed the hungry and needy; and setteth forth man poor, and destitute of consolation and necessary help, under the name of guests and bidden folks to a king's table, where is plenty of all things necessary, not only to satisfy hunger and to quench thirst, but also to expel and remove them, that the poor man shall never hunger nor thirst again; and not only that, but also for ever, world without end, this poor man shall dwell and inherit, by the mercy of his heavenly king, the joys everlasting. And this last translation or allegory is in manner not only a repetition of the first in other words, but also a declaration and more plain opening of the prophet's mind, what he meaneth in this celestial hymn.

[1]The parts of the Psalm.	The text of the Psalm.
1. Who it is that hath the cure and charge of man's life and salvation.	The Lord feedeth me, &c.
2. Wherein the life and salvation of man consisteth.	In pleasant pastures, &c.[2]
3. How man is brought to the knowledge of life and salvation.	He shall convert my soul, &c.[2]
4. Wherefore man is brought to life and salvation.	For his name's sake, &c.[2]
5. What trouble may happen to such as have life and salvation.	Although I walk through the valley, &c.[2]
6. Whereby the trouble of God's people is overcome.	For thou art with me, &c.[2]
7. What the end of God's troubled and afflicted people shall be.	I will dwell in the house of the Lord, &c.[2]

[[1] Order of the columns reversed, 1562.]
[[2] &c. omitted, 1562.]

Certeine Expo-
sitions of the constant Martyr
of Christ, Maister John Hooper, som-
time Bishop of Gloucester and Worcester, upon
the 23rd., the 62nd., the 72nd., and the 77th. Psalms
of the prophet David.

THE FIRST PART OF THE PSALM.

WHO IT IS THAT HATH THE CURE AND CHARGE OF MAN'S LIFE AND SALVATION.

THE FIRST VERSE[1].

Or, The Lord is my shepherd: as saith the common and the Geneva translation.

⁋ *The Lord feedeth me, and I shall want nothing.*

[The explanation, 1562.]

KING DAVID saith, the Lord feedeth him; wherefore he can lack nothing to live a virtuous and godly life.

In this first part some things are to be considered: first, of God that feedeth; and next, of man that is fed. God that feedeth David calleth by the name of a shepherd, and his people he calleth by the name of sheep. By this name of a shepherd the prophet openeth and discloseth the nature of God to all his miserable and lost creatures, that he is content, not only to wish and desire man, that is lost, to be found and restored again; but also doth seek and travail to restore and bring him home again: as it is written in Esay the prophet,

Isai. xl. "He shall gather together his lambs in his arm." And in
Ezek. xxxiv. Ezechiel the prophet the Lord saith, "Behold, I will require my flock of the shepherds, &c. And I will deliver my flock from their mouth, and they shall be no more their meat: for thus saith the Lord, Behold, I will search out my sheep, and will visit them as a shepherd doth visit his sheep, when he is in the midst of his scattered sheep; so will I visit my sheep, and deliver them from all places where as they have been

[1 The text, ed. 1562.]

scattered," &c. And Jeremy the prophet in the same sort declareth the nature of God towards the lost flock, saying: "He that dispersed Israel shall gather him together again, Jer. xxxi. and keep him as the shepherd keepeth his flock." Christ our Saviour nameth himself a "good shepherd," and saith that he Joh. x. was sent to call such as were not sheep of the utter mark and sign in the world, to be his sheep. This nature of the heavenly Father saw king David, when he said at the beginning of this heavenly hymn, "The Lord feedeth me," &c.

When he is assured of God's merciful nature, that seeketh the lost sheep, he openeth further the nature of God, what he will do with the sheep which he findeth: "feed him," saith the prophet David, and putteth himself for an example. Here is the mercy of the great Shepherd further declared, that he killeth not his sheep, robbeth them not, but feedeth and nourisheth them. Of this speaketh the prophet Ezechiel in the person of Almighty God: "I myself will feed my sheep, and Ezek. xxxiv. make that they shall rest quietly, saith the Lord God. That which is lost I will seek; such as go astray I will bring again; such as be wounded I will bind up; such as be weak I will make strong; but such as be fat and strong, those will I root out; and I will feed my sheep in reason and judgment." And the great Shepherd Christ saith, whether his sheep go in or Joh. x. out, they "shall find pasture."

After that this king hath opened in this hymn that God's nature is not only to seek the lost sheep, but also, when he hath found him, to feed him; then he addeth in his hymn after what sort he feedeth him: "So that I shall lack nothing," saith the prophet. Here is the declaring of the great Shepherd's pasture, wherewith he feedeth the flock of his pasture. Christ expresseth the same wonderfully in the opening of his office and doctrine unto the world in St John, saying; "I came that they might have life, and have it Joh. iv. vi. most abundantly." And talking with the poor woman of Samaria, he[2] told her that the drink he would give her should be water of life. And to the Capernaites he said, that meat which he would give them should work eternal salvation. As these properties be in God the Shepherd (as the prophet hath marked), even in the like sort be the contrary conditions in man, the sheep he speaketh of: for as

[2 He, not in 1562.]

the nature of God is to seek, so is the nature of man to go astray; as the prophet saith, "I have strayed like a wandering sheep." And even so doth Esay write of all mankind, "All we have erred," saith he, "as sheep going astray." Christ our Saviour also, in St Matthew, doth bewail the people of the world, that stray as sheep that had no shepherd. St Peter likewise saith unto his countrymen that he writeth unto, "Ye were as sheep that went astray; but ye be converted now unto the Shepherd and Pastor of your souls." And as the nature of man is to stray from God, so is it likewise to feed upon all unwholesome and infected pastures; to believe every false prophet that can do nothing but lie. In the prophet Esay the Lord saith, "The nature of sheep is to be deceived, and their pastors to be drunk, that neither know nor see the pastures of the word of God." And in the same prophet there is a most horrible plague upon man for sin; for, "The pastors shall be unable to feed, and all the food of life shall be as a book fast clasped and shut."

Ps. cxix.
Isai. liii.
Matt. ix.
1 Pet. ii.
1 Kings xxii.
Isai. xxviii.
Isai. xxix.

This going astray and feeding upon evil pasture is wonderfully set forth by St Paul: for when men will not feed upon the truth, it is God's just judgment they should feed upon falsehood. And as God's nature is not only to feed, but fully to satisfy and to replenish with all goodness, so that nothing may lack for a godly and virtuous life; in like manner, the nature of man is not only to feed, but also to replenish itself with all infected and contagious doctrine, until such time that he despise and contemn God and all his wholesome laws. This we may see in the holy prophet Esay: "The people (saith the Lord) provoketh me unto anger, a lying nation that will not hear the law of God; they say to their prophets, Prophesy not, look not out for us things that be right, speak pleasant things unto us," &c. And this replenishing of man with corrupt pasture is horribly set forth in St John, when the wicked priests and Pharisees would not believe the Shepherd's voice Christ, no, not their own servants that told them the truth, nor yet Nicodemus, one of their own court and profession. Thus in the first part of this celestial hymn is the nature of God and man described under the name of a shepherd and of sheep.

2 Thess. ii.
Joh. iv. vi.
Rom. i.
Isai. xxx.
Joh. vii.

What is to be noted out of this part of the psalm.

Of this part of the Psalm, what the prophet hath said of God and of man, we must, for our own doctrine and learning, gather some things to be the better by; for St Paul saith, "Whatsoever is written, is written for our learning." Two things we learn of this first place: the one, a certainty that God hath the cure and charge of us: and the other, a consolation and comfort that we and all ours be under his protection and governance. The first doctrine, to be certain and sure of God's defence and care over us, maketh us constant and strong to suffer and bear all adversities and troubles that God shall send us; and the second doctrine shall cause us patiently and thankfully to bear our cross, and to follow Christ. Both these doctrines the prophet David expresseth in the third and fourth verse of this psalm: "If I should (saith he) travel and pass through places contagious and infected, where appeareth nothing but the image and shadow of death, or be compelled to pass through the hands and tyranny of mine enemies, I will not fear; for thou art with me, O God, and defendest me." In the ninety-first psalm he setteth forth the assurance and felicity of all them that put their whole trust in the mercy of God; and therein also the prophet reckoneth up a wonderful sort of dangers, and layeth them before the eyes of the faithful, that he may, by the sight and knowledge of the dangers, fix and place the more constantly his faith and trust in God, that hath the charge and cure of him: "He shall (saith he) defend us from pestilence most infective, from fleeing[1] arrows in the day," &c. By the which the prophet understandeth all kind of evils that may come unto us by the means of the devil or of wicked men. And these things the faithful shall escape (saith the prophet), because they say from their hearts unto God, *Quoniam tu es spes mea*, that is to say, "For thou art my hope;" even as he said in the beginning of this psalm, "The Lord feedeth me, and I shall want nothing." Such certainty and assurance of God's defence, and such consolation in troubles of this life, we must learn and pray to have out of God's word, or else it were as good never to hear nor to read it.

Rom. xv.

Psal. xci.

The assurance of God's defence and comfort in troubles must be learned out of God's word.

And from this first part of the psalm every estate of the world may learn wisdom and consolation. If the Lord feed and govern him, he shall have God to his master and teacher, that shall give him wholesome and commodious doctrine, meet

[1 Flying, 1562.]

for the state of the life he hath chosen to live in this world. For all that shall be saved in time to come follow not one kind of life. Some be magistrates and rulers, and appointed to see both the laws of the realm, and the goods and commodities thereof, to be used and applied to the use and profit of such as be under them. Some give themselves to study and contemplation of heavenly and divine things, not busying themselves with travails of the body, but to know themselves the way of life, and to[1] be teachers of the same to others. Some be given to apply the laws of the commonwealth: some to exercise the trade and course of merchandise; some one kind of living, and some another. But of what art, faculty, science, or kind of living soever he be, that is not contrary to God's honour or honesty, he may use therein to serve God, to observe justice, to exercise truth, keep temperance, and be acceptable to God, who hath given laws meet and convenient to publicans and soldiers, servants and masters, parents and children, husbands and wives, and so to all other. But all these sorts of people must assuredly know, that in every of these vocations be more dangers than he that must live in them is able to bear: therefore from the bottom of his heart he must be assured of this beginning of king David's hymn, "The Lord feedeth me, and I shall lack nothing." And indeed the Lord hath not only said he will feed and defend him from all dangers; but also saith he will teach him how to live virtuously and reverently towards God, and honestly and quietly towards man, what state or vocation soever he choose to live in, so it be not against God's laws and the law of nature. So saith king David: "God hath appointed a law to rule and teach the man that feareth him, whatsoever kind of living he appointeth himself to live in." What treasure is there to be compared unto this, that man is not only fed and maintained by God, but also taught and instructed in every craft and science that he appointeth himself to live in? Blessed therefore is the man that in the entrails and deep cogitations of his heart can say, believe, and feel this to be true that David saith, "The Lord ruleth me, and careth for me, and I shall lack nothing.".

Psal. xxv.

But yet there is almost nothing spoken, that this king would have chiefly known. Howbeit, doubtless they be

[[1] To, not in 1562.]

wonderful things, that preserve and teach all persons, both men and women, in whatsoever kind of living honestly they appoint themselves to live in. He himself knew this to be true right well, as it appeareth when he saith: "Blessed be the Lord my strength, that taught my hands to battle:" for, if the Lord had not taught and ruled him, he had been overthrown many times, because there was not only more strength than he had of himself against him, but also more wit, more policy, more experience. Psal. cxliv.

But what things can overcome that man that is covered with this shield, *Dominus regit me,* "The Lord ruleth me?" Doubtless, nothing at all, whether it be in heaven above, or in the earth beneath, or in hell under the earth. Notwithstanding, this is not all that this doctrine, "the Lord ruleth me," doth for the poor sheep that is ruled. But here must the reader and hearer of this psalm follow king David, and desire to have the eye of his mind purged and made clean: for if the scales of infidelity and the love and delight to sin remain, or else the mind be otherwise occupied than upon the understanding of the hymn; he shall hear it, or sing it, as the ungodly colleges of priests do, that daily bo-o and roar the holy scriptures out of their mouths, and understand no more the meaning thereof than the walls which they sing and speak unto. We must therefore do as king David did, lift up the eyes of our minds into heaven, and fix our faith (as he saith) fast in the Lord; and then shall we see the unspeakable treasures and wisdom that lieth hid in this marvellous and comfortable head and beginning of this psalm, "The Lord feedeth me," &c. Psal. xxv. cxxviii. [cxxiii.]

Our Saviour Christ openeth plainly in St John what it is to be the sheep of God, and to be fed by him, and saith: "They will hear the shepherd's voice, but no stranger's voice; and because they hear the shepherd's voice, the shepherd will give them everlasting life; and no man shall take them out of the shepherd's hands." There is the greatest treasure and most necessary riches for the sheep of God uttered, which is not the knowledge of God alone to be preserved in this life, and to lack nothing that is expedient and necessary for the preservation thereof; but also to understand which ways the heavenly Father teacheth and leadeth us to the mansion and dwelling-place of life everlasting. [John x.]
The inward and spiritual comfort, treasury, and riches which this doctrine bringeth.

And if man were wise, he might soon perceive how much the life to come is better than the life present; yea, be it never so favourably fed and preserved by the heavenly Father, our shepherd and governor. For his tuition here of us, although it be sure, and so strong that none can take us out of his hands; yet is our safeguard and life troubled and mingled with adversities, subject to persecution, and also unto death: but in the life to come God's tuition is all joy, all mirth, all solace, with all perpetuity and endless felicity. And of this treasure David chiefly meant in the forefront of the psalm, when he said, "And I shall lack nothing;" for, as we see (until this life be taken from us), most troubles and most care beginneth and tarrieth in the house of God amongst his sheep, which be as lambs among wolves. Wherefore the voice and teaching of the shepherd doth heal the minds of the sheep, God's dear elect, and pulleth from them all unprofitable fear and carefulness: it quencheth all flames of lust and concupiscence: it maketh and giveth a man a noble and valiant mind to contemn all worldly things: it bringeth a man in love with God's true honour, maketh him joyful in trouble, quiet in adversity, and sure that the end of God's people shall be glorious and joyful; and also that this favour of the shepherd shall be his guide into the place of bliss, where as be crowns of everlasting glory for such as have been led by the Lord, and there they shall lack nothing: for there is neither eye can see, nor tongue can speak, nor mind can comprehend these joys and glory. And therefore the prophet both constantly and cheerfully said, "The Lord feedeth me, and I shall lack nothing:" for all things of this world be but trifles in comparison of things to come.

1 Pet. iv.

Matt. x.

Although it be a singular favour of God to understand his goodness and mercy towards us in things belonging to this life, yet is it not to be compared to the other, as David wonderfully declareth in the twenty-fifth psalm. When he hath numbered a great many of God's benefits, which he doth bestow upon his poor servants in this life, he in the end maketh mention of one specially, that passeth them all, in these words: *Arcanum Domini timentibus illum, et testamentum suum manifestabit illis:* that is to say, "The Lord openeth to such as fear him his secrets and his testament." The Lord openeth to his faithful servant the mysteries and secrets of his pleasure, and the knowledge of his laws. And these treasures, the knowledge and right understanding of God's most holy word, he saith was more sweet unto him than honey or the honeycomb, and more he esteemed the virtue of it than he did precious stones. Of all gifts this was the principal, that God gave unto him a right and true knowledge of himself. Wherefore it shall be most expedient and necessary for every christian man to labour, study, and pray, that he may earnestly, and with a faithful heart, know himself to be no better than a seely[1] poor sheep, that hath nothing of himself, nor of any other, to save his body and soul, but only the mercy of his shepherd, the heavenly Father; and to be assured also that his only mercy and goodness alone in Christ, and none other besides him, is able to feed him; so that he shall lack nothing necessary in this life, nor in the life to come.

⁋ THE SECOND PART OF THE PSALM.

WHEREIN THE LIFE AND SALVATION OF MAN CONSISTETH.

The Second Verse. [The text, 1562.]

He shall feed me in pleasant pastures, and he shall lead me by the river's side. [&c. 1562.]

[The Explanation, 1562.]

He shall set me in the pastures most pleasant and rich of his doctrine, and in the contemplation of heavenly things, wherewithal the minds of godly men are nourished and fed with unspeakable joy: and near unto the plenteous floods of the Holy Ghost, and the sweet waters of the holy scriptures he will feed me; in the which places the sheep of the Lord are nourished to eternal life, abounding with milk, and bringing forth most blessed fruit. The scripture of God useth this word "feed" in many significations: sometime to John xxi. Acts xx.

[[1] Seely: simple, harmless.]

teach and instruct; sometime to rule and govern, as magistrates rule their people, as well by law as by strength; sometime to punish and correct, &c. But in this place the prophet useth "feeding" as well for instruction by God's word, as also for defence and safeguard of God's people by God's most mighty power. He useth this word "pasture" for the word of God itself, as a thing which is the only food of a man's soul to live upon, as the meat and drink is for the body. He useth this word "lead" for conducting, that the man which is led at no time go out of the way, but always may know where he is, and whither he is going: as in many other of his psalms he useth the same manner of speaking. The "rivers of refection" he useth for the plentiful gifts of the Holy Ghost, wherewithal the faithful man is replenished. His saying therefore is as much as if he had spoken without allegory or translation, thus: "He instructeth me with his word, and conducteth me with his Holy Spirit, that I cannot err nor perish."

In this part of the psalm be many things worthy to be noted. First, it is declared, that the life of man consisteth in the food of God's word: then, that there is none that giveth the same[1] to be eaten, but God our heavenly shepherd: the next, that none can eat of this meat of God's word, but such as the Holy Ghost feedeth with the word. Our Saviour Christ declareth, that "man liveth not by bread alone, but of every word that proceedeth out of the mouth of God." Whereby he teacheth us that, as the body liveth by external meats, so doth the soul by the word of God. And no more possible is it for a man to live in God without the word of God than in the world without the meat of the world. And St Peter confesseth the same: for when the Capernaites, and many of Christ's own disciples, had satisfied their bodies with external meats, they cared not for their souls, neither could they abide to be fed, nor to hear the meat of the soul spoken of, although Christ did dress it most wholesomely with many godly and sweet words; they would not tarry until Christ had made that meat ready for them; they could be contented to feed their bellies with his meats, but their souls they would not commit to his diet, but departed as hungry as they came, through their own folly. Christ was leading them

[1 Word, 1562.]

from the five barley loaves and two fishes, wherewith they had filled their bellies, unto the pleasant pastures of the heavenly word, that shewed neither barley-loaves nor fish, but his own precious blood and painful passion, to be the meat of their souls: howbeit, they could not come into this pasture, nor taste in any case of the sweet herbs and nourishment of their souls. When Christ perceived they would not be led into this pleasant pasture, he let them go whither they would, and to feed upon what pasture they would: and then he asked of his twelve that tarried, saying, "Will ye depart also?" Peter, as one that had fed both body and soul, as his fellows had, perceived that the body was but half the man, and, that being fed, there was but half a man fed; and also that such meats as went into the mouth satisfied no more than the body, that the mouth was made for: he felt, moreover, that his soul was fed by Christ's doctrine, and that the hunger of sin, the ire of God, the accusation of the law, and the demand and claim of the devil, were quenched and taken away: he perceived likewise, that the meat which brought this nourishment was the heavenly doctrine that Christ spake of, touching his death and passion: and he understood also that this meat passed not into the body by the mouth, but into the soul by faith, and by the presence of God's Spirit with his spirit; [that][2] the body also should be partaker as well of the grace that was in it as of the life: so that he felt himself not only to have a body and a soul alive, but also that they were graciously replenished with the pastures and food of God's favour. Wherefore he said unto Christ, "To whom shall we go? Thou hast the words of everlasting life:" which words in effect sound no other thing than this psalm doth, where David saith: "The Lord feedeth me, and I shall want nothing; for he leadeth me into his pleasant pastures, and pastureth me by the river's side." Wherein it appeareth manifestly, that the word of God is the life of the soul.

The prophet David doth marvellously open this thing in the repeating so many times the word of God, in a psalm worthy much reading and more marking of the things contained therein: for he entreateth all the psalm through, that a godly life doth consist in the observation of God's

[[2] Omitted in 1562.]

laws; and therefore doth he so many times in the psalm pray God to illuminate and endue his spirit and heart with these two virtues, knowledge and love of his word, wherewith he may both know how to serve God, and at all times to be acceptable unto him. And our Saviour Christ himself, in St Luke, saith unto a woman, "Blessed be they that hear the word of God, and keep it." And in St John, Christ exhorteth all men to the reading and exercising of the scripture. For the ignorance[1] of God's word bringeth with it a murrain and rot of the soul; yet for the sins of the people God said he would send a hunger and famine amongst men, not a hunger of bread nor water, but of hearing God's word. King David, therefore, as one assured both of the author of life, and also of the food wherewith the life is maintained, stayeth himself with God's benediction and favour, that he is assured God feedeth him with his word. And he sheweth also that none is the author of this word, neither can any give it, but God alone: for when the first fall of Adam and Eve, by eating forbidden meats, had poisoned and infected both body and soul with sin and God's displeasure, so that he was destitute both of God's favour and wisdom, none but God could tell him where remedy and help lay; nor yet could any deliver him the help but God. For till God made promise that the seed of a woman should make whole and save that which the devil and man had made sick and lost by reason of sin, and also made open the remedy unto Adam, and inclined his heart to believe the remedy, Adam was dead in sin, and utterly cast away. Then the pity of the heavenly shepherd said he should, notwithstanding, in time be brought into the same pasture again, and none should deceive him, nor bring him any more out of the pastures of life.

But only God gave this meat, which was his holy word and promise, and also the mouth of faith to eat these promises of God's only gift. And the same appeareth throughout the whole Bible, that only God, by sending of his word and preachers, brought knowledge of everlasting life to the people that were in ignorance[1]: as St Paul saith, "God beforetime spake unto our fathers by the prophets, and in these latter days unto us by his Son," and after the ascension of his Son, by his apostles and evangelists; insomuch that none of

[1 Ignorancy, 1562.]

the prophets ever spake of God's word, that maintained the life of the soul, otherwise than they received it of the high shepherd, Almighty God, as St Peter saith, "Prophecy came not by the will of man; but the holy men of God spake as they were taught by the Holy Ghost:" so that God is the only author and fountain of his true word, the food of all men's souls. In like manner, he is the only giver of the same. As he is the giver of it, and none but himself; so none can eat it, but such as have the same delivered unto them by the Holy Ghost. So our Saviour Christ likewise, in the Gospel of St John, telleth Nicodemus, that it was not possible to understand and to know the grace of redemption, except he were born from above. And when St Paul preached the word of God at Philippos amongst the women by the water-side, the Lord opened the heart of Lydia to understand the things spoken of by Paul. And when Christ preached among the Jews, and wrought wonderful miracles, yet they understood nothing, neither were they any thing the better; and Christ sheweth the cause: *Propterea vos non auditis, quia ex Deo non estis;* that is to say, "Therefore ye hear not, because ye be not of God." But the fault was not in God, but in the obstinacy and frowardness of their own hearts, as ye may see in St Matthew. Christ offered himself, but yet the malice of man rebelled at all times. St Paul to the Corinthians wonderfully setteth forth man's unableness, and saith: "The natural man is not able to comprehend the things that be of God." And in St John Christ saith, "No man can come unto him, except the heavenly Father draw him; for they must be all taught of God." Now, as the prophet saw these things for himself and his salvation in God's word, even so must every christian man take heed that he learn the same doctrine; or else it were no commodity to have the scripture of God delivered and taught unto us. And every reader and hearer must learn of this psalm, that there is none other food nor meat for the soul but God's word; and whosoever do refuse it when it is offered or preached, or, when they know the truth thereof, do yet of malice, fear, lucre, and gain of the world, or any other way, repugn it, they be unworthy of all mercy and forgiveness. Let every man and woman therefore examine their own conscience without flattering of themselves, and they shall find that the most part of this realm of England in the time of our holy and blessed king Edward the sixth were fed with this holy food of God's word, or else might have been fed with it; for it was offered and sent unto them, as well by most godly statutes and laws of parliament, as by many noblemen and virtuous learned preachers. If they fed not upon it accordingly, or now their teeth stand on edge, and their stomachs be cloyed with it, to their peril be it. Thus Christ saith: "They have nothing whereby justly to excuse themselves of their sin." And likewise he saith, that whosoever hateth him hateth also his Father: by which words it appeareth manifestly, that no man can hate Christ's doctrine, but he must hate Christ himself; and no man can hate Christ, but he must also hate the Father of heaven. Wherefore it is expedient for every man to mark such places: for it was not Christ's name, nor Christ's person, that the Jews hated so mortally Christ for; but they hated him to death for his doctrine's sake; and it was Christ's doctrine that condemned the world, and shewed the life and learning of the world to be evil, and could not abide the light of God's word; and therefore in no case they could abide to hear of it, as ye see the like in his poor preachers. For his word's sake they be less passed of than dogs or brute beasts: for they be hated to death; and more favour doth Barabbas the murderer find than Peter the preacher of Christ, that would lead the flock redeemed with Christ's precious blood into the pastures of God's word with the prophet David. And yet, in this hatred of God's word, the food of God's sheep, they would be seen, and none but they, to love and honour God: but it is not so in their hearts; for they have a contempt of God, as their fruits well declare. And Christ saith, they hate both him and his Father, yea, and that without cause.

But thou, christian reader, see thou feed thy soul with no other meat than with the wholesome pastures of God's word, whatsoever the world shall say or do. Look upon this text of St John: "When the Comforter shall come, whom I shall send from my Father, even the Spirit of truth, which doth proceed from the Father, he shall testify and bear record of me." Weigh that place, and think wherefore the Son of man referred himself to the witness of the Holy Ghost; and ye shall know that it was for no untruth that was in the author, being Christ, or in the doctrine that he preached, but only to make the disciples to be of good comfort, and that they should not esteem the gospel he preached unto them any thing the less, although it had many adversaries and enemies, and was spoken against in manner every where; for against the fury and false judgment of the world, that contemned the gospel, they should have the testimony of the Holy Ghost to allow and warrant the gospel. Let us, therefore, pray to the heavenly shepherd, that he will give us his Holy Spirit to testify for the word of God, the only food of our souls, that it is true that God saith, and only good that he appointeth to feed us. And this we may be assured of, that in this heavy and sorrowful time there is nothing can testify for the truth of God's word, and keep us in the pleasant pasture thereof, but the very Spirit of God, which we must set against all the tumults and dangers of the world. For if we make this verity of God subject to the judgment of the world, our faith shall quail and faint every hour, as men's judgments vary. Wherefore, let us pray to have always in us the Spirit of adoption, whereby, when our faith shall be assaulted, we may cry, "Father, Father!" and the same help for the maintenance of the truth God promised by his holy prophet Esay, saying, "This is my covenant with them, saith the Lord: My spirit which is in thee, and my words which I have put in thy mouth, shall not depart from thy mouth, nor from the mouth of thy seed, nor from the mouth of the seed of thy seed, from henceforth until the world[1] end." Isai. lix.

Here doth the almighty God set forth what a treasure and singular gift his word is, and that it shall not depart from his people until the world's end. And in these words is this part of David's psalm marvellously opened and set forth. It is the Lord alone that feedeth and instructeth, saith Esay the prophet; it was not man's own imagination and intention, nor the wisdom and religion of his fathers (whatsoever they were); but it was the Lord that spake, and made the covenant with man, and put his Spirit in man to understand the covenant; and by his word, and none other word, he instructed man, and said that by this[2] means all men should, till the world's end, feed and eat of God's blessed promises. For in his word he hath expressed and opened to every man what he shall have, even the remission of sin, the acceptation into his fatherly favour, grace to live well in What things we receive by feeding upon God's promises in this life.

[1 World's, 1562.]   [2 These, 1562.]

this life, and, at the end, to be received into the everlasting life.

Of these things the reader may know what maintaineth life, even the word of God, as Christ saith: "If ye abide in me, and my words abide in you, ask what ye will, and ye shall have it." He shall learn also, that it is not general council, provincial council, the determination and agreement of men, that can be the author of this food, but only God. And as God is the only author of this food; even so is his Holy Spirit he that feedeth the poor simple soul of the christian man with his blessed pasture, and not the wisdom of man, men's sacrifices, or men's doings. But as touching the food of man's soul to be the only word of God, I will, if it be God's blessed pleasure (to whom, in the bitter and painful passion of Christ, I commit my will, with my life and death), open unto the sheep and lambs of God at large in another book.

<small>Matt. iv.
[John xv.]

Ps. xix.
cxix.
2 Tim. iii.
Heb. i.
1 Pet. i.
Gal. i.

John vi. xv.
Isai. liv.</small>

THE THIRD PART OF THE PSALM.

❡ HOW MAN IS BROUGHT TO THE KNOWLEDGE OF LIFE AND SALVATION: WHICH PART SHEWETH WHAT MAN IS OF HIMSELF, AND HOW HE IS BROUGHT INTO THIS LIFE, AND TO FEED IN THE PLEASANT PASTURES OF GOD'S WORD.

THE THIRD VERSE. [The text, 1562.]

He shall convert my soul, and bring me into the paths of righteousness, for his name's sake[1].

[The Explanation, 1562.]

My soul erred and went astray from the right way of godly living, but the Lord converted me from mine[2] errors and faults of living, and brought me to the observation of his holy laws, wherein is contained all justice, truth, and godliness.

Here is to be noted what degrees and orders the Lord and heavenly shepherd doth use, in bringing his sheep unto the pasture of life. First, he converteth the man that is gone

[1 'For his name's sake,' omitted in 1562.] [2 My, 1562.]

astray by his wicked ways and sinful manner of living. If he were an infidel, he bringeth him first to know, feel, and hate his infidelity, and afterwards to a true faith. If he be a persecutor, he sheweth him first his tyranny, and afterward[3] how to use himself meekly. If he be a sinful man that liveth contrary to his knowledge and profession, he bringeth him first to the knowledge and hatred of his sin, and afterwards to the forgiveness of the same. As Christ our Saviour wonderfully teacheth in St John, where he saith: "The Holy Ghost, when he cometh, shall rebuke the world of sin, justice, and judgment." By the which words he declareth, that the faithful of God cannot profit in the gospel of Christ, neither love nor exercise justice and virtue, except they be taught and made to feel the burden and danger of sin, and be brought to humble themselves, as men that be of themselves nothing but sin. And therefore the law and threatenings of God be very wholesome, whose nature and property is to cite and call men's conscience unto the judgment of God, and to wound the spirit of man with terror and fear. Wherefore Christ useth a wonderful way, and teacheth the same unto his apostles, that neither himself for that present time, nor they in time to come, could preach profitably the gospel, wherewith men are led into the sweet and pleasant fields of God's promises by his word, except they use this order, to lead them from sin to justice, and from death to life. And as justice and life cometh by Christ, shewed unto us in his bitter passion, death, and glorious resurrection; so doth sin and death both appear and be felt by the Spirit of God, shewed unto us in the law. *John xvi.*

This order also saw the holy prophet, when he said: "The Lord converteth my soul, and leadeth me into the paths of righteousness." This is a wonderful sentence, and much and deeply to be considered and weighed of the christian man. "The Lord converteth my soul," saith David. He feeleth in himself, that as long as the devil and sin have the rule and kingdom in man, the soul of man, being God's creature, is deformed, foul, horrible, and so troubled that it is like unto all things more than unto God and virtue, whereunto it was created: but when the wicked devil and deformed sin be by the victory of Christ overcome and expelled[4], the soul waxeth *The conscience that feeleth the sting of death by sin, thirsteth for life.*

[3 Afterwards, 1562.]   [4 Expulsed, 1562.]

fair, amiable, sweet, loving, pleasant, and like unto God again, and cometh into order and obeisance unto his Creator; and so, brought into the paths of righteousness, feedeth with the rest of God's well-ordered flock upon the pastures and food of his holy word, to do his blessed will.

Oh that we would, in the glass of God's word, look upon our own souls, when they be in the tyranny of the devil, under the kingdom of sin, as this king did: we should more loath and detest our own soul, and the company that our soul is accompanied withal, than if we should for all our lifetime be put into sties with hogs, and always be bound during our life to live with them, feed as they feed, sleep and wake as they do, and be as they be in all things. Look in the gospel of St Luke, and there shall ye see a man by sin so foul, so disordered, so accompanied with swine, so hungerbaned, so rent and torn, so beggarly, so wretched, so vile, so loathsome, and so stinking, that the very swine were better for their condition than he was. But see how the heavenly shepherd beheld from his heavenly throne, the place of the everlasting joys, this poor strayed sheep, feeding not amongst sheep, but amongst swine, and yet could not be satisfied therewith. And no marvel: for swine feed not upon the meat of sheep, nor yet do sheep fill themselves with hog's draff[1] and swillings; but this shepherd used his old wonted clemency, and strake the heart of his[2] sheep, making him to weep and bewail his condition—a man to come to such dishonour, to be coupled and matched with swine, to feed like swine, eat like swine such meat as swine eat, remembering that the worst in his father's house was a prince and noble king in comparison and respect of him. Then also being persuaded of his father's mercy, he returned, and his father brought him into his pleasant and sweet pastures, and gave him his old favour and accustomed apparel again, as a man to keep company with men, and no more with adulterous men and unclean swine. Howbeit, he came not to his old honour again, till the Lord had practised in him that he practised in this prophet, king David: *Animam meam convertit*, "He converted and turned my soul."

It is but a folly for a man to flatter himself as though he were a christian man, when his heart and soul is not turned unto the Lord: he shall never feed in the pastures of life, but

[1 Draff: any thing thrown away.]   [2 This, 1562.]

be an hypocrite all the days of his life; as the most part of the world be that profess Christ's name at this present day. They say they be converted from the world to God, when there is nothing within the pastures of God's word but that they will contemn, rather than to have as much as an evil look of the world for it. They say they be converted to God, when they be contented, with the world, to honour that for God that is but bread and wine in the matter and substance, as the scripture of God and the holy church of Christ have taught and believed these thousand and five hundred years and more. O Lord! be these men turned to thee? Be these the men that shall dwell with thee in thy holy mount of Sion, and stand in thy holy place? Nay, doubtless; for they be not turned to thee, but from thee; and be not with thee, but against thee. They speak with thee, and yet their deeds dishonour thee; they talk of truth, and practise lies. What, good Lord, shall thy simple and poor unlearned sheep do? Where shall they seek thy truth? for the shepherds say and sing this psalm every week, and at every dirige for the dead; and yet they be not converted in their spirits to thee, that thou mightest lead them into the paths of righteousness. But, Lord! there is no man now (in manner) that dare accuse them: they destroy themselves and thy sheep, and no man can be suffered with God's word to remedy it. Notwithstanding, good Lord, although in this world none may accuse them, yet they in the world to come shall have king David (whose psalms they daily read, and in whom they most glory) to accuse them both of heresy and blasphemy, as Moses shall accuse the wicked Jews, whom they most glory of. For as the Jews read the scripture of Moses, and yet were never the better; so these priests of Antichrist read the holy scripture, and yet neither the people nor they themselves are any thing the better. And in this they pass the abomination of the Jews and Turks: for they were, and yet be, content that their books of religion shall be used in their churches in the vulgar and common tongue; but these enemies of God and man would not have the word that God hath appointed for all men's salvation to be used in any tongue but in the Latin.

"The God therefore of peace, that brought again from death to life the great Shepherd of the sheep, by the blood of

Psal. xxiv.

the everlasting testament, our Lord Jesus Christ," convert the souls and hearts of all those that cause the sheep of God thus to eat and feed upon the carrion and infected pastures of men's traditions! Amen.

Now, as king David in this text hath wonderfully set forth the miserable nature of all God's sheep, and put himself for an example, that the nature and condition of all men is corrupt, wicked, and damnable, so that it cannot be partaker of God's benediction and everlasting grace, except it be born anew, amended, restored, and instructed; so likewise he sheweth that none converteth the soul of man but the heavenly Father, the great shepherd, that both seeth the lost state of his sheep, and willeth of his mercy the salvation and calling of the sheep home again: and then he proceedeth further, and sheweth what the heavenly shepherd will do with his sheep. He saith, "He will lead them into the paths of justice." Wherein the prophet declareth, that it is not only God that converteth the man from evil, but also he alone that keepeth him in goodness and virtue. And therein is shewed a wonderful misery and wretchedness in the soul and body of man, that can neither begin nor yet continue in a life acceptable unto God, except that God wholly worketh[1] the same himself.

And as it declareth the wonderful wretchedness of man, so doth it manifest and set forth a wonderful and unspeakable mercy and compassion of God towards man, that so marvellously and graciously he can be content to help and save his enemy and very adversary. But herein is required of as many as the Lord converteth from iniquity and sinful living, that they walk in the same law, and use their conversation in equity and justice, as it becometh obedient men and women redeemed with the Shepherd's most[2] precious blood. For the Lord doth not teach his sheep the truth, that they should live in falsehood; neither giveth he them the remission of their sins, that they should return to the same again: but because they should studiously apply and diligently exercise themselves in virtuous works, to the honour of Almighty God.

Psal. i.
Matt. v.

There be two sorts of people that the Lord will judge and punish in the latter day with extreme ire and justice. The one sort be called upon to learn the knowledge of God, and of

[1 Work, 1562.]   [2 Most, omitted in 1562.]

God's honour, as God's word commandeth: but they will not hear, nor obey the calling, but know God and learn God as the custom and manner of the world is to know him and learn him, though it be never so far from the truth. And the other sort be contented to hear and learn to know God and to serve him as he teacheth in his holy and most pure word, but in their hearts consent not to their knowledge; but, contrary to it, they do outward service to a false god, and frame their conversation, both in religion toward³ God and their manners toward men, as men of the world do: so that God hath no more reverence of him that knoweth the truth than of him that is ignorant of the truth. *Woeful are these days when in so clear light of the truth the professors thereof are so faithless and fruitless.*

Esay the prophet speaketh against the first sort of men, that will not hear when they be called, nor learn when they be taught, and saith: "When other men shall laugh, they shall weep; when other be merry, they shall be sorry; when other be whole, they shall be sick; when other men shall live, they shall die; and when other men rejoice in mirth, they shall lament in sorrow." And good cause why, saith St Paul; "for the Lord hath stretched forth his hand always to a rebellious and obstinate people, that will not learn nor know his holy will." Again, the other sort, that know and have learned the Lord's will and pleasure, and yet prepare not themselves to do his will, "shall be beaten with many stripes," saith our Saviour Christ. And the Lord in St Matthew doth wonderfully charge both such as ignorantly do offend, and those that do with knowledge offend, those also that be called upon to amendment in faith and charity, and those that be not called upon by preaching of the truth, and saith the greater damnation is upon such as know, or might know, or else when they do know, they be nothing the better for their knowledge. He putteth forth these four cities, Chorozaim and Bethsaida, Tyre and Sidon, two of them many times admonished by Christ to amend, the other two not so called upon; nevertheless, both of them the Lord will judge, but most severely such as neglect the word of God when it is offered. Therefore it is not enough for a man to hearken or hear, read or learn God's word; but he must be ruled by God's word, frame his whole life after God's word, and, before all things, avoid idolatry by God's *Isai. lxv.* *Rom. x.* *Luke xii.*

[³ Towards, 1562.]

word: as king David saith in this psalm, that the Lord did not only convert his soul, but brought him into the paths of justice.

Let every man and woman therefore think with themselves, what knowledge they have received of God: for he that hath received most shall make account for most; and the more he knoweth, and abuseth his knowledge, the more shall be his damnation: and in case they know nothing at all, and be never the better for all the preaching of the Lord's word, let them take heed what persons they be, and in what place they have dwelled. In case their poverty was such that they could not hear, and their dwelling where as was no preaching at all; yet be they under the judgment and damnation of God, because they know not, as Tyre and Sidon were. If they were of such state as they might have come if they would, and had preachers to tell them the truth, in case they would have heard the truth, such men and women shall be the more in danger of God's severe and just judgment. For God doth not only take an account of that which[1] men have received, if they use not God's gifts well, but also straitly requireth of them that might have learned the thing that either willingly or obstinately they refused to learn; as ye may see by Chorozaim and Bethsaida. God will as well take an account of him that refused to receive the gift of God's word, as he requireth an account of him that hath received it, and abused it. Whereby we learn, that not only the man that abuseth God's word shall be damned, but also he that will not learn God's word. King David had the word offered; he received it, and was carried thereby into the paths of justice, and lived godly thereafter. Now he goeth forth and sheweth wherefore man is brought to life and salvation.

[¹ Which, omitted in 1562.]

THE FOURTH PART OF THE PSALM.

WHEREFORE MAN IS BROUGHT TO LIFE AND SALVATION.

THE THIRD VERSE continued. [The text, 1562.]

For his name's sake.

[The Explanation, 1562.]

He brought not me to life and salvation (saith the prophet) for any merits or deservings of mine, but for his own infinite goodness' sake. And whatsoever evil hath been done, and sin committed, all these things I ascribe to my corrupt nature, and accuse myself to be the doer of them: but if any thing have been thought, said, or done, that is virtuous and godly, that I wholly ascribe and attribute unto the mercy of God, that gave me a good mind to wish to do well, and also strength to do the things that he gave me will to wish.

Of this part of the psalm we learn, that man can neither wish nor speak nor do any thing, nor yet understand any thing that good is, but only through the mercy of God, who maketh of an ignorant man a man of knowledge, of an unwilling man a willing man, of an evil speaker a good speaker, and of an evil doer a good doer. Therefore St Paul, when he seeth that the nature of man will take upon her to be the author of any good thing, he accuseth and condemneth her of arrogancy and pride, saying, "What hast thou that thou hast 1 Cor. iv. not received? If thou hast received, why dost thou glory as though thou receivedst not?" And in the same epistle he saith, that he "preached Christ crucified, which was a slander to 1 Cor. i. the Jews, and a foolishness to the Gentiles;" "yet (saith he) the foolishness of God is wiser than men, and the weakness of God is[2] stronger than men." And that had king David good experience of, when he said, "The Lord ruleth me, and I lack nothing: he putteth me in a sweet pasture, and leadeth me by the river's side; he turneth my soul, and conducteth me into the way and path of justice, for his name's sake, and for his mercy's sake." He saw the devil, the world, his flesh, and sin, all conquered by the power of God, and for his name's

[² Is, omitted in 1562.]

sake brought both to live, and also virtuously to live, to his honour that gave the life, and to his own salvation that received the life.

All our teaching a great many of years, and also your whole labours, have been chiefly to know the misery of man, and the mercy of Almighty God. Wherefore it shall not need long to tarry in opening of this place of the psalm; for ye be rich in God in these two points; God give you grace well to use them. Yet in any case we must remember that our souls be turned from sin, and we accepted as the people of everlasting life, only for God's mercy's sake. So doth king David _{Psal. xxxii.} wonderfully open unto us in the 32d psalm, where[1] he saith, "Blessed be they whose sins are forgiven, and whose transgressions be covered: blessed is the man to whom the Lord imputeth not his sin." Of the which words we learn that the godly king called those happy and blessed, not that be clean and pure without sin (for there is no such man in this life); but those be blessed, whose sins the mercy of God forgiveth: and they be only such as unfeignedly acknowledge their sin, and stedfastly from their hearts believe that the death and passion of Jesus Christ is the only expiation and purging _{Rom. iv.} thereof: as St Paul wonderfully expoundeth David's words in his epistle to the Romans.

As the prophet by these words, "For his name's sake," declareth that there is nothing in him, nor in any other man, wherefore God should turn the soul of man from death to life, from error to truth, from the hatred of God to God's love, from wandering astray to a stablished continuance in the verity of God's word, but only God's mercy; so doth he in other of his psalms always, when he entreateth of God's mercy and of man's sin, set forth man so naked and vile, as a thing most destitute of all health and salvation, and sheweth that none of these gifts, remission of sin, acceptation into God's love and favour, pasturing of them with his most blessed word, can happen unto any other, saving unto such as do know, and earnestly confess, that they be sinners, and infected with many contagious and dangerous infirmities. And therefore he saith in the second verse of the _{Psal. xxxii.} psalm above mentioned, "Blessed is he to whom the Lord imputeth no sin, and in whose spirit there is no guile." For

[1 Where as, 1562.]

there is no greater guile nor more danger in man, than to think himself to be somewhat, when he is nothing indeed; or else to think himself to be of such purity of mind, as though he needed not this free remission and favour of God. And as there is nothing more proud and arrogant than such a mind; so there is nothing in man more detestable and miserable. Of the contrary part, they be blessed that hunger and thirst for justice; for "God filleth the hungry with good things, but the proud he sendeth away empty." And that knew this holy prophet right well, that it was humility, and the casting down of himself, that was most acceptable unto God, and the seeking of health[2] and salvation only for his name's sake, that is to say, for his mercy promised in the death and passion of his only Son our Saviour Christ. In the end of the 32d psalm king David, that had thus humbled himself, bringeth in God, that speaketh unto him, whiles he is thus making his complaint of his corrupt nature and sinful life, saying in this manner, *Intellectum tibi dabo, &c.*, that is to say, "I will give thee understanding, and instruct thee in the way thou shalt go, and will have mine eyes ever upon thee." Wherein he declareth that such humbled men and lowly persons as know their iniquity shall have understanding of God, and shall not swerve from the right ways, not for their deeds and their deservings, but for his mercy that vouchsafeth to instruct and teach them. And so likewise doth this godly king shew in this psalm, "The Lord ruleth me, and I lack nothing: he feedeth me in sweet pastures, and leadeth me by the river's side; he turneth my soul, and bringeth me into the paths of righteousness; and all for his name's sake." When he hath opened the salvation of man, and also the cause thereof, and wherein it consisteth, he proceedeth to the fifth part of his oration and holy hymn.

_{Matt. v.}
_{Luke i.}
_{Psal. xxxii.}

[2 Wealth, 1562.]

THE FIFTH PART OF THE PSALM.

WHAT TROUBLE MAY HAPPEN TO SUCH AS GOD GIVETH LIFE AND SALVATION UNTO.

THE FOURTH VERSE. [The text, 1562.]

Although I walk through the valley and shadow of death, I will fear no evil; for thou art with me, thy rod and thy staff comfort me[1].

[The Explanation, 1562.]

Seeing I have such a guide and defender, there is no difficulty of peril, nor fear of death, that I will pass of. For what harm can death do to him that hath God the author of all life with him? Or what can the tyranny of man do, where as God is the defender?

In this fifth part king David sheweth how the Lord God doth exercise his sheep, whom[2] he feedeth with his blessed word, in dangers and troubles; and also, how he will defend them in the midst of their troubles, whatsoever they be. In the first words of the fifth part of this sacred[3] and holy hymn, the prophet declareth that the life of God's sheep and people in this world cannot be without dangers and troubles. Therefore Christ saith that he came to put fire in the world, and that the same fire should burn; meaning, that he came to preach such a doctrine as should move dissension and discord between friend and friend, the father and the son, and set them at debate. Not that his word is a learning or doctrine of dissension and discord of itself, but that by the malice of men, that cannot abide to be rebuked by the word of God, they will be always at discord and variance with the word of God, and with any friend or foe that teacheth it. And the same doth Christ our heavenly shepherd shew us, both in his doctrine and in his life, who was hated and troubled more than any man before or sithens his time, and assureth all his to have troubles in this world, yea, and death also. But it forceth not; for he saith, "I have overcome the world." And whatsoever the dangers be, and how horrible soever they seem, Christ being with us, we need not to fear. Therefore in this point the prophet correcteth the foolish opinion of man,

The wicked make the Gospel of peace an occasion of discord.

Luke xii.

John vii. viii ix. x. xvi.
The cross is the sure badge of God's children.

[1 Thy rod and thy staff comfort me, omitted in 1562.]
[2 That, 1562.]   [3 Sacrate, 1562.]

that would live as one of the sheep of God in this world without troubles. It is contrary both to the person that professeth God, and also to the religion that he is professed unto; for in the world both shall be (as Christ saith) hated: of which hatred cometh persecution and troubles, so that the people of God shall, whether they will or will not, pass through many dangers, and no less perilous than the shadows and very image of death, as here king David sheweth in this wholesome and blessed hymn.

And as he seeth right well, that the state and condition of God's people and sheep is to be troubled for Christ and his word, even so did Zachary the prophet speak of Christ and his people, how that not only the sheep should be troubled and scattered abroad, but also the shepherd should be stricken with the sword, that both sheep and shepherd should be condemned in this world. But now, as David and Zachary declare that the life and condition of Christ and his sheep be troublous in the world; so do they both declare that whatsoever the troubles be, they be both known and appointed upon whom they shall fall, and in what time they shall trouble the sheep of God: so that they can come no sooner than God appointeth, nor do any more harm than the heavenly shepherd shall appoint them to do. And this we may see and learn as well in Christ as in his sheep. How many times did the priests and Pharisees conspire Christ's death! Yet because his time was not come, they had not their purpose; but when the time of God was come, Christ said to his sheep: "Ye shall be all troubled this night for my cause; for the shepherd shall be stricken, and the sheep shall be scattered abroad." Then, as God had appointed the time, it could be no longer deferred. And because they should not miss of him whose death they sought, he came and met them, and offered himself unto them, and said that he was the same man, Jesus of Nazareth, whom they sought. And when they had taken him, and used as much cruelty towards him as their wicked malice and devilish hatred could devise, they killed him, and made him to pass not only the shadow and image of death, but also death itself. They thought then they had him where as they would, and said, "He hath saved other; let him now save himself, if he can."

Zech. xi.[4] Matt. xxvi.

John xviii.

Matt. xxvii. Mark xv. Luke xxiii. John xix.

[[4] Zech. xiii. 1562, which is the correct reference. See v. 7.]

When he was laid in the grave with his fathers, they thought to execute their plagues and tyranny towards him being dead, purposing that, as they had brought him to death and killed him, so likewise they would keep him down still, that he should never see life again, but rot in the earth like a wretch, until worms had eaten him. And for the performance of this purpose, to do all their whole wills to the uttermost, they came to Pilate, and said that the deceiver of the people, that lay in the grave, made his boast whiles he was alive, that the third day after his death he would rise again; but if it should be so, it would be worse with them after than it was before. "Appoint therefore soldiers (said they) and watchmen to keep the sepulchre till the third day be past." Whiles they yet minded to lay as much evil and contempt upon Christ our shepherd as they meant unto him, came the heavenly Father, that suffereth no more ignominy to fall upon his, nor will suffer them to continue any longer than him pleaseth, with this inhibition and stay of further proceedings in dishonouring and persecuting his only Son, and said: *Jam rediit lux tertia, surge sepulte meus:* that is as much to say, "Now is come the third day; arise, mine own dear Son buried." And then was the sorrow and contempt of this our persecuted shepherd not only ended, but also turned into endless and unspeakable joys: he passed with his forefather David most bitter pains, and also most vile death; but he feared not, because God was with him. The same appointment also hath the heavenly Father made with all dangers and troubles that shall happen unto us his poor and afflicted sheep, taken daily as it were to the shambles, to suffer what God's enemies can devise. But the heavenly shepherd doth see all their doings out of heaven, and mocketh them to scorn: for they shall never do as much as they would against Christ and his people, but as much as God will suffer them. David afterwards, in his thirty-seventh psalm, teacheth us the same with marvellous words and divine sentences: *Committe Domino viam tuam et spera in eum, &c.* "Lay (saith he) thy care upon the Lord, and trust in him, and he shall help thee."

It is most necessary therefore for every troubled man to know in his mind, and feel in his heart, that there are no troubles that happen unto man, whatsoever they be, come

Matt. xxvii.

A doctrine of God's providence most comfortable to all his afflicted.

Psal. ii.

they by chance or fortune, as many men say and think, but that they come by the providence of God; yea, the very winds of the air, tempests in the clouds[1], trembling of the earth, rages in the sea, or any other that come, how sudden or how unlooked-for soever they appear: as ye may read in the twenty-ninth psalm of this prophet, wherein[2] be *Psal. xxix.* wonderful tempests and troublesome things spoken of, as well done in the waters as upon the dry land.

But here, alas! is our nature and knowledge much to be lamented and complained upon: for as the knowledge we have of God's favour and gentleness towards us in Christ (for the most part) consisteth in the understanding of the mind and talk with the mouth, but the virtue, strength, and operation of the same favour of God is not sealed in our hearts and consciences; even so be the troubles and adversities which *The cause why there be* God threateneth for sin spoken and talked of with the *so few sincere and true pro-* tongue, and known in the mind, but they be not earnestly nor *fessors of the gospel.* feelingly sealed in our conscience and heart. And of this cometh it, that we neither love God, nor rejoice in his promises, as we ought to do, when we hear or read them; neither yet hate sin, nor be sorrowful for God's displeasure, as sin and God's displeasure should be sorrowed and mourned for of christian men[3]. Hereof also cometh it, dearly beloved, that we love no further than in knowledge and tongue, nor hate vice but in knowledge and tongue. But, alas! how miserable is this our state and condition, that knoweth neither life nor death, virtue nor vice, truth nor falsehood, God nor the devil, heaven nor hell, but half as much as they ought of christian men to be known. Read you therefore and mark the thirty- *Psal. xxxvii.* seventh psalm, and you shall know that it is not enough for christian men to understand and speak of virtue and vice, but that the virtue must be sealed in the conscience and loved, and the vice kept out of the conscience and hated; as David saith, "Leave doing of evil, and do good." So likewise he speaketh of a feeling christian man, whose conscience hath tasted how sweet and amiable God is: "Taste and feel (saith [*Psal. xxxiv.* the prophet) how sweet the Lord is." And this assure 8.] yourselves, that when ye feel your sins, and bewail the danger and damnation of them, the Spirit of God hath

[1 Cloud, 1562.]   [2 Where as, 1562.]

[3 Man, 1562.]

wrought that feeling, and that troubled and broken heart God will not despise. And there is no doubt nor mistrust of a sensible and feeling sinner: but in case he can find in himself no love to the obedience of God, nor desire to do his will by hearing of his word, nor any feeling at all of sin, nor desire to be rid from it by hearing of the law; he hath knowledge in the mind, and speech in the mouth, but no consent and feeling in his heart and conscience. And this knowledge liveth with sin, and speaketh with virtue: whereas the heart and conscience consenteth to good, and abhorreth evil, if the virtue and nature of God's word by God's Spirit be sealed in the conscience (and[1] this doth St Paul teach wonderfully), as well by faith, that cometh by hearing of God's word, as also of his precious supper, the sacrament of his body and blood and passion. He saith, that "the heart believeth to righteousness;" that is to say, the conscience and heart of him that is sealed, and assured of the virtue and grace of God's promises in Christ, believeth to righteousness, or is ascertained and knoweth itself to be righteous and just before God, because it hath consented and received the mercy of God offered in the gospel through the merits of Christ: and then the same faith which God hath sealed in the heart breaketh forth by confession; which confession is a very fruit of faith to salvation, as it is written by St Paul in the same place. And where this faith is so kindled in the heart, there can be none other but such a fruit following it. And as possible it is to have fire without heat or flame, as this virtue, faith, without the fruit of well-doing. And that is it that St Paul saith to the Corinthians: "As often as ye eat of this bread, and drink of this cup, shew ye the Lord's death until he come." Wherein St Paul requireth a knowledge of Christ in the receiver, not only in his mind that he know Christ died for his sin and the sin of the world, and to speak and declare the same death with his tongue unto others: but this is the chiefest and most principal commodity of Christ's holy supper (which men now ungodly call the mass), that the virtue and benefit of Christ's death, as it is appointed for the remission of his sins, be sealed and fully consented unto in his conscience. And this knowledge of Christ's death, with the assurance of the virtue, strength, and power thereof in the

[1 So in 1562. The punctuation is different in 1580.]

heart, will and ought to inflame us to thanksgiving, and to preach and teach unto others those commodities of Christ's death, that we know and feel first in ourselves within our own spirit and heart. *mercy are joined together, note what they work.*

Thus I have tarried longer than I thought in this matter, because I would bring myself and all others (as much as lieth in me) to feel, that knowledge and talk of virtue and vice, of God's favour and of God's punishment, is not sufficient; and to bring myself and all men from knowledge and talk to feeling, consenting, and a full surrendering of ourselves unto the profit and vantage of the things which we speak and know; or else knowledge and speaking please not God, nor profit ourselves, as Christ saith: "Not every man that saith, Lord, Lord, shall enter into the kingdom of heaven." Therefore did David both know, speak, and feel signed in his heart, the favour, help, and assistance of God to be with him into what troubles soever he should fall, and in that feeling did say[2] he would not fear. But it may fortune I have so written of virtue and vice to be known of in the mind, spoke of with the mouth, and felt in the heart, that ye may judge and feel in yourselves never to have come to this perfection. For this is out of doubt, he that hath God's love and fear thus sealed in his heart, liveth in this life rather an angelical life than the life of a mortal man: and yet it is evident by king David in this psalm, and by his 121st psalm, and in many more, that he was so sure and so well ascertained of God's present help in his troubles, that he cared nothing for death, or any other adversities that could happen. And doubtless, we perceive by his psalms in many places, that his faith was as strong as steel, and he trembled not nor doubted anything, but was in manner without all kind of mistrust, and nothing troubled, whatsoever he saw contrary to God's promises; and he passed over them, as things that could not once withdraw his cogitations from the truth and verity of God's promises, which he believed. As Abraham likewise did, he "staggered not," but with constancy of faith would have killed his own son, so strong was his faith. *Knowledge and talk without the feeling of God's fruitful working Spirit is not of God.* *Matt. vii.* *Psal. cxxi.[3]* *Gen. xxii.*

But as the gift of faith is a treasure incomparable, thus to know and feel faith to overcome all dangers; so maketh

[2 Said, 1562.]   [3 Ps. cxxi, not in 1562.]

it the heart of him that is sealed with such a faith to feel the joys and mirth unspeakable. But as this faith is the gift of God, and cometh only from him; so is it in him only to appoint the time when it shall come, and how much and how strongly it shall be given at all times, which is not at all times like, but sometimes so strong, that nothing can make the faithful man afraid[1], no, not death itself; and sometimes it is so strong that it maketh the man afflicted to be contented to suffer, yea, death itself, rather than to offend God. But yet it is with much conflict, great troubles, many heavy and marvellous cogitations, and sometime with such a fear, as the man hath much ado to see and feel, in the latter end of his heavy conflict, the victory and upper hand of the temptation.

The state of God's children beaten down with the sense and horror of sin and dread of God's judgments.

And at another time the christian man shall find such heaviness, oppression of sin, and troubles, that he shall not feel as much (in manner) as one spark of faith to comfort himself in the trouble of his mind (as he thinketh;) but that all the floods and dreadful assaults of desperation have their course through his conscience. Nothing feeleth he but his own mind and poor conscience, one so[2] to eat the other that the conflict is more pain to him than death itself. He understandeth that God is able to do all things; he confesseth with the knowledge of his mind, and with his tongue in his head, that God is true and merciful; he would have his conscience and heart to agree thereunto, and be quiet: but the conscience is pricked and oppressed so much with fear and doubtfulness of God's ire for sin, that he thinketh God can be merciful unto other, but not unto him. And thus doth his knowledge, for the time of temptation, rather trouble him than ease him, because his heart doth not, or rather cannot, consent unto the knowledge; yet would he rather than his life he could consent unto God, love God, hate sin, and be God's altogether, although he suffered for it all the pains of the world. I have known in many good men and many good women this trouble and heaviness of the spirit for the time, as though God had clean hid himself from the afflicted person, and had clean forsaken him: yet

The comfort of the afflicted even when God seemeth to have forsaken them.

at length, the day of light from above and the comfort of the Holy Spirit hath appeared, that lay covered under the veil and covert of bitter cogitations of God's just judgments

[1 Afeard, 1562.]   [2 So one, 1562.]

against sin. Therefore, seeing that faith at all times hath not like strength in man, I do not speak to discomfort such as at all times find not their faith as strong as David did in this psalm: for I know in the holy saints themselves it was not always like, but even in them as in others. And although we cannot compare with them in all things in the perfection of their faith, yet may they compare themselves with us in the weakness of our faith, as ye may see by the scriptures[3].

In this psalm and in many other ye shall perceive that David, by the constancy and surety he felt in the promises of God, was so strong, so joyful, and comfortable in the midst of all dangers and troubles of death, that he did not only contemn troubles and death, but also desired death, and to be dissolved out of this world, as St Paul and others did. At another time ye shall perceive him to be strong in faith, but not so joyful, nor yet the troubles so easy unto him, but that he suffered great battle and conflict with his troubles, and of the cause of all troubles, sin and transgression of God's laws, as ye may see in the sixth psalm: where as he cried out and said, "Lord, chasten me not in thy fury, nor punish me in thy wrath; my soul is sore troubled; but how long, Lord, wilt thou defer help?" And of such troubled consciences with conflicts ye shall find oftentimes in the book of psalms, and in the rest of God's scriptures; yet shall ye find the end of the temptation to be joyful and comfortable to the weak man that was so sore troubled: for, although God suffer a long fight between his poor soldier and the devil, yet he giveth the victory to his servant, as ye may see in king David. When he cried out, that both his body and soul was wearied with the cross of God's punishment, yet he said at the last, *Discedite a me operarii iniquitatis, quoniam exaudivit Dominus vocem fletus mei:* "Depart from me, ye workers of iniquity; for the Lord hath heard the voice of my weeping." And in other of his psalms ye shall perceive his faith more weak, and his soul troubled with such anguish and sorrow, that it shall seem there is no consolation in his soul, nor any shew of God's carefulness towards him. In this state ye may see him in the thirteenth psalm, where, as a man in manner destitute of all consolation, he maketh his

Psal. vi.

Psal. vi.

[3 Scripture, 1562.]

complaint, saying, "How long wilt thou forget me?" The same may ye read also in the forty-third psalm, where he sheweth that he, his most just cause, and the doctrine that he professed, was like altogether to have been overcome, so that his spirit was in manner all comfortless. Then he said to his own soul, *Quare tristis es, anima mea, et quare conturbas me?* "Why art thou so heavy, my soul; and why dost thou trouble me? Trust in the Lord," &c. And in the forty-second psalm he setteth forth wonderfully the bitter fight and sorrowful conflict between hope and desperation; wherein he complaineth also of his own soul that was so much discomforted, and biddeth it trust in the Lord. Of the which two places ye may learn that no man had ever faith at all times like, but sometimes more strong, sometimes more weak, as it pleased God to give it. Let no man therefore despair, although he find weakness of faith; for it shall make him to humble himself the more, and to be the more diligent to pray to have help, when he perceiveth his own weakness: and, doubtless, at length the weak man by the strong God shall be brought to this point, that he shall in all troubles and adversities say with the prophet, "If I should go through the shadow and dangers of death, I would not fear what troubles soever happen." And he sheweth his good assurance in the text that followeth, which is the sixth part of this holy and blessed hymn.

[margin: Psal. xlii. xliii.]

THE SIXTH PART OF THE PSALM.

WHEREBY THE TROUBLES OF GOD'S ELECT BE OVERCOME.

The fourth Verse continued, and the fifth Verse expounded.
[The text, 1562.]

For thou art with me; thy rod and thy staff comfort me. Thou shalt prepare a table before me against them that trouble me: thou hast anointed my head with oil, and my cup shall be full.

[The Explanation, 1562.]

Seeing thou art with me, at whose power and will all troubles go and come, I doubt not but to have the victory and overhand of them, how many and dangerous soever they be; for thy rod chasteneth me when I go astray, and thy staff stayeth me when I should fall:—two things most necessary for me, good Lord; the one, to call me from my fault and error, and the other, to keep me in thy truth and verity. What can be more blessed than to be sustained and kept from falling by the staff and strength of the Most Highest? And what can be more profitable than to be beaten with his merciful rod, when we go astray? For he chasteneth as many as he loveth, and beateth as many as he receiveth into his holy profession. Notwithstanding, whiles we be here in this life, he feedeth us with the sweet pastures of wholesome herbs of his holy word, until we come to eternal life; and when we put off these bodies, and come into heaven, and know the blessed fruition and riches of his kingdom, then shall we not only be his sheep, but also the guests of his everlasting banquet; the which, Lord, thou settest before all them that love thee in this world, and dost so anoint and make glad our minds with thine holy Spirit, that no adversities nor troubles can make us sorry.

In this sixth part the prophet declareth the old saying amongst wise men,

Non minor est virtus quam quærere parta tueri;

that is to say, it is no less mastery to keep the thing that is won than it was to win it. King David perceiveth right well the same: and therefore, as before in the psalm he said, the Lord turned his soul, and led him into the pleasant pastures, where as virtue and justice reigned, for his name's sake, and not for any righteousness of his own; so saith he now, that being brought into the pastures of truth and into the favour of the Almighty, and accounted and taken for one of his sheep, it is only God that keepeth and maintaineth him in the same state, condition, and grace. For he could not pass through the troubles and shadow of death (as he and all God's elect people must do) but only by the assistance of God; and therefore he saith he passed through all peril because he was with him.

Of this part of the psalm we learn, that all the strength of man is unable to resist the troubles and persecutions of God's people; and that the grace and presence of God is able to defend his people, and nothing but it. Therefore doth St Paul bid the Ephesians "be strong through the Lord, and through the might of his strength;" for he saith, that great and many be our adversaries, strong and mighty, which go about not only to weaken us, but also to overcome us; and we of ourselves have no power to withstand: wherefore he willeth us to depend and stay only upon God's strength. And St Peter also, when he hath declared the force and malice of the devil, he willeth us to "resist him strongly in faith." And St John saith, that "This is the victory that overcometh the world, even our faith." And our Saviour Christ, when the time was come that he should depart out of the world corporally, and perceived how maliciously and strongly the devil and the world were bent against his disciples, that he should leave in the world as sheep amongst wolves, and how little strength his poor flock had against such marvellous troubles; he made his most holy and effectual[1] prayer for them present, and them in trouble, and likewise for us that be now, and also in trouble, in this sort: *Pater sancte, serva eos per nomen tuum, quos dedisti mihi;* that is to say, "Holy Father, keep them for thy name's sake, whom thou hast given me."

Here hath every one of God's people such learning as teacheth that "our help is only in the name of the Lord, who made heaven and earth." And in this learning we[2] shall understand two necessary lessons: the first, that none can defend us but God alone, who is our protector, and none but he. And by this learning he will beware to ask or seek help any other where, saving of God, as we be instructed by his holy word: and herein we honour him, to know and confess that there is none that can preserve nor save us but he alone. The other lesson is, that our conscience, understanding that God can and will help us, shall cause us in all trouble to commend ourselves unto him, and so more strongly and patiently bear and suffer all troubles and adversities, being assured that we shall overcome them through him, or else be taken by them from this world into a world where as is no trouble at all. So said this holy prophet and king David: "If I walk in the shadow of death, I will not fear, for thou art with me." Now in that he saith, he "will not fear," he meaneth not that a

[1 Effectuous, 1562.]   [2 He, 1562.]

man may see and suffer these perils without all perils[3] (for then were a man rather a perfect spirit than a mortal creature); but he meaneth that[4] fear shall not overcome him. For Christ himself feared death; neither is there any man that shall suffer imprisonment for Christ's sake, but that he shall feel the pains: nevertheless, God's Spirit shall give strength to bear them, and also in Christ to overcome them. There is no man that can have faith, but sometimes and upon some occasion it may be troubled and assaulted with mistrust; no man such charity, but that it may be, yea, and is, troubled with hatred; no man such patience, but that it may at times feel impatience[5]; no man such verity, but that it may be troubled with falsehood: howbeit, in the people of God, by God's help, the best overcometh the worst, and the virtue the sin. But in case the worst prevail and overcome, the man of God is never quiet until he be restored unto God again, and unto the same virtues that he lost by sin: as ye may see in this king by many of his psalms, that he believed, and found God to defend him, howsoever his state was; and therefore attributeth unto him the whole victory and praise of his deliverance, saying, "Thou art with me, and dost overcome."

Matt. xxvi.

But now the prophet declareth how and by what means God is with him, and doth deliver him from all troubles. And this means of God's presence and defence he openeth by divers allegories and translations, wonderful meet and apt to express the thing that he would shew to[6] the world. The first translation, or allegory, he taketh of the nature of a rod; the second, of a staff, and saith they did comfort him and defend him; the third he taketh of a table, which he saith the great Shepherd prepared before his face against as many as troubled him; the fourth he taketh from the nature of oil, and of a cup that was always full, wherewith he was not only satisfied, but also joyfully replenished in all times and all troubles, whatsoever they were.

By the rod is many times in the scripture understanded the punishment and correction that God useth to call home again and to amend his elect and beloved people, when they offend him. He punisheth them, and yet killeth them not; he

[3 Probably a mistake for *fear*.]   [4 The, 1562.]
[5 Impatiency, 1562.]   [6 Unto, 1562]

beateth them until they know their faults, but casteth them not away: as he said to king David, that when he died his kingdom should come unto one of his own children; and in case he went astray from his law, he would correct him with the rod of other princes, and with the plagues of the sons of men; "But my mercy (saith God) I will not take from him, as I did from Saul." This same manner of speech may ye read also in his 89th psalm; and in the Proverbs of his son king Salomon ye have the same doctrine: "He that wanteth a heart must have his back beaten with a rod." And in the same book he saith, "He that spareth the rod hateth the child." So doth king David here confess, that it is a very necessary and requisite way to keep the sheep of God from perishing, to be chastened and corrected when they wax wanton, and will not hear the voice of their shepherd. And it is the part of every wise godly man to love this correction and chastisement of the Lord, as Salomon saith, "He that loveth discipline and correction loveth knowledge; he that hateth to be rebuked is a fool." And king David saith, "It is to my great good commodity[1] that the Lord chasteneth me." This rod of correction, David saith, is one of the instruments and means wherewithal God preserveth his sheep from straying. Now in the scripture sometimes the rod is taken, not for a correction that amendeth a man, but for the punishment and utter destruction of man, as David saith of Christ, "Thou shalt break them with an iron rod;" and in the Apocalypse ye may see the same. But I will speak of the metaphors and translations none otherwise than David doth use them in this place for his purpose.

The staff which he speaketh of in the scripture is taken for strength, power, and dominion; which staff is spoken of, as ye may see, in the books of the Kings, how the ambassadors and men of war sent from the king of the Assyrians to Ezechias at Jerusalem called the strength and power of the Egyptians, and also of the Almighty God, a staff of reed, and a broken weapon, not able to withstand the king of the Assyrians. And of such manner of speech ye may read many times in the prophets. But in this place David confesseth that the staff of the Lord, that is to say, God's

[1 Good and commodity, 1562.]

power, is so strong that nothing is able to overcome it; his wisdom is such that no man can make it foolishness; his truth is so true that no man can make it false; his promise is so certain and sure that no man can cause him to break or alter it; his love is so constant that no man can withdraw it; his providence is so wise that no man can beguile him; his care is so great for his flock that they can want nothing; his fold is so strong that no beast can break it; he letteth his sheep so in and out that no man can deceive him; he hath such a care of all as he neglecteth not one; he so loveth the one that he hateth not the other; he so teacheth all as none is left ignorant; he so calleth one as all should be advertised; he so chasteneth one as all should beware; he so receiveth one as all should take hope and consolation; he so preserveth one as all the rest may be assured; that[2] he useth his staff and force to comfort one king David (as he saith, "Thy rod and thy staff, they comfort me,") as all other should assure themselves to be safe under his protection. In this metaphor and translation, under the name of a staff, king David hath declared the power of God to be such that, in case he should pass by and through thousands of perils, he would not care, for God is with him with his rod and staff.

Then he setteth forth the third allegory, and expresseth another means which God useth for the defence and consolation of his poor sheep, and saith that God hath "prepared a table in his sight against all those that trouble him." By the name of a table he setteth forth the familiar and (in manner) fellow-like love that the God omnipotent hath towards his sheep, with whom he useth not only friendship, but also familiarity, and disdaineth not (being the King of kings) to admit and receive unto his table vile and beggarly sinners, scabbed and rotten sheep. That friendship and familiarity is marvellously set forth in this, that he made a table for David: as though David had said, "Who is he that can hurt me, when the Lord of lords doth not only love me, but admitteth me to be always familiarly in his campany?" The same manner of speech is used of king David towards Miphiboseth, Jonathan's son, when he said he should not only have the fields again of Saul his grandfather, but also be

The friendship and familiarity of God the heavenly Shepherd towards his sheep.

2 Sam. ix.

[2 That, omitted in 1562.]

entertained at his own table, that is to say, used friendly, honourably, and familiarly. This word "table" is diversely otherways taken many times in the scripture, but in this place it is nearest to the mind of king David to take it in this signification that I have noted. And our Saviour Christ taketh it in the same signification in St Luke's gospel, where he saith, his disciples shall eat with him at his table in the kingdom of God.

[Luke xxii. 30.]

The fourth means that the heavenly shepherd useth in keeping of his sheep the prophet setteth forth under the name of oil, and a full cup. In the word of God these words have also comfortable significations and meanings, extending to David's purpose. Isaac, when he had given the blessing from Esau to Jacob, said to Jacob: "God shall give thee of the dew from heaven, and from the fruitful ground thou shalt have abundance of corn, of wine, and oil," &c. By the which blessing he meaneth that Jacob should lack nothing to serve his needs, and to make him merry. And if we take David, that he meaneth by oil, as Isaac did, that at the Lord's table was all plenty, mirth, and solace, we take him not amiss: for so many times oil is taken for consolation and joy in the scriptures[1]. When Christ had purged the hurt man's wounds first with smarting wine, he afterwards put into them sweet oil, to ease the smart and sharpness of the wine. And so likewise saith our Saviour Christ to Simon the Pharisee, that gave him meat enough to his dinner, but gave him no mirth: "Since I came into thy house, thou gavest me no water for my feet, nor oil for my head: this poor woman never ceased to wash my feet with the tears of her eyes, and to anoint them with oil." But in many psalms king David useth this word "oil" to signify the Holy Ghost, as when he speaketh of our Saviour Christ: "Thou hast loved justice, and hated iniquity; therefore hath God anointed thee with the oil of joy above thy fellows." And this oil is not the material oil that kings and priests were anointed withal in the old time of the law, of whose confection we read in the book of the Levites: but this is the oil by whose efficacy, strength, and power, all things were made, that is to say, the Holy Ghost. And in his 89th psalm

Gen. xxvii.

Luke x.

Luke vii.

Ps. xlv.

[Exod. xxx. 22, &c.]

Ps. lxxxix.

[1 Scripture, 1562.]

he speaketh of the[2] oil in the same signification. Therefore I take king David here, when he saith God hath anointed his head with oil, that God hath illuminated his spirit with the Holy Ghost. And so is this place taken of godly men, his head taken for his mind, and oil for the Holy Ghost. And as oil nourisheth light, mitigateth labours and pains, and exhilarateth the countenance; so doth the Holy Ghost nourish the light and knowledge of the mind, replenisheth it with God's gifts, and rejoiceth the heart: therefore the Holy Ghost is called the oil of mirth and consolation. And this consolation cometh unto king David, and to all God's lively members, by the means of Christ, as St Peter saith: "We be people chosen, and a princely priesthood, &c." *The work of the Holy Ghost in the hearts of the faithful.* 1 Pet. ii.

By the word "cup," in this verse, he meaneth that he is fully instructed in all godly knowledge to live virtuously and godly for the time of this[3] mortal life: and so is the cup in the scripture taken for any thing that can happen unto us, whether it be adversity or prosperity; for they be called cups: as Christ said of his death, "Father, if it be possible, take this cup from me." And David in the sixteenth psalm useth it for man's prosperity in God: "The Lord (saith he) is the portion of mine inheritance, and of my cup." And therein he speaketh in the name of Christ, whose inheritance is the whole number of the faithful, and saith that his inheritance, which is the church, by God's appointment is blessed and happy; for no adversity can destroy it. This is meant by David's words, "the rod, the staff, the table, the oil, and the cup:" and he useth all these words to declare the carefulness, love, and defence of God towards miserable man. And he could the better speak thereof unto others, because he had so many times felt and had experience, that God was both strong and faithful towards him in all time of danger and adversity. Matt. xxvi. Psal. xvi.

And here is to be noted, that the dangers that man is subject unto in this life be not alone such as heretofore king David hath made mention of, as sickness, treason, sedition, war, poverty, banishment, and the death of the body; but he felt also (as every man of God shall feel and perceive) that there be greater perils and dangers that man standeth in

[2 The, omitted in 1562.]
[3 His, 1562.]

jeopardy of than these be, by occasion of sin, the mother of all man's adversity. Sin bringeth a man into the displeasure and indignation of God; the indignation of God bringeth a man into the hatred of God; the hatred of God bringeth a man into despair and doubtfulness of God's forgiveness; despair bringeth a man into everlasting pain; and everlasting pain continueth and punisheth the damned creature with fire never to be quenched, with God's anger and displeasure, which cannot be reconciled nor pacified.

What sin bringeth a man unto.

These be the troubles of all troubles, and sorrows of all sorrows, as our Saviour Christ declareth in his most heavenly prayer, in St John. *Non rogo ut tollas eos e mundo, sed ut serves eos a malo;* that is to say, "I do not (saith Christ to his heavenly Father) pray that thou shouldest take those that I pray for out of the world, but that thou preserve them from evil." And in this prayer he hath wonderfully taught us, that a christian man is subject to two troubles: one of the body, and another of the soul; one of the world, and another of the devil. As for the troubles of the world, he saith it is not so expedient that christian men be delivered from them, lest in idleness we should seek ourselves, and not God, as the children of Israel did: but this he knew was most necessary, that the Father should preserve us in the midst of these troubles with his help from all sin and transgression of his holy laws; and this he assured his disciples of, and all other that put their trust in him, not that they should in this life be preserved and kept from troubles and adversities, but that the heavenly Father should always give unto his such strength and virtue against all the enemies of God and man's salvation, that they should not be overcome with troubles that put their trust in him. For God suffereth and appointeth his to fight and make war with sin, and with all troubles and sorrows that sin bringeth with it: but God will never permit his to be deadly and mortally wounded. It is therefore expedient that man know who be his greatest foes, and do work him[1] most danger.

John xvii.

It is not expedient that we be without troubles, lest we seek ourselves and forget God.

There be divers psalms wherein he setteth forth the peril that he was in, as well in his body as in his soul: as when he complaineth of his banishment amongst not only cruel people, but also ungodly, that sought to take both his

[1 Him, omitted in 1562.]

mortal life from him, and also his religion and trust that he had in God's word. Wherefore he compareth them to the Tartarians and Arabians, men without pity or[2] religion. And the like doth he afterwards in another psalm, where as, giving thanks for his delivery, he saith that sinners trod upon his back, and many times warred against him, and he should have been overthrown, if God had not holpen him. Wherein he speaketh, not only of battle with the sword against the body, but also of heresy and false doctrine against the soul: as ye may see how Senacherib and Julius the apostate, two emperors, fought against the people of God, not only to take from them their lives, but also their religion and true honouring of God. And of all battles that is the cruelest, and of all enemies the principal, that would take the soul of man from God's word, and bring it to the word of man. And that persecution and trouble openly against God's word continued many years, until Christ was preached abroad, and princes made Christians. Then thought the devil his kingdom to have been overthrown, and christian men might live in Christ's religion without any trouble or war for religion: howbeit at length, for sin, the devil entered by subtle means, not only to corrupt true religion, but also persecuted the true professors thereof under the name of true religion, and therein used a marvellous policy and craft by men that walked inordinately amongst the Christians themselves: from whose companies, sects, and conversation, St Paul willed us to refrain by these words: "We command you, brethren, in the name of our Lord Jesus Christ, that ye refrain from every one that is accounted a brother, that useth himself inordinately, and not according to the institution he received of us."

Psal. cxx.
Psal. cxxix.
2 Thess. iii.

And because ye have not taken heed of this holy commandment, and kept yourselves from danger and peril of heresy, sin, idolatry, and superstition, by the rod and staff of God, nor have not eaten your meat of religion at God's table, nor your minds have been anointed with the Holy Ghost (as David in this psalm saith that he was against all troubles by these means defended and maintained, that no peril of the body by the sword, nor peril of the soul by false doctrine, could hurt him); therefore mark a little, and see the dangers that have hurted both you and your conscience also not like to be

[2 And, 1562.]

healed (as far as I can see), but more hurt hereafter. For the way to heal a man is to expel[1] and put away sickness, and not to increase and continue the sickness. From whom think ye that St Paul commanded you to refrain in the name of our Lord Jesus Christ? He saith, "from him that behaveth himself inordinately." Who is that, think ye? St Paul saith, he that ruleth not himself after the rule and institution that he himself had taught the Thessalonians. So that we must refrain then from all such as conform not themselves to the institution of St Paul; yea, although he be an angel from heaven.

Gal. i.

This departure from such as have ruled and put forth errors and lies is not new, but hath been used in England of Englishmen more than twenty years since we departed from the see of Rome, for the ambition of the Romish bishops that transgressed both this ordinance of St Paul and also of Christ. Of the which deadly and pestilent ambition the prophet Ezechiel prophesied, and so did also St Paul; if prophecies by God and commandments by his holy apostles had any thing prevailed in our dull and naughty hearts. Read the places, and see yourselves what is spoken of such a wicked shepherd. I do put you in mind of this wicked see, because I do see that, contrary to the word of God, contrary to the laws of the realm most godly against the pope's supremacy, against all our oaths that be Englishmen, and against all the old godly writers, this antichrist and member of the devil is not unlike to have the regiment of your souls again, which God forbid. I do exhort all men, therefore, to beware of him, as of one that came naughtily to such usurped authority, and whose authority is not only the trouble of all christian realms and princes, but also of all christian souls. And as he hath been always a trouble unto the one, so hath he been a destruction to the other: as I will a little declare unto you, that ye may know him the better, and so by the rod and staff of God's word defend yourselves from him.

Ezek. xxxiv.
Acts xx.

The Greek church, for this ambition of the Romish bishop, separated herself from the church of Rome, and would not have to do with her; for after that the Greeks knew that the bishops of Rome meant to take from them their liberties, they would not endure it: yet did the Romish

[1 Expulse, 1562.]

bishops always, to come to the supremacy, pick quarrels and matters to fall out upon, first with the clergy, and then with the laity. Platina writeth how Pius bishop of Rome, being deceived by one Hermes, a very evil man, began a new order about the keeping of Easter-day, and altered the time that the apostles and their disciples used until Pius' days, which was, to celebrate and keep the day of the resurrection of our Saviour Christ the fourteenth moon of the first month, which is with the Jews our March[2]. And although it be well done to keep it upon the Sunday, yet was this an horrible presumption, upon so light a cause to excommunicate the Greek church, and to make division where before was union. It came to pass in Victor's time the first, which was about the year of our Lord two hundred, and in the time of Irenæus, the bishop of Lugdune, the disciple of John the evangelist, this Victor would have condemned the Greek church, and proceeded with excommunication against it, had not Irenæus[3] letted it: yet was it the elder church, and had continued in the doctrine of the apostles from Christ's time, and had John the evangelist amongst them for the space of threescore and eight years after Christ's ascension. And notwithstanding the Greek church was the elder church, yet they took[4] the Roman church to be equal with them, according to the doctrine of Christ and his apostles, and also according to the decree that was made in the general council at Nice. And the Greek church never contended with the Romish church for the supremacy, until a proud and arrogant monk, that feigned humility, was preferred to be bishop of Constantinople; which came to such arrogancy of spirit that he would have been taken for the universal head of the church, which was a very mark to know that he was of antichrist, and not of

Antoninus, Histor. Tit. 13. 3. 23. 13.[5]

[2 Hoc tempore Pius Pontifex consuetudinem, et quidem magnam, cum Hermete habuit, qui librum scripsit titulo Pastoris insignitum; quo quidem in libro Angelus pastoris personam induens ei mandat, ut omnibus persuadeat pascha die Dominica celebrari, quod etiam fecit.— Platinæ Vit. Pontif. Pius I. Colon. 1551. p. 18.]

[3 See Euseb. Eccles. Hist. Lib. v. cap. 23, 24.]

[4 'They took' supplied from 1562.]

[5 This should be Tit. XII. cap. III. sect. 13. Triste tamen valde est, ut patienter feratur quatenus despectus omnibus prædictus frater et coepiscopus meus solus conetur nuncupari episcopus. Sed in hac ejus superbia quid aliud nisi propinqua jam Antichristi tempora esse

Christ, as Gregory the Great writeth to Constantia the empress: and at length this proud monk, at a synod kept at Constantinople, created himself the universal head of the church. Although before his time one Menna, and other archbishops of Constantinople, for the dignity of the imperial state being there, were called universal patriarchs; yet that was by name alone, and without execution of authority in any foreign bishoprick or church. But such was the ambition of these bishops, that walked (as St Paul saith) inordinately, that they would have the head and principality of religion and of the church at Constantinople, because there was the head and principality of the worldly kingdom; and so they began betime to confound the civil policy with the policy of the church, until they brought themselves not only to be heads of the church, but also lords of all emperors and kings, and at the last of God and God's word: as ruthfully it appeareth in men's conscience at this present day. Which abomination and pride Pelagius[1] the second, bishop of Rome, both spake and wrote against, and would that he nor any man else should have the name of a general bishop. And St Gregory[2] doth confirm the same godly sentence of his predecessor Pelagius, and would not, when he was commanded by the emperor, whom John the bishop had abused, take the archbishop of Constantinople for the universal head, nor condescend unto the emperor's commandment, and wrote to the empress that it was contrary to the ordinance of Christ and his apostles, and contrary to the council of Nice. He said also, that such new arrogancy was a very token that the time of antichrist drew nigh. And Gregory did not only write and speak against this arrogancy and pride, but suffered also great danger (as Platina writeth[3]), and so did all Rome, by the Lombards, that Mauricius the emperor made to besiege Rome, because Gregory refused to obey the archbishop of Constantinople as the head of the church.

Distinct. 99. Nullus.

Antoninus, Tit. 12. cap. 3.

designat?—Secund. Part. Histor. Anton. fol. 74. Nuremb. 1484. See also Carion. Chron. fol. 153. Francof. 1543.]

[1 Nullus Patriarcharum *universalitatis* vocabulo unquam utatur, &c.—Corp. Juris Canon. Decret. I. Pars. Distinct. 99. c. 4. Decretal. Grat. col. 565. Venet. 1604. Also Conc. Binii. Tom. IV. p. 477. c. 1. D. Lut. Paris. 1636.]

[2 Ibid. Distinct. 99. c. 5.]

[3 Platinæ Vit. Pontif. Gregorius I. Colon. 1551. p. 74. See also Anton. Hist. Tit. XII. cap. III. sect. 13. fol. 75.]

But although Pelagius, Gregory, and other godly men, detested and abhorred this wicked arrogancy to be the universal head of the church, yet the bishop of Ravenna began amongst the Latins to prepare the way to antichrist, as Paulus Diaconus saith, and separated himself from the society of other churches, to the intent he might come to be a head himself. But what at length came of it, Platina writeth[4]. And within a short time after, Boniface the third being the bishop of Rome, about the year of our Lord six hundred and seven, Phocas the emperor judged him to be head of the church, against both the bishop of Constantinople, and also of Ravenna: and such a sentence was meet for such an arbitror[5]. Phocas was a wicked man, a covetous man, an adulterer, and a traitorous[6] murderer of his lord and master, Mauricius; and this man, to make God and the Romans amends, gave sentence that the bishop of Rome should be the universal head of the church. But here was contemned the sentence and doctrine of Christ and his apostles, and also the decrees of the holy council of Nice. And no marvel: for they condemned both parties of arrogancy and usurpation; and not only these councils, but all other for many years, which decreed that[8], although one seat was named before the other, yet the bishop of the principal seat should not be the

_{De gestis Longobard. Lib. iii. cap. 12.
In Leon. 2.

Platina in Bonifac. 3.
Paulus Diaconus de gestis Long.[7] Lib. iv. cap. 11.}

[4 Contudit etiam superbiam præsulum Ravennatum, quod Agatho inchoaverat. Instituit enim ne electio cleri Ravennatis valeret, nisi eadem Romanæ sedis auctoritate confirmata fuisset.—Platinæ Vit. Pontif. Leo 2. p. 87.]

[5 Bonifacius III. patria Romanus, a Phoca Imperatore obtinuit, magna tamen contentione, ut sedes beati Petri Apostoli, quæ caput est omnium ecclesiarum, ita et diceretur et haberetur ab omnibus: quem quidem locum ecclesia Constantinopolitana sibi vindicare conabatur, &c.—Idem. Bonifa. 3. p. 75.]

[6 Carion. Chron. fol. 154.]

[7 Hic, rogante Papa Bonifacio, statuit sedem Romanæ et apostolicæ ecclesiæ primam esse, cum prius Constantinopolitana se primam omnium ecclesiarum scriberet.—Paul. Diac. De gestis Longobard. Lib. IV. cap. 11. fol. 20. Paris. 1514. See also Corp. Jur. Can. Decret. I. Pars. Distinct. 22. cc. 3-6. Decretal. Grat. coll. 564, 565. Venet. 1604.]

[8 Ex concil. Afric. Primæ sedis episcopus non appelletur princeps sacerdotum, vel summus sacerdos, aut aliquid hujusmodi, sed tantum primæ sedis episcopus.—Corp. Jur. Can. Decret. I. Pars. Distinct. 99. cap. 3. coll. 564, 565. Decret. Gratian. Also Conc. Carth. III. cap. 26. Binii. Tom. I. p. 711.]

De Simplicitate clericorum.

chiefest priest or head of the rest, but only he should be called the bishop of the chiefest seat. And how much it is against St Cyprian, they may see that will read his works[1], and also against St Hierome[2]. But what law can rule wickedness?

This wicked see contended still. After Phocas had given sentence with it for the supremacy, yet were the bishops of Rome always subject to the emperors, as well of Constantinople as of France, for the time of their reign; yea, four hundred years and odd after the judgment of Phocas they were in this obedience, and were made by the emperors, until the time of Gregory the seventh, who, in the time of great sedition, translated the empire into Germany; and never used jurisdiction in emperors and[3] kings, nor yet in the citizens of Rome; but only desired to have all bishops' causes to be discerned by the see of Rome; yet could not obtain so much at those days, as[4] appeareth by the council of Africa[5], where as Boniface the first could not obtain with craft, nor with his lies that he made of the canons decreed in the council of Nice, to have causes deferred to the see of Rome.

To be called pope was at the first general to all bishops.

And as for this name, pope was a general name to all bishops, as it appeareth in the epistles of Cyprian[6], Hierome[7], Augustine[8], and of other old bishops and doctors, which were more holy and better learned than these latter ambitious and glorious enemies of Christ and Christ's church.

[1] Cypr. Tract. de Simplic. prælatorum. Tom. I. Tract. 3. p. 248. Antw. 1541.]

[2] Hieron. Ep. ad Evag. Ubicunque fuerit episcopus, sive Romæ, sive Eugubii, sive Constantinopoli, sive Rhegii, sive Alexandriæ, sive Tanis, ejusdem meriti, ejusdem est et sacerdotii, &c.—Epist. Lib. II. Tom. II. fol. 117, G. Paris. 1534. See also his Commentaries on Ezekiel, Zephaniah, Galatians and Titus.]

[3] Nor, 1562.]   [4] It, 1562.]

[5] See Epist. Conc. Afric. ad Bonif. Binii, Tom. I. p. 925.]

[6] Cypriano Papæ Presbyteri et Diaconi Romæ consistentes sal. The superscription of the seventh epistle in St Cyprian's works.—Epist. Lib. II. Ep. 7. Op. Tom. I. p. 98.]

[7] See Hieron. Epp. ad August. Lib. II. Tom. II. foll. 113. F, 123. G, 125. G, K, 129. G.]

[8] See Epp. XIII, XXXIV, LXXVI. August. Op. Tom. II. and Ep. ad Aurel. Tom. III. col. 238, B. Basil. 1569. Also Hieron. Bignonii not. ad Marculfum, ap. Baluz. Capitul. Reg. Franc. Tom. II. col. 865. Paris. 1677.]

Read the text[9], distinct. 50, c. *De eo tamen, &c. Absit;* and there shall ye see that the clergy of Rome in their letters called Cyprian pope; and Clodovius, the king of France, named the bishop of Rome, as he did other bishops, a bishop.

<small>Histor. Lib. ii. cap. 27.</small>

This was the state of the primitive church, which was both near unto Christ in time, and like unto him in doctrine, and kept St Paul's equality, where as he saith, he was appointed amongst the gentiles, as Peter was amongst the Jews. And although the bishops in the time of Constantine the Great obtained that amongst bishops there should be some that should be called archbishops and metropolitans; yet all they were not instituted to be heads generally of the church, but to the end they should take more pains to see the church well ordered and instructed: and yet this pre-eminence was at the liberty and discretion of princes, and not always bound unto one place, and one sort of prelates, as the wickedness of our time believeth; as ye may see in the councils of Chalcedon and Africa. So that it is manifest, this superior pre-eminence is not of God's laws, but of man's, instituted for a civil policy; and so was the church of Constantinople equal with the church of Rome. And in our days Erasmus Roterodame[10] writeth and saith, this name (to be high bishop of the world) was not known to the old church: but this was used, that bishops were all called high priests; and that name gave Urban[11] the first unto all bishops, as it is written in Distinct. 59, cap. *Si officio.* Anno Dom. CCXXVI. But as for one to be head of all, it was not admitted. And the Greek church did never agree to this wicked supremacy, nor

<small>Gal. ii.</small>

<small>Conc. Nicen. Can. 6.</small>

[9 Corp. Jur. Canon. Decret. Pars I. Distinct. 50. capp. 35 and 26. Decretal. Grat. coll. 289, 297. Ven. 1604.]

[10 Apol. ad concl. Stun. Hoc argumentum illi eripio; quum id cognomen (summus Pontifex) non esset auditum illo seculo. p. 321. Ego dico nomen hoc (summum orbis pontificem) non fuisse auditum illis temporibus. p. 322. Op. Tom. IX. Basil. 1540.]

[11 Jure inde *summi Pontificis* locum sperare debebit.—Corp. Jur. Can. Decret. I. Pars. Distinct. 59. cap. 2. Decret. Grat. col. 349.

N. B. This is attributed to Zozimus, Ep. 1. ad Isichium Salonitanum Episcopum, A.D. 418, instead of to Urban, A.D. 226. Emendata est inscriptio ea plerisque vetustis Gratiani exemplaribus. See also Dagoberti Regis Capitulare III. Tit. I. cap. 11. Baluz. Capit. Reg. Franc. col. 99.]

obeyed it, until the year of our Lord one thousand two hundred and two; compelled thereunto by one Baldwin[1], that brought the Frenchmen, by the help of the Venetians, unto Constantinople, to restore one Alexius unto the empire, upon this condition, that he should subdue the Greek church to the church of Rome. But this came to pass, that the pope never, after he had gotten by alms and help of princes to be over them, passed one iota for the emperor of Constantinople further than he served his turn. So that ye may see both his beginning and proceedings to be of the devil; which if ye kill not with the staff of God's word, and beat him from your conscience, he will double kill your souls.

Now, within one hundred and fifty years after Phocas had made the bishop of Rome head of the church, the bishop of Rome contemned the emperor of Constantinople, and devised to bring the empire into France, and to give the king of France the same authority over the bishop of Rome that before the emperor had, as it appeareth in Charles the Great[2], and his successors a long time; and yet was the bishop of Rome under the princes, and not (as he is now) an idol exempt from all order and obedience. For princes made the bishops of Rome, and all other bishops within their realms; and so continued the making of the pope in the emperor's authority, until it was about the year of our Lord one thousand one hundred and ten. After that[3], Henry the fifth, being sore molested by sedition moved against him by the pope, Paschalis the second, was constrained at length to surrender his authority unto him, who turned the face of his bishoprick into manifest wars. What followed when the pope was thus free, and lived without obedience to the christian magistrates, I will not in this treatise make mention, but put you in remembrance that for certainty there followed such

He meaneth here authority to elect bishops, and to have power of both swords.

[1 See Guntheri Hist. Constantinop. Sect. 11. ap. Canisii Antiq. Lect. Tom. v. Par. II. p. 372. Ingolds. 1604.]

[2 See Corp. Jur. Can. Decret. Greg. Lib. I. De elect. Tit. vi. cap. 34. coll. 188, 189. Venet. 1604. Innoc. III. Duci Caring. Apostolica sede—quæ Romanum imperium in personam magnifici Caroli a Græcis transtulit in Germanos. This was done by pope Stephanus, A.D. 776. The coronation of the emperor, however, was delayed for some time, and was performed by pope Leo. See also Carion. Chron. fol. 161. Francof. 1543.]

[3 See Carion. Chron. fol. 196.]

trouble amongst christian princes as never was before; as it is to be seen by the doing of the wicked man Gregory the seventh, who took then upon him to have authority to use two swords[4], the spiritual and the temporal; insomuch that Henry the fourth was compelled threescore and two times to make war in his life by the means of the bishop of Rome. And, as it is written[5], this wicked bishop stirred up the emperor's own brother-in-law, Radulphus the duke of Suevia, to war against him, and sent him a crown of gold, with this verse graven in it: Albertus Crantzius, Ecclesiast. Histor. Lib. vi.

Petra dedit Petro, Petrus diadema Radulpho;

that is to say, "Christ gave the empire to Peter, Peter giveth it to Radulph:" meaning that Christ had given the empire worldly to the bishop of Rome, and he gave it to Radulph. Ye may see what a rod the emperors made for their own tail. For, after they had made the bishop of Rome head of the church, the bishops[6] made themselves shortly after the heads of emperors and kings; a just plague of God for all them that will exalt such to rule as God said should be ruled.

These bishops be not only proud, but also unthankful. For, whereas all the world knoweth the bishop's authority to come from the emperor in worldly things, and not from God, but against God; this monster, Gregory the seventh, said Abbas Uspergensis in suo Chronico.

[4 Corp. Jur. Can. Extravag. Comm. Lib. I. De majorit. et obed. Bonifac. VIII. cap. 1. In hac ejusque potestate duos esse gladios, spiritualem videlicet et temporalem, evangelicis dictis instruimur.—Uterque ergo est in potestate ecclesiæ, spiritualis scilicet gladius et materialis. Col. 227.]

[5 Quod cum ille religiose cœpisset implere, videntes cardines orbis quia præ timore sedis apostolicæ contremiscant potestates, et sub eo curventur qui portant orbem, suggessisse summo Pontifici, ut, dejecto degenere qui publicam peregisset pœnitentiam, alium curaret in regno sublimari: percontante autem Pontifice, quis dignus videretur? Rodulphum Suevum esse prætensum: cui illico Papa miserit coronam cum elogio, Petra dedit Romam Petro, tibi Papa coronam; mandaveritque Moguntino et Coloniensi Archiepiscopis, ut illum eligerent, consecrarent, tuerentur.—Crantz. Saxon. Hist. Lib. v. c. 7. p. 296. Colon. 1574.—See also Carion. Chron. fol. 193. Also Vit. Greg. Papæ VII. Conc. Binii. Tom. VII. Par. 2. p. 309. Lut. Paris. 1636.]

[6 See Corp. Jur. Can. Decret. I. Pars. Distinct. 96. capp. 9, 10, 11. Decret. Gratian. coll. 551, 552, 553.]

that Christ gave him the empire of Rome, and he giveth it to the duke of Suevia, Radulph, to kill his good brother Henry the fourth. He that will know more of this wicked man, and of his brethren bishops of Rome, let him read Benno the cardinal, that writeth in his history of the popes that he saw, of John the twentieth, Benedict the ninth, Silvester the third, Gregory the sixth, Leo the ninth, Alexander the second. But in his old days he saw and writeth horrible and execrable things of Gregory the seventh[1]. Yet was England free from this beast of Rome then, in respect of that it was before the idol was expelled[2] in king Henry the eighth's time. But Alexander the third never rested to move men to sedition until such time as king Henry the second[3] was content to be under him as other were. And all this suffered England for Thomas Becket, the pope's martyr[4].

When they were crept up into this high authority, all their own creatures, bishops of their sect, cardinals, priests, monks, and friars, could never be contented to be under the obedience of the princes: and, to say the truth, princes durst not (in manner) require it; for they were in danger of goods and life. And the emperor[5] Henry the seventh was poisoned by a monk, that poisoned the idol of the mass,—both a god and minister meet to poison men, and both of the pope's making. And what conscience did they make of this, think ye? Doubtless none at all; for the pope saith, and so do[6] all his children, that he can dispense and absolve themselves and all men from what oaths soever they have made to God or man. This enemy, with his false doctrine, is to be resisted and overcome by the word of God, or else he will destroy both body and soul. Therefore against all his crafts and abominations we must have the rod, the staff, the table, the oil, and the cup, that David speaketh of, in a readiness to defend ourselves withal.

Now followeth the last part of this holy hymn.

[1 See Brown's Fasciculus Rerum, Vol. I., where Cardinal Benno's character of Gregory VII. will be found.]
[2 Expulsed, 1562.]
[3 Seventh, edd. 1580 and 1562.]
[4 Platinæ Vit. Pontif. Alexander 3. p. 176. Colon. 1551.]
[5 Carion. Chron. fol. 218. Francof. 1543.]   [6 Doth, 1562.]

⁋ THE SEVENTH PART OF THE PSALM.

WHAT THE END OF GOD'S TROUBLED PEOPLE SHALL BE.

THE SIXTH VERSE.   [The text, 1562.]

Thy loving kindness shall follow me all the days of my life, and I will dwell in the house of the Lord for ever.

[The Explanation, 1562.]

I WILL, in the midst of all troubles, be strong and of good cheer: for I am assured that thy mercy and goodness will never forsake me, but will continually preserve me in all dangers of this life; and when I shall depart from this bodily life, thy mercy will bring me into that house of thine eternal joys, where as I shall live with thee in everlasting felicity.

Of this part we learn, that the dangers of this life be no more than God can and will put from us, or preserve us in them, when they come unto us, without danger; also that the troubles of this world be not perpetual nor damnable for ever, but that they be for a time only sent from God, to exercise and prove our faith and patience. At the last we learn that, the troubles being ended, we begin and shall continue for ever in endless pleasure and consolation, as David sheweth at the end of his psalm. So doth Christ make an end with his disciples, when he hath committed them, for the time of this life, to the tuition of the heavenly Father, whiles he is bodily absent: he saith, at length they shall be where he is himself, in heaven for ever. For in this life, albeit the faithful[7] of God have consolation in God's promises, yet is their joy very dark and obscure by reason of troubles both without and within; outwardly by persecution, inwardly by temptation. Therefore Christ desireth his Father to lead and conduct his church in truth and verity, whiles it is here in fight and persecution with the devil, until it come to a perfect and absolute consolation, where as no trouble may molest it. For then, and not before (to what perfection soever we come), shall we be satisfied: as David saith, "The plentifulness of pleasure and joy is Psal. xvi.

[7 Faithfuls, 1562.]

in the sight and contemplation of thee, O Lord!" For then shall the mind of man fully be satisfied, when he, being present, may presently behold the glorious majesty of God: for God hath then all joys present to him that is present with him, and then man knoweth God as he is known of God. These joys in the end of troubles should give the troubled man the more courage to bear troubles patiently, and be persuaded (as St Paul teacheth) that the troubles of this present life be not worthy of the joys to come, which shall be revealed to us when Christ cometh to judge the quick and the dead: to whom, with the Father and the Holy Ghost, be all honour and praise, world without end. Amen.

(∴)

marginal notes: 1 Cor. xiii. / Rom. viii.

[FINIS. 1562.]

⁋ An Exposition

upon the Sixty-second Psalm, made by

the constant Martyr of Christ, Master

John Hooper, Bishop of Glo-

cester and Worcester.

The Argument.

The prophet in this psalm doth declare (by his own experience) how the truth of God's word, and such as favour and follow the same, be esteemed and used in the world of worldly men; the truth itself rejected, and the lovers thereof slandered and persecuted. And seeing truth and true men before the prophet's time, in his time, and after his time, were thus miserably afflicted, in this psalm he writeth his own condition and miseries, with certain and most comfortable remedies, which ways the afflicted person may best comfort himself, and pass over the bitterness and dangers of his troubles, and suffer them, as long as God layeth them upon him, patiently. So that whosoever from the feeling of his heart can say this psalm, and use the remedies prescribed therein by the Spirit of God, doubtless he shall be able to bear the troubles both of the devil and man patiently, and contemn them strongly.

⁋ The parts of the psalm be in number generally two.

I. In the first is contained, how that the favour of God, and his help, is able to remedy all adversities.

II. In the second is contained, how that the favour of man, and his help, is able to redress no adversities.

The first part comprehendeth eight verses of the psalm.

The second part containeth the other four verses, that next follow, to the end of the psalm.

⁋ These two general parts do contain
more particular parts in them, in
number six.

I. First, what is to be done by the christian man that is afflicted.

II. The second part sheweth why the troubled man in trouble looketh for help of God.

III. The third part declareth how suddenly God can destroy the persecutors of the truth.

IV. The fourth part containeth the repetition of the first and the second part; with more causes shewed why patiently trouble is to be borne, and faithfully to be believed that God can and will remedy it.

V. The fifth part declareth that man's power is not to be feared, nor his friendship to be trusted unto; for no man is able to damn or save.

VI. The sixth part setteth forth how that God hath promised to help the afflicted, and will assuredly perform it.

⁋ *The psalm with the parts before named,*
where they begin, and where
they end.

1. "My soul truly waiteth still upon God."

The first part teacheth a man to fly unto God in the time of oppression and trouble.

2. "For of him cometh my salvation. He verily is my strength and my salvation; he is my defence, so shall I not greatly fall."

The second part of the psalm, that declareth why the troubled man trusteth in God.

3. "How long will ye imagine mischief against every man? Ye shall be slain all the sort of you: yea, as a tottering wall shall ye be, and like a broken hedge.

4. "Their device is only how to put him out whom God will exalt: their delight is in lies: they give good words with their mouth, but curse with their heart. Selah."

The third part of the psalm, wherein is shewed that suddenly the persecutors of the innocent shall perish.

5. "Nevertheless, my soul, wait thou still upon God, for my hope is in him.

6. "He truly is my strength and my salvation; he is my defence, so that I shall not fall.

7. "In God is my health and my glory, the rock of might; and in God is my trust.

8. "O put your trust in him always, ye people; pour out your hearts before him, for God is our hope. Selah."

In these four verses is contained the fourth part; wherein is mentioned the repetition of the two first verses.

9. "As for the children of men, they are but vain; the children of men are deceitful upon the weights; they are altogether lighter than vanity itself.

10. "O trust not in wrong and robbery; give not yourselves to vanity: if riches increase, set not your hearts upon them."

Here is the fifth part, that teacheth no trust to be put in man; for he is not able to damn nor save.

11. "God spake once, and twice I have also heard the same, that power belongeth unto God:

12. "And that thou, Lord, art merciful, for thou rewardest every man according to his work."

In these two verses is comprehended the sixth part, which is, that God hath promised to be merciful in helping the afflicted, and that he will perform his promises.

A BRIEF EXPLANATION OF THE PSALM GENERALLY.

"My soul doubtless waiteth still upon God," &c. Be my troubles never so great and dangerous, yet my soul shall trust continually and constantly in the Lord, that can and will remedy them. For he is my strength and my salvation; and he is my defence. "So shall I not greatly fall." Although, good Lord, by reason of mine infirmity and sin, which is in all men, my soul is weak and feeble, that it will be oppressed with the lightest of all thy troubles which thou layest upon man for his sin; yet, when it taketh hold of thy mercy, it waxeth strong: and although it be weak and trembling by reason of infirmity, yet doth it not clean fall from the trust of constancy and hope.

And let the wicked imagine their wicked imaginations against thy poor servants, O God; yet at length shall they come to shame and destruction, as the tottering wall doth fall, and the rotten hedge is consumed with fire. For that they go about they shall never bring to pass; because they devise to put him to shame that God hath purposed to exalt and magnify. And whatsoever doubleness they use, to speak fair with their mouth, and yet have false and hollow hearts, it shall not bring their intent to their purposed end. Selah. God be thanked, of whom dependeth all the hope of my salvation. And he is my strength, my salvation, and my defence; so that I shall not fall.

Wherefore, all christian and afflicted persons (saith the prophet), follow mine example, and put all your hope and trust in the mercy of God; who only save us from evil, and bless us with all goodness. Pour out therefore before him all your cares and heaviness, and look assuredly for help from him; for doubtless the help of man is nothing worth. For "if man and vanity were both weighed in a pair of balance, vanity itself would be weightier than man. How then can so light a thing as man is help in the time of trouble?" And as a man is but vanity, or else rather more vain than vanity; so be all worldly riches that man possesseth, and as little or less able to help an afflicted man, as man is unable to help himself.

And this I know (saith the prophet), not by man's wisdom, but by the mouth of God, that whatsoever help man looketh for besides God, he may be assured at all times to be both helpless and comfortless; and, trusting to God, he shall be at all times both holpen and comforted: for so saith the Lord, whose sayings no power is able to falsify nor to resist.

¶ *What things are to be noted out of every particular part of this psalm, for the edifying and comfort of him that shall use to say, sing, or meditate this psalm.*

THE FIRST PART.

"My soul truly waiteth upon God."

Out of the first part (wherein is contained what the Christian should do in the time of trouble) is to be noted what it is for a man to have his soul waiting still upon God, or else to have silence always in his soul towards God, in the days of adversity, as this psalm speaketh.

When the christian man or woman in the time of sorrow and heaviness without grudge or impatience looketh for the help of God, and giveth not himself to quarrelling or complaining of God, as though he did him wrong, and punished him too much; then doth the soul wait upon the Lord, or else hath silence towards God, as we may see by Job, where his soul attended still upon the Lord. When his goods, cattle, house, and children were taken from him, he said after this sort: "The Lord gave them, the Lord hath taken them away; as the Lord is pleased, so is it done. The name of the Lord be blessed." All this while he bore the cross of God without murmur or grudge, and had his soul still waiting upon God, as this prophet here saith. But when he was burdened further, and from the sole of the foot to the top of the head was stricken with sores and botches, he cursed the day that he was born in, and the night wherein he was conceived, with many more unquiet and lamentable words, as it appeareth in his book. *[margin: When doth the soul of man wait upon the Lord in the days of trouble, or else hath silence? Job i. Job iii.]*

The like example we have before of king David in the book of the psalms, where be these words: "In trouble and adversity I said, I was cast away from the sight of thine eyes, O God:" and as Job sometime said, if he should die, yet he would trust in the Lord; so said David a little before, if he should go in the midst of the shadow of death, he would not fear. In the which psalm ye may see how constantly his soul waited upon the Lord: yet in the thirty-first psalm his *[margin: Psal. xxxi. Job xiii. xvii. Psal xxiii.]*

troubles were so great that in them he said, "I am cast from the sight of thee, O God." So that these testimonies and examples of the scriptures do declare, that to have the soul to wait upon the Lord is to be assured that God will help in trouble, and patiently to bear the trouble without grudge, until God send remedy and help for it.

<small>*What it is to have the soul wait upon the Lord in the time of trouble.*</small>

The second thing to be gathered of the first part is to mark and see that in the very elects of God, and most excellent personages amongst holy men, there is sometime quiet, patient, and thankful sufferance of adversity strongly, that it seemeth in the soul of him that is troubled there is so constant and strong faith that it maketh all sorrows and troubles rather pleasant and sweet than heavy, burdenous, or painful. At another time troubles seem unto them so heinous and grievous, that the burden of them is as great a pain as death, not only unquieting the body, but also very sore vexing of the spirit with these and like cogitations: "God hath cast me out of his sight; God will have mercy upon me no more; my soul is heavy and troubled." And this diversity of increase and decrease of faith and hope of holy men and women before our time teacheth us great wisdom and consolation: wisdom, in that we see faith and hope be not natural qualities in man, although he be never so virtuous, or never so graciously elected by God to eternal salvation; but they be the merciful gifts of God, given unto man for Christ's sake, and wrought by the Holy Ghost above man's deservings. We learn also that the gifts of God, faith, hope, and charity, patience and sufferance, with such like virtues, be not at all times of like condition and strength in man; but at some time so strong that nothing can fear us, and at another time so weak that all things do make us dismayed and fearful. Now and then it is so doubtful that we cannot tell whether it were best to suffer for the truth, or else to be released, consenting unto falsehood. Thus God useth his gifts in us not always after one sort; partly for our sins, and partly to prove us, and to bring us to a certain knowledge of our infirmity and weakness. From Saul, Judas, and Cain he took his Spirit clean, to punish their iniquity and wickedness; and from Job, to attempt his patience, and to make him feel that of himself he could bear nothing.

<small>*Psal. xxxi. xlii. xliii. lxxvii.*
Increase and decrease of faith in the faithful.
Wisdom to be learned of the premises.
Faith, hope, charity, &c. be not at all times of like strength.</small>

<small>*Consolation.*</small>

We learn consolation out of this text in this, that in our

troubles the Lord forsaketh us not, but comforteth us; and the more our troubles and adversities be, the more is his grace and favour towards us: as the prophet saith in another of his psalms: "As adversities oppressed my heart, so thy consolations, Lord, rejoiced me:" in the which psalm ye may see what consolation the afflicted conscience taketh in adversities. The psalm is made against the wicked oppressors and persecutors of the poor; wherein they say, As the tyranny of the wicked troubleth us, so thy consolations, good Lord, do rejoice and comfort us. And the same saith St Paul to the Corinthians: "As the afflictions of Christ do abound in us, even so by Christ aboundeth our consolation." *The Lord forsaketh not his people in trouble. Psal. xliv. [xciv. 19.] 2 Cor. i.*

There is also to be noted, in that the prophet saith, his "soul waiteth upon the Lord," many men can dissemble injuries, wrongs, and oppressions outwardly; sometimes, when they be not able to revenge; and sometimes, when they dare not revenge, for lack of opportunity and occasion, lest more harm might ensue of that their enterprise: as the Jews durst not kill Christ a great while, for fear of the people; yet were they murderers in their hearts before God, the fact outwardly not then being done. Some again revenge not, because they think dissembled patience will gain worldly commodities and riches. Howbeit, this quietness and refraining from revenging is nothing worth before God. But when the heart and soul waiteth upon God, and is contented to be as God maketh it, that waiting and service of the soul the Lord delighteth in, and is pleased withal. This is a godly doctrine, and much to be desired, to have the mind contented with such things as be troublesome and painful to the body outwardly. And where the mind waiteth not patiently upon the Lord in trouble, it will appear divers ways. Sometime, many years after the displeasure is done, the man that suffered the displeasure revengeth it wrongfully and cruelly: as the Pharisees and the high priests deferred the bloody fact in the killing of Christ until they had gotten time and opportunity for their purpose. Sometime the impatience and unquietness of the mind appeareth with checks and taunting answers unto God; as, when God asked Cain where his brother Abel was, he asked God again, whether he were his brother's keeper, or no? The same ways appeared Pharaoh's unquietness. When God would have had him to dismiss his people, he asked what *Matt. x. xxvi. John xi. xviii. Luke xix. Note. The impatience of the mind is many ways known. Cain. Gen. iv. Pharaoh. Exod. v.*

God he was, unto whom he should do such homage and service. Sometime it appeareth by desperate weighing the greatness of trouble, not considering the mercy of God, that is greater than sin: as Cain's unquieted soul for the killing of Abel brought his tongue to blaspheme the mercy of God, saying that his iniquity was greater than the mercy of God could forgive. So did the wicked soul of Judas, that betrayed Christ, make his tongue confess before the Pharisees his treason and wickedness, and never to call upon Christ for the remission thereof. Sometime the impatience of the mind is known outwardly by finding fault with God's works: as, when Adam's mind was unquieted for the eating of the apple, he said unto God that his wife, the woman that he gave unto him, deceived him. Achab the wicked king, being impatient with the scourges that God sent upon his realm for his own sins and the people's, picked a quarrel with the good prophet Elias, and said that he troubled all his realm. So said the Jews against Paul: "This is he that troubleth all the world."

Abel. Gen. iv.

Judas. Matt. xxvii.

Adam. Gen. iii.

Ahab. 1 Kings xviii.

Jews. Acts xxi. xxiii. xxiv.

This is daily seen, whensoever the mind and the soul is unquieted, the fault is laid upon God's work: as, if the higher powers hang a true man, and save a thief; deliver Barabbas, and hang Christ; straightway the tongue walketh, that he is set in authority by God. Indeed so he is, but yet to punish the evil, and to maintain the good; and not to molest the good, and maintain the evil, as commonly now-a-days is seen. Simon Magus shall be at liberty, and Simon Peter in chains: Annas and Caiaphas shall rule like lords, Christ and St Paul shall be ruled and suffer death; although not personally in their own bodies, yet in their members and disciples. Let the mind of the thief be touched for theft; straightway poverty, the work of God, beareth the blame. Let whoredom vex the whoremonger's mind; immediately the tongue complaineth upon God's work, youth, strength, and such other. Let the mind be troubled with covetousness; by and by God's work, wife, children, be alleged for excuse; for they must be provided for, saith the covetous man; when he hath enough for himself and ten times as many more children as God hath sent him, if it were thankfully used towards God, and liberally towards the world. So that if any man be touched with anguish or heaviness for sin, immediately the

Simon Magus. *Annas and Caiaphas.*

Thief.

Whoremongers.

Covetous men.

tongue saith, he was born under an evil planet, or in an evil hour, and so findeth fault with the work of God, which God made excellent good. Thus may ye see, where as the soul of man waiteth not upon God, the impatient man accuseth God and all his works, both in heaven and in earth. But the godly, feeling the rod of God for sin and iniquity (as God never punisheth without just cause), he first accuseth himself, and acknowledgeth his own offences; and then saith with the prophet Micheas, "I will suffer the indignation of God, for I have deserved it." Gen. i.
Prov. xviii.
The godly feeling the rod of God do accuse themselves, acknowledging their offences to have merited the same.
Mic. vii.

To this waiting upon the Lord without quarrelling and desperate lamenting exhorted Jeremy the prophet the children of Israel for the time of their being in servitude and captivity of Babylon; bidding them to plant and graft trees, and so to provide for themselves, until the time were expired of their affliction and captivity.

Men may mourn and lament their sins and troubles that they suffer for sin; as we may see how the psalm of the prophet containeth the bewailing and weeping of the people, that sate heavily and lamentably by the river side in Babylon. And the like may ye read in the Lamentations of Jeremy. But this mourning was without desperation and quarrelling, as the letters and books do record. Besides these things, the cause of their bewailing and lamenting, whiles their souls waited upon the Lord, differeth from the most sort of mourners and bewailers now-a-days. For we may see now-a-days, if the wife bewail the death of her husband, it is most commonly because she hath taken from her a loving head and governor. If the husband lament the departure of his wife, it is because he is bereaved of a faithful helper. If the son mourn for the death of his father, it is because there is taken from him, not only his father, but also his patron and defender. If the parents be sorry for the taking away of their children, it is because they want their dalliance, sport, and pastime with them, or such other worldly affections. If the prince take grievously the calling away of his subject from this world, it is because he lacketh a trusty soldier, a faithful captain, a wise counsellor, or profitable officer. If the subject lament the death of his prince, it is because he hath lost his advantage, authority, or estimation. If the servant weep for his master, it is because with his master is departed his commodity, and trust of worldly riches and friendship. If the master mourn for his servant, it is because there is taken from him a skilful, a diligent, or a faithful doer of his business; and such-like causes as men grievously of every sort feel and lament. If the parson lament his parishioner, it is most commonly because he seeth the breach of an honest household decayeth his tenths and profit. And if the parishioner mourn for his pastor, most commonly it is because he lost a good companion or profitable friend. If the bishop bewail the death of such as die in his diocese, it is most commonly because he is destitute of such a one as favoured much affection to set forth and do such things as he worldly desired should go forwards; or else perchance such manner of one as could excuse him, what negligence or fault soever he should perpetrate or commit for the time he were in office. If the diocese be sorry for the death of the bishop, it is because the one part (which is the clergy) doth fear lest there shall come another that will be more diligent and quick in doing his office, and see that they shall do the same: the other party (called the temporalty) lament, because they have lost such a one as peradventure fed well their bellies with bread and beef; or else was so remiss that he would suffer all sin unpunished, and rather be a bearer of the evil than a maintainer of the good. Now this is such bewailing and mourning as ethnicks, publicans, and infidels may have. But wherefore the christian soul, that waiteth upon the Lord without quarrel or desperation, doth weep and lament, read you the psalm before named, and the Lamentations of Jeremy; and there shall you find in the psalm these words: "We sat by the rivers of Babylon and wept, when we remembered thee, O Sion." The chiefest cause of their weeping was, because the word of God was not preached, the sacraments ministered, nor the Almighty God lauded and praised in the temple of Hierusalem, as God had commanded by his word. This is a most just and also a most worthy cause to weep for, whiles God punisheth us; that, for our sins, not only our quietness and wealth, but also the word of God (which is greater) is taken away, and his due honour given unto idols. For the children of Israel, perceiving that God's honour was defaced for their sins, they wept as often as they remembered it; as God give us grace

Why sat the people by the river side of Babylon.

A just cause of lamentation.

to do the same! The like did St Peter: he lamented not _{Peter.} because he left all his goods for Christ's sake; but wept that by his denial of Christ he felt himself not constant in the _{Matt. xxvi.} faith and love of his master. So did Mary Magdalene bewail _{Mary Magdalene. Luke vii.} that she had offended Christ, and not because the world knew her to be a sinner.

St John Chrysostom hath a notable saying: "He that _{Jo. Chrysost. in Epist. ad Rom. cap. 2.} feareth more hell than Christ is worthy of hell[1]." And that meant the prophet when he cried out, "What is there in _{Psal. lxxiii.} heaven or in earth, that I prefer before thee, O Lord?"— as though he had said, there is nothing can make me as glad as thy love towards me, nor anything so sorry as thy displeasure, good Lord. Thus doth the soul of the very Christian wait upon the Lord in all troubles and adversities, and patiently doth bear the punishments of sin; and not only bear patiently the pain, but also considereth what is the greatest loss that may happen unto him by reason of troubles: _{What is the greatest loss that a Christian considereth.} not the loss of worldly riches, lands, and promotions, nor the loss of health of body by sickness, neither the loss of the body itself by death, ne yet the loss of the soul into eternal pains. But the greatest loss that he weigheth is the loss of the good will of him that made him, and of great mercy redeemed him, and with much kindness always nourished him. That is to be seen in the prodigal son, which when he _{The prodigal son. Luke xv.} had spent all his goods lecherously, and brought himself to most miserable poverty, and to such extreme famine that he would have been glad to have eaten the meat prepared for the pigs, besides the great heaviness of heart, that weighed the time of prosperity, and conferred it with his estate of so extreme misery; yet nothing made him so sorry and pensive as the calling to his remembrance how unreverently he had used his most gentle, loving, and benign father, who was not only liberal and free to his children, but also to his hirelings that lacked nothing. This consideration of his offence towards his father made him a great deal more sorry than all the pains he otherwise sustained. And thus must every Christian wait upon the Lord, and then doubtless consolation shall

[1 Διόπερ εἰ καὶ μηδενὸς ἕνεκεν ἑτέρου, τούτουγε ἕνεκεν γεέννης ἂν ἦμεν ἄξιοι, τὴν γέενναν μᾶλλον τοῦ Χριστοῦ φοβούμενοι.—Joh. Chrysost. Εἰς τὴν πρ. Ρωμ. ἐπιστ. λόγος ε. Tom. III. p. 35. Eton. 1613.]

follow, as it appeareth by the same prodigal son, and by this psalm of the prophet.

Moreover, if we mark with what dangers and troubles the soul seeketh her Lord and spouse Jesus Christ, in the mystical book of Solomon's Ballads, we shall see with what attendance, diligence, and patience, the soul waiteth upon Christ. "I sought him (saith the soul), but I found him not. I called him, and he would not answer me. The watchmen of the city found me, and beat me, and wounded me. They took my robe from me, that kept the walls. I require you, ye daughters of Hierusalem, if ye find my spouse, tell him that I am sick with love." Note these words, "I sought him (saith the soul), and found him not. I called him, and he answered not." Was not this enough to have clean discomforted the heavy, sick, and troubled soul, that ran and cried to her love and husband Jesus Christ, and yet for the time never the nearer? Further, in running and calling for him, the soul fell into the hands of her enemies, that robbed her of her mantle; and yet, notwithstanding these dangers, she cried out unto all that she met, that in case they found her spouse, they would tell him that she was sick with his love.

Ponder these things altogether: first, to travail and cry, and not to profit; next, in travailing and crying, to lose all her goods, yea, the mantle that she went in; thirdly, to put her life in danger with confessing Christ to be her spouse before such as hated him mortally. And yet how did this christian creature? Doubtless, waited upon the Lord without murmur or grudge. And in all these troubles, note there is no complaint nor quarrel made of her prayers that were not heard, of the pains that for the time profited not, of the loss of her goods and apparel, nor yet of the danger that she was in of her and Christ her spouse's enemies. But here was the weeping, lamentation, and sorrow, that Christ her spouse could not be found; in whose love she burned so ardently that all adversities grieved her not, neither did she any thing at all esteem them; but only the want of Christ was her grief and sorrow: yet was she patient, and trusted still in the Lord.

The like may ye see by the woman of Canaan, how she called upon the Lord for her daughter; unto whom Christ made no word of answer. Further, his disciples were troubled and wearied by her importunate suit. Also Christ called her in manner no better than a dog: yet was there neither the bitterness of his words nor the inhumanity of his apostles that she passed for, but she waited still upon the Lord, and was nothing sorrowful for all the sharp words she suffered, but only because the help of the Lord was not extended and bestowed upon her daughter, as she desired. But what ensueth of such a patient expectation and sorrowfulness of God's absence? Mark what the prophet saith.

Patient expectation of redress taketh all scourges and troubles in good part.

THE SECOND PART OF THE PSALM.

1. "For of him cometh my salvation.
2. "He verily is my strength and my salvation: he is my defence, so shall I not greatly fall."

The second part declareth why the troubled person seeketh health of God.

Here first be three doctrines to be noted: First, to know by God's word that God can help: the second, that God will help: and the third, that the afflicted is bound boldly to require help of God. Whereof the troubled person must be assured by the scripture, or else he shall never find consolation.

Three doctrines to be noted.

Now to the first part, that God can help: this scripture is to be marked, that saith, God is omnipotent, that is to wit, able to do all things. So said he to Abraham, when he eftsoons promised him the land of Canaan: "I am the God omnipotent; walk before me, and be perfect." The same said Jacob, when Benjamin his young son was so instantly desired by his brethren to go into Egypt, when they lacked corn: "My God omnipotent (said Jacob) can make the prince of Egypt favourable unto you." So did God tell Moses that he was the Lord that appeared unto Abraham, Isaac, and Jacob, even the Almighty God. The like is in the same book, when God had drowned Pharaoh and his host: Moses gave thanks, and said his name was Almighty. Thus in the word of God we may learn every where, as well by his name, as by his most marvellous works, that he is omnipotent, and there is nothing impossible unto him.

God is omnipotent.
Gen. xvii.
Gen. xliii.
Exod. vi.
Pharaoh. Exod. xv.

Even so doth the word of God declare, that, as he is omnipotent and can save, in like manner is he willing and

As God is able, so is he willing to save.

will save. King David saith, that "he saveth both man and beast." In another psalm he saith, "God saved him from all adversities." And again he saith, he will save all that trust in him; and not only save, but also save for nothing. So God saith by the prophet Esay: "I will save thy children." And in the same book it is declared, that God's hand is not weakened; but that he can save, and will save. This willing nature of God to save is manifestly opened unto us in all the prophets. And in St Matthew Christ saith, he "came to save such as were lost." The same is to be seen in St Luke, how that "the Son of man came not to damn, but to save." St John the evangelist saith, his coming was to save the world. And St Paul saith, "He would all men to be saved."

<small>Psal. xxxvi.
Psal. xxxiv.
Psal. xxxv. lvi.
Isai. xlix.
Isai. lix.

Jer. xv. xxiii.
Ezek. xxxiv.
Dan. xii.
Hos. i.
Zeph. iii.
Zech. viii. ix. x.
Matt. xviii.
Luke ix.
John iii.
1 Tim. ii.</small>

Now as the word of God, and the examples contained in the same, declare that God can and will help in the time of trouble and adversity; so doth it declare that men be bound to call and seek for help in the time of adversity. As we read in Esay the prophet, where God crieth out in this sort: "Ye that be athirst, come to the waters," &c. In St Matthew Christ commandeth all men that be troubled to come unto him. Also in the psalms he biddeth all men call upon him in the days of their heaviness, and he will hear them, and deliver them. Again, he willeth us to ask, and it shall be given unto us.

<small>As God can and will help, so doth he command us to call unto him for help.

Isai. lv.
Matt. xi.
Psal. l.

Matt. vii. xviii.
Mark xi.
Luke xi.
John xiv. xv. xvi.
1 John v.</small>

Now as these three doctrines are to be marked in the Almighty God, so must they be grounded in the heart of the troubled person. And, first, he must give this honour unto God, that he alone is able to save, and none but he; as the prophet Esay saith of him. Then, being thus persuaded, the afflicted person will not seek help at dead saints, nor at any other creature's hand, but at God's only. And as none giveth God the strength able to help, but is of itself in God and with God; so is there none that can give God a will to help; but he of himself is inclined to have mercy upon the afflicted; and his mercy is most prone and ready to help the poor and miserable.

<small>God alone is able to save, and none but he.
Isai. xlv.
No help to be sought at dead saints, &c. but only of God.

God is inclined of himself to have mercy.</small>

Hereof learneth the afflicted Christian, that none inclineth God to be merciful, but his own gentle and pitiful nature: so that the sinners may boldly in Christ resort unto him first, because he is mercy itself; and not to go astray to seek first mercy at dead saints' hands, and by their means at last find God merciful and ready to help him. And when the afflicted perceiveth by the word of God, that he commandeth him to call upon him, and upon none other, he may take a courage and audacity to be bold to come unto him, be his sins never so many, horrible, or filthy; yea, if in number they exceeded the gravel of the sea, yet be they fewer always than his mercy: if they be as red as scarlet, yet shall they be made as white as snow. The book of Wisdom saith even so: "Although we have sinned, Lord, we be thine, knowing thy greatness." *The afflicted by the commandment of God taketh audacity to approach to his mercy. Isai. i. Wisd. xv.*

And where as these doctrines be grounded, see what followeth. In all the depth of anguish and sorrow this followeth, as this psalm saith: "Of him cometh my salvation. He is my strength, my salvation, and my defence," &c. The same may we see also in the dialogue between the christian soul, or Christ's church, and Christ, in the book of Solomon's ballads: were she never so black and burned with the sun, were she never so troubled with the vanities of the world, she cried out and said boldly unto Christ, "Draw me; we will run after thee." And although the poor wretched soul be environed and compassed about with sin, troubles, and adversities, as the fair lily is hedged about with thorns; yet she trusteth in her husband, that he will help her. And indeed most comfortably her spouse Christ comforteth her with these marvellous words: "Arise, haste thee, my spouse, my fair one, and come. Now winter is past, the rain is gone and ceased." *Psal. lxii. Cant. i. Consolation.*

That book of Solomon is to be read, to see how mercifully God comforteth a troubled and deformed soul by sin: and yet God layeth it not to the soul's charge, that hath Christ to her husband. Also there is to be seen that the soul is bold to seek and call for help of God her husband, and goeth to no strange god for aid or succour, although she be burned with the sun, and a miserable sinner. The like is to be seen in the prodigal son. Although he was never so beggarly, miserable, sinful, wretched, and unkind to his father; yet he said, Even as I am with my miseries, I will go to my father, and tell him that I have offended against him and against heaven. The father, when he saw him, spat not at him, reviled him not, asked no accounts of the goods he had *Read the book of Solomon's ballads. Prodigal son. Luke xv. Let us not be ashamed to go to our heavenly Father, and confess our sins, be they never so*

[HOOPER, II.]

horrible: for whensoever we return from our wickedness, he remembereth no more our transgressions, but embraceth us as his dear children.

viciously spent, laid not to his charge his filthy conversation with whores and harlots; neither did he cast into his teeth how he had dishonoured him and his family: but when he saw him afar off, he was moved with compassion towards him, ran to meet him, took him about the neck, and kissed him. The son confessed his fault; and the father, minding more the comfort of his lousy and beggarly son than the repetition of his transgressions, commanded his servants speedily to fetch him robes and to clothe him, gave him a ring upon his finger and shoes to his feet, killed his fat calf, and made merry and rejoiced with his lost son, that he was found again. Here is the state and condition of a soul that waiteth (as Asaph saith) for a time upon the Lord in trouble and heaviness, marvellously set forth. See this wretched man spoiled of all his goods, destitute of all friends, shut out of all honest company, of a gentleman become a swineherd, of one that had once men to wait upon him become now a waiter upon pigs; once he gave others meat, and now all men refuse to feed him; erst a man that scarce delicate dishes could content his appetite, now his stomach irketh till it be filled with swine's food: yet moreover than that, he saw nothing behind him nor before him but misery and wretchedness. Behind him he left all his goods spent riotously, his estimation, parentage, such friends as he had; when money was plenty, lost; and also (as far as reason could see) his father's utter displeasure, and the reproach and ignominy of his alliance and kinsfolk purchased for ever. Before him he saw hunger and scarcity, a sort of filthy swine, and the best meat draff and chaff, for the sustenance and maintenance of his piggish life, in case he might have been so maintained: yet, in the midst of these sorrows, attending in his spirit upon the mercy of his father, marvellously in the filth of a pig's sty, and in the pains and anguish of misery, hark what a wonderful doctrine he bloweth out: "Oh, what abundance of bread is there in my father's house, and I starve here for hunger! I will arise, and get me to him, and confess my fault," &c. He saith not, Oh, what abundance of bread hath my brother and my kinsfolk; but, "What abundance of bread is there in my father's house!" He said not, I will make my complaint to my brother; but said, *The heavenly Father is to be resorted* "To my father." Whereof is learned, that all penitent christian sinners do know that the heavenly Father hath the bread of mercy, to satisfy their hungry desire; and that he is to be resorted unto in such sinful and troublesome state, and not any other in heaven, but he alone through Jesus Christ, who was killed to redeem and save the penitent faithful sinners of the world. *unto in the days of necessity and hunger, for he only hath the bread of mercy to feed his children.*

See now how this prodigal and outrageous son knew why he should seek help of his father in the time of his vile misery and wretchedness. *What caused the prodigal son to resort unto his father in the time of misery.*

First, he knew his father's power, and therefore said: "Oh, how great plenty of bread is there in my father's house!" believing that his father was able to give him meat sufficient. Next, he was assured that his father was merciful, and would give him such things as he lacked; and being thus persuaded, boldly he returned unto his father, and to him he uttered all his grief; who was a great deal more prest[1] and ready to help, than his son was ready to ask help. Of the same mind was the woman of Canaan: for although she found little comfort at the first, yet she argued so from the nature of man to the nature of Christ, that Christ cried out upon her, and said, "O woman, great is thy faith; be it unto thee as thou desirest." For when she said, the dogs did "eat of the crumbs that fell from their masters' table," she knew that she herself and all men in respect of God were no more, nor yet so much as dogs in the respect of man. And when she perceived that man could be contented to spare his crumbs to the dogs, she knew right well that man was not so merciful and liberal unto dogs as God unto sinners. Wherefore she stood still with Christ constantly, and left not calling, until Christ gave her to wit that she was indeed a very well persuaded woman, both of his power able to help, and of his good will ready to help. For indeed, although she was a Canaanite, she knew that, if a man shut not out dogs from his table, Christ would not shut from his mercy a sinful Canaanite. The same persuasion made Mary Magdalene creep under the board to his feet with tears, there to receive and eat of his mercy, to quench the hunger and smart of her sins. These examples do declare, why the troubled may put their trust in God: because he is omnipotent, and can do all things; and he is merciful, and will help all penitent and faithful sinners. And so said this prophet Asaph: "Of him cometh my salva- *The woman of Canaan.* *They that come unto Christ must debase themselves with humility.* *Mary Magdalene.* *God is both omnipotent and merciful.*

[1 Prest: prepared.]

tion." And he sheweth the cause why: "For he is my rock, my salvation, and my defence."

These three words declare marvellously the nature of God, that alone helpeth, and also the faith of him that calleth for help.

<small>Rock.</small>

As for God, whom the prophet calleth first his "Rock:" by this word he openeth marvellously how strong, firm, and sure, and how invincible he is, against all troubles, adversities, and tempests, as well of the body as of the soul. In

<small>Matt. vii. He that buildeth upon the rock is wise.</small>

St Matthew, the man that buildeth his house upon the rock or stone is called wise; and the cause is, that what winds soever blow, and what tempests soever arise, they cannot cast down the house, nor overthrow the building; for it is grounded upon the stone. The stone is God and his word, the builder

<small>What is the rock.</small>

is the christian man, and the building is the religion that he hath learned of God by his word. And although we see God, our rock and sure stone, is not assaulted with stormy

<small>If the rock were not sure, the builder and building would come to ruin.</small>

and tempestuous showers and rain; yet the builder and the building, that is to say, the christian man and his religion, be blown at, and such showers of trouble fall upon them, that, were not the rock firm and sure, all the building and the builder also (for man's part) would surely fall and come to

<small>To build the house of God is to teach salvation in Christ.</small>

utter ruin. The experience of the same winds and floods we may see in the Acts of the Apostles. For when Peter and the rest builded the house of God, that is to say, taught men their salvation by the merits and passion of Christ, there

<small>Acts v.</small>

arose such winds and floods, that the builders were put into prison, and the building in great danger. When St Stephen builded the congregation with God's word in Christ, whiles

<small>Acts vii.</small>

he was building, such winds and floods of malice assaulted him, that his brains were knocked out. When Ananias and the rest planted and builded the house of God, that is to say, converted the infidels unto the faith of Christ at Damascus, there arose such winds and tempests at Jerusalem, that Saul

<small>Acts ix.</small>

came from thence towards Damascus with commission from the high priests to kill the builders, and to overthrow all they had builded.

Let us leave off the examples of holy men, and see what happened to the head and chief Captain of all saints and

<small>If Christ had not been the rock of</small>

good builders, our Saviour Jesus Christ. When he called the world from ignorance to knowledge, from death to life, and from damnation to salvation, there arose such winds and storms, that, had he not been the rock itself of strength and invincible power, he had been overthrown clean, and his buildings turned upside down. For before he was of age to be born, in his mother's belly, the devil went about to slander him as a bastard, and would have persuaded the same to the godly man Joseph, spoused in marriage to the blessed virgin Mary. He had no sooner put his head out of his mother's belly, but straightway Herod's sword was whet and bent to kill him. Within a little while after, the devil stirred up his own kinsfolk and countrymen to cast him down from a hill-top, and to break his neck; and at length killed him indeed. But what was the outgoing of this builder? Forsooth, "Father, into thy hands I commend my spirit." And what was the assurance of his building? that is to say, in what surety stood his disciples and followers in the midst of these winds and great storms? Doubtless, Christ commended them to the custody and protection of his heavenly Father, the rock and sure stone of all salvation; from whom winds, floods, temptations, persecution, death, sin, nor the devil himself with all his company of wicked spirits, be able to remove the simplest of all Christ's flock. In the Revelations of St John there is a marvellous doctrine, what winds and floods shall blow and overflow this rock in the building and builders for the time of this life. There is a woman that had brought forth a man child; and by and by there was a foul great red dragon with seven heads and seven[1] horns, that would have devoured this child, before he had come to his inheritance and kingdom appointed unto him. And when he saw he could not prevail against the child, he cast out of his mouth water, as it had been a great stream, after the mother: but there was given her wings to escape. For the rock that she was builded upon was sure; that whatsoever winds or waters (that is to say, what troubles soever) should happen, nothing could overthrow her. And so saith Asaph here: 'God being my rock and sure fortress, my soul nor my body shall never be confounded.' As he declareth more openly by the two words that follow: "He is my strength and my salvation also," saith the prophet: as though he had said, I do not

strength itself, he had been cast down.

Christ was slandered before he was born. Matt. i. ii.

Christ persecuted as soon as he was born.

Christ's own kinsfolk were raised against him. Luke iv.

Christ slain. Luke xxiii.

Christ commended his disciples to the protection of his Father. Matt. vi. John xvii.

Rev. xii.

He that hath God for his rock is assured of a Saviour.

[¹ Ten. See Rev. xii. 3.]

only know God to be sure, strong, and invincible; but also I know this his might, strength, and sureness, is my wealth and my salvation. For many men know that God is the rock and strength of all powers; but none doth know that his power and strength is salvation for himself, but such as be God's indeed.

<small>Application of God's strength by faith to his own defence.</small>

Therefore, seeing this faith, that believeth God particularly to save a private person, is only God's gift, and cometh not of man; let us pray, that when we see how God hath been the rock of salvation to others, that he will be so unto us likewise. For it is a singular gift of God to say boldly, stedfastly, and merrily, from the bottom of the heart unto him, "Thou, Lord, art my rock, my salvation, and my comfort." And he that feeleth in himself, for himself, God to be his salvation, hath such a treasure, that all treasures beside it are nothing to be esteemed; and he will not pass of goods, lands, nor life, for this faith's sake.

<small>Faith is the gift of God.</small>

<small>He that feeleth in himself God to be his salvation, hath the greatest treasure of all.</small>

But faith, as long as it cometh no nearer the heart than the ear, the lips, the teeth, or the tongue, it is but an easy matter to believe; as we see these rumblers up of the psalms and the rest of God's word at this time in the church, where they that say them, nor they that hear them, understand any thing at all, or be any deal the more edified for that which is done or said in the church. And I am assured, if the priests felt in their hearts the vengeance of God to come for this abusing the word of God, and the people knew what an incomparable treasure they have lost by the taking away of the word of God in the vulgar tongue, the priest would weep water of his eyes, as often as he said his service, and the people would sigh full heavily, as oft as they heard it, and understood not what it meant. Wherefore let every man pray to God that he may know him, as the prophet Asaph doth, that he is the rock and salvation to him that so calleth upon him.

<small>The abuse of God's word provoketh his vengeance.</small>

<small>God's word in an unknown tongue amongst the people to be lamented.</small>

The third word is "Defence:" by the which the prophet noteth two marvellous doctrines; the one touching God, and the other touching man. The thing touching God is this: look, as in himself God is omnipotent, so is he of power both in body and soul to do all things for his creatures in general. And as, generally, he can do all things for his creatures, so, particularly, he is salvation to all that by faith believe in him.

<small>Defence. Two Doctrines.</small>

And as he is also salvation, particularly, to such as believe in him; even so, particularly, is he a defence, buckler, and protection of such as shall be saved: that neither sin, the devil, or any troubles of the body, nor troubles, doubtfulness, anguish, perplexity, or heaviness of mind shall hurt or damn him. The doctrine touching man by this word, "Defence," is this: look, as the faithful man hath in himself this general knowledge with all men, that God is almighty to do all things as he lust with his creatures generally; so, particularly, he believeth, that he is able, and will save, such as particularly believe their salvation in him. And as the faithful particularly believeth his salvation to be only in God; so doth he also believe and challenge particularly, with the rest of his brethren in Christ, maintenance, perfection, and defence from all misadventures, jeopardies, and dangers that may happen in this life, before he come to everlasting joys. God, therefore, give us grace with the prophet Asaph to say faithfully unto him, "Thou art my strength, my salvation, and my defence:" then, doubtless, we shall be assured of that which followeth, "So shall I not greatly fall." *[Note. Nothing can hurt him that is in Christ Jesus.]* *[The faithful believeth that as God is able to save generally, so is he to save particularly.]*

Of these words, "So shall I not greatly fall," we be also taught and instructed very necessary lessons and doctrines. First, what difference there is between the defence of God towards his people in this life, and in the life to come.

As touching the defence of God towards his people in this life, it is marvellously set forth by Christ in his prayer a little before his death; where he prayed unto his Father not to take his apostles out of this world, but to preserve them in this world from sin. So that he would his friends, with God's defence, should abide for a time in the world. And what they should have in the world, for all God's defence, Christ told them: "In the world (saith he) ye shall suffer affliction; and ye shall weep, and the world shall laugh." Again he said unto them, that he sent them forth "as sheep amongst wolves." Whereby we may see that God's favour and God's defence saveth not his very elects in this life from troubles and afflictions: for St Paul saith, "As many as will live godly shall suffer persecution." Therefore the Holy Ghost placeth the faithful congregation, the spouse of Christ (whom God loveth and defendeth), amongst thorns and brambles; and sometime likeneth the faithful congregation unto a *[Defence of God towards his people in this life. John xvii.]* *[They that will live in Christ must suffer persecution. John xvi. Matt. x. 2 Tim. iii. Cant. ii.]*

The faithful congregation is likened to a ship, a house, and a woman travailing with child, &c. Matt. vii. xiii. Rev. xii.
ship tossed upon the sea with danger of drowning: sometime unto a house, whereupon bloweth all winds and weather: and sometime to a woman travailing with child, before whom standeth a foul dragon ready to devour both child and mother. So that by this prophet Asaph's words, that saith, "he shall not greatly fall," and by these other places, we learn, that in this life such as God loveth and defendeth from the eternal fire of hell be, notwithstanding, for this life under

John xvi.
great crosses and wonderful troubles: yet Christ willeth us to be of good comfort, for he hath "overcome the world." And the prophet saith, "God is my rock and my salvation: I shall

Who do suffer in this world greatest troubles. Prov. iii. Heb. xii. Rev. iii. 1 Pet. iv. Rom. viii.
not greatly fall." And to consider the truth, such as God most strongly defendeth, and best loveth in this world, suffer many times greatest troubles. Yea, and God beginneth with his friends sometimes first and most sharply, as St Peter saith. And St Paul saith, "We be predestinate to be made like unto Christ in troubles, whiles we be in this troublesome world."

Consolation Cant. ii.
But the defence of God and his love in the world to come is void from all bitterness and pain, and from all troubles and adversities; as it is most comfortably and joyfully written in the ballads of Solomon, where (for a time) the Lord defended his spouse that stood in the midst of sharp and prick-

They whom God calleth of mercy out of this life be void of all troubles.
ing briers and thorns: at length he calleth her to perpetual rest and consolation, assuring her that the winter is gone, and the tempestuous showers past; the sweet flowers do appear, and the pleasant voice of the turtle is heard: meaning, that such as be loved and kept by God in the world of bliss to come be sequestered and departed from all troubles and adversities. The like may you see in the Revelations of St John, wherein he, mystically to set forth the pleasantness and

Rev. xxi.
unspeakable joys of heaven, saith, "It is paved with precious stones, and the gates thereof be also of pearls." And more-

The description of the heavenly joys.
over, "There is a light more lighter than the sun or moon; for the clarity[1] of God lighteneth it, and the brightness is the Lamb of God. There shall the elects dwell for ever, and the gates shall never be shut, neither shall there be any night

The defence of God towards his in the life to come. Isai. lxvi.
there to trouble it." The same is to be seen also in Esay the prophet, how in that life God's defence is, in such as be saved, without all kinds of troubles and adversities.

[1 Clarity: brightness.]

Now here is to be noted, that as God's favour and defence in the world to come, in such as be saved, is void of all troubles and adversities; even so God's favour and his defence in this world, in such as shall be saved, is joined and annexed with troubles and adversities. Let us therefore be content with trouble and persecution in his favour here in this life, or else doubtless we shall never have his favour and defence in the life to come in joy and everlasting consolation.

The favour of God towards his in this world is annexed with troubles.

There is yet another learning in these words, "I shall not greatly fall:" that is, that the children of God shall not perish for any kind of trouble, and yet in this world they can lack no kind of affliction. All shall they suffer; and yet at length overcome all, as this prophet Asaph did: he was troubled, but yet not overcome: he fell, but not so far that he arose not again; and he was so troubled with the cross that God sent him, that he could speak nothing for the time; yet at length he said, God was his sure rock and his salvation. Thus God tempteth his, but desperation he leaveth to his enemies. God suffereth his to feel in this world the punishment of sin, but he reserveth the pain thereof in the world to come to his enemies and to the reprobates. He maketh his to be sorry for sin in this world; but such as be not his he suffereth to be careless and painless of sin in this life, that their damnation may be the more dolorous in the world to come. Therefore, blessed be such as fall and fear, as the prophet Asaph saith, but not too far, unto all wickedness and wantonness of life.

Trouble shall not overcome God's children.

Desperation God leaveth only to his enemies.

Note the difference between God's children and such as be not his.

THE THIRD PART.

3. "How long will ye imagine mischief against a man? Ye shall be slain all the sort of you: yea, as a tottering wall shall ye be, and like a broken hedge.
4. "Their device is only how to put him out whom God will exalt; their delight is in lies; they give good words with their mouth, but curse with their hearts."

The third part sheweth how the persecutors of the innocent shall suddenly perish.

By the similitude and metaphor of a tottering or quivering wall, the prophet declareth how lightly and suddenly the Lord will destroy the persecutors of his people: for as the

The wicked persecutors be as a tottering wall, suddenly

wall that is tottering and quivering with every wind and weather is easily and suddenly overthrown; even so be the wicked and tyrannical persecutors suddenly destroyed; yea, when they be in their own conceits most strong and valiant: as it may be seen by the mighty host of Senecharib and Benedab, the army of king Pharaoh and such other, that persecuted the people of God, verily supposing their strength to have been able utterly to have oppressed God's people, whom they hated. The like is to be seen where Hesther and Judith, two seely and poor women, were instruments to overtumble and destroy the wicked Hamon and proud Holofernes. So by this we learn, that the strength and persecutions of the wicked be not permanent nor strong, but transitory and feeble, destroyed and vanquished with the presence of God's favour towards his, as often as it pleaseth him to punish the malice and mischief of the wicked.

overthrown in their most prosperity.

Sennacherib.
Benhadad. 1 Kings xx. 2 Kings viii. xviii. xix. Exod. xiv.
Esth. vii.
Judith xiii.
Holofernes.
The presence of God's favour towards his is the destruction of the wicked.

But there is one learning particularly to be noted in this similitude of a trembling or tottering wall, wherewithal the prophet setteth forth the fall and confusion of the wicked, which is this, that when the wicked persecuteth the godly, and that the least resistance of the world is stirred up by God against them, the Lord, that stirreth up the plague to punish them, striketh also their hearts with such trembling and fear, that one man in a good cause shall be able to withstand ten such wicked persecutors, whose conscience God hath so feared, that they are not able to bear the countenance of a man; no, not able to overcome the terror of their own spirit, which beareth them record, that, as they in time past have fought against God and his cause, so now God justly fighteth against them, both with the fear of hell-fire towards their souls, and with outward adversities towards their bodies. So God said he would send such trembling and fear unto such as neither loved nor kept his laws, as it is written by the holy prophet Moses. The example whereof ye may read also in Daniel the prophet, that the emperor of the Chaldees, when he was in the midst of his strength, mirth, banquets, and jollity, saw no more but a poor little hand write in the wall of his palace, that never spake word, shewed no terrible sight of men of war, nor gave any blow in his palace; yet fell the emperor into such a trembling and fear at the sight thereof, that all his limbs (in manner) stood him in no stead. Christ never

God doth so strike the hearts of the wicked with fear, that one man in a good cause is able to withstand ten.

Note.

Deut. xxviii.

Dan. v. A handwriting in the wall feared the emperor of the Chaldees in his most jollity.

gave blow, but modestly asked his murderers whom they sought for; and yet fell they flat and prostrate to the ground. So that the wicked persecutors of the godly be aptly and properly likened and compared to a tottering and trembling wall. For as soon as ever the blasts of God's ire and judgment be moved and kindled against them, they be so quivering and comfortless, that they would take them to be most their friends that soonest would dispatch them out of the world; as Christ said aptly of them, they should pray the mountains to fall upon them. As long as God feigneth himself asleep, and suffereth the blessed to fall into the hands of the wicked to be crucified and slain as they please, they be more strong and more cruel than lions; but when God ariseth, and taketh the defence of his poor people, then they be more fearful than the hart or trembling hare: as we may see when seely, harmless Jacob passed homeward into his country from Mesopotamia, such as he never gave blow nor spake foul word unto trembled at his coming, as though he had been in battle with thousands of soldiers. The like may we see by the brothers of Joseph; when he spake most gently unto them, yea, and told them that he was their brother, there was such a terror and fear strake their consciences for persecuting of him, that they could make no word of answer. When the children of Israel should come into the land of Canaan, the Lord said he would send before them his fear, to amaze and astonish the people of the country, that their strength should do them no harm.

 The fury of the wicked may seem in his own eyes to be stable, firm, and constant, but indeed there is nothing more trembling nor tottering; as we may see at this present day. Such as persecute the lively and seely flock of Christ, and tyrannously hold the neck of the godly under the yoke of idolatry, they have no ground, no certainty, nor any assurance more than flesh and blood that favour them, by whose favour they oppress the truth, and persecute the lovers of it: so that, in case flesh and blood should fail them, then would they be in such trembling and quivering, that they would do whatsoever they were commanded to do, to be delivered from fear and terror. As we may mark and see in the bishop of Winchester, Gardiner, and also Bonner, the bishop of London. When king Henry the eighth suspected

[margin:] John xviii. Christ asking his murderers whom they sought, they fell upon the ground.

[margin:] Luke xxiii.

[margin:] Note diligently.

[margin:] Jacob. Gen. xliii. [xxxv.]

[margin:] Joseph.

[margin:] The children of Israel. Exod. xxiii.

[margin:] They that persecute Christ's flock at this present have no assurance but flesh and blood.

[margin:] Stephen Gardiner. Edmund Bonner.

them both to be favourers of the pope (the capital enemy of Christ and his church), Winchester fell into such a trembling and fear, that with all haste he wrote his purgation in a book named, *True Obedience*[1]; and Bonner set an epistle before it, both they crying out against the pope, as against a tyrant and false usurper of authority in this realm, although they thought nothing less. Thus we may see how inconstant, trembling, and quaking these tottering, wicked persecutors of God's word be. I could declare more of their religion to be of the same conditions; but because these two, and Tunstall, the bishop of Durham, be known openly to the world by their books to be such, I speak only of them.

<small>A Book De Vera Obedientia.</small>

<small>Read Tunstall's sermon against the bishop of Rome and the treason of Cardinal Pole.</small>

When the prophet hath declared that the persecutors of the godly shall suddenly perish, he telleth the cause why they shall perish: "Because they devise how to put him down (saith he) whom God will exalt." And after that the prophet hath shewed that the cause of their fall and punishment is their conspiracy against God's elect, he setteth forth by what means the wicked use to depose, persecute, and tumble down the people of God: "By lies (saith the prophet), and by imagining of falsehood and untruth." And when he hath declared that the wicked do purpose to bring their case and matter against the godly with lies, he sheweth after what sort and fashion lies by wicked men be used: "to bring mischief to purpose." This is the letter of the psalm concerning the third part of it. Now there is in every of these sentences profit to be gathered by the reader or hearer of it.

<small>Why shall the persecutors of the godly perish.</small>

<small>By what means do the wicked put down the people of God.</small>

First is to be noted the conspiracy and treason of the wicked against God. If it please the Lord to favour and advance one, the nature of the wicked is, as much to deface that God would have honoured as may be. As God bare favour and advanced Abel, Cain wrought treason, and killed his brother, for the love that God did bear him. The Lord appointed Samuel to rule; the wicked misliked that which God best approved. God would exalt David; Saul, Absalom, and Achitophel would prefer themselves. Again, the Lord appointed Noah to teach the people to beware of the universal flood; the people preferred liars, unto whom God never gave

<small>Cain. Abel. Gen. iv.</small>

<small>1 Sam. viii. xviii. 2 Sam. xv.</small>

<small>Gen. vi. vii.</small>

[1 See Brown's Fasciculus Rerum, Vol. II. Also Burnet's Hist. of Reform. Vol. I. Book III. and Vol. II. Book II.]

his holy Spirit. God elected Jeremy the true prophet; the people advanced Passur the false prophet. The Lord exalted his dear Son, and willed the world to learn of him; the people preferred the Pharisees, and desired the judge to hang Christ. God commanded his word only to be taught; but the world plucketh it so down, that either they clean refuse the word, or else they will have it none otherwise than it is authorised and made true by man. God saith, "That which is wisdom before the world is foolishness before him:" the world recompenseth most arrogantly God with the like, and accounteth all his wisdom and learning foolishness, in respect of worldly wisdom, counsel, and religion. But what saith the prophet Asaph shall become of these Nemrods and controllers of God? "They shall (saith he) quickly fall, and be destroyed as a tottering wall." Here we see how controlling and amending of God's works at length speedeth, and what is the end of these persecuting giants of God's afflicted. They fight, they fare foul, they move heaven and earth to alter the purpose and mind of God; but "He that sitteth in heaven laugheth them to scorn." And they themselves that thus wickedly use Christ and his members fall down and come to nought, as old, rotten, and dusty walls.

<small>Jer. xx.</small>

<small>Matt. iii. xvii. xxvii.</small>

<small>John v. 1 Cor. i.</small>

<small>What shall become of the controllers of God.</small>

<small>God laugheth the intent of the wicked to scorn. Psal. ii.</small>

And in the other part, that these shameless tyrants conspire thus against Christ and his people by lies and falsehood, is declared the filthiness of their conscience, that be so far past shame and honesty, that they care not (so they may obtain their wicked purpose) how craftily or falsely they lie or calumniate any sayings or doings of God or man: as the devil, their father, when God had exalted man into paradise, he wished him out of it, and began to work man's destruction with calumniating and false lying upon God's own word. When God had set up David to reign, Absalom, his own son, thinking the better to pull his father down, lied falsely upon him to the people, and said that there was no judge appointed in Israel to hear causes and to end them between man and man. So slandered he his father, a man of good justice, and advanced himself, that never knew what justice meant. The good prophet Elias likewise, whom God appointed to warn the people to beware of sin, king Ahab, to disgrace him, lied falsely upon him, and said that he was the troubler of the commonwealth. So Christ, whom God had elected to save

<small>So the wicked may obtain their purpose, they care not by what means.</small>

<small>Gen. iii. By what means the devil deceived Adam.</small>

<small>David. Absalom. 2 Sam. xv.</small>

<small>Elias. Ahab. 1 Kings xviii.</small>

<small>Christ.</small>

the world from death and damnation, the wicked sort of the world said, "He hath saved others, but he cannot save himself." Again, God sent him to be amongst the troubled to comfort them; but such as wanted consolation, when they saw him, prayed him to depart out of their country; because with his presence they lost their swine. God said that Paul was the chosen vessel, to bear the name of him through all the gentiles: Tertullus and the other Jews said he was one that molested all the world. Even so at this time there is neither honest nor virtuous man, that God exalteth to speak the truth, but the wicked saith he is an heretic, a schismatic, and a traitor. But seeing it is none other than always hath been accustomed falsely to be laid to such as God loveth, it must be borne patiently.

But now the prophet sheweth how these liars and envious persecutors use their lies: "They give fair words with their mouth (saith the prophet), but they curse with their heart." By these words we may learn that there are three manner of ways that lies do harm: the one, when they be openly and plainly used; the other, when open falsehood outwardly is cloked with pretended truth; and the third, when they be dissembled outwardly, and yet in the heart they lie hid, tarrying for a time when they may be put abroad to do mischief, and to work the destruction of the godly. But forasmuch as the devil, the father of all lies, knoweth that such as he inspireth with lies cannot do harm with his lies, except they be used as the persons be qualified amongst whom the lies must be sown, he teacheth his disciples to use them as opportunity and occasion shall serve.

Manifest and uncovered lies he causeth to be used amongst such as do not know nor love the truth; for those lies shall stablish and confirm the wicked in their error and wickedness. As for example: Absalom and Achitophel told the people as many lies (in manner) as they did words, against king David; and when they were by Absalom's fair words alienated from king David, and bent unto his son, because he promised to use justice to every man and lawful favour; after Absalom came to Hebron, and had of his side Achitophel, his father's chief counsellor, he lied openly, and the people more and more were stablished in error and treason.

The like is to be seen in the book of the Numbers, that when such as returned out of the land of Canaan, whither they were sent to view the goodness and strength of the country, ten of the twelve espies brought the people into such a terror and fear, that they thought it impossible to recover the land. Thus being in an error, manifest lies against God, Moses, Joshua, and Caleb, might be used well enough and prevail. *Numb. xiii. Moses. Joshua. Caleb.*

In matters of religion is the same, amongst such as be deceived and in error; manifest lies do take place, and do as much harm as the devil requireth to be wrought by them. As amongst the Chaldees, such as most commended the idol of fire were most esteemed. Amongst the Egyptians, such as most blasphemously could speak in the defence of witchcraft and sorcery were taken for the best men. Such as could best defend the honour of Baal, amongst the idolatrical Jews, had most reverence and honour. Amongst the Pharisees, he that could most speak for the maintenance of men's traditions was taken for the worthiest man. And now amongst the papists, he that can best defend papistical idolatry and superstition is highest preferred. But (as I said) this use of lies and falsehood takes place in none but in such as the devil (the god of this world) will not suffer to have the word of truth known. And this use of lies and falsehood doth not train men unto error and heresy, but stablisheth men in them that do not know the truth. *Manifest lies in matters of religion. Gen. xi. Exod. vi. vii. viii. 1 Kings xvi. xvii. xviii. Matt. xv. Amongst the papists, defenders of idolatry be preferred. 2 Cor. iv.*

There is another sort of people, which be the faithful, at whom the devil hath indignation, and laboureth with all diligence to deceive; against whom the use of manifest lies, he knoweth, cannot prevail: for such as do know and love the truth do abhor falsehood. Wherefore, if the devil prevail against them, it is by another use of lies than he used to the other sort of the world.

This use of lies is of two sorts; as we see by the word of God. The one is to make an evil thing to appear good, under the pretence of good; and a false thing to appear true, under the pretence of truth. As we may see how the devil, under the pretence of good and profit unto Eve, made her eat of the apple which was forbidden. Cain, under the pretence of friendship, brought Abel into the field, and killed him. Saul, under the pretence of amity, bade David to *The use of lies amongst the faithfulless. Gen. iii. iv. Eve. Cain. 1 Sam xviii. Saul.*

feast, and so meant to have slain him. Absalom, under the colour of justice and love to the commonwealth, sought his father's death, and made his subjects traitors: with many more such examples in the word of God. Whereby is declared, that the devil, by his disciples, useth lies many ways: sometime to stablish men in error that be in error already: sometime to deceive such as be in the truth; but then manifest lies be not used, but rather lies conveyed, covered, and cloked with the mantle of truth and verity; as we may see by the examples before specified: howbeit, many times this use of lies, howsoever it pretendeth truth, cannot deceive men. Then, rather than the devil will miss of his purpose, he teacheth another use of lies, which is more dangerous and painful to the godly than any yet before mentioned of: of the which use the prophet Asaph speaketh in this place, saying, "They speak fair with their tongues, but think evil in their hearts." This is a perilous kind and use of lies; for it doth one of these two great mischiefs, or else both of them: that is to say, either at length it overcometh the truth, or else mortally persecuteth the truth that will not be overcome. As we may see by Esau: he used a great while fair speech and gentle manners with Jacob his brother; but in his heart he said, "If my father die, I will kill my brother." Again, Absalom spake fair to his father, and asked him leave to go to Hebron, to pay there the sacrifice that he promised, whilst he was in Gessur of Syria, unto God; but, in his heart, he went thither to raise king David his father's subjects against him. Certain came to Christ, and said, "Master, we know that thou art true, and that thou teachest the ways of God in truth;" yet, in their hearts, they came to trip him in a case of treason, if they could.

This use of lies is very dangerous; for it lieth in the heart hid secretly, expecting and looking for time convenient, when and how it may break forth to serve the turn: yet is the devil the father of lies, and the temple of the devil the wicked man's and woman's hearts, wherein they lie ashamed or afraid to utter them; but holdeth outwardly with the truth, which inwardly they mortally hate, until they may take occasion to do outwardly as they would. And we see it in Cain, Esau, Absalom, the Pharisees, and others. Yea, our own age hath too good experience of this use of lies: for how many within this twelvemonths spake fair of God and his word, and shewed themselves outwardly as friendly as could be unto them; but what their conscience and hearts were inwardly, now it appeareth. Doubtless, that they hated deadly in their spirits that they most extolled with their mouths; for now they be gone from the truth outwardly, which inwardly they never loved. And by the use of their lies they train as many as they may to be partakers of their evils; and such as they cannot by the use of lies draw unto their sect, by violence and tyranny they persecute, and compel with extreme punishment and hatred in lands, goods, and body. *The amiable countenances of the papists in king Edward's days be turned now into fiery faces.*

Thus may we see by this prophet Asaph, which way the wicked persecuted the godly, and molested the seely members of Christ, that wished all men good, and no men harm, even with lies and falsehood, and used many crafty and subtle ways. Whereof we be not instructed by the prophet only to know this poison of the devil concerning lies, and the divers and manifold use and practice of them; but also, that the Christians be most in danger of them, yet must be contented for Christ's sake to bear them, and circumspectly to beware they be not deceived by them.

THE FOURTH PART.

5. "Nevertheless, my soul, wait thou still upon God; for my help is in him.
6. "He truly is my strength and my salvation; he is my defence, so that I shall not fall.
7. "In God is my health and my glory, the rock of might; and in God is my trust.
8. "O put your trust in him always, ye people; pour out your hearts before him: for God is our hope. Selah."

The fourth part repeateth more at large the declaration of the first and the second part.

The fifth and sixth verses be word for word as the first and the second were: only there is left out in these two verses this word "greatly;" for before he said, he should not "greatly" fall. The which word may be taken two ways very comfortable of the reader and hearer, if it be well marked and believed.

<small>The people of God do fall.
Prov. xxiv.
1 John i.</small>

The first way is, that the prophet meaneth not that the people of God shall not fall, for that is against the scripture; for "The just man falleth seven times in the day." Again, "If we say we have no sin in us, we deceive ourselves, and the truth is not in us." Now, whereas sin inseparably dwelleth (as it doth) in all men, whilst they live upon the earth, there be faults and falls before God of the man's part, in whom

<small>The sins of the faithful be not imputed unto them for Christ's sake.</small>

this sin dwelleth: yet God of his mercy, for the blood and death of Christ, doth not account these inseparable sins to be falls; but loveth the person, preserveth him, and will not impute nor lay any of those falls or faults unto his charge, but in Christ esteem him justified and clean, as though he were of

<small>Rom. viii.
Justification.
Note.
Rom. viii.</small>

himself so indeed. And thus the prophet saith, that of God's part, and by our acceptation into his favour through Christ, the faithful falleth not: that is to say, his sin is not accounted damnable, nor laid to his charge, for Christ's sake: as St Paul writeth to the Romans.

<small>He that standeth fast of God's election cannot fall to damnation.</small>

Another way it may be taken: that a Christian hath testimony in his spirit by the Spirit of God, that he is so elected, chosen, and ordained of God to eternal salvation, that whatsoever the world, the flesh, the devil, or sin shall do, yet standeth he assured of God's election, grace, strength, and fidelity, that he shall never fall to damnation, but arise again, and be called from his falls, whatsoever they be. And yet this most sure and comfortable knowledge will not give him licence nor liberty to sin, but rather keep him in a fear and love of the strong and mighty God, in whose hands he is, and kept from the great fall of eternal damnation, from the which he was delivered from the beginning with God. So that ye may learn of this place, what perseverance is in the meditation and contemplation of God's most holy word and promises. At first they seem unto the flesh things impossible, as we may

<small>Nicodemus.
John iii.</small>

see by Nicodemus, who was as ignorant as could be at the beginning, when he came first to school to Christ. But when

<small>The longer a man is at school, the more sweetness in learning doth he feel.</small>

a man hath been exercised awhile in it, he feeleth more sweetness in the promises of God: as we see by this prophet. For after he had borne the cross of affliction a little while, and learned the nature of God, how merciful he is to sinners, he said, "Although I fall, yet it shall not be greatly." But when he had tarried in the school of Christ, and learned indeed what he was, and how that he was able to perform his mercy, he said plainly, whatsoever sin, the devil, the world, the flesh, hell, heaven, or the earth would say against him, he should not fall. These two interpretations are to be noted; for whichsoever we use, we may find comfort and unspeakable consolation.

Now, when he hath declared that he shall not fall into God's eternal ire and displeasure, he sheweth how this certainty of eternal salvation came unto him; and why God so mercifully and strongly hath warded and fenced him against all temptations and perils of damnation. It is (saith he) because God is his health; that is to say, one that hath not only taken him from the sickness and danger of sin, the tyranny of the devil, and damnation of the law, but also preserveth him in the same state, that he fall not again into the sickness and peril that he was delivered from. Whereof we learn, that it is not man's labours, nor man's works, that helpeth a sinner, and saveth a damnable soul; but it is the free work and undeserved mercy of Almighty God. Wherefore we be taught that there is no health but in God alone. *Why shall not the godly fall.* *Health.* *The mercy of God, and not man's work, saveth a sinner.*

Then saith the prophet also, that in God is his "glory." Of the which word he noteth two things; the one, touching God alone, and the other, touching God and himself. The glory that toucheth God alone is, that this troubled prophet pondered, in the heaviness and anguish of his mind, the number and strength of his enemies, the devil, the flesh, sin, the world, and the bitter accusation of God's laws, that truly accused and painfully grieved his conscience for sin. Of the other side, in faith he considered how the scripture declared that God was merciful, even unto the greatest sinners of the world. And he learned also by the word of God, that God had made promise unto sinners to be merciful. He considered further, that God had many times used and practised his mercy towards sinners. And he found likewise by the scripture, that God, to perform his mercy, would not spare his own dearly beloved Son, to redeem man from his sin with his own precious blood and painful death. *Glory.* *Note.*

Thus weighing the strength of the devil and sin in the one part to damn, and the strength of God's mercy in Christ *The afflicted Christian that believeth the*

Jesus on the other part to save; and perceiving the riches, abundance, and strength of God's mercy to be more available to save than all the power and strength of the devil and sin to damn, for the great victory that God taketh over such strong enemies; the prophet triumpheth in the glory of God joyfully and thankfully; extolling him for his mercy and power, that hath broken the serpent's head, and spoiled him of his prisoners. So we use to do, when any man by valiantness defendeth us from our enemies: we extol and magnify him for his victory and conquest. This glory gave the prophet Asaph in this psalm to God, when by faith he saw God conquering of hell, sin, the devil, the accusation of the law, desperation, the flesh, and the world. And the same glory giveth every faithful creature unto God at the end of the Lord's prayer, when he saith: "For thine is the kingdom, the power, and the glory." By the which words we know that, howsoever the devil and wicked people take upon them to usurp by violence, war, and tyranny, and live never so princely in pomp and pride, they be but usurpers, if they come to it wrongfully; for the kingdom appertaineth unto God: and howsoever they extend their power, in God's sight they be no stronger than a bruised reed or broken staff; for the power is God's: and what glory soever they feign and flatter themselves to have, it is but withered hay and vile dust in the sight of God.

But now the prophet, by the eye of faith seeing this glorious triumph, strength, and power in God, saith, that in this glorious, almighty, and triumphant God is his glory, and desireth to have part of that victory and of that marvellous majesty. And as the psalm saith, he calleth and nameth the God of glory his glory. O marvellous and unspeakable boldness and constancy of faith! A man, nothing but sin by nature, in the sight of God nothing but earth and ashes, replenished with all misery and wretchedness, by nature corrupt, the very enemy of God, a vessel prepared unto all dishonour, ignominy, shame, and perdition, contemned through sin, and shamed before all creatures; and yet now, with all these dishonours, by faith saith the King of glory is his glory, and the conqueror of all dishonour is his shield and buckler. Of the other part, who can think or speak any thing thankful to such a King of glory and most mighty conqueror, that abhorreth not, of mercy, to be the honour and glory of so vile, sinful, and wretched a thing as man is? whose eyes abhor no filth of sin in penitent sinners, whose presence refuseth not the company of the sick and miserable, whose strength comforteth the weak, whose mercy rejoiceth the comfortless, whose life expelleth death, whose health banisheth sickness, whose love vanquisheth hatred, whose immortality giveth everlasting life, and who crowneth us with endless pity and compassion in joys perpetual. Consolation.
Psal. ciii.

Thus the prophet, after he had espied the Almighty God in himself gloriously to be void of all troubles, dolours, and other adversities, and that he had also conquered gloriously the captains of all adversities, hell, death, Satan, and sin, he challenged by faith, and craved by God's promise, to be partaker of God's glory in this point. And doubtless, he that can feel in his heart that God is his glory, he shall take no dishonour nor shame by all the works of the devil, sin, or the world. Therefore many times, in reading or thinking of the psalms, or other part of the holy scripture, it is expedient to meditate and pray, that the word we speak or pray may be unto us as much salvation, comfort, and glory, as we perceive God hath appointed in it for us. And when we say with our mouth to God, "Thou art my salvation, my glory, my rock, and my trust;" let us cry, "Lord, increase our faith; help us for thy name's sake constantly to believe thee to be unto us indeed in spirit, as we speak of thee outwardly with our mouth." For in case the heart understand not, nor believe the word we speak with our mouth, we honour God in vain, as the scripture saith. Let us therefore pray, as St Paul teacheth us, saying, "I will pray with the spirit, and I will pray with the mind also." O lively faith!

Luke xvii.

Isai. xxix.
Matt. xv.
1 Cor. xiv.

When the prophet hath by faith assured himself of God's favour, he exhorteth all the christian congregation to do the same, saying: "O put your trust in him always, ye people," &c. Here the prophet teacheth what the minister of the church, bishop, and others should do, when they understand the scripture, and learn by it fear and faith, love and hope in God: they be bound to teach the congregation the same scriptures for her salvation. Whereby is condemned the use of the scripture in an unknown tongue; which is directly against God's word. And here be kings and rulers also Exhortation.

What is the office of the pastor when he understandeth the scriptures.

1 Cor. xiv.

taught to see their subjects, tenants, and servants to understand the word of God; likewise the father and the mother, the master and the mistress, who be bound to know for their salvation the word of God, and to teach it unto others under their governance. Therefore, in the end of the verse is put "Selah"; as though he had said, Happy be those that put their trust in the Lord, and teach other to do the same; and cursed be those that trust not in the Lord, and teach others to do the like.

Marginal note: The office of kings and magistrates, parents and masters.

THE FIFTH PART.

9. "As for the children of men, they are but vain: the children of men are deceitful upon the weights; they are altogether lighter than vanity itself.
10. "O trust not in wrong and robbery; give not yourselves to vanity: if riches increase, set not your heart upon them."

The fifth part sheweth, how man's power is not to be trusted unto.

The prophet by no means would have men to put their trust in flesh and blood; in case they do, they must needs perish. For when miserable man shall trust in vain vanity, which is man, he can be no less than vanity itself, in whom he hath trusted. And this is one misery and wretchedness, a man to be deceived of help and succour, where as he most trusted to have been holpen and succoured. Thus must it needs happen to them that trust in men. For men of most excellency and greatest authority, riches, and power in the world, be but vanity, as the prophet saith. Now as they be, so is their help; and as their help is, so is the comfort and consolation of such as seek help at their hands. Those that be trusted unto be but flesh and blood: the best of flesh and blood is but vanity: the consolation and help of vanity is misery and wretchedness: wherefore the prophet exhorteth all men to beware they seek not aid and comfort of man, for he is but vain. The Israelites used for their help against their enemies the Egyptians; but the more flesh conspired together, the worse success had all the battles they fought. Now as we see, men that have their trust in men suffer much trouble and misery in the world, because their help they

Marginal notes: No trust in flesh and blood. Note. As man is, so is his help. Note diligently. The Israelites used the Egyptians for help.

trust in is of inferior strength and power to the troubles and adversities that they be cumbered withal. So doth the word of God declare, that such men as trust in vanity have not only worldly adversities against them, but also for their so doing (trusting in flesh) they be accursed of God, as the scriptures say: "Cursed be he that trusteth in man." So that we see marvellous and unspeakable harms come of the trust in man: first, miseries of the world; and next, the enmity and curse of God: for he that putteth his trust in man with the same one fact and doing doth two horrible evils: the one, he deceiveth himself; for the vanity that he trusteth in cannot save him: and the other, he dishonoureth God, that only can save, in putting his trust in mortal man, that cannot save, and so maketh of man God, to God's high displeasure and dishonour. Every christian man therefore should forsake flesh and blood, and trust in the Lord Almighty, maker of heaven and earth, as the prophet Asaph did a little before, when he said, in God was his glory, who could defend him from all hurts present, past, and to come, whatsoever they were. The like may we see in St Paul, that said: "God forbid that I should glory in any thing, saving in the cross of our Lord Jesus Christ, by whom the world is crucified unto me, and I unto the world:" that is, because I put all my trust of salvation (saith St Paul) in him that was crucified, the world taketh me for an heretic, and so persecuteth me; but yet it overcometh me not, neither taketh it away my glory, my consolation, and my crown of eternal joys. For even as the world persecuteth me with fire, sword, and all other crucifyings, so I crucify the world again, testifying by the word of God, that their living is naught, and their faith and trust worse. So that, as they crucify me with worldly trouble, in like manner I crucify the world again with the word of God, and speak against it, bearing testimony that it is the enemy of God, and shall perish eternally: but this I do (saith Paul), "because I glory in nothing, saving in Christ crucified." Thus doth the prophet Asaph teach all men to put their trust in Christ, and not in sinful man; which is not only vanity, but also, 'if vanity were laid in one balance, and man in the other, yet, of both, man were the more vanity. Therefore man is not to be trusted unto,' saith the prophet.

An inferior medicine to the disease cannot cure the patient.

Jer. xvii.

What doth come of the trust in man.

Two evils.

Gal. vi.

A goodly explanation of Paul's words, "God forbid that I should glory in, &c."

Man more vain than vanity.

<style>.marginalia { float: left; font-size: small; width: 10em; }</style>

Why man is more vain than vanity.

And for a further declaration that man is more vain than vanity, he openly declareth in the process of his psalm, that man is given, besides vanity, to wrong and robbery, which two evils do increase man's miseries. For man is not only born vain vanity, but also by process of time in wicked living addeth wrong and robbery unto vanity, and so maketh vanity more vain and damnable than it was before.

Whoso trusteth in anything saving in God, doth dishonour God. Wrong done unto God.

Hosea ii. Jer. xliv.

Now this robbery and wrong is done two manner of ways, to God and to man. He that putteth his trust of salvation in any other thing, saving in God, loseth not only his salvation, but also robbeth God of his glory, and doth God (as much as lieth in him) manifest wrong: as the wicked people amongst the Jews did, that said, as long as they honoured and trusted unto the queen of heaven, all things prospered with them; but when they hearkened to the true preachers of God's word, they said all things came into worse state, and that with scarcity and trouble they were overwhelmed.

What doth he that believeth any doctrine besides God's word.

He that putteth also his trust and confidence in any learning or doctrine besides God's word, doth not only fall into error, and lose the truth; but also, as much as lieth in him, he robbeth God's book of his sufficient truth and verity, and ascribeth it to the books of men's decrees; which is as much wrong to God and his book, as may be thought or done: in the which robbery (or rather sacrilege) no man should put his trust, as the prophet saith.

Wrong done unto man.

Another way wrongs be done unto man, when the rich and sturdy of the world, by abusing of friendship, oppress, rob, and spoil the poor. And by his thus doing, first, he deceiveth himself; for evil-gotten goods cannot long prosper, neither can any family advanced by fraud, craft, or subtlety, long time endure. Then, he deceiveth the simple and poor that trusteth upon the outward shew of his port and estimation, which glittereth in the world as a vain-glorious and deceivable beauty and honour; and marketh neither how wickedly the glory of the robber and doer of wrong sprang up, nor how miserably God hath ordained it to fall again: but seeing carnally, he seeth a vain man in vanity prosper for a time; he trusteth in this vanity, pampered up with robbery and wrong, until such time as vanity vadeth, and he much lamenteth that put in vanity so much vain hope. But grant that honour and riches by God's gift and truth abound; yet were they not given for men to trust in, but for men to give God more thanks, and to help the poor with them from injuries of oppression, and need of hunger, thirst, and poverty. Therefore the prophet saith: "Although riches do abound, yet men should not put their hearts upon them:" that is to say, men should not trust in them, nor keep them otherwise than their use or keeping should serve to the glory of God; in abundance to be liberal, and in time of need to be careful; not to keep them for a private commodity, but, as Joseph did say, to save the multitude from scarcity and penury. Thus doth the prophet exhort all men to beware they put not their trust in men; for both they and all that they have of worldly things be transitory, vain, and inconstant. *(margin: Why riches are given unto man.)* *(margin: Gen. xli.)*

THE SIXTH PART.

11. "God spake once, and twice I have also heard the same, that power belongeth unto God:
12. "And that thou, Lord, art merciful; for thou rewardest every man according to his work."

The sixth part containeth how that God hath promised to help the afflicted, &c.

Job hath the same phrase and manner of speech: "The Lord spake once, and will not repeat the same again:" that is as much to say, as that the word of God is so sure, that it cannot be made frustrate, nor changed by any means. So saith this prophet Asaph, "God spake once," which standeth sure for ever, and cannot be altered. *(margin: Job xxxiii. Note.)*

This word of God hath relation to the verses before: wherein be opened the vanity of man, or insufficiency to help himself or others in trouble, which cannot be changed, nor ever shall be, but as¹ flesh is vanity, be it never so holy: as Adam called his best son and holy martyr Abel, that is to say in the Hebrew tongue, vanity; perfectly knowing that all flesh by sin was vile and vain, and therefore not to be trusted unto. *(margin: Gen. iv. Abel in Hebrew in English is vanity.)*

This "once" speaking of God is also referred unto the text that followeth, which declareth two virtues in God,

[¹ As, probably a misprint for *all*.]

How God doth reward every man after his works.

power and mercy; power to punish his enemies, and mercy to recompense his faithful afflicted. And this is so true, that it shall never be made false; the wicked to feel God's strength in damnation, and the faithful to feel God's mercies in salvation; not because their works deserve it, but because God of his mercy so contented to bless the poor faithful workman. So he giveth each man after his works, the evil hell-fire by justice, and the good heaven's bliss by mercy.

Now the prophet saith he heard it twice at God's mouth; that is to say, he knew God had made promise of mercy to save the faithful penitents, and of justice to punish the impenitent sinner. And this he heard in the time of the law of nature, by reading of Moses' books, and also by the Holy Ghost in his own time, when by the inspiration of the Holy Ghost he wrote this psalm and the rest of his prophecies. The same have we likewise heard, first, by reading of the books of Moses; next, by reading of the scriptures of the prophets; and thirdly, by reading of the new testament: the which I pray God give us grace to believe and follow. Amen.

❡ An Exposition
upon the seventy-third psalm, made by the constant martyr of Christ, Master John Hooper, Bishop of Glocester and Worcester.

The Argument.

The matter and argument of this psalm is a consolation for them that are wont much to be moved and afflicted, when they see the ungodly flourish and prosper in all wealth and pleasure; and contrariwise, the godly and good people oppressed with poverty, and all other calamities and afflictions; as ye may see the prophet Asaph entreat of this matter in this his first psalm. The same ye may see also in king David, in his 37th psalm; wherein he exhorteth men not to judge amiss of God, nor to leave off godly conversation, although the best be punished, and the worst scape quit. These two psalms, entreating of one matter, are to be read and known of us in these perilous days, lest the hatred and persecution that happeneth to God's truth, and to the lovers thereof, might unhappily make us to judge of God, and to forsake his truth, as many have done, and daily the number of them increase, with the decrease of God's honour, and the increase of their own damnation. For now Christ trieth the chaff from the corn, the rust from the metal, and hypocrisy from truth. If we will not or cannot abide the hammer, or trying-pot that God setteth us in, to explorate and search whether our faith will abide the fire of trouble and persecution, or not; if we suffer not, all our religion is not worth a haw. For it is not words that prove faith, but deeds:

_{Psalm xxxvii.}

_{Matt. xxvi. 1 Tim. i. 2 Tim. iv. 1 John ii. 1 Cor. iii. Heb. xi. Matt. x. James ii. Gen. xii. xv. xvii. xxii. Rom. iv. Matt. vii.}

    if it abide the trial, it is true; and the more it is tried,
       the finer it will be, and at length brought into
          such fineness, as corruption shall never hurt
            nor harm it in the world of grace
              and virtue. God therefore grant
                us grace to suffer his trial,
                  and search strongly,
                    patiently, and
                      thankfully.
                        Amen.

⁋ THE ORDER OF THE PSALM.

I. *The text and letter of the psalm.*

II. *The paraphrase, or plain explanation of the text and letter of the psalm.*

III. *The principal parts, and most notable doctrines contained in the psalm.*

⁋ The Text and Letter of the
Psalm of Asaph.

The First Verse.

1. "Truly God is loving unto Israel; even unto such as are of a clean heart."

⁋ *The Paraphrase, or plain Explanation.*

<small>Matt. v.
Luke vi.
Rev. iii.
Prov. iii.
Heb. xi.</small>

God loveth the godly, although they be afflicted; and hateth the ungodly, although they be in prosperity. The Lord is loving and merciful to such as be afflicted, and specially if their hearts be pure and clean, and judge nothing of God amiss, whether they see the good oppressed, or the evil exalted. In their hearts they murmur nothing at God's doings, nor in their minds they find no fault with God's order and providence.

The Second and Third Verse.

2. "Nevertheless, my feet were almost gone; my treadings had well near slipt.
3. "And why? I was grieved at the wicked; I do see also the ungodly in such prosperity."

⁋ *The plain Explanation.*

<small>Psal.
xxxvii.
lxxiii.
Hab. ii.</small>

Yet notwithstanding, when I saw the good afflicted, and the evil prosper, it troubled my mind; so that in manner I was forced and compelled, through indignation, to judge of God as other evil men did; and grievously offended his high majesty, in thinking his doings not indifferent in troubling the good and quieting of the bad.

The Fourth Verse.

4. "For they are in no peril of death, but are lusty and strong."

⁌ *The plain Explanation.*

I perceived further (saith the prophet), that the wicked lived not only quietly and pleasantly, but also died in manner without heaviness or any great torments. Besides all these felicities, pleasures, and ease for their own parts in this world, it happeneth, when they die, they leave also pleasant and delectable mansion-houses, great riches, and large possessions to their children.

The Fifth and Sixth Verse.

5. "They come into no misfortunes like other folk, neither are they plagued like other men.
6. "And this is the cause that they be so holden with pride, and overwhelmed with cruelty."

⁌ *The plain Explanation.*

If any miss of loss and damage in this world, it is they: if sickness flieth from any, it flieth from them: so that much felicity and little adversity causeth them to know neither God, their neighbours, nor themselves.

The Seventh Verse.

7. "Their eyes swell for fatness, and they do what them lust."

⁌ *The plain Explanation.*

Such as flourish with riches and authority wax proud and arrogant; for all things come so abundantly unto them, that they have more than they look for.

The Eighth Verse.

8. "They corrupt other, and speak of wicked blasphemy; their talk is against the Most Highest."

⁌ *The plain Explanation.*

They afflict and cruelly persecute the good and innocent, and they are come to this insolency and pride, that they would not only their abomination should be known, but also they themselves boast of it, and in most abomination most extol and magnify themselves.

The Ninth Verse.

9. "For they stretch forth their mouth unto the heaven, and their tongue goeth through the world."

ℭ *The plain Explanation.*

They be so blinded and deceived with the felicity and trouble of this world, that they spare not God nor godly men; but speak against both, and do their wills and pleasures.

The Tenth, Eleventh, Twelfth, Thirteenth, Fourteenth, Fifteenth, Sixteenth, and Seventeenth Verses.

10. "Therefore fall the people unto them, and thereout suck they no small advantage.
11. "Tush, say they, how should God perceive it? Is there knowledge in the Most Highest?
12. "Lo, these are the ungodly; these prosper in the world; these have riches in possession.
13. "Then have I cleansed my heart in vain, said I, and washed my hands in innocency.
14. "All the day long have I been punished, and chastened every morning.
15. "Yea, I had almost said even as they: but lo, then should I have condemned the generation of thy children.
16. "Then thought I to understand this, but it was too hard for me,
17. "Until I went into the sanctuary of God: then understood I the end of these men."

ℭ *The plain Explanation.*

Because the wicked men prosper so well in this world, the people of God conform and apply themselves to do as they do, and frame their lives and manners unto the rule and fashion of such wicked people as prosper; and they suck and draw into their minds the wicked men's opinions and conversations, and so replenish themselves with iniquity, as the thirsty man doth replenish himself with water. And when the people see the best part turn unto the manners of the worst, and be as evil or worse than the worst, they muse and think whether there be any God, or knowledge in God, that suffereth these abominations. And not only the common people (saith the prophet Asaph) stood in a mammering whether God took any heed or cared for the world, seeing that wicked men did so prosper, and the godlier sort so vexed: but I myself also, considering these things with myself, fell into such madness and error of judgment, that I had done evil so to apply myself to virtuous and godly life; seeing I was vexed and turmoiled with continual miseries, and seeing that there was never a day that did not bring her cross and trouble to the servants of God and virtuous people. These things (saith the prophet) fondly and foolishly I spake to myself many times; but when I weighed the thing with more judgment, and considered the matter more deeply with myself, I thought, If I thus judge and speak of God, do I not improve[1], reprehend, and condemn the life, conversation, and labours of all godly men? the which will not be drawn nor enticed from godly life and the love of virtue by no misadventures nor afflictions in this world; neither do they judge that they have studied and followed godliness in vain, whatsoever trouble hath happened to them in this world. And therefore, when I assayed to compass the cause and verity of these things, the greatness thereof brought me into much fear and carefulness. And further, I perceived that I could not come to the knowledge of these things, except the Almighty God would reveal and open unto me the mysteries and secrets of his providence and wisdom, that I might see and understand what end and outgoing these wicked men should have, that with most abomination and blasphemy in this life had most felicity and pleasure. And by tarrying in the thoughts and cogitations of this case and matter, at last I found that these wicked men and women, whose felicity and prosperous estate tormented me, their end was most miserable, full of wretchedness and pain.

The Eighteenth and Nineteenth Verses.

18. "Namely, thou settest them in slippery places, and castest them down, and destroyest them.
19. "O how suddenly do they consume, perish, and come to a fearful end!"

[1 Improve: reprove, cast a slight upon; Lat. improbare.]

⁋ *The plain Explanation.*

Doubtless the felicities and pleasures, Lord, that thou gavest to these wicked doers, are slippery and brittle: for so may I well call them, because such as enjoy them for the most part so abuse them in this life, that they lose the life everlasting.

The Twentieth Verse.

20. "Yea, even as a dream when one awaketh, so shalt thou make their image to vanish out of the city."

⁋ *The plain Explanation.*

These wicked men's felicity vanished as the dream of him that is awaked. For as the dream for a time seemeth to be true, and as long as he sleepeth he supposeth it to be as he dreameth; but as the dream passeth, the sleep being broken; so doth these wicked men's felicity, when they depart out of this life.

The Twenty-first, Twenty-second, Twenty-third, and Twenty-fourth Verses.

21. "Thus my heart was grieved, and it went through my reins.
22. "So foolish was I and ignorant, even as it were a beast before thee.
23. "Nevertheless, I am always by thee: for thou hast holden me by the right hand.
24. "Thou shalt guide me with thy counsel, and after that receive me with glory."

⁋ *The plain Explanation.*

Before (saith Asaph) that I saw such wicked men as flourished in all felicity and pleasure cast down headlong from their places, I was wonderfully troubled: and no marvel; for I was but a fool and an idiot, that perceived not the judgment of the Lord, but as a beast before thee in that respect, O Lord; yet didst thou conduct me, such a fool as I am, to the understanding of thy pleasure in such difficile and hard causes. And in their pleasures thou shewedst me their loss and damnation; and in mine own adversity and trouble shewedst me my salvation and perpetual health.

The Twenty-fifth and Twenty-sixth Verse.

25. "Whom have I in heaven but thee? And there is none upon the earth that I desire in comparison of thee.
26. "My flesh and my heart faileth: but God is the strength of my heart, and my portion for ever."

◘ *The plain Explanation.*

When the prophet hath weighed God's judgment towards such as with iniquity lived in all pleasure, and perceived that their pains were for ever, and their joys but for a time, he is now inflamed with the love of God, and breaketh forth into these godly words and sentences: Who can delight me in heaven but thou, O Lord? Whom shall I love upon the earth, whom shall I reverence and honour, but thee? Doubtless, of all things except thee I pass nothing of, nor set store by. Thee only I embrace, thee only I desire, and thee only I covet and wish for; for only thou art to be beloved, to be honoured, and to be wished for: so that both my soul and my body be ravished with the love of thee; for thou art the strength and foundation of my soul and body; thou art my riches, my treasure, and my everlasting inheritance.

The Twenty-seventh and Twenty-eighth Verse.

27. "For lo, they that forsake thee shall perish: thou hast destroyed all them that commit fornication against thee.
28. "But it is good for me to hold me fast by God, to put my trust in the Lord God."

◘ *The plain Explanation.*

And good cause have I, O Lord, to love thee: for they shall perish and be destroyed, as many as love any thing besides thee, and forsake thee. Therefore, as I know it profitable only to prefer thee, O Lord, in all love and favour; so
is it meet that I, being thus saved by thy mercy, and
receiving so many benefits at thy hand, should
continually with laud and praise
celebrate and magnify the
marvellous works of
thy goodness
and provi-
dence.
(∴)

The end of the Paraphrase or plain Explanation.

⁋ The principal parts of the Psalm LXXIII.

Verse 1. "Truly God is loving to Israel, &c."

The first part is contained in the first verse; and it declareth that God loveth the good, although he punisheth them.

Verse 2. "My feet were almost gone, &c."

The second part is contained in the second verse; and it declareth how weak and frail a thing the nature of man is, and upon how small an occasion it is in danger to fall from God.

Verse 3, 4, 5, 6, 7, 8. "I was grieved at the wicked, &c."

The third part is contained in six verses that follow; wherein the felicity of wicked men consisteth, that good men be so sore grieved at.

Verse 9, 10, 11. "Therefore fall the people unto them, &c."

The fourth part is contained in other three verses next ensuing; and it declareth how frail, brittle, and weak a thing man is, that for every trifle turneth and withdraweth himself from God.

Verse 12, 13. "Then have I cleansed my heart in vain, &c."

The fifth part is contained in two other verses next following; and it declareth how soon men repent their well-doings.

Verse 14. "Yea, and I had almost said even as they, &c."

The sixth part is contained in one verse next following; and it declareth how great a danger it is temerously[1] to judge of God, or of God's people, without the word of God.

Verse 15, 16, 17, 18, 19, 20, 21. "Then thought I to understand this, but it was too hard for me, &c."

The seventh part is contained in seven verses next following; and it declareth that man's reason is but ignorant and beastly in considering of God's works,

[1 Temerously: rashly.]

Verse 22, 23, 24, 25, 26, 27. "Nevertheless I am alway by thee: for thou hast holden me by my right hand, &c."

until it be illuminated by God and his word; and then is made open, how vain all things be that wicked men possess in this world.

The eighth part is contained in six verses next following unto the end of the psalm; and it declareth a wonderful and unspeakable consolation. For although we be grievously tempted, yet we be not forsaken of God, but preserved and lift up, when else otherwise we should fall. And in this part, in setting forth the multitude and number of God's consolations, he draweth near the end of the psalm, and concludeth it with this text, "I will set forth thy works:" wherewith he declareth that he will be thankful unto God for his great gifts and mercy.

¶ The end of the parts and chiefest matters in the psalm.

WHAT THINGS ARE TO BE MARKED OUT OF THESE PARTS AND MATTERS OF THE PSALM.

☙ *Out of the first part are many things to be noted.*

First, the nature and condition of God (forasmuch as he hath prepared for men a place of joy permanent and everlasting) is not to reward such as be his, and ordained to the life to come, with so slender and small a recompence in the blood of his Son Jesus Christ as these worldly and transitory things be of this world; but with riches and treasures that shall not corrupt nor be eaten with vermin, nor yet taken from us by thieves: as St Paul saith, "He hath made us to sit with him in the glory of heaven;" and as Christ said unto Peter, that

Matt. vi.
Coloss. iii.
1 Cor. xv.
Matt. xxv.
Cantic. iv.
John xvii.
Ephes. ii.

became a beggar with the rest of the apostles in this world for Christ's sake, "Ye shall (saith Christ) sit upon the twelve seats, judging the twelve tribes of Israel." Matt. xix.

We must therefore note out of this place of the prophet's psalm, that God, although he whip and scourge us, as we have most worthily deserved, yet he loveth us, and will not take his mercy from us, but once[1] leave beating of us, and burn the rod, and then in Christ reward us with everlasting life. In any case, therefore, we must well assure ourselves in the days of God's punishments, that the end of his crosses and afflictions be the beginning of everlasting joys. For "he receiveth none but such as he first correcteth and chasteneth." Rom. viii. Luke xxiii. Psal. cxix. Rev. vi. xxvii. [? vii.] xxii. Isai. liv. Hos. i. Heb. xii.

The second learning in this part is, to be persuaded that God doth not punish without just cause, for that he delighteth in punishing of his people; as the wicked Pharaoh, Nemroth, Saul, and Julian the apostata said. When he had drowned all the world with water for sin, the wicked people judged that God had punished of a partial and choleric passion in his fury, without just matter and cause: and therefore they went about, in contempt of God, to build a tower so high that God should never have been able to wreak his wrath upon them again. So did cursed Pharaoh; he asked what God that should be that could plague him and his realm? and in the time of his punishment railed and spake most unreverently. Wicked Saul also, when God for his disobedience punished him, he, in despite of God, sought remedy to withstand the punishments of God by witchcraft and necromancy. And Julian the emperor, when Christ gave him in the wars his death-wound, took an handful of his own blood, and hurled it in despite of Christ into the air, and said, "Thou hast overcome, thou Galilean[2]:" and so in mockery he called Christ, and christian men Galileans. Wherefore, in any case, this beginning of the psalm is to be marked, and used in the time of all men's punishments, and to say with heart and mouth unto the heavenly Father, whatsoever he layeth upon us, "Truly God is loving unto me," &c. And so doth king David cry Isai. liii. Rom. iii. Exod. xiv. Gen. x. 1 Sam. xxviii. Trip. Hist. Exod. v. 1 Sam. xxviii. Trip. Hist.

[1 Once: at some time or other.]
[2 Aiunt enim quod, cum fuisset vulneratus, mox manum sanguine suo compleverit, et in aërem projecit, dicens, Galilæe, vicisti.—Trip. Hist. Cassiod. Lib. vi. cap. 47. See also Theodoret. Hist. Eccles. Lib. iii. c. 25.]

out, when God was most severe and busy in punishing both him and his people, saying, "Thou art just, Lord, and right; and just is thy judgment." So did the emperor Maurice say, when his wife and children were killed before his face, "Thou art just, Lord, and thy judgments are righteous[3]." Job likewise was of the same mind: although his wife and kinsfolk provoked him to speak unpatiently and unreverently of God, yet he said, that he and all his were the Lord's, and that if he had taken them of him, why should not he be contented, that God should have them again at his pleasure? *Psal. cxix. Carion. Job i. ii.*

These two notes are to be marked and used, whatsoever happen: first, that God purposeth to bestow heavenly pleasures and treasures upon his people; and therefore he will not reward them with the trash and wicked mammon of this life, and transitory vale of misery: the second, when he punisheth his in this world, it is of love; and that the person afflicted must both take it so, and also say so with this prophet Asaph, "Truly God is loving unto Israel," that is to say, to him that professeth his religion. *John xvi. Gal. v. Col. i. 1 Thess. i. Heb. xii. James i. 1 John i.*

The third note is, to mark that God is known and felt, in the time of punishment and persecution, to be loving but of such as be of a clean heart. Whereof we learn, that all men that bear the name of Israelites and of christian religion judge neither reverently nor yet patiently of God's punishments, but such christian men as be of clean hearts. Out of this place we may learn the cause why, in this troublesome time, so many wax weary and fall from the truth of God's word, whiles God is a punishing of us that have been unthankful unto him, and did not live according to his word—the Lord forgive us! Doubtless, now they mislike, and start back: no, not start back, but openly in the face of God's enemies sware and stare, as Peter did (God send them Peter's repentance!), that they never passed nor cared a jot for God's word. And all is because they be not nor ever were of a clean heart; that is to say, so persuaded in their hearts that God's holy word is the only truth, what punishment soever God lay upon them that profess it. God give us this clean heart, that we may unfeignedly say, Doubtless, the Lord is loving unto *Psal. cxix. Deut. iv. 2 Sam. xxii. Neh. ix. Psal. xviii. xci. cxviii. Rom. v. xii. 1 Cor. iv. 2 Cor. i.*

[3 Carion. Chron. fol. 154. Francof. 1543. He does not give the expression here ascribed to Mauricius. See Gibbon, Decline and Fall, ch. xlvi. Vol. IV. p. 493. Lond. 1788.]

his word, and to them that profess it, although he lay thousands of crosses upon them in this world.

Out of this place we be admonished, dearly beloved, to beware of the greatest and abominable evil (one of them) that can be done against God; that is to say, witchcraft, and calculation by astronomy, and such other like. How heinous an offence is this, when we see the heavens rain, the clouds wholly bent to storms and tempests, the winds roaring and in such rage as all should go asunder, thunder and lightnings as men wonder at; and under all these plagues, tempests, and foul weather, the young springing corn, the sweet root of herbs, the little withered grass lie buried and covered under weather and storms, frost and snow, whilst God suffereth winter, and maketh cold to continue. Were it not now witchcraft and very abomination to say and divine of these stormy and winterly tempests, that summer should not be green, parched blades of grain should not come again in the harvest to corn, bitten and buried roots should not at the spring bring forth sweet and pleasant flowers, that shaken and wind-torn trees by tempests should not, in the calm coming of the summer, bud forth their leaves? What witch and cursed man would thus judge of earthly things, that have their times of vading and losing of all beauty for the sin of man? If this be abomination, for the bitterness and storms of winter to condemn and curse the summer to come, because summer's fruits and the spring's beauty be stained and all defiled with winter's barrenness and dim clouds; what is this but ten times more abomination, for the bitterness and storms of persecution to condemn and curse the life to come of God's people, because truth's fruits and the resurrection's glory be stained and all dishonoured with worldly scarcity and dim persecution? But as Asaph the prophet saith, "All eyes see not these things, but such as be of a clean heart." All men have eyes, for the most part, and all men have hearts, but they be such as the worms of the earth and birds of the air can eat and devour; but he that will live in God and see these things must have immortal eyes and an incorruptible heart, which cometh by grace in God's Spirit, to see by faith and honour with reverence God's doings, as well in the winter and cold storms of persecution, as in the summer of felicity and pleasure; and to remember that all men and women have this life and this world appointed unto them for their winter and season of storms. The summer draweth near, and then shall we be fresh, orient, sweet, amiable, pleasant, acceptable, immortal, and blessed, for ever and ever; and no man shall take us from it. We must therefore, in the mean time, learn out of this verse to say unto God, whether it be winter or summer, pleasure or pain, liberty or imprisonment, life or death, "Truly God is loving unto Israel, even unto such as be of a clean heart."

❡ *Out of the second part are divers things also to be noted.*

2. "My feet were almost gone, &c."

First, the prophet noteth, how wretched and miserable man is, and how soon inclined to do evil. He saith, that he was ready and prest to have slipped from God, even with the beholding of God's own works, when he saw God give unto the wicked felicity and prosperity; which things be only God's riches to give to whom he will. Although he bestowed none of his upon the wicked, yet was he offended that he should bestow his own where he lusted. The same occasion took the workmen in the vineyard to murmur against God; as it is in the gospel of St Matthew. So that we be natu- Matt. xx. rally given to this, that God giveth always too much unto other, and too little unto us; yea, although he would give us all the world, and yet keep any one thing for himself (even his very Godhead), in case he will not give also that unto us, we be ready to bid him farewell. And in case he will not also give us as much as is in him, such is our nature, that we will by some means or other seek to have it: as we may see, when he had made Adam, and given him both knowledge Gen. iii. and power above all other creatures made for his use, because he was not made God altogether, he fell most heinously from God; and slipt not only in his feet, but also in soul and body, to his utter ruin and destruction, and of us all that come of him. For this is our condition: let God give us never so much, we think it too little (except we have a singular grace to consider it); and let us surrender unto God never so little homage or service, we think it all too much. Such is our cursed nature and first birth, to be ready to slip from God upon the lightest occasion of the world; yea, when God doth other men good, and us no harm. But this nature we have of the devil our forefather, to disdain and malign at other men's profit and preferment, as he did: for when God made Adam, and put him in paradise, the devil never rested envying Adam's prosperity, until he had brought him to the loss of all together, and to slip clean from the Lord. This doctrine therefore, touching the brittleness and frailness of man's nature, is to be marked; lest that, whereas the prophet said, "My feet were almost gone," we slide and fall altogether from God.

Gen. iii.
John viii.

There is also to be noted, that the prophet said he was "almost gone," and not altogether. Here is the presence, providence, strength, safeguard, and keeping of man by Almighty God, marvellously set forth: that although we be tempted and brought even to the very point to perpetrate and do all mischief, yet he stayeth us, and keepeth us, that the temptation shall not clean overcome us. And so St Paul saith of God's providence and present help, that "he will not suffer us to be tempted further than we shall be able to bear:" and many times when we be brought into the greatest danger and peril both of body and soul, before we fall and be overcome, the Lord preserveth us and preventeth the evil: as when Abraham went into Egypt, and perceived that the Egyptians would put him in danger for his wife Sarah (for she was a fair woman), he desired her to say she was his sister; and by that means thought to save himself from danger, and to win favour at the Egyptians' hands. The chastity of this godly matron, Sarah, and wife of Abraham, came into such extreme peril, that neither Abraham nor she knew how to stand fast in the state and chaste condition of matrimony; for she was coupled to the king as his wife. But lest the woman should have fallen, and her feet slipped, the Lord rebuked the king, and told him that Sarah was another man's wife, and unlawful for him; and so, by his merciful defence and goodness, kept all parts from falling in that respect. The like may ye see also in Judith, the godly woman, that, without a singular grace of God, had fallen with Olofernes, and abused womanhood and widowhood: had not the Lord stayed in time, the fall was imminent and (in manner) at hand. And ye may read the same likewise of the people that were within the city of Bethulia at the same time, how near they were fallen,

[1 Cor. x. 13.]

[Gen. xii.]
Gen. xx.

Judith xiii.

Judith vii.

when they appointed God a time to help them, the space of five days; in case he deferred his help any longer, they would yield themselves into the hands of their enemies: but God stayed their fall, and that by the hands of a woman; and if there had not been more mercy in God than faith in them, their feet had not only slipped, but also all the whole land, country, and city. The like ye may see also in the notable history of Hesther, where as the very rock and chief stay of the Jews' health, Mardocheus, made suit to the queen for Asuerus' pardon for the life of the Jews, when sentence and judgment was past against them of death: so that, if faith in the promises of God had not stayed him, he had slipped and fallen down, to see all things against him and his countrymen. But before men utterly fall, the Lord is with them, and preserveth them with his mercy; as David said, "When my feet were moved, thy mercy, O Lord, stayed me." *Esther iv.* *Psal. xciv.*

The third thing to be noted of these words is the manner of the prophet's speaking, which must be marked and understood, or else the reader or hearer of the psalms shall take no profit.

"My feet were almost gone, and my treadings had well nigh slipped."

By the "feet" he understandeth the mind, and by the "treadings well nigh slipped" he understandeth the judgment and wisdom of the mind. As foul and slippery ways be dangerous for the feet, so be the works of God to the mind that is not illuminated with the light of God's word; and as the slipping and running away of the feet causeth all the body to fall, even so the ignorance of the mind causeth both body and soul to fall, and grievously to misjudge the works of God: and as the fall of the body souseth and defileth itself with mire and dirt, even so doth the fall of the mind defile both body and soul with impatience and envious indignation at God's works. So that the prophet saith by these words, "My feet were almost gone, and my treadings had well nigh slipped," my mind was so troubled to see God suffer the evil in such prosperity, and the good in such adversity, that my judgment almost slipt from the right sentence of thee, O Lord; and very scarcely I avoided most heinous sin towards thee, in controlling of thy most wise and just doings.

If we marked the pith and wisdom of the scripture, we should see many things more in ourselves than we do, and doubtless grow to an excellency in wisdom, and find out what evils we be most inclined unto. Amongst all other, hatred and indignation of other men's prosperity is not the least, nor the most seldomest. And indeed, the father of sin, the devil, hath that in him. First, he disdained God and his felicity; but he won nothing thereby but everlasting pains. Then he envied man and his felicity; yet the wicked spirit gained nothing to himself but double damnation and loss of us all. And this seed of the devil descended into our nature (as we may see), and made Cain to kill Abel his brother; made Ismael to persecute Isaac; Esau, Jacob; Dathan and Abiron, Moses and Aaron; Aaron and Mary his sister, Moses; Jacob's children, Joseph; Saul, David; Herod and the Pharisees, Christ and John the Baptist; the ten apostles, John and James; Peter, St John the Evangelist; and the members of the devil and Antichrist in this our time, the members of Christ: so that they be not only almost fallen, but also (the Lord help them and us all!) altogether slidden to envy and indignation, and likewise to violent oppression of God's holy word. But let us not slip ne fall into indignation that they prosper and we are afflicted; but say in the midst of these oppressions of the good, and prosperity of the evil, "Truly God is loving unto Israel;" and let us pray also for their amendment.

Gen. iii.

Gen. iv. xxi. xxvii. Numb. xvi. xii.

Gen. xxxvii. 1 Sam. xix. Matt. xiv. xxvii. xx. John xxi. xvi.

⁋ *The third part.*

3. "And why? I was grieved at the wicked, &c."

Herein is contained what the felicity of the wicked is, and wherein it consisteth, that the godly be offended withal, when they flourish and be in honour, and the poor members of Christ persecuted and without all honour, and be rather worms than men: yea, the dogs and brute beasts of the enemies be in more estimation than the poor believers in Christ.

Psal. xxii.

Out of this part is to be noted, first, a great fault and oversight in the people of God, for lack of judgment and true knowledge wherein truth and very felicity indeed consisteth: the lack of the which knowledge maketh men both impatient and lewd judges of God's holy works. The prophet therefore herein amendeth his own and our ignorance, and willeth us to know perfectly wherein felicity and happiness doth rest. The Christian must understand and assure himself, that the felicity and everlasting beatitude of man is wrought by quietness of conscience and innocency of life: of which two parts and virtues in this tract I will speak more hereafter, as well what they be, what be the causes of them, as what is the effect of them. I will assure you, if we know not these things well, our religion will be but awhile permanent and true unto God.

To enter therefore into the knowledge of the matter, wherein the beatitude and felicity of man consisteth, it is requisite to cast some clouds and darkness upon these worldly things that wicked men possess, and godly men think them thereby to be happy. Look, as the sun, at the rising and passing over the earth, doth hide and cover the globe and sphere of the moon, and darkeneth also the light and clearness of the stars; even so doth the tranquillity of conscience, and the brightness of faith and charity, that dwelleth in the heart of the faithful, darken and hide all things that seem beautiful and voluptuous to the world and carnal lusts of man. And he that hath a testimony at home in his own conscience, that he is in the favour of God, will not greatly pass of other men's judgments, whether they save or damn, laud or dispraise; nor yet greatly pass, although he lack such notes of riches and glory as worldly men judge and know felicity by. For he that knoweth surely wherein felicity doth consist will not take the worldly opinion of men for his record, nor for his reward; neither will he greatly fear for any damnation or punishment that the world can annex and join unto his life for this mortal time. It is therefore Christianity to know that felicity and beatitude resteth in the riches of the mind, by God's grace, wrought by the Holy Ghost for the merits of Christ.

There was amongst the philosophers great diversity of opinions in this matter, wherein felicity and beatitude should consist. Some said it rested in this, a man still and continually to be void from anguish and sorrow. Other said it consisted in the knowledge of things. Some said, in pleasure and voluptuousness. Aristotle and Theophrastus, and such other as were of the sect of the Peripatets, did hold that a blessed and fortunate life did consist in honesty; and said that the same might be accomplished with the voluptuous pleasures of the body, and with external riches, honour, and felicity. But both these opinions and all the rest are confuted by our Saviour Christ and his holy word. He saith, "This is life everlasting, that men know thee, O Father, the only and true God, and whom thou hast sent, Jesus Christ." And in another place he saith, "Every one that forsaketh house, brothers, sisters, father, mother, wife, children, or possessions, for my name, shall receive an hundredfold, and possess life everlasting." By these places we know that beatitude and felicity consisteth in knowledge and working of God's will, which be the causes of quietness of conscience and innocency of life; wherein felicity doth consist, as I said before. The right knowledge of God bringeth faith in Christ. Faith in Christ bringeth tranquillity of conscience. Tranquillity of conscience by faith worketh charity and love, to do and work the will of our heavenly Father. This may ye see also in the book of the Psalms, that felicity and bliss resteth not in these trifling things that glitter to the eye, wherewith the prophet was so sore offended; but in knowledge and working of God's will. "Blessed is the man whom thou teachest, Lord, and whom thou instructest in thy law." And in another psalm he saith, "Blessed is the man that feareth the Lord, and desireth to work his will." In these psalms, if ye read them with judgment and prayer to God, ye shall find both knowledge and consolation, far above the common sort of such as read and use them in the churches now, to the dishonour of God, and to the destruction of their own souls.

And in this matter of felicity and beatitude of man and woman in this life, I would have you judge by the scripture of God, or else ye shall be deceived, what it is, wherein it consisteth, and what it worketh: for only the word of God teacheth and sheweth it, and nothing but it. The scripture of God plainly declareth that nothing can be profitable which is not honest and virtuous. And virtue is blessed and very felicity, in what condition or state soever it be: neither can it be increased with any external or bodily goods or honour; neither yet can it be diminished with any adversities or troubles. And nothing can be blessed but that which is void from iniquity, full of honesty and the grace of God: as ye may see in the book of the Psalms, where as this matter is plainly set forth. "Blessed is the man that hath not walked in the counsel of the wicked, nor stood in the way of sinners, nor sate in the chair of scorners; but his delight was in the law of God," &c. And in another psalm he saith, "Blessed are they that be clean of life, and walk in the law of God." Out of these places we learn, that knowledge and innocency of life worketh felicity and beatitude. We must therefore beware that we judge not felicity to be in these inconstant and uncertain riches of the world; but we must contemn them, and also beware we fear not the trouble that may happen for such virtues wherein felicity doth stand. And we must understand also, that although these virtues, wherein felicity consisteth, and such as be friends of God dwelleth[1], be afflicted and troubled, that neither the felicity, nor the person in whom it dwelleth, is anything the worse for troubles and adversities before God, but rather the better: as ye may see by the word of God, that saith, "Blessed be ye when men speak evil of you, and persecute you, and speak all evil against you, lying, for justice sake. Be glad and rejoice; for your reward is great in heaven. So did they persecute the prophets before you." And in another place it is said: "He that will come after me, let him deny himself, and take his cross and follow me." The psalm therefore, in this part, amendeth the judgment of weak and wavering christian men, that be offended with the prosperity of the wicked, because they do not know, nor mark by God's word, wherein felicity doth consist, and that it remaineth in such virtues as be not diminished nor drowned in the adversities of this world, whatsoever dangers happen. When was Moses stronger than when he saw of the one side the mountains of Egypt, and of the other side Pharaoh and his army, and before him the Red Sea, and, in the midst of these enemies, he and his people standing like sheep ready for the wolves to be slain? He was never more strong, nor in this life more blessed, than at that time. Daniel was never better than amongst the lions. We must therefore know the virtues wherein felicity doth consist to be nothing

Psal. i.

Psal. cxix.

Matt. v. x.

Matt. xvi.

Exod. xiv.

Dan. iii.
[Dan. vi.]

[1 There seems to be an omission here; probably we ought to read, 'and such as be friends of God, in whom it dwelleth.']

diminished by sorrow and trouble, nor anything increased by voluptuous pleasures and brittle honours of this world: as St Paul most godly setteth forth in his Epistle to the Philippians: "The things (saith he) that I thought profit and gains, for Christ's sake I esteem as hurt and damage; for whose love I esteem all things as nothing, so that I may win Christ." And Moses esteemed the treasures of Egypt hurtful, and preferred them not before the reproaches and rebukes of the Lord: neither thought he himself rich nor blessed with the riches of Egypt, ne cursed when he was in need and lacked them. Elias the prophet, if he had considered his need and danger, he might have accounted himself very miserable and unhappy: but because he knew it was appointed him of God, he complained not of God's doings; for he was as well contented to have bread from God by the raven in the morning, and water at night from the fountain, as though he had had all the world; and he was nothing the less blessed, although he was poor, but rather more blessed, because he was rich to God-ward.

_{Phil. iii.}

_{Heb. xi.}

_{1 Kings xvii.}

Read the gospel of St Matthew, and see the practice of this felicity. Moses, that was so destitute of all worldly help, and Elias void of all worldly consolation, do talk with Christ in the mount of Thabor, where as Peter would have tarried with all his heart, although he knew both Christ and those that he talked with in the estimation of this world were accounted most unhappy and miserable of all men; yet he saw that transitory honours, riches, and felicity, holp nothing to the life everlasting: as Christ plainly teacheth in St Luke, "Blessed are the poor; for theirs is the kingdom of God. Blessed be they that hunger and thirst for justice; for they shall be satisfied. Blessed be ye that now weep; for ye shall laugh." Therefore the poverty, misery, and affliction that the prophet was in, when he spake this psalm and most godly hymn, hindered nothing at all his felicity and blessing of God; but rather furthered it, if he had wist wherein truly and verily felicity had consisted: as ye may see hereafter how he came to the knowledge of it.

_{Matt. xvii.}

_{Luke vi.}

Another thing is to be noted out of these six verses, containing the third part of the psalm: that such treasures, riches, and honours, as men set most by in this world, be rather (unto men that have not grace) lets and impediments

_{1 Tim. vi.}

to everlasting felicity, and to the attainment of virtue in this life, than furtherers: as the scripture saith: "Woe be unto you, rich men, which have your consolation. Woe be unto you that are now full, for ye shall hunger. And such as laugh shall weep." Achab the wicked king, not contented with his kingdom, would take Naboth's vineyard from him: but it had been better for him that he had been a swineherd; for his lands and riches abused made him to kill an innocent man and his true subject. Plentifulness of God's gifts abused bringeth contempt of God and man: as ye may see how Nabuchodonozer, in wealth and riches, envied the living God, and came into bestiality. The children of Israel, when they had filled themselves with gifts, were not thankful, but unthankful; and fell from unthankfulness to idolatry and all abomination. And as men contemn God in prosperity, so do they also their neighbours: as ye may see by this part of the psalm, where as the prophet saith: "Their eyes swell for fatness;" that is to wit, their riches and honour puffeth them up in such pride, that they contemn and despise all men. *[Luke vi. 1 Kings xxv. [xxi.] Dan. iv. Exod. xxxii.]*

The third thing to be noted is, that all things that the felicity and joys of wicked men consist in be but worldly and transitory things, and as uncertain as man is himself; which is to be marked: because no man can be happy or blessed by any such vading and inconstant things; neither can any man come to the beatitude of joys permanent by such things as God giveth indifferently as well to the bad as to the good, and to the vicious as to the virtuous: as Solomon in the book of the Preacher marvellously setteth forth, and matcheth equally the good with the bad, in such things as happen under the sun: "The good and the bad (saith he) be rich and poor, in trouble and in prosperity, have friends and foes, be merry and sorry, do live and die all in like." But neither the things that bring them to life everlasting, nor yet life everlasting itself, be one thing. For there is nothing that leadeth to everlasting life but the knowledge and fear of God, and the doing of his blessed will: the which virtues come not by nature, but by grace: as Solomon declareth, when he prayed so earnestly to have wisdom and understanding from God. And as these virtues come not from nature, even so be they not the riches of all men, but of virtuous and *[Deut. xl. Psal. xcii. Isai. xl. Matt. vi. 1 Pet. i. Eccles. iii. iv. v. 1 Kings viii. [iii.]]*

godly men only. And as they dwell and inhabit only in such as fear God, so do they only conduct and lead such as be godly (and none other) to eternal life: the which differeth as far and as much from the wicked's eternal life, as joy differeth from sorrow, ease from pain, pleasant consolation from fiery flames, love from hatred, God from the devil, and heaven from hell. For these riches wherewith the ungodly are endued in this life be not the things that can make any man blessed or cursed before God: therefore no more to be cared for than need is: to have them, if God will; if not, to lack them: to have them with God's grace well to use them; or else to pray to lack them, lest they abuse us. Better it were to have too little in the world with God's favour, than too much with his displeasure. If we have meat, drink, and clothe, let us be contented with it, as with sufficient things to pass this life: if any more than these come, to take heed they make us not to swell in pride, and take from us the remembrance and service of God.

_{1 Tim. vi.}

O that godly eyes would look upon this psalm, and namely upon this part of it, that declareth wherein the glory, honour, and felicity of wicked men consisteth! then I know his eyes shall hardly escape tears and weepings, to see and hear a wicked and cursed creature of God pampered with such a sort of vain fleetings, that when he would most gladly flee from sorrow, the least be able to carry him away. Mark the wicked man's riches, and ye shall perceive that God hath given no more than he hath unto the clay, mould, and stony earth, wherein lieth both gold and precious stones. His beauty and amiableness of vesture and apparel is not like the rose of the garden, nor the lily of the field; his strength much inferior to brute beasts; his wisdom less than horse or mule, that use in meats and drinks enough for necessity, and not too much for sensuality. If lack and need oppress them, patiently they lack until order provide for them: but if the wicked lack, he beareth not lack with patience, nor seeketh enough by truth. The courageous horse fiercely in fight contemneth death; and the meek swan, feeling the life to pass, with sweet tunes welcometh Atropos, and striveth not, but willingly is contented to surrender that which will not be kept with force. But what doth the rich wicked man? Forsooth, as the wise man saith: "O death! how bitter is the remembrance of thee to

_{Luke xii.}

_{Matt. vi.}

_{That is to say "death."}

_{Ecclus. xli.}

such as have confidence in their riches!" Lord! what a charnel-house of stinking carrion is this body and life of wicked man puffed up with riches; inferior, with all that ever he hath, to the birds of the air, the beasts of the fields, and unto the barren clay that he was made of; and the soul itself within that wicked body cursed of God, and ordained to eternal pains! Who is he that can read or behold the state and honour of man, in whom is not mentioned one virtue to dwell, without sorrow and heaviness? What a cursed nature is man made of, that can see another thus pampered up with God's displeasure, and cannot rather bewail and mourn to see his brother by these riches lost and cast away, than to envy or disdain at his person! Oh, woe befall them that fall into this sin of ours, that thus rather with malice and disdain envy the miseries and curses of God upon other, than charitably do go about to amend them, or ruthfully to bewail them! Read, my dear beloved in the Lord, this place, and mark well the wicked men, and learn to pray for them; as God give us all grace to do.

⁋ *The fourth part.*

10. "Therefore fall the people unto them, &c."

Out of this part is to be noted, how dangerous a thing it is to be continually assaulted with temptation; and that the end of it (for the most part) is the conquest and overthrow of as many as be assaulted: as we may see by the examples of our forefathers. Temptation not resisted at the beginning prevailed against the innocent fathers Adam and Eve in paradise; against Cain in murder; against Aaron and the people in idolatry; against Nimrod in pride; against David in adultery; against Judas in avarice; against Aaron and Mary his sister in envy; against Esau in gluttony; against Pharaoh in pride; against Herod in hypocrisy; against the Pharisees in blindness and obstinacy of mind; against the Jews in the slander of Christ's death; against the Gentiles in ignorance of God's word; against the most part of Christians now-a-days in cowardness and fear; and against all the world in looking more how to profit itself, than to serve and fear God. The prophet said before, he was "almost gone," to see the wicked so prosper: but he saith now, that the people fall utterly unto them, and learn both wicked opinions and wicked life of the wicked.

Gen. iii.
Gen. iv.
Numb. xvii.
[? Exod.
xxxii.]
2 Sam. xi.
Matt. xxvi.
Heb. xi.
[? xii.]
Exod. iii.
Matt. xiv.
John vii. viii. ix.
1 Cor. i.
Rom. i.

The second is, that the people fall not into the wicked blasphemy of iniquity one by one, but by clusters in great number. Wherein is much to be noted, that so few so hardly turn to God, and so many so quickly to abomination. But, as Christ said, "The way to heaven is narrow and strait, and few enter; and the way to hell is broad and plain, and many enter in it."

Matt. vii.

¶ *The fifth part.*

14. " Then have I cleansed my heart in vain, &c."

Out of it we be admonished, that our nature is to be offended by and by with troubles for the glory of God. And even as we be unquiet with the troubles, so be we inconstant and unstable in the knowledge and truth that we suffer trouble for; and begin to repent that ever we began to favour or embrace the truth; and wish also that we had used ourselves as other men did, and then to have suffered with other men the common lot and fortune of the world, and not thus to have been given to a singular knowledge of God's word, which bringeth with it a singular hatred and punishment in this world. Such is our nature, if we be by afflictions and troubles but for a day's space made like unto Christ, we think it too long; but if we be by sin for all our lifetime made like unto the devil, we think the time too short, and wish longer to live, because we would longer work and delight in sin and abomination. Great and heinous is our offence in this respect: for a little time spent in well-doing we judge too long; and all time spent in evil-doing we judge too short. All labours and pains be too little, if they be bestowed in worldly things; but if they be appointed to heavenly things (be they never so few and slender), we think them too much. There is not sea nor land, with all the perils within them, but men dare adventure both their goods and their lives to win increase of worldly goods; but to win towards God and godliness, scarce one of a great many without danger will labour or take pains to gain it. So doth the prophet say in this place, that "he had cleansed his heart in vain;" because he saw cleanliness and virtue persecuted, and filth with iniquity honoured and exalted. Christ in the gospel of St John, perceiving that, when virtue and well-doing should be troubled, men would wax weary of well-doing and virtue, he said unto his disciples,

Jer. xx.

"Remember, when they come, that I spake of them, and warned you before." *John xvi.*

⁋ *The sixth part.*

15. "Yea, and I had almost said even as they, &c."

Out of it we learn, that no man should judge of God's works, nor God's people, but by the word of God. In this behalf we do many times grievously offend the Almighty God. For when the world damneth God's word, then doth the most part of men the same. If the world say it is true, we say so too. If the world say it is untrue, we say it is untrue: and if the world condemn it, we condemn it also. Likewise if the world account them cursed and damned that be persecuted for God's sake, and for the testimony of his name, we do so too. Yea, and moreover, if the world slander and lie upon poor men and poor women that suffer for God's sake, we speak as they do, and sometimes persecute also the good with them. This is an horrible thing, to reprove (after such a carnal and worldly sort) God and all his blessed people; which will be at length, doubtless, a just condemnation of the world.

⁋ *The seventh part.*

16. "Then thought I to understand this, but it was too hard for me, &c."

We learn out of this part, that, until reason be amended and removed from her natural blindness, it can do none other but condemn both God and God's people. And no marvel; *Psal. lxxxiii. xxxi.* for the prophet, in the eighty-third psalm, and also in the thirty-first psalm, hath these words: *consultaverunt adversus absconditos tuos,* "they have consulted against thy hidden people." As though he had said, The merciful Father of heaven keepeth the godly people in most sure and strong defence and protection; but this kind of protection is hid from the eyes of man's reason: so that it seemeth many times, that God hath the less care of the godly, and passeth more of the wicked than of them. Yet, howsoever the world judgeth, God sleepeth not. Further, how blessed the state and life of the godly is, and how cursed the life and state of the wicked is, only the virtuous and godly do perceive. Therefore the scripture calleth those that be godly and virtuous the hidden of God. Moreover, the godly do perceive, that all the vanity of worldly things, which be the treasures of the wicked, and the permanent state and condition of heavenly things, which be the treasures of the godly, be only seen of such as enter into the holy sanctuary and secret treasures of God's most holy word, without the which worldly things seem to be riches, and heavenly things poverty,—wicked men to be blessed, and godly men cursed,—falsehood to be truth, and truth falsehood,—death to be life, and life death.

⁋ *The eighth part.*

23. "Nevertheless, I am alway by thee, for thou hast holden me always by my right hand."

<small>Rom. viii.</small> The prophet out of this part declareth that which St Paul writeth to the Romans: "If God be with us, who can be against us? If he love us, what is he that can separate us from his love? which spared not his only Son for our redemption, but gave him for us unto the death. Therefore, there is neither life nor death, things present nor things to come, that can separate us from him."

Unto this place is referred all the deliverance from trouble and danger that God used from the beginning of the world unto our time. And when we understand and know God's mercy towards ourselves and others, we must give ourselves
  wholly to laud and praise his holy name, and be thank-
    ful: for there is nothing more unnatural in man
      than forgetfulness of God's great and
        innumerable gifts towards us.
         To whom be all honour
          and praise, world
           without end.
            Amen.

⁋ An Exposition
upon the seventy-seventh psalm, made by the constant martyr of Christ, Master John Hooper, Bishop of Glocester and Worcester.

The Argument.

When this prophet Asaph (being a man appointed to the service and teaching of God's word unto the people) perceived that such as were under his cure and charge were many times troubled and brought into great heaviness, for the fear and dread they had conceived of God's most just ire and strait punishment for sin and transgression of his holy laws, and in himself felt especially the burden of God's displeasure against sin intolerable, he received from the Holy Ghost, the Spirit of consolation, what was the best remedy and help for every troubled conscience, to appease and quiet the poor spirit of man, that knoweth and feeleth not only that God is justly angry for sin, but also will straitly punish the iniquity and abomination of the same. And when he had learned himself by God, how a troubled and desperate conscience might be quieted, he spake it to such as were alive and with him, and wrote it to all such as should come after him until the world's end; that troubled sinners might
see their sins forgiven in the mercy of
God, and they themselves accepted,
as God's most dear chil-
dren, into eternal friendship and endless
joys of sal-
vation.

⁋ THE PARTS OF THE PSALM.

I. *In whom a man should put his trust, and to whom he should resort in the days of sickness, troubles, and adversity.*

II. *How a man should use himself towards him in whom he putteth his trust in the time of trouble.*

III. *What great and perilous dangers the man that is troubled shall suffer for the time of his trouble.*

IV. *How a man taketh consolation in the time of his trouble.*

⁌ THE TWO FIRST VERSES OF THE PSALM, CONTAINING THE TWO FIRST PARTS.

1. "I will cry unto God with my voice; even unto God will I cry with my voice, and he shall hearken unto me.

2. "In the time of my trouble I sought the Lord; my hand I held up all night, and it was not weary: my soul refused comfort."

⁌ THE FIRST PART.

⁌ *In whom a man should put his trust, and to whom he should resort in the days of sickness, troubles, and adversity.*

1. "I will cry unto God with my voice; even unto God will I cry with my voice, and he shall hearken unto me."

First out of this text it is to be noted, that God only is to be trusted unto in the days of trouble, as our Saviour Christ exhorted in heaviness and anguish of body and soul all people to resort unto him, saying: "Come unto me all ye that be laden and burdened, and I will refresh you." And the same is spoken of God by Isaiah the prophet: "Ye that be athirst, come unto the waters; and ye that have no money, come and take it freely." St John likewise, in the midst among troubled and afflicted persons, reciteth the words of Christ, saying, "If any be dry, let him come to me, and drink. He that believeth on me (as the scripture saith), floods of water of life shall flow out of his belly."

Of this knowledge and surety in the soul of man, that God is, can, and will be an ease and remedy for the troubled conscience, cometh justice, peace, and joy of the conscience. Not that any man shall be by and bye without all fear, trembling, and dread of his sins, and of God's just judgment against sin, but that this fear and trembling shall not come to desperation; neither shall he be more afraid of his

Matt. xi.

Isai. lv.

John vii.
Isai. xii.

Rom. v. xiv.

sins than comforted by God's mercy and grace in Christ. Therefore saith our Saviour Christ, "Blessed be they that weep, for they shall be comforted. Blessed be they that hunger and thirst for justice, for they shall be replenished." In this that he saith, "Blessed be they that weep," he noteth such as do know and feel with sorrow and heaviness of conscience that they be sinners, and the filthiness of their sins maketh them sorrowful and heavy-hearted; yet shall they in Christ be comforted. Again, the poor, sensible, feeling, and troubled sinner doth wish his sins away, and would gladly have virtue and justice to rule and do altogether in him God's holy will and pleasure. This hunger and thirst (saith Christ) shall be quenched for the merits of his own death and passion: as it shall not miss, if men, in their thirst, hunger, persecution, and trouble, do know and use only God for their help and consolation, as this prophet did, and teacheth us to do the same in this psalm. *Matt. v.*

Of those that weep and mourn who be blessed.

In this first part be two sorts of people condemned. The one is such as plainly despair, and in their troubles neither look for consolation, nor yet believe that there is any consolation to be hoped for in Christ; the other is such as seek consolation, but not only at God's hand and power, but at the saints departed, at witches, conjurors, hypocrites, and the works devised and done by man. The first sort be left comfortless, because they seek no consolation; and the second sort find no comfort, because they seek it where it is not, contrary unto God and his holy word. Happy therefore is the troubled that seeketh consolation at God's hands, and nowhere else. "For he is (as it is written by the prophet Esay) the God alone that doth save, and none but he." But there be two manner of impediments that keep the Almighty God from the helping and comforting of people that be in trouble. The one is ignorance of God's nature and property towards the afflicted; and the other is fear and dread, whereas God is most justly angry for sin, lest that in his anger and just punishment he will not be merciful. *Two sorts of people condemned.*

Isai. xlv.

Two impediments keep God from helping the troubled. 1. Ignorance. 2. Fear of God's justice.

Of the first impediment, which is ignorance, is sprung into the world horrible blasphemy, that neither seeketh help at God's hand, nor yet is thankful unto God for anything that God giveth; but rendereth all things to such gods and *Of ignorance is sprung horrible blasphemy.*

saints as he hath devised out of his own imagination, or else learned (as St Peter saith) out of the traditions of his elders: so that ignorance taketh away the honour of God, and also the salvation of them that be ignorant. The remedy against this great impediment is only the reading, meditating, hearing, and learning of God's holy word, which is as a candle-light in a dark place, to keep and preserve a man from danger and peril. And so saith king David, that it is a candle unto his feet, and a light unto his steps. And in another place of his psalms he saith, "The law of God is so perfect, that it turneth souls unto the Lord." Wherefore (saith he) it is the part of every man that will be virtuous and godly, to have his desire and cogitations in the law of God both day and night. And, to preserve the people from this horrible impediment of ignorance, God spake by his prophet Esay these words: "My Spirit, which is in thee, and my words, which I put in thy mouth, shall not depart from thy mouth, and from the mouth of thy seed, saith the Lord, from henceforth for evermore." And in the same prophecy Christ prayeth the heavenly Father to seal his word in his disciples, whereby the dangerous impediment of man's salvation, which is ignorance, might be eschewed and avoided. The same remedy against ignorance commandeth Almighty God also by Moses in Deuteronomy, and by St Paul to the Ephesians; where as the fathers and the mothers be not bound themselves alone to know the law of God, but also bound to teach it to their children, that by ignorance they offend not God.

Of the second impediment, which is fear and dread of God's justice, cometh trembling and terror of the conscience, and many times also the extremest evil of all evils, very desperation, that never looketh who can help, neither yet trusteth to find any help. But of these fruits of terror and fear, and also of their remedies how they may be cured and holpen, it shall be shewed hereafter in the psalm, as it followeth, where as both terror of conscience and tranquillity of the same be marvellously and divinely set forth. Only, until I come to those points, I do note that this fear and terror of conscience in the faithful be the very hunger and thirst that Christ saith shall be quenched, and they that feel them shall be replenished with grace and consolation, as the blessed virgin, the mother of Christ, saith; and they that feel them not shall depart empty without grace. And the cause of this terror and fear is the Spirit of God, that worketh the knowledge of our sin by preaching, reading, or thinking of God's law, that openeth and detecteth how wretched and sinful we be by nature in the sight of God. But of this matter is better occasion ministered afterwards in the psalm than in this place. *Luke i.* *Rom. iii. v. vi. vii. viii. God's Spirit worketh the knowledge of sin by preaching of the law.*

❡ THE SECOND PART.

❡ *How a man should use himself towards him in whom he putteth his trust in the time of trouble.*

2. "In the time of my trouble I sought the Lord: my hand I held up all night, and it was not weary: my soul refused comfort."

In this part is taught us, both by doctrine and by example, how we should use ourselves in the time of trouble. When we know there is no help nor helper but God alone, it is not enough for a man to know that God can help; but also we must believe constantly, that he hath as prompt a will to help, as a sufficient power able to help: and then, being assured that he both can and will help, we must call upon him for help, according to his commandment unto us: "Call upon me in the days of trouble," &c. *How we should use ourselves in the time of trouble.* *Psal. l.*

Out of this place we may mark and learn what an intolerable burden and unspeakable sorrow the terror and fear of sin is, and how grievous a thing the sight and contemplation of God's displeasure and just judgment is against every sinner, for his sin and transgression of God's most holy law. The text saith, that the prophet, when he felt the displeasure of God against sin, cried out with a loud voice unto the Lord: whereby we learn, that the conscience of man, admonished by the word of God of the filthiness and abomination of sin, bringeth all the body into a trembling and fear, lest God should use rather justice, and justly punish sin, than mercy, and mercifully forgive sin. And thus being made afraid thoroughly of sin, the mind is occupied with sorrowful and heavy cogitations, and the tongue by vehemency of the spirit brought into clamours and cries: *The fear and terror of sin is an intolerable burden.* *The conscience being admonished of the filthiness of sin bringeth the body into a trembling and fear.* *What ensueth after the fear of conscience for sin.*

as we may see commonly by examples left unto us in the word of God, that where sin is thoroughly felt in the conscience, the feeling sinner is not only troubled within in spirit, but also outwardly in all the members and parts of his body, as it is to be seen most manifestly in king David. In what a sea of heaviness was king David in his conscience, when he spake to his own soul: "Why art thou so heavy and sorrowful, O my soul, and why dost thou thus trouble me?" Again: "How long wilt thou forget me, O Lord? for ever?" And in other psalms we may see into what trembling and fear outwardly he was brought by the knowledge and feeling of his sin. In one place he saith, the fear of his sins did not only overlay his conscience, but also crushed and (in manner) all-to broke his bones. And in another place, his visage was all defaced with weeping tears, and so abundantly they gushed out of his eyes, that he watered, or rather overflowed, his bed with them where he lay. Into what horrible cries and wailings many times he fell for fear of sin, this psalm and many other do declare. The like horror and fear also of the sight and feeling of sin we see to have been in St Paul, when he cried out upon himself, "O wretched man that I am! who shall deliver me from this body subject unto death?" And Mary Magdalene, with the sight and feeling of God's displeasure against her sin, made tears and weepings enow to wash the fountain of mercy's feet, Jesus Christ. But blessed is that conscience feared[1] by the law, whose fear by the sweet promises of the gospel is turned into mirth; and blessed be those tears and weepings that end in consolation; and happy is that troubled body whose end is immortality in the resurrection of the just. Further, as we see here king David, a sinner, for fear of God's judgment brake out into loud cries for help and preservation, the same anguish and trouble of mind and of body for fear of God's punishment for sin towards man was likewise in Christ without sin, which said, "My soul is heavy unto death;" and in such an agony was his body, that he burst out and sweat both water and blood.

So that of this second part first we learn, that such as be truly and unfeignedly brought to a knowledge, feeling, and

[1 Feared: frightened.]

repentance of their sins have it with great heaviness of mind, terror of conscience, and trouble also of the body many times; that no sickness nor troubles may be compared to the trouble of the conscience for fear of due and condign punishment for the sin perpetrated and committed against God's laws. *No trouble to the trouble of conscience.*

The second doctrine that we be taught out of this second part is, to declare what difference there is between the penitent Christian in adversity, and the desperate person that looketh for no help, or else the presumptuous person that contemneth help. *Difference between the penitent, desperate, and contemptuous man.*

The penitent afflicted calleth unto the Lord; and although he find his burden never so intolerable, do weep and lament never so sore, yet he despaireth not, but in adversity he hath hope, and is not confounded, as in prosperity he hath faith, and yet presumeth not. The desperate man feeleth all troubles and no consolation, is wholly overcome with mistrust, full of incredulity, and clean void of hope, as Saul, Judas, and others. The contemner of admonition hath hope in prosperity, with all presumption, as Cain and Pharaoh; and in adversity desperation, with all mistrust and diffidence. The Christian afflicted calleth in faith and hope upon the Lord, and is heard: the wicked afflicted calleth not upon the Lord, but is clean rejected and comfortless by God's most just judgment. The Christian afflicted seeth all his sins less than the least mercies of God: the wicked afflicted seeth the least of his sins greater than the greatest mercies of God. The one in trouble by faith glorifieth the Lord, and by mercy findeth salvation: the other in trouble by mistrust dishonoureth the Lord, and by justice findeth damnation. The one by troubles, through faith in Christ, is made like unto the Son of God, and cannot be separated from him in eternal life: the other by troubles, through desperation of Christ, is made like unto Satan, and cannot be separated from him in eternal death. The one in eternal life findeth everlasting joys: the other in everlasting death findeth endless pains. Almighty God therefore grant us grace in all our troubles and afflictions penitently and faithfully to call upon him, and to find him merciful unto us his wretched creatures. Amen. *The penitent man. The desperate man. The contemptuous man. Note. The christian afflicted. The wicked afflicted. Note.*

The third thing to be noted in this second part is, that God's nature and man's differ much one from the other. For *God's nature and man's differ much.*

316   EXPOSITIONS ON CERTAIN PSALMS.

Man for the most part is unstable, and followeth religion as the world favoureth.

Idols set up again in Queen Mary's time.

man (for the most part) is no more serviceable unto God, nor longer friendly unto man, than God's condition upon the earth is fortunate and quiet with the world: for if storms arise for God's cause, and troubles happen where quietness erst had place, the men of the world alter their love, service, and reverence, and will neither make nor meddle with God nor his cause; no, although ten thousand idols be brought in for one God, as Englishmen have seen in former time. As long as Christ had a king in this realm to hold of his part, and that great livings, gains, friendship, and love of the world rose for God's sake, they dissembled towards his word; and so long as fair words could please God, he lacked none: but now even such as God did most for do know neither God nor his word, but had rather hear ten times spoken of the falsest tradition that ever man brought into the church, than once of Christ's most holy gospel; so that now men's natures for adversities' sake be clean turned from God.

How long man's love continueth towards man.

How long the love of man continueth towards men, daily experience sheweth within one month. If a man fall into trouble for the most just cause, he that was his friend will not only alter his love from him, but also all the notes and tokens of the same. Whereas in prosperity he was assured both of friendly words and friendly works, in adversity he shall find neither words nor works, except words and works of displeasure. In prosperity fair looks and amiable countenances were as common as the cartway: in adversity there shall neither look nor countenance be shewed, except it be frowning and bending of brows; yea, and moreover, adversity taketh from the dissembling friend all knowledge that ever he had of his friend afflicted, that if[1] the poor afflicted (although he be even under the nose of his feigned friend) with courtesy and all obeisance cannot be known.

God loveth and helpeth the poor afflicted.

Psal. lxxvii.

Consolation.

O God! blessed be thy name, that withdrawest neither thy knowledge, love, nor yet thy help from the poor afflicted, but hearest them, and grantest them their godly and honest requests; as here this prophet most godly and comfortably writeth of thee; for he saith, "The Lord shall hearken unto me, when I seek him in the time of my trouble." And also the Lord abhorreth not to be present with the afflicted, be his

[1 This is the exact reading: the sense is, so that the poor afflicted, &c.]

troubles never so great: "For I am (saith the Lord) with him in trouble; I will deliver him, and set him in honour," &c.

<small>Psal. xci.</small>

Of this doctrine we learn two things: the one, that God hateth not the troubled man for his trouble, but for his sins. Men do clean contrary for the most part; for they hate the man for trouble, and not for sin: for let the wickedest man alive have prosperity, and all wicked men will love him for his prosperity's sake. God turneth not his favour from man for trouble, but for sin. The world for trouble's sake will not know the most dear and honest friend: but let the most wicked that liveth by breath have prosperity, and wicked people will not fail to know him with beck and du-gard, if he come into company; yea, rather than fail, the most wickedest man alive shall be narrowly sought out, that wicked men may have acquaintance of him. But he that hath God to his friend is sure of a Saviour, as well in adversity as in prosperity, as the prophet here declareth, which can in troubles send ease, and in quietness continue joys for ever. To him therefore be all laud and praise, worlds without end. Amen.

<small>God hateth not the troubled for his trouble, but for his sin. Man hateth man for trouble, and not for sin.</small>

The fourth thing to be noted in this second part is, the continuance of the faithful afflicted in prayer unto God. For the prophet saith, that he "lifted up his hands all night, and waxed not weary." Of this continuance in prayer we learn two things: the one, perseverance in prayer; and the other, patient expectation and willing sufferance until God send redress and ease. To the first the scripture exhorteth us, that we pray both heartily and continually unto God, not because he is ignorant of our troubles, but because we should thoroughly be brought to understand that there is none can help us out of trouble but he; and also that by continuance in prayer we may the better know, and more earnestly repent, our sins, that be the cause of our troubles: thirdly, that by often remembrance and divers rehearsals of our iniquity unto God we may the sooner bring both our souls and bodies into the service and homage of Almighty God, whom we have by sin most grievously displeased.

<small>Continuance in prayer.</small>

The second virtue, patient expectation in troubles, declareth that we be much bound unto God, that chasteneth us in this life, and deferreth not our punishment to the eternal pains in the world to come. Also it maketh the mind of men

<small>Patient expectation.</small>

to understand the wisdom of God, and also the foolishness of man, that many times, for lack of patient expectation and thankful sufferance, waxeth weary of his cross and punishment, and also murmureth against God, because he helpeth not when man's wisdom judgeth most meet to be holpen. But patient expectation prescribeth God no time when to help, nor yet means how to help; but saith, "Thy will be done in earth as it is in heaven;" also, "Lord, if thou wilt, thou canst deliver me:" as the prophet useth here in this psalm; he called and cried upon the Lord all the night, and attended patiently when God would help, leaning altogether to his blessed will and pleasure, to do or not to do, as him best pleased.

Matt. vi. viii.

ℭ THE THIRD PART.

What great and perilous dangers the man that is troubled shall suffer for the time of his trouble.

2. "My soul refused comfort.
3. "When I am in heaviness, I will think upon God: when my heart is vexed, I will complain. Selah.
4. "Thou holdest mine eyes waking: I am so feeble, I cannot speak.
5. "I have considered the days of old, and the years that be past.
6. "In the night I called to remembrance my song, and communed with mine own heart; and my spirit searched diligently.
7. "Will the Lord absent himself for ever? and will he be no more entreated?
8. "Is his mercy clean gone for ever? and is his promise come utterly to an end for evermore?
9. "Hath God forgotten to be gracious? and will he shut up his loving-kindness in displeasure?"

Here in these verses it appeareth, what terrible and fearful things a man that is in trouble shall suffer and be vexed withal. And the first that the prophet mentioneth is in the end of the second verse, and it is this, "My soul refuseth comfort."

Of this adversity and anguish of the soul we may learn

many things: first, that as long as sin appeareth not nor is felt, the mind of man is quiet, jocund, and pleasant; and the mirth and pleasure of the mind rejoiceth the body, and maketh it lusty and pleasant; not feeling at all the breach of God's commandments, neither passing anything at all of sin nor evil conversation, but rather delighting in things that displease God than in any virtue or honesty. But when trouble, sickness, or death cometh, then most commonly, though men see not the horror of their sins to repent, yet feel they the horror thereof to desperation; and, that once felt in the soul, all the joys of the world cannot comfort the troubled person: as Adam, with all the solace of paradise, could not rejoice, when his soul felt the abomination of his offence towards God: Cain could never pluck up merry countenance for the cruel killing of his brother Abel: Peter could not stint weeping for his denial of Christ, until Christ looked upon him: Mary Magdalene could not pull up her head from under the table for shame of her sin, until Christ had forgiven her; nor the poor woman that was taken in adultery, until her offences were pardoned: neither yet could this prophet's spirit take any consolation, as long as his sins were felt and not pardoned. Whereof followeth this saying,—a small trouble of conscience putteth away all joy and mirth of the world. Wherefore it is wisdom, and also the duty of all christian people, to avoid sin and the enmity of God, which only troubleth the conscience; and to put the body to all pains possible, yea, and to death itself, rather than to put the soul in danger towards God: as St Paul writeth to Timothy his disciple, and not without cause. For as the spirit that contemneth God, and feeleth for his contempt God's displeasure, cannot take comfort, but is full of anguish and heaviness inward, and in the outward man full of pain and sorrow; so likewise shall the soul in the life to come inwardly feel unspeakable grudgings and sorrows, and outwardly the unquenchable and everlasting fire of hell. And here is to be noted, that the very elect and dearest friends of Christ be not free from trouble and anguish of mind for their sins perpetrated and committed against God. But this is a consolation, that the elect, as they find anxiety and anguish of mind for sin in this life, so in this life is the conscience that is troubled by grace quieted, that it may after this life find eternal rest. And it is a common

An ordinary way that God useth to call sinners to repentance, and from repentance to forgiveness.
Psal. li.

order and ordinary way, whereby God useth to bring the sinner to acknowledge and repent his sin, and so from knowledge and repentance to the forgiveness of his sin, to shew and set before the conscience of the sinner his sin; as the example of king David and others do declare: "My sin (saith David) is always before me." As though he had said, In case I could hide mine iniquity from all the world, yet can I not excuse it before God, nor hide it from mine own conscience. And every man's sins thus open before God, and known and felt in his own conscience, bringeth the soul into this discomfort and heaviness, that it refuseth all consolation and comfort; as this prophet Asaph saith marvellously in this second verse of his psalm.

Two manner of discomforts.

There is to be noted out of this comfortless spirit of the prophet Asaph another most necessary doctrine for every christian creature, which is this: that there is two manner of discomforts, or two sorts of heaviness in the word of God, that is appointed to lead us in the time of this wretched life; as there is in it also two manner of consolations. There is two manner of brightness and clearness, and two manner of darkness and obscureness in it; as it shall appear in the treatise of this psalm hereafter. And because the diversity is not marked, the word of God doeth many times and in many places and persons no good at all.

An inward discomfort.

There is a discomfort inwardly, and a discomfort outwardly, in the scripture. The discomfort inwardly is, when the sinful man or woman seeketh and suffereth the same discomfort in his soul that the law of God doth open and proclaim against him for his sins committed against God and his law: so that, as the law commandeth after this sort, *Agite*

Matt. iii. Mark i.

pœnitentiam, "Repent ye," so the man that is commanded by the law to be sorry and heavy for his sins is sorry and heavy indeed by the working of God's Spirit: as we may see in Adam, what inward fear and discomfort he had, when he

Gen. iii. iv. 2 Sam. xi. [xii.] Matt. xxvii. [xxvi.] Acts ix.

heard the voice of God after the doing of his sin: Cain the like, David the same, with Peter, Paul, and others in the word of God.

This discomfort inwardly is felt of all God's elect that be able to learn and know the nature of God's law, and the damnation and curse of God upon sin; for this is a general commandment to all flesh born and conceived in sin, *Agite pœnitentiam*, "Repent ye." It is also many times felt of such as die, and lived wickedly; as Saul and Judas, whose spirits in their discomforts refused all consolation, and so died without comfort in great anguish and perturbation of mind. But that is not general in all wicked and damned persons: for many times they feel no discomfort nor heaviness of spirit inwardly in this world; but God, of his unspeakable wisdom and justice, maketh them (for their sins) alive, and in security of conscience, to go to hell: as Pharaoh, whilst he followed the Israelites in persecution into the Red Sea, suddenly was drowned; Korah, Dathan, and Abiram[1], whilst they were doing their sacrifices, God killed them in opening the earth, that swallowed them alive down into hell. Now this inward discomfort, although it end not in joy but only in such as believe their sins to be forgiven in the death and passion of Christ, yet we see by the examples of the scripture that both good and bad suffer and feel this, that their spirit will take no comfort. Matt. iii.
Mark i.
1 Sam. xxxi.
Matt. xxvii.
Mark xiv.
Saul and Judas.

Pharaoh.
Exod. xiv.

Numb. xvi.

Rom. iii. v.

But now as concerning outward and external discomfort, which is felt as well of such as have the word of God, as such as have not the word of God, but only the law of nature: as we may see in the time of the law of nature how Noah shewed the discomfort of all men, and the destruction of the world for sin; but this discomfort did not enter into the spirits of the hearers. Christ complaineth of the same, that the people had both discomfort and comfort preached unto them; and yet they received none of them both. "To whom (saith Christ) should I compare this generation? It is like boys that sit in the streets, and cry unto their fellows, and say, We have played upon our timbrels to you, and you have not danced: we have sung mourning songs unto you, and ye have not wept." God, by his prophet Esay, saith the same: "All the day long have I extended forth my hand unto an unfaithful and intractable people;" meaning, that whatsoever he threatened, or gently offered unto the Jews, it came no further than the outward ear. Whereof both the prophets and Christ himself grievously complain, in this sort: "They have ears, and hear not; and they have eyes, and see not." Outward discomfort.

Gen. v. vi.

Matt. xi.
Luke vii

Isai. lxv.

Isai. liii. vi.
Matt. xiii.
John xii.
Rom. xi.

[1 Dathan and Abiram were destroyed by the earthquake: but Korah was consumed by fire whilst offering incense at the door of the tabernacle.]

Rom. i.

St Paul rebuketh men also that by the law of nature knew good, whereof they should have rejoiced, and evil, whereof they should have lamented, and yet did not. And, to leave off the examples of our fathers mentioned in the scriptures, we may see the same by daily experience amongst ourselves. We read in the book of God, we hear by preaching, we know in our own consciences, the displeasure and anger of God against us for our sins: God outwardly sheweth us the same with many horrible plagues; as by sickness, war, sedition, scarcity, enmity, and hatred; by the deliverance and surrender of a whole realm (to the utter destruction thereof) into the hands and rule of a stranger; and by the delivery and giving over of christian souls into the hands and rule of the antichristian pope and his wicked clergy: and yet this discomfort cometh no further than our outward ear. If Asaph, the author of this psalm, were amongst us, he would say his spirit would take no consolation. And this is an horrible plague, that weekly this psalm is read amongst the popish clergy; and yet it bringeth their spirits to no sorrow nor feeling of God's displeasure. Wherefore our own experience teacheth that there is an inward and an outward discomfort in this psalm, and in the rest of God's most holy word. The one penitent sinners feel, and by it amend their lives; and the other some wicked men feel, and yet despair: but of the most part of the world it is not felt at all; whereof cometh the contempt of God, the love of ourselves and of the world, and the loss of our sinful souls in the world to come. Let us therefore mark the scripture that teacheth this discomfort, and pray to God, that as we see it in the letter, so we may feel it in the spirit. Of the two manner of consolations it shall be said in the next verse; and of the brightness and darkness also in the psalm hereafter.

Sin not felt bringeth the contempt of God, &c.

Now in the trouble of the spirit is another thing to be considered, whereof the text also maketh mention: that is, how the discomfort of the spirit had continuance all the night. Whereof is to be gathered the greatness of discomfort. For as the night is a very image of death, and the bed a very similitude of the sepulchre and grave; even so is the discomfort of the spirit in the night, that will not suffer the body to take rest, but to be unquieted with itself: the which unquietness of the spirit is a very similitude and image of eternal discomfort in the world to come, that both body and

Unquietness of the spirit is a very image of eternal death.

soul, which were created first to inherit the heavenly bliss, after the fall of Adam should rest by night (as king David saith), and after this life, for sin unforgiven, should for ever be disquieted in the unquenchable fire of hell. *Psal. civ.*

Here may we learn the circumstances and causes, how the trouble of the prophet Asaph's spirit was increased. It was trouble engendered by sin (the occasion only of all men's miseries), opened and revealed unto the conscience by the law, condemned by justice to eternal fire; and it continued all night: yea, how much more, the scripture declareth not. In the which night, the darkness thereof represented unto his eyes outwardly the horror of hell prison; and also his bed the grave and sepulchre, wherein all flesh is clad, after the spirit departeth. The sheets of man's flesh after this life be nothing but earth above and earth underneath: as, whilst it liveth, it is clad with such vain things as grow upon the earth. *The cause of all trouble is sin. Psal. xxxix. Rom. v. vii. viii. The night representeth hell prison. The bed representeth the grave. The sheets of man's flesh is earth.*

This whole night in discomfort of the spirit declareth two notable things: first, how earnestly God is angry indeed with sin, that putteth man to such long pain for it; and the next, how gracious a God he is, that will not yet suffer the discomforted spirit to despair in his discomfort, as it followeth marvellously in the next verse. *Two things to be noted.*

3. "When I am in heaviness, I will think upon God: when my heart is vexed, I will complain. Selah."

Whilst Asaph was thus troubled in spirit, he remembered the Lord, and called unto him for help. First, out of this verse it is to be considered, that nothing can quiet the comfortless spirit but God alone. But forasmuch as it seemeth by the parts of this psalm that followeth, that this verse came in by occasion, rather than to shew a full remedy for the prophet's trouble, I will not write what I think thereof, but defer the remedy against trouble to such other verses as follow: because the prophet said before, that his spirit could take no consolation, and that a great many of troubles follow, as the psalm declareth. It sheweth that he was not able to bear the troubles of the mind alone, without the invocation and help of God. Wherefore, before he expresseth by writing all his troubles, he writeth also, how in the midst of them he did remember and put his trust in the Lord. *No comfort to the afflicted but God alone.*

21—2

Out of this we learn how necessary it is in time, at the beginning of troubles and temptations, to remember the Lord, and to call unto him for mercy. For the more temptations do grow without present assistance of God's grace, the greater is the damnation, and the more is the danger thereof: as we may see in the examples of the scripture. Adam fell into anxiety and discomfort of spirit, and God immediately told him of his fault, and by God's grace his discomforted spirit was quieted in the promises of God: Cain, by the murder of his brother Abel, felt the discomfort of the spirit, and by neglecting of God's calling died in the same. David, being admonished by God's grace, found rest for his unquieted spirit: Saul, in deferring the remedy of God's grace, died comfortless. Peter at the beginning, through God's grace, with one look of Christ put away discomfort: Judas, with contemning Christ's admonitions, died in horrible despair.

<small>Note. Gen. iii. Gen. iv.</small>

<small>2 Sam. xii.</small>

<small>1 Sam. xxxi.</small>

<small>Matt. xxvii.</small>

Whereof we learn to beware, as much as may be, that temptations grow not so far, that God's admonition, or the remembrance of God's name, be forgotten; but that we do, in the midst of discomforts, as Asaph the prophet did, remember and call upon the Lord for help. There is also by this remembrance of God in the discomfort of the spirit to be noted, what a vanity all the world and worldly things be for man in time of trouble, when God shall shew and reveal unto man his sins.

This Asaph, as we read in the scripture, was a man whom, for his virtues and good qualities, king David appointed to be a musician for the comfort of many, until the building of the temple of Hierusalem: yet now, as we see, he is not able to solace himself with his music, nor yet with any worldly thing; but his only comfort is in the Lord. And here the prophet declareth the truth of Christ's sentence written in St Luke: "What doth it profit a man to win all the world, and to lose his own soul?" What external riches can comfort the inward spirit, troubled with sin and transgression of God's law? None at all, doubtless; as the scripture sheweth examples everywhere. All king David's kingdom was not able to appease his troubled and discomforted spirit, when he said to his troubled soul, "Why art thou so heavy and sad, my soul, and why dost thou trouble me?"

<small>What manner of man Asaph was. 1 Chron. vi.</small>

<small>Luke ix.</small>

<small>Note.</small>

<small>Psal. xlii. xliii.</small>

Now this one thing more I will mark in this verse, and no more, because it is more fully used by the prophet for the comfort of discomforted spirits in the verses that follow. I said there was two kind of consolations in the word of God: the one outward, in the face and lesson of the letter; and the other inward, in the understanding and feeling of the spirit. And of this division must great heed be taken: for it is not every man that readeth and heareth that Christ died for the remission of sin, that shall have the consolation of the redemption promised in Christ's blood. For we see and read (God give us grace to learn it!) that Adam caused his sons to hear of his own fall in paradise, and the redemption of his fall in the blood of Christ to come[1]; as Abel, his younger son, right well perceived: yet did Cain, hearing the same consolation, perish in his sin. There was consolation and rest promised unto all them that came out of Egypt: but none took the benefit thereof but Josua and Caleb. There was in the outward letter promised consolation unto all Abraham's children: but none received the commodity thereof but such as in spirit followed the faith of Abraham. The scripture saith in the letter, that God would all men to be saved; yet we see such as follow not the Spirit offered be damned. God by his word, in the time of holy and blessed king Edward the sixth, offered consolation unto all this realm; yet none shall enjoy it but such as in their spirits have learned, kept, and do follow the word of consolation. So our Saviour Christ in St Matthew doth say: "Not every man that calleth me Lord, Lord, shall enter into the kingdom of God;" but he that followeth in Christ God's commandments. There be a great many at this day (as there were before our time) that know and speak of such consolation as is contained in the letter and utter[2] bark of God's word; but in their consciences they feel not indeed the consolation thereof: as Judas preached abroad, with the rest of his companions, consolation to the lost sheep of the house of Israel; but he shewed unto others that he felt not himself. So did the Pharisees, when the scripture was read every Saturday in their synagogues, shew that Messiah should come to redeem the world; yet they themselves (for the most part) felt not the consolation indeed that the scripture did testify of Christ. Even so at

Two kinds of consolations in the word of God.

Gen. iv.

Who be the children of Abraham.

Consolation offered unto England in King Edward's days.

Judas.

Pharisees.

[1 This is inferred from the nature of the offering brought by Abel. See Heb. xi. 4.]

[2 utter: outer.]

this present many read this psalm (and daily almost in the letter), whereof, if it be in English, he that understandeth not but the English tongue seeth great consolation in the letter, and also in the prophet Asaph, that used the psalm; yet when need should be, the inward consolation of the psalm of many is nothing felt. The cause is, that either they understand it not, or else mark it not: either they think (as the papists do teach) that to say or sing the psalm, without understanding and feeling of it in the spirit, is sufficient for the work itself, and that it pleaseth God *ex opere operato,* as they term it.

It is too evident, and also too horrible (if it pleased God), that men be contented only with the external consolation contained in the word of God. For if they hear that God's commandments be true and full of consolation, they be contented to hear of them in the letter or by speech, and never learn them or feel them by heart. The like is in the articles of our christian religion. They be thought to be true and godly; and yet the most part that so judge neither learn them nor feel them in their conscience: wherefore they do outwardly and inwardly as much idolatry contrary to their creed, by the commandment of men, as can be devised; for their consolation of faith is no more but such an outward knowledge as the most men hold withal, without any proper judgment or singular feeling of their own spirits. The same is likewise in prayer: for in the external letter there is so much consolation as may be; but in the heart of him that prayeth is there no understanding nor feeling of the consolation that outwardly is spoken and talked of. Therefore, mark this order of the prophet Asaph. He said that his spirit could take no consolation in all the night-time, whilst he held up his hands. And as there is not only discomfort and unquietness spoken of, but also felt; not only noted and written in the letter of the psalm, but also thoroughly felt inwardly in the spirit with heaviness and anguish, without comfort and consolation; so in this verse is there consolation in the letter, in the voice, and in the mouth mentioned of, and inwardly the same consolation felt in the spirit. And as outwardly God's displeasure troubled him, so inwardly God's holy name and promises comforted him. And this is to be noted, lest we should hear of consolation outwardly, or

Prayer.

read it in the book of the holy Bible, and yet inwardly neither feel nor know any consolation at all.

In the end of this verse is put this word "Selah." And it doth note unto the reader or hearer, what a miserable and comfortless thing man is in trouble, if God be not present with him to help him. It is also put as a spur and prick for every christian man and woman to remember and call upon God in the days of their troubles. For, as the Jews say, wheresoever this word "Selah" is, it doth admonish and stir up the reader or hearer to mark what was said before it: for it is a word always put after very notable sentences. *Man in trouble without God's presence is miserable.*

Then followeth the rest of such pains and troubles as this prophet suffered whilst the Lord laid his cross upon him, after this sort:

4. "Thou holdest mine eyes waking: I am so feeble I cannot speak."

Before, he said his spirit could take no consolation, which was a grief unspeakable; for no thought is able to comprehend the anguish of the mind, much less is the tongue able to express it. But now, he sheweth a further increase of discomfort, and saith that the terror of his mind was such, that he was not only comfortless, but the Lord also, to the increase of sorrow, kept sleep from him. And as the greatness of God's punishment suffered him not to sleep, so would it not permit him to speak, but made him speechless: such was the great punishment of God towards him. *Note.*

Here is the tyranny and violence of sin to be perceived and seen, which is first in this verse to be noted. It taketh all mirth from the spirit, and bringeth in heaviness and discomfort. It taketh away sleep, and placeth for it tediousness and sorrowful watch. It taketh away also the speech of the tongue, and leaveth the man mute and speechless. *What sin worketh in man.*

If sin can do so painful things in the body and soul, whilst they be yet conjoined together, and there is hope of remission; what can it do, when the one is in the earth, and the other in hell separated, or else both of them conjoined again in the resurrection of the wicked, where there is no hope of redemption, but assurance of everlasting pain? Besides this, it is to be noted in this verse containing the increase of the prophet's heaviness, what a precious jewel *A peaceable conscience a precious jewel.*

man or woman hath, that hath a quiet heart and peaceable conscience. For wheresoever they be, there be all the members of man and woman wholly bent unto the service and honouring of God. The eyes shall never be turned from their service; neither shall the tongue cease (if it be able to speak) to sound forth always the glory of God, as David saith: "Mine eyes be always towards the Lord." Again, "I lifted up mine eyes unto the Lord. As the eye of the handmaid attendeth upon her mistress, so our eyes attend upon the Lord." Again, "Mine eyes, Lord, be not proud." And in another psalm he saith, there should come neither sleep ne slumber in his eyes, until he had provided a place for the ark of God to rest in. In case the spirit be troubled, or in a contempt of God's laws, not liking his holy devices, the eyes be either troubled with overmuch watch (as in this psalm we see), or else bent to see vanity, the lusts and concupiscence of the flesh and the world. Wherefore David prayed the Lord to turn his eyes that they looked not upon vanity. For the eye of him that hath not a right spirit is insatiable. And many times the eye (where as the spirit is without the favour of God) abhorreth God's own good gifts: as the eyes of the Israelites loathed manna in the desert, saying, "Our eyes see nothing but manna." Even so the tongue also of the godly-spirited man will sound the glory of God, as king David used his tongue, and will not hinder it by naughty speech.

If the spirit be void of God's fear, then doth it speak of malice falsely to slander the good, as king David doth declare; or else for trembling or quaking it can speak nothing at all, as ye may perceive by the prophet Asaph in this place. He that will therefore consider accordingly the greatness of this fear in the spirit, and how it taketh away the office of every member external, doubtless must labour to have the spirit that David prayeth, in this sort: *Cor mundum crea in me, Deus, et spiritum rectum innova in visceribus meis;* "Create in me a clean heart, O Lord, and renew in me a right spirit!" In the which verse the prophet prayeth, first, to have such an heart as by faith in Christ may be clean and purged from sin; and next, to have a certain and sure spirit, that doubteth nothing of God's promises towards him. For such a spirit within the body of man or woman maketh the heart so joyful, that no sorrow can molest it; and it strengtheneth so every member, that they will be given to nothing so much as to the service of God. But if the spirit be wicked, doubtless the outward members will serve nothing but iniquity: if it be troubled, the outward members cannot be quiet. For as the soul giveth life to the body, so doth the virtue of God in the soul draw the outward parts of the body unto the obedience of virtue. And contrariwise, the vice of the soul draweth the members of the body unto the service of sin and iniquity. And as the ears and eyes of man were made by God to be instruments to hear and see God's will and pleasure, and by them (sith man fell in paradise) knowledge might come into the soul and spirit of man by hearing God's word preached, and seeing his sacraments ministered; so by them abused in hearing and seeing of sin and abomination there entereth into the soul much vile filthiness and transgression. The prophet Asaph, therefore, doth admonish us to beware that we bring not our spirits into discomfort by sin and transgression of God's laws: for if we do, whether the offence be done in the spirit by the evil that naturally is in it, by original sin, by the temptation of the devil, or by the means of any member of the body, doubtless the trouble of the spirit shall not only take away the office of the members (as ye see in this place the speech of the tongue and the closing of the eyes be taken away); but at the length also, God shall make the same body and the same members to rise again at the general resurrection, and they shall suffer with the wicked spirit eternal pains. Let this doctrine, therefore, teach all men to know and feel the cruelty of sin, that so painfully unquieteth both body and soul; and think that,—if these grudgings, discomforts, terrors, and fears be so great, that death itself is more tolerable and easy to bear,—how much more intolerable and unspeakable be the pains of hell, which God hath ordained for all impenitent sinners!

Note.

Rom. vii. viii. xii.

Unto what use the eyes and ears of man were created.

Rom. x.

James xix.[1] 1 Cor. xv.

Isai. lxvi. Matt. xxv.

After this verse of trouble and anguish, where as we see sleep taken from the eyes, and speech from the tongue, followeth next how these great sorrows were mollified and somewhat diminished.

[[1] So in ed. 1580: intended perhaps for Jam. v. 1, 2, 3.]

5. "I have considered the days of old, and the years that be past.

6. "In the night I called to remembrance my song, and communed with mine own heart: and my spirit searched diligently."

I did (saith the prophet), in this great discomfort and heaviness, consider with myself the times and worlds of old, wherein the Lord had holpen and delivered my fathers before my time from such troubles as I am in, and also from greater. And in the night, while I was sleepless, I remembered that many times I lauded and exalted the goodness of God in my psalms and hymns, giving him thanks for his great mercy and goodness used towards his church at all times; and in remembering God's accustomed clemency and pity my spirit was much given to debate things.

Consolation in trouble.

Out of these two verses we may note divers doctrines for our consolation in the days of our trouble. And the first (after my mind) shall be concerning the two brightness and the two darkness in the word of God. The one brightness is in the letter outwardly; and the other brightness is in the spirit and heart of the reader of the scripture. This brightness or clarity of the letter is this, when by reading, hearing, or thinking of God's word, men learn and know that God made all things, and that he preserveth all things, and that Jesus Christ his only Son is the Mediator between God and man, and that he pacified God's just ire against man by his bitter death and passion. Also he knoweth by the external histories of the scripture, that God hath delivered many times his people from dangers and perils in manner impossible to be holpen.

This clarity and brightness of the scripture, although it be necessary, yet it is not sufficient; for it standeth alone in bare and naked knowledge, which before God saveth not, neither illuminateth the man that hath the knowledge in a sufficient clarity and brightness of faith, and of God's promises due in Christ unto faith: as we may see how the children of Israel had the external clarity and brightness of God's

Gen. xii. xiii. xv. xvi. xvii.

promises unto Abraham, Isaac, and Jacob, that they and their posterity should inherit the land of Canaan, that flowed with all plenty and abundance; yet, notwithstanding, such as came out of Egypt for the most part perished in the desert and wilderness. The Pharisees and learned men amongst the Jews had the clearness and brightness of Christ's coming, and of the place he should be born in, and told in that part the truth unto Herod; yet did they, for all this knowledge and clarity, abhor Christ when he came, and put him to death most wrongfully. The people in like sort saw an external brightness in Christ, that by his miracles and wonders they thought him worthy to be made a king; and yet, for all this, they cried out against him, *Crucifige eum, crucifige eum,* "Crucify him, crucify him." The devil himself said he knew who Christ was, the Son of the Most Highest; and yet, for all this knowledge and clearness, shall he never be saved. And Christ himself also perceived that this external brightness was amongst a great many that called him Lord, Lord: yet notwithstanding he said they should not enter into the joys of heaven. So likewise be there very many at this present time, that see the clarity and brightness of Christ outwardly in the letter, and yet follow it not here in living, neither shall they have the effect of their knowledge in the life to come: for their clearness is only knowledge, without feeling or practice of the brightness inwardly, which deserveth more stripes than obscurity or darkness doth.

_{Numb. xiv.}
_{Micah v. Matt. ii.}
_{Matt. xxvii. Mark xv. Luke xxiii. John xix. John vi. Luke iv.}
_{Matt. vii.}
_{Luke xii.}

There is another clarity or brightness, which is an inward understanding and spiritual knowledge and sight of God's truth; which no man hath but he that is possessed with the Spirit of God, that whatsoever he readeth in God's word himself, or heareth preached of other men, he understandeth it, and consenteth unto it gladly and willingly. As for example: God spake unto Adam, and his words made him afraid, so that he trembled for fear. Christ spake unto Paul, and he fell down flat, and could not abide the peril of Christ's voice. So that, as the law rebuked sin in the voice and letter, it wrought also rebuke and discomfort in the hearts of Adam and Paul, and made them afraid inwardly, as the voice and letter was terrible outwardly. Wherefore they had not only an external clearness of God's hatred against sin, but also an internal sight and feeling of the same, as the scripture doth record.

_{Gen. iii.}
_{Acts ix.}

The like is also in the promises of God, when they be preached or read, that promise remission of sin. The inward clarity and brightness of the same is to feel privately, every man and woman in his own conscience, through faith in Christ, that the same promises do appertain and belong unto himself: as the prophet Abacuc saith: "The just man liveth by his own faith." Also, when Christ said unto the woman of Canaan, that it was not good to cast the bread that appertained to the children unto dogs, she said, "Yes, Lord; for the dogs do eat of the crumbs that fall from their master's table." And so doth Christ himself use the brightness of his promises to Mary Magdalene, "Thy sins be forgiven thee;" applying the clearness of the letter unto the inward comfort of her soul.

The same is likewise marvellously expressed in the common creed, where as every man saith, he believeth in God the Father, God the Son, and God the Holy Ghost, and that he believeth the remission of sins; meaning, that whosoever saith his creed should see and feel in his soul the clarity and brightness of his salvation, that is contained in the letter and words of the creed. But this clearness is not seen of all men, nor yet of the most part of men, as Christ declareth: "Many be called, and few chosen." Many say, Lord, Lord, and few do the Lord's will. Therefore Christ saith marvellously concerning the clarity and brightness of God's word inwardly, in St Luke: "Blessed be they that hear the word of God, and keep it:" by the which words he declareth, that many hear and see the outward light and truth of God's word, but very few there be that see the inward light and profit thereof. Of this is learned what the cause is that Christians bear the name of Christ, and yet be not Christ's indeed; for because a great many be contented with the name, and few do understand what the name truly and verily containeth in it.

And as there is in the scripture this double brightness, whereof the one lieth in the letter, and many see what it meaneth by the external word, and the other lieth in the meaning of the letter, and is perceived only by such as have the Spirit of God; so is there two kinds and sorts of darkness and obscurity in the scripture; the one in the letter, and the other in the sense and taking of the letter. The outward obscurity is to be seen in such as contemn the word of God, and will not read it nor hear it: as the Turks and heathen, and also the common sort, that bear the name of Christ, be christened in Christ's name, and outwardly be taken to be very Christians indeed, and yet they know not so much as the letter of Christ's laws, that prescribeth them what they should do, and what they should not do. And this obscurity is a brutish, beastly, and external darkness.

The other is obscurity or darkness inwardly in the text: for although the letter be well known, and the sound thereof seemeth to be plain, yet the sense is not so common nor so manifest as the letter soundeth. Whereupon St Paul bindeth all men in the understanding of the letter unto the analogy and proportion of faith, that no one place be taken contrary to many places: whereof was gathered the abridgement of our common creed, accepted at all times and of all christian men for an infallible truth; so that whosoever believed it was accounted a good christian man. And of this obscurity of the scripture in the sense and spirit is risen this troublesome contention about transubstantiation of bread and wine in the sacrament of Christ's body and blood. For the ungodly sort would have no substance of bread and wine to remain in the sacrament, and yet a corporal presence of body and blood, contrary not only to the articles of our faith, that telleth us he is in heaven, and shall abide there until he come to judge the quick and the dead, but also contrary to many other places of the scripture. *The inward obscurity.*

Matt. xxvi. Mark xiv. Luke xxii. 1 Cor. x. xi. Acts iii. Coloss. iii.

And this is no new thing, to have and record the text and letter of the scripture, and yet lack the effect and the very consolation of the scripture indeed. For here in these two verses the prophet Asaph doth record and remember God's doings mercifully in time past, and yet taketh no more consolation thereof than he findeth in the bark of the letter, or in the rehearsal of the histories. And the same he doth of his own psalms and hymns, whereof he maketh mention; and yet by the same mean his spirit is brought into no further considerations of God's truth than it was before, with much heaviness and sorrow, as the verses following do declare: so that, in the affliction of the spirit, he could repeat and call to his remembrance the truth, how God had dealt mercifully with his forefathers, but felt not at that present the like mercy of God towards himself; neither could he see nor feel for his consolation the ease and succour of God's promises which he saw in others, as all the elects of God at length shall doubtless feel: as it is said by the prophet, *Sicut audivimus, sic vidimus*, " As we have heard, so have we seen;" and at length

Psal. xlviii. (as the psalm saith) he felt himself. Whether he wrote the psalm of his own sorrows and troubles, or of the sorrows and troubles of the Israelites, it maketh no matter: let every man in that case use his own judgment, so that he mark the doctrine of the psalm.

There is to be noted of these verses also this doctrine, that whatsoever trouble the spirit was brought unto, whatsoever watch had taken his eyes, and whatsoever vehemency of disease had taken his speech from him, yet under all these crosses he cursed not God, nor grudged against his plagues; but, as a man contented, gave himself to record and to call to memory how God was wont to be unto men afflicted, and took account how in times past he had spent his years, and found that he had made certain psalms or hymns to the glory of God, and to the praise of his holy name. Of the which we learn not only patience in the time of trouble and persecution, but also how to spend our youth and transitory life in doing or making some things that may be records and remembrances, when we be gone, that we lived here to serve God, and not to serve ourselves. And it is a great help and no small consolation for a man that is in trouble and heaviness, to think that he in his life before sought the glory of God; and that testimony of conscience is more worth in the time of trouble than all other men's deeds for him. Not in that his seeking God's glory and setting forth of the same can be his gage and ransom before God; but because it is a very testimony that God once loved him, and gave him of his blessed Spirit, to indite something to God's praise and honour. And as godly psalms and virtuous hymns be testimonies of a virtuous spirit, so be wanton and adulterous ballads records of a vicious and sinful spirit. And as the remembrance of good and virtuous works in the time of sickness and trouble be joyful and comfortable, so is the remembrance of wicked doings sorrowful and painful. We be therefore taught by this prophet to be circumspect and wary, how we accumulate and heap upon our souls infidelity and the wicked works thereof: for as they be the only cause of trouble, so do they not only work trouble, but also increase trouble, and augment the heaviness of the spirit and pains of the body; as is declared marvellously by the grave and profound sentences following, wherein he declareth what it was that his spirit searched so diligently for. It was this:

7. "Will the Lord absent himself for ever, and will he be no more entreated?
8. "Is his mercy clean gone for ever, and is his promise come utterly to an end for evermore?
9. "Hath God forgotten to be gracious, and will he shut up his loving-kindness in displeasure?
10. "And I said, It is mine own weakness, but the right hand of God can change these things."

These verses declare what minds and cogitations do happen to men that be in sickness or trouble, and how grievous they be unto the patient. *The troubled spirit is overwhelmed with grievous cogitations.*

Out of these verses first we see a common rehearsal of the great terror and fear of the feeling of God's displeasure and anger towards the woeful spirit for sin. The first meditation of the sinful spirit was this: "Will the Lord absent himself for ever?" This may be understood two manner of ways; for this English word "ever" hath two meanings in the Hebrew tongue: sometime it is taken for continuance and time everlasting; sometime for certain years, and the life of men. If it be taken in this place for time everlasting, the sorrows of the prophet were the greater, when he revolved with his spirit that God justly for sin might cast him into everlasting pains, the remembrance whereof is greater pain than the mortal death of the body. If this word "ever" be taken for a certain time, and the life of man, then meaneth the prophet thus: "Will God as long as I live absent himself, and thus continue me in heaviness of spirit and sorrows as long as I live?" Which sense soever be taken, there be profitable things to be learned of it. But I suppose the latter sense to be the better for divers causes: first, in this, that the psalm containeth the complaint and prayer of the prophet, a man of God, that cannot be brought to this desperation, that he should be cast away for ever from the favour of God unto eternal pains. And the text that saith, "It is mine own infirmity, and the right hand of the Lord can change this," doth bear with this latter sense and explanation. For the words be of great weight, and of marvellous wisdom and consolation, and do declare, that although the prophet felt the judgment of God against sin, and was in a marvellous terror and fear with the horror and sight of his sins, yet the Spirit *The remembrance of God's justice for sin is greater than the death of the body.*

of God did testify with his spirit, that he was the child of God, and that it was a pain and punishment of the soul and body, and not a desperation and thorough casting away and absenting of God's mercy. For the very elects of God be so chosen, so ordained, so preserved and kept, that nothing is able to take them out of God's hand. For the godly men in the scripture did rejoice with the assurance of God's certain promise, and did not presume to do evil, as St Paul in sundry places doth give testimony: once to the Romans, where as he felt and perceived the filthiness of sin, and the just judgment of God against the same; as it appeareth by his woeful cry and complaint, "O wretched man that I am! who shall deliver me from this body subject unto death?" He felt (as we may perceive) the heavy burden and weight of God's displeasure; and yet, in the midst of terror and fear, he stayed assuredly in the mercy of God through Christ. And the same he writeth also to the Corinthians, and to his disciple Timothy, that his death was at hand, and that he knew, although his quarrel were never so good, that he of himself was a sinner, and by sin worthy rejection and casting away from God; yet he said that Christ had in keeping for him a crown of justice, which he should assuredly receive at the day of his death. God is contented that his chosen people shall suffer and bear the burden and heaviness of temptation and fear of everlasting pain, as Adam did first in paradise, David many times, Job, and others; yea, Christ himself, that said his "soul was heavy even unto death," which made him sweat both water and blood. But these temptations and terrors shall never overcome and cast away the person that hath his faith in Christ: for none is able to take his sheep out of his hand.[1] Yet God withdraweth his hand many times, and suffereth his to be tempted and to be comfortless and, as it were, clean overthrown: not that indeed their election can be altered, or they themselves left comfortless until the end of their lives, but for a time; as ye may see by Job, who spake as horrible words, and as desperately, as might be: yet see in the end of this book, and mark what a joyful outgoing his grievous temptations had. What pitiful cries were these of Christ our Saviour upon the cross!

[¹ The reference may be to John vi. 39; but the words seem to point rather to John x. 28, 29.]

"My God, my God, why hast thou forsaken me?" Yet the end was, "Father, into thy hands I commend my spirit." Matt. xxvii.
Mark xv.
Luke xxiii.
John xix.

It is written, that we must enter into heaven by many troubles. Now, of all troubles, the trouble of the mind and of the spirit is the greatest. Who then can enter into heaven without such troubles? Doubtless, no man; for the judgment of God must begin at his house, as St Peter saith; that is to say, none shall in this life more feel God's displeasure for sin in the spirit, nor suffer more adversity in the body, than such as be of God's own household and very elects. Wherefore we be admonished, in the troubles and sorrows that this prophet Asaph sustained in his soul that could not rest, and in his body that could not sleep nor speak, that good men be not free from adversity, and that adversities, be they never so great, shall not separate men from God for ever, but for a time he punisheth sin, and hideth the consolation of God from us; as the scripture saith: "For a time a little while I have forsaken thee; but I will gather thee together in wonderful mercies. In a short time of my wrath I hid my face awhile from thee, but I will have mercy upon thee for ever, saith the Lord thy Redeemer."

Psal. xxxiv.
Acts xiv.
The trouble of the mind is the greatest.

1 Pet. iv.
Prov. xii.[1]
Heb. xii.

God hideth his consolation for a time to try us.
Isai. liv.

All men that shall profitably know and feel the certainty of God's promises in this life, and enjoy them in the life to come, shall be troubled with some pain of doubtfulness of them, before he come to perfection. For as by sin death entered into the flesh, and also the flesh is subject unto sickness and adversity, so is there entered into the soul and powers thereof, by reason of sin, great imperfection. As the mind of all men is burdened with ignorance, the heart with contumacy, and the will with frowardness, so that as they be, before regeneration and knowledge of God, in all godly matters stark blind, very obstinate, and naturally altogether froward; even so, after regeneration and the knowledge of God, they continually resist and fight against the spirit, not only of man, in whom these powers dwell, but also against the Spirit of God, that teacheth and leadeth the spirit of man to eternal salvation: so that it is not man that is able to overcome the wickedness of his own soul. And therefore, seeing life through grace dwelt in a body naturally full of sin, St Paul said, "I do live; yet not I, but Christ liveth in me."

Gen. iii.
Rom. v.

Rom. vii.
viii.
Eph. ii.
Psal. liii.

Rom. viii.
John iii.

Philip. i. ɑ.
Gal. ii.

[[1] The reference should probably have been to Prov. iii. 11, 12.]

[HOOPER, II.]

So this prophet Asaph seemeth in words to be stark dead from grace, but it was not for ever; for he felt the Spirit of God, that told him that such heavy and ungodly thoughts of his spirit came of his own infirmity, and that God's right hand could alter and change them. And this is the difference between the affliction of the godly and ungodly, as it is wonderfully set forth in the psalm next before this saving one, where it is said, "There is a cup in the Lord's hand full of red wine, and he poureth out of it; but the wicked shall drink the dregs thereof, and the ungodly of the earth shall receive the bottom of it." The cup in the scripture is taken many times for adversity, whereof God filleth a quantity and a certain measure unto all his elect and chosen servants; but the wicked shall drink the bottom and all, and never come to rest nor ease.

Out of this temptation we may learn how foolish and how impatient we be. When God sendeth troubles, we think such to be best at ease that want them; whereas the Lord's book declareth that it is necessary, and also very expedient, that we should have them. Again, there is to be noted, how that the prophet in the cogitations of his mind maketh no mention of the grief of the body, whereof he spake before at the beginning of his troubles. For in the second and fourth verse he declareth how he held up his hands all night, cried with his voice until he was speechless, and lay waking, and could not sleep: of the which sorrows now he maketh no rehearsal, but saith his spirit was searching and inquisitive whether God would absent himself for ever, with divers like interrogatories of God's nature, as follow in the psalm. Whereof we learn the vileness of our own nature, and also the treason and subtlety of the devil: for as long as we sin, we have such delight and pleasure therein, as though it were but a play to transgress and break God's holy commandments; but when sickness and trouble have laid the wicked body abed, and made it weak and feeble, our conscience is waked by the law of God, and we put in such terror and fear that nothing can quiet us. Also, as long as we do sin, the devil beareth us in hand that God is so merciful, do what we will, that he will not be angry; but when sickness or death invadeth, then turneth the devil his tale, and persuadeth with us that God is only extreme just, and nothing at all merciful.

And this grief of the mind is so sore and vehement, that all the pains of the body seem nothing in comparison thereof; as we see in this place by the holy prophet Asaph, that was very sore unquieted in his body, yet did his spirit make no account of it, but still he stayed and staggered, trembling and quaking at the heaviness and sorrow of the spirit, that could not feel, for the time of his trouble, any certainty or consolation in the promises of God.

Of this we be admonished, that whatsoever we have, if God's favour lack, we have nothing able to rejoice us: and of the other side, if we lack all things, and have assuredly God's favour, there is nothing able to make us heavy and sorrowful. As we see king Saul, having a noble kingdom, 1 Sam. xvi. xxiv. and lacking the favour of God, was always unquieted: poor 2 Sam. xv. xvi. David, having the grace and favour of God, was quiet and contented with all things, saying, "If God will, he may restore me; if he will not, his will be done." The assurance of God's promises made Paul glad to die; and the mistrust 2 Tim. iv. and desperation of God's promises made Judas weary to live. Matt. xxvii. The certainty of God's truth made St Stephen quietly to die Acts vii. in the assurance of eternal life; the uncertainty and doubtfulness of God's mercy caused Saul to die in the fear of 1 Sam. xxxi. eternal death. Riches of this world be treasures much esteemed and made of, friends and lovers much sought for and warily kept, and health of body highly regarded and preserved with much care; yet, if the soul be destitute of the assurance of God's grace, the rest seem to be of no valure at all: as we see Saul in his kingdom, with riches, strength, and 1 Sam. xvi. friendship; yet, his mind vexed still [with] an evil spirit, and God's Spirit departed, his sorrows were incomparable. So that we learn, that not only the goods appertaining to the body be nothing worth where as the spirit wanteth the grace of God, but also, where as the spirit is troubled, the goods of the body be little felt, and nothing passed of; as we see by this prophet in this psalm.

The other part of his cogitations in the time of his sickness was this: "Will he be no more entreated?" This grievous temptation, whether God would be entreated to forgive sin any more, may have two understandings; the one generally, and the other particularly: generally, in this sort, whether God, once offended, will be merciful and forgive, or

22—2

not; particularly, whether God, whose nature is merciful, will forgive the private man that seeketh by faith mercy, as he hath in time past forgiven all men that asked it with repentance in faith. The first sense and taking of the text generally is marvellous wicked and blasphemous, to think that God, once offended with any man, will never forgive again. Of this opinion was Cain, when he said his sins were greater than they might be forgiven; and he thought God would be no more entreated, because he judged his fault greater than the mercy of God that forgiveth faults. And wheresoever this judgment of the spirit is, this sentence is verified, God will be entreated no more. And as every man that is privately thus minded, that his own sins be greater than can be forgiven, even so hath he the like mind and judgment also of all other men's sins that be like unto his, thinking them to be greater than they may be forgiven; for he that despaireth of his own faults cannot think well that other men's faults as great as his own be remissible: as Judas, that hanged himself for betraying of Christ, could not think well of Peter that denied Christ, but rather judged of Peter as he did of himself, saying, God will be entreated no more.

marginal: Gen. iv.
marginal: A wicked judgment.
marginal: Matt. xxvii. xxvi.

Of this wicked judgment of God's mercy, whether he will be entreated any more of a sinner, after that he hath sinned, I will speak no more; but they that lust to read how horrible a thing it is may have many psalms that do declare it; namely Psalm x. and lxxiii. In the one of them it is said by the wicked, that God hath forgotten the earth, and careth neither for the godly life of the godly and virtuous, nor the ungodly life of the ungodly and wicked: and in the other psalm they make a doubt whether there be any knowledge in God of man and of his life, or not. But these sorts of people be too horrible and blasphemous, and not to be rehearsed or much spoken of.

marginal: Psal. x. lxxiii.

The other sense of this place, that is more particular, is the better sense for the argument and meaning of the psalm; that is, to ask whether God will be entreated no more, as touching the remission of his own sin; or else, whether God will be no more merciful to help him out of trouble, that specially and particularly suffereth the trouble. And this question so asked is very common and familiar to the Christians, and putteth them to great trouble and heaviness. As we may see that this prophet Asaph considered the years before him, and what God did to his elders, and found that they received remission of their sins, and great benefits in this world at God's hand: so do a great number of men, in hearing and reading the scripture of God, see and perceive the remission of many men's sins, and how mercifully God dealt with them; yet when they feel their own sin, and suffer their own cross and trouble, they have much ado, and with great difficulty do they believe that God will be as good unto them, being private sinners and privately afflicted, as he was unto the great number of those, of whom they read in the scripture that God forgave them their sins, and preserved them in most horrible and dangerous troubles.

Therefore, this is a common wisdom and daily experimented sentence: *Omnes, cum valemus, bonum consilium ægrotis damus:* "When other men be sick, we can give good counsel patiently to bear it." When other men be afflicted and troubled, we can speak of many means to quiet them. When they be in any mistrust of God's promises, we can comfort them with many arguments of faith: but most commonly, if we be sick ourselves, troubled, or in mistrust of God's promises, we can ease or comfort ourselves very little. And good cause why; for God that giveth, of his own gift and only free liberality, wisdom, knowledge, learning, and consolation, giveth also the grace that the said virtues may work their operation, and expel the infirmities and diseases wherefore these wisdoms and virtues were ordained: as it is marvellously noted of St Paul: "I have planted, and Apollo hath watered, but God gave the increase." The word of God is a means to teach truth, and to condemn falsehood; to place virtue, and to remove vice; to give consolation, and to banish and put away diffidence and distrust: but God giveth and worketh the effect thereof. Meat is made to preserve the body; but if God giveth not strength, it misseth the purpose. The horse and man be means to overcome; but in battle God giveth the victory. The preacher preacheth God's word; but God openeth and teacheth the mystery thereof: man heareth, but God giveth the understanding. Asaph remembered God's works, and had in mind his own godly psalms; but God must give the consolation: he saw the truth, and knew that God was faithful; but the joy and profit thereof lay in the distribution and gift of God,

A whole man can give good counsel to the sick, but being sick himself cannot apply the same to his comfort.

1 Cor. iii.

Rom. i.
Matt. x.
xxviii.
Acts xvi.

Prov. xxi.

as we may well perceive by this sorrowful interrogatory, "Will he be entreated no more?"

When we hear or read God's promises, we ought to pray.
Mark ix.
Luke xvii.

Of this part we learn how we ought, when we read or hear God's promises for our salvation, to pray; and how necessary a thing this prayer is that godly men made in the scripture: "Lord, help my incredulity; Lord, increase our faith." The poor man that heard and saw Christ's mercy and liberality in healing of others desired also health for his own child. Christ said, if he believed, all things were possible. The poor man said, "I believe, Lord; help mine unbelief." The apostles, when they heard Christ speak of forgiveness of one to the other, they said, "Increase our faith, good Lord:" as though they had said, Except thou give us strength to believe and credit thy godly lessons, we shall take no commodity nor profit by them. Therefore let the preacher of God, the reader of God's word, the hearer of God's word, and the thinker upon the same, many times before, also whilst they be speaking, thinking, reading, or hearing of God's word, pray in their spirits, that the word of God may work in them the thing wherefore the word was instituted and appointed of God;

2 Tim. iii.

or else we shall be (as St Paul saith) always learners, and yet never come to the knowledge of the truth. And I do verily think, and am truly persuaded, that for lack of earnest and continual prayer, with lifting up of my heart unto God, whilst I preached his most holy word unto the people, God judgeth me not worthy to see such fruits of my labours as I hoped for. And for this, that the people did not heartily pray to understand God's pleasure by his word preached, they be accounted unworthy of such salvation as God did offer them by his word and the true preaching of his mysteries. Let all men therefore pray to God in Christ, that they may be the better for the hearing, recording, remembering, or reading of God's word. For, notwithstanding they have amongst them the book of God, yet shall they be troubled (without God's singular grace) with one of these two evils: either to mock and scorn at the scripture, caring not whether they learn it or no; or else, when they have learned it, to doubt whether it be true or no. And then followeth these questions: "Will God absent himself for ever?" and, "Will God be no more entreated?" with such other doubts as do follow in this psalm; with much heaviness unto the spirit where such demands rest and have place.

Then followeth the third demand by this troubled prophet, "Is his mercy clean gone for ever?" Here in this demand first be two things to be noted; the one declaring a fault in the prophet's faith, and the other expressing a verity in the prophet's knowledge. The fault in his faith was to doubt or to stand in a mammering of God's mercy, which is most sure, and endureth for ever and ever, and to ask this question, whether his mercy were clean gone for ever? The verity of his knowledge was to judge and say, that it was his mercy that forgave sins, and not his or any other men's merits that could deserve the pardoning of sin: as ye may see how sinful Saul for his sin thought to have appeased God with sacrifice, and the proud Pharisee with his pretenced good works. But here in this knowledge, that the prophet complained of the departure of God's mercy, is set forth that only mercy appeaseth God's ire in Christ for the sin of man. And what works soever be done, except God's mercy pardon the sin, they all can neither please God, nor quiet the conscience and troubled spirit of him that doth the works: as it may be seen in the example of St Peter, and the rest of the apostles. When that Saint Peter walked upon the sea coming towards Christ, and felt the wind strong and tempestuous, he began to fear: and when he began to sink, he cried, "Lord, save me." And the Lord put forth his hand and took him, and said unto him, "Thou of little faith, why doubtest thou?" 1 Sam. xv.
Luke xviii.

Exod. xxxiv.
Deut. v.vii.
Psal. xxxiii.
li. lvi. lxxxv.
cxxx. cxliii.

Matt. xiv.

Here we see, if God did help us no more of his mercy than our own merits deserved, or else no more than the gifts of God, faith, hope, and charity, as they be qualities in us, we should surely perish. Therefore this place of the prophet Asaph, where he demandeth this question, whether God's mercy be gone for ever, doth teach us, that of all things we should be most assured of this, that only mercy is the help of man's troubles and damnation. But as I said before there were two manner of clarities and brightness in the word of God, so now I say there is two manner of mercies of God mentioned in the scripture: the outward mercy is in the letter, which men read and sing every day, and speak and talk of; but the other is inward. *Note.*

Two manner of mercies mentioned in the scripture.

When that men cannot feel God's mercy in their conscience as they hear it spoken of, and as they read it in the book, they be troubled and full of anguish and pain; and as long as they be in this case, without God's mercy, they can do nothing that pleaseth God, or content themselves. But as soon as the spirit is assured and feeleth that God for his mercy doth forgive and forget the iniquity that the spirit and body have committed and done against God, it rejoiceth and is so glad, that it will do nothing but that which pleaseth and is acceptable unto God, and in Christ shall content and quiet his own conscience. As for example: Adam, before he inwardly felt the mercy of God promised in Christ to forgive and remit his sin and offence, in what heaviness was the poor man! He hid himself, and could not abide the voice of the living God; for he felt that his doings pleased neither God nor himself. But when grace had assured him of God's mercy, he fell in the spirit to quietness. For, where the Spirit of God testifieth and beareth record with the spirit of man that he is the child of God, there is joy and consolation, with this joyful song and melody, *Abba, Pater,* "Father, Father:" so that wheresoever this song is felt in the spirit, there are such joys as no tongue can express, as all the book of Solomon's ballads marvellously do declare. And where as the mercy of God is not, there is either abomination of sin, and continuance therein, without any fear or grudge of conscience at all; or else such heaviness of spirit, that desperation utterly quaileth and oppresseth the spirit for ever. Yet shall the spirit and soul of man feel this for a time, while God hideth his merciful face: " Is his mercy clean gone for ever?" which cogitations of the mind be full bitter and sorrowful, as all men of God do know that have felt them, and as the prophet declareth in the process of his psalm, in this sort: " And is his promise come utterly to an end for evermore? Hath God forgotten to be gracious? And will he shut up his loving-kindness in displeasure?" These demands and questions of his own mind and spirit that was troubled be no more in effect than troubles that he named before. But in this, that he calleth the trouble by so many names, it declareth that his spirit was for the time so disquieted, that the pains in manner could not well be named and expressed: as it is to be seen always when the mind of man is brought into an excellency and profoundness of mirth or sorrow, then it is so ravished with the vehemency of them both, that the tongue is not able to express the inward joy nor the inward sorrow; as it is to be seen as well in profane writers as in the holy word of God. Read ye the eighteenth psalm of king David, which he sung to the Lord when he was quit and delivered from all his enemies; and ye shall see what shift and copy[1] of words he used to name God, and to express what he thought of God in his heart, and with what metaphors he expresseth the strength of God, that overcame all his enemies. The psalm is to be read and marked. Again, read ye these psalms, xlii. xliii., where ye shall perceive the prayer of David, wherein is described a vehement agony and most bitter battle between faith and desperation; and there mark what words he hath found out to express the sorrows of his heart, that was so sore put in doubt by desperation and weakness of faith: "The hart (saith he) being wounded was never more desirous to come to the water than my soul desireth to come to thee, O God!" And at length, when he can find no more words to utter the pensiveness of his heart, he turneth his words inward to his own soul, and asketh why she is so heavy and sad. Ye may see also the very same joyful and sorrowful spirits in the ballads of Solomon, and in the Lamentations of Jeremy the prophet. In the one it seemeth that the soul annexed unto Christ is in such joy as the tongue cannot express it; and in the other, for sin the soul is afflicted in such sort, that it cannot tell how to express the heaviness thereof.

Psal. xviii.

Psal. xlii. xliii.

There is to be considered also in these demands of the prophet that he made to himself in his spirit (as the text saith, he revolved the matter with his own spirit) this doctrine, how easy a thing it is to teach and comfort other men, and how hard a thing it is for a man to teach and comfort himself in the promises of God. St Paul found fault therewithal, and said to the Jew: "Thou teachest another man, and teachest not thyself." And Judas went forth with the eleven other of his fellows to teach God's mercy in Christ unto the lost sheep of the house of Israel; but he neither followed his own doctrine, nor yet took any comfort of remission of sins in the promises of God, but hanged himself desperately. Wherefore it is very expedient for every man and woman that hath learned and doth know the truth of God, to pray that they themselves may follow the truth; and for such as know and

Rom. ii.

Matt. x. xxvii.

[1 Probably in the sense of copiousness.]

teach others the consolations of the scriptures of God, that they may, with knowledge of them, feel them indeed, and, with speaking of them to others for their learning, they may speak them to themselves for their own edifying.

But doubtless it is an easy matter for a man to speak of comfort and consolation to others, but a hard thing to feel it himself. Virtue is soon spoken of to other men's instructions, but the putting thereof in practice and use is very hard; yea, not only in the scholar that is taught, but also in the master that instructeth. Beware of despair, can every man say; but to eschew despair in great conflicts of the mind is an hard matter. Read the book of the Psalms well, and ye shall see the experience thereof to be most certain and true. In the sixty-second psalm ye shall have this commandment to all men: "Trust ye always in him, ye people:" yet when it came to the trial in himself, ye may see with what heaviness and great trouble of mind he came to the trust in the Lord. Ye may learn by these psalms indited by king David, that easily he taught God's religion, and how men should put their trust in the Lord, and yet how hard it was to do and practise the thing himself that he taught unto others. Asaph also declareth the same; for in the seventy-third psalm he teacheth what men should think and judge in adversity, that God would be good unto Israel. But in this psalm he himself, being under the rod and persecution of God, is come to questioning and demanding: "Will God absent himself for ever? Will he be no more entreated? Is his mercy clean gone for ever?"—with many other demands, declaring unspeakable troubles and difficulties of the mind, before it be brought to a perfect consent and full agreement unto the promises of God. So that we see the excellent prophets, and most virtuous organs and instruments amongst sinful men, knew it was an easy matter to speak of faith and virtue, and yet a very hard thing to practise true faith, and to exercise virtuous living. St Paul sheweth the same to the Romans to be in himself: for he had more ado in Christ to get the victory of sin in himself, than to speak of the victory unto others by mouth; and more ado to mortify and kill the flesh, and to bring it in subjection to the spirit, than to practise the death of the flesh in himself, and to follow the spirit. He spake and uttered with his mouth most godly doctrine to the destruction of sin; but with what prayers, tears, and clamours to God, he did the same in himself, read 2 Cor. xii.

The old saying is, Knowledge is no burden, and indeed it is a thing easy to be borne; but to put knowledge in experience the body and the soul shall find pain and trouble. And yet Christ's words where he saith, "My yoke is light, and my burden easy," be most true to such as have wrestled with sin, and in Christ got the upper hand. To them, I say, the precepts of virtuous living be easy and sweet, as long as the Spirit of God beareth the overhand in them. But when faith waxeth faint, and the flesh strong, then cannot the Spirit of God command nor desire anything, but both body and soul be much offended with the hearing thereof, and more grieved with the doing of it. St Peter likewise maketh mention of the same: for when Christ bade him follow him (meaning that he should die also for the testimony of his word), he liked not that, but asked Christ what John should do; being doubtless in great perplexity, when Christ told him that he should suffer the pains of death. But here are to be noted two things: the one, that as long as affliction is talked of generally, and other men's pains spoken of, so long can every man and woman hear of affliction, yea, and commend the persons that suffered affliction; as we see at this day, all men be contented to hear of the death of Christ, of the martyrdom of his saints, and of the affliction and imprisonment of his godly members: but when the same or like should be experimented and practised by ourselves, we will none of it, we refuse it, and we abhor it; yea, so much that, where Christ, and those saints whose names be most common and usual in our mouths, suffered the vilest death that could be devised, we will not suffer as much as the loss of a friend, or the deceivable goods of this unstable and transitory world: so that in the generality we be very godly, and can commend all godly martyrs and sufferers for God's sake; but, alas! in the particularity we be very ungodly, and will follow no martyr, nor suffer at all. Also, as long as we be without danger for Christ's sake, we can speak of great dangers, and say that we will suffer all extremity and cruelty; but when it cometh to pass, that an enemy to God and his word shall say indeed, Forsake thy religion, or else thou shalt die, (as Christ said unto Peter, "When thou art old, another shall gird thee, and lead thee

To such as have wrestled with sin, and in Christ got the upper hand, God's precepts be easy and sweet. Matt. xi.

Rom. vii.

John xxi.

We can praise other men for welldoing, but we be loath to put it in experience ourselves.

John xxi.

whither thou wouldest not,") then a little threatening of another man stark quaileth this man that said he would suffer all troubles: as Peter said, "If he should lose his life, he would not refuse his Master;" but when another, yea, a poor maid, but asked him whether he were one of Christ's servants, and made no mention at all of loss of life or goods, he would not hazard himself to bear so much as the name of Christ's disciple.

<small>Matt. xxvi.</small>

Thus we see the vileness and frailty of our own nature, how weak we be to suffer indeed, when of necessity we must bear the cross, and can by no means avoid it. How troublesome also it is both to body and soul, this psalm and place of the scripture declareth; and therefore in the end of these temptations is put "Selah," a word that maketh, as it were, an outcry against the corrupt nature of man for sin: as St Paul said: "I know that there dwelleth in my flesh no good thing." To admonish therefore man thereof indeed, and to shew him his own damnation, the word is put there to cause the reader or hearer of the place to mark and bewail the wretchedness thereof: as the prophet himself doth in the next verse.

<small>Rom. vii.</small>

⁋ THE FOURTH PART.

How a man taketh consolation in the time of his trouble.

10. "And I said, This is my infirmity: but these things the right hand of God can change."

Here is life and death, and the occasions of both, marvellously set forth. He said that it was his infirmity that caused him to question and doubt of God's mercy; wherein he hath disburdened God, and charged himself with sin and doubtfulness. And so much all men see and find in themselves, that damnation is of ourselves, and salvation only of God. There is also to be noted in this infirmity, that it occupieth not only the body, but also the soul: for he saith these cogitations and questions (as touching the doubtfulness of God's mercy) were the devices and acts of his mind; so that both his body and soul were comfortless. And good cause why; for in both of them were sin and abomination against God. And of these two parts of man, the body and the spirit, came these dubita-

<small>Hosea xiii.</small>

tions of God and of his promises: the which fruits of corruption engender (except sin be forgiven) eternal death. And here is the wisdom of the flesh seen to be very enmity unto God, working continually the breach of God's commandments, and the destruction of man's salvation, as much as lieth in it. But in the second part of the verse is life, and the occasion thereof; which is a sure trust that God can remove despair, and put in place thereof faith, hope, and sure confidence. And the occasion of this help is not man's merits, but the right hand of God, that is to say, God's power inclined to save man by mercy. *Rom. viii.*

The occasion of man's help is God's right hand.

Of this doctrine be certain things to be marked of every reader and hearer of this psalm. First, in this verse is declared how man taketh consolation in time of his trouble, which is the fourth part of the psalm; and in the same part the psalm endeth. He saith it was his infirmity that made him to question and demand in his spirit so doubtful things of God, and of his promises: whereof we learn, that consolation beginneth where sorrow and heaviness is first felt; for the spirit can take no solace by God's promises, until such time as it feeleth by God's law how sinful it is for the transgression thereof. Therefore Solomon saith: "The just man is the first accuser of himself." And so doth the prophet Asaph in this place confess that these cogitations and profound thoughts against God came of his own infirmity and sin. And the knowledge of a man's own wickedness from the bottom of the heart, although it be a shame to speak or remember the vileness of sin, wherewith [the] sinner hath most grievously transgressed God's commandments, yet is this knowledge and confession of our sin and iniquity very necessary, and is, as it were, an induction to the remission thereof, as it is to be seen in this prophet, and in the prophet David. For here is first confessed that all sins in him came of his own infirmity, and all consolation against sin came of God's right hand. And the prophet David saith, when he was in like trouble for sin, "I determined (saith he) to confess against myself mine own iniquity; and thou, Lord, forgavest the wickedness of my sin." But here is to be noted in this, that the confession of sin is, as it were, an induction and beginning of consolation; that confession of sin is not the beginning of consolation, except he that maketh *Prov. xviii.*

True confession of sin is in manner an induction to the remission thereof.

Psal. lxxiv. [lxxvii.] xxxii.

the confession be assured in his heart of God's promises in Christ, that, of mercy in Christ's death, his sins be forgiven; as ye may see in these two prophets. The one said, "It is mine infirmity that worketh this doubtfulness in my soul;" and the other said, "I determined to condemn myself of sin."

Thus far it is death, and an increase of diffidence in God's promises, and an induction to desperation, to feel sin, to bewail sin, to speak of sin, and to remember sin. But where as knowledge and confession hath a certainty and assurance of God's forgiveness annexed unto it, there is confession and knowledge of sin partly a beginning of consolation against sin. I call it partly, or as an occasion, because, first of all, God by his word, or by his punishments, through the operation of the Holy Ghost, openeth the soul of the sinner to see and know his sin, also to tremble and quake at sin, rather than to hate and abhor sin. And from these principles and originals cometh the humble and lowly confession of sin, not to man, but unto God; except it be such an open sin done against man, as man knoweth of that the sin is committed against: then must the offender of man also reconcile himself to man that is offended, according to the commandment of God. Therefore we must mark what confession and acknowledging of our own infirmities is: for every confession is not acceptable before God, nor the beginning of consolation, as these examples declare. Judas said openly in the face of the court where Christ our Saviour was arraigned, that he had offended in betraying innocent blood; but there followed no faith nor hope of forgiveness: so that, for lack of faith in Christ's blood, desperation and hanging of himself ensued his confession: whereby it is evident that confession of sin without faith is nothing worth, but a testimony of a desperate man's damnation. King Saul, after long impulsion by the prophet Samuel, was brought to confess that he had offended in preserving alive Agag, king of the Amalekites, and the fattest of his cattle. "I have offended (saith Saul); for I have broken and transgressed the commandment of God." But what followed? "God's right hand can remedy my sin," as this prophet Asaph saith? or, "God hath forgiven the iniquity of my sin," as David said? or else, "God be merciful unto me a sinner," as the publican said? No; but this ensueth: "I pray thee (saith Saul to Samuel) bear thou my sin." In this man's confession of sin was not the beginning of consolation, but of more sorrows; for his heaviness from that day more and more increased with his sins, until he was slain. And the cause thereof was this: he would that Samuel, being but a man, should have pardoned his sin; whereas none can do it but God, as it is notably to be seen in king David; for when he said he had offended the Lord, Nathan the prophet said, "And God hath taken away thy sins." Wherein is declared, that the minister can but pronounce to the sinner, that God in Christ forgiveth sin. So that we see Judas' confession of sin was nothing worth, because he found no faith nor trust for the remission thereof; and Saul's confession was of no valure, because he trusted and desired consolation at man's hand, and not at God's. Yet in Saul's confession was something good, in that he confessed (although it were long first, and in manner wrested out of his mouth by the prophet Samuel) his fault to God; and in that point he did as David did, who said, "I have offended the Lord." And this is to be noted, because now-a-days men be taught to confess their sins to the saints departed, that know not what the outward works of men be upon the earth, much less the inward and sinful cogitation of the heart. So that in this part the papists' confession is worse than Saul's, and in the other part it is like: for as Saul trusted to the merits of Samuel, and would have him to bear his sin; so do the people trust that the priest's hand upon their head, and the penance enjoined them by the priests, shall be a clean remission and full satisfaction for all their sin: but before God their sins be as much forgiven them as Saul's were, that is to say, nothing at all.

But where as sin is known and confessed from the very heart unto God, although it be a bitter thing, and also a shameful thing, to feel and bear God's displeasure for sin, the burden whereof is very death, and more grievous than death itself; yet where as confidence and trust in the mercy of God is annexed with it, there followeth great consolation and comfort: as it is to be seen in this prophet, that spake with a strong faith boldly, "The right hand of God can change these things;" so that the latter part of this verse hath more comfort than the first part hath discomfort. And it is a plain doctrine, that although the sins of man be many and horrible, yet be they fewer and less in estimation many thousand folds than God's mercies. Death is declared in the first part of the verse in this, that man's infirmity is not only sinful in body and soul, but also doubtful of God's mercy and holy promises: yet in the second part by grace is set forth life and clean deliverance from the tyranny of the devil, the servitude of sin, the accusation of the law, and the infirmity of nature, by the strong and mighty power of God, whose mercy in Christ is always ready to help poor afflicted and troubled sinners.

Isai. i.

Ezek. xviii. 1 John i.

After this confession of sin, and the great confidence that the prophet had in God for his mighty power and mercy's sake, that was both able by power and ready with will to help and remedy this troubled spirit and great adversities of the prophet, he goeth forth in the consolation, and taketh yet more and more of God's benefits, used in times towards such as were afflicted, after this sort.

11. "I will remember the works of the Lord, and call to my mind thy wonders of old time.
12. "I will think also of thy works, and my talking shall be of thy doings.
13. "Thy way, O God, is holy; who is so great a God as our God?
14. "Thou art the God that doth wonders, and hast declared thy power amongst people.
15. "Thou hast mightily delivered thy people, even the sons of Jacob and Joseph. Selah.
16. "The waters saw thee, O God; the waters saw thee, and were afraid: the depths also were troubled.
17. "The clouds poured out water, the air thundered, and thine arrows went abroad.
18. "The voice of thy thunder was heard round about; the lightnings shone upon the ground; the earth was moved, and shook withal.
19. "Thy way is in the sea, and thy paths in the great waters, and thy footsteps are not known.
20. "Thou leddest thy people like sheep by the hand of Moses and Aaron."

Of these means, how men take consolation in adversity, that the prophet now maketh mention of, first we learn, what difference is between the consideration of God's works advisedly and by faith, and the consideration of God's works rashly and without faith. The which diversity is to be seen in this prophet. For the one part, as touching the remembering of God's works out of faith and in faith, he spake before in the second verse, and in the fourth verse, how that he considered the works and old doings of the Lord when he was troubled. But, as ye have heard, because his spirit was in a doubtfulness and mammering upon the certainty of God's doings, he felt no consolation thereof, but much heaviness and anguish of mind. For those demands, " Will God absent himself for ever ? Will he be no more merciful?" and such-like heavy and doubtful complaints, could never proceed but from a sorrowful and much troubled conscience. But now, after that God's Spirit hath wrought in his spirit this assurance and judgment, that God can in him change the conditions of his miseries (as ye may see), he maketh no more complaint of doubtfulness, neither remembereth any more the fearfulness of his conscience; but goeth forth with repetition and rehearsal of all things comfortably, how that God in time past help troubled spirits and afflicted personages, that put their trust in him. So that of this we learn, that whosoever hath a sure faith in God taketh consolation of God's word and works; and such as have not first true faith in God cannot in the spirit receive comfort of God's word or works. Outwardly men may marvel at God and his works, but inwardly it easeth not the heaviness, nor yet quieteth the grudge of conscience.

Wherefore it behoveth us all that we pray earnestly unto God to give us faith to believe his word and works, when we hear, read, or see them. For the word and works of God do nothing comfort the unfaithful; as we may see by the scripture, where God saith he stretched forth his hand all day long to a people that believed not; for such as have ears and hear not, eyes and see not, be rather the worse for God's word and works than the better. Ye shall see, where the spirit of David was replenished with faith, he was so assured and ascertained of God's present help, that he said he would not fear, although a thousand men environed and compassed him round about: no, he would not fear, though he should walk in the shadow of death. At another time, when faith quailed and waxed faint, he was trembling in his spirit, and fearful in his body : as we may see, when he felt his spirit wax faint, he said, " My

Exhortation to prayer.

Isai. lxv.
Rom. x.
Isai. vi.
John xii.

Psal. iii.

Psal. xxiii.

Psal. vi.
xxxviii.

soul is troubled very sore, and my bones be weakened." And in other of his psalms he sheweth that his soul was very heavy and comfortless, and could take no consolation. Also, when the spirit is assured of God's grace, then the eyes cannot look upon any work of God but the mind taketh by the contemplation and sight thereof unspeakable consolation; as David declareth in his psalms, and saith he would see the heavens the works of God's fingers, and would mark how one day was an induction to another, and how the heavens praised the Lord. At another time, when the consolation and life of the spirit was overwhelmed with troubles, he could not see at all with his eyes, but cried and complained that he was stark blind. And also in that marvellous psalm, in number lxxxviii., where as prayer is made to be delivered from the horror and feeling of sin, the prophet saith that his eyes waxed dim and blind. The same is to be seen likewise in the crosses and afflictions that God sendeth. As long as true faith and confidence remaineth in the heart, all troubles be welcome and thankfully taken; as we read, when Job had news that his goods and children were taken from him in manner suddenly, he most patiently said, " God gave them, and God hath taken them away; as God would, so it is done." But when faith quailed, and the spirit was troubled, then followed these impatient words: " I would my sin were laid in one balance, and my pain in another;" as though God had laid more upon him than he had deserved. When the spirit was quieted, for all his poverty and nakedness, he rejoiced, and was contented with his birth and coming into the world, and also with the state in the world appointed unto him by God, saying, "Naked I came out of my mother's belly, and naked I shall depart hence again." But when faith fainted, then came out these words: " The day, the night, and the time be cursed wherein I was born;" with many more horrible words, as the text declareth. So that we see, where as God's Spirit wanteth, there is no learning nor consolation to be had of anything; as it is opened in this psalm, in that at the first time the prophet recorded God's works, and was so troubled in his mind, that he occupied his cogitations this way: " Will God be no more merciful? Hath God shut up his mercy in his ire?" But now, in the second record of God's works, he beginneth his entrance clean contrary, and saith God's right hand can change his sorrow, and turn his heaviness into mirth. And upon this ground and sure hope of God's promises he proceedeth forth to a consideration and deep record of God's facts in this sort: "I will remember the works of the Lord," &c.

In this verse and in the next following it be contained three kind of words; remembrance, meditation, and speech. By the first we learn, that it profiteth nothing to read or hear God's word, except we remember it, and bear it away with us: by the next we learn, that it availeth us not to learn and bear the word of God in remembrance, except by meditation and thinking upon it we understand what it meaneth: and by the third we learn, that neither the remembrance of it nor the understanding thereof profiteth, except we teach and instruct other in the same, of whom we have charge, if we may.

Now to consider further, we see how the prophet beginneth with this word 'remembrance:' whereof it appeareth that he had learned before out of God's word God's nature towards penitent sinners, to forgive them; and towards wilful, obstinate, and impenitent sinners, to be a just judge to punish them. Here is the ignorance of all people condemned, that never learn to know God's word in sickness nor in health; but when they be troubled or sick, they send for such as they think and fancy have learned and do remember how God's word doth comfort in adversity: and then, if he that is sent for be not learned in God's word, he cannot remember how God is wont to comfort the troubled or sick; then all that ever the sick man heareth of an ignorant comforter or counsellor is as clean void of consolation or counsel as though he had never sent for a counsellor or comforter. For no man can have more of another than the other hath himself, which is neither knowledge, counsel, nor consolation out of God's word: therefore he is not able to give knowledge, consolation, nor comfort to another. If the prophet Asaph had been as the most part of people now-a-days be, that fall sick and into many kinds of trouble, and had sent for an ignorant fool (which commonly is called a ghostly father), he had been in as good taking as these wretched souls be, that, being comfortless, seek comfort where none is to be had, seek knowledge where none is, and seek counsel where ignorance aboundeth. Let all men therefore remember this verse, that when the prophet was in trouble, he remembered the wisdom and marvellous works of God (for he knew them before): so let all men and women learn, before they come into trouble, a true knowledge of God, that in the time of trouble they may remember it to their consolation.

But now to the second word, where he saith he will meditate in all the works of God. Here is another notable doctrine, that neither the learning of God's word nor the remembrance thereof profiteth anything, except it be understanded and applied to the use that God hath appointed it for. And here be two sorts of people wonderfully condemned. The one sort be those that, for custom or bondage to their profession, do learn without the book a great part of the scripture; or else, by daily use in singing or saying their service (as it is called), they learn to sing and say a great part of the bible. But this availeth nothing; for they understand it not in the sense and meaning that the Holy Ghost appointed it for, nor perchance the grammatical construction thereof. And these remembrances of God's word be nothing but lip-labour, and honouring of God with the mouth, but the heart is far away; which before God is in vain, and of no estimation. The other sort of people be such as profess the gospel, that have learned much, and can remember much, but follow very little; so that they be nothing the better for it.

<small>Isai. xxix.
Matt. xv.</small>

The third word is, that the prophet saith he will speak of God and his works, as outwardly and inwardly he remembereth them, and with his spirit doth meditate them: as it is likewise the part and duty of all christian men so to do; for as they believe in the heart to justice, so will they confess it to salvation, as St Paul saith to the Romans. Here in this word be three sorts of people condemned: the one, that will not confess and teach the truth for fear of losing their advantage; the other will not confess and teach the truth for sluggishness and sloth; and the third will not confess and teach the truth for timidity and fear.

<small>Rom. x.
Three sorts of people condemned.</small>

In the first sort be such as know doctrines for the soul, or medicines for the body, and yet, because they get gain thereby, they would not have too many know thereof, lest their own gains should be the less: as we see, such a one as knoweth a good method and order to teach would be loth it should be common, because his estimation and gain (as he thinketh) should diminish and decrease. The excellent physician would not have his cunning common, lest many men, as cunning as he, should part his gains amongst them.

The second sort of men be those that come to great livings by their learning, and, when they have the reward of learning, they teach no more, as bishops and ministers of the church; whom the prophet calleth dumb dogs that cannot bark, their mouths be so choked with the bones of bishopricks and benefices. I speak of such as know the truth and love it, and not of such as neither know it nor love it: for although those men speak but seldom, yet it is too much; for better it were never to speak, than to speak falsely. *Note well. Isai. lvi.*

The third sort be our Nicodemes, that can speak of Christ in the night, or to their friends, but openly they will confess nothing with the mouth, nor do anything outwardly, for fear of the world, that should sound to God's glory. And these men be assured they shall have their reward, that Christ will deny them before his Father which is in heaven. *Nicodemes. Matt. x.*

Of this we learn wherein our profession consisteth: first, to learn God's word; secondly, to bear it in our heart and remembrance; thirdly, to understand it; and fourthly, to speak of it to the glory of God and the edifying of our neighbours: and God's word this ways used shall keep us humble and lowly in prosperity, and patient and strong in adversity. *Wherein doth our profession consist.*

But in these two verses be more words necessary to be considered, if we will take consolation in adversity: the first, "I will (saith the prophet) remember the works of the Lord, and that of old time" (or, 'from the beginning'): the second, "I will think also of all the works of the Lord," &c. In this that the prophet saith, he will remember the works of the Lord of old time, or from the beginning, we learn that it is expedient to know, or (at the least way) not to be ignorant of any book in the scripture: for whereas we find not consolation in the one, we may find it in the other. And where he saith, he will remember all the works of the Lord (meaning as many as the scripture maketh mention of), we be instructed, that we cannot see these works for our erudition, neither yet give the Almighty God thanks, except we learn them from one of his books or[1] the other. And here is to be noted, that seeing we be bound to know and to be thankful for all the works of God contained in the scripture, we be much in danger, *We ought not to be ignorant of any book in the scripture.*

[1 To, in the original edition.]

as well for ignorance as unthankfulness, that we know not the principal works of our own creation or redemption. We be therefore admonished to have books to read the works of God, and to be diligent to ask better learned than we be, what God's works do mean: as the children by God's law be bound to ask the parents, and the parents bound by the same to teach them; then shall both fathers and children find comfort and consolation against all temptations in the time of trouble and heaviness: as we see this man's remedy (by the Spirit of God) riseth from recording, meditating, and speaking of God's word and works.

Deut. iv. vi. xxxi.

Here hath this prophet marvellously opened, how a man in trouble cometh to consolation and comfort. First, that the spirit and heart of man must have such strong faith as may credit God's power, and also his good will, and believe that God both can and will for his truth's sake help the troubled conscience. Therefore Solomon giveth a godly and necessary commandment: "Keep thy heart with all circumspection, for of it proceedeth life." So did David: when the prophet Nathan had made him afraid for the murder of Urias and the adultery with Bersaba, his conscience was in great anguish and fear, and, among other things that he prayed for to God, he desired that God would create and make him a new heart; that is to wit, to give him such a stedfast and burning faith, that in Christ his sinful heart might be purged. And secondarily, he prayeth to have so right and sure a spirit, that should not doubt of God's favour towards him. Thirdly, that God would always preserve his Holy Spirit with the heart regenerated, that from time to time the heart might be ruled in obedience towards God. Fourthly, he prayeth to be led with a willing spirit, that quietly and patiently he may obey God in adversities, without impatience or grudge against God. And where as this knowledge and feeling of the favour of God is in the spirit, there followeth recording and remembrance of God's works, meditating and thinking upon heavenly things; and the tongue ready also to speak forth the glory of God, to God's honour and praise, and to the edifying of God's people and congregation, after this sort:

Prov. iv.

Psal. li.

Note.

13. "Thy way, O God, is in holiness: who is so great a God as God, even our God?"

Here is a consolation much worthy to be learned and received of all troubled men; and it is this, to understand and perceive that all the doings and facts of Almighty God be righteous, although many times the flesh judgeth and the tongue speaketh the contrary, that God should be too severe, and punish too extremely; as though he did it rather of a desire to punish, than to correct or amend the person punished: as we see by Job's words, that wished his sins laid in one balance, and his punishment in another balance, as though God punished more extremely than justly. The same it seemeth king David also felt, when he said, "How long, Lord, wilt thou forget me? for ever?"—with like bitter speeches in the scripture, complaining of God's justice, judgment, and severity. The same we read of Jeremy the prophet: he spake God's word truly, and yet there happened unto him wonderful great adversities, the terror whereof made him curse the day that he was born in. And doubtless, when he said, "Why hast thou deceived me, Lord?" he thought God was rather too extreme than just in his punishment, to afflict him in adversity, and to suffer Passur the high priest and his enemy to be in quiet and tranquillity.

Consolation.

Job vi.

Psal. xiii.

Jer. xx.

Pashur.

This prophet Asaph was before in great trouble (as ye heard), and especially of the mind, that felt not a sure trust and confidence in God's mercy, and thought of all extremities that to be (as it is indeed) the greatest, a mind desperate and doubtful of God's mercy; yet now he saith, "God is holy in his way, and all that he doth is right and just."

We learn hereby that the pot cannot say to the potter, "Why hast thou made me after this sort?" Neither may the mortal man, in whom is nothing but sin, quarrel with the Lord, and say, What layest thou upon me? but think that, although he had made us both blind, lame, and as deformed as monsters, yet had he made us better than ever we deserved. And in case he laid all the troubles of the world upon one man, yet are they less than one sin of man doth deserve. Thus hath the prophet learned now and felt, and saith, "The doings of God be holy and right, and there is none to be compared unto him;" and sheweth the cause why none is to be compared unto God. In the declaration whereof he continueth seven verses, and so maketh an end of the psalm.

Potter.

Jer. xix. [xviii.] Rom. ix.

The first cause why he saith none is to be compared unto God is this:

14. "Thou art the Lord that doth wonders, and hast declared thy power amongst people."

<small>God is the doer of wonders.</small>
First, he noteth generally, that God is the doer of wonders and miracles; and afterwards he sheweth, wherein God hath wrought these miracles. Of this we learn three doctrines: the one, that some men know generally that God worketh all things marvellously; the second, that other some know that God worketh in some men marvellously; the third, that other also know that God worketh in themselves marvellously.

<small>Three doctrines.</small>

Of the first sort be such as know by God's works generally that God hath, and doth dispose all things upon the earth, and nothing hath his beginning nor being but of God: of whom St Paul speaketh to the Romans, that by God's works they knew God, and yet glorified him not. Of the second sort be such as more particularly know and speak of God's miracles; as such be that read how God of his singular favour preserved Noah and his family, and drowned all the world besides; how he brought the children of Israel out of Egypt, and delivered the people from the captivity of Babylon, with such-like: and yet, when they be in troubles themselves, these marvellous works and mercies shewed unto others cannot comfort themselves. Of the third sort be such as know generally the marvellous works of God, and perceive that in some God is particularly merciful; and from some he findeth it in himself singularly the mercy of God; and from the remembrance of God's benefits unto others he findeth in himself the working of God's mercy, and findeth in his conscience such comfort indeed, that he remembereth others before him, that had of God's mercies in their time of troubles.

<small>Rom. i.</small>

<small>Gen. vii.
Exod. xiv.</small>

<small>Note.
The true Christians take consolation themselves of God's miracles wrought upon others.</small>
The most part of men consider generally that God is the worker of miracles; the common sort of Christians consider that God hath wrought miracles particularly upon others; but the very elects and Christians indeed see the miracles of God wrought particularly upon others, and take consolation singularly of God's mercies themselves: as we see this prophet marvellously declareth God's wonders, and putteth the general working of God's miracles between a singular working of wonders and a particular working of wonders.

The generality is this: "Thou art God that doth wonders, and hast declared thy power amongst people." The singularity and particularity of God's working of wonders is the one before, and the other behind. The singularity is in this, that he perceived that it was his own infirmity that made him doubt of God's promises; and yet God's singular grace made him singularly feel and perceive that God singularly would be good unto him. The particularity is in this, that he saith, "With God's right hand God delivered the posterity of Jacob and Joseph from the servitude of Egypt," &c. The way to consider the marvellous works of God is a profitable consideration and sight of them, as well to know them as to be the better for them: for there is no man can take commodity or profit by God's goodness shewed unto a multitude, except he singularly receive gain thereby himself: as we see, when a whole multitude was fed marvellously with a few loaves and fewer fishes (almost five thousand people), he taught the consolation and health of man's soul in his own blood; but none was the better for it but such as believed every man for himself that which Christ spake. The miracles and merciful help of Christ unto others had nothing profited the poor woman of Canaan, except she herself had been partaker of the same. Jacob and Joseph.
John vi.
Every man must believe for himself.
Matt. xv.

And as it is in the works of God that do comfort the man afflicted, so is it in the works of God that bring men into heaviness and sorrow for sin. Generally, the word of God rebuketh sin, and calleth sinners to repentance; particularly, it sheweth unto us how that David, Peter, Mary Magdalene, and others, repented. But to us those sorrows and repentance do no good, except we every man singularly repent and be sorrowful for his sins. For it is not another man's sickness that maketh me sick, nor another man's health that maketh me whole: no more is any other man's repentance my repentance, or any other man's faith my faith; but I must repent, and I must believe myself to feel sorrowfulness for sin by the law, and remission thereof by faith in Christ: so that every private man must be in repentance sorry with the true repentant sorry, and faithful with the true faithful. For as God himself is towards man, so be all his works and promises: for look, to whom God is merciful, to the same be all his promises comfortable; and to whom God is severe and Repentance.
Notable doctrine.
Note.

rigorous, to the same God's threatenings be terrible, and his justice fearful: as king David saith, "With the holy thou wilt be holy, and with the innocent thou wilt be innocent; with the chosen thou wilt be chosen, and with the perverse thou wilt be perverse."

_{Psalm xviii.}

Such as follow virtue and godliness God increaseth with gifts and benefits; and such as have wicked manners, and by false doctrine decline from the truth, in those God is severe and sharp. And except such persons repent, God will spoil them from all judgment of truth; and, being blind and destitute of knowledge, permit them to the power and dominion of most filthy lusts and abominable desires: so that such as would not love the beauty and excellency of virtue shall tumble and wallow themselves like swine in the filth and vomit of sin; of the which abominations and just judgments of God St Paul speaketh in the epistle to the Romans. For this is to be noted; look, as every man is, even so he thinketh of God. And as the good and godly man thinketh well of God, so doth the evil and wicked man think evil of God. Some think that man and all worldly things be ruled and governed by God with great justice and inscrutable wisdom, with all mercy and favour. Others think that God ruleth not this world and worldly things; and in case they think he do, yet do they condemn his administration and rule of injustice and partiality, because God doeth as it pleaseth himself, and not as man would have him do. And upon these diversities of judgments in men's minds, God is to the godly merciful, and to the ungodly severe and rigorous. If the spirit of man judge truly and godly of him, by and bye the spirit of man shall perceive and feel the heavenly influence of God's Spirit stirring and impelling his spirit to all virtue and goodness. If the spirit of man be destitute of the Spirit of God, and judge perversely and wickedly, the spirit of man shall feel the lack of God's Spirit and true judgment to blind the eyes of his mind, and cast himself into all abomination and sin, as the iniquity of the man justly hath deserved. Of the which thing cometh this, that as the virtue and godliness of godly men daily increaseth, even so doth the iniquity and abomination of the ungodly also increase.

_{To whom God is merciful, and to whom severe.}

_{Rom. i.}

_{A wicked judgment of God's doings.}

_{O horrible blindness!}

And look, what place and preeminence God obtaineth with any man, in the same place and preeminence is the man with

_{Look, what preeminence God obtaineth of man,}

God. And such as do godly, after God's word, honour and reverence the almighty God, judging aright of God's might and providence, they give most humble thanks unto the mercy of God, that alone, and none but he, can teach or instruct the mind of man in true knowledge, nor incline his will to godly doings, nor inflame the soul with all her powers to the desire and fervent love of godliness and virtue: as we see by this prophet Asaph in this place, that, as long as his spirit wanted the help of God's Spirit, it judged doubtfully of God's mercy and promises; but, when the Spirit of God had exiled and banished doubtfulness, and placed this strong fortress of confidence, "The right hand of God can change this my woeful and miserable estate," with the judgment and feeling thereof, he was rapt and stricken with a marvellous love of God's wonders, and repeated them with great joy and consolation, what God had done generally to all men; after that, what he had done to some particular men and private nations, naming Jacob and Joseph, whose offspring and succession he brought out of the land of Egypt, as it followeth in the psalm:

the same place hath man with God.

A strong fortress.

15. "Thou hast mightily delivered thy people, even the sons of Jacob and Joseph. Selah."

Of this verse we learn two consolations: the one, that every Christian troubled may see his elders and also his betters troubled: not that it is a comfort to a man that is afflicted to see another in trouble: but to mark that God loved none so well but in this world he sent trouble unto, and excepted not his dear Son. Wherefore it is a consolation to the afflicted to be made like unto the godly fathers, that were before his time, by tribulation, and to remember that, although all christian men be not brought under the captivity of Pharaoh in Egypt, nor under Nabuchodonozer in Babylon, yet there is an Egypt and a Babylon for every christian member; that is to say, the captivity of sin, the bondage of the flesh, the severity of the law, the danger of the world, the enmity of infidels, the treason of dissembling friends, the wickedness of evil and devilish ordinances, the dissimulation of hypocrites, the perjury of inconstant persons, the breach of faithful promises, the inconstancy of the weak, the cruelty of papists, the love of man, and the hatred of God, with many others; as, the ignorance of God's laws, the rebellion of the heart against it, frowardness

Two consolations.

Whom God loved he always corrected.

Every christian member hath an Egypt and a Babylon.

of the will to consent unto it, diffidence and mistrust of God's mercy, boldness to sin in the time of health, faintness and mistrust of the remission thereof in sickness, love of vice and sin, hatred of virtue and godliness, sudden falling from grace, slow rising unto it again, loathsomeness to die mortally, readiness to live wickedly, sorrowfulness to forsake this world, great delight to use it evil whiles we have it, loath to seek heavenly things, glad to seek earthly things, nothing feeling the poverty and trouble of the soul, always grudging at the poverty and trouble of the body; with innumerable other captivities that every Christian is entangled withal, as every man may judge by his own life.

The greatest consolation in trouble.

The next consolation is to see the truth of God's help promised to all men, when they be troubled, to have been declared, opened, and verified in others in time past. For this is the greatest consolation that can be to any man in trouble or in sickness, when he is assured of such help and such medicines as never were used but did help the afflicted and heal the sick. Now against all the troubles of man, and also against all the sickness of man, God hath promised his present and helping mercy: the which medicine and help never failed, but did help as many as put their trust therein. Therefore doth this prophet Asaph establish and assure himself of God's help against his grievous temptations and troubles that he suffered, by recording that his griefs were no greater, nor his troubles more dangerous, than Jacob's, Joseph's, and their posterity's, nor yet so grievous: insomuch

From the greater to the lesser.

that, seeing the mercy of God could help the greater troubles in his predecessors, he could help and ease the less in him that was presently troubled. And, being so assured of God's

Selah.

help, he spake at the end of this verse, "Selah:" as though he had said, It is most true that God can help and comfort me, as he holp and comforted my forefathers. And, for the better consolation and more firm assurance, he sheweth how marvellously he did help the posterity of Jacob and Joseph, after this sort:

16. "The waters saw thee, O God, the waters saw thee, and were afraid; the depths also were troubled."

Unto insensible things be attributed sensible qualities.

In this that he saith, the waters were afraid when they saw God, first, the manner of speech in the scripture is to be noted, that attributeth unto insensible things sensible qualities;

as in this place is attributed unto the water sight and fear, whereas indeed properly the water cannot see nor fear. But when the scripture useth any such phrase or speech, there is to be marked divers doctrines of edifying: first, of God; then, insensible creatures; and thirdly, of man, for whose sake the scripture sometime speaketh unto insensible creatures as though they were sensible, and worketh miracles in them for the instruction and amendment of sensible and reasonable man. *Three doctrines.*

The learning touching God is, that he worketh his will, and useth his creatures, as it seemeth unto his wisdom inscrutable most meet and convenient; as here he troubleth and altereth the condition of the seas and waters. These waters were appointed by God, in the third day of the creation, to be in one place, and was called the sea, a pleasant element, and a beautiful thing to see: and God said, "It was good," as the effect thereof sheweth indeed; for it nourisheth the earth with necessary moisture by privy veins and secret passages secretly passing through the earth. And when the floods, that do moisture the earth, have done their office, they return into their old lodging the sea again; from whence riseth the matter of showers and rain to moisture from above, that floods beneath cannot be conveyed unto. And it serveth for transporting the necessaries of one realm to the other, quietly suffering the ships to pass with great gain and pleasure. These and many more commodities God worketh by this insensible creature, when it is calm and navigable: but when he moveth it with his winds and tempests, it is so horrible in itself, that no man may without peril and death travel within it, so raging and fearful is that pleasant element of the water, when God moveth it. It hath (by God's appointment) his time of calm, and time of storm; time to profit men, and time to undo men; time to be a refuge for men in the days of peril, and time to be a grave and sepulchre for men; time to conjoin strange nations together, and time to separate them again, as it pleaseth the Creator Almighty God to appoint and direct it. *The first doctrine touching God.* *Gen. 1* *Time.*

The doctrine that toucheth the insensible creature itself is, that it can be no longer calm, nor any longer troubled, than it pleaseth the heavenly Governor to dispose it. And here is to be noted against such men as attribute storms and calms to fortune; whereas only the voice of the Lord moveth tempests, and sendeth fair weather. It is also a doctrine *The second doctrine touching the insensible creature.* *Psalm xxix.*

against all men that do think the waters and seas may be moved and cease at their own pleasure; which is contrary to this prophet's doctrine, that saith, "The waters saw the Lord, and were afraid:" so that their trouble riseth from the commandment of the Lord, and they cannot do what they lust, but what God biddeth them to do. It is godly set forth afterwards in another psalm, wherein the passage of the children of Israel is mentioned, as it is in this psalm.

<small>Ps. lxxvii.</small>

<small>Ps. cxiv.</small>

<small>The third doctrine touching man.</small>

The doctrine touching man in this verse is a declaration of man's obstinacy and stubbornness. The insensible creature the water, that lacketh both life and reason, at every commandment be as the Lord their Maker commandeth them to be: with every tempest they be troubled, and with every calm so plain and quiet, that it seemeth rather a stablished land than a variable sea. But let God send his word unto man, and the contents thereof threaten the tempest of all tempests, eternal death, hell-fire, and God's everlasting displeasure; yet man will not hear nor see them, nor yet be moved any thing at all: or let God gently and favourably offer his mercies unto man, and by his word exhort him never so much to repentance, it is for the most part in vain. Therefore God by his prophets Moses and Esay called heaven and earth to witness against man's stubbornness and hardness of heart.

<small>O rebellion of man!</small>

<small>Insensible creatures shall be a condemnation unto man.</small>

<small>Deut. xxxii. Isai. i.</small>

<small>Mark most diligently.</small>

There is also out of this trouble of the water this doctrine to be learned, how to receive consolation, and how to learn fear, by the creatures of God that bear no life, and yet be thus troubled. Consolation in this sort, when the penitent man that suffereth affliction and trouble seeth insensible things moved and unquieted, that never offended, he shall judge the less wonder at his own trouble. When he seeth that a sinner and wretched offender of God is punished, he shall learn fear. When he seeth God doth punish his creatures that never offended, for the sin of man, what punishment is man worthy to have, that is nothing but sin itself? And what fear should this bring into christian men's consciences, to know that no creature deserveth punishment, no creature disobeyeth God, but the devil and man? O! what man or woman can with faith look upon the least flowers of the field, and not hate himself? In summer-time, when men shall see the meadows and gardens so marvellously

<small>The devil and man be only disobedient unto God.</small>

apparelled with flowers of every colour, so that he shall not be able to discern whether their beauty better please the eye, or their sweet savour the nose; what may they learn, in thinking of themselves (as the truth is) that there is nothing in them but filth and sin, that most heinously stink before the face of God! And when man shall perceive that flowers vade, and lose both beauty to the eye and sweet savour to the nose, that never transgressed; what may miserable man think he is worthy to lose, that is nothing but sin, and ever offendeth! Again, when man shall perceive that God thus marvellously, after long winter and great storms, doth raise out of the vile earth so beautiful flowers, plants, and trees, what consolation may the man take that hath his faith in Christ, to think that all his sins in his precious blood be forgiven, and, after long persecution and cruel death, he shall come to eternal life! After this sort did the prophet consider the works of God and the troubles of his creatures, and received great consolation thereby. O take heed, miserable man.
Consolation.

In the end of this verse the prophet saith, "The depths were troubled." In the which words he hath aptly shewed the mighty power of God, and perceiveth how the record of God's fact may be his consolation. In this that he saith, "The depths were troubled," there be divers understandings. If he mean of the seas, when they are troublesome and tempestuous by foul weather, he speaketh rather after the judgment of such as suffer the trouble and peril of the waves, that think at one time they fall to the bottom of the sea, and at another time they be rather upon high mountains than upon the waters, the rages thereof be so extreme: yet indeed, the bottom of the seas be not felt, neither doth the ship that is saved descend so far; but the tempests be so sore, that it seemeth to the sufferers thereof that no extremity can be more. In this sense it serveth marvellously the prophet's purpose: for, as they that endure the tempests of the sea think there could be no more extremity than they sustain, so do they that suffer the tempest of mistrust and despair (for a time) of the conscience think they could endure no more extremity of conscience: whereas indeed, if God should suffer them to feel the extremity, it were eternal death, as the extremity of the sea in tempests is shipwreck and loss of man and goods. But if it be understood as it standeth in the letter, then hath the Depths.

A goodly similitude.

prophet relation to the mighty hand of God, that brake the Red Sea even unto the very bottom, and also the water of Jordan, that his people might have both a nigh way, a safe way, and a glorious way towards the land that the Lord had promised them. And then in this sense we learn, that although water and wind, with all troubles else, cover the face of the earth in the bottom of the sea, and is not possible to come to the use of man, even so the troublesome temptations and great terror of God's wrath against sin covereth the soul of man, that, unto the judgment of the flesh, it shall never come to have the use and fruition of God's holy favour again.

<small>Exod. xiv.
Josh. iii.</small>

But now, as we see by miracle God maketh dry the depth of horrible seas, and turneth the bottom of them to the use of man, so doth he in the blood of Christ (by the operation of the Holy Ghost) dry up and clean lade out the ponds and deep seas of mistrust and heaviness out of the soul, and turneth the soul itself to the use of his own honour, in the joys everlasting. And as the water covereth the beauty of the land, so do sin and temptation cover the image and beauty of man's soul in this life. But, as with a word God can remedy the one, so with the least of his mercies he can redress the other. And for the better experience and more certainty thereof we see it proved by this prophet Asaph in this place. For the ground was never more overwhelmed with water, nor the bright sun with dimmy clouds, than was this poor prophet's spirit with heaviness and sorrow of sin and temptations. Therefore he feeleth how God easeth the heart, and recordeth how he banished floods and waters, to make his people a way to rest and tranquillity.

<small>O the merciful goodness of God towards man inscrutable!</small>

17. "The clouds poured out water, the air thundered, and thine arrows went abroad."

The prophet remembereth the marvellous inundation and drowning of the world in the days of Noah, that drowned all the world for sin, saving such as were in the ark or ship with Noah. And he remembereth also the horrible thunder that was heard of the people, when God gave his law unto them upon mount Sinai. Likewise, he calleth to remembrance the plagues of Egypt, wherewithal God punished Pharaoh, his people, and the whole land; which pains and plagues he calleth (after the phrase of the scripture) arrows and darts.

<small>Noah.
Gen. vii.
Exod. xix.
Note.
Exod. v. vi. vii. viii. ix. x. xi.</small>

These remembrances may be comforts to the hearers and to the readers two manner of ways. First in this, that God, when he punisheth, punisheth justly, as he did the whole world for sin. Whereof the prophet gathereth, If sin justly merited to[1] trouble all the generation of man, it is no great marvel though sin trouble me, that am but one man, and a vile sinner. If sin brought all flesh unto death, saving those that were in the ship, is it any marvel though sin make me to tremble and quake? Again, if God, when he gave the law to Moses and to the people, spake out of thunder, declaring what a thing it was to transgress that law, insomuch that all the people were afraid to hear the Lord speak, and desired that Moses might supply his room; what marvel is it that my conscience trembleth, feeling that my soul hath offended the laws of God? And if Pharaoh and his realm were sore afraid of God's outward plagues, what cause have I to fear the inward dread and sorrowful sight of sin, shewed unto me by God's law! So that we may take this consolation out of this place, that God is a just judge to punish sin, and not a tyrant, that punisheth of affection or wilful desire. And so said David, "Whensoever or howsoever thou punish (let men say and judge as they list), thou art just, and righteous be all thy doings."

God punisheth justly for sin.

Exod. xix.

God is no tyrant.

Psal. li. x. cxix.

The other consolation is, that in the midst of all adversities God preserved penitent and faithful sinners: as, in the time of the universal flood, the water hurted not Noah, nor such as were in the ship: in the time of Pharaoh's plagues, the Israelites took no harm: at the giving of the law, the Israelites perished not with lightning and thunder. Even so sorrows and anguish, diffidence and weakness of faith, they are plagues and punishments for all men by reason of sin; yet penitent sinners, by reason of faith in Christ, take no hurt nor damnation by them: as it appeareth by this prophet, that was troubled in the spirit and in the body as marvellously as could be, but yet in Christ escaped the danger, as all men shall do that repent and believe. Whereof we learn, that as the rain falleth generally, and yet bettereth no earth to bring forth her fruit but such as is apt to receive the rain (stony rocks and barren ground being nothing the better); even so doth the plagues and rain of God's displeasure plague

God always preserveth penitent sinners.

Rom. viii.

[¹ Old edition, *do*.]

[HOOPER, II.]

all mankind, but none be the better therefore but such as
Heb. vi. x. repent and bewail their sins, that gave God just occasion
thus to punish them. The same is to be considered also of
the verse that followeth, which is this:

18. "The lightning shone upon the ground, the earth was
moved, and shook therewithal."

By these manner of speeches, "the lightning shone, and
the earth quaked," the prophet setteth forth the strength and
might of God's power, and willeth men to love him and to
fear him; for he is able to defend and preserve his faithful,
and to punish and plague the wicked. And the like he saith
in the verse following:

19. "Thy way is in the sea, and thy paths in the deep
waters; and thy footsteps are not known."

The Israelites were conducted by God through the Red sea. Pharaoh and his were drowned. Exod. xiv.

He taketh comfort of this miracle, that God brought the
Israelites through the Red Sea, in this, that the waters knew
the Israelites, and gave place unto them, that they might dry-
footed go through them: but when king Pharaoh and his
people would have followed in the same path, persecuting
God's people, the sea would make no way for him, nor yet
shew the steps where the Israelites trod, but overwhelmed

Psal. cxxi. cxxv. xiii. xlvi. liv. lxxi.

them in most desperate deaths. So in the seas of temptations,
such as put their trust in the Lord pass, and never perish by
them; whereas such as put not their trust in the Lord perish

Exod. xiv.

in temptations, as Pharaoh and his army did by water. And
the next verse that concludeth the psalm sheweth by what
means the Israelites were, under God, saved in the Red Sea
by the hands of Moses and Aaron; as it appeareth:

20. "Thou leddest thy people like sheep by the hand of
Moses and Aaron."

The best is not able of himself to resist temptations.

Of this verse the afflicted may learn many consolations.
First, that the best people that be are no better able to resist temptations, than the simple sheep is able to withstand
the brier that catcheth him. The next, that man is of no
more ability to beware of temptations, than the poor sheep is
to avoid the brier, being preserved only by the diligence of

Shepherd.

the shepherd. The third, that as the shepherd is careful of
his entangled and briered sheep, so is God of his afflicted

faithful. And the fourth is, that the people of Israel could take no harm of the water, because they entered the sea at God's commandment. Whereof we learn, that no danger can hurt when God doth command us to enter into it; and all dangers overcome us, if we choose them ourselves, besides God's commandment: as Peter, when he went at God's commandment upon the water, took no hurt; but when he entered into the bishop's house upon his own presumption, was overcome, and denied Christ. The Israelites, when they fought at God's commandment, the peril was nothing; but when they would do it of their own heads, they perished. So that we are bound to attend upon God's commandment, and then no danger shall destroy us, though it pain us.

<small>They that do things at God's commandment can take no harm.</small>

<small>Matt. xiv.</small>

<small>Matt. xxvi.</small>

<small>Numb. xiv.</small>

The other doctrine is in this, that God used the ministry of Moses and Aaron in the deliverance of his people, who did command them to do nothing but that the Lord did first bid. Whereof we learn, that such as be ministers appointed of God, and do nothing but as God commandeth, are to be followed; as St Paul saith, "Follow me, as I follow Christ." And these men can by the word of God give good counsel and great consolation, both for body and soul: as we perceive this prophet, in marking God's doings unto the Israelites, applied by grace the same wisdom and helping mercy
   unto himself, to his eternal rest, through Jesus
     Christ, in the world to come. To whom,
      with the Father and the Holy
       Ghost, be all laud and
        praise world without
         end. Let all Chris-
          tians say,
           Amen.

<small>Such as be ministers of the church ought to attend only upon the voice of God.</small>

<small>1 Cor. xi</small>

FINIS.

A table declaring as well the
general as the special contents of this
whole book.

	PAGE[1]
The Argument of the twenty-third Psalm . . .	187
⁋ Of this Psalm there are seven parts . . .	189
1. Who it is that hath the cure and charge of man's life and salvation	190
2. Wherein the life and salvation of man consisteth. .	197
3. How a man is brought to the knowledge of life and salvation: which part sheweth what man is of himself, and how he is brought into this life, and to feed in the pleasant pastures of God's word . .	204
4. Wherefore man is brought to life and salvation .	211
5. What trouble may happen to such as God giveth life and salvation unto	214
6. Whereby the troubles of God's elect be overcome .	222
7. What the end of God's troubled people shall be .	241
The Argument of the sixty-second Psalm . . .	243
⁋ Of this Psalm there are two general parts and six particular	243, 4
⁋ The first general part containing four particular parts.	
1. How that the favour of God and his help is able to remedy all adversities	243
⁋ The second general part containing two particular parts.	
2. How that the favour of man and his help is able to redress no adversities	243
⁋ A brief paraphrase upon the whole Psalm. .	245
⁋ The six particular parts as they follow in their order and place.	
1. What is to be done by the christian man that is afflicted	247

[1 The numbers of the pages are adapted to the present edition.]

TABLE OF CONTENTS OF CERTAIN PSALMS.

		PAGE.
2.	Why the troubled person seeketh health of God	255
3.	How the persecutors of the innocent shall suddenly perish	265
4.	Why trouble is patiently to be borne and faithfully to be believed that God can and will remedy it	273
5.	How man's power is not to be trusted unto	278
6.	How that God hath promised to help the afflicted	281

The Argument of the seventy-third Psalm . . 283
ℂ A paraphrase upon the whole Psalm . 284, 5, 6, 7, 8, 9
ℂ Of this Psalm there are eight parts . . . 290

1.	That God loveth the good, although he punisheth them	291
2.	How weak and frail a thing the nature of man is	295
3.	Wherein the felicity of wicked men consisteth, &c.	298
4.	How frail, brittle, and weak a thing man is, &c.	305
5.	How some men repent their well doings, &c.	306
6.	How great a danger it is temerously to judge of God, &c.	307
7.	That man's reason is but ignorant and beastly in considering of God's works, &c.	307
8.	The multitude and number of God's consolations, &c.	308

The Argument of the seventy-seventh Psalm . . 309
ℂ Of this Psalm there are four parts . . 309, 10

1.	In whom a man should put his trust, and to whom he should resort in the days of sickness, troubles, and adversities	310
2.	How a man should use himself towards him in whom he putteth his trust in the time of trouble	313
3.	What great and perilous dangers the man that is troubled shall suffer for the time of his trouble	318
4.	How a man taketh consolation in the time of his trouble	348

ℂ Other points of christian doctrine are referred to the consideration of the reader.

A BRIEF TREATISE

RESPECTING

JUDGE HALES.

[The "Brief Treatise" respecting Judge Hales is extracted from Strype's Ecclesiastical Memorials, Vol. III. Part II. Catal. xxiv. The Editor has not been able to meet with an earlier edition. Strype says, "This treatise, as I met with it among the Foxian MSS., I have cast into the Catalogue. It was written by Bishop Hoper, as may appear by one of his letters[1] preserved in the volume of the Martyrs' Letters." Strype, Eccles. Mem. Vol. III. Part I. p. 275. Oxf. 1822.]

[[1] See Letters, number xxix.]

A brief Treatise,

wherein is contained the truth, that Mr Justice Hales never hurt himself until such time as he condescended unto their papistical religion, and waxed weary of the truth. But now there is hope he[2] will repent, and continue in the same as he did before. Yet be there many that daily labour him to the contrary.

ST PETER the apostle, good christian reader, doth teach that we that are Christians are Christians to this end, "to shew forth the virtues of him that called us unto his unspeakable light;" meaning that we should always be setters forth of as many things as we could to his honour and praise. And that is a very kind of ingratitude, and a certain degree of injustice, not to propulse and defend any man from violence and oppression; and a greater ingratitude and more injustice, not to propulse and defend the just cause of God, when unjustly by violence it is slandered and oppressed. For in times past the condition of the ungodly was always to speak slanderously and falsely by God's doings: insomuch as, when Christ wrought the salvation of the people, they said he wrought all things by the power of Belzebul, the chiefest of the devils. St John could fast; but he was counted to have a devil. Christ could eat and drink; but he was counted a friend to sinners and publicans: so that hatred unto the truth did always falsely report and calumniate all godly men's doings. Again, there was never evil that happened to any country or commonwealth, although it were the just plague of God for the sin of the people of the country, but it was always laid to the good people's charge: as when the Lord took away corn, wine, oil, fruits, and other things necessary, from the Israelites, the wicked people said that the word of God and his true preachers

1 Pet. ii.

Matt. xxii. [xii.]
Luke xi.
Mark iii.
[Matt. xi. 18, 19.]

Hos. ii.

Tertull. in Apolog.[3]

[2 He shortly afterwards destroyed himself. See Strype, Eccl. Mem. Vol. III. c. xxi.]

[3 Si Tiberis ascendit ad mœnia, si Nilus non ascendit in arva—statim Christianos ad leonem.—Tertull. Apol. cap. 40. Op. p. 36. c. Lutet. 1641.]

were the causes thereof. If the water in Egypt called Nilus did not accustomably flow over Egypt, the wicked Egyptians laid the fault to such as professed Christ. If that flowed too much also, the fault was imputed to the good Christians. So the Romans, if Tiber the flood waxed either too high in flowing, or too low by drought, none bare the blame but the poor Christians. So at this time, if any mischief happen, our ungodly papists put the fault still in the gospel of Christ, or in the professors of it. Yea, and if a man should kill himself, there is none burdened with the cause thereof but God's gospel and God's people: which false reports all good men from the beginning hath written and spoken against, as it appeareth by the holy scripture, and also by the old ancient doctors and others.

Forasmuch therefore as upon the thirteenth day of April, anno 1554, the bishop of Winchester, lord chancellor of England, and a very enemy and persecutor of God's most true religion, and a murderer of his elect and chosen people, said in the reproach of God's most true and catholic religion, set forth by the blessed king of noble memory, Edward the Sixth, that it was a religion that brought men to despair and murdering of themselves, falsely accusing the truth of God's word, that comforteth and most preserveth weak consciences from heaviness and desperation; and also most untruly reporting the professors thereof to be most desperate and wicked persons; whereas indeed it is most false; (for from the beginning of Christ's church both the apostles and many thousands of martyrs have boldly and willingly contemned the tyranny of all persecutors, and most patiently suffered most cruel deaths; and if the ungodly man were not clean blinded and given over, as I fear me he is, to a reprobate mind, he might judge this rather to be true, that such as he himself hath most cruelly put to death, or been the chiefest cause of their deaths, as John Frith, D. Barnes, Jerom, Garret, A. Askew, Jos. Lascelles[1], and a great number more, known for their learning and virtues to have been holy men upon the earth, and now blessed saints through Christ in heaven, did likewise profess the said true doctrine, and suffered their bodies to be burnt for the same, without any

[[1] For an account of the martyrdom of these persons see Foxe, Acts and Mon. B. VIII. pp. 1036, 1201, 1240, 1241. Lond. 1583.]

desperation; and yet the wicked man, sitting chief judge in the Star-chamber, to discomfort and to drive back all men from their salvation, which cometh by the true word of God, named it the doctrine of desperation, and the professors thereof desperate people;) and the occasion of this ungodly and untrue talk was the doing of one Judge Hales, Sir James Hales, knight, that the same thirteenth day of April, being a prisoner in the Fleet, wounded himself in divers places of his body; and, saving the providence of God (that stopped the devil's malice that it came not to pass, and to so devilish an end as he intended), very like the man would have killed himself; but God provided his own servant to be sooner at hand with him than his master thought of, belike;—but now, forsomuch as upon this man's hurt my lord chancellor hath not only spoken uncharitably by the hurt man (whose learning, equity, and wisdom, all England honoureth), but also upon this man's fault he maketh faulty God's word and all the professors thereof;—therefore, to certify the truth unto the world, how this man, Mr Judge Hales, came to this ungodly mind to destroy himself, (for that I do know the truth,) I can do no less of duty than to open it unto all the world; that men may beware how they wax weary of God in denying him in the time of trouble. And God I take to record, I will write no more than that I have perfectly learned, and leisurely searched the truth and prison where Judge Hales did this deed upon himself. And besides this, I will not write the truth of this matter for any hatred I bear to my lord chancellor, whose body and soul I wish to do as well as mine own body and soul; nor for any love that I bear in this respect to any that is of a contrary religion to my lord chancellor; but only for the love and zeal I bear unto God's word, which is slandered by my lord chancellor through this man's ungodly fact, which he much repenteth at this time, and I trust God will forgive him. The matter is this.

Mr Hales, as all men know, is imprisoned for the testimony of Jesus Christ, and persecuted because he will not conform himself to the false and most untrue religion set forth at this time by the bishops. And although the papistical sort seem not to care whether Mr Hales return to their part or no, yet all men may see by their crafty doings, that very gladly they would have men recant and conform themselves to their false faith and doings. And to compare[1] this matter, and to bring it to pass, Mr Hales was divers times exhorted by one Mr Forster, a gentleman of Hampshire, and also a prisoner in the Fleet, that he should give over his opinion, and conform himself to the proceedings now-a-days set forth: and, as the same Forster hath reported to others that are prisoners with him, Mr Hales condescended unto his advice, and resolved himself to leave his former truth, and to cleave unto the error that was offered by this man's persuasion unto him, because the error was without danger that he should depart unto, and the truth full of peril that he should depart from. Thus the good man, Mr Hales, waxing faint and feeble in the truth, was increased more and more with anguish and anxiety of mind, his conscience rebuking him of his timorousness and fear. But as soon as it was known that Mr Hales was minded to relent from the truth, and to consent to falsehood, the twelfth of April in the morning came the bishop of Chichester into the Fleet, where he had long talk with Mr Hales in the garden; the contents whereof I cannot learn: but, as many of the prisoners have said openly in the Fleet, the bishop had made up all together, and clean removed Mr Hales from his first faith, and established him in the latter opinions allowed now by the bishops. The same day at afternoon came there to the Fleet Judge Portman, a Somersetshire man, and had great talk and long with Mr Hales; after whose departure, supper-time being at hand, Mr Hales came into the parlour, and sat at the table very heavily, eating little or nothing, but full of cogitations, and heavy with pensiveness; and soon after supper gat him to bed, where as he had no rest, but watch with heaviness and sorrow till the next morrow towards six of the clock; at what time he commanded his servant to fetch him a cup of beer, who saw the butler as he was coming to the stair-head, and prayed him to bring up a cup of beer for his master to his chamber; and immediately he returned to his master, who in that short time (whiles his man was calling at the stair-head for a cup of beer) wrought to himself this displeasure in putting of himself in danger of his life, and gave occasion to my lord chancellor, and to the rest of the ungodly generation, to slander and deface the true word of God and the professors thereof.

[1 Compare: procure, or, perhaps, a misprint for *compass*.]

But now let all men judge indifferently how this man, Mr. Hales, came to this desperation of mind, and then all men shall perceive it came into heart when he had surrendered himself to accomplish the commandment of man. For as long as he was constant in the truth, he endured, and strongly passed ever more cruel imprisonment. For he was first imprisoned in the King's Bench, and very christianly endured it: then was he for all the time of Lent in the Counter of Bread Street, and strongly endured it: at length he came to the Fleet, and bare it almost for the space of three weeks strongly; till at length by persuasion he waxed weary of the truth, and then denying Christ, that was made man of the substance of the blessed Virgin Mary, and crediting a false Christ, that was and is made (after the papistical opinion) of bread, was it any marvel though the devil entered into this man? No, doubtless; for his new-made Christ is not able to keep the devil away. For he cannot come out of the box, although he should rot there, and be burned, as it many times happeneth. Therefore it is no marvel though such as trust in that false Christ fall into desperation. For Judas, although he chose not a new-made Christ when he betrayed the old, yet the devil entered into him, and he hanged himself for betraying his old master. It is no marvel therefore to see men that forsake the truth of God to be vexed with evil spirits, and many times to kill themselves. But this we may see most evidently by Mr Hales, that until such times as he consented to forsake God's truth, which of long time he had most godly professed, he never fell into this danger and into this peril, to kill himself. So that the papistical doctrine, by this man's example, is a very worm, that biteth the conscience, and never leaveth till it have killed the man that forsaketh the truth, and turneth unto lies.

Wherefore my lord chancellor might rather of this horrible fault done by Mr Hales have learned to have detested and abhorred his own false and popish religion, that as soon as any of Christ's members fall from the truth into it, they either despair, or kill themselves most commonly, as evidently it was, as is proved by Mr Hales; for whose salvation all Christians most earnestly pray unto God. Further, my lord chancellor might learn by this man's deed, what horrible and devilish ways be used towards Christ's members by himself and others, that the like was never used among the Turks, by villainy and compulsion to drive men and compel men to such a religion as the word of God never knew of. In case it were true, as it is most false, when did ever the bishop of Winchester read in God's word that any outward law made by man could enforce faith, which is *the only gift of God*, and should be truly and charitably taught to all men by God's word? But all men may see that like as their doctrine they preach is none of God's, so may they perceive that they have none other arguments to defend it withal but the tyrannical sword and fire: for fear whereof many dissemble with God in outward obedience to idolatry, with so much striving and anguish of conscience as many, after that they had condescended for fear unto this wicked and condemned religion by God's word, the old doctors, and the laws of this realm, they never be merry in spirit afterward; and many times, for very desperation of God's mercy, kill themselves. If the bishop and his generation did not delight in blood, and pass for nothing but for their own kingdom of antichrist, they would learn by this man's hurting of himself to beware how they persuade men to do against their consciences.

But let all men pray to God for strength, and that he will of his mercy mitigate this bondage and servitude, more cruel than ever was the servitude in Egypt or Babylon. For then were the children of God in captivity in strange lands, and under strange kings; but we poor Englishmen be in captivity in our own land, and under our own countrymen, that make us commit more vile idolatry than ever did the Israelites in Egypt. From the which the Lord Almighty in the blood of Christ deliver us, and amend our persecutors, if it be his will. Let all good men say, Amen.

EPISTOLA

AD

EPISCOPOS, DECANOS, ARCHIDIACONOS, ET CETEROS CLERI ORDINES

IN SYNODO LONDINENSI CONGREGATOS.

[THE Epistola ad Episcopos, Decanos &c, the Appellatio ad parlamentum, and the treatise De sacratissimæ cœnæ Domini vera doctrina et legitimo usu, are reprinted from Foxe's work entitled, "Rerum in ecclesia gestarum &c commentarii," which was published at Basle, 1559.

Foxe, in an address to the christian reader, at page 298 of the above work, states that Hooper, " præter ceteras privatim ad amicos non parvo numero epistolas, bina *hæc* insuper syntagmata elucubravit, alterum de re et veritate eucharistica, ad sublimem parlamenti curiam, alterum ad Vigornienses et Glocestrenses suos, de vero et falso discernendo cultu ; utrumque opus Latine suaque manu scripsit." Yet notwithstanding this statement the latter treatise does not appear in his work.

Hooper designed the two treatises for presentation to parliament, and wrote letters[1] to Cardinal Pole and Day, bishop of Chichester, begging them to undertake the charge of them : but, meeting with a refusal from both, he sent them to Bullinger[2], requesting that he would have them printed at Zurich by Froschover ; or, if Froschover were otherwise engaged, send them to Basle to Oporinus. Oporinus was Foxe's printer, and hence probably they came into that writer's hands[3].]

[1] See Apology against the untrue and slanderous report &c. : also Letters, number XXXVII, and, further, Rerum in ecclesia gestarum &c. p. 393. Foxe says that Pole, in his reply, confessed that the request was not unfair, but that he was afraid to comply with it : Day altogether refused. Bale mentions Hooper's letters to Pole and Day, and quotes the commencement of each of them. See Script. Illustr. p. 680. Basil. 1559.
[2] See Letters, number XXXVII.
[3] The Editor is indebted for this suggestion to an article on " The Marian Exiles" in the Edinburgh Review, No. CLXXII, April, 1847.

Episcopis, Decanis, Archidiaconis,
et ceteris cleri ordinibus in synodo Londinensi congregatis,
gratiam et pacem a Domino[1].

Non vos latet, viri doctissimi, in rebus arduis, ambiguis, et difficilioribus [2] judicium apud veteres, juxta mandatum Dei, delatum fuisse semper ad sacerdotes Levitas, et ad præsidem qui pro tempore judicis munere fungebatur; ut omnes hi causas et lites difficiliores explicarent ex præscripto legis Dei. Ita qualescunque controversiæ fuerunt, ex sententia sacerdotum et præsidis ad normam et præscriptum legis Dei lata componebantur; et ab eo quod judices partibus litigantibus statuissent nullo modo erat declinandum. Quod si quis contumacius sacerdoti aut præsidi non paruisset juxta legem Dei sententiam pronuncianti, pœnas contumaciæ morte luebat; quo populus hac ultione et contumaciæ vindicta admonitus metueret, et deinceps insolescere desisteret. Quam difficiles, imo quam periculosæ inter nos et vos de re eucharistica lites agantur, vestræ conciones, scripta, et libelli testantur: nos vero, qui meliorem, veriorem, et antiquissimam fidem sustinemus, confiscatione omnium bonorum nostrorum, dura et inhumana carceris servitute sentimus. Quare mei ipsius nomine ac omnium fratrum qui mecum eandem catholicæ ac sanctæ religionis veritatem profitentur vos omnes in Christo Jesu obtestor, ut causam hanc, vel aliam[3] quamcunque ob religionem ortam inter nos et vos, deferre dignemini ad supremam curiam parlamenti; ut ibi utraque pars coram sacro et excelso senatu sese religiose et animo submisso judicio et auctoritati verbi Dei subjiciat. Et si vestram religionem, quam sanctam, orthodoxam, ac catholicam esse contenditis, ex verbo Dei asserere potestis, illam et nos libenter amplexabimur, nostram, quam modo pro sacrosancta defendimus,

[[1] This letter was reprinted in the eighth edition of the Acts and Monuments, 1583, the last published during Foxe's life-time: the texts of the two editions have been collated, and the variations of the later given in the notes.]

[[2] Causis difficilioribus, 1583.]   [[3] Aliquam, 1583.]

repudiantes; gratias item Deo et vobis agentes quam maximas, quod per vos ab erroribus liberati ad veritatis cognitionem revocemur. Non solum autem hoc a vobis obtestamur, ut vos vestramque causam judicio verbi Dei coram summo parlamento deferatis; verum etiam, ut nobis commodum detur tempus quo veterum scripta et sacras literas evolvamus, a sacro[4] senatu impetrare dignemini: et si ibi justas ac legitimas rationes fidei nostræ non reddiderimus, judicio magistratus nos ipsos submittimus, ut debitam ultionem nostri sceleris et impietatis nobis infligat.

Si hæc facere non recusaveritis, religio, quam castam, illibatam, et salvam, ac ab omnibus amplectendam esse contenditis, gloriosius de nostra fide et religione ac de nobis ipsis (qui illam impiam esse et falsam contestamur) victoriam reportabit. Nam si vestra religio et cultus in causa eucharistiæ fontem et originem ducunt ex verbo Dei, proculdubio sanctam et sempiternam esse oportet. Et scitis quod res sancta et vera, quo magis examinatur, et per verbum Dei exploratur, eo fit illustrior et purior: et quanto purior et illustrior fit, tanto magis ab omnibus desideratur, et obviis ulnis excipitur. Quis enim non desideraret et amplecteretur religionem et cultum a Deo mandatum, et ab illius verbo sancitum ac confirmatum? Quare si vestra religio et cultus Dei res sit vera[5], sancta, et a Deo mundo exhibita, non est quod ei metuatis. Nam quod variis modis tentatur ac probatur, modo pium ac sanctum fuerit, jacturam ab hostibus nullam sentit, sed potius hostes conculcat ac interficit. Solis radii sterquiliniorum sordibus non coinquinantur; veritasque divini verbi errorum tenebris et caligine non offunditur.

Nec est quod vobis ipsis metuatis, modo re ipsa id præstetis quod ubique jactatis. Nam quotquot vestras partes non sequuntur, aliquo gravissimo ignominiæ genere nimis superbe afficitis; nos omnes omnino indoctos esse prædicatis, aut plane dementatos affirmatis. Vobis autem plus quam divinam vindicatis prudentiam: nobis vero plus quam belluinam stoliditatem tribuitis. Jam quam facile erit doctis indoctos, hominibus sanæ mentis insania percitos, ingenio et prudentia flagrantibus stolidos et ignaros vincere, sacer parlamenti conventus nullo negotio intelliget. Ideo si omnino ob Christum et illius causæ gloriam, quam nos defendimus, aut ob salutem nostram, ut vestra prudentia nos stultitiæ arguamur, vestraque doctrina

[4 Sancto, 1583.]   [5 Adeo vera, 1583.]

et eruditione nos ignorantiæ accusemur, hoc facere non vultis; tamen ut publice impietatis convincamur coram summo senatu, hoc præstate.

Et si istis rationibus nihil moveamini, tamen vestra ipsorum causa certe postulat, ut palam eæ lites inter nos componantur, idque coram competenti judice; ne apud omnes pios male audiat, et fortassis hac suspicione laboret, quasi lucem et publicum examen fugiat, ne impietatis et idololatriæ per verbum Dei rea[1] deprehendatur; et vos, qui malam causam, imo pessimam, ferro et igne defenditis, non tam docti nec pii, ut omnino videri et haberi vultis, inveniamini, sed potius ignorantiæ et stultitiæ, quas nobis impingitis, redarguamini. Non vos fugit, quomodo publice, palam, et in facie ac præsentia omnium statuum hujus regni, in summa curia parlamenti veritas verbi Dei per fidos, doctos, et pios ministros de vestra impia missa gloriose victoriam reportavit, quamvis per trecentos annos non solum locum et templum Dei occupaverit, verum etiam corda hominum (tanquam Deus) inhabitaverit. Sed quocunque titulo, nomine, honore, reverentia, sanctitate, tempore, patronis, universalitate splenduit, ubi per sanctissimum regem Edouardum sextum, sanctissimæ memoriæ, ad vivum lapidem Lydium verbi Dei examinari per proceres, heroes, ac doctos hujus regni viros[2] erat mandatum, statim evanuit, et nihil aliud apparuit quam spurcissimum et immundissimum idolum sub pallio et nomine Dei impie contectum.

Æqua et justa petimus, ut palam et publice lites inter nos componantur. Si igitur vestræ causæ et vobis ipsis non diffidatis, una nobiscum apud sanctum senatum agere dignemini, ut coram illo auctoritate verbi Dei quis nostrum veriorem partem defenderit dignoscatur. Nullis enim legibus sanctis et justis unquam fuit permissum, ut una pars litigans de altera parte judex constitueretur. Nam in omnibus controversiis et causis difficilioribus (maxime in religione) medius aliquis, et neutra litigantium pars, in judicem eligendus[3] est. Nec Christus ipse, quamvis ipsa Veritas, æterni Patris filius, hanc potestatem et imperium judicandi sibi vindicavit, quandocunque lites de ejus doctrina inter illum et Pharisæos vel quoscunque alios contigerunt; sed semper ad legem appellavit, adversariosque suos ut legis præscripto et sententia [John v.] starent rogavit, "Scrutamini (inquiens) scripturas." Nos

[1 Rea, wanting in 1583.]   [2 Viros, omitted in 1583.]
[3 Eligenda, 1583.]

etiam a vobis nihil aliud in nomine Domini nostri Jesu Christi supplices petimus et rogamus, nisi ut causa, de qua inter nos litigatur, sententia et auctoritate verbi Dei decidatur ac finiatur. Et si per verbum Dei fidem nostram parum candidam et piam ostendere valetis, porrigemus vobis herbam, dabimusque dextras. Ne[4] in impios Arrianos pii et sancti patres hanc judicandi potestatem sibi assumpserunt; sed adfuit disputationi pius princeps Constantinus imperator, qui rationes partium litigantium diligenter perpendit, et sententiam atque judicium causæ soli auctoritati verbi Dei detulit.

Quid hoc est igitur? Quo jure contenditis? Vultis et nostri et causæ nostræ testes, accusatores, et judices esse? Nos tantum legem et evangelium Dei in causa religionis judicem competentem agnoscimus: illius judicio stet vel cadat nostra causa. Tantum iterum atque iterum petimus, ut coram competenti judice detur nobis, qui vincula et carceres sustinemus, amicum christianumque auditorium: tunc haud dubitamus quin nostras rationes et argumenta auctoritate verbi divini simus stabilituri, ac vestra plane subversuri. Hactenus præjudicio injuste gravamur: nec mirum, cum una pars litigantium alterius partis judex[5] constituatur. Quapropter ad verbum Dei, tanquam unicum et solum competentem in causa religionis judicem, appellamus. Si præter et contra hanc legem Dei falsa et impia (ut cœpistis) vi et dolo promovere non desistetis, sed fratres vestros truculenter persequendo pergetis, nos in tantis periculis constituti ad misericordiam Dei confugiemus, qui solus et possit et velit nos a vestris erroribus incolumes et salvos conservare. Præterea, ut olim aliqui ex nobis pro salute et incolumitate aliquot vestrum apud magistratum civilem intercessimus, sic et nunc pro omnium vestrum salute in Christo Jesu apud Patrem cœlestem intercedere non desistemus, ut tandem ad meliorem et sinceriorem mentem reversi unicum Christum Jesum, quem præcinuerunt prophetæ, prædicaverunt apostoli, quemque omnes pii agnoscunt, jam quoad humanitatem sedentem ad dextram Patris in cœlis, amplectamini et exosculemini, repudiato conficto et ementito illo Christo ex pane confecto, quem non solum juvenes, virgines, et senes, verum etiam oves et boves pecoraque campi, volucres cœli et pisces maris, panem agnoscunt ac sentiunt, et non Deum.

Desistite, rogamus igitur enixe, ulterius oculos piorum per-

[4 Nec, 1583.]   [5 Judex alterius partis, 1583.]

stringere. Verus enim Christus, quatenus homo, jam amplius sursum ac deorsum per manus sacerdotum agitari et immolari non potest. Infernum vicit, peccata nostra[1] in cruce expiavit, mortem destruxit, et jam astra tenet; quem olim videbitis venientem in nubibus cœli cum potestate magna et gloria, sempiternisque pœnis vos plangetis, nisi hic pœnitentiam falsæ et impiæ vestræ doctrinæ egeritis. Si Deus autem pro sua inexhausta bonitate et clementia per verbum suum lites istas inter nos et vos[2] componi dignetur, non dubito quin oculos vestros ita sit aperturus, ut quam horribiliter et impie Dei ac hominum testimonio et scriptis abutamini[3] videatis. Sed si furioso et excandescenti spiritu vestras partes citra auctoritatem verbi Dei defendere velitis, actum est omnino de vestra æterna salute: quod Dominus propter Filium suum unicum avertat.

Cogitate etiam apud vos ipsos an hoc sit piorum ministrorum ecclesiæ officium, vi, metu, et pavore corda hominum in vestras partes compellere. Profecto Christus non ignem, non gladium, non carceres, non vincula, non violentiam, non confiscationem bonorum, non regineæ majestatis terrorem, media organa constituit quibus veritas sui verbi mundo promulgaretur; sed miti ac diligenti prædicatione evangelii sui mundum ab errore et idololatria converti præcepit. Vos non Christi sed antichristi armis utimini, quibus populum invitum ad vestra scelera[4] compellitis, et non volentem et instructum verbo Dei trahitis. Sed quam malus custos perpetuitatis sit timor, non ignoratis. Certe qui timet, nisi Dei Spiritu semper revocetur, odit. Tradite igitur saluberrima præcepta legis et evangelii populo Dei, ut pro Christi ministris per verbum Christi ab omnibus agnoscamini. Ideo enim ministri ecclesiæ Christi estis constituti, ut tantum Christi doctrinam populum Dei doceretis, et non ut novam et a Christo alienam obtruderetis. Quæ jam vos in ecclesia agitis, si coram æquo judice amicam ac christianam disputationem non recusaveritis, ex verbo Dei ostendemus vel a lege Mosaica mutuata, vel per antichristum et pseudo-ministros in ecclesiam fuisse introducta, ut hoc brevi tractatu excelsæ parlamenti curiæ destinato[5] facile constabit.

Scio inter vos esse tam turgido et invido[6] spiritu præditos,

[1 Vestra, 1583.]   [2 Et vos, omitted in 1583.]
[3 Abuti, 1583.]   [4 Sacra, 1583.]
[5 Destinato, omitted in 1583.]   [6 Iniquo, 1583.]

qui putant nos tantum inanis gloriæ, superbiæ, arrogantiæ, et famæ nostræ fumo duci, et ideo velle potius semper male currere quam admonitos de errore bene recurrere. Sed hoc Deus novit, quod tantum illius gloriam nostramque salutem in Christo quæramus[7], dicant adversarii quicquid[8] velint. Meminerint autem nostri adversarii et cogitent, quanquam apud illos nec pro doctis nec piis hominibus habemur[9] (et haud dubie nos ipsos omnis impietatis et peccati apud Deum quotidie accusamus), tamen homines sumus ratione præditi. Et quis, nisi insanus, jactura et amissione omnium bonorum suorum, uxoris, liberorum, libertatis, et vitæ redimeret famæ aut inanis gloriæ titulum? Profecto tanti pœnitere (ut dicitur) non emeremus. Igitur illius verbi veritatem nostris bonis omnibus ac vitæ ipsi præferimus: et si centies (Deo nos adjuvante) moriendum nobis fuerit, ad idololatriam et impium cultum Dei, quæ Dei misericordia hactenus reliquimus, non revertemur. Domini sumus, sive vivimus sive morimur: ejus igitur voluntas in vobis et in nobis cum misericordia fiat. Amen.

Vestræ salutis in Christo studiosissimus Joannes Hoperus, nuper Vigorniensis et Glocestrensis episcopus[10].

[[7] Quæerimus, 1583.] [[8] Quid, 1583.] [[9] Habeamur, 1583.]
[[10] This designation omitted in 1583.]

APPELLATIO AD PARLAMENTUM.

Joannis Hoperi
appellatio ad Parlamentum: ex carcere.
Anno 1554. Mens. August. 27.

QUANQUAM, viri illustrissimi, cœlestis Pater sæpius suam voluntatem patefecit absque studio, auctoritate, et consensu magistratus, nihilominus aliquando contingit, ut hoc fiat magistratus auxilio, industria, et auctoritate, ut veritas divini verbi gloriosius ac celerius inter populum propagetur: quemadmodum legimus factum sub Josia, rege Judæorum, qui sua ipsius industria et opere suo populo Dei verbum (uti ipse accepit ex libro Deut.) diligenter proposuit ac promulgavit. Et ubi verbum Dei malorum superstitione vel impietate improborum impeditur, vel qui illud promotum esse cupiunt opprimuntur et affliguntur, ad supremam auctoritatem et magistratum appellari solet: ut Paulus ad Cæsarem et illius tribunal appellavit, ut illic potius apud divini verbi penitus ignaros causam suam ageret, humanitate et æquitate ethnicorum confisus, quam apud suos; qui tamen alioqui omnem eruditionem et cognitionem verbi Dei jactitabant, cum revera nihil illis superstitiosius aut magis tyrannicum usquam esset expertus. Qua quidem ad Cæsaris tribunal appellatione non solum ad aliquot annos vitæ suæ consuluit, verum etiam doctrinam Christi, quam religiose ac diligenter promotam esse cupiebat in universum orbem, commodius et ocius propagavit, non solum viva voce, dum per duos annos integros libero servaretur in carcere, verum etiam per epistolas multas ac præclarissimas, quas in carcere et vinculis scripsit, quæ ad hunc usque diem ad nostram eruditionem et consolationem Dei bonitate et singulari providentia conservantur.

[2 Kings xxiii.]

Acts xxiv. xxv.

[Acts xxviii.]

Quare cum per magistratus imperium et auctoritatem sæpe divina doctrina et quicquid est orthodoxum ocius et latius spargatur, et pii concionatores verbi Dei a tyrannide et malitia impiorum melius muniantur, hoc nomine ego hunc sanctum ac venerandum conventum parlamenti appello, ut publice, præsentibus piis fratribus qui carcerum et vinculorum molestias sustinent, coram vestra claritate, honore, et prudentia quæstionum contentio, quæ inter nos et neotericos agitatur, juxta verbi Dei veritatem ac sanctorum patrum testimonia componatur: quo tandem nos ipsos apud vestrum tribunal æquissimum ab hæretici dogmatis infamia, quam injustissime nostri Christique adversarii nobis impingunt, liberemus: quod scilicet veram panis et vini substantiam in sacra cœna Domini cum apertissimo verbo Dei ac omnium veterum patrum testimoniis semper retinemus; deinde, quod corporalem Christi præsentiam a signis cœnæ Domini auferimus, et tantum spiritualem et sacramentalem præsentiam in vere ac rite signis utentibus constituimus, quam fide demum qui signis recte utuntur percipiunt; ceterum illius corporis corporalem præsentiam juxta sacras scripturas cœlo tantum tribuimus: postremo, quod nullum sacrificium propitiatorium, quo placetur ira Dei erga peccatores, et cujus pretio ac dignitate recipiamur in gratiam et favorem Dei, agnoscimus, præter unicam mortem Christi in cruce semel peractam, et hoc solum per Christum ipsum ante 1500 annos.

Hanc fidem nostram, quam omnibus modis neoterici expugnare et ab omnibus ecclesiis deturbare conantur, sanctam ac salutarem esse testantur omnia sacrarum literarum volumina, patriarchæ, prophetæ, Jesus Christus Salvator mundi, evangelistæ, apostoli, veteres canones et concilia, atque omnes sancti patres prope per mille annos a Christi ascensione in cœlos. Et hoc coram vestro sacrosancto cœtu et concilio evidentissimis argumentis et rationibus nos evicturos pollicemur periculo nostri capitis; modo nobis, qui carceres et vincula diu admodum summa cum difficultate sustinuimus, tempus concedatur quo memoriæ vires, agilitas, et solertia redintegrentur, et quo sanctorum patrum libros evolvere liceat. Hoc tantum postulamus, ut coram sacro vestro cœtu una cum adversariis nostris æquis animis, positis affectibus, audiamur, et sint sacri libri judices inter nos et nostros adversarios; quibus nosmet ipsos causamque sanctissimam quam defendimus omnino submittimus. Quod si per sacrosancti senatus et excellentissimæ curiæ parlamenti auctoritatem et gratiam quæstiones de quibus inter nos controvertitur examinari, disputari, ac finiri licuerit ex auctoritate verbi Dei et sanctorum patrum testimoniis, tunc haud dubie per Dei bonitatem vincet pars melior, et sancta catholica fides atque religio ecclesiis Christi restituetur, et neotericorum superstitio atque idololatria, quibus horribiliter et magno cum periculo æternæ iræ Dei ecclesiæ Anglicanæ jam laborant, nullo negotio deturbabuntur.

Quam gratum et acceptabile opus Deo sacer senatus præstaret, si divina ac cœlestia ecclesiis Anglicanis restitueret, et humana atque terrestria removeret, non opus est pluribus dicere. Satis est enim scire, quod ab exordio mundi qui divina restituerunt, et humana a populo (quo ad religionem) amoverunt, maximam inde a Deo laudem sint adepti; et qui vel veram religionem contempserunt, vel segniter et pigre eam provehendam curaverunt, ignominiam sibi accersiverint sempiternam. Si igitur pius senatus jam supplices nostras preces admiserit, ut coram sublimi et excelsa curia parlamenti causam nostram agamus, facillime omnes pii intelligent ea quæ jam fiunt a neotericis in ecclesiis esse mera mendacia, et antichristi Romani commenta, non solum præter verbum Dei superinducta, verum etiam ex diametro pugnantia cum verbo divino; ac pontificis omnes privatas missas defendentes transgredi mandata Dei [Matt. xxvi. Mark xiv.] propter traditiones hominum. Nam Christum dixisse scimus, "Accipite et manducate;" "Accipite, bibite ex hoc omnes:" Romani vero deuterotæ, spretis ac contemptis hisce Dei mandatis, incomitati, singuli seorsim ac soli, panem et vinum accipiunt. Christus autem jussit ecclesiam accipere, manducare, et bibere sacramenta corporis et sanguinis sui: hæc vero divina præcepta Romanistæ rejiciunt, et nova ac impia ab hominibus excogitata et inventa in medium protulerunt; quæ in ecclesiis Christi tyrannice et violenter mandantur ac imperantur sub pœna capitis; videlicet, ne quis ex plebe gustet ex sacro calice et vino consecrato; sed ut omnes in genua procumbant, panemque et vinum pro Deo optimo maximo adorent. Christus sacramenta eo nomine instituit, ut sui pacti ac fœderis initi per mortem suam cum humano genere essent testimonia, obsignacula, et sacra signa, quibus ex æquo omnes qui Christo nomina sua dederunt, modo vere illos pœniteret male actæ vitæ, veraque fide instructi accederent[1], et

[[1] Fors. instructi essent, accederent, &c.]

communicarent, tam minister ecclesiæ quam populus: neoterici communicationem corporis et sanguinis Christi a populo subduxerunt, quam Christus toti ecclesiæ mandavit; et in illius locum sacramentorum adorationem introduxerunt, quam Christus Jesus nunquam præcepit.

Nec vero solum hanc Christi veram cœnam ex ecclesiis Christi profugarunt, ut suas impias missas privatas statuerent; verum etiam quicquid præterea in ecclesiis factitant ex adverso cum Dei mandatis pugnat. Deus enim omnia jubet fieri in ecclesiis ad ædificationem; sive concio habeatur, sive oretur, aut sacramenta ministrentur in publico cœtu, omnia nota et cognita lingua fieri debent; ut expresse et liquido ex verbo Dei constat: isti autem neoterici contemptim, neglecto aperto mandato Dei, omnia in ecclesiis Anglorum Romana agunt lingua, quam paucissimi intelligunt. Sed prætendunt neoterici Romani inter cetera inepta et ridicula se hoc facere, quo Romanam linguam semper in ecclesiis inter doctos conservent, sacraque Biblia in nostram linguam male versa calumniantur. Sed quam puerilis (ne dicam impius) sit hic prætextus, cæci vident. Si vero oscitanter vel parum candide interpretes in vertendis Bibliis sunt suo functi munere, meminerint eos ipsos qui jam ecclesias Anglicanas verbo Dei ne Anglice audiatur spoliant majorem partem Bibliorum transtulisse: et mirum est quod jam proprios fœtus ac partus non agnoscant, sed crudeliter enecent. Si quid desiderent amplius, omni studio et opera, quæ nimis obscure, improprie, vel non sufficienter reddita animadverterint, rogamus ut corrigant et eméndent: interim permittant populo hujus regni, juxta mandatum Dei, ut omnia fiant in lingua illi cognita. Et ubi Biblia per illos clarius, elegantius, et vicinius Ebraicæ et Græcæ veritati fuerint conversa in Anglicam linguam, removeantur quæ jam in ecclesiis extant, et clariora et elegantiora in illorum loca substituantur. Sed ridiculum plane est, et quod Christiani diutius ferant indignum, ut verbum Dei apud indoctos ignota lingua tractetur; ut D. Paulus testatur: "Si quis videtur propheta aut spiritualis, agnoscat quæ scribo vobis, quod Domini sint præcepta." Et si neoterici cæcitate et insania, quod irreligiosius legunt et tractant verbum Dei, non essent cœlitus tacti, qui fieri posset ut decimum quartum caput 1 Corinth. (ubi luce ipsa clarius Paulus ostendit, mandat, ac divino jussu imperat, ut omnia publice in ecclesiis agantur, doceantur, le-

[margin: 1 Cor. xiv.]
[margin: Ignota lingua in cultum sacrum non inducenda.]
[margin: 1 Cor. xiv.]

gantur, orenturque cognita lingua) non intelligerent? Nisi etiam amentia et spiritus vertigine agitarentur neoterici, cum missas suas celebrant, quomodo non animadverterent hæc Dei mandata, quæ quotidie legunt et recitant, "Accipite et manducate?" Quis vero nesciat verba ipsa, quæ ab illis quotidie recitantur, docere hoc esse Dei mandatum, ut sacra mysteria corporis et sanguinis Christi toto cœtui et illis qui sacris Domini adsunt proponantur, distribuantur, accipiantur, comedantur, et bibantur? O satanicam et deplorandam cæcitatem, quæ quotidie negligit, contemnit, violat, ac hostili odio persequitur eadem ipsa Dei mandata quæ quotidie in suis missis recitant et legunt! Sed tale est Dei tremendum judicium, ut qui semel sese traditionibus humanis obstrinxerunt verbum quidem Dei legant et audiant, sed tamen non animadvertant nec intelligant. Hoc est, juxta diras illas Dei comminationes et execrationes in prophetis sanctis, oculos habere, et non videre; aures habere, et non audire. Rideant audacter neoterici nos et alios omnes qui Christum pure ac illius mysteria et sacra rite, religiose, et legitime docuimus et ministravimus juxta normam ac incommutabilem regulam verbi Dei; nos vero illorum miseriam et insaniam vehementer deplorabimus, qui, relictis Dei præceptis, siliquis humanarum traditionum (quæ cibus sunt porcorum) vesci gaudeant, quæ nec illis qui in ecclesiis ministrant, nec iis quibus ministrantur, famem peccati eximunt, neque territas conscientias tranquillant; sed potius omnia Christi mortis merita penitus sepeliunt, et mentes eorum, quos Christus suo sanguine est mercatus, cæcitate, superstitione, et idololatria satanica perstringunt ac corrumpunt.

[Isai. vi. Jer. v. Ezek. xii.]

Sed ad propositum revertatur oratio. Quod isti Neoterici omnia Latine in ecclesia agi volunt, non id eo faciunt vel quod translationis vitio tam vehementer offendantur, vel quod misellus grex Christi illis adeo curæ sit; sed ut ex lingua Romana, Anglis plerumque ignota, hæc duo sacrificuli neoterici assequantur: primum, ne quod impie contra mandata divina in suis missis agunt detegatur; quod omnino fieret, si vulgari lingua omnia quæ impia sunt in missa mundo paterent: secundum, ut suam auctoritatem salvam ac incolumem semper apud indoctum vulgus, cui misere per suas missas imponunt, tueantur. Nam verbum Dei cognita lingua populo propositum illorum idololatriam proderet, et illos an-

Duplex causa, cur ignota lingua res suas tractent papistæ.

tichristianismi in faciem argueret. Hinc illæ reprehensiones, minæ, et condemnationes Anglicorum Bibliorum. Hoc enim sacrosancto senatui et excelsæ curiæ parlamenti sub judicio capitis mei polliceor, me ex Ebraicis probaturum Anglicanam versionem multo esse viciniorem Ebraicæ veritati quam sit communis versio, quam neoterici jam in usu habent et D. Hieronymo falso tribuunt. Sæpius autem cum piis ac doctis fratribus antehac de recognoscendis et clarius vertendis Bibliis egi. Cuperem vero optimam et perspicuam versionem Bibliorum in ecclesiis Dei: sed ablationem et raptionem eorundem per Romanos sacrificulos ad unius diei spatium in publicis conventibus a populo Dei omnino condemnarem. Hoperi in recognoscendis Bibliis pium consilium.

Oro igitur obnixe vos omnes, principes, duces, comites, nobiles, et totum populum vestri magni et excelsi conventus in Christo Jesu, ut verbum Dei vulgari lingua populo hujus regni restituatur, omniaque in ecclesiis Anglicanis Anglice agantur, et sacramenta Dei juxta Christi institutionem rite administrentur; denique ut omnes controversiæ in religione ad verbum Dei exigantur ac decidantur. Satis enim est christiano homini Christi lex et evangelium: tyrannicum autem et plane satanicum est ad illam religionem christianum hominem compellere, quam lex Christi et evangelium penitus ignorant. Turcæ quidem dum non recedunt a suo Alcorano, Judæi perfidi dum suum Talmud studiose observant, ab omni suspicione et infamia hæretici dogmatis fiunt immunes. Quid hoc est igitur apud Christianos, ut qui sacrorum voluminum testimoniis omnem suam religionem et fidem habent ratam et confirmatam, tam misere omni infamia hæretici dogmatis per Romanos neotericos proscindantur, et quævis calamitatum genera pati cogantur? Turcæ non plus exigunt quam ut Alcorani testimonio fides Turcarum approbetur: perfidi vero Judæi satis esse putant, si illorum religio Talmudico calculo sit rata ac confirmata; et tamen illorum libri mendaciis et blasphemiis scatent: testamentum autem sanguine Christi confirmatum, cui nihil addi vel adimi per hominem debeat, nostram fidem ac religionem agnoscit, approbat, et confirmat, non implicite nec abscondite, sed clare ac lucide; et tamen quia antichristi figmenta et mendacia una cum Christi vera religione non amplectimur, pro Christianis a neotericis non agnoscimur.

Neoterici vero sibi ipsis ac aliis imponunt, cum dicunt panis et vini transubstantiationem in cœna non clare, nominatim, et aperte exprimi in sacris literis, sed implicite et obscure contineri. Sed ubi ex verbo Dei panis et vini substantiam semper manere in cœna probavimus, tunc alias rimas labendi quærunt, satisque impudenter affirmant veteres patres non solum transubstantiationem panis et vini, verum etiam realem et corporalem corporis et sanguinis Christi præsentiam, et item corporis Christi oblationem propitiatoriam, agnoscere in sacra cœna Domini. Injuriam plane ac vim faciunt isti neoterici sanctis patribus. Verba autem mutationis panis et vini ac præsentiæ corporis Christi in cœna Domini, imo verbum sacrificandi et sacrificii, scimus frequenter esse apud patres. Sed ipsi hæc vocabula usurpant eo modo et sensu quo ecclesia Christi ab ejus ascensione usurpavit, et nos nunc usurpamus: hoc est, panem et vinum in sacra cœna mutari quidem, sed in usu, non in substantia; Christum vero corpore suo adesse, sed spiritualiter et sacramentaliter contemplatione fidei recte utentium sacra cœna Domini, quoad corporis ejus gratiam, sed non quoad corporis ejus substantiam. Cœna Domini (quod impia missa non est) etiam sacrificium Christianorum vocatur, non re ipsa, sed nominis communicatione et participatione; quia recordatio et memoria sit veri sacrificii Christi semel in cruce oblati. Qualis autem injuria et tyrannis est hæc, non permittere ut sancti patres sua ipsorum verba interpretentur! Ubi enim illi sacramentaliter et figurate loquuntur, neoterici ad nudum, simplicem, ac ipsum verborum stridorem et strepitum urgent. Certe hoc non est candide agere, verba contra mentem scribentis et suam ipsius interpretationem detorquere; sed fraudulenter et superbe dominari scriptis sanctorum patrum. Sed istorum vafras et superbas mentes Spiritus Sanctus nunquam in suum sacrarium admittet: nam humiles docet, turgidas dimittit inanes. Nos quidem, qui carceres et vincula sustinemus, hoc in nos probandum suscipiemus, adjuvante Deo, omnes veteres patres, per octingentos annos, et plus a Christi in cœlos e terris ascensione, nostram fidem ac religionem agnovisse, et pro vera, sancta, et catholica docuisse, suaque morte confirmasse. Et per hanc fidem omnes qui hactenus in Christo obierunt vitam assequuti sunt æternam. Et qui hanc impiam et neotericam fidem et religionem de panis et vini transubstantiatione in Deum et hominem Jesum Christum, vel Christum per sacrificulum Deo Patri in missa impia et papistica pro remissione peccatorum offerri, sunt professi, nisi pœnitentiam tam horrendæ idololatriæ in hac vita egerunt, quantum humano permittitur (ex verbo Dei) judicio, recta ac trita via ad inferos et sempiternas miserias migraverunt. Nam missa, quæ hodie ubique sub papæ tyrannide in ecclesiis celebratur, non solum profanationem sacræ Domini cœnæ et conculcationem passionis Jesu Christi, verum etiam idolum habet impium ac satanicum. Panis enim et vinum exhibentur in missa, ut pro Deo vivo et vero adorentur ac colantur; quod ubique in sacris literis sub pœna æterni supplicii prohibetur. Quare nullo modo permittendum est nec tolerabile in ecclesia Christi: uti plurimis eisdemque verissimis argumentis in hoc tractatu, vestræ prudentiæ ac sanctitati destinato, ostendi. Illum ne respuatis, neque aversemini, priusquam ex lectione quid contineat intelligatis, valde precor pro vestra erga Dei gloriam reverentia et honore, proque vestro amore ac studio et desiderio, quibus erga regnum Angliæ estis affecti, proque illius etiam incolumitate, protectione, ac defensione contra Romanum antichristum, qui omnibus regnis, regibus, principibus ac populis suæ impietatis et superstitionis tenebras summa ope offundere nititur, ut suam tyrannidem in corpora, fortunas, et animas omnium exerceat, contra omnia jura cum divina tum humana. Nam hoc idolum (nempe recens ille Deus, quem ex pane et vino neoterici factum esse fingunt) ecclesiis Christi per papæ tyrannidem primo obtrudebatur; et ejusdem tyranni ope et industria verus cœnæ Domini usus ab ecclesiis Christi exturbabatur, dum meras nugas suas et vanissima somnia omnibus amplectenda proponeret. Ubi enim Deus per verbum suum mandat, ut omnia in ecclesiis agantur lingua vulgari ad ædificationem (ut antea dixi), quibus totus cœtus Deum Conditorem, Redemptorem, ac Confirmatorem unicum agnoscat, hic certe papæ tyrannis prohibet, et omnia fieri ignota lingua in ecclesiis jubet, etiam sub pœna ferri, flammæ, carceris, mortisque animæ et corporis. Christi verbum, omnes sancti patres, sacrique canones privatas missas damnant, et non solum usum sacræ Domini cœnæ omnibus, cum ministris tum populo, in ecclesiis permittunt ac mandant, verum etiam quo ordine sacra cœna sumi debeat ostendunt: uti canones Niceni concilii[1] *Canones Niceni concilii.*

[1 Λαμβανέτωσαν δὲ κατὰ τάξιν τὴν εὐχαριστίαν μετὰ τοὺς πρεσβυτέρους, ἢ τοῦ ἐπισκόπου διδόντος αὐτοῖς ἢ τοῦ πρεσβυτέρου.—Conc. Nic. can. XVIII. See Concil. General. et Provinc. Binii. Lutet. Paris. 1636. p. 345.]

præcipiunt; ut scilicet primum sacerdotes, deinde diaconi, postea universus cœtus sacræ Domini cœnæ communicent. Hic autem impius Romanus pontifex, primogenitus antichristi, flammis, ferro, et igne Christi cœnæ sacrum usum ab ecclesiis deturbavit, et privatas missas ejus in locum substituit. Christi verbum præcipit ut ejus mors meritaque per prædicationem sui verbi universo populo declarentur: papæ vero tyrannis hoc fieri jubet per hydromantiam, panis adjurationem, cinerum, frondium, cereolorumque incantationem. Et ut uno verbo omnia absolvam, in omnibus fere quæ jam in ecclesiis Anglicanis aguntur papistæ isti transgrediuntur mandata divina propter humanas traditiones. Ad legem enim Dei appello, quam hac in causa judicem constituo.

Si autem vestra industria et auctoritate in hoc sacro et celebri conventu divinæ voluntati morem gerere velitis, humana et impia ab ecclesiis vos amovere oportet, et divina ac sancta denuo restituere. Sin vero id facere recusaveritis, neglecti vestri officii pœnas tandem gravissimas luetis, et populi perditionem ex impiis dogmatibus prognatam de manibus vestris Deus requiret. Non satis est, nec sacrum et excelsum senatum parlamenti apud Deum excusabit, quod isti Cybeles et Corybantes, Romani sacrificuli, dicunt se certo scire ea quæ jam in ecclesiis fiunt esse sancta et divina. Nam ea tantum sunt sacrosancta, quæ Dei verbum pro sacrosanctis agnoscit; et reliqua omnia, etsi hominibus excelsa videantur, abominanda sunt coram Deo, et tandem eradicabuntur, tanquam plantæ quas Pater cœlestis nunquam plantavit. Tunc vero quisquis illas plantavit, nisi tempestive pœnitentiam egerit, æternis suppliciis afficietur. Et non solum hujusmodi pœnis affligentur idololatriæ et impietatis auctores, verum etiam omnes quotquot illorum idololatriæ et impietatis sunt participes, nisi pœnitentiam egerint: ut Christus ait, "Si cæcus cæco ducatum præstet, ambo in foveam cadunt." [Matt. xv.]

Cum igitur, viri clarissimi, tota sacrarum literarum series moneat ad beatam vitam assequendam in primis pertinere, ut eorum consilia et doctrinas fugiamus qui nos a recto et vero Dei cultu conantur abducere; restituite, restituite, inquam, denuo ecclesiis Christi suos oculos et lumina, quibus omnium hominum doctrinas, religiones, et cultus probare possint an sint ex Deo. Oculi vero et lumina Christianorum sunt verbum Dei, uti optime nostis. Si eo in vulgari lingua populus destituatur, et Latine omnia inter Anglos indoctos agantur, non est mirum si Anglia facile in omnes antichristi abominationes et mendacia impingat. Sanctius igitur erit (dicant neoterici quod velint), si ea tantum legantur, doceantur, orentur, ac ministrentur in ecclesiis Christi, quæ Christus legi, doceri, orari, et ministrari præcepit. Nam huic Deus Pater gratiam [Joh. iii.] non dedit ad mensuram, nec illius mandata a quoquam violari debent. Cum ergo a Dei voluntate ac illius mandatis tota nostra pendeat fides et religio, hac sola contenti simus; et per hanc in Christo Jesu, quo solo nostra nititur fides, non solum mendacia, calumnias, et dira hostium nostrorum verba facile devorabimus; verum etiam quæcunque tormentorum aut mortis genera, permittente Deo, in nos neoterici exercebunt, fortiter contemnemus, et gloriose pro Christo moriemur, ipso nos adjuvante. Satis etiam est, quod hactenus (testimonium perhibentibus conscientiis nostris in Christo Jesu) spe quæstus aut gloriæ non venimus ad sacram evangelii functionem et prædicationem; sed ut obedientia nostra Dei vocationi ac sanctissimi regis nostri Eduardi sexti voluntati et imperio morem gereremus.

Nec in hoc, quod impietati et falso cultui neotericorum non consentimus, divina aut humana jura offendimus. Tantum peccamus (si saltem contra antichristum verbum Dei obtendere pro animarum nostrarum salute sit peccare) in impias et tyrannicas leges Romani pontificis, cujus fictæ et ementitæ auctoritati omnes nos Angli jurejurando religiosissimo resistere obstringimur. Reginæ majestati interim nec verbis nec factis, imo ne cogitatione quidem, volente Deo, resistemus. Proceres vero omnesque status hujus regni Angliæ a Deo ordinati nostram fidem in Christo habent obstrictam; quam inviolatam illis semper servabimus. Sed si (quod Deus avertat) ad peregrinos ac impios cultus, quales sunt divorum invocationes, panis et vini adorationes, ementiti sacrificii propitiatorii in missis fabulæ et figmenta, peccatorum expiationes per hydromantiam, panis, frondium, luminum, et hujusmodi incantationes, nos adigent, nostrum est Deo magis tamen obedire quam hominibus; et omnia hujusmodi decreta, si quæ prodierint, fortiter et religiose contemnere verbo atque mandato divino tenemur.

Atque injurias quidem per alios nobis inflictas patienter ferre studebimus; aliis vero ullas molestias exhibere cavebimus. Deus est; Deus faciat quod bonum videatur in oculis illius: ipsius est ultio; ipse rependet. Nos vero, quibuscunque injuriis, miseriis, carceribus, vinculis, et calamitatibus affecti fuerimus per adversarios, rogabimus tamen Patrem nostrum cœlestem in Christo Jesu, ne illis peccata sua imputet, sed ad sanctiorem vitam reducat. Regineam etiam majestatem principesque ac omnes hujus regni Angliæ status officiose, ut debemus, assiduis precibus Deo in Christo Jesu commendabimus, ut hic pie ac sancte singuli suis fungantur officiis, et post peractam miseram istam vitam una omnes beata æternaque vita fruamur: Amen. E carcere, 27 Augusti, 1554.

Vestræ excellentiæ et dignitati addictissimus Joannes Hoperus, nuper Vigorniensis et Glocestrensis episcopus, non solum natura, verum etiam legibus ac voluntate germanus Anglus.

HYPERASPISMUS

DE VERA DOCTRINA ET USU

CŒNÆ DOMINI.

Joannis Hoperi

de sacratissimæ cœnæ Domini vera doctrina et legitimo usu contra Neotericos ad excelsam parlamenti curiam Anglicanam illustre cum primis ac divinum monumentum, e carcere conscriptum.

Præfatio.

NE cuiquam vestrum, fratres, mirum sit rogo, quod scriptis in causa eucharistiæ rationem fidei meæ notam esse cupio; quodque publice in schola eandem testari recuso. Non ideo facio quo justissimæ ac sanctissimæ causæ meæ diffidam, nec quo adversariorum argumenta metuam; sed constant aliæ multæ rationes, maxime justæ et piæ, quæ ut hoc faciam impellunt ac permovent: primum, ut fides quam in hac causa habeo inviolatam ac integram, sacrarum literarum auctoritate et sanctorum patrum testimonio comprobatam, ad vos pure et integre absque omni fuco, nævo, et papistarum fermento perveniat; quod quomodo ex publica disputatione fieri possit, non satis video: deinde, quod hi qui publicæ disputationi præsunt, et censores ad hanc controversiam finiendam sunt designati, nostri ac causæ nostræ hostes sunt et agnoscuntur infensissimi: ad hæc causæ eucharistiæ, quam nos defendendam suscepimus, ac etiam nobis ipsis, jam antehac præjudicarunt. Quis igitur dubitet quin omnia nobiscum acturi sint præjudicatione, malis artibus, et imposturis, quicquid de libera disputatione prætendant ac in vulgus spargant? Nam si liberam disputationem optarent, vel saltem cogitarent, causam nostram ante disputationem minime condemnassent; nec nos, qui damnatæ causæ merito patrocinamur, pro hæreticis ab illis haberemur, in vincula non conjiceremur, nec confiscationem omnium bonorum nostrorum pateremur.

Cum ergo causæ nostræ videamus præjudicari, et nos ipsi, qui causæ adsumus, carceris squalorem et molestiam diu et difficulter, non citra valetudinis et vitæ periculum, sustineamus; quomodo nobis in mentem venire poterit ut putemus in publica disputatione Dei gloriam et veritatis causam, de qua inter nos controvertitur, investigandam ac inquirendam esse? Nam si nostra causa, quæ vera est, imo quæ verissima, prævaleret, cogerentur adversarii errorem suum agnoscere, et leges ac acta, quæ legitimum cœnæ Domini usum de ecclesia Christi deturbarunt, revocare atque rescindere: præterea, qui jam in carcere detinentur, et qui ob impia sacra exulant, isti a carcere, illi vero ab exilio, revocarentur. Sed quam difficile sit ut hujusmodi leges aboleantur, pervicaces resipiscant, captivi in libertatem vindicentur, et exules in patriam tuto redeant, &c. ubi omnis potestas penes talem episcopum sit qui veritatem verbi Dei pejus cane et angue oderit, non est difficile cuivis judicare.

Nec me fugit etiam quam inhumaniter (ne quid dicam acerbius) scurriliterque actum sit cum doctissimis et pientissimis patribus[1], D. Cranmero, nuper archiepiscopo Cantuariensi, D. Ridleo, nuper episcopo Londinensi, et D. Hugonio Latimero, olim episcopo Vigorniensi; qui nullo non ignominiarum genere in schola sunt aspersi: quibus non dabatur facultas, ut quæ habebant dicenda dicerent; et quæ dicebant, quamvis gravissima et verissima, partim clamoribus deturbabantur, partim cachinnis eludebantur: et, quod deterius est, quæ a notariis in schola excipiebantur per præsides scholæ et disputationis censores in publicum prodibant aut mutilata ac truncata, aut corrupta, non solum in contumeliam et derogationem doctrinæ et eruditionis piorum virorum, verum etiam in odium causæ quam ipsi doctissime defenderant. Talis est enim adversariorum mens et animus, ut quæ ab ipsis prolata sunt melius et castius prodire in publicum studeant quam ab illis dicebantur, quæ vero a piis sunt dicta vitiata in lucem dentur: ut, sive vincant sive vincantur, semper vincere videantur; et nos, qui meliorem partem defendimus, victi, etsi vincamus, proclamemur. Nostrum igitur est, ne causæ nostræ dignitas male audiat, et nostra fides hac in parte papistarum fermento et sordibus coinquinetur, quid sentiamus nostris literis et laboribus propriis omnibus testatum relinquere.

Res controversa inter nos catholicos et Neotericos Romanos de eucharistia tribus constat capitibus.

1. Neoterici in cœna Domini panis et vini interitum vel conversionem in corporis Christi substantiam constituunt:

[1 See Foxe, Acts and Mon. Book x. p. 1428. Also Burnet's Hist. of Reform. Vol. II. B. ii. p. 280. Ed. 1683.]

catholici panis et vini substantiam in cœna Domini non minus post verborum prolationem et sanctificationem quam antea manere confitentur.

2. Neoterici corporalem corporis Christi et sanguinis præsentiam in cœna Domini post verborum prolationem adesse affirmant: catholici tantum sacramentalem et spiritualem corporis Christi et sanguinis præsentiam in cœna Domini esse volunt; et corporalem Christi præsentiam tantum cœlo tribuunt, sedentem ad dextram Dei Patris, unde illum expectant judicaturum vivos et mortuos.

3. Neoterici non tantum corporis et sanguinis Christi corporalem præsentiam in cœna collocant, sed etiam ipsum Christum Patri cœlesti in missa per manus sacrificuli offerri pro peccatis docent: catholici nullum præter mortem Christi esse sacrificium pro peccatis credunt et profitentur.

CAPUT I.

Contra transubstantiationem.

Rationes quibus catholici innituntur.

[Matt. xxvi. Mark xiv. Luke xxii. 1 Cor. xi.]

Christus, cum sacramentum et recordationem corporis et sanguinis sui institueret, panem accepit, et gratiis actis fregit, et assidentibus discipulis porrexit, dicens: "Accipite et manducate; hoc est corpus meum, quod pro vobis datur: hoc facite in mei recordationem." Ex quibus verbis Christi panis substantiam post verba sanctificationis semper manere luculenter constat. Nam panis substantiam quam in manus accepit fregit: quam fregit discipulis porrexit: quam porrexit corpus suum crucifigendum appellavit; nec panis substantiam ablatam ullo verbo significavit.

Hujus primæ assertionis prima probatio.

Christus panem consecratum in sacramentum corporis sui corpus suum dixit.

Cum de ipsa panis substantia ante verba sanctificationis in cœna Domini nulla sit controversia, hoc tanquam ab utraque parte concessum prætereo. Christum panis substantiam in sacra cœnæ actione discipulis distribuisse ex panis nomine, quem porrigebat, discimus: ubi, sepositis aliis creaturis, panem in sacramentum et recordationem corporis sui immolandi consecravit, et nomine corporis sui panem sanctificatum honoravit, dicendo, "Hoc est corpus meum." Quodque panis substantiam in sacra cœnæ actione nomine corporis sui honoravit, et panis substantiam non abstulit, verba ipsa a Christo prolata clare testantur: "Hoc est (inquit) corpus meum." Non dixit, Hujus panis substantiam destruo, in cujus locum corporis mei veram substantiam substituo: nec hoc dixit, Hujus panis substantiam (quem vobis manducandum exhibeo) in veram corporis mei substantiam converto, et sic sub panis involucro et forma, vera panis substantia ablata, corpus meum vobis manducandum do: sed de pane ipso quem fregit et porrigebat, absque omni fuco et transubstantiati panis suspicione, clare, aperte, panem ipsum corpus suum appellavit, dicendo, "Hoc est corpus meum."

Hujus assertionis firmissima probatio.

Divus Paulus panis substantiam in ipsa sacra cœnæ Domini actione manere clarissimis testatur verbis: "Panis (inquit) quem frangimus, nonne communio corporis Christi est?" Non dixit, Accidens, seu forma panis, quam frangimus, communio corporis Christi est: nec hoc dixit, Corpus Christi latet sub forma panis quam frangimus: sed simplicissime et apertissime dixit, "Panis quem frangimus communio corporis Christi est." Unde constat post verba sanctificationis in ipsa actione et distributione corporis Christi panem semper manere, panem frangi, panem distribui, panem a sacro cœtu accipi, panem edi, panemque sanctificatum corporis Christi esse communionem. [1 Cor. x.] *Panis sanctificatus est caro corpori Christi.*

Hujus assertionis variæ constant apud Paulum validissimæ confirmationes.

Prima: panem fractum communionem corporis Christi appellat; ergo de pane post verba consecrationis vel sanctificationis loquitur. Nam panis ante sanctificationem communis panis est, et non sacramentum, nec communio corporis Christi. Concluditur divi Pauli auctoritate post verba consecrationis in cœna Domini panem remanere, et in ipsa actione sacramenti panem porrigi: ut Paulus inquit, "Panis quem frangimus, nonne communicatio corporis Christi est?" Paulus expresse panem appellat id quod frangitur: igitur panis a consecratione manet. Neque enim Paulus tam incircumspecte loquutus fuisset appellando panem quod jam corpus Christi esset: neque accidentia panis frangi quisquam sanæ mentis dixerit. *Prima confirmatio.*

Secunda confirmatio.
[1 Cor. x.]

Secunda confirmatio: "Unus panis, unum corpus multi sumus, quia de uno pane participamus." Hic Spiritus Sanctus, verus verborum Christi interpres, per divum Paulum eucharistiam corporis Christi panem vocat, "de quo (inquit) participamus." Concludimus ergo cum Spiritu Sancto panis substantiam non tolli nec mutari, quoad ejus substantiam, sed perpetuo manere in sacra cœna Domini: et qui panis substantiam in eucharistia vel destrui vel mutari (quod ad substantiam attinet) docent, non solum scripturis divinis adversantur, sed etiam Spiritum Sanctum mendacii arguunt, qui panem frangi post verba sanctificationis verbis clarissimis testatur. Accedunt et aliæ hujus assertionis ex eodem apostolo confirmationes.

3 Confirmatio.

"Quotiescunque enim comederitis panem hunc, et de poculo biberitis, mortem Domini annunciabitis donec venerit."

4 Confirmatio.

"Quisquis ederit panem hunc, aut biberit de poculo Domini indigne, reus erit corporis et sanguinis Domini."

5 Confirmatio.

"Probet autem seipsum homo, et sic de pane illo edat, et de poculo illo bibat."

Ex istis locis Pauli agnoscere docemur verum panem ac verum vinum in sanctissima Domini cœna manere, et nihilominus et corpus et sanguinem Domini appellari.

Epilogus hujus nostræ assertionis per Jesum Christum Salvatorem nostrum.

Verba Christi perpensa.
[Matt. xxvi. Mark xiv. Luke xxii.]

"Non bibam posthac de hoc vitis fructu," sunt verba Christi post verba sanctificationis in cœna Domini, post distributionem sanctificati calicis, et post susceptionem sanctificati calicis. Quibus verbis declarat se de vera et germana vini natura fuisse loquutum, et non de externa forma vel accidentibus vini, sublata vel mutata vera vini aut fructus vitis substantia, ut neoterici dicunt. Fulcitur ergo et munitur nostra fides, quæ panis et vini substantiam in eucharistia asserit, verbis Christi evangelistarumque et apostolorum scriptis. Quare a Christo et ejus discipulis hæreseos non damnamur, nec ab illorum ecclesia et schola ut hæretici expellimur, quicquid neoterici in nos tanquam in hostes Christi detonent. Satis ergo esse putamus nostram fidem Deo approbari, apostolorum Christi calculo, et per ipsius verbi certitudinem.

Confirmatio nostræ assertionis ex appellationibus et nominibus sacramentorum vel signorum sacramentalium.

Sacramenta apud veteres ista sortiuntur nomina.

Apud Augustinum, De catechizandis rudibus[1], sacramentum signaculum appellatur. Contra Adimantum[2], in Psalm. iii[3], De Civitate Dei, lib. x. cap. 5[4], contra Maximin. lib. iii. cap. 22[5], sacramentum signum vocat.

Hieronymus, lib. iv. in Matth. cap. xxvi[6], sacramentum repræsentationem nominat.

Tertullianus, lib. iv. contra Marcionem[7], et Bertramus[8] sacramentum figuram vocant. Ambrosius[9] et Chrysostomus[10]

August.

Hieron.

Tertull.
Bertra.
Ambros.
Chrysost.

[1 De sacramento sane quod accepit, cum ei bene commendatum fuerit, signacula quidem rerum divinarum esse visibilia.—August. De Catechiz. Rud. cap. xxvi. Op. Tom. iv. col. 923. B. Basil. 1569.]

[2 Non enim Dominus dubitavit dicere, Hoc est corpus meum, cum signum daret corporis sui.—Contra Adimant. cap. xii. Op. Tom. vi. col. 187. c.]

[3 Cum adhibuit ad convivium, in quo corporis et sanguinis sui *figuram* discipulis commendavit et tradidit.—In Psalm. iii. Op. Tom. viii. col. 16. B.]

[4 Sacrificium ergo visibile invisibilis sacrificii sacramentum, id est, sacrum signum est.—De Civit. Dei. Lib. x. cap. v. p. 109. c. Paris. 1586.]

[5 Hæc enim sacramenta sunt, in quibus non quid sint, sed quid ostendant, semper attenditur: quoniam signa sunt rerum, aliud existentia, et aliud significantia.—Contra Maximin. Lib. iii. cap. xxii. Op. Tom. vi. col. 754. D. 755. A. Basil. 1569.]

[6 Ut... ipse quoque veritatem sui corporis et sanguinis repræsentaret.—Hier. in Matt. xxvi. Op. Tom. ix. fol. 36. G. Paris. 1534.]

[7 Acceptum panem et distributum discipulis corpus illum suum fecit, 'hoc est corpus meum' dicendo, id est, figura corporis mei.—Tertull. adv. Marcion. Lib. iv. Op. p. 571. A. Lutet. 1641.]

[8 Si enim nulla sub figura mysterium illud peragitur, jam mysterium non recte vocitatur. p. 4.—Cernimus quod doctor iste mysteria corporis et sanguinis Christi sub figura dicit a fidelibus celebrari. p. 18.—Bartram. Lib. de Corp. et Sang. Dom. Oxon. 1838.]

[9 Post consecrationem corpus Christi significatur.—Ambros. De Initiand. cap. ix. Op. Tom. iv. col. 351. G. Paris. 1603.]

[10 Quidnam significat panis? Corpus Christi.—Chrysost. 1 Cor. x. Hom. xxiv. Tom. x. p. 213. Ed. Benedict. In the Basle edition 1547, however, the version is, "Quidnam *est* panis?" p. 510. D. In the Greek, Τί γάρ ἐστιν ὁ ἄρτος; σῶμα Χριστοῦ. Tom. iii. p. 397. l. 22. Eton. 1613. There seems no ground for the reference to 1 Cor. xi.]

sacramentum significationem appellant, De his qui initiantur sacris, lib. iv cap 5. et in 1 Cor. xi. 1 Corinth. x.

Basilius. Basilius[1] in sua Liturgia sacramenta ἀντίτυπα vocat.

Ex istis nominibus et appellationibus discimus sacramenta omnia non esse rem ipsam, quarum sunt sacramenta; sed earum rerum obsignacula, signa, repræsentationes, figuras, significationes, et ἀντίτυπα. Discimus præterea, quod sacramenta retinent semper earum rerum terrenarum substantiam ex quibus conficiuntur: ut baptismus semper retinet aquæ substantiam eam quam prius habuit: atque ut olim sacramenta veteris legis earum rerum substantiam retinebant ex quibus conficiebantur; ut pascha agni immolati substantiam non amisit; circumcisio cultri et carnis in qua facta fuit circumcisio substantiam retinebat; ita et eucharistia panis et vini substantiam non perdit. Commentum igitur humanum est, quod asserit tantam a Deo inditam verbis virtutem, ut prolata et recitata super signa ipsam signorum substantiam vel destruant, vel in rerum signatarum substantiam immutent. Nam verba, quatenus a ministris ecclesiæ sunt prolata, panis et vini substantiam sanctificandi virtutem non habent; multo minus destruendi vel immutandi *Quomodo sanctificantur sacramenta.* substantiam vim habent: quia sacramenta non prolatione verborum Dei per ministrum, sed verbo ac mandato Dei, voluntate et institutione Christi sanctificantur; et in ipsis verbis nulla inest vis effectrix sanctificandi. Sanctificantur enim creaturæ per verba, mandata, et institutionem Domini, ubi hæc omnia cum verborum prolatione in sacramentorum sanctificatione et usu una concurrunt. Quod si millesies pronunciarentur aut sonarentur hæc verba, "Hoc est corpus meum," non observatis Christi Domini institutione et mandato de distributione panis ad ceteros qui una cum ministro communicent, nihil efficiunt illa verba. Ideo in missa, ubi verba Christi præter et contra mandatum Dei (non observata legitima *Panis et vinum in missa non sunt sacramenta corporis et sanguinis Christi.* Christi cœnæ institutione) proferuntur, nihil efficiunt: nec panis nec vinum in missa pro sacramentis corporis et sanguinis Christi agnosci debent. Verba Christi ad sanctificationem creaturarum valent, et sacramenta constituunt, ubi ipsa cum

[1 Προθέντες τὰ ἀντίτυπα τοῦ ἁγίου σώματος καὶ αἵματος τοῦ Χριστοῦ σοῦ.—Basil. in Liturg. Biblioth. Pat. Græco-Latin. Tom. II. p. 51. E. Paris. 1624. The same word is used by Theodoret. Dial. II. Εἰ τοίνυν τοῦ ὄντως σώματος ἀντίτυπά ἐστι τὰ θεῖα μυστήρια.—Op. Tom. IV. p. 125. Halæ, 1772.]

Dei mandato, Dei voluntate, ac Christi institutione concurrunt: tunc verba sanctificandi vim et virtutem habent, non a seipsis, nec ab illo qui ea pronunciat, sed a Deo, qui ad sacramentorum sanctificationem hujusmodi verba proferri jusserat, ut non solum creaturæ sanctificarentur, sed distribuerentur, et sumerentur a fidelibus juxta Christi institutionem, quo per verba et sacramenta mysterium mortis ac redemptionis Christi vere intelligerent: cui si ex animo crederent, ab omni peccatorum labe purificarentur. Sed isti neoterici parum recte de verbo Domini judicant. Ubi enim Christus de verbo prædicato et credito loquitur, illi de verbo pronunciato aut recitato intelligunt, quasi sic vim et virtutem habeat a Domino sanctificandi; quod est absurdissimum, ut Augustinus pulcherrime testatur: "Unde ista (inquit) virtus aquæ, ut corpus tangat et cor abluat, nisi faciente verbo? non quia dicitur, sed quia creditur. Nam et in ipso verbo aliud est sonus transiens, aliud virtus manens, etc[2]." "Ideo (inquit) verbum fidei est quod prædicamus, et verbo fidei consecratur baptismus[3]." Et ut Chrysostomus ait, "Virtus evangelii non est in figuris literarum, sed in intellectu sensuum[4]." Appositissime igitur patres, ut huic errori transubstantiationis occurrerent, sacramenta signacula, signa, figuras, repræsentationes, et id genus alia vocant: ut cum illis rerum terrestrium involucris mentes rite utentium ad res ipsas cœlestes et significatas eveherent, rerum terrenarum substantiam in sacramentis non tollentes nec mutantes, sed illarum substantiam rerum cœlestium signa et obsignationes esse affirmantes. Et sacramenta, quamvis res cœlestes obsignent, nec in ipsas vel in ipsum Christum migrare unquam docebant.

Confirmatio nostræ assertionis ex natura et conditione sanctificationis creaturarum panis et vini in cœna Domini per Spiritum Sanctum.

Verba quibus utitur Spiritus Sanctus, et quibus Dei sacramenta fiunt, adhibent atque asciscunt res terrestres panem

Error papistarum in verbo.

August. Tract. in Joan. 80.

Chrysost. in Matth. cap. xxiii. Verbo fidei consecrantur sacramenta.

Spiritus Sanctus et verbum consecrant res terrestres in sacrum usum.

[2 August. In Evang. Joan. Tract. LXXX. Op. Tom. IX. col. 445. A. Basil. 1569.]

[3 Hoc est verbum fidei, quod prædicamus; quo sine dubio ut mundare possit consecratur et baptismus.—Ibid. B.]

[4 Deinde ubi est virtus evangelii? in figuris literarum, an in intellectu sensuum?—Chrysost. Op. Vol. II. col. 1049. D. Basil. 1547. The writings however in which this passage occurs are pronounced by Erasmus not to be the production of Chrysostom.]

et vinum in sacrum usum et finem ex mandato Dei et Christi institutione, et corporis et sanguinis Christi nomine creaturas panis et vini induunt: ut jam non sit communis panis et commune vinum; sed ut per mandata Dei et Christi institutionem sacramenta corporis et sanguinis Christi sint mysteria nostræ redemptionis in illius corpore super crucem morte sua nobis perquisitæ. Hoc est quod Paulus ad Corinthios dixit: "Poculum cui benedicimus, nonne communicatio corporis[1] Christi est?" Poculo benedicere est vinum virtute Spiritus Sancti et Christi institutione per verbum Dei consecrare in sacramentum sanguinis Jesu Christi: ita ut vinum ejus induat nomen cujus est sacramentum, sed non mutetur in ejus substantiam cujus est sacramentum. Vinum tanquam signum vel sacramentum sanguinis Christi vini semper retinet substantiam; et signum non induit rei signatæ naturam et substantiam, sed substantia vini eadem remanet quæ fuerat antea. Accedit autem post sanctificationem alius augustior et magnificentior usus et finis vini quam antea, citra vini substantiæ jacturam aut substantialem mutationem, quam neoterici fingunt. Nam Spiritus Sanctus, verbum Dei, et Christi institutio res terrestres consecrant ad res cœlestes testificandum, approbandum, et obsignandum: sed res terrestres, quoad illarum substantiam, nunquam in rerum cœlestium naturas aut substantiam migrant vel convertuntur; ut agnus paschalis res terrestris Spiritu Sancto et mandato divino ad testificandam, approbandam, et obsignandam gloriosam populi Dei liberationem ab Ægypto institutus erat, sed in ipsam transitus substantiam et naturam non migrabat. Sic omnia Judæorum sacrificia, cum res essent sua natura terrestres, mandato et verbo Dei ad significandam, testandam, et obsignandam expiationem peccatorum in Christo venturo instituta erant; in Christi tamen naturam et substantiam mandato et verbo Dei nunquam transierunt. Mentiuntur ergo plane, et peregrinis ac ementitis laudibus verbum Dei extollunt, qui verbo Dei ultra vim sanctificandi, admonendi, et obsignandi gratiam Dei in sacramentis attribuunt. Deus universa olim ex nihilo per verbum suum creavit: sed illud verbum non erat sonus transiens, sed ipsius Dei Filius ex eadem hypostasi et substantia Patris. Moyses per verbum Dei aquas Ægypti in cruorem, solis splendorem in plus quam Cimmerias tenebras permutavit, et Petrus claudum erexit in pedes; sed non per

[1 For corporis read sanguinis.]

verbum recitatum, dictum, aut prolatum, sed potentia illius et virtute cujus munere fungebatur.

Præterea nusquam legimus in scripturis sanctis de transubstantiatione, aut conversione alicujus substantiæ in aliam substantiam, quin statim, mutata priore substantia in aliam substantiam, mutata simul fuerint prioris substantiæ forma et accidens; nec unquam manebat posterior substantia sub prioris substantiæ forma: ut Nilus in Ægypto amisit una cum priore substantia aquæ priorem aquæ formam et cetera aquæ adjacentia: costa Adami in mulierem facta et substantiam et formam costæ reliquit: sic Mosis virga versa in serpentem: et aqua in vinum conversa a Christo una cum interitu et mutatione prioris substantiæ aquæ posterioris substantiæ vini formam et adjacentia induit, ita ut admiraretur architriclinus aquam vinum factam. *Substantia nusquam mutatur, quin pariter mutentur accidentia. Aquæ Ægyptiorum in sanguinem versæ.*

Opera Dei ergo et sacramenta altius consideranda veniunt ab iis, qui Deum auctorem in his quæ facta sunt agnoscere et laudare cupiunt. Sunt enim quædam opera, quæ Deus ex nihilo produxit; ut cœlum et terra, atque ea quæ primordia erant et primaria seminaria eorum quæ jam extant. Illa fide intelligimus fuisse aptata per Patrem mediante Filio et Spiritu Sancto. Et quemadmodum intelligimus omnia in principio fuisse ex nihilo creata, sic illorum stupendam et admirandam creationem admiramur, quod jam sint quæ antea non erant, et quod Deus ex nihilo sua ineffabili potentia ea produxerit. Sunt quædam opera Dei quæ fide intelligimus fuisse facta, at non ex nihilo, sed ab alia priore existenti substantia; ut primam mulierem a Deo ex costa Adami factam, serpentem ex virga Mosis, sanguinem ex Ægyptiorum aquis, vinum ex aqua in nuptiis factum. Hæc fide etiam intelligimus a Deo facta, ubi prioris substantiæ naturam cognoscimus sublatam, et novam creaturam ex præexistenti materia subsistere; prioris substantiæ destructionem agnoscimus, et posterioris existentiam admiramur. Hæc etiam omnia per verbum Dei facta sunt; non per verbum prolatum, recitatum, aut literis sculptum, sed per verbum quod est Filius Dei et ipsa imago et character substantiæ Dei Patris. Alia sunt opera Dei facta per verbum, id est, Filium Dei, quæ non constant ex creatione existentis substantiæ mutatæ in aliam substantiam: sed quando quod prius suo vitio spurcum, tetrum, mortuum, et pollutum erat ope divina instauratur; ut mortuum cadaver Lazari ope divina vitæ erat restitutum; animæ etiam, quæ *Operum Dei rerumque productarum varia consideratio.*

vitiis et peccatis jacent sepultæ, ope Spiritus Sancti in sanguine Christi purgantur. Corporis resurrectionem vel ad vitam restitutionem fide intelligimus: et quia hoc rationi et externis sensibus constat, factum admiramur. Animæ purgationem et resurrectionem a peccatis fide credimus, et gratias Deo agimus: sed quia hoc sensibus non constat factum, non admiramur. Sunt alia opera Dei, quæ per verbum, id est, Dei Filium, et verbum simul prolatum sunt facta; ubi creaturæ nec in materia nec forma mutantur, sed in alium usum et finem per Dei verbum applicantur, quem a sua natura non habuerunt. Hujusmodi opera fide per verbum intelligimus, sed non admiramur, quandoquidem istorum operum efficacia et dignitas circa animum utentis per fidem versatur; et non subest judicio rationis vel usui sensuum, quamvis aures sonitum verborum audiant, oculi elementorum fractionem et distributionem cernant, et gustus veram elementorum naturam dijudicet. Ex isto ordine sunt opera Dei quæ sacramenta vocantur: ut in baptismo Spiritus Sanctus per verbum prolatum et elementarem aquam in animo per fidem operatur remissionem peccatorum, et baptizati acceptationem et confirmationem in gratiam et favorem Dei: in cœna Domini Spiritus Sanctus per verbum et externa elementa panis et vini recipientis animum per fidem corpore et sanguine Christi, vel potius omnibus meritis et bonis in morte sua nobis partis, pascit ac refovet. Sed hoc opus Dei nullas creaturas de novo producit, nec creaturas panis et vini, circa quas tanquam elementaria organa versatur, in alias mutat substantias; sed salvis et reservatis panis et vini pristinis substantiis ea in alium usum et finem destinat; ex quibus qui fide sunt participes non solum pani et vino elementari communicant, verum etiam de corpore et sanguine Christi, quorum panis et vinum per opus Dei sunt sacramenta, participant. Et quia circa elementa panis et vini nulla substantialis mutatio est facta, sed omnium sacramentorum mysteria, dignitates, et fructus circa animum fide recipientis et rite ministrantis versantur, intellectum capimus, et fruimur promissionibus Dei et sacrorum sacramentorum rebus significatis, quæ nos Christo et Christum nobis conglutinant et consociant. Ideo est quod Augustinus miracula nulla admittit in eucharistiæ sacramento. Ejus verba sunt hæc[1]: "Sed quia hæc hominibus nota sunt, quia per ho-

August. de Trinit. Lib. iii. cap. 10.

[1 August. De Trinit. Lib. III. cap. x. Op. Tom. III. col. 289. c. Basil. 1569.]

mines fiunt, honorem tanquam religiosa possunt habere, stuporem tanquam mira non possunt."

Abutuntur ergo populo Dei, et ejus ecclesiæ periculose imponunt, qui panis et vini substantiæ destructionem vel mutationem in cœna Domini docent per verbum Dei miraculose. Nam Augustinus constanter testatur religionem circa panem et vinum ob Christi institutionem fieri; sed miraculum aut stuporem circa eucharistiæ sacramentum fieri pernegat. Et verissimum est quod Augustinus dicit, nullum esse in cœna Domini stuporem aut miraculum. Miraculum enim est quod naturam excedit, et rationis superat judicium; ita tamen ut, quando sit factum, semper fiat et appareat in his rebus quæ sub sensuum et rationis judicium cadunt: ut miraculum formatæ mulieris ex costa Adami, aquæ Ægypti mutatio in sanguinem, virgæ in serpentem, virginis partus, et omnium creaturarum existentia et productio ex nihilo. Omnia ista præter naturam et supra rationis judicium fuerunt creata: sed postquam sunt facta, non solum sub rationis, verum etiam sensuum naturalium, judicium cadebant. Discrimen igitur servandum est inter ea opera Dei quæ fide intelligimus facta, et[1] stuporem seu admirationem, ut mira et inusitata, excitant; et ea opera Dei quæ fide intelligimus, et[2] nullum horrorem, admirationem, vel miraculum rationi et sensibus afferunt. Sub priore autem operum Dei genere continentur omnes creaturæ Dei ex nihilo creatæ, ut cœlum, terra, aer, mare, et quæ in principio Deus ex nullis præexistentibus materiis produxit; vel illæ creaturæ quæ ab aliis creaturis præexistentibus originem duxerunt, ut Eva ex costa Adami, serpens e virga, cruor et vinum ex aquis, et hujus generis quam plurima. Utriusque generis opera, quæ a fide perdiscuntur et intelliguntur, rationi et sensibus admirationem et horrorem inducunt, vel in hoc, quod ex nihilo originem suam virtute divina traxerint, vel quod supra et præter rationis judicium ex præexistentibus materiis contra naturam originem suam habuerint. Miraculum ergo, horrorem, et admirationem rationi humanæ et corporis sensibus hæc intulerunt; fidei vero nostræ, quæ circa ea solum versatur quæ rationis nostræ excellentiam et dignitatem sensuumque nostrorum perspicuitatem transcendunt, inferre non poterunt. Ideo Paulus inquit: "Per fidem intelligimus perfecta fuisse [Heb. xi.]

Miraculum quid.

[2 The relative *quæ* is here required as the subject of the verbs *excitant* and *afferunt*.]

secula verbo Dei." Non dicit, per fidem miramur vel obstupescimus perfecta fuisse verbo Dei. Nam quemadmodum Dominus ipse ob suam immensam sapientiam nullum opus quod fit in coelo vel in terra admiratur; sic et vera fides (quæ est illius donum in nobis) nihil in operibus Dei admiratur; sed discit, agnoscit, amplectitur, et gratias omnipotenti Creatori agit. Miraculum ergo rationi et sensibus post introductum peccatum horrorem et admirationem intulit (ubi ante peccatum Adam non obstupuit ad creaturas, sed commode singulis nomina attribuit) non Deo ipsi, vel fidei nostræ, ejus in nobis muneri. Et ubi horror vel admiratio facti rationem et sensus non movent, miraculum proprie vocari non potest. Qui igitur in coena Domini panis et vini substantiam per miraculum transubstantiari in substantiam corporis et sanguinis Christi affirmant, illud miraculum rationi et sensibus prodant et manifestent, et tunc miraculum omnes facile agnoscent et amplectentur: sed præexistentem panis et vini substantiam a sanctificatione semper remanere, ut antea ratio judicat, sensus arguunt atque convincunt. Nec vero sumus humano premendi testimonio, ut id asseramus in sacra Domini coena, quod sacræ literæ et sanctorum patrum scripta condemnant. Nam hactenus perspicua evicimus demonstratione sæpissime, evincemusque posthac semper, transubstantiationem panis et vini in coena Domini esse contra sacras scripturas et sanctorum patrum testimonia; modo citra causæ præjudicationem et absque omni amarulentia et odio et patienter audiamur.

In coena Domini nullum est miraculum.

Sed cum de vi et potentia verbi Dei ulterius paululum progrediendum sit, necessarium fore duxi, ut illorum impudentia obstruam ora qui dicunt virtute verborum Christi panis et vini substantiam in coena Domini vel penitus tolli, vel in ipsam corporis et sanguinis Christi substantiam transmutari. Primum, vis verbi Dei ac potentia, quatenus est ipse Dei Filius coæternus ac coæqualis Patri, nihil produxit ex nihilo vel ex præexistenti materia quam nudas et simplices creaturas, quod ad illarum substantias attinet. Et hominem, quem ex limo terræ plasmavit, ad imaginem suam fecit; et illum tamen ut Deum et hominem sibi in personali conjunctione et unitate non associavit, sed ut multis præclaris plasmatoris donis imbutus creaturæ tantum servaret dignitatem, et altius non aspiraret sub periculo tremendi Dei judicii et iræ. Ecce summam vim ac virtutem verbi Dei, scilicet Patris omnipotentis, Filii, et

Vis et potentia verbi divini.

Spiritus Sancti, creaturas tantum producentem. Unde ergo illa vis et virtus verbi a pfaffo[1] prolati, ut ex creatura panis et vini talem conficeret creaturam quæ Deo altissimo in communione, conjunctione, et unitate personali communicaret? ita ut quod heri vel nudiustertius creatura esset panis, nimirum iners et rationis expers, hodie per quinque verborum prolationem et efficaciam Deus fieret et homo unitate personali. Quis unquam talia audivit? Quis hæc vel narrando non obstupesceret? Quis credat plus posse fieri per verba Christi ab hominibus prolata quam a Christo ipso? Christus verba sanctificationis circa panem et vinum in usu cœnæ Domini efferendo panis et vini substantiam corpus et sanguinem suum appellavit: neoterici verba sanctificationis circa panem et vinum in Romana missa efferendo sub panis et vini accidentibus corpus et sanguinem Christi constituunt. Christus verba sanctificationis circa panem et vinum efferendo panis et vini substantiam in sacramentum corporis et sanguinis sui consecravit, et elementorum panis et vini substantiam non abstulit: novi Christiani verba sanctificationis circa panem et vinum efferendo panis et vini substantiam subvertunt. Christus verba sanctificationis circa panem et vinum efferendo panis et vini substantiam ita in sacramentum corporis et sanguinis sui consecravit, ut memoria essent et recordatio corporis sui immolati et sanguinis sui super crucem in remissionem peccatorum effusi: neoterici vero verba sanctificationis circa panem et vinum efferendo panis et vini substantiam ita consecrant, ut re ipsa sint corpus et sanguis Christi, imo sacrificium pro peccatis vivorum et mortuorum.

Conferamus igitur novissima primis, Christum tonsis Romanis, Christi institutionem sacræ cœnæ incantationibus papistarum, quibus ementita sua sacra peragere se confingunt. Si id fecerimus, divinarum literarum et sanctorum patrum testimoniis facile intelligemus missam Romanam non plus commercii cum sacra Domini cœna habere quam lucem cum tenebris, Christum cum Belial, præstigiatorum incantationem cum ipsa veritatis perspicuitate et splendore. Salomon quidem dicit, "Non est [Prov. xxi.] sapientia, prudentia, et consilium adversus Dominum." Si ergo Spiritus Sancti sapientia, prudentia, et consilium prævalerent (ut

---

[[1] Pfaffus, German Pfaffe, Latin Papa; priest, in a contemptuous sense.]

apud omnes pios praevalere deberent), praestaret, ut Romanis sacris relictis ad veram Christi Domini coenae institutionem juxta verbum illius accederemus. Nam quod ipse in sacra sua coena fecit, ut nos faceremus mandavit. Obtemperandum igitur est illius imperio; et, ut Salomon dixit, "Ne transgrediaris terminos antiquos, quos posuerunt patres tui," Christi institutio in causa eucharistiae nobis satis esse debet: id autem optimum et sanctissimum, imo perfectissimum, quod ipse fecit. Quis enim cum Christo vel sanctorum sanctissimus pietate et sanctitate est conferendus? Quis ei vel angelorum praestantissimus dignitate et vetustate temporum est comparandus? Quaenam ecclesia, etsi illius sanguine sine macula et ruga fuerit, consilio et religione ei praeferenda? Nonne omnes qui sana mente sunt praediti noverunt, quod qui Christi ac Dei religionem postponunt, hominisque sapientiam, consilium, prudentiam, terminos, limites, fines, et usus anteferunt, quique ipsissimam Christi institutionem, doctrinam, et distributionem sacratissimae coenae negligunt atque contemnunt, et ad hominum commenta sese convertunt, digni sunt ut omni errore et vertigine maligni spiritus ad quasvis imposturas et deceptiones impellantur? Quis autem non videt, omnes qui ista faciunt, qualemcunque catholicae ecclesiae fucum praetendant, de toga ad pallium, vel ab equis ad asinos (ut aiunt) descendere? Nam missa Romana, etsi superstitiose multam religionem ostentet, indigna est ut pro mortua umbra vel nuda figura sacratissimae Domini coenae habeatur. Christi vero institutio veram mortis Christi recordationem et memoriam reddit ac renovat, et ob oculos recte utentium fidelissime semper eandem proponit atque depingit. Consilium ergo et mandatum Christi in sacra coenae actione observemus, ne illius institutionis terminos et fines transgrediamur. Si autem id fecerimus, illius mandatorum praesidio ab omni errorum periculo incolumes servabimur, quicquid impiorum fremitus et furor contra nos Deique veritatem moliantur. Nam hoc omnibus persuasum esse cupio per Christum Jesum, postquam veritas verbi Dei et verae Christi ecclesiae ad modicum temporis spatium acerbissime ab hostibus evangelii necatae fuerint, e mortuis denuo resurrecturas gloriosius, et regnaturas cum Christo in perpetuum. Meminerimus quod semen Abrahae, quod Christus semel in utero beatae Mariae Virginis mystico Spiritus Sancti spiramine assumpsit, nunquam abjecit, quicquid mundus, mundique principes, sapientes, et prudentes erga illum conspirassent;

sed in ipsa mortis tyrannide et imperio sibi servavit nostram naturam, quam tertio die a crudeli mortis funere vitæ restituit, et paucos post dies cœlo gloriose intulit. Sic et nos, si volumus esse pii, ejus verbi sinceritatem et sacramentorum puritatem, quam ab illo suscepimus, semper retinebimus salvam et incolumem, quicquid mundus, diabolus, vel infernus ipse contra nos agitaverint.

Meminerimus præterea, quod quicquid Christus in veram corporis et sanguinis sui substantiam semel accersivit et adjunxit, vera fuit caro vel verus illius sanguis; et quia vera caro et verus sanguis, animæ conjuncta, unam personam Dei et hominis constituebant: et hanc substantiam corporis sui vel nunquam deposuit, vel ut corporis illius organici partes et substantiam deposuit; ut sacrum cruorem de cruce ex latere ejus perfosso et corpus exsangue a recessu animæ sepulturæ reliquit. Si ergo verborum sanctificationis vi ac potentia Christus panem et vinum in sacra cœna corporis sui et sanguinis substantiam effecit, vel isti neoterici vi et virtute verborum sanctificationis in missa panis et vini substantiam in corporis et sanguinis Christi substantiam transubstantient aut convertant; necesse est ut Christus illam substantiam ex pane et vino factam semper retineat ac nunquam deponat. Sed ita se res habet, ut panis ille quem neoterici in corporis Christi substantiam converti asserunt, si nimis diu a consecratione reservetur, putrescat et in vermium substantias transire videamus. Et aliquando legimus eundem panem sacrum fuisse combustum, et ex illius substantia cineres fuisse relictos; ut Cyprianus in sermone de lapsis testatur [1]. Ergo evincitur ipsa experientia et sensuum judicio ex panis sacri substantia cineres gigni. Concluditur ergo illam panis substantiam nunquam realiter et substantialiter in corpus Christi fuisse conversam. Nam Christus aliquam partem corporis sui organici vel nunquam deposuit, vel in materia et forma sui organici corporis illam partem deposuit; ut verus sanguis e latere perfosso de cruce effluxit, et vera caro Christi in sepulchro triduo jacuit. Vera autem caro et verus sanguis Christi ex combustione panis sacrati in cineres nunquam transeunt: nisi velint neoterici contra

Cyprianus in sermone de Lapsis.

[1 Et alius, quia et ipse maculatus sacrificio a sacerdote celebrato partem cum ceteris ausus est latenter accipere, sanctum Domini edere et contrectare non potuit: cinerem ferre se apertis manibus invenit.—Cyprian. De Lapsis. Serm. v. Op. Tom. I. p. 344. Antw. 1541.]

[Psal. xvi.
Acts ii.
xiii.]

scripturas, carnem Christi videre corruptionem. Panis est ergo substantia, ex qua cineres in combustione gignuntur, et non substantia corporis Christi, quæ corrumpi non potest, nec panis accidens, ex quo substantia alterius rei emergere nequit.

Sed neoterici cum vident se undique premi, et verbum Dei clare, imo clarissime, panem semper servari post verba sanctificationis, et verum panem frangi in sacra cœnæ Domini actione testari, ut apud Paulum, "Panis, inquit, quem frangimus, nonne communio corporis Christi est?" et quod Christus veram vini substantiam post verba sanctificationis remanere constanter affirmet, dicens, "Non bibam posthac de hoc genimine vitis;" cumque vident sacramentorum appellationes et nomina a patribus indita nullam posse elementorum destructionem admittere, sed per Christi institutionem, mandatum, et verbum, elementa sacramentorum tantum in excellentiorem et augustiorem usum et finem evehi; et præterea, cum in illorum transubstantiationem et elementorum destructionem vident non solum verbum Dei, sanctorum patrum testimonia, sed etiam scholas philosophorum et dialecticorum conspirare; in omnes sese vertunt formas, ut errorem transubstantiationis defendant. Nunc verba Christi, "Hoc est corpus meum," proferunt, quibus panis substantiam tollere conantur: sed ubi ostenditur Christum non panis substantiam sustulisse, sed panem ipsum vocasse corpus suum, et quod panis substantia virtute Christi in sacramentum corporis sui transiit absque omni panis substantiæ destructione et mutatione; tunc ad miracula confugiunt, et miraculose panis et vini substantiam in corpus et sanguinem Christi mutatam fingunt. Sed postquam illis ostensum fuerit nullum in sacramento exstare miraculum, miraculi præsidio destituti, ad patres et ad consensum catholicæ ecclesiæ, tanquam ad sacram anchoram, se conferunt. Sed hoc impudenter suo more faciunt, et sibi vindicant quod nostrum est: ut posthac ex testimoniis sanctorum patrum omnibus piis constabit. Sed prius ad scholam dialecticorum.

Confirmatio nostræ assertionis ex scholis Dialecticorum.

1. Christus in sacra cœna post verba sanctificationis fructum vitis dedit; ergo vinum: nam fructus vitis et vinum sunt synonyma, quæ uni rei tribuuntur. A definitione seu interpretatione nominis ducitur argumentum. Nam fructus

vitis non est (ut neoterici fabulantur) accidens vini, sed vini substantia, quæ est subjectum in quod accidentia vini cadunt; nempe color vini, gustus vini, odor vini, et ejusmodi. Et cum Christus sanguinis sui effusionem in remissionem peccatorum per poculum præsignare voluerit, vini substantiam ori recipientium sacrum illud poculum admovebat : cui scilicet substantiæ, tanquam proprio, accidentia vini vel fructus vitis innitebantur; quæ si in aliquo subjecto sese non suffulcirent, omnino per se non consisterent. Ὑπόστασις ergo et vera vini οὐσία ex Christi verbis in eucharistia semper manet.

2. Panis in sacra cœna Domini post verba consecrationis (inquit Paulus) frangitur : ergo panis in sacra cœna Domini semper manet. Argumentum valet a sufficientis testimonii auctoritate; et etiam ab accidenti panis ad suum subjectum, cui fractio innititur. Nam quamvis fractio non sit nativum accidens panis, sed accessorium et extrinsecus opera ministri in sacra cœna ad panem accedit; tamen quando actu frangitur, fractio illa est panis accidens, non solum accessorium, verum etiam inseparabile. *Cor. x.*

Fractio non est accidens accidentis, sed substantiæ.

3. Fructus vitis, qui bibi solet, est vinum : sed hic fuit fructus vitis qui bibebatur: vinum ergo fuit. "Non bibam posthac, &c." Argumentum tenet ab adjacentibus aut accidentibus inseparabilibus.

4. Panis in sacra cœna gustum servat panis, speciem panis, odorem panis, latitudinem, longitudinem, et quantitatem panis: ergo est panis. Argumentum constat ab adjacentibus nativis panis ad subjectum panis.

5. Panis in sacra cœna, tam ante verba consecrationis quam post, servat materiam panis, ut inquit Paulus i. Cor. x. et formam : ergo est panis. Argumentum valet a causa materiali et formali ad subjectum existens.

6. Si panis et vinum diu serventur a consecratione, corrumpuntur : panis in vermes et situm transit, vinum in acetum. Ideo tempore Origenis[1] reliquiæ comburebantur : et nunc cautelæ missæ panem sic corruptum et vinum quod acescit comburi præcipiunt: ergo sunt panis et vinum quæ corrumpuntur et comburuntur. Argumentum tenet a destructione nativorum adjacentium ad destructionem subjectorum, quibus adjacentia illa inseparabiliter insunt. Ex istis constat fidem nostram quam in causa cœnæ Dominicæ defendimus non solum Christum habere assertorem, ac gloriosum

[1 See "Early Writings," page 521, note 8.]

apostolorum testimonium, qui sparsim in suis scriptis panis et vini nomen et substantiam retinent ac docent in ipsa sacræ cœnæ actione (ubi Christus vinum vocat fructum vitis, et Paulus panem dicit frangi); verum etiam dialecticorum argumentis illam habemus ratam atque confirmatam: ita ut in hac parte nec Christi theologiam, nec ipsam dialectices censuram offendamus.

Confirmatio nostræ assertionis ex indicio brutorum animantium.

Mures panem illum a sacrificis reservatum sæpe rodunt. Ideo cautum est decretalibus legibus[1], ut panis ille in pixide (obsignata pixide) diligenter servetur. Præterea cautum est, ut si panes, ad situm tollendum, ad solem vel gratum aërem exponantur, sacerdotes illos rete muniant, ne a volucribus cœli deportentur et devorentur. Sed bruta animalia hujusmodi injurias corpori Christi inferre non valent: ergo quod roditur a muribus, et devoratur a volucribus cœli, non est corpus Christi, sed verus panis et vera panis substantia.

Confirmatio nostræ assertionis a rebus inanimatis.

Ignis tempore Origenis et Esichii, et tempore Cypriani (ut constat in sermone de lapsis), panem consecratum consumpsit, relictis ex pane cineribus.

Aër, si nimis diu panis servetur, eum inficit et corrumpit: quemadmodum vinum acescit nimis diu servatum.

Si panis sanctificatus in aquam incidat, fertur, ac in superficie natat. Si panis in terram cadat, citius corrumpitur, ut communis panis. Ideo cautum est papistarum legibus, ut panis a missatoribus relictus in eminentiori loco reponatur, ut immunis a corruptione reservetur. Ignis panis substantiam agnoscit, et quod humidum est evaporari facit; quod vero siccius est relinquit, nempe substantiam panis in cineres redactam. Aër panis substantiam etiam agnoscit, quam inficit et corrumpit, si diu servetur. Aqua panis substantiam etiam agnoscit, quam in superficie desuper sustentat. Et terra panis substantiam agnoscit, et citius corrumpit quam si a terra

[1 See Corp. Jur. Can. Decretal. Greg. Lib. III. Tit. 44, c. 1. col. 1554. Venet. 1604. Also Binii, Conc. Lateran. cap. 20. Tom. VII. par. 2. p. 812. Lutet. Paris. 1636.]

sustolleret[2]. Hinc constat cum verbo Dei, tum scholis dialecticorum, atque brutorum animantium indicio, necnon elementorum inanimatorum effectis, manere panis substantiam, nostræque fidei sinceritatem stabiliri. Adversarii igitur nostri, transubstantiationis panis et vini in eucharistia assertores, et Christum ipsum, evangelistas, atque apostolos habent adversantes; et sacramentorum etiam nomina, dialecticorum scholam, bruta animantia, ac ipsa denique elementa.

Alia confirmatio nostræ assertionis ex auctoritate sanctorum patrum.

Irenæus: "Sed et suis discipulis dans consilium primitias Deo offerre ex suis creaturis, non quasi indigenti, sed ut ipsi nec infructuosi nec ingrati sint, eum qui ex creatura panis est accepit, et gratias egit, dicens, 'Hoc est corpus meum.' Et calicem similiter, qui est ex creatura quæ est secundum nos, suum sanguinem confessus est[3]." Irenæus hic testatur panem et vinum, a Christo in sacra cœna post verba sanctificationis discipulis distributa, fuisse, quod ad substantiam attinet, tales creaturas quales in nostris mensis communiter ministrari videmus. Et in eodem libro idem docet his verbis: "Offerimus enim ei quæ sunt ejus, congruenter communicationem et unitatem prædicantes carnis et spiritus. Quemadmodum enim qui est a terra [panis] percipiens vocationem Dei jam non communis panis [est], sed eucharistia, ex duabus rebus constans, terrena et cœlesti[4]." Hic Irenæus non solum sensu, sed etiam verbis, cum Christo Jesu Salvatore nostro idem dicit. Christus panem in sacra cœna corporis sui appellatione honoravit dicendo, "Hoc est corpus meum:" Irenæus dicit, "Panis qui a terra est, percipiens vocationem Dei." Christus dixit, "Hæc facite in memoriam mei," ubi panem in sacrum usum, videlicet, mortis ejus recordationem, accommodavit: Irenæus inquit, "Jam non communis panis est, sed eucharistia." Christus dixit de pane, "Hoc est corpus meum:" Irenæus idem dicit, sed aliis verbis: "eucharistia, constans ex duabus rebus, terrena et cœlesti." Christus panem fuisse et corpus suum asseruit: Irenæus panem dicit a consecratione rem esse

Irenæus adversus Valentinum. Lib. iv. cap. 34.

[2 Rather *sustolleretur*.]
[3 Iren. adv. Hæres. Lib. IV. cap. 32. Ed. Nic. Gallas. 1570. p. 261. § 3, 4.]
[4 Ibid. cap. 34. p. 264.]

constantem ex re terrena et cœlesti. Christus dixit de pane, "Hoc est corpus meum, quod pro vobis frangitur;" ubi spiritualem et sacramentalem conversionem panis in corpus suum tradendum asseruit: Irenæus eandem spiritualem conversionem panis in corpus Christi exprimit, sic inquiens; "Et corpora nostra percipientia eucharistiam jam non sunt corruptibilia, spem resurrectionis habentia[1]." Unde constat non aliam esse mutationem panis et vini in eucharistia quam nostrorum corporum eucharistiam percipientium in immortalitatem: nostra autem corpora eucharistiam percipientia re ipsa, quoad corporis substantiam, non sunt immortalia: quare ex Irenæo recte concludimus, quoad substantiam panis in eucharistia, nullam esse mutationem; sed ut nostra corpora, quantum ad spem futuræ resurrectionis attinet, sunt immortalia; ita et panis in eucharistia, quantum ad contemplationem fidei attinet, est ipsum corpus Christi. Irenæus vixit circa annum Domini 150.

Justinus Mart. Apolog. 2.
Justinus Martyr[2] dicit, cibum et potum in eucharistia in nostram carnem et sanguinem converti, et quod nostra corpora alant. Quod si panis et vini substantiam verba consecrationis tollerent (ut neoterici dicunt), haud dubie in eucharistia corpora nostra non alerentur. Corpus enim Christi nostram carnem non pascit, nec in nostrum corpus converti potest. Nam si hoc fieret, non solum σαρκοφάγοι essemus, verum etiam corpus Christi per nostri corporis corruptionem videret et pateretur corruptionem. Quæ enim corpora nostra pascunt in corporis nostri substantiam convertuntur, et cum corporibus nostris fiunt corruptibilia. Multa alia præclara habentur apud hunc sanctissimum virum de perpetua panis et vini existentia in eucharistia: sed quia illius opera jam mihi desunt, illum candido lectori commendo; a quo plus discat qui plura hac in re discere cupit. Et hoc in me recipio probandum sub periculo capitis, sanctum patrem ac martyrem Justinum asserere panis et vini substantiam in eucharistia post verborum sanctificationis prolationem in ipsa cœnæ actione semper manere: sit liber judex. Justinus vixit circa annum Domini 200.

[[1] Iren. adv. Hæres. Lib. IV. cap. 34. p. 264.]
[[2] Οὕτως καὶ τὴν δι' εὐχῆς λόγου τοῦ παρ' αὐτοῦ εὐχαριστηθεῖσαν τροφήν, ἐξ ἧς αἷμα καὶ σάρκες κατὰ μεταβολὴν τρέφονται ἡμῶν, κ.τ.λ.—Just. Mart. Apol. II. p. 98. A. Lutet. Paris. 1615.]

Origenes idem testatur materiam panis nihil prodesse, verum in ventrem vadere, et per secessum exonerari; sed verbum Domini supra panem prolatum prodesse[3]. Hæc et multo plura apud Origenem contra errorem transubstantiationis panis et vini a studioso lectore reperiri possent, modo pio et candido animo illius opera perlustrentur: quæ et ipsemet annotarem, si vel libros meos haberem, vel saltem quæ antehac ex eo in meum usum excerpsi. Sed quæ dico vera sunt: ipsum auctorem pro judice appello. Origenes vixit circa annum Domini 220.

Origenes in Mat. cap. xv.

Cyprianus inquit, "Vini utique mentio est, et ideo ponitur, ut Domini sanguis vino intelligatur[4]." Et paulo post: "Non bibam a modo ex ista creatura vitis usque in diem illum quo vobiscum bibam novum vinum in regno Patris mei:" et statim sequitur, "et vinum fuisse, quod sanguinem suum dixit[5]." Et iterum: "Per saporem vini redolet sanguis Christi[6]." In capite fere Epistolæ hæc habentur verba: "Ego sum vitis vera: sanguis Christi non aqua est utique, sed vinum: nec potest videri sanguis ejus, quo redempti et vivificati sumus, esse in calice, quando vinum desit calici, quo Christi sanguis ostenditur[7]," etc. Et paulo post: "Unde apparet sanguinem Christi non offerri, si desit vinum calici[8]." Et iterum: "Quomodo de creatura vitis novum vinum cum Christo in regno Patris bibemus, si in sacrificio Dei Patris et Christi vinum non offerimus[9]?" Metuo ne isti neoterici contra conscientiam et cognitam Dei veritatem hanc metamorphosim et transubstantiationem panis et vini defendant. Rogo, christiane lector, ut verba Cypriani martyris alta mentis cogitatione perpendas, et vide an quis excogitare poterit aliquid apertius contra transubstantiationem.

Cyprianus lib. epistolarum. Epistola 3.

Primum, quod sanguis Domini vino intelligitur. Quæ verba duo nobis declarant: unum, quod vinum semper manet a consecratione, quo sanguis intelligitur; alterum, quod san-

---

[3] Τὸ ἁγιαζόμενον βρῶμα διὰ λόγου Θεοῦ καὶ ἐντεύξεως, κατ' αὐτὸ μὲν τὸ ὑλικὸν, εἰς τὴν κοιλίαν χωρεῖ, καὶ εἰς ἀφεδρῶνα ἐκβάλλεται—καὶ οὐχ ἡ ὕλη τοῦ ἄρτου, ἀλλ' ὁ ἐπ' αὐτῷ εἰρημένος λόγος ἐστὶν ὁ ὠφελῶν τὸν μὴ ἀναξίως τοῦ Κυρίου ἐσθίοντα αὐτόν.—Origen. Commentar. in Matth. xv. Tom. xi. Pars I. p. 254. B. C. Rothomagi, 1668.]

[4 Cyprian. Epist. Lib. II. Epist. 3. Op. Tom. I. p. 81. Antw. 1541.]
[5 Ibid. p. 83.]
[6 Ne per saporem vini redoleat sanguinem Christi.—Ibid. p. 87.]
[7 Ibid. p. 79.]   [8 Ibid. p. 83.]   [9 Ibid.]

guis Christi re ipsa non adest, sed intellectu fidei cernitur. Ita vides divum Cyprianum una sententia binos neotericorum errores subvertere : nempe, vini in cœna conversionem in sanguinem Christi, et realem sanguinis Christi præsentiam. Nam inquit, " Vino intelligitur sanguis Domini :" et non dixit, sub accidentibus vini intelligitur sanguis Christi. Et iterum, "Sanguis Domini intelligitur," inquit; et non dicit, sanguis Domini realiter adest.

Secundum, "Non bibam ex ista creatura vitis." Perpende : divus Cyprianus vinum a verborum sanctificatione in cœna Domini creaturam vitis appellat, non aliquod adjacens vitis, sed germanam vitis naturam, quæ est vinum. Quid potest dici apertius ? Et quis tam obcæcatos habet oculos, quos hæc Cypriani sententia non aperiat? Pergit adhuc divus Cyprianus in hunc modum:

3. "Vinum fuit quod sanguinem suum dixit." Ergo a sanctificatione vinum semper mansit, vel bis mentitus est Cyprianus : antea enim, quod in calice est a sanctificatione creaturam vitis vocavit; nunc vero vinum esse affirmat. Et ne quis vini ablationem in calice per visus deceptionem imaginaretur (quandoquidem visus judicium variæ aliquando illudunt species), subjunxit aliorum sensuum, olfactus et gustus, judicium, qui exactius vini naturam expendunt et explorant. Nam color vini nonnunquam homini imponit, aliquando præ se ferens bonum et generosum vinum, quum sit tenue et dilutum : et sæpenumero vinum ostendit, cum non sit vinum. Ne igitur vini substantiam et naturam in calice sancto abesse putaremus, Cyprianus subjunxit :

4. "Per saporem vini (inquit) redolet sanguis Christi." Qua unica sententia et vini naturam semper tenet in calice, et sanguinis Christi substantiam a calice, quoad ejus substantiam, abesse testatur. Sapor enim vini (inquit) redolet sanguinem Christi : quod fieri nequit, nisi redolentia vini figurate intelligatur. Nam sapor vini non gustum sanguinis nec sanguinis redolentiam refert : sed quemadmodum gustus vini et vini redolentia sitim extinguunt, et sitientis vires recreant; sic sanguis Christi in cruce effusus peccatorum sitim extinguit, et sitientis vires redintegrat.

5. Adhuc clariora habet Cyprianus : "Sanguis Christi (inquit) non est aqua, sed vinum." Si sanguis Christi sit vinum, ergo vinum in cœna non tollitur. Propterea addit : "Non potest videri sanguis Christi in calice, si desit vinum calici."

Iterum utrumque errorem transubstantiationis panis et vini, et realis præsentiæ corporis Christi et sanguinis, subvertit. Primum, quo ad existentiam substantiæ vini in cœna Domini post verba sanctificationis, dicit, "Non potest videri sanguis Christi in calice, si desit vinum calici:" ergo nec abesse nec converti in aliam substantiam vinum in cœna Domini potest; sed vinum semper manet vinum.

6. Nam si desit (inquit) vinum, sanguis Christi non potest offerri. Sed quomodo verba divi Cypriani realis sanguinis præsentiam pernegant, in proximo capite, ubi hanc quæstionem tractavero, indicabo.

7. "Quomodo (ait) de creatura vitis novum vinum cum Christo in regno Patris bibemus, si in sacrificio Dei Patris et Christi vinum non offerimus?" In hisce verbis mirum est quam aperte divus Cyprianus affirmet, non solum vini substantiam in cœna Domini semper remanere, verum etiam corporalem sanguinis Christi substantiam abesse a cœna Domini; et nullum sacrificium propitiatorium in remissionem peccatorum in cœna Domini offerri. Sed duo posteriora sequentur suis locis. Hoc ad præsens negotium spectat, ut probemus elementorum substantias nec tolli nec mutari in sacra cœna, sed semper existere. Nam (inquit) si vinum in sacrificio Dei Patris ac Christi non offerimus, quomodo de creatura vitis novum vinum cum Christo in regno Patris bibemus? Erubescant igitur neoterici, et resipiscant, qui alteram partem sacramentorum (hoc est, rem terrestrem) docent vel perimi, vel in aliam substantiam transmutari; Cyprianus enim plane testatur vinum semper manere et offerri in cœna Domini.

Multa alia præclarissima hac de re videre potest diligens lector, si humili et candido animo discendique cupido epistolam sancti patris evolvere diligenter voluerit. Sed si hunc patrem Cyprianum vel alios quoscunque veteris ecclesiæ scriptores eo animo evolveris, ut illorum scripta tuo errori stabiliendo applices; et ubi apud illos reperieris vini substantiam in calice a sanctificatione remanere, panisque substantiam, quæ ex ea creatura quæ est secundum nos, in ipsa cœnæ actione ministrari et distribui; et ubi patres vini et panis nomina semper retinent, tu vel ex tuo cerebro, vel ex scrinio et pectore neotericorum, appellationem et nomina panis et vini abjicies, atque panis et vini accidentia vel adjacentia tantum retinebis; non tu veritatem sanctorum patrum discis, sed patrum veritati, quantum in te est, injuriam facis: et, quod pejus et periculosius est, ubi sanctorum patrum veritas a tua malitia vel ignorantia non sit intellecta, tuum errorem altius confirmabit. Nam, ut Augustinus ait, "Panis hominem alit, accipitrem necat." " Sol aquilarum oculos vegetat, nostros sauciat inspectus et obtenebrat[1]." Simplices et humiles sanctorum scripta ædificant ac instruunt; callidos et superbos inficiunt ac destruunt. Sic sacræ scripturæ legentibus sunt tanquam helleborum, quod "alio modo cibus est, alio medicamentum, alio vero venenum." Piorum autem mentes ex sacris literis incredibili afficiuntur voluptate, et scientia atque doctrina pascuntur: afflicti, miseri, et calamitosi ex eorum lectione rerum divinarum cognitionem et Dei promissionum certitudinem assequuntur: mali vero ex eorum lectione in deterius merguntur. Qui igitur animum ad sacras literas perdiscendas applicat, illarum testimoniis discat, quid Deus a se exigat, quid mandet, quidve vetet; et ex illis Dei voluntate patefacta et cognita, illius mandato obtemperabit, et a veritatis via nunquam aberrabit. Qui autem sanctorum patrum scripta pure et sinceriter perdiscere cupit, duo observare diligenter oportet: primum, ut quicquid in scriptis patrum invenerit, judicio et calculo sacrorum voluminum subjiciat; ac illos ut testes et interpretes divinorum librorum (et non ut auctores et judices) legat et audiat: deinde, qui per sanctorum patrum scripta errorem sibi eripi cupit, oportet illum (ut est in proverbiis) crapulam erroris prius edormire. Nam si ad veterum patrum scripta vigilante animo et cognoscendi veritatem cupido non accesserit, oleum perdet et operam.

Pergam jam ad reliquos patres, qui panis et vini substantiam in eucharistia manere semper testantur. Cyprianus vixit circa annum Domini 250.

Theodoretus hæc habet verba: "Volebat enim eos qui sunt divinorum[2] participes non attendere naturam eorum quæ videntur, sed propter nominum permutationem mutationi quæ fit ex gratia credere. Qui enim quod natura corpus est triticum et panem appellavit, et vitem rursus seipsum nominavit, is symbola et signa quæ videntur appellatione corporis et sanguinis honoravit, non naturam quidem mutans, sed naturæ

[[1] August. De Mor. Manich. Lib. II. cap. viii. Oper. Tom. I. coll. 781. D. 782. B. Basil. 1569.]

[[2] Supply mysteriorum.]

gratiam adjiciens³." Hic discimus perlucide, quod verba sanctificationis naturam panis et vini non mutant; sed quod verba ex mandato et institutione Christi creaturis panis et vini gratiam addunt. Et in secundo dialogo idem clarius testatur ad hunc modum: "Neque enim signa mystica post sanctificationem recedunt a sua natura. Manent enim ἐπὶ τῆς προτέρας οὐσίας καὶ τοῦ σχήματος καὶ τοῦ εἴδους, in priore substantia, figura, et forma, et videri et tangi possunt sicut prius⁴." Theodoretus inquit panem et vinum in coena Domini non exuere suam substantiam, sed retinere ut prius; ita ut possint a sanctificatione et videri et tangi, quemadmodum ante consecrationem. Idem testatur Gelasius contra Eutychen: "Sacramenta quæ sumimus corporis et sanguinis Christi divina res est, propter quod et per eadem divinæ efficimur consortes naturæ; et tamen non desinit substantia panis et vini. Et certe imago et similitudo corporis et sanguinis Christi in actione mysteriorum celebrantur⁵." Duo affirmat Gelasius: alterum, quod substantia panis et vini in coena non desinit esse; alterum vero, quod imago et similitudo corporis et sanguinis Christi in sacra actione mysteriorum celebrantur. Quisnam apertiora desideraret in hac causa eucharistiæ quam Gelasius profert, qui dicit panis et vini substantiam non desinere?

Gelasius.

Augustinus hæc habet: "Panis ad hoc factus in accipiendo sacramento consumitur⁶." Consumitur panis accipiendo sacramento, ait, non conficiendo: quare a consecratione panis substantia remanet, quod accipiendo et comedendo consumitur. Duo neotericorum errata hic subvertuntur: primum, illorum

August. de Trinitate Dei, Lib. iii. cap. 10.

[³ Theodoret. Dialog. I. Ἠβουλήθη γὰρ τοὺς τῶν θείων μυστηρίων μεταλαγχάνοντας μὴ τῇ φύσει τῶν βλεπομένων προσέχειν, ἀλλὰ διὰ τῆς τῶν ὀνομάτων ἐναλλαγῆς πιστεύειν τῇ ἐκ τῆς χάριτος γεγενημένῃ μεταβολῇ. Ὁ γὰρ δὴ τὸ φύσει σῶμα σῖτον καὶ ἄρτον προσαγορεύσας, καὶ αὖ πάλιν ἑαυτὸν ἄμπελον ὀνομάσας, οὗτος τὰ ὁρώμενα σύμβολα τῇ τοῦ σώματος καὶ αἵματος προσηγορίᾳ τετίμηκεν, οὐ τὴν φύσιν μεταβαλών, ἀλλὰ τὴν χάριν τῇ φύσει προστεθεικώς.—Oper. Tom. IV. p. 26. Halæ. 1772.]

[⁴ Id. Dial. II. Οὐδὲ γὰρ μετὰ τὸν ἁγιασμὸν τὰ μυστικὰ σύμβολα τῆς οἰκείας ἐξίσταται φυσέως· μένει γὰρ ἐπὶ τῆς προτέρας οὐσίας καὶ τοῦ σχήματος καὶ τοῦ εἴδους, καὶ ὁρατά ἐστι καὶ ἁπτά, οἷα καὶ πρότερον ἦν.—Op. Tom. IV. p. 126. Halæ. 1772.]

[⁵ Biblioth. Patr. Cont. Hæres. Tom. IV. col. 422. D. E. Paris. 1624.]

[⁶ Aug. De Trinit. Lib. III. cap. X. Op. Tom. III. col. 289. C.]

transubstantiationem rem esse fictam ostendit; dein, verum panem accipi et dentibus teri in sacramento confirmat. Nescio quid apertius dici potuerit pro panis essentia in cœna Domini post verba sanctificationis. Proferam adhuc plura testimonia ex Augustino, quæ panis et vini substantiam semper manere in cœna Domini confirmant. Contra Faustum Manichæum: "Noster autem (ait) panis et calix non quilibet, quasi propter Christum in spicis et sarmentis ligatum, sicut illi desipiunt, sed certa consecratione mysticus fit nobis, non nascitur[1]." Ecce, Augustinus dicit, " panis certa consecratione fit mysticus:" et non dicit, panis certa consecratione amittit suam substantiam, et fit verum et reale corpus Christi. De Baptismo contra Donatistas inquit: " Nam quando Dominus corpus panem vocat de multorum granorum adunatione congestum, populum nostrum quem portat indicat adunatum; et quando sanguinem suum [vinum] appellat de botris atque acinis multis expressum atque in unum coactum, gregem item nostrum commixtione adunatæ multitudinis copulatum[2]." Hæc verba Augustinus recitat e Cypriano: quæ si diligenter perpenderentur a neotericis, cito errorem suum deponerent, et veritatem agnoscerent. Quid enim desiderant amplius? Augustinus dicit Christum corpus suum panem vocare: quare abhorrent neoterici ab hoc loquendi modo, et novum fingunt; scilicet, panis non est corpus, sed, destructa panis substantia, sub specie et forma panis corpus Christi latitat? Hæc loquendi forma nusquam in scripturis sanctis nec apud patres primitivæ ecclesiæ invenitur; sed tantum apud neotericos scholasticos, quorum scripta, si cum scripturis sacris et veteribus patribus conferantur, nihil sunt præter nugas et mera somnia. Præterea Augustinus hoc addit, quod panis multorum granorum adunatione congestus a Christo corpus suum sit vocatus. Quis diceret panem multis granis congestum esse accidens vel formam panis, et non panis substantiam? Idem dicit De Consensu Evangelistarum: " Ne quisquam se agnovisse Christum arbitretur, si corporis particeps non est, id est, ecclesiæ; cujus unitatem in sacramento panis significavit apostolus, dicens, 'Unus panis, unum corpus

[1 August. Contra Faust. Man. Lib. xx. cap. xiii. Oper. Tom. vi. col. 370. a.]

[2 Id. De Baptism. contra Donat. Lib. vii. cap l. Oper. Tom. vii. col. 490. d.—where corpus suum,—quem portabat,—sang. su. vinum app. —greg. it. nos. significat, &c.]

multi sumus³,'" etc. Divus Augustinus in sacramento eucharistiæ illum semper retinet panem, qui corporis Christi mystici, id est, ecclesiæ, repræsentat unitatem. Ille panis est qui ex multis granis et seminibus constat; et non qui tantum panis formam retinet, ut neoterici dicunt. Nam ut verus panis a consecratione in cœna Domini ex multis constat granis; sic vera ecclesia, quæ est corpus Christi mysticum, constat ex multis membris, quæ uno glutino fidei unum corpus conficiunt in vitam æternam; quique panis substantiam in eucharistia tollunt, hanc mysticam unitatem ecclesiæ et ejus conjunctionem cum Christo destruunt, et sic præcipuos fines sacramenti subvertunt. Christus enim non solum nostram redemptionem in morte sua per sacramentum docet, verum etiam nostram cum illo conjunctionem, ut ei semper a susceptione sacramenti serviamus, et omnes illius sanguine redemptos amemus, foveamus, et diligamus ut fratres, quibuscum in Christo Jesu communicamus. Et quemadmodum per Adam sumus omnes ex eadem massa carnis prognati ad mortem; sic et per Christum sumus omnes ex eodem ejus Spiritu regenerati ad vitam.

Quam multa etiam utilissima doctrinarum genera et summæ consolationes ex vero usu Dominicæ cœnæ piis contingant, ipsi soli sciunt, qui interne per Spiritum Dei instructi in ipso usu cœnæ mortem Christi et sua peccata vere meditantur. Et quam horrenda doctrinarum genera et frigidas cæremonias (imo impias blasphemias) populo obtrudant qui, relicto vero Domini cœnæ usu a Christo mandato et exhibito, præscribunt ecclesiæ de papistarum et neotericorum lacunis, omnes noverunt qui tetram et abominandam missam diabolicam cum sacra cœna Domini conferre dignantur. In sententiis Prosperi Divus Augustinus hanc rem clarius adhuc ostendit. "Nam, inquit, sicut Christi persona constat ex Deo et homine, ita sacramentum ex re visibili et invisibili, sacramento et re sacramenti: quia, inquit, omnis res illarum rerum naturam et veritatem in se continet ex quibus conficitur⁴." Quid clarius desiderari potest ad probandum nullum esse interitum vel mutationem panis substantiæ in eucharistia? Primum dicit, quod ita se habent res in sacramento eucharistiæ ut in persona Christi. Sed Christi

De Consecratione, distinctione 2.

[³ Id. De Consens. Evang. Lib. III. cap. XXV. Oper. Tom. IV. col. 513. D. where si ejus corp.—commendat Apost., &c.]

[⁴ Corp. Jur. Canon. Decret. III. Pars. De Consecr. Dist. II. cap. 48. Decretal. Gratian. coll. 2278, 2279. Venet. 1604.]

persona retinet tum Dei tum hominis veram et genuinam naturam et conditionem: ita et sacramentum Christi continet tum rei coelestis tum terrestris genuinam naturam atque conditionem. Sed per assumptionem humanitatis in Deum Christus nullius naturæ substantiam destruxit aut permutavit, verum utriusque naturæ veritatem Dei et hominis servavit. Quare per institutionem Christi assumptio panis et vini in sacramentum sui corporis et sanguinis panis et vini substantiam non destruxit aut permutavit, sed utriusque naturæ veritatem panis et vini servavit. Deinde dicit, quod "omnis res illarum rerum naturam et veritatem in se continet ex quibus conficitur." Cum ergo sacramentum conficitur ex Dei gratia et panis et vini substantia, oportet, juxta Augustini sententiam, panis et vini naturam et veritatem in se, cum sit sacramentum, retinere, et non abjicere vel mutare, ut neoterici dicunt. Et paulo post idem dicit, " Sicut ergo coelestis panis, qui Christi caro est, suo modo vocatur corpus Christi, cum revera sit sacramentum corporis Christi, illius videlicet quod visibile, quod palpabile, in cruce positum est; vocatur ipsa immolatio carnis, quæ sacerdotis manibus fit, Christi passio, mors, crucifixio, non rei veritate, sed significante mysterio[1]," etc. Ecce dicit, suo modo panis vocatur corpus Christi, non quod revera sit corpus, sed sacramentum corporis; et quod vocatur ipsa immolatio carnis quæ sacerdotis manibus fit, etc. non rei veritate, sed significante mysterio. Et quomodo hæc intelligenda sint Augustinus præclarissime docet in libro de doctrina Christiana: "Ut autem literam sequi, et signa pro rebus quæ his significantur accipere, servilis infirmitatis est; ita et inutiliter signa interpretari male vagantis erroris est[2]."

Deum obsecro in visceribus Christi, ut tandem mentes neotericorum aperiat ad sacra sua oracula intelligenda. Mirum enim est tam multa de patribus jactitare, cum nihil sub sole magis illorum errorem perimat hac in causa quam sanctorum patrum testimonia. Panem in sententiis Prosperi sacramentum corporis Christi appellat Augustinus: hic autem dicit, quod signum pro re quæ hoc significatur accipere servilis infirmitatis est. Non sunt igitur signa in locum rerum signatarum extollenda, nec inutiliter interpretanda: sed suum honorem a Christo desig-

[1 Ibid. col. 2279.]
[2 August. De Doctr. Christ. Lib. III. cap. IX. Oper. Tom. III. col. 50. A. Basil. 1569.]

natum retineant; nos nihil vel addamus vel auferamus: ne ultra quam tutum est progrediatur nostrum judicium; et ubi nobis ex scripturis sanctis constat panis et vini substantiam a consecratione in eucharistia manere, illam non destruamus, ne inutiliter analogiam et naturam sacramenti auferamus, et ex creaturis panis et vini Deum ipsum et hominem nobis confingamus; quod citra Dei blasphemiam et periculum animæ nostræ fieri non potest. Satis est, si signorum substantias semper retinemus; et si agnoscimus quod ex verbo et institutione Christi fiunt sacramenta corporis et sanguinis Christi; quodque fidei et menti nostræ seipsum communicat, ut nos participes omnium bonorum suorum faciat quæ in morte sua super crucem paravit. Relinquamus etiam neotericorum fabulas de transubstantiatione panis et vini: nam nihil afferunt præter mendacia et apertissimam ac detestandam idololatriam. Hoc autem docet Augustinus religiosissime his verbis: "Figura est ergo, præcipiens passioni Domini esse communicandum[3]." Non dicit, sacramentum est ipsum corpus Christi, sed est modus et ratio, operante Spiritu Sancto, quo passioni et morti ejus communicamus hoc quo certi simus et persuasi nostra omnia peccata virtute et potentia mortis Christi nobis condonari, nosque in favorem Dei et gratiam recipi.

De doct. Christi. Lib. iii. cap. 15.

Unum adhuc caput pulcherrimum contra neotericorum sententiam (qui elementorum, hoc est, panis et vini, substantiam tolli asserunt) annotabo, ex libro de fide ad Petrum Diaconum: "Firmissime tene et nullatenus dubites, ipsum unigenitum Deum, Verbum carnem factum, se pro nobis obtulisse sacrificium et hostiam Deo in odorem suavitatis: cui cum Patre et Spiritu Sancto a patriarchis, prophetis, et sacerdotibus tempore veteris testamenti animalia sacrificabantur; et cui nunc, tempore novi testamenti, cum Patre et Spiritu Sancto, cum quibus ille una est divinitas, sacrificium panis et vini in fide et caritate sancta ecclesia catholica per universum orbem terræ offerre non cessat. In illis enim carnalibus victimis figuratio fuit carnis Christi, quam pro peccatis nostris ipse sine peccato fuerat oblaturus, et sanguinis, quem erat effusurus in remissionem peccatorum nostrorum. In isto autem sacrificio gratiarum actio, atque commemoratio est carnis Christi, quam pro nobis obtulit, et sanguinis, quem

Cap 19.

[3 Id. ibid. Lib. III. cap. XVI. Oper. Tom. III. col. 53. B.]

pro nobis idem Deus effudit," etc.¹ Et statim post pauca hæc sequuntur: "In illis ergo sacrificiis quid esset donandum figurate significabatur: in hoc autem sacrificio quid nobis jam donatum sit evidenter ostenditur. In [illis] sacrificiis prænunciabatur Filius Dei pro impiis occidendus: in hoc autem pro impiis annunciatur occisus," etc. Augustinus dicit, "offerimus sacrificium panis et vini:" non dicit, per verba sanctificationis tollimus panem et vinum, ut neoterici dicunt. Religiosius ergo nobis erit, cum scriptura sacra et cum sanctis patribus, panis et vini substantiam retinere et offerre Deo nostro, ut ait Augustinus, quam cum neotericis novam mutationem et destructionem panis et vini in sacra cœna Domini inducere, et creaturam panis et vini pro Deo ipso colere ac venerari, cum nulla creatura sit vel possit esse eadem cum Deo; ut idem Augustinus eodem libro testatur cap. 22.²

Eusebius Emissenus. De consecratione, distinct. 2.

Hanc panis et vini substantiæ destructionem vel in corpus Christi mutationem Eusebius Emissenus etiam doctissime subvertit. "Quomodo, inquit, tibi novum et impossibile esse non debeat, quod in Christi substantiam terrena et mortalia convertuntur, teipsum qui in Christo es regeneratus interroga. Dudum alienus a vita, peregrinus a misericordia et a salutis via, intrinsecus mortuus exulabas. Subito initiatus Christi legibus, et salutaribus mysteriis innovatus, in corpus ecclesiæ, non videndo, sed credendo, transiluisti; et de filio perditionis adoptivus Dei filius fieri occultata puritate meruisti: in mensura visibili permanens, major factus es teipso invisibiliter, sine quantitatis augmento," etc.³ Emissenus talem ponit mutationem panis et vini in sacra cœna Domini qualis nostri sit in baptismo. Sed, ut idem dicit, nostra mutatio in baptismo nihil ad destructionem vel substantialem corporis nostri mutationem pertinet; sed per Spiritum Sanctum peccata nostra delentur, novo Spiritus afflatu regeneramur, et inferne⁴ omnino mutati sumus. Talis est creaturarum panis et vini mutatio in corpus et sanguinem Christi, inquit Emissenus. Et ut hoc

[¹ August. De Fide, ad Petr. Diac. cap. xix. ibid. col. 230. c. d.]
[² Neque angelos neque aliam quamlibet creaturam ejusdem naturæ esse, cujus est secundum naturalem divinitatem summa Trinitas.—Ibid. col. 231. c.]
[³ Corp. Jur. Canon. Decret. iii. Pars. De Consec. Dist. ii. cap. 35. Decretal. Gratian. col. 2268. Venet. 1604.]
[⁴ Qu. interne?]

apertius indicet, statim subjunxit, " Et cum reverendum altare cibis spiritualiter satiandus ascendis, sacrum Dei tui corpus et sanguinem fide respice, honora, mirare, mente continge, cordis manu suscipe, et maxime totum haustum[5] interioris hominis assume." Corpus Christi, inquit, in altari fide respiciendum est, fide honorandum, mente contingendum, manu cordis suscipiendum, et haustu interioris hominis assumendum. Ne verbum quidem habet de panis et vini substantiæ mutatione in corpus et sanguinem Christi, vel de corporali Christi præsentia in cœna Domini: sed mutationem sacramentalem ponit, quemadmodum in baptismo est; et tantum sacramentalem præsentiam corporis et sanguinis Christi, quam fidei et menti præsentem facit, et non corporalem externo homini exhibendam. Retinet enim hic Emissenus veram panis et vini substantiam in cœna; sicut in baptismo nostra vere retinetur substantia. Panis tamen et vinum per Spiritum Sanctum et Christi institutionem sacramenta fiunt corporis et sanguinis Christi; ut nos in baptismo facti sumus ex filiis iræ filii Dei, non substantialiter mutati, sed Spiritu Christi regenerati.

Idem asserit D. Hieronymus: "Hoc autem triticum (inquit) et hoc vinum, quod non comedunt nisi laudantes Dominum, et non bibunt nisi in atriis sanctis ejus, de quo Dominus in passione dicebat, 'Non bibam de hoc genimine vitis hujus, donec illud bibam novum in regno Patris mei[6].'" Ecce, quod comedunt fideles in atriis Domini triticum appellat D. Hieronymus; uti et Paulus panem: quod etiam in atriis Domini bibunt vinum vocat; ut Salvator noster fructum vitis nominavit. Mirum enim est quod neoterici, qui quotidie veterum scripta et testimonia revolvunt ac perlustrant, non animadvertunt. Sed inde est, quod priusquam sacras literas vel veterum patrum libros discunt, superstitione et errore papismi librorumque eorum cæcitate et spurcitia seducti et coinquinati, quicquid in sacris literis vel sanctorum scriptis invenerint contaminant, et Harpyiarum more contactu immundo omnia fœdant; quodque in sacris literis et veterum patrum scriptis sanctum atque purum fluit, ipsi prius polluti omnia immundo polluunt animo. Hieronymus etiam ait, quod " comedentes et bibentes corpus et sanguinem Domini

Hieronymus, Libro 17 in Esaiam. cap. 62.

Libro 7 in Esaiam cap. 21.

[5 toto haustu.]
[6 Hieron. in Esai. lxii. Lib. XVII. Oper. Tom. v. fol. 104. E. F. Paris. 1534.]

vertuntur in principes ecclesiæ[1]." Sed hæc conversio ad animum pertinet, et non ad corporis et sanguinis substantiam: nam quantum ad corpus attinet, manent pii a susceptione eucharistiæ æque miseri atque antea; sed quoad animum et fidem, fortiores fiunt et potentiores quam ut vel a mundo vel ab inferno vincantur. Eusebius conversionem panis et vini in sacra Domini cœna nostræ conversioni ad obsequium Dei in baptismo comparavit: Hieronymus vero videtur panis et vini substantiam in corpus et sanguinem Christi per verba sanctificationis extollere; sed eo modo quo rite utentes sacramento eucharistiæ ad regiam perferantur dignitatem. Jam fideles et recte utentes eucharistia reges facti sunt, non quod ad substantiam attinet, sed quia fide nacti sunt a Christo potestatem, dominationem, et imperium super peccatum, carnem, mundum, infernum, mortem, atque diabolum; et non quod utentes eucharistia substantialiter transeunt vel migrant in reges. Et panis igitur et vinum nacta sunt ex Christo et ejus institutione nomina corporis et sanguinis sui (ita ut quisquis illis abuteretur indigne, vel pro communi pane et vino haberet, reus esset corporis et sanguinis Christi), non quod substantialiter panis et vinum transeant vel migrent in substantiam corporis et sanguinis Domini, sed quod ea repræsentent.

Facessant ergo et procul fiant a cogitationibus et fide omnium piorum hæc vana, falsa, puerilia, et neoterica de transubstantiatione elementorum panis et vini in ipsam corporis et sanguinis Christi substantiam. Christianorum enim est agnoscere, gratias quoque agere Deo Patri nostro cœlesti, quod per Christum Jesum Filium ejus facti sunt reges, quibus datur potestas conculcandi et premendi peccatum, diabolum, mortem, et infernum; et quod panis et vini substantiam in eucharistia Christi institutio in sacramentum corporis et sanguinis sui evexit: in cujus sacramenti vero usu a Christo ecclesiæ suæ tradito fides recte utentium sacramento utentium animos et mentes ad æthera trahit; ubi corpore et sanguine Christi pascuntur atque aluntur efficaciter: hoc est, qui rite et religiose sacramento corporis et sanguinis Christi communicat est vere in Christo, et Christus vere in illo. Esse autem in Christo, est omnium meritorum ejus esse participem: Christumque in nobis esse est virtute Spiritus sui se nobis ostendere esse vitæ auctorem, causamque ejusdem, atque nostro spiritui

[1 Hieron. in Esai. xxi. Lib. VII. Ibid. fol. 42. D.]

testificari, quod sumus filii Dei. Fides enim christiana contemplatur mortem Christi amarissimamque illius passionem, quam pro expiatione nostrorum peccatorum in cruce sustinuit. Et hinc Dei Patris erga nos ineffabilem dilectionem discimus, qui unico suo Filio non pepercit, sed pro nobis omnibus illum tradidit. Hac etiam Dei immensæ clementiæ et bonitatis contemplatione nos in amorem ejus qui vitam nobis restituit, et odium nostrorum peccatorum, quæ Christum ab omni peccato immunem cruci et crudelissimo mortis generi affixerunt, inflammamur. Hinc præterea discimus peccatorum atrocitatem, horrorem, et magnitudinem nullis aliis rationibus, viis, et mediis expiari potuisse quam unica morte Filii Dei. Hæc et mille alia utilissima ex vero usu Domini coenæ discuntur, ubi vera doctrina de utraque parte sacramenti (scilicet, terrena et coelesti) retinetur. Sed ad alia testimonia sanctorum patrum, quæ panis et vini substantiam retinent a verbis sanctificationis in eucharistia, redeo.

Basilius Magnus de institutione Monachalis regulæ, cap. 70, docet, quod sumptio eucharistiæ fieri debeat cum timore et fide. "Timorem (inquit) apostolus docet, dicens, 'Qui manducat et bibit indigne judicium sibi manducat et bibit,' etc. Fidem vero nos edocet sermo Domini dicentis, 'Hoc est corpus meum, quod pro vobis datur: hoc facite in meam commemorationem.'" Concludit orationem suam Basilius et caput in hunc modum: "Talem ergo affectum et fidem præparare debet in animo suo, qui de pane et de calice participat[2]." Etsi Basilius plus æquo monachalem vitam extulit, et multas occasiones ut idem alii facerent præbuit; ad hanc tamen impietatem non pervenit, ut panis et vini substantiam in eucharistia tolleret, et panem et vinum adorandum in missa populo exhibendum doceret: sed a verborum sanctificatione in ipsa coenæ actione panis et vini substantiam retinuit, ut ex responsione sua ad monachum constat, qui quali timore, fide, vel affectu percipere debeamus corporis et sanguinis Christi gratiam interrogavit. "Talem ergo (respondit Basilius) affectum et fidem præparare debet in animo suo, qui de pane et calice parti-

[2 Ποταπῷ φόβῳ ἢ ποίᾳ πληροφορίᾳ ἢ ποίᾳ διαθέσει μεταλάβωμεν τοῦ σώματος καὶ τοῦ αἵματος τοῦ Χριστοῦ; Τὸν μὲν φόβον διδάσκει ἡμᾶς ὁ ἀπόστολος λέγων, κ.τ.λ. Τὴν δὲ πληροφορίαν ἐμποιεῖ ἡ πίστις τῶν ῥημάτων τοῦ Κυρίου εἰπόντος, κ.τ.λ. Τοιαύτην διάθεσιν καὶ ἑτοιμασίαν ὀφείλει ἔχειν ὁ μεταλαμβάνων τοῦ ἄρτου καὶ τοῦ ποτηρίου.—Regul. Brev. Interr. 172. Oper. Tom. II. pp. 682. B. 683. A. Paris. 1638.]

cipat." Verba etiam monachi ad Basilium sunt animadvertenda. "Quo affectu (inquit) percipere debemus corporis et sanguinis Christi gratiam?" Non quærit quomodo sint elementa panis et vini formanda in ipsam corporis et sanguinis Christi substantiam: nec quærit quo affectu percipere debeamus corporis et sanguinis Christi substantiam, sed corporis et sanguinis Christi gratiam. Unde omnibus constat, quod tempore Basilii Magni istud figmentum et somnium de transubstantiatione panis et vini in ipsam naturam et substantiam corporis et sanguinis Christi, atque commentum hoc Romanum de corporali corporis et sanguinis Christi præsentia, non fuerunt cognita nec audita ecclesiæ Christi; sed panis et vini sacramentalem et spiritualem mutationem in eucharistia agnoscebant, quam nos etiam omni religione, reverentia, et honore profitemur. Præterea spiritualem corporis et sanguinis Christi præsentiam in eucharistia agnoscebant. Nam Christus a suis sacramentis nunquam abest: ideo timore et fide muniendi sunt qui sacramentis Christi communicant. Sed corporalem sui præsentiam non agnoscebant: nam monachus sciscitatur a Basilio præceptore suo quo affectu percipere deberet corporis et sanguinis Christi gratiam.

Satis absque dubio manducat et bibit in eucharistia qui corporis et sanguinis Christi gratiam efficaciter manducat et bibit, licet corporis substantiam non apprehenderit ore et ventre; sed satis est, quod fides Christo vescitur sedente superne ad dextram Dei Patris. Nos vero utrumque confitemur, et Christi præsentiam et ejus-absentiam in cœna Domini. Præsens quidem est spiritualiter et sacramentaliter contemplationi nostræ fidei, dum sacramentis utimur: absens vero est corporaliter in suo corpore contemplationi externi visus, ita ut in nostrum corpus, dum sacramentis communicamus, corporaliter non intret. Fides nostra, dum sacra peragimus, Christo toto et Deo et homine, corpore et anima fruitur, ita ut corpus et anima rite utentium participent toto Christo Deo et homine per internam operationem Spiritus Sancti; qui semper (ut dixi) et adest et præest sacramentis Dei, atque corda illorum recte utentium Christo conjungit et adglutinat; in quibus Spiritus Sanctus habitat, clamans et vociferans, "Abba, Pater," ac testificans spiritibus sacramentis rite utentium, quod sunt filii Dei, per gratiam corporis et sanguinis Christi pro nobis super crucem partam: ut Basilius docet, nec realem corporis illius perceptionem in cœna Domini somniat. Rogo igitur pium lectorem, ut diligenter perpendat verba et sententias hujus venerandi patris Magni Basilii in causa eucharistiæ. Primum, quod dicit nos gratiam corporis et sanguinis Christi sumere in cœna Domini; et non dicit, corpus ipsum in quo meruit nobis hanc gratiam præsens sisti. Deinde substantias sacramenti eucharistiæ (quod ad res terrenas spectat) servat, panemque et vinum vocat, ut sacræ scripturæ nominant et testantur. Jam quia sacræ scripturæ elementa panis et vini in sacra cœna agnoscunt; hoc est, panis substantiam in cœna frangi, distribui, et manducari; ut Paulus inquit, "Panis quem frangimus, nonne communicatio corporis Christi est?" et vini substantiam discipulis in ultima cœna exhiberi, distribui, et participari; ut Christus inquit, "Non bibam ex hoc fructu vitis, donec illud bibam novum vobiscum in regno Patris mei;" videamus an liceat Christianis ab hac doctrina Christi, quæ panis et vini substantiam in cœna asserit, ob quamcunque causam deflectere. 1 Cor. x.

Basilius in libro prius citato hæc habet verba: " Quis potest in tantum temeritatis progredi, ut audeat a se quicquam loqui vel cogitare[1]?" Basilius vocat temeritatem aliquid loqui vel excogitare a seipso citra sacrarum scripturarum testimonia. Temeritas ergo est, et non sacrosancta religio, hæc panis et vini mutatio in corpus et sanguinem Christi, quam neoterici in cœna constituunt. Proferant vel ostendant ex sacris literis transubstantiationis nomen et doctrinam; quod si fecerint, illorum sententiis subscribemus: si non possint, ut revera est impossibile, meminerint verborum patris Magni Basilii, non licere cuiquam ex proprio dicere quod sibi videtur bonum, absque testimoniis divinarum scripturarum. Nam Spiritus Sanctus (ut inquit Christus), cum venerit, non loquetur a seipso; sed quæcunque audierit, hæc loquetur. Et Christus de seipso dicit, "Ego a me ipso non sum loquutus; sed qui misit me Pater, ipse dedit mandatum quid dicam et quid loquar," etc. Quum ergo Christus, ipsa veritas, nihil loquutus sit nisi quæ a Patre audivit, absque dubio ecclesia, quæ est vera Christi sponsa, dicit et loquitur tantum quæ didicit a Christo marito. Si autem Romana ecclesia, Christi hostis infensissima, a Christo didicit panis et vini interitum, vel Cap. 13.

[[1] Τίς ἂν εἰς τοσαύτην ἐξέλθῃ μανίαν, ὥστε ἀφ' ἑαυτοῦ τολμῆσαί τι καὶ μέχρις ἐννοίας λαβεῖν;—Regul. Brevior. Interr. I. Oper. Tom. II. p. 624. A. Paris. 1638.]

illorum mutationem substantialem in substantiam corporis et sanguinis sui, proferant e sacris literis testimonia, et herbam illis porrigemus. Sed nos scimus, et ipsi quidem sacrifici non sunt nescii, quod sacræ literæ ne gry quidem de transubstantiatione elementorum in cœna Domini meminerint: sed elementorum tum nomina (ut dixi) tum substantias semper retinent post verba sanctificationis æque ut antea. " Quare (ut inquit Basilius) de his quæ scripta sunt in divinis scripturis nulla prorsus licentia permittitur cuiquam vel admittere quod prohibitum est, vel omittere quod præceptum est; quum ipse Dominus ita præceperit, dicens, ' Et custodi verbum hoc quod ego mando tibi hodie: non adjicies ad illud, nec auferas ab eo.' Sed et terribilis quædam expectatio est judicii et ignis zeli, qui consumpturus est adversarios, et eos qui ausi sunt tale aliquid operari[1]." Hæc Basilius.

Quam horrenda est igitur papistarum impudentia, qui panis et vini nomina et substantias abhorrent ac destruunt in sacra cœna Domini, cum scripturæ sanctæ utrumque clarissime testentur, ut supra demonstravimus! Sed frontem illam meretricis induerunt impii illi neoterici, quæ erubescere nescit, ut tandem commeritas pœnas ipsorum impudentiæ et impietatis luant. Legatur 14 caput Basilii Magni ejusdem libri, et constabit hujusmodi impostoribus non esse obtemperandum in iis quæ contra mandatum Dei præcipiunt. Nam illic hæc habentur verba: " Commonitionum sane non parva est diversitas. Aliæ namque contrariæ videntur esse mandatis Dei: aliæ autem interrumpere mandatum, vel contaminare videntur: aliæ vero ad explendum id atque ædificandum veniunt, etc[2]." Et paulo post: " Si autem contrarium aliquid mandatis Christi, vel quod illa corrumpere videatur aut contaminare, jubemur ab aliquo facere, tempus est nobis dicere, ' Obtemperare

[1 Ibid. Ἐπεὶ δὲ τῶν ἐν ἡμῖν στρεφομένων πραγμάτων τὰ μέν ἐστιν ὑπὸ τῆς ἐντολῆς τοῦ Θεοῦ ἐν τῇ ἁγίᾳ γραφῇ διεσταλμένα, τὰ δὲ σεσιωπημένα, περὶ μὲν τῶν γεγραμμένων οὐδεμία ἐξουσία δεδόται καθόλου οὐδένι οὔτε ποιῆσαί τι τῶν κεκωλυμένων, οὔτε περιαλεῖψαί τι τῶν προστεταγμένων, τοῦ Κυρίου ἅπαξ παραγγείλαντος καὶ εἰπόντος, κ.τ.λ.—p. 624. B. C. See also Interr. 303, p. 736.]

[2 Τῶν δὲ ἐπιταγμάτων διαφορᾶς οὐκ ὀλίγης οὔσης· τὰ μὲν γὰρ ἐναντίως ἔχει πρὸς τὴν ἐντολὴν τοῦ Κυρίου, ἤ τι παραφθείροντα αὐτήν, ἢ μολύνοντα πολλαχῶς ἐπιμιξίᾳ τοῦ κεκωλυμένου· τὰ δὲ συνεμπίπτει τῇ ἐντολῇ· τὰ δὲ κἂν μὴ συνεμπίπτει κατὰ τὸ προφανές, ἀλλὰ συμβάλλεται, κ. τ. λ.—Ibid. Interr. 114, pp. 663. E. 664. A. &c.]

oportet Deo magis quam hominibus;' et rursus meminisse Domini dicentis, 'Alieni autem vocem non sequuntur, sed fugiunt ab eo, quia nesciunt vocem alienorum.' Sed et sancti apostoli meminisse debemus, qui ad cautelam nostram ausus est ne angelis quidem parcere, dicens, 'Etiamsi aut angelus de cœlo evangelizaverit præterquam quod evangelizavimus vobis, anathema sit.' Ex quo docemur, etiamsi valde nobis carus sit aliquis, si magnificus habeatur, et in admiratione sit positus, qui prohibet nos facere quod a Domino præceptum est, vel rursus imperat quod Dominus fieri prohibuit, execrabilis debet esse ejusmodi omnibus qui diligunt Deum[3]." Unde discimus, quæ sunt contra mandata Dei, vel corrumpunt aut contaminant præcepta divina, non esse facienda. Vide igitur, scriptura sacra panis et vini substantiam aperte, imo apertissime, in cœna Domini semper retinet: isti tamen neoterici contra scripturam sanctam panis et vini substantiam destruunt. Scriptura autem sancta non solum utriusque elementi (panis scilicet et vini) conservat substantiam; verum etiam præcipit ac mandat, ut utriusque elementi panis et vini substantia in cœna Domini per ministrum distribuatur, atque etiam a populo suscipiatur: neoterici vero satis esse dicunt unius elementi substantiam (id est, panis) distribui; et sic institutionem Christi, qui utramque speciem panis et vini distribuit et distribui jussit, mutilant ac truncant. Sed quid ait Basilius? Execrabilis debet esse ejusmodi, quamvis carus sit (ut parens), qui hoc docet et mandat: quamvis magnificus (ut princeps vel magistratus), quamvis in admiratione positus (ut qui in ecclesia sanctitate et pietate pollere videatur), qui prohibent nos facere quod a Domino præceptum est, vel rursus imperant quod Dominus prohibuit. Et hoc, inquit, facere debent omnes qui diligunt Christum. Optarem igitur hæc duo capita, 13, 14, Magni Basilii a magistratu et a populo melius intelligi, ut hic nihil contra mandatum Dei populo mandet, et populus, si imperetur, non obtemperet. Satis est ut Cæsar ea mandet et præscribat suo populo quæ sunt Cæsaris; Deo autem relinquat et verbo illius quæ sunt Dei: et si quæ Dei sunt Cæsar a suis exigat, meminerint oportet, obediendum esse Deo magis quam hominibus. Deus quidem in verbo suo panis et vini substantiam et nomine et re in sacra cœna retinet: non est igitur illis credendum, obediendum, vel obtemperandum, qui

[[3] Ibid. B. C.]

illorum substantiam tollunt et destruunt. Nam verbi Dei sanctitas et auctoritas præferenda est omnibus, etiam ipsis cœlestibus spiritibus, ut Paulus docet. Basilius etiam Magnus ad Chilonem discipulum de vita solitaria idem dicit: "Omnis scriptura divina ex Deo est, ac admodum fructuosa, nihilque per se immundum atque impurum retinet aut præbet, nisi ei qui illud esse putaverit impurum," etc.[1] Sive ergo parens, sive princeps, sive pastor, sive angelus de cœlo fuerit, qui aliud evangelizaverit quam verbi Dei sanctitas et puritas evangelizavit, anathema sit. Audiatur jam Joannes Chrysostomus, quid contra istos neotericos dicat.

<small>Homil. lxxxiii. in Mat. cap. 26.</small> Joannes Chrysostomus: "Sed cujus rei gratia non aquam sed vinum post resurrectionem bibit? Perniciosam quandam hæresim radicitus evellere voluit, eorum qui aqua in mysteriis utuntur: ita ut ostenderet quia et quando hoc mysterium tradidit vinum tradidit; etiam post resurrectionem in nuda mysterii mensa vino usus est[2]." Quid apertius desiderent neoterici contra vini transubstantiationem? Quando (inquit Chrysostomus) Christus hoc mysterium tradidit, vinum tradidit, quod etiam post resurrectionem in nuda mysterii mensa bibit. Quod post consecrationem tradidit vinum fuisse affirmat; ut id quod post resurrectionem in nuda mensa bibebat. Miror igitur neotericos non erubescere, ac vereri tam clara et perspicua verba et testimonia divinarum literarum ac sanctorum patrum illudere. Si hoc enim non sit illudere divina et humana testimonia, nescio quid sit illudere. Christus vero, apostolica ecclesia, et sancti patres in cœna Domini elementis et signis sacramenti nomina et substantias panis et vini tribuunt: isti autem illusores et impostores neoterici, jurati in Romanum antichristum, elementis et signis sacræ cœnæ Domini et nomina et substantias signorum tollunt et destruunt, tantumque signorum adjacentia et formas panis et vini conservant et retinent. Quod autem Christus retinet et sancti

[1 Πᾶσα γραφὴ θεόπνευστος καὶ ὠφέλιμος, καὶ οὐδὲν κοινὸν δι' αὐτῆς, εἰ μὴ καὶ τῷ λογιζομένῳ κοινὸν εἶναι ἐκείνῳ κοινόν.—Basil. Ad. Chilon. Disc. Op. Tom. III. p. 4. E. Paris. 1638.]

[2 Καὶ τίνος ἕνεκεν οὐχ ὕδωρ ἔπιεν ἀναστὰς, ἀλλ' οἶνον; ἄλλην αἵρεσιν πονηρὰν πρόρριζον ἀνασπῶν. Ἐπεὶ γὰρ εἰσί τινες ἐν τοῖς μυστηρίοις ὕδατι κεχρημένοι, δεικνὺς ὅτι καὶ ἡνίκα τὰ μυστήρια παρέδωκεν οἶνον παρέδωκεν, καὶ ἡνίκα ἀναστὰς χωρὶς μυστηρίων ψιλὴν τράπεζαν παρετίθετο οἴνῳ ἐκέχρητο.—Chrysost. Hom. LXXXIII. in Matth. XXVI. Op. Tom. II. p. 511. l. 12. Eton. 1613.]

patres, neoterici non retinent; quodque Christus et sancti patres affirmant, isti negant : appello Christi et sanctorum patrum libros. Isti tamen neoterici clamant ad ravim usque, quod catholica Christi ecclesia hoc docet, hoc mandat, hoc etiam per mille quingentos annos servavit, retinuit, et servari ac retineri jussit. O miram et detestandam ecclesiam! quæ nec Christum pro capite, nec evangelistas, apostolos, aut sanctos patres pro membris habeat, sed ex diametro pugnet et bellum moveat, ut Christum et eos qui sunt Christi penitus trucident ac perdant! Consulite Tertullianum adversus Marcionem, Tertull. Libro I. "Per panem (ait) repræsentavit Christus corpus suum[3]." Non dixit, panis substantiam fecit corpus suum, neque quod panis substantiam abstulit per verba sanctificationis, et corpus suum pro ea substituit. Idem dicit adversus Judæos: "Sic enim Christus revelavit, panem corpus suum appellans[4]." Idem quoque habet Tertullianus, Lib. IV. adversus Marcionem.

Hieronymus hæc habet : "Nos audiamus, panem quem fregit Dominus deditque discipulis suis esse corpus Domini Salvatoris, ipso dicente ad eos, 'Accipite et comedite; hoc est corpus meum[5].'" Hieronymus hic plane testatur Christum panem fregisse ac dedisse discipulis suis in ultima cœna, quem corpus suum nominabat. Hoc pulcherrime etiam affirmat Augustinus de Trinitate Dei Lib. III. cap. 4. "Potuit (scilicet Paulus) tamen significando prædicare Dominum Jesum Christum aliter per linguam suam, aliter per epistolam, aliter per sacramentum corporis et sanguinis ejus. Nec linguam quippe ejus, nec membranas, nec atramentum, nec significantes sonos lingua editos, nec signa literarum conscripta pelliculis, corpus Christi et sanguinem dicimus ; sed illud tantum quod ex fructibus terræ acceptum et prece mystica consecratum rite sumimus ad salutem spiritualem in memoriam pro nobis Dominicæ passionis[6]." Augustinus dicit, id quod est ex fructibus terræ prece mystica consecratum dicimus esse corpus et sanguinem Domini, quæ sumimus ad salutem spiritualem in memoriam pro nobis dominicæ passionis. Non dixit, ut neoterici docent, fructus terræ substantiam converti in corpus et sanguinem Domini

Hieron. Hedibiæ quæst. 2.

[3 Nec panem, quo ipsum corpus suum repræsentat.—Oper. p. 440. A. Lutet. 1641.]

[4 Ibid. p. 222. A. See also p. 493. D.]

[5 Hieron. Hedib. Quæst. 2. Oper. Tom. III. fol. 49. Paris. 1534.]

[6 August. De Trinit. Lib. III. cap. 4. Oper. Tom. III. col. 284. A. B. Basil. 1569.]

prece mystica, sed quod mystica prece fructus terræ induit nomen corporis Christi, quem in memoriam Dominicæ passionis in cœna mystica sumimus.

Subscriberem verba Epiphanii quæ habentur Lib. III. contra hæreses, Tom. II, et in Anchorato: præterea Joannis Chrysostomi ad Cæsarium monachum: et verba Ambrosii de iis qui mysteriis initiantur capite ultimo, et de sacramentis Libro IV. cap. 4: item Cyrilli verba in Joan. cap. 6: Origenis Homil. 7, in Levit. Homil. 16. in Numer. in Matth. cap. 26: contra Celsum Lib. VIII: Hesychii Lib. XX. super Levit. cap. 18: nam apud istos multa sunt præclarissima ac sanctissima, quæ panis et vini substantiam in eucharistia retinent et asseverant. Sed talis est mea sors, et hujusmodi me detinet locus, ut istorum sanctorum patrum librorum copia mihi fieri non possit: nec ego, pro honore ac reverentia quibus sanctos patres prosequor, et candore quo erga fratres meos afficior, ausus sum mutilata, manca, aut mutata illorum verba et sententias citare; quod fortassis facerem, si illorum sententias meis verbis exponerem. Ideo mihi satis esse puto in hac librorum penuria loca patrum demonstrare, et pios ac studiosos lectores ad ea exploranda et perpendenda relegare; certa ac bona fide pollicens piis lectoribus istos patres a parte nostra omnino stare contra neotericos, qui transubstantiationis panis et vini errorem dolo malo et tyrannide in ecclesiam primo induxerunt, et introductum mendaciis, ferro, et igne in ecclesia retinent. Sed hoc unum, priusquam absolvero tractatum hunc, pro panis et vini substantiæ existentia in cœna Domini a christiano lectore postulo, ut nos et hanc causam quam in nos defendendam suscepimus ad amussim et regulam sacrorum librorum et veterum patrum scripta examinet, probet, et judicet; et si in hac causa non aliter loquimur quam sacræ scripturæ et sancti patres loquuntur, non pro hæreticis, sed pro iis qui non aliter loquuntur quam Spiritus Sanctus suggerit, impellit, et docet nos loqui, habeamur. Jesus Christus enim, Filius Dei vivi, panem quem tenebat sacris manibus corpus suum appellavit; vinum quod discipulis in cœna impertivit sanguinem suum vocavit. Spiritus Sanctus in divo Paulo corpus Christi panem, et panem corpus Christi, quinquies nominavit. Patres vero sub initium ecclesiæ panem et vinum in cœna Domini corporis et sanguinis Christi nomine honorabant, quemadmodum audistis.

Idem et nos facimus: utrumque nomen panis et corporis, vini et sanguinis, retinemus in sacratissima Domini cœna; illorum substantiam in Christum Deum et hominem non extollentes, nec illorum usum ut sacramenta et mysteria corporis et sanguinis Christi deprimentes: qua in parte, quoad nomina signorum et signatorum, nihil a Spiritu Sancto et usitato modo loquendi in scripturis sanctis dissentimus. Sumus igitur, judice Spiritu Sancto in sacris literis nobiscum pronunciante, absolvendi ab omni schismatis et erroris suspicione et culpa. Deinde, quod panis et vini substantiam in cœna Domini una cum illorum nominibus semper retinemus, id etiam cum Spiritu Sancto in sacris literis et scriptis patrum facimus: Christus enim et nomen et substantiam panis in cœna retinet, dicendo, "Hoc est corpus meum." Quantum ergo ad substantiam elementi, panis erat: quantum ad memoriæ et sacramenti mortis Christi mysterium, corpus Christi erat. In substantia vero panis erat: in memoria et mysterio autem corpus Christi erat. Idem Christus pronunciat de calice, dicendo, "Non bibam posthac ex hoc fructu vitis, donec bibam illud novum in regno Patris mei." Quoad substantiam, vinum et fructus vini erat in mystico calice: quoad mysteria et sacramentum mortis Christi, sanguis erat Christi. Sic etiam Paulus, quoad substantiam, panem frangebat in cœna sacra: quoad sacramentum et mysteria, panis communio erat corporis Christi. Patres idem testantur: quoad substantiam, panis creatura est secundum nos, ut inquit Irenæus; quoad mysteria et sacramentum, corpus Christi est. Quoad substantiam, panis et vinum sunt; sed quoad usum, mysterium, et sacramentum, figuræ sunt, symbola, obsignacula, et ἀντίτυπα veri corporis et sanguinis Christi, ut omnes veteres testantur. Quoad substantiam, panis et vinum sunt; sed quoad mysteria et res significatas, sunt gratia corporis et sanguinis Christi, ut Basilius Magnus dicit.

Quid ergo peccavimus, quid commeruimus, nomina et rem ipsam panis et vini retinendo in sacra Domini cœna? Nonne Christus, Paulus, et omnes veteres idem faciunt? Si illi ergo veritatem Dei et naturam sacramentorum agnoscebant, et nos agnoscimus. Nam quod dicimus et credimus ipsi prius ante nos dixerunt et crediderunt: sint illorum libri judices inter nos et neotericos, Christi ac nostri implacabiles hostes. Judicet jam æquus lector an liceat Christiano, relictis Christo, apostolis, evangelistis, et sanctis patribus, neotericis istis consentire et subscribere, qui et nomina et substantias panis et vini in eucharistia abhorrent et perimunt. Nam quod Christus, evangelistæ, apostoli, et sancti patres panem et vinum vocant, ipsi nova, ficta, et ementita voce transubstantiationis elementorum inducta (Christo, apostolis, evangelistis, et sanctis patribus nunquam audita), panis et vini accidentia vocant. Hoc autem illis polliceor, quod si ostenderint ex sacris literis vel scriptis priscorum patrum intra 600 annos post Christi assumptionem in cœlos, vel nomina tantum transubstantiationis elementorum panis et vini in substantiam corporis et sanguinis Christi in cœna Domini; vel quod sub involucris et accidentibus panis et vini lateant corpus et sanguis Christi, quemadmodum antea dixi nunc dico, illorum subscribam judicio et sententiæ. Sed nos scimus, et ipsi non sunt inscii, quod hæc puerilia, papistica, et ementita nuper sunt introducta in ecclesiam per Romanos pontifices, qui non solum Christi instituta in ecclesia permutarunt, verum etiam totius Romani imperii et status christianorum principum legesque omnes violaverunt et contempserunt; et seipsos non solum hominum, verum etiam Dei ac illius verbi, judices fecerunt: ut illorum lex testatur, quæ incipit, "Si Papa."

Meminerimus ergo ea observare quæ a Christo nobis præscribuntur, et eo modo quo nobis ab eo sunt tradita; nec nova ex nostro pectore cudamus, nec ab aliis excusa curemus. Deus enim Saddai[1] ipse est Deus noster: sequemur ergo illum, et felices perpetuo (quamvis ad tempus afflicti) erimus. Judicent itaque pii an æquum sit, ut neoterici, qui peregrinas voces et nova vocabula finxerunt (nempe transubstantiationem panis et vini, et corporis et sanguinis Christi præsentiam realem et corporalem sub formis et accidentibus panis et vini latitantem), judices ac censores sacrarum scripturarum constituantur; an vero ut divinis literis et sanctorum patrum testimoniis subjiciantur. Sed utri parti tutius, sanctius, et melius nos ipsos concredere possimus, sanctarum scripturarum et veterum patrum testimoniis, an neotericorum mendaciis et figmentis, facile est cuivis Spiritu Christi prædito dijudicare: sacrorum enim librorum auctoritas omnibus, cum veteribus, tum neotericis, est præponenda: veteres vero neotericis sunt præferendi. Sed

Neotericorum nova vocabula.

[1 From the Hebrew שַׁדַּי, Almighty.]

schola neotericorum auctoritatem in sacras literas et in omnes patres usurpat; ita ut utrumque pro suo arbitrio interpretentur; et sensum quem neoterici ex scripturis sanctis et priscis patribus eliciunt scripturis ipsis et sanctis patribus præferunt; quod est impiissimum. Nam sensum ac mentem Spiritus Sancti, quam in sacris literis semper quærere ecclesia Christi deberet, suis interpretationibus subjiciunt; et ubi per verbum Dei jubemur omnium spirituum dogmata probare, neoterici verbum Dei et sanctorum patrum scripta per illorum calculum et interpretationem probari contendunt. Ideoque in ecclesiis quæ a Christo et Spiritu ejus Sancto mandantur et docentur negliguntur et contemnuntur; et quæ a neotericis imperantur et docentur omnes amplectuntur et venerantur. Et hoc est Christum in ecclesiis propulsare, et antichristum erigere; mandata divina in sacramentorum usu contemnere, et mandata hominum venerari et colere: ut in sacra cœna Domini superius ostendi; ubi nunc in ecclesiis quæ tyrannidi papæ subjiciuntur non solum verus usus sacræ Dominicæ cœnæ exulat, verum etiam vera et legitima cœnæ Domini doctrina expellitur. Dominus igitur et Deus Pater noster cœlestis in Christo Jesu pro sua immensa misericordia ecclesias suas a lupis et mercenariis liberet, et det illis veros pastores, qui gregem Christi tam misere dissipatum colligere studeant ad sanctæ et apostolicæ ecclesiæ veritatem, ut sub Spiritu Christi Sancto pusillus grex pascatur pabulo vitæ æternæ. Amen.

Capitis primi finis.

CAPUT II.

Contra corporalem Christi præsentiam in eucharistia.

Secundum caput in quo a neotericis dissentimus consistit in hoc: illi corporalem corporis et sanguinis Christi præsentiam in cœna Domini affirmant: nos tantum spiritualem et sacramentalem corporis et sanguinis Christi præsentiam in cœna Domini agnoscimus, credimus, docemus, et confitemur; corporalem vero Christi præsentiam tantum cœlo tribuimus ad dextram patris omnipotentis, unde illum spe exspectamus, ut judicet vivos et mortuos. Et usque ad illud tempus restaurationis omnium, cum sacris literis, tum sanctorum patrum testimoniis, et communi symbolo, quod vulgo symbolum apostolorum vocatur, edocti, carnem Christi e nostra carne assumptam in cœlo collocamus. Nam Christus post quadraginta dies, devicta mortis et inferni tyrannide, illam carnem a nobis receptam in altum subduxit, ut amplius in terra locum non habeat.

Rationes quibus movemur, ut a neotericis hac in parte dissentiamus.

Christus, ut suos discipulos de morte sua jam imminente consolaretur, non solum promisit se tertio die a morte resurrecturum, et mortis imperium et tyrannidem destructurum; verum etiam, quod a morte corpus suum gloriosum a terra elevaret in cœlum, [et][1] relictis hujus mundi sedibus cœlestem inhabitaret orbem, donec dies ille adveniret quo cum magna gloria descenderet judicaturus vivos et mortuos. Verba illius sunt hæc: "Exivi a Patre, et veni in mundum: iterum relinquo mundum, et vado ad Patrem." Relinquere autem mundum, et ire ad Patrem, non solum est humani corporis infirmitates a resurrectione deponere, et immortalitatem induere; sed etiam carnem immortalitate donatam, quam mortalem et infirmam in utero sacræ virginis e nostra carne assumpsit, a terris in cœlum subducere: ut, quemadmodum in cruce mundus a carne Christi crudeliter vitam eripuit, ita et ipse a resurrectione post quadraginta dies eandem, per mundum vita spoliatam, vivam et immortalem e mundo in altos cœlos gloriose subtraheret.

Prima probatio hujus assertionis.

Christus dicebat se relicturum mundum; et, ut majorem certitudinem sui abitus animis discipulorum infigeret, ante mortem, quasi jam jam hoc esset facturus, dixit, "Relinquo mundum." Relinquere mundum est a mundo recedere, a mundo abesse, et in alium locum extra mundum se conferre atque locare. Relinquere autem mundum non est seipsum invisibilem reddere, et modo invisibili esse in mundo: nam qui invisibilis vel modo invisibili adest non abest; et qui non abest a mundo mundum non reliquit. Si igitur Christus, quantum ad corporis illius veri et organici præsentiam, mundum impleret; vel invisibilis et modo invisibili aliquot loca, ubi panes in sacra cœna consecrantur, corporaliter occuparet; falsum esset dicere, Christum mundum reliquisse: nam

[1 The conjunction seems to be required here.]

qui corpore est præsens in aliquo loco non abest ab eo loco. Cogimur ergo, si volumus esse pii, dicere, Christum, quoad ejus humanitatem, reliquisse mundum. Et postquam desiit corpore esse in mundo, tum efficacissime adfuit suo Spiritu; aderitque suæ ecclesiæ omnibus diebus, usque ad consummationem seculi. Nos igitur Christi verbis muniti fideliter ac constantissime credimus Christum, quoad humanitatem, hunc mundum reliquisse.

Secunda probatio hujus assertionis.

"Pauperes (inquit Christus) semper habebitis vobiscum; me autem non semper habebitis." Me, inquit Christus, non habebitis. Quoad ejus humanitatem hæc intelligi oportet, quod illum in mundo nobiscum habere non possumus; sed quoad divinam ejus naturam nusquam abest: "In ipso enim vivimus, movemur, et sumus;" et præterea per prophetam inquit, "Cœlum et terram ego impleo, dicit Dominus." His autem Christi verbis, "me non semper habebitis vobiscum," compellimur ejus corporis præsentiam a nobis abesse fateri, nisi Christum mendacii arguere velimus; quod absit: ipse enim est "via, veritas, et vita." Non sunt igitur audiendi contra Christum qui dicunt ipsum corporaliter adesse, et corporaliter exhiberi in sacra cœna Domini per ministros ecclesiæ; nec decet fidum et verum Christi ministrum id affirmare quod Christus negat. Hæc sunt verba negativa Christi, "Me non semper habebitis vobiscum." Injuriam ergo faciunt Christo qui dicunt nos Christum, quod ad corpus ejus attinet, habere. Verba autem negativa Christi sunt perpendenda, ne fraude interpretationum neotericorum eludantur. Non dixit Christus, me sub hac forma, mole, vel quantitate corporis non habebitis; vel, me qualiter videtis nunc non habebitis; vel, qualiter me interfecturi sunt Judæi non habebitis, verum modo invisibili, supernaturali, cœlesti, non vero corporali aut locali modo, ut neoterici dicunt; sed de corpore suo simpliciter et aperte dixit, "Me non habebitis;" hoc est, me, quantum ad humani corporis præsentiam attinet, non habebitis. Quare et nos religiose ac vere dicimus, quicquid neoterici (Christi ac ejus verborum correctores) in contrarium oggannient et latrent. Cum Christo vero nostro capite loquimur et credimus, "me non habebitis;" cujus præsentia et fruitione gloriosissima satiabimur, ubi hanc mortalem vitam deposueri-

Matt. xxvi.

Christus, quoad divinam naturam, ubique est: sed, quoad humanam, in uno loco esse oportet.

mus. Interim satis est quod fide illo satiemur, quem spe exspectamus, ut tandem facie ad faciem illum videamus.

Probatio tertia hujus nostræ assertionis.

"Si quis (inquit Christus) dixerit, Ecce hic, ecce illic est Christus, nolite credere." Rursus admonet suos Christus, ut ne credant, imo ne cogitent, eum corpore adesse huic mundo: quicunque enim (inquit) locum, sive hic sive illic, corpori meo assignaverint, nolite credere. Qui ergo Christum supra caput sacerdotis, vel intra ejus manus, aut in pixide denotant, assignant, et demonstrant, gravissime peccant, hoc mandatum Christi "nolite credere" contemnentes; et tandem hujus mandati violationem infernalibus flammis (nisi resipuerint) luent in perpetuum. Et revera Christus Salvator noster, quoad corpus ejus jam gloriosum, nec sursum nec deorsum per manus hominum jam agitari, moveri, nec elevari potest; sed, ut dixi, cœlum gloriose obtinet, et terram (hoc est fidelium mentes) sursum suo Spiritu elevat, ut superna quæramus et curemus, et non terrestria. Nostræ autem mentes, dum hic vivimus, a peccati maculis et rerum caducarum nimio amore elevantur, ut æterna agnoscant et amplectantur: et tandem etiam corpora nostra convivificabit, ut sint conformia corpori suo glorioso. Illius autem Spiritu nos movemur et sumus: sed ejus corpus movere non possumus. Ideo caute et diligenter præmonuit ecclesiam, ut ab hujusmodi insaniis et præstigiis caveret.

Probatio quarta nostræ assertionis.

Marc. xvi.
Rom. viii.

"Itaque Dominus, postquam loquutus esset eis, receptus est in cœlis, et consedit a dextris Dei." Idem dicit et divus Paulus: "Qui et suscitatus est, qui etiam est ad dextram Dei," etc. Ubi vero Christus sæpius admonuisset suos, ne crederent corporalem ejus præsentiam futuram super terram; et si quis id affirmaret ac assereret dicendo, ecce hic, ecce illic, non esse ei credendum; et cum verbis non obscuris docuisset, quod pauperes secum semper haberent, sed non ipsum; et præterea palam dixisset, "Ego relinquo mundum;" jam ne admonitio et doctrina ejus de abitu suo parum animis eorum insideret, admonitionem et doctrinam suam confirmat actu et ipsa corporis ablatione non solum a terris, verum etiam ab illorum aspectibus, quibus illum ad nubes usque prosequebantur: ut Marcus evangelista et Paulus apostolus liquido testantur. "Receptus est, inquit Marcus, in cœlum." Heb. iv. ix. Et alio in loco Paulus dicit, quod Christus penetravit cœlos. Et iterum: "Non enim in manu facta sancta ingressus est Christus," etc. Ex istis vero locis admonemur, ut duo credamus: primum, quod Christus, quantum ad carnem, mundum reliquit; secundum, quod carnem, quam in mundo assumpsit, in cœlo collocavit; ita ut jam, quoad carnem, Christus ubi factus fuit homo non sit; et in cœlo, ubi prius non erat quoad carnem, jam (relicta terra) resideat: quemadmodum alii loci sacræ scripturæ testantur.

5. *Probatio nostræ assertionis.*

"Qui consedit ad dextram throni majestatis in cœlis." Marc. xvi. Heb. viii. x. Et iterum: "Perpetuo sedet ad dextram Dei." Christus, ut corporalem sui absentiam ab hoc mundo suis discipulis persuaderet, variis ac gravissimis usus fuit argumentis. Primum, jussit ut non crederent iis qui dicerent, Ecce hic, ecce illic est Christus: secundum, quod pauperes cum illis semper haberent, sed ipsum non haberent: tertium, quod relinqueret mundum, et iret ad Patrem. Jam vero ne quis de illius orationis veritate, quam de abitu suo sæpius cum discipulis habuit, dubitaret, adest tempus quo id præstaret factum quod hactenus verbis prædixit. "Receptus est (inquit Marcus) in cœlum." Et ne quis putaret phantasma aut spectrum fuisse quod in cœlos ascendit, S. Lucas in Actis Apostolorum modum et certitudinem Christi ascensionis fidelissime annotat et nobis commendat. "Cum essent (inquit) defixis in cœlum oculis, eunte illo, ecce viri duo astiterunt illis amicti vestibus albis, qui et dixerunt, Viri Galilæi, quid statis intuentes in cœlum? Hic Jesus, qui assumptus est a vobis in cœlum, sic veniet quemadmodum vidistis eum euntem in cœlum." Duo docet S. Evangelista: primum, quod vere et visibiliter Jesus ascenderit; quod et angeli cœlestes et oculi discipulorum testantur: deinde, quod eodem visibili modo venturus sit in extremi temporis articulo. Et donec dies ille advenerit, cœlum et non terra Christum, quoad humanitatem, servabit ac retinebit: ut quemadmodum ante ascensionem Christus juxta humanitatem suam tantum erat in terra, et non in cœlo; ita post resurrectionem juxta carnem suam tantum sit in cœlo, et non in terra.

6. *Probatio hujus assertionis.*

Act. iii.

"Illum oportet cœlum suscipere usque ad tempus restaurationis omnium." Petrus de Christo (quatenus homo est) loquitur: quem juxta carnem oportet cœlum suscipere usque ad novissimam diem. Petrus autem non dicit, quod cœlum suscipiet illum quantum ad formam ejus visibilem et corporis ejus dimensiones, quantitates, et qualitates, sed in terris erit secundum carnem forma invisibili et modo non quantitativo, vel erit in eucharistia non ut in loco, non corporali modo, ut neoterici misere et pueriliter dicunt: sed Lucas claris et evidentissimis verbis testatur, quod Christus terras reliquit, et nubes suscepit illum ab oculis eorum; et Petrus lucidissime dicit hunc Jesum qui assumptus est in cœlum, oportere cœlum suscipere usque ad tempus restaurationis omnium.

7. *Probatio hujus assertionis.*

Act. iii.

"Quemadmodum vidistis illum euntem in cœlum, sic veniet." S. Lucas ut omnem suspicionem corporalis Christi præsentiæ ab ecclesia tolleret, dicit, quod quemadmodum vidistis illum euntem in cœlum, ita veniet; hoc est, eadem visibili forma. Duo saluberrima dogmata in hisce verbis continentur: unum, de Christi Salvatoris nostri corporis e terris elevatione et ablatione; alterum vero de ejus corporis adventu in novissimo

Act. iii.

die; usque in quem diem et horam nunquam terris corpore aderit, ut Petrus testatur.

8. *Probatio hujus assertionis.*

1 Cor. xi.

"Mortem Domini annunciate, donec venerit." Duo D. Paulus hisce verbis ecclesiam Christi docet: primum, quod sacra cœna Domini sit recordatio et memoria mortis et passionis Christi; nam (inquit) quoties cœna rite celebratur, mors Christi, qua a morte æterna sumus redempti, ob oculos mentis et fidei nostræ ponitur: secundum, Christum ipsum, cujus mortem per cœnam hanc exprimimus, re ipsa corpore cœnæ suæ non adesse. Dicit enim, "Donec venerit." Quasi diceret, quamvis miranda et ineffabilis futura sit persecutio et tyrannis in ecclesia Christi, dum Christus corpore ab ecclesia abest residens in cœlis, talis est tamen Dei amor et $\phi\iota\lambda\alpha\nu\theta\rho\omega\pi\iota\alpha$ erga suam ecclesiam, ut usque ad Filii ejus in corpore adventum duratura sit vera ecclesia, ut inter electos Christi mors semper vigeat et refricetur. Quod si Christus corporaliter adesset sacræ cœnæ, ut neoterici Romani docent, Paulus non diceret, "mortem Domini annunciate donec venerit;" sed, mortem Domini annunciate, quia, quoties cœnam sanctificatis, toties Christus corpore suo adest. Quid autem desiderent neoterici apertius, contra corporalem Christi præsentiam in cœna, quam hoc quod Paulus dicit, "donec venerit?" "Donec" hoc loco indicat tempus futurum quo Christus corpore venturus est, et non præsens tempus quo nunc adest quoties sacra cœna peragitur, vel aliquot verba a ministris recitantur.

Nona probatio hujus assertionis.

"Superna quærite, ubi Christus est ad dextram Dei Colos. iii. sedens." Jubemur per D. Paulum superna quærere, quia superne Christus est quoad corporis ejus præsentiam: quo autem ad divinam ejus naturam ubique est, et ima summaque implens, ut propheta testatur. "Quo ibo (inquit) a spiritu [Psal. tuo, et quo a facie tua fugiam? Si ascendero in cœlum, tu cxxxix.] illic es: si descendero ad infernum, ades," etc. Ne igitur cum neotericis Romanis πανταχουσίαν, hoc est, ubiquitatem illius corporis constituamus. Paulus unum locum (nempe sedes beatas et cœlestes) nobis corpori Christi assignat; ubi Christus corpore suo solum residet superne (inquit) et non inferne. Viderint isti neoterici, qui corpus Christi ita distendunt et dilatant ut cœlos et terras impleat, quomodo Christo (qui dixit quod mundum relinqueret, quod ad ejus humanitatem spectat) et Paulo (qui per adverbium loci, "ubi," tantum cœlo superne corpus Christi tribuit) respondeant. Viderint, inquam, quomodo in novissimo illo calamitatis et miseriæ die Christo respondeant, qui jam ipsum, quod ad humanitatem ejus attinet, παντότοπον faciunt, hoc est, omnem locum implentem; cœlum corporali modo et veris corporis organici dimensionibus; terras vero absque omnibus veri corporis conditionibus et qualitatibus. Duplicem autem Christum faciunt; verum hominem suis qualitatibus imbutum in cœlis, monstrum vero hominis in terris absque omnibus qualitatibus et conditionibus hominis.

Decima probatio nostræ assertionis.

"Quid si videritis Filium hominis ascendentem ubi erat Joan. vi. prius?" Capernaitæ (ut nostri neoterici) carnis Christi manducationem dentibus oris somniabant. Christus autem multis ac sanctissimis rationibus illam comestionem ad fidem et mentem hominis referebat, ut Joannes, cap. vi. testatur; et inter alias rationes hanc tanquam epilogum omnium aliarum præcedentium adduxit: "quid si videritis (inquit) Filium hominis ascendentem ubi erat prius?"—ac si dixisset, Quid de ventre aut dente cogitatis, quasi meam carnem manducandam, devorandam, aut concoquendam dentibus, stomacho, aut ventri donarem? Aliud est genus manducandæ carnis meæ quod volo, nempe mentale et spirituale; non per dentes, sed per fidem, quæ hominis mentem sursum in cœlum attrahit, quo ego hoc corpus quod videtis sustollam; ubi tantum fuerit loci spatium inter me et vos quantum est inter cœlum et terram. Quomodo igitur ii qui terras incolunt corpus assumptum et locatum in cœlis ore et dentibus assumerent? Fide autem eo veniendum est, non pedibus: ibi fide corpus meum est manducandum, et non hic in terris ore et dentibus. Nescio quid neotericorum oculos aperiat, ut veritatem hac in parte perspiciant, nisi hæc sacræ scripturæ loca illud fecerint: quod ut faciant, Deum Patrem nostrum cœlestem propter Jesum Christum Filium ejus sedulo noctesque diesque fatigo.

Undecima probatio nostræ assertionis.

"Spiritus est qui vivificat; caro non prodest quicquam." Christus nostræ redemptionis τὸ λύτρον et pretium persolvebat in carne; et nunc dicit illam carnem non prodesse, si accipi deberet ut Capernaitæ carnem Christi accipiebant; cogitabant enim carnem Christi omnino corporaliter esse manducandam: Christus igitur dixit carnem suam ita corporaliter manducatam nihil prodesse. Et hac gravissima oratione Christus Capernaitarum stultitiam mire perstringit et reprehendit: primum, quod adeo stulti essent ut cogitarent humanam carnem esse comedendam; quod multo crudelius esset quam humanam carnem occidere: deinde, quod tam imprudentes essent ut vel ipsi id optarent, vel[1] quod ipse Christus id faceret quod nihil prodesset. Quare inquit, Quid vel vos expectatis quod vobis non prodest; vel quid me inutilem nuncium Patris cœlestis cogitatis? Ideo autem veni, ut mundo prodessem et benefacerem: sed si carnem meam corporaliter (ut vos putatis) vobis comedendam imper-

[1 *Cogitarent* appears to be wanting to complete the sense.]

tirem, ego ipse bene novi quod caro mea ita comesta nihil vobis prodesset. Ergo hoc intelligite, quod caro mea est occidenda; quam si quis fide et spiritu manducat, non morietur in æternum. Sic autem caro mea est cibus mentis, non ventris: fide suscipitur, non ore. Nam carnem meam a mundo in cœlum extollam; quo oportet qui velit meam carnem manducare et sanguinem meum bibere fide ascendere. Qui vero humi jacent, et crassam atque corporalem præsentiam mei corporis cogitant, nihil fructus aut utilitatis inde percipiunt. Hic apud Joannem duobus validissimis argumentis corporalem corporis sui præsentiam in sacra Domini cœna Christus pernegat (non dico, in impia Romana missa, quia nec Christus nec Christi sacramentum est, sed idolum et belphegor[2]). Hoc autem primum probat argumento ab inutili hisce verbis: "Caro (scilicet, corporaliter comesta, ut vos cogitatis) non prodest quicquam:" deinde, ab impossibili hisce verbis: "Quid si videritis Filium hominis ascendentem eo ubi erat prius?" hoc est, in cœlum; quo fides sola pii hominis ascendit, ut Filium Dei Patri cœlesti sistat quotidie pro remissione peccatorum suorum; in quem locum caro et sanguis non penetrant, quamdiu hoc mundo fruuntur."

Duodecima probatio nostræ assertionis.

"Cum domi sumus in corpore, peregrinamur a Domino." 2 Cor. v.
Domi esse in corpore est hac vita, quæ miseriis et calamitatibus variis jacet obnoxia et afflicta, frui. Peregrinari autem a Domino est, non solum æterna beatitudine et felicitate ad tempus carere, dum hic vivitur; verum etiam corporis illius præsentia carere qui morte sua cœlos et immortales glorias nobis meruit. Tendimus autem ac contendimus, ut post hanc vitam in cœlis cum eo vitam degamus, qui per mortem suam non solum mortem exuit, verum etiam mortalium hominum secula deseruit, et immortale suum corpus a nostro consortio subduxit in cœlos; ut ipse a nobis, et nos ab ipso, ad tempus peregrinaremur, ut Paulus inquit. Quatenus autem Christus Deus est, ab eo non peregrinamur: nam piis semper sua providentia et gratia præsens est, et piorum conversatio in cœlis est, ut Paulus inquit; impiis vero sua providentia et justitia, vel ut emendet vel puniat, absens non est. Si hanc peregrinationem neoterici intelligere volunt liberationem ab

[² Probably from the Hebrew בַּעַל פְּעוֹר Baal-Peor.]

omni calamitatum et afflictionum perturbatione et sensu, perperam D. Paulum torquent. Nam dum peregrinamur a Domino, et maximis calamitatibus afficimur pro illius nomine, maximam illius gratiæ et fortitudinis abundantiam præsentem esse sentimus; ita ut ejus Spiritus præsentia quæ jam patimur non solum contemnamus, verum etiam gravissima et periculosissima quæ ventura esse putamus in Christo non curemus: quod fieri non posset, si hospites et peregrini essemus a Domino Deo nostro, qui nos consolatur in omni tribulatione nostra; ita ut non solum patienter, verum etiam gratanter, omnia feramus. Hostes enim et adversarios patienter ferimus, et illorum salutem æque Deo ut nostram sedulo dies ac noctes commendamus: Deo perpetuas canimus laudes, quod nos dignetur pro sui nominis gloria aliquid pati: et tantum rogamus in nostris precibus, ut vel vincat illius verbi veritas quæ opprimitur, vel nos per mortem cito ad se revocet. Nam satis diu nos vixisse putamus, si in hac vita neotericorum idololatriam fortiter usque ad mortem contemnamus: quod facturi sumus Deo protegente, qui magna sua misericordia nos primum eripuit per Christum e morte æterna; deinde, ab hæreticorum et papistarum impia doctrina; et transtulit nos in lucem claritatis suæ, quam nunquam expungi patietur iis qui illam in verbo suo studiose precibus quærunt.

Decimatertia probatio nostræ assertionis.

oan. xvi.

"Ecce aperte loqueris, nec proverbium ullum dicis." Postquam Christus dixisset, "Relinquo mundum et vado ad Patrem," apostoli dicebant illum aperte fuisse loquutum, nec proverbium ullum protulisse. Aperte autem loqui est ita rem de qua agitur clare et perspicue enunciare et proferre, ut ab iis quibus res commendatur absque omni dubitatione, hæsitatione, et ambiguitate intelligatur et cognoscatur. Sic Christum fuisse loquutum de ejus abitu ex hoc mundo ad Patrem discipuli ejus testantur hisce verbis, "Ecce aperte loqueris:" quasi dixissent, satis lucide intelligimus quæ dicis et doces, quod abiturus es a mundo. Jam neoterici Romani, quæ Christus aperte et lucide protulit, suis technis, vafritiis, imposturis, et præstigiis obfuscant et obumbrant; ut nec veritas nec perspicuitas verborum Christi intelligi aut percipi possint. Ubi enim Christus liquido dicit, "Relinquo mundum," quod omnes discipuli (quamvis rudes et satis adhuc carnales) perspicue intellexerunt, neoterici dicunt quod non reliquit mundum; hoc est, non penitus abstulit corpus suum ex hoc mundo, sed invisibilem se fecit mundo, et modo invisibili mundo semper adest, ac in mundo se continet, ad quatuor vel quinque verborum prolationem per presbyterum in papistica missa; et modo visibili residet, ac se juxta corpus continet in cœlo: juxta veras corporis sui qualitates et quantitates corporaliter cœlum occupat; juxta autem corpus quod nullas humanas conditiones habet corporaliter cœnam Domini occupat, ac in ea continetur. Visibile corpus Christi corporaliter locant in cœlis: invisibile vero Christi corpus corporaliter docent esse in eucharistia. Sed hoc non est aperte et liquido, sed obscure et ænigmatice loqui. Christus autem nullum משל, quod est proverbium, dixit. Proverbium enim est quod non facile ab omnibus intelligitur, vel quia verba ex quibus constat sunt rara, inusitata, aut variæ significationis; vel quia talem in se proverbium continet eruditionem et doctrinam, ut raro vel difficulter comprehendamus: quemadmodum sunt sententiæ Salomonis, quas משלי, id est, proverbia, vocat; in quibus non solum sunt multa difficilia verba, verum etiam sententiæ quam plurimæ intellectu admodum difficiles. Christi autem oratio quam habuit ad suos de discessu corporis sui e terris, quæ erat ista, "Exivi a Patre, et veni in mundum; iterum relinquo mundum, et vado ad Patrem," nihil ambiguitatis, difficultatis, vel obscuritatis (ut apostoli testantur) in se habuit; sed palam et aperte quæ fuerunt dicta in hac oratione de corporis ejus recessu intellexerunt. Parum igitur candide et minus Christiane faciunt neoterici, qui perspicuitati et lumini verborum Christi suis interpretationibus tenebras et nebulas obfundunt.

Nos igitur perspicuitatem et lucem verbi divini assequentes Christum (quod ad carnem ejus attinet) mundum reliquisse docemus et credimus; Spiritu tamen suo tam bonos quam malos sustentare; hos quidem, ut pie vivant; illos autem, ut impie vivere desistant. Et in sacra actione cœnæ suæ mysticæ piis ita semper adest, ut illis seipsum totum tum corpore tum anima communicet; non ut in corpus per os descendat, sed ut in animam per fidem sese infundat, ejusque vi et virtute cum corpus tum anima pie recipientis sacramentum sanctificentur ad vitam æternam; modo non secundum carnem, sed secundum Spiritum, qui se Christo sacramentis obstrinxere vivant et ambulent. Hæc est nostræ fidei ratio ex sacris literis deducta, rata, et obsignata, quam veram ac sinceram coram Deo et sanctis angelis ejus ex verbo Dei scimus, agnoscimus, tutamur, et defendimus; pro qua vitam hanc mortalem deponere (si ita Deo visum fuerit) sumus parati; certo persuasi quod animas nostras sic deponendo bene facturi simus, et cum Christo per Christum victuri imperpetuum. Jam ad alias rationes quibus movemur ut a neotericis dissentiamus descendam.

Decimaquarta probatio nostræ assertionis.

<small>ebræ. ii. iv.</small> "Similis est fratribus per omnia excepto peccato." Si Christus similis sit fratribus per omnia, juxta D. Pauli testimonium, injuriam faciunt Christo qui illum dissimilem fra- <small>imilem esse atribus uid.</small> tribus reddunt. Similem esse fratribus est, non solum carnis sanguinisque et animæ fratrum naturis et substantiis communicare, verum etiam illarum veras qualitates, quantitates, et dimensiones naturæ et substantiæ fratrum semper retinere et nunquam deponere: quod si deposuerit, tunc desinit esse similis fratribus. Jam talis est nostra natura et substantia, ut semper locum occupet; et dum in uno loco fuerit, pro eodem temporis instanti in alio loco esse non possit: ut natura et <small>Reg. ii.</small> substantia corporis Eliæ, dum esset in terris et hæc loca inferiora mundi teneret, in cœlis non agebat, nec turbine ab Elisæo fuit ablatus; et ubi Elias ascendit turbine in cœlum, cernente Elisæo et ita clamante, "O pater, pater, Israelitarum currus et equites," in terris cum Elisæo tunc desiit esse. Talis autem est natura et conditio omnis seminis Abrahæ, ut semper unum locum pro uno temporis instanti occupet; ita ut simul et eodem tempore diversa loca occupare non possit. Cum Christus juxta carnem ab Abrahami semine assumptam similis sit fratribus, ut qui veras, nativas, et genuinas conditiones et naturas humani corporis retineat, oportet ut eisdem naturæ legibus constringatur et contineatur (quod ad humanitatem ejus spectat), ut sit in uno loco pro uno temporis instanti, et, dum superna et cœlestia loca occupat, a terrenis et inferioribus absit; quemadmodum, dum terras hasce incoleret, a supernis sedibus abfuit. Ita quoad corporis ejus veritatem et substantiam simul cœlum et terram implere vel occupare non possit, quin fratribus statim futurus dissimilis. Quod si corporis ejus naturam et substantiam, quam ex Abrahami semine Christus in utero beatæ virginis assumpsit, ita extendat ac dilatet, ut cœlum et terram simul impleat vel occupet, naturam

et conditionem seminis Abrahæ exuit ac deponit, nec (ut dixi) fratribus similis est. Nam hominis non est nec angelorum naturæ, sed solius Dei, duos simul vel occupare, vel omnes simul locos implere. Hominum vero et angelorum est, ut, quando uni loco adsunt, ab aliis pro eodem temporis instanti absint: ut Christus, cum esset juxta carnem trans Jordanem, ubi Joannes fuerat baptizans primum, non erat Bethaniæ, ubi Lazarus erat mortuus, ut ipsemet testatur: "Et gaudeo propter vos, ut credatis, quod non fuerim ibi." Ita cum esset juxta carnem in monte Tabor, non erat Hierosolymis; et cum esset in terris, non erat juxta carnem in cœlis: et jam cum sit in cœlis, non est juxta carnem in terris. Cum igitur Christus Deus sit et homo, et, quatenus Deus, retineat et nunquam deponat veri Dei substantiam et naturam, ut sit et maneat in perpetuum verus Deus, similis Patri et Spiritui Sancto; ita cum sit verus homo, quatenus est homo, retinet et nunquam deponit veri hominis substantiam et naturam, ut sit et maneat imperpetuum verus homo, similis fratribus, juxta D. Pauli doctrinam.

Joan. x. xi.

Matt. xvii.

Nam Christus Salvator noster, verus Deus verus et homo in una persona, in hac unitate personæ naturas et substantias veri Dei et veri hominis semper retinet ac servat: et quamvis natura humana assumpta sit in Deum, ut unam personam Christi Dei et hominis constituat; Christi tamen Deitas humanæ naturæ substantiam et veritatem non absorpsit, non annihilavit, non destruxit, non confudit, neque commiscuit: sed utriusque substantiæ et naturæ veritas, tum Dei tum hominis, in Christi persona manet semper discreta et distincta, nec una in alteram convertitur; nec præstantior et dignior natura in Christo (nempe Dei) minorem et inferiorem (nimirum hominis) destruit, consumit, aut in naturæ divinæ conditionem, proprietatem, aut dignitatem mutat vel convertit. Et juxta divinæ suæ naturæ veritatem (quatenus est similis Deo Patri) nobis in terris adesse confitemur; sed juxta humanæ naturæ certitudinem (quatenus similis est fratribus) nobis in terris adesse credere non possumus. Nam ita Deus et homo in una persona Christi conjunguntur, ut neutra natura veritatem suam amittat, nec alterius proprietates et conditiones altera induat, sustineat, aut vindicet. Cum enim solus natura esset Deus, ut homo fieret, divinitatem suam in carnem non convertit; sed per assumptionem humanitatis in Deum Deus factus est homo.

Et quemadmodum in terris humanam naturam mortalem assumpsit in Deum, et tamen mortalis naturæ humanæ conditionem non destruxit, nec divinæ naturæ adæquavit, sed utrique naturæ, Dei et hominis, semper suas servavit conditiones et qualitates (excepto peccato), ut Christus, quatenus homo, juxta naturam divinam in cœlis esset et in terris; juxta naturam humanam in terris esset et non in cœlis: ita et a resurrectione a mortuis tertio die veram humanam naturam jam factam immortalem semper servavit, et tandem in cœlos a terra sustulit, ut jam in cœlis Deus fieret et homo, ubi ante solus Deus erat; et in terris usque ad consummationis tempus Deus tantum esset (sublata corporis sui substantia) ubi ante Deus erat et homo. Ita sicuti post incarnationis suæ mysterium in utero virginis in terris egit juxta utriusque naturæ, divinitatis et humanitatis, substantiam, virtutem, et efficaciam; pari modo jam post illius ascensionem in cœlos in terris agit juxta divinitatis substantiam et humanitatis (per divinitatem) efficaciam (hoc est, Spiritu suo), et non substantiam. Nam quemadmodum nostra conversatio per Spiritum Sanctum in cœlis est, unde expectamus Redemptorem nostrum, qui reformabit corpora nostra, ut sint conformia corpori suo glorioso; et tamen quoad corporis nostri substantiam in terris deorsum solum degimus et versamur, et non in cœlis; ita et Christi mortis, resurrectionis, et ascensionis virtus et efficacia per Spiritum Sanctum nobis qui in terris vivimus adsunt; et tamen quoad ejus corporis substantiam in cœlis superne degit et versatur, et non in terris: unde illum expectamus, ut tandem Spiritu Dei Patris sui e mortuis resuscitati substantialiter et corporaliter illi in aëre occurramus, qui substantialiter et corporaliter descensurus est ad judicandum vivos et mortuos. Interim quia fratribus suis est (uti Paulus dicit) similis, corporis illius substantiam in cœlis ad dextram Dei Patris collocamus, ut quoad illius corporis et sanguinis præsentiam nec in cœna nec in terris quæramus, sed superne, ubi est ad dextram Dei sedens. Illic eum quærimus, dum hic vivimus: illic eum inveniemus, cum hoc corporis ergastulo fide ipsius liberati fuerimus.

Recognoscamus verba D. Pauli, " Similis est fratribus per omnia dempto peccato." Non dicit Paulus, Similis fuit fratribus per omnia: sed, "est (inquit) similis fratribus per omnia." Paulus hanc epistolam post Christi ascensionem in cœlos scripsit, cum jam omnes mortalis corporis deposuisset conditiones, et immortalitate donatus esset; et tamen dicit, "Similis est fratribus:" unde constat, quod Christus, quoad humanitatem ejus attinet, non exuit humanas conditiones per resurrectionem, quamvis immortale, incorruptibile, gloriosum, et spirituale corpus induisset; humanam naturam per resurrectionem ad incorruptionem restituens, non ejus veritatem auferens. Humana autem natura post resurrectionis magnificentiam eadem quæ erat (quod ad veram humanæ naturæ substantiam attinet) semper permansit; sed immortalitatem naturæ humanæ, quam antea non habuit, in resurrectione assumpsit. Sed mutata jam corporis Christi mortalitate, et immortalitate donata, adhuc (inquit Paulus) Christus est fratribus similis; hoc est, verus homo ex anima rationali et humana carne subsistens, ut Athanasius dicit. Præterea dixit quod Christus non solum similis est fratribus, verum etiam, "per omnia, inquit, similis est fratribus:" ac si dixisset, Exceptis peccati sordibus et maculis, Christus quoad humanitatis suæ substantiam et naturam in omnibus convenit et similis est fratribus. Illi autem veram corporis humani naturam, hoc est, corpus et animam, habent: eadem ergo et Christus habet. Illi eandem corporis humani naturam non ubique vel pluribus in locis simul habent; sed in uno loco pro uno temporis instanti semper retinent: idem et Christus facit. Nunquam enim legitur Christum (quod ad veram humani sui corporis substantiam attinet) simul in pluribus locis fuisse. Fratres autem ejus, quos corpore e terra sustulit, ut Enoch et Elias, quoad corporis illorum et animæ substantiam jam non sunt in terris: sic et Christus, qui illis est similis, quoad corporis et animæ ejus substantiam jam non est in terris; nam e terris in cœlos corpus et animam suam subduxit.

Nos igitur, qui corporalem ejus præsentiam in cœna negamus, cum D. Paulo illum similem per omnia fratribus facimus. Neoterici autem, qui corporalem ejus præsentiam in cœna asserunt, cum Marcione, Eutyche, et aliis hæreticis, per omnia dissimilem fratribus suis faciunt; nam omnia quæ naturæ humanæ semper et inseparabiliter adsunt, sive sit morti obnoxia, sive a morte libera, neoterici tollunt. Sed sive sit natura humana in Christo in Deum assumpta, sive natura humana quæ ex puris naturalibus constat, semper natura humana suas nativas et inseparabiles qualitates retinet ac servat; non nomina, verba, et titulos tantum, sed res ipsas. Nam quemadmodum in essentia divina consistit unitas, ac in personis pluralitas; ita in persona Christi (quoad personæ proprietatem) est unitas, et in unitate personæ consistit essentiæ pluralitas. Christus enim utriusque naturæ veras essentias, Dei et hominis, in unitate personæ retinet; ita ut in Christo nec naturarum commixtionem nec personæ divisionem confiteamur. Utriusque autem naturæ essentias in Christi persona ponimus; sed commixtionem naturæ, vel divisionem personæ non agnoscimus. Et ideo est quod Paulus dicit, Christum, quoad ejus naturam humanam, similem esse fratribus.

Viderint isti neoterici, qui corporalem Christi præsentiam in sacramento constituunt, qualenam corpus et qualem naturam humanam Christo tribuant. Paulus quidem tale corpus talemque naturam humanam Christo semper ascribit, qualia nos portamus et circumferimus, excepto peccato: et jam a Christi resurrectione, excepta ejus immortalitate, Christi corpus nostram naturam nunquam exuit, nec deponit suas nativas et inseparabiles qualitates, quæ essentiæ naturæ indivulse cohærent. Semper, ubicunque fuerit, corpus humanum in loco est, et habet suas longitudines, profunditates, altitudines, ac alias dimensiones. Habet etiam humanum corpus sua membra discreta, separata, et disjuncta, quæ mira proportione, harmonia, et consensu corpus ipsum constituunt. Membra vero humani corporis ad constitutionem totius concurrunt; sed discretim, disjunctim, et separatim sua loca in corpore humano retinent. Non sunt autem confusa, ut alterum alterius locum occupet, vel ut simul omnia confuse confundantur: sed in corpore humano caput suum locum et dignitatem in eminentiore parte corporis vindicat; collum, scapulæ, brachia, venter, pedes, et cetera quæ ad humani corporis constitutionem concurrunt, singula membra seorsim in corpore loca propria et dignitates conservant. Et quemadmodum membra humani corporis mutuo sibi ipsis non invident, sic nec unum membrum alterius membri locum et dignitatem usurpat; sed singulatim ac discretim suis sedibus et locis jure hæreditario in humano corpore gaudent et fruuntur. Jam D. Paulus dicit quod Christus, quatenus homo, sit similis suis fratribus: hoc est, quod tale habeat corpus humanum, quod humanis proprietatibus (hoc est, longitudine, latitudine, et profunditate humani corporis) absolvitur. Et in hoc corpore vero et organico membra habet discreta, disjuncta, ac separata, ut singula discretim in suo corpore suas proprias sedes et dignitates vindicent et occupent, et nullum membrum alterius membri locum usurpet, ut antea dixi. Trutinemus igitur et æqua lance libremus an humana Christi natura, quam neoterici fingunt ad quatuor verborum prolationem adesse in cœna Domini, has retineat conditiones, vel non. Ipsimet vero id pernegant, et dicunt verum corpus Christi in cœna adesse; sed tamen non localiter. Dicunt etiam naturale corpus Christi confici ex pane, sed illud naturale corpus in sacramento nullas habere naturales proprietates. Habere autem corpus Christi in cœna singula membra humani corporis dicunt; sed non disjunctim et separatim posita, propter panis formam, quæ arctior et angustior est quam ut sub ea singula membra Christi corporis propria loca et naturales sedes vindicent atque possideant. Totum tamen et integrum Christum, quatenus est verus homo, intra bini pollicis mensuram et ambitum (ut aiunt) continent; ita ut caput et pedes, brachia et venter, unum locum in corpore Christi teneant.

Hæc vero et infinita alia stulta, absurda, et puerilia habent neoterici, quibus errorem suum in hac causa muniant et defendant. Est verum corpus, sed non simile corporibus fratrum: est naturale corpus, tamen naturalibus corporibus dissimile. Vera natura humana in cœna adest, sed omni naturæ humanæ dissimilis. Quam horrenda sunt ista, et quam periculosa christiano homini, talem naturam humanam et tale corpus humanum Christo (qui verus est Deus et homo) attribuere, quæ nullas humanæ naturæ conditiones habeat! Si hoc non sit humanitatem Christi penitus tollere et destruere, judicent omnes qui Christum ex animo norunt et diligunt. Hoc autem firmiter credimus, et nullatenus dubitamus, quod Christus Jesus Salvator noster, quantum ad humanitatem ejus attinet, similis sit nobis, excepto peccato: et illam similitudinem, quam juxta humanam naturam habet nobiscum, nunquam (quocunque in loco fuerit) deposuit, sive in terris sive in cœlis fuerit. Cum igitur doctrina et fides neotericorum tale corpus Christi in cœna constituant quod corporibus nostris per omnia sit dissimile, ab illis merito, verbo Dei coacti, dissentimus, et corpus Christi esse quod prædicant omnino negamus; nam (Paulus inquit) similis est fratribus per omnia. Ejus verbis credimus et firmiter adhæremus; a quibus, adjuvante Deo, nec ferro nec igne dimovebimur, certo persuasi, quod ille Christus, pro quo tam strenue neoterici in missa contendunt, sit fictitius, et nihil aliud quam somnium aut phantasma: nam verus Christus, ubicunque sit, similis est fratribus. Et quem illi fingunt in missa, fratribus dissimilem, nos ignoramus. Satis autem est quod similem nobis agnoscimus, quem in cœlis sursum colimus et adoramus; unde venturus est in novissimo die, ut causas omnium rectissimo judicio discernat: apud quem nihil dubitamus quin adversarii nostri, antichristus Romanus cum suis rasis, ipsorum impietatis rationem reddituri sint, nisi in hac vita hujus hæreseos et idololatriæ illos pœnituerit. Quod ut concedat ille qui solus corda hominum ad pœnitentiam convertit, obnixe in Christo precor. Amen.

Decimaquinta probatio nostræ assertionis.

Luc. xxii.
1 Cor. xi.

"Hoc facite in mei commemorationem." Si quis recte horum verborum naturam et Christi sententiæ proprietatem perpendat, nullo negotio animadvertat Christum sui corporis in mortem traditi memoriam per sacram cœnam instituisse, et non corporalem sui præsentiam. Nam jussit cœnam sanctam celebrari ad recordationem mortis illius, et non ut corpus ipsum ex pane conficeretur; ut liquido ex verborum Christi natura et propositionis proprietate constabit. Primum, dicit, "Facite." Non dixit, Create de novo corpus meum; nec dixit, Transubstantiate panis et vini substantiam in meum corpus et sanguinem; nec, Corpus meum ex pane factum sacrificate in remissionem peccatorum. Nihil horum dixit; sed, "Hoc facite" (inquit), nempe, quod me jam videtis facere.

Facere cœnam Domini quid.

Facere autem cœnam Domini est ita agere in sacra cœnæ actione ut Christus agere præcepit, et ut in hoc sacræ cœnæ mysterio unius Domini sola auctoritas valeat. Facere cœnam ergo est Domini institutione, verbo, atque exemplo panem et vinum communi usu exuere, et in sacrum usum applicare; et non panis et vini substantiam vel penitus destruere, aut in aliam substantiam, nempe corporis Christi, transubstantiare.

Mirum est quod hujus dictionis, "facite," naturam neoterici aliquando, saltem missando, non perpendant. Sed, quemadmodum ex verbis Christi, ita et ex sententiis ejus nihil certi constituunt. Præstaret omnino potius naturam vocum perpendere et explicare quam contra vocum naturam et veritatem voces detorquere, et in peregrinam significationem urgere. Nam ubi de vocis natura et proprietate nihil certi constat, sursum ac deorsum, Euripi more, quicquid disputatur vagatur.

Rectam ergo definitionem vocis in omnibus controversiis constituant; et tunc facile elici possit cuinam sententiæ et utri parti vocis proprietas magis conveniat. Quis autem hanc vocem, "facite," in Christi sententia, "Hoc facite in mei commemorationem," diceret idem significare quod, "hoc corpus meum sacrificate," non ad memoriam, sed re ipsa? Hoc equidem Christianum non est, sed potius Protea aut Vertumnum agere; vocesque a Christo simpliciter prolatas a simplici et genuina natura detorquere, maxime cum nullum similem loquendi modum ex sacris libris proferre possint. Neque vero, si id etiam possent, firmum argumentum inde conficeretur, tota scriptura testante Christum semel immolatum esse. *Facite.*

Idem etiam neoterici faciunt in hac voce, "memoria." Proprietatem et naturam memoriæ, quæ absentium tantum contemplationem comprehendit, præsentium naturas, proprietates, ac substantias comprehendere volunt: ut Christi absentis a terra memoria sit idem atque ipsum corpus Christi jam præsens habere. Primum, memoriæ naturam ac proprietatem tollunt, quæ circa rei memoratæ substantiæ absentiam versatur: quod est non solum ignorantia finitionis memoriæ vocis naturam præterire, sed etiam et partes et membra memoriæ non intelligere. Nam memoria est vel naturalis, vel artificialis, vel spiritualis. Naturalis retinet absque omni externo adminiculo quæ antea intellectu vel sensuum perspicuitate sunt comprehensa. Artificialis ea retinet quæ vel ex intellectus industria vel sensuum perspicuitate comprehendit; sed non absque aliquo adminiculo, vel sensibus externe objecto, aut de novo intrinsecus animo concepto. Adminiculum autem externum est annulus, liber, vel hujusmodi quibus solent uti qui amicorum immemores esse nolunt. Spiritualis vero memoria ea retinet spiritualia quæ ex Spiritus sancti afflatu comprehendit; et tamen, ne apprehensa ex memoria elaberentur, spiritus ac fidei contemplationi Deus optimus adminicula spiritualia adjunxit. Hasce omnes memoriæ species circa earum rerum substantias quæ absunt versari constat; sive per se memoria res absentes contemplatur, sive aliquo alio medio vel naturali aut spirituali memoria adjuvatur: sed res memorata nunquam re ipsa adest. Naturalis memoria vel amici absentis præsentiam, aut lectionis ac studii notitiam et cognitionem, retinet. Artificialis nec absentium nec intermissi studii notitiam retinet, nisi aliquo externo adminiculo adjuta. Ideo Cicero et alii multi, ne ab- *Memoria.* *Naturalis memoria.* *Artificialis memoria.* *Adminiculum.* *Spiritualis memoria.*

sentium et lectionis memoria præterflueret, locos et imagines invenerunt, quibus memoria naturalis parum retenta adjuvaretur: in ipsis tamen locis et figuris, quibus memoria versaretur, res memorata corporaliter non extitit. Memoria autem spiritualis ne hebescat ac obliteretur, Spiritus sanctus summa ope cavet, et adminicula addit, videlicet, verbum ac sacramenta Dei, quæ memoriæ Spiritu sancto præditæ Christum corpore absentem modo spirituali præsentem faciunt; sed non ita ut Christus, cujus memoriam sacramenta et verbum Dei refricant, corporaliter adsit; sed, quemadmodum memoria in rebus caducis ac evanidis aliquibus modis (nempe locis ac figuris) adjuvatur, ita in rebus maxime seriis et spiritualibus verbo ac sacramentis memoria adjutatur. Et sicut substantialiter res mortales atque caducæ figuris ac locis, quorum præsidio memoriæ infiguntur, non insunt; sic res divinæ et spirituales substantialiter verbo ac sacramentis non adsunt, quod ad illarum corporalem substantiam attinet.

Quemadmodum autem isti horum verborum, 'facite,' et, 'in memoriam facite,' naturam ac proprietatem vel ignorant aut contemnunt; ita et totius propositionis et sententiæ Christi conditionem subvertunt. "Hoc (inquit Christus) facite in memoriam mei:" quod si exponas, sonat, "Facite hæc quæ me videtis facere; non ut me ex pane faciatis de novo; sed ad recordationem mei antehac in utero matris meæ facti, et jam pro vestra[rum] animarum salute immolandi, et in memoriam corporis mortis meæ facite." Et quemadmodum naturam et proprietatem istorum verborum, "Hoc facite in mei commemorationem," plane neoterici subvertunt, et aliter interpretantur quam orthodoxi patres omnes; ita et istorum verborum, "Hoc est corpus meum," naturam ac proprietatem penitus destruunt, et novum ac peregrinum sensum fingunt omnibus orthodoxis patribus ignotum. Et ideo satis equidem admirari non possum neotericos tam obfirmate ac pertinaciter ita verborum et sententiarum Christi naturam, veritatem, ac proprietatem obumbrare atque obfuscare, cum omnes veteres sanctique patres aliter verba et sententiam Christi interpretentur quam neoterici, ut in hoc tractatu manifestissime apparebit.

Augustinus tropicam loquutionem in verbis cœnæ ubique fere constituit, ubicunque de ejus rei argumento tractat: ut ad Bonifacium epistola 23[1]: Contra Adimantum Manichæum

[1] Si enim sacramenta quandam similitudinem earum rerum qua-

cap. 12[2]: De doctrina Christiana libro 3, cap. 16[3]: In Psalm. 99[4]. Apud veteres hæc sacra Domini cœna aliquando missa vocatur; non ideo quod ministri Christum Deo Patri mittant et sacrificent, sed quia gratiarum actiones laudesque perennes Deo pendant, quod unigenitum Filium suum pro salute mundi ipse in mundum miserit, ut morte afficeretur. Apud Tertullianum cœna sacra ἀγάπη vocatur, quia, dum cœna ministraretur, in pauperes divites suorum bonorum erogationem facerent. Aliquando cœna Domini immolatio, celebratio, oblatio, et sacrificium nominatur; non quod re ipsa immolatio esset, sed quia in cœna immolationis Christi semel pro nobis oblati et immolati celebris fieret commemoratio; ut iidem sancti patres testantur. Vocatur etiam cœna Domini aliquando eucharistia, propter gratiarum actiones, quas ecclesia impendit pro morte Christi. Nonnunquam cœna Domini apud patres vocatur sacramentum seu mysterium: sed hoc fit, non quia in sacramento et mysterio Christus corporaliter comprehendatur, sed quia in sacramento et mysterio commemoratio fiat de ómnibus beneficiis quæ Christus in morte sua pro nobis persolvit. Appellatur etiam aliquando cœna Domini viaticum; non ut Christus corporaliter manu ducat mysteria cœnæ percipientem in cœlum, sed quia qui fide mysteria mortis Christi suscipit fide ab æterna morte liberatur, et cum Christo regnabit in perpetuum. Sit igitur sacra Domini cœna mortis Christi sacratissima memoria, juxta sacras scripturas et sanctorum patrum testimonia; et non ultra creaturas panis et vini ad adorationem exponant. Nam nisi resipuerint qui hoc faciunt, tandem idololatriæ pœnas gravissimas luent.

Et quemadmodum verborum et sententiarum Christi natu-

Sacra cœna variis nominibus appellata.

rum sacramenta sunt non haberent, omnino sacramenta non essent. Ex hac autem similitudine plerunque etiam ipsarum rerum nomina accipiunt.—Op. Tom. II. col. 93. c. Basil. 1569.]

[2 Non enim Dominus dubitavit dicere, Hoc est corpus meum, cum signum daret corporis sui.—Id. Op. Tom. VI. col. 187. c.]

[3 Figura est ergo, præcipiens passioni Domini esse communicandum.—Id. Op. Tom. III. col. 53. B.]

[4 Id. in Psalm. xcviii. (xcix.) Spiritualiter intelligite quod locutus sum. Non hoc corpus quod videtis manducaturi estis, et bibituri illum sanguinem quem fusuri sunt qui me crucifigent. Sacramentum aliquod vobis commendavi: spiritualiter intellectum vivificabit vos.— Tom. VIII. col. 1105. B. C.]

ram ac proprietatem neoterici contemnunt; ita et ipsam sacram Christi coenæ institutionem truncant ac mutilant. Nam contra expressum mandatum Dei, "Bibite ex hoc omnes," neoterici panem sine calice distribuunt; quod non solum est Christi institutum mutilare, verum etiam sanguinis Christi effusionis memoriam e memoria expellere. Sacro enim calice rite juxta Christi institutionem ministrato et populo distributo, virtus utique effusi Christi sanguinis conscientiis fide recipientium obsignatur. Igitur qui unicam tantum eucharistiæ partem (nempe panem) accipiunt, non sacramentum Christi, sed fructum panis et satanicum idolum percipiunt; et ministri qui sic panem absque calice distribuunt sacrilegium committunt, et idolum pro Deo vero ad adorationem ostentant. Nam in recta administratione sacramentorum Christi institutio et auctoritas tantum valere debent. Præterea, quemadmodum veram naturam et proprietatem verborum et mentis Christi una cum Christi vera institutione sacræ coenæ ab ecclesiis Christi neoterici deturbarunt; ita frigidis et impiis cæremoniis jam sua, et non Christi, sacra in ecclesiis ornant atque magnificant. Nam quod nunc faciunt Christus prohibuit; et quod omittunt ac negligunt Christus omnino fieri præcepit: ut ex collatione sacræ Domini coenæ cum his quæ jam in missa papistica fiunt apertius constabit; si modo sacra cum profanis componere liceat.

Collatio.

Quomodo Christus, Filius Dei, sapientia Patris, sacra coena usus sit; et quomodo alios uti docuerit.

Sub initium sacræ coenæ concionem habuit gravissimam, quo multis argumentis Judam proditorem suum ad poenitentiam revocaret. Admonuit illum primo indiscriminatim, ne illius impietatem ceteris apostolis palam faceret, inquiens, "Unus vestrum me proditurus est." Deinde, ad meliorem mentem revocare studet, argumentum ducens a religione mensæ; ubi inter omnes probos, ut una mensa qua omnes pascuntur, ita et una esse debet mens quæ omnibus bene velit. "Qui intinxit (inquit) mecum manum in catino, hic me proditurus est." Tertio, deterret proditorem a proditione sceleris metu et poena quæ proditionem comitarentur. "Væ (inquit) homini illi per quem Filius hominis proditur. Bonum erat ei, si natus non fuisset homo ille." Finita sanctissima concione, dum epulum typici agni comederent, accepit Jesus panem, et, cum egisset gratias, fregit, deditque discipulis, et ait, "Accipite, comedite; hoc est corpus meum."

Huc usque de panis distributione in sacra Domini cœna juxta institutionem et mandatum Christi. Jam sequetur,

Quomodo papa, primogenitus antichristi, impia missa (quam impie sacram cœnam Domini vocat) utatur, et alios uti doceat.

Conciones ex verbo Dei de pœnitentia nullas habent, imo omnino abominantur: etsi quæ aliquando fuerint sunt tales quæ veram pœnitentiam obscurent aut etiam sepeliant; nam humana et impia doctrina conscientias stupefaciunt ac conturbant sub specie veræ doctrinæ. In ipsa missæ actione panem accipiunt, gratias tamen non agunt; sed tantum digitis panem crucibus signant: panem vero non frangunt, nec ecclesiis distribuunt: verba autem, "Accipite et manducate," recitant, sed mentiendo: nemo accipit, et nemo panem comedit: "hoc est enim corpus meum," tacite susurrant.

Huc usque de pane missali juxta institutionem Romani pontificis. Videamus jam quomodo sacer panis in usu sacræ Domini cœnæ juxta institutionem Christi conveniat cum impio pane in missa juxta institutionem Romani antichristi.

1. Christus in sacra cœna accepit panem, et publice gratias egit.	Romani neoterici in impia missa panem accipiunt, et secreto atque tacite panem crucibus signant.
2. Christus panem publice aliis fregit.	Neoterici arcane sibi ipsis panem frangunt.
3. Christus in cœna dedit panem discipulis.	Neoterici sibi ipsis solis panem in missa impertiunt.
4. Christus aliis in cœna palam dixit, "Accipite et manducate."	Neoterici sibi ipsis in missa tacite dicunt, "Accipite et manducate."
5. Christus panem consecratum dedit manducandum.	Neoterici panem elevant adorandum.
6. Christus panem corporis sui immolandi sacramentum fecit.	Neoterici Christum se dicunt re ipsa sacrificare.

[HOOPER, II.]

7. Christus cognita lingua in sacra cœna omnia peregit.   Neoterici ignota lingua in missis omnia agunt.

Priusquam ad alteram speciem sacramenti progrediar, rogo ut pii omnes propter Christum cogitent ac perpendant, quantum in usu et distributione panis in sacra cœna juxta institutionem Christi discriminis sit ab usu et distributione panis in impia missa: et ubi discrepantiam et antithesin animadverterint, statim perspicient panem in diabolica missa ita cum sacro pane in cœna Domini convenire ut frigida cum calidis, humentia cum siccis, mollia cum duris, et sine pondere habentia pondus. Et ubi hæc discrimina intellexerint, ad mentes illos redire admoneo, et cogitare apud se quis horum sit præferendus, Christus unigenitus summi Patris, an neoterici hac in causa antichristi filii. Et si Christi personam neotericis præferunt, judicent ipsi num etiam usus panis in sacra cœna juxta institutionem Christi non sit præferendus usui panis in impia missa juxta institutionem antichristi. Et ubi hæc omnia mature deliberaverint, dicant mihi bona conscientia, num quemadmodum Christi persona omnibus personis est præferenda, an non ita et usus sacræ Domini cœnæ a Christo institutus omnibus aliis usibus sit anteferendus. Hæc piis animis altius consideranda relinquo, et ad collationem alterius partis sacræ cœnæ me conferam.

Collatio.

1. Christus Dei Filius in sacra cœna accepit poculum, et gratias egit.   Neoterici in impia missa poculum accipiunt, et crucibus digitorum notatis signant.
2. Christus Dei Filius poculum quibuscum sedebat dedit.   Neoterici illis qui adsunt non dant.
3. Christus dixit, "Bibite ex hoc omnes."   Neoterici omnes ex poculo bibere prohibent.
4. Christus palam dixit, "Hoc facite in mei commemorationem."   Neoterici dicunt se idem facere et offerre quod Christus fecit et obtulit.

Hunc etiam poculi usum in sacra Domini cœna juxta Christi institutionem cum usu poculi in impia missa conferant; et nullo labore Christi institutionem cum impia missa omnibus modis pugnare facile percipient. Et ubi repugnantias intellexerunt, dicant hic, ut coram Deo in novissimo die responsuri sunt, uter horum anteponendus sit, usus poculi in sacra Domini cœna juxta institutionem Christi, an usus poculi in papistica missa juxta antichristi tyrannidem. Hoc autem ex verbo Dei apertissime constat, quod impia missa et sacra Domini cœna inter se non conveniant: et qui hoc noverint, si missis hisce diabolicis adhærere voluerint, suo periculo facient; tandem reddituri rationem quod mandata Dei propter traditiones hominum neglexerint; et tunc demum sentient quam horrendum sit incidere in manus Dei viventis.

Sed scio quid prætexant neoterici, et quomodo Christi institutionis in sua cœna violationem conentur excusare: nempe catholicam ecclesiam missarum privatarum usum tanquam sacrum admisisse, et catholicos patres verbum Dei sic interpretatos fuisse. Quibus sic respondere oportet: ecclesiam quæ privatarum missarum usum admisit esse catholicam, sed impiam, et non sanctam; ideoque tanquam catholicam et universalem meretricem Babylonicam, antichristi sobolem, ab omnibus contemnendam. Sancta enim catholica ecclesia Christum auctorem et sponsum suum tantum audit. Nam Christus, qui est in sinu Patris, ipse ecclesiæ catholicæ sanctæ enarravit, quomodo sese in omnibus quæ ad fidem et usum sacramentorum spectant gereret. Et hanc suam voluntatem absolute et perfecte in verbo suo patefecit: quod (scilicet verbum) certitudinem, auctoritatem, ac sufficientiam habet, nec ab ecclesia catholica christiana, nec a Romana et antichristiana, sed a Deo ipso: et tantum propter hunc auctorem Deum sancta catholica ecclesia audiri debet. Noluit enim Deus in causa fidei a primi hominis lapsu hominibus credi sine certis et evidentissimis ipsius verbi testimoniis: imo, quod hominum conditionem superat, etiam angelis de cœlis credi noluit præter vel contra verbi sui certitudinem: multo minus istis personatis asinis, qui impiis missis hodie in sua catholica ecclesia inserviunt; quæ nova catholica ecclesia nec auctor nec testis est divinæ veritatis. Non auctor; quia quæ jam docet et agit omnibus modis pugnant cum verbi Dei certitudine: nec vero testis; quia totam narrationem sacrarum literarum, imo ipsam historicam commemorationem, vel abstulit vel mutavit, ut in hac causa eucharistiæ paulo ante per antithesin ostendi. Si autem ista Romana ecclesia, cujus tyrannide hodie Anglica ecclesia jacet oppressa, testis esset verbi Dei, proculdubio testis officium observaret; quod est, nec addere nec demere quicquam verbo Dei, sed bona fide quod verbum Dei in se continet tantum testificari. Sed, ut jam ostendi, ista

Ecclesia catholica, sed non sancta.

catholica meretrix neotericorum ecclesia non solum verba et narrationes, verum etiam doctrinas verbi divini mutavit: quare non audienda tanquam judex, nec admittenda tanquam testis. Nam judicis officium est sententias ex legibus proferre, et secundum leges judicare: et testis est ea in testimonia producere quæ certo et indubitato cognita habet. Judicet igitur neotericorum ecclesia secundum leges divinas, et ei nos ipsos omni honore ac reverentia subjiciemus: proferat adversum nos ex verbo Dei testimonium, et illud omnino humiliter admittemus. Sed ita se res habet: tyrannice leges Dei usurpant, et falsissime in verbi Dei professores testimonium dicunt: quare talem ecclesiam, licet catholicam, pro sancta catholica ecclesia non agnoscimus.

Negamus etiam omnibus modis orthodoxos patres unquam verbum Dei ita fuisse interpretatos, ut illorum interpretationibus vel panis et vini substantiæ destructionem vel in naturalem corporis Christi substantiam conversionem constituerent: nec usquam ex sanctorum patrum interpretationibus constat, Christum corporaliter sacramentalibus signis adesse, vel sub signis sacramentalibus in remissionem peccatorum offerri: sint illorum libri judices. Quemadmodum igitur neotericorum catholicam ecclesiam pro vera et sancta Christi catholica ecclesia multas justissimas ob causas non agnoscimus; ita et illorum interpretes pro piis ac fidelibus verborum Dei interpretibus non admittimus. Nam, quemadmodum officium pii judicis est semper secundum leges judicare, et pii testis est vera audita et cognita in omnibus controversiis proferre; ita et veri ac fidi interpretis est ea quæ interpretanda sibi sumit, non solum verba, verum etiam mentem, auctoris quem interpretandum sumpsit, religiose et summa fide reddere. Conferamus ergo verba et mentem Filii Dei in sacra cœna cum interpretatione neotericorum. Quod si fideliter verba ac mentem Spiritus sancti retineant, pro veris ac fidelibus interpretibus illos agnoscemus: sed si et verba et mentem Spiritus sancti subvertant, et ad impietatem et superstitionem trahant atque obtorqueant, absit ut illorum interpretationes pro veris admitteremus. Faciemus jam in paucis periculum: quod si in illis fide reperiantur digni, bona spes est fore ut etiam in reliquis illis tuto credere possimus.

Christus accepit panem in sacra cœna, et gratias egit: neoterici in missis panem accipiunt, gratias tamen non agunt, sed panem digitis, ut dixi, crucibus consignant. Jam gratias agere non est digitis cruces facere; sed corde, animo, et voce Dei beneficia agnoscere, illumque omni honore quo possumus pro collatis in nos beneficiis afficere. Quare neoterici mysteriorum Dei interpretes primum vocis Dei naturam offendunt. Nam textus habet Matthæi xxvi. εὐχαριστήσας; et Marci xiv. εὐλογήσας; quod omnes fere "gratias egit" et "benedixit" vertunt. Benedicere autem est aliquando, laudare et gratias agere, ut David inquit: "Benedicam Dominum in omni tempore:" aliquando, bene precari, ac omnia fausta optare; ut Jacob benedixit Pharaonem, id est, salutem imprecabatur: et aliquando, aliquid profanum in sacros ac pios usus consecrare: sic Deus sub initio creaturarum piscibus maris et volucribus cœli benedixit; hoc est, virtutem multiplicandi illis concessit. Homini etiam et mulieri benedixit Deus sub initio, dum adhuc in statu innocentiæ permanebant; hoc est, ut semper sese et suas proles ad opus et servitium illius applicarent. Deinde benedixit diei septimo; hoc est, diem septimum in sacros usus designavit. Sic in hoc loco S. Marcus evangelista dicit quod Christus in ultima sacra cœna panem benedixit; id est, panem in sacrum usum, ut mortis ejus esset sacramentum, consecravit; vel, omnibus faustis ac laudibus Patrem suum cœlestem prosequebatur, quod morte sua mundum sibi reconciliaret; quod est gratias agere, ut Matthæus inquit. Benedicere igitur panem in sacra Domini cœna non est crucibus panem notare, sed per verbum et institutionem Christi gratias agere, et panem a profano usu ad sacrum deputare et consecrare. Et idem dicendum est de benedictione poculi. Errant ergo toto cœlo interpretes neoterici in hoc, quod benedicere pro cruces facere interpretentur. Quare istam interpretationem tanquam a vocis analogia peregrinam rejicimus, et genuinam vocis naturam retinemus.

    Præterea, cum Christus benedixisset, vel gratias egisset, panem fregit, ac discipulis distribuit. Frangere panem quamvis in sacris literis pro pascere sæpius usurpetur, hic tamen panem frangere est panem in multas partes rumpere vel dissecare, ut singulis sua pars panis contingat. Et hoc fecit Christus, ut panis fractionis analogiam et mysterium discipuli intelligerent. Nam immolationem et mortem sui corporis sub fractionis panis involucro ob oculos illorum ponebat; atque hunc panem fractum illis impertivit, ut per panis exhibitionem intelligerent quod Christus fracti, mortui, et immolati sui corporis merita illis etiam impertiretur. Neoterici istorum verborum

[marginalia: Benedicere est aliquando laudare. [Psalm. xxxiv.] [Gen. xlvii.] Panem frangere.]

Christi interpretes non solum naturam verborum, verum etiam illorum mysticam ac sacramentalem significationem, plane destruunt. Nam vocem, fregit, proferunt; sed re ipsa (ut Christus jussit) non frangunt: et verbum, dedit, sonant; sed nihil dant. Hoc non est interpretem, sed oppressorem verborum Christi agere. Ad hæc Christus palam discipulis suis de pane dixit, "Hoc est corpus meum:" neoterici interpretes tacite sibi ipsis ac parietibus hæc dicunt. Christus jussit omnes qui sacræ cœnæ interfuerunt sacrum panem accipere et manducare, his verbis: "Accipite et manducate ex hoc omnes:" neoterici vero hæc Christi verba et mandata voce recitant, et factis contemnunt; nullus enim cum ministro accipit, nullus panem comedit. Judicent jam qui ex corde Christum amant, an hoc sit pii hominis, in sacris Dei mysteriis voces mandatorum Dei proferre, et ipsa Dei mandata contemnere.

Addiderunt papistæ "enim" verbis Dei.

Sed hac de re plura in suo loco postea. Et quod deterius est, isti neoterici interpretes Christi verbis sua etiam addiderunt. Ubi enim Christus de pane dixit, "Hoc est corpus meum," ipsi sic proferunt, "Hoc est enim corpus meum;" "enim" addendo: quod apertissime est contra mandatum Dei. Si Christus sapientia Patris satis dixit, quare non sunt contenti his quæ ab illo dicebantur? Si satis non dixit, illum insufficientiæ et stultitiæ arguunt: quod est maxime impium, ut vel cogitemus illum quicquam imperfectum reliquisse. Si autem discipuli Christi sunt (ut videri volunt), quare illius præceptis semet non subjiciunt? Ipse enim voluit atque mandavit (ut D. Paulus testatur) ut, quoties sacra cœna perageretur, mysticus panis omnibus frangeretur ac distribueretur. Quamobrem igitur privatas suas missas non abjiciunt? et cur sacram communionem juxta Christi institutionem non restituunt? Si sunt veri discipuli Christi, quare de pane dicunt, Manducate ex hoc omnes, cum Christus verbi "omnes" in distributione panis non meminit? Quamobrem etiam de poculo verbum "omnes" expungunt cum Christus de poculo diserte dixerit, "Bibite ex hoc omnes?" Et quare, si sunt discipuli Christi, et veri verborum Christi interpretes, quod Christus expresse fieri jubet, "Bibite ex hoc omnes," ipsi manifeste fieri prohibent, "Non bibite ex hoc omnes, sed soli sacerdotes?" Non est profecto nec pii hominis nec fidi interpretis hoc mandare quod Christus vetat; nec hoc prohibere quod Christus præcipit. Et tamen neoterici sæpissime hoc faciunt, ut liquido innotescet, si quis impias illorum privatas missas æqua ac diligenti consideratione et collatione cum sacra Domini cœna conferre voluerit. Si sint veri interpretes verborum Christi, cur ausi sunt idem memoriam et rem memoratam, signum et signatum, facere? Christus cœnam fieri in memoriam sui jussit: neoterici interpretes dicunt, non tantum memoriam Christi fieri in missis suis, verum etiam Christum ipsum corporaliter adesse et sacrificari. Hic neoterici Spiritum sanctum, optimum oratorem, qui rectissime mentem suam exprimere possit, corrigunt; nam quod ipse memoriam Christi vocat, isti Christum ipsum appellant. Non est igitur mirum, quod nos cum Christi sponsa sanctaque catholica ecclesia ab istis neotericis dissentiamus, ut Christo capiti nostro indivulse adhæreamus. Christus hanc propositionem, "Hoc est corpus meum," refert, non ad sui ipsius corporis substantiam, sed mortis sui corporis commemorationem: nam statim prolata propositione, "Hoc est corpus meum quod pro vobis frangitur," subjunxit, "Hoc facite in mei commemorationem." Unde ex circumstantiis a Christo ipso prolatis constat corpus Christi non realiter, sed spiritualiter et sacramentaliter verificari de pane in sacra cœna; cui semper adest, non corpore, sed spiritu, et corporis sanguinisque et animæ meritis ac virtute: et sacer panis qui est in ore fide recipientium est quodammodo Christus ipse: id est, cum illa visibili forma et substantia panis vere et non ficte, efficaciter et non inutiliter, adest Christus, qui nunquam a recte utentibus sacra cœna corporis ac mortis ipsius memoria, ac denique spiritu suo, abest. Figurata autem sive sacramentali loquutione et sermone improprio panis est corpus Christi. Ac de veritate quidem hujus propositionis, "Hoc est corpus meum," nihil dubitamus: quemadmodum de multis aliis paribus loquutionibus in scripturis pie sentimus; ut, "Petra erat Christus;" "Ego sum vitis;" "Agnus est transitus;" "Circumcisio est fœdus," etc. in quibus non solum phrasis et circumstantiæ sacrarum literarum tropum admittunt; verum etiam veri interpretes sacrarum literarum passim hanc interpretationem tam in illis quam in hac sententia, "Hoc est corpus meum," et, "Nisi manducaveritis carnem Filii hominis," figurative et tropice interpretantur: ut Augustinus ad Bonifacium; Contra Adimantum Manichæum, cap. xii.[1]; De Doctrina Christiana, libro

Lucæ xxii.
1 Cor. xi.

[1 Vide supra, pp. 462, 463; notes 1, 2.]

III. cap. 9[1]; Hieronymus in Matthæum[2]; Tertullianus contra Marcionem[3], et alii quam plurimi ex veteribus, veri sacrarum literarum interpretes.

Sed altius paululum perpendamus, primum, corticem et nudam pellem verborum Christi in sacra cœnæ actione: deinde, verborum verum sensum eliciamus atque expendamus: postea, neotericorum interpretationes verborum et sententiæ Christi cum Christo ac sanctis patribus conferamus. Primum, Christus panem quem manibus tenebat benedixit, hoc est, in sacrum usum consecravit et applicavit, ut non solum corporis sui esset sacramentum, verum etiam nomen ipsum corporis sui, cujus erat sacramentum, indueret. Nam Christus in ultima cœna accepit panem, atque illum benedixit; hoc est, panem acceptum in sacrum usum sacramenti sui corporis consecravit: ideoque fit, quod Christus eundem panem in sacrum usum consecratum nominis sui titulo honoravit dicendo, "Hoc est corpus meum." Jam judicet verbum Dei, an hæc verba, "Hoc est corpus meum," a ministro prolata panis substantiam convertant in corpus Christi; vel indicent ac declarent potius non panis substantiam annihilari aut transubstantiari in corporis Christi substantiam; sed ipsam panis substantiam ostendant esse, suo modo, corpus Christi. Textus vero non habet, quod Christus panem accepit, cujus substantiam mutavit in substantiam corporis sui, quem corpus suum appellavit: sed manifeste dicit, "Accepit panem et benedixit," quem corpus suum appellavit. Et ne nimium cortici vocum discipuli adhærerent, quasi re ipsa corpus suum lateret sub cortice et forma panis, quia dixit, "Hoc est corpus meum;" statim hujusmodi suspicionem amovit, dicens, "Hoc facite in meam commemorationem." Jam inter hasce duas propositiones, Benedixit, et, Facite hoc in mei memoriam, media interseritur hæc propositio, Hoc est corpus meum. Et cum benedicere panem in sacro usu cœnæ Domini non sit panem destruere, sed reservare et in sacrum usum applicare; et facere in memoriam sit absentis amorem ac benevolentiam animo revolvere, et non corpore absentis frui; quo jure quove auctore neoterici interpretes contra præcedentia et subsequentia mediæ propositionis ejus sententiam ad literam trahant, cum verus et germanus sensus hujus propositionis, Hoc est corpus meum, ab his quæ præcedunt et subsequuntur plane depen-

[[1] Vide supra, p. 429.]   [[2] Vide supra, p. 406, note 6.]
[[3] Vide supra, pp. 406, note 7; 440, note 1.]

deat? Circumstantiæ textus sacramentalem sensum hujus propositionis, Hoc est corpus meum, urgent: hunc sensum omnes amplecti tenentur, et non de novo alium et peregrinum inferre. Neoterici quidem mira fingunt, falsa inducunt, et impia defendunt. Nam dicunt verborum istorum, Hoc est corpus meum, vi panis substantiam mutari in ipsum corpus Christi. Perpende igitur verba Christi. In tota propositione, Hoc est corpus meum, tantum unicum est verbum substantivum, Est; quod nec factionem nec passionem significat, sed existentiam ejus rei de qua dicitur. Jam quod hisce verbis testatur, pronunciat ac palam declarat esse corpus suum. Neoterici interpretes naturam verbi, Est, quod subsistentiam et existentiam significat, interpretantur per verba vel activæ vel passivæ significaticnis; quasi virtus verborum de novo panem in corporis Christi substantiam mutaret, aut panis passive corpus Christi fieret. Qualis autem sit hæc dexteritas et candor in explanandis sacris literis, nativam proprietatem vocum tollere, nullus ignorat. Isti tamen neoterici impudenter hæc verba semper crocitant, Hoc est corpus meum: quibus verbis nihil in tota sacrarum literarum serie potest esse apertius contra panis et vini transubstantiationem, et corporalem corporis Christi præsentiam in sacra Domini cœna. Nam Christus de pane dixit, " Hoc est corpus meum:" non dixit, Sub hujus panis cortice latet corpus meum. Dixit præterea, "Hoc est corpus meum:" et non dixit, Hoc transubstantialiter in corpus meum converto; nec dixit, Hoc fit istorum verborum virtute corpus meum; ut stolide ac impie neoterici interpretantur.

Dicunt etiam isti novi interpretes panem illum in altari converti in corpus Christi, manentibus semper prioris panis forma et accidentibus: hisque mendaciis, tanquam sint oracula Apollinis, credi volunt ab omnibus; et qui credere recusaverit pro hæretico habendus est. Sed quid responderent neoterici, si quis quæsierit, num panis ille quem Deum et hominem conficere nituntur ante consecrationem sit prima substantia an secunda? Primam esse responderent, non dubito; quandoquidem ex Aristotele didicerunt primas substantias individua esse, ut hunc lapidem, hunc hominem. Jam sic instarem: At destructis primis substantiis nihil earum remanet; hoc est, simul primæ substantiæ accidentia perirent; nam accidentia solum in individuis locum habent. Sed accidentia prioris substantiæ (ut antea dixi) semper manent: ergo et illorum prima substantia. Nam est axioma in omnibus scholis, Destructis primis substantiis nihil est reliquum. Dicant neoterici interpretes an corpus Christi, quod suis missis adesse contendunt, sit prima vel secunda substantia. Si sit prima, ergo oportet habeat sua accidentia, quia accidentia tantum sunt in individuis seu primis substantiis. Sed accidentia veri corporis Christi in missis adesse negant: quare credimus nec substantiam corporis Christi adesse posse. Restat igitur, ut corpus Christi, si aliquod sit in missa, sit substantia secunda: et tunc non est homo, sed species hominis, hoc est, idea hominis, et nihil extra intellectionem: quod Marcionicum plane est.

Sed quam mira neoterici fingant et excogitent, ut hunc suum novum Christum asserant, non est praesentis instituti meminisse: qui illorum libros evolvit eorum non potest esse inscius. Sed unum novum et egregie confictum testimonium, quo jam Deum suum super verticem sacerdotis elevatum suffulciant, non praeteribo. Nam non ante multos menses unus ex neotericorum secta et haeresi non infimus (videtur enim sibi omnia scire et nihil ignorare) me gravabat quodam loco Davidis ex Psalmo LXXII; ubi iste neotericorum maximus fautor dicebat apud Targum Chaldaeum paraphrasten mentionem apertissime fieri istius novi Christi latentis sub panis specie supra verticem sacerdotis extensi, hisce verbis: "Et erit placentula panis supra caput sacerdotis." Ubi autem Chaldaeum paraphrasten consuluissem, reperi apud illum idem quod Ebraei et Graeci habent; nempe, "Erit placentula frumenti in capite montium." Quod Chaldaeus sic scribit, בריש תוריא, *Beresh turaia*, quod est, in capite montium; et concordat cum Ebraeo בראש הרים, *Beroshe harim*, in capite montium; et Graeci ἐπ' ἄκρων τῶν ὀρέων. Quod Ebraei, Chaldaei, et Graeci vocant montes, hic neotericorum patronus sacerdotes vocavit. Si ita legeretur apud Chaldaeos, nihil neotericos adjuvaret, cum omnino negent illic quicquam panis esse. Sed non est mirum. Nam usurpant potestatem, non solum sententias mutandi, verum etiam ad placitum nomina omnibus rebus imponendi: quod nec pii hominis, nec fidi interpretis est. Vae igitur indocto vulgo, quibus quod libet licet mentiri absque omni reprehensione!

Sed neoterici hic mihi forte objicerent, vitandam esse nimiam subtilitatem, et causam eucharistiae non tam rigide ad rationis præcepta esse urgendam. Respondeo, me hæc vera et infallibilia præcepta rationis non adducere, quibus mihi ipsi aut aliis fidem et verum usum sacræ cœnæ persuadeam; quæ tantum ex verbo Dei discenda sunt : ubi, quantum in me est, omnes in Christo Jesu exhortor, quibus vita æterna est curæ, ut investigent atque explorent hanc rem penitius : quod si non fecerint, aut ignorantiæ tenebris aut superstitionum præstigiis a veritatis cognitione perpetuo impedientur. Sed in hunc finem huc retuli aliquot certos canones ex philosophicis præceptis, ut clare ostenderem neotericorum impia sacra et vesanam doctrinam nec cum præceptis sacrarum literarum nec canonibus philosophorum convenire. Nam quid iniquius contra doctrinam Christi vel philosophorum excogitari potest quam substantiam corporis organici longitudine, latitudine, et profunditate spoliare; et magnitudinem corporis Christi tollere, quæ, tum juxta sacras literas (quæ dicunt, "Verbum caro factum est;" et, "Similis est fratribus per omnia,") tum juxta omnes scholas philosophorum, ita hæret in substantia corporea, ut nunquam prorsus eam magnitudinem substantia corporea exuere possit? Neoterici vero in missis magnitudinem corporis Christi abstractam ab omni vera et continua quantitate esse fingunt, ut mathematici quantitates absque materia considerant. Quid hoc est aliud nisi phantasticum corpus Christi imaginari, et verum corpus penitus destruere?

Sed forte neoterici interpretes meo me hic stringent vinculo. Nam objicient aliam fuisse conditionem corporis Christi adhuc mortalis, aliam a resurrectione immortalis, aliam vero in eucharistia existentis. Quibus facile annuo, ac divisionis membra lubens amplector. Nam, morte corporis nondum persoluta, corporis conditione erat mortalis, tamen veri corporis substantiam semper retinens : mortis tyrannide devicta, immortalis est; tamen veri corporis substantiam non amisit : in eucharistia existit; sed ut Spiritu suo ac meritis passionis sacramentis suis adsit, et corpore absit. Et quemadmodum mortalem ejus naturam ac immortalem eandem substantiam semper esse confitemur; sic eandem naturam (quoad substantiam) omnino a terra abesse in cœlis confiteri compellimur auctoritate divinarum scripturarum impulsi. Quare Christus, sive mortalis sive immortalis (quoad ejus humanæ naturæ substantiam), rationis judicio semper fuit obnoxius; et ejus naturæ humanæ veritatem argumentis ac rationibus rationis captui manifestavit: sed naturæ suæ dignitatem et merita tantum judicio et contemplationi fidei patefecit. Quoad corporis ejus substantiam nunquam nec majus nec minus Christus recipit; perinde autem est jam factus immortalis verus homo atque antea, cum esset morti obnoxius: et quoad corporis ejus substantiam jam immortalis, ratione ac sensibus comprehensibilis est, ut Lucas testatur. Nam apostolis seipsum exhibuit viventem, postquam supplicio fuisset affectus, idque quam plurimis argumentis; nempe miraculis, familiaribus colloquiis, ostensione vulneris, comestione cibi, et aliis modis: unde Joannes dicit, " Quod audivimus, quod vidimus oculis nostris, quod perspeximus, et manus nostræ contrectaverunt de sermone vitæ," etc. Ex hisce et similibus locis sacrarum literarum constat Christum semper a virginis conceptione et partu habuisse et semper habere talem humanæ naturæ substantiam, quæ rationis et sensuum judicio est obnoxia, ubicunque fuerit: et quod aliquando, cum esset in terris, rationis ac sensuum judicium in corporis sui substantia superavit; ut cum jejunaret quadraginta dies et quadraginta noctes, et cum super mare ambularet, et ejusmodi; ita placuit uti natura sua humana ad gloriam Patris sui: tamen nullas conditiones veræ humanæ naturæ, cum hæc faceret, deposuit, sed semper incolumes servavit. Et idem sæpius actum est cum reliquis hominibus quibus Deus utitur ad suam gloriam. Moyses enim absque humanæ naturæ jactura, quemadmodum Christus, jejunavit quadraginta dies et noctes: Elisæus totum exercitum Sennacherib incognitus duxit in Samariam[1], ut Christus duos discipulos euntes in Emmaus incognitus comitabatur, tamen nullas substantiæ sui corporis partes deposuit: Petrus, ut Christus, super mare ambulavit, et veri corporis sui essentiam non amisit: Elias raptus est in cœlum turbine, tamen verus homo. Ita, utcunque Deus corpus Filii sui vel piorum hominum applicaverit, nunquam corporum veris qualitatibus illa spoliavit. Ideo nec majus nec minus corpus Christi, sive mortale sive immortale, recipit, sed semper (quoad corporis ejus substantiam) idem est. Mortalitatis conditiones per mortem exuit: veri autem corporis organici conditiones per resurrectionem non deposuit, sed incolumes ac intactas semper servat, non solum ut sacris literis ac fidei nostræ, verum etiam rationi et sensibus, illas comprobaret ac

[1 This occurred to the army of Benhadad, king of Syria. 2 Kings vi. 19.]

affirmaret, devicta mortis tyrannide. Neoterici interpretes sacrarum literarum cum nullis conveniunt nisi perfidis Judæis. Nam, quemadmodum ipsi in suis commentariis in prophetas mordicus defendunt quod Messias, quem adhuc expectant, præsentia sua corporali Gog et Magog, hoc est, universum mundum, sit subjugaturus, ut ipse hujus mundi imperio potiatur; ita neoterici suum Messiam corporaliter adesse volunt; cujus præsentia non solum corpora et animæ hominum salvæ fiant, verum etiam ut a canibus morbos expellat, incendia extinguat, porcos sanet, quasvis animalium pestes profliget, et ut omnes corporaliter in hac vita conservet.

Sed relinquamus has imposturas et scelera Deo; et investigemus qua ratione et quibus mediis Christus, quatenus homo, possit nobis esse salutaris. Scimus quod, quatenus est homo, amicis et inimicis notus erat, Judæ æque ut Petro: sed uni erat saluti, alteri vero damnationi. Quare dupliciter Christus, quatenus homo, considerandus venit: uno modo, quatenus est odor vitæ ad vitam, et positus in resurrectionem multorum; alio modo, quatenus est odor mortis ad mortem, ac positus in ruinam multorum. Quatenus sit odor vitæ ad vitam et resurrectio multorum, solis fidei oculis conspicitur, sola fide agnoscitur et apprehenditur. Quatenus est odor mortis ad mortem et ruina multorum, judicio carnis conspicitur, agnoscitur, et apprehenditur. Fide exultavit Abraham ut videret diem Christi; vidit, et gavisus est: judicio carnis Judæi, Pharisæi, et quam plures alii exultabant ut viderent diem nati Messiæ; viderunt, et tristati sunt, et odio habuerunt. Magi fide natum Christum adoraverunt: Herodes judicio carnis natum Christum interficere conatur. Pontifices et scribæ populi ex cortice prophetiæ Micheæ ubi Christus nasceretur; magi sub cortice stellæ quare nasceretur, fide intellexerunt; nempe ut omnes nationes terræ nato Christo obtemperarent: ideo inquiunt, "Accessimus, ut adoremus eum." Jam conferamus quid fides comprehendat et nobis applicet de Christo vero homine. Primum, per Spiritum sanctum ex verbo agnoscit Christi veram humanæ naturæ substantiam, quam ex nostræ carnis substantia in utero beatæ virginis e semine Abrahæ susceptam agnoscit. Deinde, id nobis e Christo vero homine applicat, quod ex nobis Christus non accepit; nempe puritatem, innocentiam, et sanctificationem, quam semper Christus in nostræ carnis substantia habuit. Et hæc omnia fides impetrat et exorat propter mortem quam

Christus in nostræ carnis substantia sustinuit, ut hæc per gratiam nostram immunditiam et fœditatem abluerent, et in nobis habitarent; quibus ad vitam æternam sanctificaremur. Exempla hujus fidei, quæ merita ac virtutes animæ, carnis, et sanguinis, mortisque Christi nobis applicat sine corporis Christi præsentia, passim in sacris literis occurrunt: ut Abraham Christi nondum nati merita ac virtutes fide est assequutus: centurio virtutem ac merita Christi in sanando milite suo, et non corporalem Christi præsentiam, fide exoravit hac oratione, "Domine non sum dignus ut intres sub tectum meum; sed tantum dic verbum, et salvabitur puer meus." Christi sympatriotæ et cognati illum corpore præsentem habuerunt, et tamen illius meritis destituebantur, et illum omni honore spoliabant; de quibus Christus in hunc modum conqueritur: "Non est propheta expers honoris nisi in patria sua et domo sua." Et hoc est quod D. Joannes in Revelationibus Jesu Christi dicit: "Ille erat agnus occisus ab origine mundi." Nam omnibus ætatibus ab exordio mundi his qui fide illum vera expectabant Christus efficaciter (quamvis non corporaliter) semper adfuit, etsi non juxta corporis humani præsentiam, tamen juxta corporis gratiam. Nobis autem, postquam corpus suum in cœlum sustulit, semper ex mera sua gratia meritis passionis suæ nostra expiavit peccata, Patri suo nos reconciliavit, corda et corpora nostra pavit, ac aliis virtutibus et donis Spiritus sancti illustravit: sed nunquam corporis sui substantiam manducandam aliquibus communicavit. Quod enim a nobis accepit, veram substantiam, in mortem pro nobis dedit; et virtutes quas cum corporis sui substantia semper retinet per fidem nobis impertit. Sed quod a nobis accepit si nobis impertiret, non prodesset: quemadmodum dixit, "Caro non prodest quicquam." Sic quod a nobis accepit apud se semper retinet, nempe corporis sui substantiam: et quod a nobis non accepit nobis impertit, nempe omnia bona quæ in nostræ carnis substantia in vita et in cruce nobis promeruit. Si quis oculis fidei orationem Marthæ pro Lazaro fratre suo defuncto contempletur, facile intelliget quæ dico: verba autem orationis sic habent: "Domine, si fuisses hic, frater meus non fuisset mortuus." Ex quibus verbis fidem Marthæ intelligimus omni ex parte non fuisse integram. Bene credidit quod Christus mortis ac morborum imperium haberet: sed male credidit, quod putabat

Matt. xiii.

Apoc. xiii.

[Joan. xi.]

Christum non potuisse morbos depellere et mortuos suscitare, nisi corpore suo adesset. Martha enim credere debuisset quod absens, quoad id quod a nobis accepit, tantum potuit contra morbos et mortem quantum præsens. Sic et nos etiam nunc credere debemus quod absens, quoad id quod a nobis accepit, tantum potest quantum præsens. Et, quod ad nostram salutem attinet, expedit ut in eo quod a nobis susceperit sit absens, quemadmodum ipsemet testatur, "Expedit vobis ut ego vadam," etc. Eruamus ergo oculos rationis et carnis, qui circa corporis Christi substantiam versantur carnaliter; et oculos fidei obtendamus in Christum Salvatorem nostrum, qui merita passionis Christi vident, ac eadem nobis applicant. Hisce vero oculis fidei Christum et verbo et sacramentis suis semper præsentem contemplamur, sed Spiritu et non carne; et qui oculos in carnalem corporis illius præsentiam intendunt, non solum ipsi decipiuntur, verum etiam alios decipere conantur. Nam Christi corpoream substantiam, quæ est finita, infinitam constituunt, ut cœlum et terram impleat: quod ipsis substantiis incorporeis, nempe animabus, angelis, et spiritibus, non est concedendum. Si ergo in sacra cœna Domini totum Christum fide recipimus, nec opus nec utile erit corporis ejus substantiam corporaliter et realiter per gulam trajicere: quod nunquam fuit factum, nec fieri potest. Et ne fieret, dixit, "Quid si videritis Filium hominis ascendentem eo ubi erat prius? Spiritus est qui vivificat; caro non prodest quicquam." Ex quibus discimus nos non posse eum carnaliter recipere; nec vero prodesse quicquam, ut illum carnaliter recipiamus.

Decimasexta probatio nostræ assertionis.

"Ascendit ad cœlos, sedet ad dextram Dei omnipotentis; inde venturus est judicare vivos et mortuos." Hanc fidem ut veram, sanctam, illibatam, indubitatam, et catholicam a nascentis ecclesiæ Christi primordiis omnes patres servabant, ut commune symbolum, quod apostolis Christi tribuitur, testatur; et hodie ab omnibus tanquam certissimum compendium et regula verissima, qua fideles ab infidelibus, veri Christiani ab iis qui hæreseos notis et maculis contaminantur[1], suscipitur. Ideo in apostolica ecclesia, et sanctorum patrum cœtu, qui hanc fidem illibate et religiose contestabantur, non pro hære-

[[1] The sense is incomplete. Supply *discerni possunt*.]

ticis, sed fidelibus, habebantur. De transubstantiatione vero panis et vini per ministrum in corporis et sanguinis Christi substantiam, vel quod Christus (qui secundum humanitatem in cœlos ascendit) hic in cœna corporaliter adesset, nunquam in sacris literis vel sanctorum patrum scriptis, per mille ferme annos ab ascensione Christi, legitur. Sed isti Romani et neoterici illos tantum igne et gladio persequuntur, qui hanc fidem catholicam profitentur. Nam si Christum impanatum, per pfaphum genitum et factum, in missis suis adesse credant et confiteantur, et si Christum ad dextram Dei Patris assidentem in cœlis nesciant, vel haud curent, satis esse pfaphi putant. Hoc enim scio (nec audita refero, et mœrens ac dolens scribo) quam pauci (imo paucissimi) episcopi sunt vel pastores ecclesiæ in hoc regno Angliæ, qui articulos fidei suis parochiis fideliter doceri curant. Quod si veri articuli christianæ religionis promulgarentur, absque dubio pfaphorum figmenta cito deprehenderentur a populo, ac perirent in ecclesia Christi. Quid autem potest excogitari contra corporalem Christi præsentiam in cœna clarius quam hoc quod symbolum apostolorum habet: "Ascendit ad cœlos," etc.? In scholis vero dialectices duo in hoc articulo concederentur, terminus a quo, et terminus ad quem. A quo Christus ascenderit, jam in articulis fidei dicitur, quod a terris ascenderit: terminus vero ad quem; "et in cœlum, inquit, ascendit." Jam quoad corporis ejus substantiam, terras, a quibus ascenderat, reliquit; et cœlos, in quos corpus suum transtulit, retinet. Ab infernis igitur abest quoad humanitatem, et supernas sedes quoad humanam naturam inhabitat. Præterea, plura adhuc continentur in hisce articulis, quod "sedet ad dextram Dei Patris," etc.: ubi terminus in quo Christus residet secundum humanitatem discitur, nempe cœlum supernum. Et ne quis hunc terminum, in quo Christus juxta carnem residet, putaret ubique extendi et protrahi, articulus fidei miro et admirando epilogo fidem nostram, quod ad Christum Filium hominis attinet, absolvit in hunc modum: "Inde venturus est judicare vivos et mortuos:" ac si diceretur, cœlum oportet Christum recipere (quoad ejus humanitatis substantiam) donec tempus aderit quo judicaturus sit vivos et mortuos. Hoc autem adverbium loci, Inde, docet nos non aliunde Christum esse venturum, ut judicet vivos et mortuos, quam e cœlis. Cœlum igitur (ut scholastici loquuntur) terminus est a quo Christus extremo die venturus est. Cum cœlum terminus sit a quo Christus veniet ac descendet ad nubes in novissimo die juxta carnem, terra certe, ubi Christus ex panis substantia (juxta neotericos) conficitur, terminus a quo Christus veniret ac ascenderet ad nubes in novissimo die esse non potest: quod si fieret, idem corpus simul et una ascenderet et descenderet, et simul terram infra nubes et coelum supra nubes incoleret; quod nihil nisi sola Dei essentia facit, non diaboli. Nam ipsi simul unum locum occupant: ideo Deus hunc in modum diabolum alloquitur: "Ubi fuisti? Circuivi, inquit diabolus, terram, et perlustravi eam." Unde discimus simul et in eodem instanti, quoad ejus substantiam, diabolum ubique esse non posse. Circuire enim et perlustrare terram est terram opere et industria successive et per successivos labores invisere; et qui sic circuit simul totum non implet. Angeli hoc non faciunt. Nam qui cum Jacobo certabat rogabat ut dimitteretur, quia aurora et tempus instabat quo ad sua rediret. Praeterea, angelos in scala videbat Jacob, illos quidem ascendentes, istos autem descendentes: ita ut ex scala illa Jacobaea liquido constet, quod angeli, quoad illorum substantiam, superna ac inferna simul non occupant. Christus vero, quatenus homo, hoc non facit. Nam quando in utero erat virginis matris, extra uterum ejus non erat: et quando egressus est ex utero, in utero non mansit. A resurrectione, quando tumulum reliquit, in quo corpus ejus triduo jacuit, in tumulo non erat; ut angeli testantur, "Resurrexit: non est hic: ecce locus ubi posuerunt eum." Quando in monte Oliveti cum discipulis suis colloquebatur de ipsius ablatione, quoad corporis ejus praesentiam testificans, non erat in nubibus; quas statim penetravit, ut astra teneret. Et cum nubes suscepissent illum ab oculis discipulorum, cum ipsis corporaliter praesens in terris non erat. Falsum est igitur quod neoterici dicunt, Christum, quoad ejus corporalem praesentiam, in terris sub speciebus panis et vini contineri. Nam coelum tenet ac possidet; unde veniet judicaturus vivos et mortuos: ut Paulus tamen inquit, qui sacram Domini coenam peragunt mortem Domini annunciant, donec venerit. Sed corporis Christi corporalem praesentiam, in quo redemptionem humani generis persolvit in cruce, hic adesse tota sacrarum literarum series et auctoritas pernegat; et in coelis illum, quoad corporis ejus praesentiam, collocat; ibique et nos illum sub poena aeternae Dei irae quaerere mandat, nec alibi, ne sub nomine et pallio Christi deci-

Job i.

Talia Deo etiam per prosopopæiam tribuantur.

[Gen. xxxii.]

[Gen. xxviii.]

Matth. xxiv. piamur: ut Christus ait, "Multi venient in nomine meo, dicentes, 'Ego sum Christus;' et multos seducent." "Sed si quis vobis dixerit, Ecce hic, ecce illic est Christus; nolite credere."

Confirmationes nostræ assertionis ex testimoniis sanctorum patrum, qui Christum jam [im]mortalitate[1] donatum (quatenus est homo) in cœlis collocant, et non in terris.

Cyprianus de symboli apostolorum expositione.

"Placuit autem, ut corpus quod mortale et corruptibile susceperat, de sepulchri petra levatum, et immortale atque incorruptibile effectum, jam non in terrenis, sed in cœlestibus, et in Patris dextra collocaret[2]." Caro Christi, quæ deposita erat in sepulchro, post tres dies juxta scripturas sanctas immortalitatem induit: et ut carnis Christi vera resurrectio discipulis et aliis indubitato constaret, Christus hanc multis argumentis et signis per quadraginta dies patefecit: et postea immortalem carnem de petra (inquit Cyprianus) sepulchri levatam jam non in terrenis, sed in cœlestibus, et in Patris dextra collocavit. Si Christus autem, quoad corporis ejus substantiam, non sit in terrenis, sed in cœlestibus, miror neotericos contra Cyprianum Christum, quoad corporis præsentiam, in terrenis constituere: id enim affirmant neoterici quod D. Cyprianus pernegat. Cyprianus autem dicit quod non est in terrenis: neoterici vero in terrenis esse dicunt. Cyprianus dicit, Non est in terrenis, sed in cœlestibus: neoterici autem aiunt illum in terrenis et in cœlestibus simul esse. Cyprianus, primum, negat Christum esse jam in terrenis; et, secundum, asserit quod sit in cœlestibus: neoterici vero et primum et secundum asserunt, et Christum, quod ad humanitatem ejus spectat, simul in terrenis et cœlestibus collocant. Et ut hæc manifesta et clara D. Cypriani verba (quæ negant Christum juxta carnem esse in terrenis) eludant, dicunt terrena et cœlestia, apud Cyprianum, significare terrenas et cœlestes conditiones et qualitates, et non loca terrena sive cœlestia: et ita interpretantur Christum non habitare in terrenis, sed in cœlestibus: id est, Christus post resurrectionem terrenas exuit conditiones, miserias, afflictiones, ignominias, et mortem; et[3] induit conditiones, proprietates, glorias, et immortalitatem:

[1 In Foxe, mortalitate.]
[2 Cyprian. Expos. in Symb. Apost. Op. Tom. II. p. 180. Antw. 1541.]
[3 *Cœlestes* appears to be wanting to complete the sense.]

sic vivere in terrenis esse hujus vitæ miseriis et calamitatibus
esse subjectum; et vivere in cœlestibus esse ab hujus vitæ
miseriis et calamitatibus liberari. Hæc equidem aliquo modo
vera sunt: sed nec verbis nec argumento D. Cypriani conveniunt. Nam non solum docet Christum per gloriosam suam *Papistici*
resurrectionem corporis mortalis conditiones deposuisse; verum *cavilli dilutio.*
etiam articulum Christi ascensionis in cœlos interpretatur, et
corpus Christi immortalibus et gloriosis conditionibus donatum
e terrenis locis ad cœlestia loca fuisse sublatum : et id testatur
illius verbum, "In Patris dextra collocaret;" quod non est
Christum post resurrectionem suam in altiore et digniore conditione tantum collocare, verum etiam in altiore et eminentiore
loco collocare: alioqui frustra poneretur articulus de Christi
ad cœlos ascensione. Si enim Patris dextra, et cœlestia, de
quibus Cyprianus meminit, nihil significarent præter cœlestes
et divinas qualitates, has Christus induit statim a resurrectione,
devicta et conculcata mortis tyrannide. Sed cœlestis Pater
sepultum suum Jesum Christum a resurrectione non tantum
præstantioribus, gloriosis, et immortalibus conditionibus dona-
vit; sed etiam præstantiora et digniora loca et habitacula illi
dedit et contulit, juxta sanctam ac catholicam fidem, "Ascendit
ad cœlos; sedet ad dextram Dei Patris omnipotentis." Sed
non constitui apud me aliorum rationes subvertere, nec illis
argumentis quibus neoterici veritatem expugnare conantur
respondere; verum rationes ac certitudines meæ ipsius fidei
omnibus Christi fidelibus simpliciter, nude, aperte, ac vere
proponere. Satis enim esse judico illorum nugas et infrugi-
fera somnia damnari et expugnari per Christi, evangelistarum,
apostolorum, sanctorumque patrum scripta, et catholicæ ecclesiæ Christi testimonia.

"Non super terram, nec in terra, nec secundum carnem, *Ambrosius*
quærere debemus, si volumus invenire[4]." Et paulo post: *lib. 10. in Luc. cap. 24.*
"Stephanus non super terram quæsivit, qui stantem ad dex-
tram Dei vidit." Ambrosius jubet nos cavere, ne Christum
super terram, in terra, vel secundum carnem, quæramus,
si volumus illum invenire. Neoterici autem jubent, mandant,
et ferro flammisque imperant, ut Christum, quoad carnem,
super terram et in terra latentem et delitescentem sub panis
et vini formis et speciebus quæramus: quod nisi fecerimus,

[4 Ambros. In Luc. xxiv. Lib. x. Oper. Tom. III. col. 229-230. A.
Paris. 1603.]

ut hæreticos nos proscindunt et flagellant. O miseranda, deploranda, ac calamitosa ecclesiæ Christi conditio, in qua tales dominantur et imperant qui catholicam Christi fidem a Christo, apostolis, et evangelistis traditam, sanctorumque patrum testimoniis confirmatam, profligant et persequuntur, ut peregrinam, fictam, et ementitam inducant et defendant! Quod autem Ambrosius dicit, non super terram nec in terra quærendum esse Christum juxta carnem, Christus apud evangelistas aliis verbis expressit. "Si quis, inquit, dixerit, Ecce hic, ecce illic est Christus; nolite credere." Quid est quærere Christum super terram vel in terra, nisi panem in altum a pfapho sublatum supra caput suum, vel eundem panem in altari repositum, pro Christo adorare? Nam ipsi semper hoc habent in ore, si supra caput in missis panis formam elevamus et extollimus, Ecce hic est Christus; et si panem in altari deposuerint, ogganniunt, Ecce ibi est Christus. Et si in ecclesia plures missæ fiant simul, panis per unum pfaphum factus est Christus Deus et homo: per alterum, statim ubi ad canonem venerit, fiet Christus Deus et homo; per alium vero jam panis factus Deus et homo consumptus est in stomacho pfaphi, et Christus hominem et mundum relinquens avolavit in cœlum: ut est De consecratione, distinctione secunda, in glossa[1]. Præterea, in una ecclesia simul et eodem tempore unus pfaphus Christum suum impanatum seorsum erigit: alter eodem tempore deorsum deprimit. Hic Christum incipit ex pane conficere; ille vero Christum confecit. Iste autem Christum comedit: alius comedendum adorat. In hoc altari forma panis recepta stomachum pfaphi implet: in illo vero altari forma panis adhuc jacet, sub qua statim Christus corpore est comedendus. In alio autem altari Christus trophæum agit; et sursum (quantum pfaphi vires extendunt) supra caput ejus extollitur. Ita ut pfaphi neoterici, dum unus Christum e supernis revocat, alter ad cœlos mittit; dum unus sursum elevat, alter eundem deorsum detrahit; dum hic hodie conficit Christum, ille eodem tempore eundem in pixide reservat; dum iste in pixide servat, alius vero eundem vermibus pollutum comburit; mirum in modum Christianam deformant religionem.

Hæc omnia scimus fieri in ecclesiis quæ tyrannidi Romani

[[1] Certum est quod species quam cito dentibus teruntur, tam cito in cœlum rapitur corpus Christi.—Corp. Jur. Can. de Consec. Dist. II. gloss. in cap. xxiii. Decret. Grat. col. 2261. Venet. 1604.]

pontificis subjiciuntur: sed quam procul absint ista a christiana religione, articuli fidei catholicæ testantur. Nos autem credimus Christum Jesum semen Abrahæ semel in utero beatæ virginis assumpsisse: illud ad mortem juxta carnem in cruce obtulit: idem tertio die immortale fecit; et post quadraginta dies illud e terris subduxit, ac sustulit in cœlum; quod in cœlo semper permanebit usque ad consummationem seculi: ita ut jam per manus sacrificuli illud semen Abrahami in Christo non possit amplius seorsum aut deorsum moveri vel agitari. Viderint ergo neoterici, qui Christi humanitatem indies ex pane conficiunt, et sub panis specie sursum ac deorsum dicunt se illum corporaliter agitare et movere, quid respondeant Christo, cum venerit in gloria majestatis suæ ad judicandum vivos et mortuos. Profecto si neoterici illorum scriptorum doctrinæ essent memores, qui dicunt Christum a resurrectione omnes hujus mundi conditiones deposuisse, et alias spirituales et cœlestes induisse; non dicerent, imo horrerent dicere, corpus Christi, immortalitate et cœlestibus conditionibus præditum, sursum ac deorsum per manus hominum agitari. Quod enim sursum ac deorsum movetur per hominem certe ultra mortales conditiones non induit. Præterea, de novo indies fieri non est cœleste et immortale, verum terrestre et caducum. Si autem ex pane qui hodie nec Deus nec homo erat fit Deus et homo, profecto hoc non est divinum nec humanum, sed plane phantasticum et abominandum. Quis enim, nisi omni fide et ratione destitutus, diceret vel crederet quod panis, qui hodie ex tritico conficitur, cras futurus sit Deus et homo? Rogo igitur enixe Dominum nostrum Jesum, ut omnes qui Christo nomina dederunt sedulo et alta mente secum perpendant hoc, an quod hodie nec Deus nec homo sit crastino sit futurus utrumque Deus et homo. Porro, quod neoterici dicunt, hoc fieri virtute et omnipotentia verbi divini, cogitent apud se, an sit possibile vel credibile, ut hodie id Deus fiat quod heri Deus non erat. Scriptura autem sancta nos docet Deum nec principium nec finem habere. Quomodo igitur erit cras Christus quod hodie est panis? Sed ad reliqua sanctorum patrum testimonia redibo.

Alia confirmatio nostræ assertionis.

"Dupliciter vero sanguis Christi et caro intelligitur: vel spiritualis atque divina, de qua ipse dixit, 'Caro mea vere est   <small>Hieronymus in primum cap. Epistolæ Ephes.</small>

cibus, et sanguis meus vere est potus;' et, 'Nisi manducaveritis carnem meam, et sanguinem meum biberitis, non habebitis vitam æternam:' vel caro et sanguis Christi quæ crucifixa est, et qui militis effusus est lancea, etc.[1]" D. Hieronymus unam carnem Christi spiritualem atque divinam facit, quam cibum fidelium Christus appellavit ab omnibus comedendum: alteram vere ac positive naturalem et crucifixam facit. Ita et sanguinem Christi duplicem facit; unum a fidelibus bibendum, alterum militis lancea effusum. Neoterici vero contra Hieronymum affirmant, eandem carnem crucifixam in suis missis esse comedendam, atque eundem sanguinem militis lancea effusum esse bibendum. Quod autem D. Hieronymus negat ipsi affirmant. Nam inquit, Alia est spiritualis atque divina caro, de qua Christus dixit, "Caro mea vere est cibus;" et alia caro, quæ a Judæis est crucifixa. Eandem etiam divisionem ponit de sanguine; unum ad potandum in sacra cœna, alterum vero effusum in dira cruce. Idem et nos dicimus, quod spiritualis atque divina caro Christi ab omnibus fidelibus recte cœnam Domini manducantibus sumitur, sed non carnalis et humana caro: hoc est, caro Christi in hunc spiritualem ac divinum usum a Deo Patre destinata, ut illius morte super crucem nostra omnia peccata perlitaret, ab omnibus edi debet; non ut carnis Christi substantia stomachum recipientis symbola sacræ cœnæ impleat; sed ut mortis ejus meritis, quam in carne est passus, conscientiæ maculas abstergat, atque peccatores Deo Patri reconciliet. Hæc caro Christi fide sumitur, et non ore: totum hominem (id est, corpus et animam) implet, et non unam hominis partem, scilicet stomachum. Hæc autem non per hominem cum externis symbolis exhibetur; verum per Spiritum sanctum, quando symbola juxta institutionem Christi rite ministrantur. Idem dicendum est etiam de sanguine Christi, qui spiritualis est potus fidelium: sed sanguis Christi militis lancea effusus in cœlis est, et non in terris. Et hoc idem Hieronymus clarius ostendit in libro Ecclesiast. cap. iii. hisce verbis: "Porro quia caro Domini verus est cibus, et sanguis verus est potus, juxta ἀναγωγήν; hoc solum habemus in presenti seculo bonum, si vescamur carne ejus, cruoreque potemur, non solum in mysterio, sed etiam in scripturarum lectione[2]." Duo D. Hieronymus his verbis docet: primum,

Hieronymus in Eccles. cap. 3.

[1 Hieron. In Ephes. c. i. Oper. Tom. ix. fol. 90. k. Paris. 1534.]
[2 Id. In Eccles. cap. iii. Op. Tom. vii. fol. 31. m.]

quod caro Christi et ejus sanguis juxta ἀναγωγὴν sunt cibus et potus; secundum, quod non solum in mysterio, sed etiam in scripturarum lectione, caro et sanguis Christi percipiuntur.

Perpendamus altius hanc divi Hieronymi doctrinam. Juxta, inquit, ἀναγωγὴν caro Domini est verus cibus, et sanguis ejus verus potus. Quis vel abecedarius[3] ignorat quod ἀναγωγὴ non historicum vel literalem, sed allegoricum ac reconditum sensum in sacris literis exigat? Si ergo caro Christi juxta ἀναγωγὴν sit verus cibus, quare non anagogice Christi verba, "caro mea vere est cibus," accipiunt? Sed quod Christus atque omnes sancti patres spiritualiter et juxta ἀναγωγὴν loquuntur, neoterici, ut novum atque ementitum Christum suum protegant, omnia ad strepitum atque verborum stridorem urgent: quod omnino nec pium nec sanctum est. Deinde, inquit Hieronymus quod caro et sanguis Christi æque in sacrarum literarum lectione atque in mysterio percipiantur. Nemo autem dubitat quin in lectione sacrarum literarum caro Christi non carnaliter et corporaliter, sed spiritualiter et efficaciter percipiatur. Mirum ergo est, quod corporalis et carnalis corporis Christi perceptionem in mysterio Domini cœnæ constituant. Sed isti neoterici, ut suum novum Deum masculo pectore defendant, diruunt, ædificant, mutant quadrata rotundis[4], ut solent dicere. Christi quidem spiritualem et sacramentalem manducationem corporis sui diruunt, atque carnalem impie ædificant; et bene quadrata in verbo Dei suis rotundis præstigiis et circulatoriis mutant. Nos credimus tamen, quod juxta ἀναγωγὴν caro Christi verus sit cibus, et sanguis ejus verus potus, sed non juxta literalem et historicum sensum. Et hoc credimus, non solum sanctorum patrum testimoniis admoniti, verum etiam Christo ipso mandante, qui dixit, "Verba quæ ego loquor vobis spiritus et vita sunt: caro non prodest quicquam." Spiritualem ergo, juxta ἀναγωγὴν, exigunt sensum, et non sermonis aut literarum stridorem et strepitum; quem semper neoterici contra sacras scripturas et sanctorum patrum scripta insulsissime urgent. Neoterici valde conqueruntur, quod populus hujus regni adeo abominatur ac detestatur illorum impia sacra; quodque diligentius et religiosius templa non frequentant. Sed ego certe magis miror, quod qui illorum missis intersunt subito ac repente vel in furorem vel in mortem

[3 Abecedarius, qu. *learner of A B C D?*]
[4 Hor. Epist. I. i. 100.]

non incidant. Quis enim non horresceret, et judicium Dei non metueret, quando quod ante missam triticum, simila, et panis erat, in missa pro Deo ipso adoratur; et quod jam juxta illos Deus est, erat aliquando, nempe ante semihoram, quando Deus non erat? Quam horrenda sunt ista quæ a neotericis ad ravim usque clamitantur, quam tremenda; quod ante consecrationem panis erat, post consecrationem fiat Deus! Deus misereatur nostri atque ecclesiæ suæ, et liberet illam ab isto idolo abominationis. Profecto gravissime in Deum peccant, qui hujusmodi impiis sacris intersunt. Si tamen de rebus adiaphoris, mediis, vel ceremoniola aliqua ageretur, non tantum esset periculum illis qui intersunt: sed res agitur de novo Christo, et novo sacrificio, de quibus nec prophetæ nec evangelistæ unquam audierunt vel prædicaverunt; ut postea manifestius ostendam.

<small>August. in Jo. tract. 30. Corpus Christi in uno loco.</small>
"Sursum est Dominus; sed etiam hic est veritas Domini. Corpus enim Domini in quo resurrexit uno loco esse oportet: veritas ejus ubique diffusa est[1]." Hic D. Augustinus cum Cypriano et Ambrosio, item cum sacris literis, idem dicit. Dominus, inquit, quatenus homo, sursum est: sed quatenus Deus, hic est; cujus vi ac potentia vivimus, movemur, et sumus: præterea omnes creaturæ ab eo a corruptione conservantur. Et Dominum, quod ad corpus ejus attinet in quo resurrexit, in uno loco esse oportet (sic vetera exemplaria Augustini legunt, et sic in canonico jure, De consecratione, distinctione secunda, Augustinus citatur; et non, potest esse, ut posterior editio Augustini habet[2]). Hic duo Augustinus animadvertit: unum, quod Christi corpus in quo resurrexit (hoc est, corpus Christi immortale et gloriosum) in uno loco esse oporteat; alterum vero, quod simul et semel idem corpus gloriosum plura loca occupare vel implere non possit. Hæc Augustini verba premunt ac flagellant neotericorum errorem, qui dicunt corpus Christi reale esse in sacramento, tamen non localiter (ut aiunt), vel non ut in loco. Quod si non sit in loco, haud dubie non est corpus, ut statim ostendam. Sed contra illos aperte testatur Augustinus: "Corpus in quo resurrexit in uno loco esse oportet."

<small>August. Tract. in Joan. 50.</small>
Idem Augustinus affirmat Tractatu in Joannem L[3], ubi tam perspicua et manifesta habentur verba, ut omnes hunc errorem

[1 August. in Evang. Joan. Tract. xxx. cap. vii. Op. Tom. IX. col. 247. c. Basil. 1569. Where *veritas Dominus*, and *esse potest*.]

[2 Corp. Jur. Can. de Consec. Dist. II. cap. xliv. col. 2276. Venet. 1604.]

[3 Tract. L. cap. xii. Op. Tom. IX. coll. 367. D. 368. A.]

de corporali corporis Christi præsentia facile agnoscant; nisi velint in clara luce oculos suos obserare, et volentes ac scientes agnitam et apertam veritatem impugnare. Verba ejus sunt hæc, commentantis in hunc locum Joannis evangelistæ, "Et loquebantur inter se, Quid putatis, quod non venit ad diem festum? etc." "Nos indicemus modo Judæis ubi sit Christus; utinam velint audire et apprehendere, quicunque sunt ex semine illorum qui dederant mandatum ut indicarent eis ubi esset Christus. Veniant ergo ad ecclesiam, audiant ubi sit Christus, et apprehendant eum. A nobis audiant, et ex evangelio audiant. Occisus est a parentibus eorum, sepultus est, resurrexit, a discipulis agnitus, ante oculos eorum ascendit in cœlum, ibi sedet ad dextram Patris: qui judicatus est venturus est judex. Audiant et teneant. Respondent, Quem tenebo? Absentem? Quomodo in cœlum manum mittam, ut ibi sedentem teneam? Fidem mitte, et tenuisti. Parentes tui tenuerunt carne; tu tene corde: quoniam Christus absens etiam præsens est: nisi præsens esset, a nobis ipsis teneri non posset. Sed quoniam verum est quod ait, Ecce ego vobiscum sum usque ad consummationem seculi, et abest, et hic est; et rediit, et nos non deseruit: corpus enim suum intulit cœlo, majestatem non abstulit mundo." Hæc Augustinus. Quis desiderare vel excogitare potest quicquam clarius et apertius contra errorem de corporali corporis Christi præsentia in terris quam hæc quæ ab Augustino notantur? Rogat Augustinus Judæos ut ad ecclesiam veniant, et audiant ubi sit Christus. Sed rogat Augustinus ut in ecclesia hoc discant Judæi per illum et alios, qui Christum indicarent; non ex umbris et tenebris humanarum literarum, verum ex stella et luce evangelii; quod indicat, inquit, Christum a Judæis occisum, post mortem fuisse sepultum, post sepulturam e mortuis resurrexisse, et agnitum fuisse a discipulis, ante quorum oculos ascendit in cœlum, et ibi sedet ad dextram Patris; et tandem qui judicatus est veniet judicaturus vivos et mortuos. Hæc rogat Augustinus ut audiant et teneant. O utinam neoterici nostri hoc a populo Christiano rogarent, ut ex evangeliis discerent ubinam esset Christus noster, qui semel pro nobis vitam suam deposuit: tunc absque dubio audirent, intelligerent, et tenerent, Christum (juxta humanam suam naturam) esse in cœlis, et non in terris. Sed neoterici humana dogmata tantum produnt, ex quibus fingunt Christi humanitatem invisibiliter latere in terris sub speciebus panis et vini; contra manifesta testimonia omnium evangelistarum et apostolorum, ac etiam D. Augustini, qui dicit, Fidem mitte, ac tenuisti: ac si dixisset, Post assumptionem carnis Christi in coelum non opus est ut manum mittas in coelum, quo illum teneas. O si ista verba neoterici diligenter perpenderent! Si autem Augustinus credidisset corporis Christi realem praesentiam in eucharistia, quam apposite potuisset dicere, Manum ministri ad altare astantis contemplare, et illic Christum latentem sub speciebus panis et vini invenias et teneas! Vel sic dixisset, Recipe panem sanctum et consecratum; et sub ejus forma Christum ore percipies, et per gulam in stomachum trajicies. Sed pius Augustinus omnem corporalem corporis Christi praesentiam a Judaeis tollit, sic inquiens: "Parentes tui tenuerunt carne; tu tene corde: quoniam Christus absens etiam praesens est: nisi praesens esset, a nobis teneri non posset." Non dicit Augustinus ad Judaeum, Parentes tui tenuerunt carne et carnali modo; sed carne, simpliciter. Nec dicit, Tu corporaliter Christum corde tene; sed simpliciter dicit, Corde tene: hoc est, ut antea dixit, Mitte fidem, et tenuisti; id est, crede in Jesum Christum, et illum tenes, et ipse te tenet. Nam quamvis quoad corporis ejus praesentiam absit, virtute tamen, efficacia, et meritis suae gratiae ac passionis praesens est: et sic corpore abiit, et spiritu hic est; et rediit, et nos non deseruit: corpus enim suum intulit coelo, majestatem autem non abstulit mundo. Qui haec Augustini verba diligenter candidoque judicio legeret, facile errorem de corporali corporis Christi praesentia in terris intelligeret: quod ut omnes semel intelligant, Deum suppliciter oramus, et ut errorem cognitum ex animo deponant. Tunc tandem ad gremium sanctae matris ecclesiae Christi redirent, et cum illa firmiter crederent Christum adesse suis sacramentis, non carnaliter, corporaliter, aut realiter; sed sacramentaliter spiritualiter, et potentialiter.

Annotabo etiam illum insignem locum ex libro de essentia Divinitatis, qui inter libros Aurelii Augustini computatur.

August. de essentia Divinitatis.

Circa finem istius libri haec habentur verba: " Sed quia Filius Dei, qui in substantia divinitatis cum Patre unum est, ob reparationem humani generis, quod in Adam lapsum fuerat, prope finem mundi in uterum Mariae virginis illapsus, veram carnem ex ejus substantia creavit, atque in singularitate personae suae ita univit, ut Deus pariter esset et homo; simplici vero persona, ut dictum est, genuina vero substantia ex eadem virgine incorrupto pudore nasceretur; ut qui erat et est in divinitate verus Deus a Patre genitus, invisibilis et incorporeus atque incomprehensibilis, sicut et Pater, ipse esset et verus homo, visibilis, corporeus, et circumscriptus; atque idem ipse, non alius Deus et alius homo, sed Deus et homo, unus est Christus Dei Filius; passus pro salute nostra, in sola carne mortuus, et sepultus in eadem carne; in qua etiam die tertio per virtutem divinitatis suæ de sepulchro resurgens ascendit in cœlum, et sedet ad dextram Patris: quem inde venturum ad judicandum vivos et mortuos in ea carne in qua ascendit, sed glorificata, universalis expectat ecclesia; quemadmodum et in symbolo universi decantant fideles. Et idcirco eundem Dei Filium secundum substantiam divinitatis suæ invisibilem et incorporeum et immortalem et incircumscriptum[1] nos credere et confiteri oportet: juxta humanitatem vero visibilem, corporeum, localem, atque omnia membra humana veraciter habentem credere convenit et confiteri. Quoniam, sicut eundem Dei Filium et Redemptorem nostrum secundum divinitatem invisibilem et incorporeum, sicut et Patrem et Spiritum Sanctum, non credere impium est; ita eundem Dei Filium in homine assumptum visibilem, corporeum, atque localem post resurrectionem non credere et profiteri profanum est[2]." Hæc Augustinus: vel igitur Augustinus vel neoterici male et perperam de humanitate Christi jam immortali facta sentiunt. Augustinus enim dicit, quod, sicut Christus verus Deus est, invisibilis et incorporeus atque incomprehensibilis; ita et verus homo est, visibilis, corporeus, et circumscriptus. Verba Augustini sunt notanda. Christus autem, inquit, ut verus homo, est corporeus et circumscriptus: neoterici vero dicunt ac docent Christum in sacramento (ut est verus homo) esse corporeum, tamen incircumscriptum. Sed qualis sit ille Christus, qui est juxta humanam naturam incircumscriptus, viderint qui hoc prædicant et docent. Profecto non ille est quem patriarchæ, prophetæ, et apostoli agnoverunt: igitur nullus est. Nam verus Christus, quatenus homo, est (inquit Augustinus) circumscriptus. Præterea addit, Et idcirco eundem Dei Filium secundum substantiam divinitatis suæ invisibilem et incor-

[[1] (Sicut et Patrem et Spiritum Sanctum) August.]
[[2] August. de Essent. Divinit. Op. Tom. IV. coll. 974. C. D. 975. A. Basil. 1569. Where for *genuina, gemina.*]

poreum et immortalem et incircumscriptum nos credere et confiteri oportet: juxta humanitatem vero visibilem, corporeum, localem, etc. Augustinus dicit quod Christus (quatenus est verus homo) non solum est visibilis et corporeus, verum etiam localis. Quomodo igitur cohæret hæc fides S. Augustini et sanctorum, qui Christum a resurrectione, quatenus est homo, localem faciunt, cum fide neotericorum, qui Christum in eucharistia illocalem reddunt? Omnes enim neoterici dicunt quod Christus est sub forma panis et vini in sacramento, sed non ut in loco: Augustinus vero ait quod, sicut Christus, quatenus verus Deus, est incircumscriptus; ita, ut verus homo, est circumscriptus et localis. Addit etiam, A resurrectione. "Quoniam (inquit), sicut eundem Dei Filium et Redemptorem nostrum secundum divinitatem invisibilem et incorporeum, sicut et Patrem et Spiritum Sanctum, non credere impium est; ita eundem Dei Filium in homine assumptum visibilem, corporeum, atque localem post resurrectionem non credere et confiteri profanum est." Miror igitur qua temeritate et audacia isti neoterici audeant Christum verum hominem constituere incircumscriptum et illocalem, idque pro veritatis assertione defendere; cum Augustinus dicat "eundem Christum Dei Filium in homine assumptum visibilem, corporeum, atque localem non credere ac confiteri post resurrectionem profanum esse." Quare autem non insurgunt bellaque movent contra hunc sanctum patrem Augustinum, qui dicit Christum (quoad humanitatem) localem non credere ac confiteri profanum esse? Neoterici vero dicunt Christum (quoad ejus humanitatem) in cœna credere adesse, et non localem, sanctum esse; imo sanctissimum vocant ac docent: sed Augustinus profanum esse ac impium affirmat. Eligant ergo pii lectores quem velint instructorem et judicem habere in hac causa; sanctissima Dei verba et sanctorum patrum scripta, an Papæ tyrannidem et neotericorum mendacia. Quod autem sacræ literæ veterumque patrum testimonia profanum vocant, isti neoterici sanctum esse jactitant.

Aliud testimonium ex Augustino subjiciam, quo (juxta corporalem sui præsentiam) Christum a nobis abesse confitetur: sed interponam unum locum D. Gregorii, qui habetur homilia xxi. Paschatis, ne alias seorsim per se positus huc non tantum facere crederetur. Hæc habet verba, commentans in hunc locum evangelistæ, "Surrexit; non est hic:" "Non est hic dicitur per præsentiam carnis, qui tamen nusquam deerat per præsentiam majestatis¹." Ex quibus verbis cognoscimus Christum, quod ad divinitatem ejus attinet, ubique esse; quod vero ad humanitatem, locum semper retinere, et esse (ut Augustinus dicit) circumscriptione et localiter in loco: quod neoterici Romani omnibus modis pernegant. Nam pro hoc maxime contendunt, ut Christum verum hominem sub speciebus panis et vini corporaliter habeant, non tamen circumscriptum aut localem: quod est penitus humanitatis Christi substantiam destruere atque annihilare. Legant igitur sacras literas sanctorumque patrum scripta cum judicio, absque ulla præjudicii temeritate: et tunc tenebræ falsæ doctrinæ, quæ illos in errore detinent, luci evangelii proculdubio cedent; et ipsi, ab humanarum traditionum servitute liberati, Domino Deo nostro de fontibus Israel (hoc est, ex divinis scripturis, et non hominum) laudes gratis animis cantabunt. Nam (ut Augustinus inquit) "sanctæ scripturæ non temerarios et superbos accusatores, sed diligentes et pios lectores desiderant²." Quid autem arrogantius superbiusve contra scripturas divinas per Spiritum sanctum ecclesiis traditas, ac morte et sanguine Christi obfirmatas et consignatas, excogitari possit quam id affirmare quod ipsæ apertissimis verbis pernegant; idque negare quod omnibus modis illæ affirmant? Propterea rogo æquum lectorem ut judicet quæ dico testimonio verbi divini. Verbum enim Dei per Spiritum sanctum mundo proditum dicit, "Si quis dixerit, Ecce hic, ecce illic est Christus; nolite credere." Et iterum, "Pauperes semper habebitis vobiscum; me non semper habebitis." Iterum, "Relinquo mundum, et vado ad Patrem." Iterum, "Quem oportet cœlum suscipere usque ad tempus restaurationis omnium." Ad hæc, "Quid si videritis Filium hominis ascendentem ubi erat prius?" Neoterici tamen, contra ista apertissima loca, et multa alia testimonia, quæ negant Christum juxta carnem esse in terris, affirmant, docent, ac prædicant Christum (quoad humanitatem) præsentem esse in terris; atque hanc affirmationem ferro et igne in ecclesiis stabiliunt; ubi sacræ vero literæ ecclesiis apertissimam negationem tradunt. Præterea sacræ literæ (ut hactenus est

August. contra Adimant. Manichæi discipulum. cap. 12.

Matth. xxiv.

Matth. xxvi.

Joan. xvi.

Act. iii.

Joan. vi.

[¹ Greg. Magn. Hom. xxi. Oper. fol. 325. c. Paris. 1533.]
[² August. contra Adim. cap. iii. Op. Tom. vi. col. 178. A. Basil; 1569.]

ostensum) asserunt notissimis ac clarissimis verbis panem dari, panem frangi, panem edi in cœna Domini. Nam Christus de pane accepto et benedicto dixit, "Hoc est corpus meum, quod pro vobis datur." Iterum, "Panis quem frangimus, nonne communio corporis Christi est?" Adhuc sæpius, "Quotiescunque comederitis panem," etc. Et de calice Christus dixit, "Non bibam amplius ex hoc fructu vitis," etc. Neoterici autem hanc notam ac clarissimam assertionem panis et vini in sacra cœna, quam sanctæ literæ testantur, omnibus modis, etiam ferro et igne, oppugnant. Quod Christus per sacrum suum verbum affirmat, ipsi vero per leges papales negant: et quod Christus per verbum suum negat, illi per jus pontificum affirmant. Sed si neoterici (ut videri volunt) multum fuissent versati in veterum patrum scriptis, non urgerent unum locum sacræ scripturæ, "hoc est corpus meum," contra multa et clarissima loca, quæ supra fideliter annotavi. Imo hoc audeo affirmare, nullum locum (si germane intelligatur) in tota divinarum literarum serie plus facere contra transubstantiationem panis in cœna, quam hic locus facit, Hoc est corpus meum. Nec sum nescius quam mirabiliter se torqueant neoterici in hac propositione interpretanda. Augustinus vero in libro De Doctrina Christiana docet unum locum per plura intelligi debere, et non unum contra plura[1]. Et, ut inquit contra Adimantum Manichæi discipulum, capite tertio: "Intelligenda sunt, non temere accusanda, quæ imperitis videntur esse contraria[2]." Quid est hoc igitur nisi arrogantiæ, vel potius insaniæ, indicium, semper recurrere ad petitionem principii, dicendo, "Hoc est corpus meum: vel est realiter corpus Christi, aut Christus arguendus et accusandus est mendacii; nam ipse dixit, Hoc est corpus meum?" Nos quidem Christum hoc dixisse non ignoramus: et Christum atque propositionem veros esse credimus atque testamur. Dicimus tamen, et semper probabimus, nec Christum corpus suum naturale in sacramento constituere voluisse, nec propositionem talem habere sensum qualem neoterici falsissime

---

[1 Nihil enim fere de illis obscuritatibus eruitur quod non planissime dictum alibi reperiatur.—August. de Doctr. Christ. Lib. II. cap. vi. Op. Tom. III. col. 23. c. Basil. 1569.

Ubi autem apertius ponuntur, ibi discendum est quomodo in locis intelligantur obscuris.—Ibid. Lib. III. cap. xxv. col. 57. A.]

[2 Id. Contra Adim. cap. III. Op. Tom. VI. col. 176. B.]

fingunt et jactitant. Imo judicet æquus lector, an verba ipsa propositionis non ostendant panis substantiam remanere in cœna, quam Christus corpus suum appellavit. Nam Christus dixit de pane quem tenebat in manibus, Hoc est corpus meum: non dixit de alia substantia quam panis. Nec dixit, Sub hac, in hac, supra hanc, vel cum hac forma, panis est corpus meum, quod vobis manducandum exhibeo: sed de pane dixit, Hoc est corpus meum; et sacramentali modo panis substantiam corpus suum fecit, et ita vocavit. Et sic de sacramento sacramentalis loquendi modus non est contemnendus. Omnia enim sacramenta eorum induunt nomina quorum sunt sacramenta: ut non solum sacræ literæ, verum etiam sanctorum patrum testimonia testantur. Sacramenta tamen non transeunt in naturas ipsas earum rerum quarum sunt sacramenta; sed sacramenta et res sacramentorum distinctas ac discretas naturas semper retinent. Neutra vero substantia, vel signi aut signati, perit, nec in alterius substantias transit; sed utraque manet: ut omnia sacramenta Christi ab origine mundi ecclesiis suis tradita testantur. Augustinus vere in Psalmum xcviii. pulchre et erudite naturas signorum et signatorum discretas ac distinctas retinet, hisce verbis: "Non hoc corpus quod videtis, inquit, manducaturi estis, neque illum sanguinem quem effusuri sunt Judæi, qui me crucifigent, bibituri estis: sacramentum aliquod vobis do: id spiritualiter acceptum vivificat[3]." Hæc et hujusmodi verba quam plurima habet Augustinus in eodem Psalmo: sed quia liber mihi non adest, rogo pium lectorem ut Augustinum legat, et bene perpendat ac cogitet apud se verba Augustini, qui dicit, Non hoc corpus quod videtis manducaturi estis. Simpliciter enim dicit, quod corpus Christi quod videbatur non esset manducandum. Non autem dixit, Hoc corpus, quale vel qualiter videtis, non estis manducaturi (ut neoterici Romani dicunt); sed, Hoc corpus quod videtis, dixit, non estis manducaturi. Augustinus autem dicit, Nec illum sanguinem bibituri estis quem effusuri sunt qui me crucifigent. Neoterici vero e contrario repugnant, dicentes, Omnino bibituri estis sanguinem illum quem Judæi effusuri sunt, sed non eo cruento et tyrannico more. Augustinus corporis et sanguinis Christi substantiam per hominem manducari vel bibi negat; nam dicit, Hoc corpus non estis manducaturi, nec illum sanguinem bibituri.

[3 Vide supra, p. 463, note 4.]

Hæc pronomina, hoc, quis, ille, vel hujusmodi, omnes qui vel elementa grammatices norunt haud ignorant quod substantiam corporis et sanguinis significent, quam non sumus suscepturi cum sacramenti perceptione. Duo dicit Augustinus hoc in loco: unum autem, quod corporis et sanguinis Christi substantia, quæ est res sacramenti, non sit præsens, nec corporaliter lateat sub externis formis sacramenti; alterum vero, quod sacramenti et rei sacramenti naturæ et substantiæ non confundantur, commisceantur, aut annihilentur in sacramento. Neoterici multa et varia docent, scribunt, et disputant de signi et signati conjunctione et unione, an sit personalis, realis, vel rationalis: sed quia rem per se perspicuam ac planam ex sacris scripturis cognoscimus, non opus erit circa tales argutias et circulationes, quæ rem perlucidam ac planam implicatam, obscuram, ac nodis et difficultatibus plenam reddunt, immorari. Satis enim est, quia verum, quod scimus ex verbo Dei signum et signatum uniri et conjungi institutione divina, contemplationeque ac usu divino, cœlesti, ac fideli; præterea significatione et rerum similitudine. Nam quemadmodum externa aquæ lotio corpus abluit et mundat, ita interna Spiritus sancti operatio animam abluit et purgat; et quemadmodum panis et vinum corpora nostra alunt ac sustentant, ita corpus et sanguis Christi animas fide recipientium nutriunt et refovent; ut integer homo, cum corpore tum anima, per integrum Christum corpore et anima, quem contemplatione ac consideratione fidei percipit, vivat in Christo ad vitam æternam. Sed signum et signatum uniri naturaliter, ita ut signum in sacramento fiat aliquorum verborum prolatione quod signatum est sua substantia et natura, credere non possumus. Christus enim testatur vinum in sacramento esse fructum vitis; quod verum non esset, si per verba sanctificationis vinum sua natura et substantia fieret significatum, hoc est, verus sanguis Christi. Idem docet Paulus de pane ad Corinthios, ut est antea. Institutione tamen Christi, ac contemplatione et consideratione fideli, coeunt et conjunguntur signum et signatum in sacramentis; sed non aliter, ut neoterici dicunt: qui non solum signi naturam et substantiam (id est, panis et vini) in sacra cœna destruunt ac perimunt; sed etiam semper res signatas per signa ita præsentes faciunt, ut qui unum recipit et alterum necessario recipiat: ita ut, sive impii, sive pii, vel bruta animantia (ut sunt canes, mures, et hujusmodi) signum externum capiant, et res signatas capere oporteat, propter signi et signati inseparabilem ac indivulsam unionem, conjunctionemque naturalem, quam ipsi constituunt: quod non solum falsum, verum etiam impium esse, constanter testamur. Nam Israelitæ sub Mose manna, qui erat typus Christi, omnes manducabant: sed non manducabant manna Christum, quia plures illorum non approbavit Deus, ut inquit Paulus. Sic Simon Magus tinctus erat baptismo Christi: sed non erat tinctus baptismo Christo; et, ut Augustinus dicit, "Judas manducabat panem Domini; sed non manducabat panem Dominum[1]." Quæ loca testantur quod significata non semper sunt præsentia externis signis; sed illis tantum una adsunt qui vera fide ac pœnitentia (modo adultæ sint ætatis) externa signa juxta mandatum et institutionem Christi percipiunt. Et malos non comedere carnem Christi ipsemet Christus testatur, dicens, "Qui manducat meam carnem, et bibit meum sanguinem, in me manet, et ego in illo." Manere autem in Christo est participem esse omnium meritorum Christi: et Christum manere in homine est ei quem inhabitat per Spiritus sancti efficaciam ostendere quod ipse sit auctor et causa illius vitæ in quo manet. Jam impii qui non agunt pœnitentiam vitæ præteritæ non sunt participes omnium meritorum Christi; nam hujusmodi margaritæ non solent projici ante porcos et canes, quorum fœditatem et conspurcationem impii induerunt. Propterea (ut Sapientiæ liber testatur) in malevolam animam non introibit sapientia, nec habitabit in corpore subdito peccatis. Si quis cupit hac de re plura cognoscere, quod mali non comedant corpus Christi, legat Cyprianum in sermone De Cœna Domini[2], Augustinum De verbis Domini, sermone xxxiii.[3], trac-

[1 In Joan. cap. xiii. Tract. LIX. August. Op. Tom. IX. col. 402. c. Basil. 1569.]

[2 Quamvis ab indignis se sumi vel contingi sacramenta permittant, non possunt tamen spiritus esse participes quorum infidelitas vel indignitas tantæ sanctitudini contradicit.... Verum his qui verbo tenus corde sicci et mente aridi sacris intersunt, vel etiam participant donis, lambunt quidem petram, sed inde nec mel sugunt nec oleum, qui nec aliqua caritatis dulcedine nec Spiritus sancti pinguedine vegetantur, sed sicut cibis communibus irreverenter sacris utuntur muneribus.—(Arnold. ap.) Cyprian. Op. Tom. II. pp. 294, 298. Antverp. 1541.]

[3 Nolite parare fauces, sed cor. Inde commendata est ista cœna, Ecce credimus in Christum, quem fide accipimus....Modicum accipimus, et in corde saginamur. Non ergo quod videtur, sed quod creditur, pascit.—August. Op. Tom. X. col. 128. D.]

tatu in Joannem xxvi.[1], Hieronymum in Esaiam cap. lxvi., libro iv.[2], in Hieremiam[3], cap. xxii. Et dicere etiam quod canes et mures, si externum signum sacramenti acceperint, quod una cum externo signo significatum (hoc est, corpus et sanguinem Christi) recipiant (ut dixi), plane impium est. Panis angelorum factus est munificentia Dei panis et cibus piorum hominum, sed non impiorum, nec canum nec murum: nec a Deo Patre in mundum Christus erat missus, ut impios, canes, et mures pasceret; sed ut peccatores ad pœnitentiam converteret, et pœnitentes corporis et sanguinis sui meritis adimpleret. Quod autem neoterici dicunt, quod impii cum sacris signis corporis et sanguinis Christi signata (hoc est, ipsum corpus et sanguinem Christi) accipiant, sed indigne, et ad judicium et condemnationem, non admittimus; propterea quod de suo scrinio et pectore loquuntur, et non ex verbo Dei. Paulus enim clare testatur, quod qui panem signum indigne accipiunt judicium manducent. Hæc sunt illius verba: [1 Cor. xi.] "Itaque quisquis ederit panem hunc, aut biberit de poculo Domini, indigne, reus erit corporis et sanguinis Domini." Non dicit Paulus, Itaque quisquis ederit corpus Domini et biberit sanguinem Domini indigne: sed quia indigne sumentes sacramenta corporis et sanguinis Christi signis cœlestibus contumeliam faciunt, ea contumelia signorum rebus signatis imputatur, ut Paulus dicit; ita ut sint corporis et sanguinis Christi rei: ut Israelitarum, Judæ, ac Simonis Magi exempla testantur; qui externa signa, manna in deserto, sacrum panem in cœna Domini, externamque lotionem baptismatis receperunt, quos tamen Christus non approbavit.

Hic subjicerem plura testimonia contra realem Christi præ-

[[1] Ac per hoc qui non manet in Christo, et in quo non manet Christus, proculdubio nec manducat spiritualiter carnem ejus, nec bibit ejus sanguinem, licet carnaliter et visibiliter premat dentibus sacramentum corporis et sanguinis Christi.—August. Op. Tom. IX. col. 230. D.]

[[2] Omnes voluptatis magis amatores quam amatores Dei... comedere cibos impietatis, dum non sunt sancti corpore et spiritu: nec comedunt carnem Jesu, neque bibunt sanguinem ejus.—Hieron. Op. Tom. v. fol. 114. D. Paris. 1533.]

[[3] Et ipsi quidem (hæretici) passionem Domini et sanguinem pollicentur; sed in perpetuum non regnant.... Quodque infert, Non comedent et non bibent, subauditur, corpus et sanguinem Salvatoris.—Ibid. fol. 140. I.]

sentiam in eucharistia ex Origene in Matthæum Homilia xxxiii., ex Augustino ad Dardanum, ex Cyrillo in Joan. libro vi. cap. 14. et cap. 21. Sed quandoquidem istorum librorum copia mihi fieri non potest, satis est, cum non datur ultra, loca tantum annotare, et lectorem ad auctores ipsos relegare, ut suo studio illos perlustret; propterea quod hanc impiam et idololatricam doctrinam de corporali præsentia in cœna Domini detestentur atque expugnent. Jam ad tertium caput, in quo a neotericis dissentimus, descendam; quod tam paucis quam potero absolvam, ne tractatus nimium crescat. Sed ne videamur vel ignorantia aut dolo malo sanctorum patrum modos et formulas loquendi de corporis et sanguinis Christi præsentia in cœna Domini præterire, brevi epilogo omnes (quantum possum) fideliter annotabo.

1. Dicunt nos carnem Christi manducare, et ejus sanguinem bibere.
2. Panis et vini substantiam converti in substantiam carnis et sanguinis Christi.
3. Quod cum pane et vino idem recipimus quod pependit in cruce.
4. Quod Christus carnem suam nobiscum reliquit; vel quod sit totus hic, et totus in cœlo.
5. Quod id quod est in calice fluxit ex latere Christi.
6. Quod idem recipitur ore quod fide creditur.
7. Quod panis et vinum post verba sanctificationis sint corpus et sanguis Christi.
8. Quod nutrimur corpore et sanguine Christi.
9. Quod Christus abiit, et hic manet.
10. Et quod se ipsum ferebat suis manibus.

Tales vero loquutiones apud patres agnoscimus: et quomodo ipsi se ipsos etiam interpretentur non ignoramus; spiritualiter vel figurate, ut omnes patres testantur, et non secundum literam: ut Origen in Levit. Homilia vii.[4] Chry-

[[4] Carnibus enim et sanguine verbi sui, tanquam mundo cibo ac potu, potat et reficit omne hominum genus.... Agnoscite, quia figuræ sunt quæ in divinis voluminibus scripta sunt; et ideo tanquam spiritales, et non tanquam carnales, examinate et intelligite quæ dicuntur.... Si enim secundum literam sequaris hoc ipsum quod dictum est, 'Nisi manducaveritis carnem meam, et biberitis sanguinem meum,' occidit hæc litera.—Orig. Op. Tom. ii. p. 225. Paris. 1733.]

sostomus in Joan. Homilia xlvi.¹ Tertullianus lib. I. et IV., contra Marcionem², Contra Adimant. cap. xii.³ Cyprianus libro Epistolarum II., epistola 3.⁴ Intelligunt enim Christum juxta suam divinitatem hic in terris nobis adesse, vel spiritualiter in omnibus qui fideliter in Christum credunt, et pie vivunt; vel quod panis et vinum in sacra cœna figurative pro corpore et sanguine Christi accipiuntur. Hæc autem vera esse quæ dico, non ignorabit qui veterum patrum scripta perlustrare dignabitur.

Finis.

CAPUT III.

Contra sacrificium missæ.

Tertium caput in quo a neotericis dissentimus consistit in hoc; quod ipsi corpus Christi in Romana missa Deo Patri pro remissione peccatorum vivorum et mortuorum offerunt; hoc est, volunt Christum ex pane factum esse sacrificium propitiatorium pro vivis ac mortuis. Nos autem privatam Romanam missam pro aliquo opere a Deo ordinato, vel pro sacramento mortis et passionis Christi non agnoscimus; sed humanum commentum ac profanationem sacræ Domini cœnæ esse credimus ac profitemur, ut antea est ostensum. Et nullum a morte Christi esse sacrificium propitiatorium credimus atque confitemur; hoc est, a morte et præter mortem Christi nullum tale esse sacrificium vel opus, quod iram et indignationem Dei erga peccatum placare, atque illius gratiam in remissionem peccatorum peccatoribus impetrare possit. Hoc enim Christus semel per seipsum in cruce fecit; nec in hoc sacrificii propitiatorii genere, quod est pretium nostræ redemptionis ab æterna ira et damnatione, socium aut successorem Christus patitur. Nam solus ipse omnia, semel ipse omnia, in se ipso omnia, per se ipsum omnia, super crucem omnia per sui ipsius sanguinis effusionem ac mortem (quoad pretium et solutionem nostræ redemptionis) perfecit ac absolvit imperpe-

[¹ .... μέμνηται τροφῆς πνευματικῆς, p. 745. Ἀπὸ τῆς τραπέζης ταύτης ἄνεισι πηγὴ ποταμοὺς ἀφιεῖσα πνευματικούς, p. 747.—Chrysost. Op. Tom. II. Eton. 1610.]

[² Vide supra, p. 406, note 7; and p. 440.]

[³ Vide supra, p. 406, note 2.]   [⁴ Vide supra, p. 422.]

tuum : ita ut hoc sacrificii genus propitiatorii sit indescendens et immigrabile : ita etiam ut extra ipsam Christi mortis actionem, et cruentam ejus sanguinis effusionem, atque illius sanctissimæ animæ a corpore ejus in cruce expirationem, migrare non possit.

Rationes quibus impellimur ut hoc firmiter credamus sunt istæ.

"Atque hic, quod idem maneat in æternum, perpetuum habet sacerdotium : unde et salvos facere ad plenum potest qui per ipsum adeunt Deum, semper vivens ad hoc ut interpellet pro illis. Talis enim decebat ut esset nobis pontifex, pius, innocens, impollutus, segregatus a peccatoribus, et sublimior cœlis factus ; cui non sit quotidie necesse, quemadmodum illis pontificibus, prius pro propriis peccatis victimas offerre, deinde pro peccatis populi : nam id fecit semel, cum se ipsum obtulit." Hic D. Paulus multis præclaris ac perspicuis evincit argumentis Christi sacrificium non solum unicum esse et perpetuum, verum etiam semel oblatum. Primum argumentum petitur a natura et dignitate personæ Christi : quia, inquit, Christus, jam factus immortalis, nulla morte ab officio suo impediri potest. Itaque quemadmodum ipse in perpetuum manet, ita et ejus sacerdotium nullum habiturum est finem. Adhuc alia ratione probat unicum et perpetuum esse Christi sacrificium. Christus unicus et perpetuus est sacerdos : quare unicum et perpetuum esse oportet ejus sacerdotium et sacrificium. Hoc ex natura et dignitate personæ Christi sequi et concludi Paulus docet, a comparatione sacerdotum legalium cum sacerdote novi testamenti Christo. Illi quidem plures fuere, quia mors illorum sacerdotium impediebat ac finiebat : at Christus sacerdos in æternum secundum ordinem Melchizedech, immortalis, morti amplius nihil debet. Apud dialecticos Pauli ratiocinatio concludit a disparatis. Propter mortis enim tyrannidem veteres plures fuere sacerdotes : sed propter immortalitatis perpetuitatem Christus sempiternus est sacerdos. Deinde a natura et conditione sacerdotii Christi probat sacerdotium et sacrificium Christi unicum esse ac perpetuum. Christi vero sacrificium est (inquit) ἀπαράβατον, hoc est, intranscendens et immigrabile. Non transit (inquit Paulus) nec migrat hoc sacerdotium a Christo in alium. Non dicit (ut neoterici dicunt) Christi sacerdotium non esse migrabile in alios per mortem, quemadmodum sacerdotium Aaronicum sub lege migrabat in alios ; verum

Hebræ. vii.

hoc sacerdotium Christi immortale transit immortaliter in Christi successores et vicarios, quos episcopos ac alios ministros ecclesiæ vocant. Sed quam procul hoc sit a veritate, qui tantum elementa Christi religionis didicerunt non ignorant. Paulus enim primum vocat Christi sacerdotium immigrabile in perpetuum et intranscendens. Si autem Christi sacerdotium aliquo modo (fingant neoterici qualem modum velint) in alios transcendit vel migrat, non est immigrabile et intranscendens, ut Paulus ait. Nam hoc est immigrabile, quod nec migrat nec migrare potest in alium: ut hoc est immortale, quod nec moritur nec mori potest. Usurpant igitur et tyrannice in se recipiunt neoterici hanc potestatem interpretandi sacras scripturas, ut Christi sacrificium aliquo modo migrabile faciant, quod sacræ scripturæ omnino immigrabile et intranscendens constituunt. Adhuc alio modo D. Paulus probat hoc Christi sacrificium unicum esse et semel oblatum, ab effectu et fine Christi sacrificii. "Unde," inquit, "et salvos facere ad plenum potest qui per ipsum adeunt Deum, semper vivens ad hoc, ut interpellet pro nobis." Et quemadmodum antea ab impossibili probavit Christi sacerdotium esse immigrabile, ex natura et conditione tum personæ tum officii Christi; ita nunc idem probat ab utili et commodo sacerdotii et sacrificii sacerdotii Christi. Fructus vero æterni sacerdotii Christi est nostra salus; quæ cum semel a Deo per Christi mortem sit nobis parta et acquisita, non opus est ut amplius vel alio modo inquinatur[1] aut perficiatur. Nam inquit Paulus non solum, Salvos fecit, verum etiam, Ad plenum salvos fecit. Ad plenum autem salvos facere est omnibus modis, numeris, ac rationibus salvos facere; ita ut amplius a quoquam nihil desiderari, addi, adjungi possit. Cum ergo Christus solus, semel, et hoc etiam super crucem præstiterit plene ac absolute, in immolatione et morte sui ipsius, profecto nihil superest; nec quicquam absolvendum pro peccatorum condonatione ac remissione aliis sacrificiis vel sacrificulis reliquit. Quod si quid ad plenam satisfactionem peccatorum reliquisset, ad plenum (ut inquit Paulus) salvos non fecisset. Sed nihil vel sacerdotibus vel sacrificiis hac in parte reliquit: sed in se, per se, ac propter se solum, in cruce omnia pro redemptione humani generis morte sua persolvit et absolvit; ut Paulus hic inquit, "Ad plenum nos salvos fecit." Et ut adhuc signifi-

Probat Paulus sacerdotium Christi esse immigrabile, ab utili sacerdotii et sacrificii Christi.
Fructus sacrificii Christi est nostra salus.

[1 So in Foxe. Qu. inquiratur?]

cantius et clarius hoc Paulus intimaret, addit, "Qui per ipsum adeunt Deum." Verba sunt perpendenda. Non dicit, Salvos fecit ad plenum eos qui Christum denuo et ex novo Patri offerunt ac sistunt; sed dicit, Eos ad plenum salvavit qui per ipsum Patrem coelestem adeunt: hoc est, qui Christi fiducia et meritis Deum adeunt, ac solicitant pro remissione peccatorum et acceptatione, vota sua nanciscentur. Iterum verba Pauli resumo: "Qui per ipsum Deum adeunt." Oportet igitur accedere et adire Deum per Christum; et non sistere vel offerre Christum Deo. Accedere autem et adire Deum per Christum, est per ea et propter ea quæ Christus ipse præstitit in morte sua remissionem peccatorum et acceptationem in ejus gratiam quærere. Nostrum ergo est per Christum Deum Patrem adire; et non Christum Deo offerre vel sacrificare: et proculdubio, si nos Christum, qui est ab omnibus peccatis atque peccatorum maculis et suspicione immunis et alienissimus, Deo offerremus ac sisteremus, Deus Pater a nobis oblatum in sacrificium non admitteret. Ideo Paulus subjicit gravissimas sententias atque doctrinas, "Semper vivens ad hoc, ut interpellet pro illis." Christus vero jam non vivit, ut amplius cruento vel incruento (ut novi Christiani dicunt) sacrificio sistatur vel offeratur Deo per ministros ecclesiæ; sed ut ipse ab immolatione sui ipsius, et immortalitate donatus, interpellet pro nostra salute apud Patrem coelestem. En verba Pauli: Ideo vivit ut ipsemet interpellet, et non alter ipsum sistat vel sacrificet. Sed ulterius contra istos neotericos pergit D. Paulus in hunc modum: "Talis enim decebat ut esset nobis pontifex, pius, innocens, impollutus, segregatus a peccatoribus, et sublimior coelis factus," &c. Si hæc verba probe ac candide a pfaphis et Romanis sacrificulis intelligerentur, ne unus quidem illorum Christum Deo Patri sisteret vel sacrificaret, sub poena tremendæ iræ divinæ. Verba Pauli jam introspiciamus: "Talis enim decebat ut esset nobis pontifex, pius, innocens," etc.

Postquam Paulus ostendisset vim, efficaciam, ac virtutem sacrificii Christi, quod fructus illius esset salus nostra; iterum redit ad descriptionem personæ Christi, qui sacrificium obtulit, quod sit pius, innocens, etc. Quibus verbis Paulus testatur quod non satis est, ut id quod offertur sit purum et innocens; sed ut ipse etiam qui offert sit innocens et ab omni peccato immunis; ob cujus sacrificium Dei Patris ira et indignatio

Quod purum est per impurum oblatum a Deo non acceptatur.

contra peccatum placetur. Quod si Deo offertur quod a maculis et peccatorum sordibus purum sit, modo per impurum et peccatis obnoxium et pollutum offeratur, a Deo non acceptatur nec admittitur: nam nec offerentem nec oblata, peccatis conspurcata ac vitiata, Deus dignatur respicere. Et ut res clarior fiat, exemplis quibusdam illam illustrabo. Quid purius, sanctius, ac magis divinum excogitari poterit oratione Dominica, quam ipsemet Christus nos orare docuit? Tamen propterea quod nos, qui hanc orationem Deo Patri nostro cœlesti fundimus, obnoxii simus peccato, illam ipsam orationem Jesu Christi, quatenus a nobis oblatam, Deus Pater negligit, contemnit, et non admittit. Ideo Christus docuit, ut, quando aliquid sanctum, bonum, aut salutare a Deo impetrare velimus, uti illius nomine, hoc est, illius fiducia, dignitate, et honore, id faceremus. Nam etsi bona et pura sua natura essent quæ Deo tribueremus; tamen, propter offerentis impuritatem et imperfectionem, Deus ea nec magni æstimaret, nec reciperet: et ratio hæc est; propterea quod ea quæ sua natura perfectissima sunt, atque a Deo mandata, nunquam a nobis, qui obnoxii sumus congenitis et nativis malis, pure et absolute possint præstari. Quamobrem Paulus dicit legem [Rom. vii. 12, viii. 3.] ipsam, Dei inviolatam ac perfectissimam voluntatem, per nostram infirmitatem infirmari. Igitur, etsi Deo offeramus quæ Deus nobis præcepit ac mandavit ut a nobis offerantur, propter nostram tamen imperfectionem sunt imperfecta; imo si nostra ipsorum corpora morti propter Christum sponte et ultro daremus, nihil nobis prodesset. Pulchrum est igitur quod Augustinus dicit: "Non pœna, sed causa facit martyrem[1]:" ac si dixisset, Etsi sexcenties homo sese morti tradat, ac vivum sacrificium se Deo consecret, non in hoc Deo placet, quod sese offert mille mortibus cruciandum; sed quia ob Christi causam, cujus meritis ac passione est redemptus, nulla mortis genera timet aut formidat. Ideo si neoterici Christum ut sacrificium propitiatorium in suis sacris (vel potius, profanis missis) offerre velint, meminerint oportet, quod Deus non solum purum et immaculatum sacrificium, verum etiam innocentes homines, puros et ab omni peccatorum macula et suspicione, qui offerant, exigat. Nam Deus sua non curat (licet sanctissima ex sese), si per impurum offerantur.

[[1] Epist. LXI. col. 310. A. Epist. CLXVII. col. 762. B. Op. Tom. II. and elsewhere.]

Quare dico nos Christum Deo Patri non offerre: sed Christus nos et omnia nostra, quæ Deo placent, offert. Quod si neoterici papistæ Christum haberent suis manibus corporaliter (ut se fingunt habere), et Deo illum sexcenties offerrent pro peccatis vivorum et mortuorum, oporteret Deum Patrem Filium suum, sic per peccatis obnoxios oblatum, non agnoscere. Ipse enim solus, qui in corpore suo nostra peccata perlitavit super crucem, se ipsum semel obtulit, et recte potuit offerre, Deo Patri in odorem bonæ fragrantiæ, et amplius offerri non potest. Quapropter omnia nostra a Deo petimus per Filium, et propter Filium: sed Filium non offerimus nec sacrificamus Deo. Nisi enim per Christum prius fuerimus Deo reconciliati, omnia sane, quæcunque facimus, coram Deo sordent atque vilescunt. Christus igitur nos prius propter merita suæ passionis ac mortis Deo Patri cœlesti offert et consecrat; deinde nostra omnia, preces, eleemosynas, afflictiones, et quicquid tandem in nomine Christi facimus: ipseque Pater propter Christum recipit, ac tandem coronabit tanquam merita sua: ut Augustinus dicit: "Offerre in remissionem peccatorum solus Christus potuit, et non aliud quam sui ipsius corpus[2]." Veteres multa sacrificia habuerunt sub lege Mosaica, quæ sacrificia pro peccatis appellabantur, sed re ipsa peccata non tollebant, nec expiabant: "nam (ut inquit Paulus) lex nihil ad perfectionem [Heb. vii.] adduxit." Tamen sub lege patres peccatorum remissionem fuerunt nacti, non ob alicujus operis vel sacrificii dignitatem aut meritum, quæ sub lege fiebant; sed tantum propter Christum venturum, qui immolationem sui ipsius pro remissione peccatorum in cruce perlitavit: quod admirando amore bona fide præstitit ante mille quingentos annos; ita ut non sit necesse quotidie offerre: "nam id semel fecit, cum se ipsum obtulit," [Heb. vii.] inquit Paulus. Tanta est autem illius unici sacrificii, semel peracti in cruce per Christum ipsum, vis et potentia, ut per illud, et propter illud, omnia peccata omnium vere pœnitentium, qui sacrificii mortem præcesserunt, et qui illam sequuntur usque ad finem seculi, fuerunt, sunt, et erunt remissa. Impium ergo est vel aliud sacrificium præter mortem Filii Dei substituere, vel idem sacrificium repetere. In illo enim sacrificio, quo Dei ira et indignatio contra peccatum placatur, oportet ut hæc omnia simul in uno concurrant: primum, ut

[[2] For a similar sentiment see Aug. De Trin. Lib. IV. cap. xiv. The exact passage given in the text has not been found.]

qui offert, et quod offertur, sint immunes, puri, immaculati ab omni peccatorum labe et contagione : deinde, ut tanta sit virtus illius sacrificii semel peracti, ut omnem peccati atrocitatem et impietatem expurget ac debellet : præterea, ut ista peccatorum purgatio sit facta per mortem et sanguinis effusionem illius sacrificii quod offertur : deinde, quod qui tale sacrificium offert, destructa mortis tyrannide, vivat in perpetuum, ut interpellet pro illis quos sacrificii sui fecit participes. Et quemadmodum Christus se ipsum semel tantum obtulit, et post oblationem offerri semper desinit; ita nullo modo pro remissione peccatorum aliis sese commendavit offerendum. Impium igitur est quod neoterici dicunt, Christum se ipsum obtulisse sacrificio cruento; sed per sacrificulos offerri sacrificio incruento. Nam sacrificium incruentum Deus pro remissione peccatorum non admittit. Propterea Paulus dicit, quod "absque sanguinis effusione non fit remissio." Hunc igitur Christum pro unico sacerdote et unico sacrificio in remissionem peccatorum agnoscimus et confitemur : plures vero sacerdotes pluraque sacrificia quam Christum ac illius mortem pro remissione peccatorum prorsus rejicimus. Præterea Christo in suo sacrificio nec socium nec successorem tribuimus vel admittimus ; sed Christum solum, Christumque semel offerentem atque oblatum, quærimus ac profitemur.

Secunda probatio nostræ assertionis.

"Per proprium sanguinem ingressus est semel in sancta, æterna redemptione reperta."

Hic D. Paulus unicam placandi Deum ob peccata offensum rationem præscribit; quæ fit per sanguinis expiationem, quam Christus solus et semel pro omnibus in cruce absolvit ad æternam redemptionem comparandam, ut in eodem capite Paulus testatur. "Nam si sanguis taurorum et hircorum, et cinis juvencæ aspergens inquinatos, sanctificat ad carnis purificationem; quanto magis sanguis Christi, qui per Spiritum æternum se ipsum immaculatum obtulit Deo, purgabit conscientiam a mortuariis operibus ad serviendum Deo viventi!" Sanguis Christi per se ipsum Deo oblatus purgat conscientias nostras a mortuariis operibus ad serviendum Deo viventi. Unde constat, quod omnis peccatorum venia collocanda est in morte Christi, quam semel ipse in cruce per se ipsum sustinuit; et non expectanda est per crebras ac repetitas oblationes Christi incruentas, quas falso et impie neoterici fingunt. Illa enim unica Christi oblatio satis est, quam ipse, et non alius, per mortem suam fecit: ad quam si fide confugimus, repulsam non patiemur; nec peccatorum pondere ac tyrannide, vel legis divinæ accusatione et servitute, opprimemur. Satis vero, abundeque satis, iræ et indignationi Dei opponit qui unicam Christi mortem opponit: et satis, abundeque satis, tutus est a peccatorum fœditate, legis accusatione, mortis et inferni damnatione et tyrannide, qui Christi mortis ac passionis dignitate, honore, ac meritis sit munitus ac defensus. Non dico, ut qui hoc unico mortis Christi præsidio a mortis damnatione sint liberi, uti carnis curam agant, et mortis Christi securitate perdite vivant, ut neoterici falso in nos calumniantur; sed ut hac fide præditi verbum Dei audiant, cui etiam credant, vitamque suam ad illud componant, et adversa pro Christi veritate non abhorreant; Christi, apostolorum, ac martyrum exempla imitantes ac assequentes. Omnia vero a Christianis quæ Dominus jubet, quantum humana infirmitas præstare poterit, sunt facienda; semper tamen dicere oportebit, "Remitte nobis peccata, quia servi sumus inutiles." Strenue autem agendum est quod possumus: sed fiducia nostra tantum meritis Christi nitatur oportet, ut intrepide stemus ante thronum Dei; in cujus quidem conspectu nullus vivens justificatur, ut David dicit. Omnes tamen pii, qui sentiunt se opprimi ira et indignatione divina propter peccata, per fidem in Christi meritis Deum adeunt, atque illum semper placatum invenient. Ideoque, ut nos a Patris sui ira et judicio defendat, "in ipsum cœlum (inquit Paulus) ingressus est, ut appareat nunc in conspectu Dei pro nobis: non ut sæpius offerat se ipsum, quemadmodum pontifex ingreditur in sancta singulis annis per sanguinem alienum; alioqui oportuisset illum sæpius passum fuisse a condito mundo: nunc autem semel sub consummationem seculorum ad profligationem peccati per immolationem sui ipsius apparuit. Et quatenus illud manet omnes homines ut semel moriantur, post hoc autem judicium; ita et Christus, semel oblatus ut multorum peccata tolleret, rursus absque peccato conspicietur iis qui illum expectant in salutem." Duo Paulus hic præcipue docet: unum, quod unico mortis Christi sacrificio ad plenum a peccatorum condemnatione liberemur; alterum vero, quod semel tantum illud sacrificium Christus per se ipsum obtulerit; ita ut per

[Mors Christi sola firmum adversus omnia mala præsidium.]

[Psal. cxliii.]

[Heb. ix.]

se, nec per alium, amplius offerri queat. Per alium autem offerri in sacrificium non potest, quia omnes sumus peccatis obnoxii: et qui hac impietate gravantur nihil possunt (ut dixi) meritorie per ipsorum ministerium offerre. Et cum nullus, Christo solo excepto, super terram omnibus modis mundus et innocens unquam apparuerit, vel appareat, in conspectu Dei; ideo nullus sacrificium expiatorium vel propitiatorium Deo Patri coelesti offerre potest: sed soli et uni Christo hoc convenit, et hanc gloriam alteri Christus non est daturus. Hoc vero sacrificium non fit nisi morte; quia peccata non expiantur quin sanguis sacrificii effundatur, et mors sacrificantis interponatur. "Nam (ut inquit Paulus) testamentum in mortuis ratum est; quandoquidem nondum valet cum vivit testator." Testamentum omnes sciunt esse apud Paulum promissiones humano generi factas propter Christum; hoc est, remissionem peccatorum, acceptionem in gratiam et favorem Dei, et vitam æternam. Hæc, inquit Paulus, non sunt valida nec rata, nisi Christi morte obsignentur. Si hæc igitur per Christum quotidie in missis papisticis offeruntur, quotidie Christum crucifigunt. Paulus enim dicit, "Siquidem ubi testamentum est, mors intercedat necesse est testatoris." Si autem fit remissio peccatorum, acceptatio in favorem Dei, et certitudo vitæ æternæ per Christum oblatum a ministris, mors Christi, qui offertur, intercedat necesse est. Quare, ut uno verbo omnia absolvam, scatet plane missa ista Romana sacrilegiis. Non solum autem Christi mortis ac passionis dignitatem conculcat; verum etiam sacratissimam Christi mortis memoriam in coena Domini violat ac profanat. Juxta enim scripturas divinas unus et solus Christus est ad se offerendum idoneus. Et scripturæ sanctæ non modo unicum Christi sacrificium asserunt, sed etiam semel tantum oblatum. Neoterici autem non solum docent Christum in missa per alienas manus offerri; verum etiam quotidie fieri, imo centies, si tot fiant in ecclesia per diem missæ. Quid desiderent apertius vel fortius contra illorum fictam Christi oblationem in missa quam quod Paulus dicit, "Non ut sæpius offerat se ipsum?" Et iterum, "Nunc semel sub consummationem seculorum ad profligationem peccati per immolationem sui ipsius apparuit." Ad hæc, "Christus semel oblatus, ut multorum peccata tolleret." Hæc vero et hujusmodi testimonia de sacerdote Christo, et illius sacrificio validissimo, quivis a Paulo audire potest, a quo discet hujus controversiæ veritatem. Sed si velit plus neotericis quam sacris literis tribuere, respondeat Deo in novissimo die suo. periculo. Deus autem verbum suum lucernam constituit suæ ecclesiæ, et non humana dogmata. Si igitur, relicto verbo divino, hominum doctrinæ adhæreat, et tandem justum Dei judicium pro contemptu illius verbi sentiat; sibi ipsi hoc imputet, et non Deo. Nam Deus ab humanis traditionibus revocat, et suum verbum proponit: si quis igitur revocantem negligit, sua ipsius culpa pereat necesse est.

Qui transgrediuntur mandata Dei propter traditiones hominum gravissimas tandem luent pœnas.

Tertia probatio nostræ assertionis.

"Sanctificati sumus per oblationem corporis Jesu Christi semel peractam." Et iterum: "Hic vero, una pro peccatis oblata victima, perpetuo sedet ad dextram Dei; id quod superest expectans, donec reddantur inimici ipsius scabellum pedum ejus. Unica enim oblatione perfectos effecit in perpetuum eos qui sanctificantur." Et, "Ubi peccatorum est remissio, non est amplius oblatio pro peccato." Apostolus Paulus nullum præter sanguinem et mortem Christi agnoscit sacrificium expiatorium. Unde igitur habent neoterici illorum sacrificium propitiatorium incruentum et absque sanguine, nisi a spiritu diaboli et antichristi? Apostolus enim Paulus divino Spiritu afflatus, cum de impetranda peccatorum venia et condonatione agit, nos ad unicum illud sacrificium quo defunctus est Christus in cruce confugere jubet. Quonam spiritu agitantur igitur neoterici, qui docent ac imperant, quod si velimus et cupiamus mortem Christi nobis fore efficacem et utilem, ut hoc faciamus per crebras ac reiteratas applicationes sacrificii, quæ per sacrificulos in missis privatis fiunt? Dominus tandem pro sua inexhausta clementia populum suum a tyrannide Romani pontificis liberet, et suo sancto verbo ecclesias ubique illustret. Amen. Cogitet pius lector quid Paulus per hæc verba ad Hebræos docere voluerit, "Ubi horum est remissio, non est amplius oblatio pro peccato." Hac unica sententia Spiritus sanctus duos expugnat errores: primum, Judæorum, qui per sacrificia legalia peccata expiari volebant; secundo, neotericorum errorem, qui dicunt se in missis non aliud sacrificium offerre, sed idem quod Christus super crucem obtulit; tantum hoc discriminis retinentes, quod Christus sacrificium cruentum obtulit, illi vero incruentum. Paulus utrumque negat posse

Heb. x.

In quo differat Christi in cruce et sacrificorum in missa sacrificium.

fieri, et aliud sacrificium per Judæos, et idem sacrificium per Christianos: "nam (inquit) ubi horum est remissio, non est amplius oblatio pro peccato." Negat et aliud, idem sacrificium a quoquam præterquam a Christo ipso, idque semel, oblatum esse. Paulus quidem per Spiritum sanctum simpliciter negat oblationem. Neoterici vero Pauli simplicem negationem arguunt ac reprehendunt, affirmantes adhuc superesse oblationem incruentam pro remissione peccatorum. Si autem hoc non sit bellum gerere cum Deo, nescio quid sit. Metuo igitur ne multi illorum agnitam veritatem (quod absit) odio persequantur. Si enim dociles mentes sacrarum literarum lectioni afferrent, non esset possibile quin statim veritatem in hac controversia assequerentur.

Quarta confirmatio nostræ assertionis.

<small>Psal. xl.</small> "Holocaustum et hostiam pro peccato non postulasti: tunc dixi, Ecce, venio."

Hanc partem hujus psalmi D. Paulus in Epistola ad Ebræos, cap. x., refert ad Christum Jesum Salvatorem nostrum: qua probat unica Christi oblatione et victima super crucem humanum genus a servitute diaboli et peccati fuisse liberatum. Nec alio Deum placatum fuisse David testatur.

<small>Psal. li.</small> "Si voluisses (inquit) sacrificium dedissem: utique holocaustis non delectaberis." Omnia autem sacrificia, quorum sanguis juxta legem effundebatur, peccati atrocitatem indicabant, atque ob oculos offerentium ponebant quod qui talia peccata et scelera designassent digni essent morte æterna; sed peccatorum ac scelerum sordes non abluebant: peccatores ad venturum Christum relegabant, qui sanguine suo labes peccatorum expungeret: quod sanguis taurorum et hircorum præstare non valebat. Et ideo sanctus vates, anxius atque sollicitus de

<small>Psal. li.</small> suorum peccatorum venia, rogavit ut illum hyssopo aspergeret: non quod aspersione hujus herbæ peccatorum maculæ expiarentur; sed quod aspersione sanguinis Messiæ, cujus typus hyssopi aspersio erat, omnia ejus peccata ita eluerentur, ut nihil in illius animo et corpore resideret quod oculos summi Dei offenderet. Et quemadmodum ante Christi mortem nullum exstabat sacrificium cujus dignitate ac pretio peccata condonarentur; ita præter ipsam mortem semel in cruce peractam nullum restat pro peccatorum expiatione aliud

<small>Heb. x.</small> sacrificium: ut D. Paulus superius dicit: "Sacrificium et

oblationem et holocaustomata pro peccato noluisti, neque comprobasti, quæ juxta legem offeruntur: tunc dixi, Ecce, adsum, ut faciam, Deus, voluntatem tuam (tollit prius ut posterius statuat); per quam voluntatem sanctificati sumus per oblationem corporis Jesu Christi semel peractam." Duo D. Paulus Ebræis proponit: unum, quod sub lege Moysis nullum erat sacrificium vere propitiatorium, cujus pretio et dignitate peccatorum ac scelerum labes expiabantur; alterum vero, quod jam inter Christianos nullum sit sacrificium propitiatorium præter mortem Christi, quam semel in cruce pertulit. Ita ut non solum omnia alia sacrificia Judæorum et Christianorum a dignitate et pretio sacrificii propitiatorii excludat; verum etiam ut sacrificium a Christo oblatum pro remissione peccatorum iterum offerri perneget. Nam nos (inquit), a legis sacrificiis liberati, sanctificati sumus per oblationem corporis Jesu Christi semel peractam: quibus verbis unicum Christi sacrificium populo Dei commendat, Christumque semel pro omnibus oblatum docet. Cum igitur clare ex verbo Dei constet, quod semel Christus se ipsum pro omnibus in remissionem peccatorum obtulerit, scimus nec per alios offerri posse, nec sæpius posse offerri, ut neoterici fabulantur: et quantumvis neoterici in oculis suis videantur sapientes, et prudentiæ suæ egregie Prov. iii. innitantur contra mandatum Dei; nos tamen scimus illorum prudentiam stultitiam esse apud Deum. Quare illorum doctrinam et impia sacra tanquam pestem, toxicum, et venenum redemptionis nostræ in Christo Jesu abhorremus ac detestamur; satis esse credentes nostram salutem ex verbo Dei cognitam ac confirmatam habere.

Quinta confirmatio nostræ assertionis.

"Et sanguis Jesu Christi Filii ejus emundat nos ab omni 1 Joan. i. peccato." Et iterum: "Lavit nos a peccatis nostris per san- Apocal. i. guinem ipsius, et fecit nos reges et sacerdotes Deo et Patri suo."

Satan ab exordio mundi, pro hostili suo odio quo erga humanum genus flagrat, duobus modis homini imponere maxime consuevit: primo, ut Christum, per quem cœlestis Pater mundum sibi reconciliari constituit, ignotum penitus mundo faceret: secundo, ut quamobrem Christus sit passus mundus ignoraret; certo sibi persuasus alterum istorum duorum utrumque rectissimam esse viam ad infernos et sempiternas miserias.

Ex altera vero parte (quamvis impius sit, et æternus Dei ac omnium hominum hostis) probe novit, quod qui mortem Christi mortisque ejus dignitates et merita intellexerint, atque firma fiducia omnem culpæ et pœnæ impietatem et atrocitatem soli sanguini illius amovendam assignaverint, tyrannidem suam tuto contemnere et omnino vincere possint. Nam qui Christum fide assequuntur, illis Christus suo sancto Spiritu mortis suæ merita in salutem æternam applicat. Cum vero Christi vera cognitio humano generi adeo sit necessaria et utilis, sine qua nemo peccati, mortis, et inferni tyrannidem effugere potest; non est mirum quod tantas caligines ac tenebras Satan mundo offundat, ut Christi vera cognitio sese non proderet. Hasce autem tenebras et caligines Satan sparsim offundit partim per antichristos, qui mundo persuadent aliud esse sacrificium præter mortem Christi, quo homines salvi fiant; partim vero has tenebras per pseudochristos, qui se ipsos pro Christo venditant, spargit; et partim etiam per pseudoprophetas, qui falsa et nova dogmata fingunt, et vera veteraque vi et dolo opprimunt et persequuntur. Per hæc tria hominum genera Christi sanguinis effusionem incognitam, vel prorsus et funditus male et perperam intellectam, flagitiose, impie, ac profane inter homines esse studet, ac summa ope curat. Antichristi autem sunt omnes qui missas privatas hodie celebrant in ecclesiis Christi, quique pro vivis et mortuis sacrificant. Pseudochristi vero sunt papa et episcopi, qui sese pro Christo venditant. Nam quod Christus ipse manifeste mandat ipsi manifeste vetant. Christus enim dixit, " Venite ad me omnes qui laboratis et onerati estis: ego reficiam vos:" pseudochristi episcopi hoc prohibent, et jubent ut, relicto Christo, divos corporibus exutos adeant. Christus dixit, " Torcular calcavi solus:" pseudochristi dicunt, Christus hoc non solus fecit; sed partim ipse in cruce; partim vero et nos obscœnis, teterrimis, ac fastiditis missis privatis torcular pro remissione peccatorum conjunctim atque divisim calcamus ac premimus. Pseudo autem prophetæ sunt, qui Christi nomen et doctrinam jactitant, et tamen utrumque subvertere conantur: quales sunt qui hodie concionantur sub prætextu, nomine, et doctrina Christi; Christum tandem[1] atque ejus doctrinam universam sub papæ tyrannidem cogere conantur.

Exemplum vero neotericorum impietatis aliud non quæram

[1 Qu. tamen?]

quam hoc, quo dicunt Christum quotidie in illorum missis ac illorum opera pro peccatis vivorum et mortuorum offerri. Joannes dicit quod Christus emundat nos ab omni peccato. Ergo totum redemptionis omnium peccatorum nostrorum pretium sanguini Christi super crucem effuso assignat; et sacrificulis nullam partem relinquit. Quod si objiciant non aliud sacrificium et pretium pro peccatis offerri in missis, sed idem quod Christus obtulit in cruce, sic illorum impietati respondeo. Christum se offerre impudenter asserunt (sive cruentum sive incruentum, nihil pensi habeo; perinde mihi est:) verum si aliquo modo quod Christus fecit vel per se vel per alium facere possit, quoad sacrificium pro redemptione peccatorum et redemptionis pretio attinet, omnino ejus sacrificium in cruce factum invalidum et minus sufficiens ad placandam Dei iram erat. Repetitio enim ejusdem sacrificii pro redemptione peccatorum et redemptionis pretio duo semper comprehendit: unum, quod qui offerunt peccatis semper sunt obnoxii; alterum vero, quod offertur non satis esse pro æterna peccatorum expiatione. Hæc autem vera esse quæ dico, Paulus testatur, qui dicit[2]: "Propter peccata offerentis et eorum pro quibus sacrificia quotannis offeruntur, pontifices per sanguinem in sanctum sanctorum ingrediebantur. Et quia sanguis taurorum et hircorum peccata auferre non valebat, quotidie sacerdos astitit, sacra peragens, et easdem sæpius offerens hostias," etc. Utrumque D. Chrysostomus pulchre ostendit: primum, ut per illorum crebras ac repetitas oblationes accusatio, et non solutio, (inquit) esset peccatorum; secundum, quod infirmitatis accusatio, et non virtutis ostensio (scilicet sacrificii), esset. Ideo subdit Chrysostomus: "In eo quod offerebantur, redargutio peccatorum; in eo autem quod semper, redargutio infirmitatis. In Christo autem contrarium habetur: semel oblatus est. Nam quæ formam habent alicujus, tantum exemplar ostendunt, non autem virtutem[3]," etc. Si neoterici easdem offerunt in missis hostias, nempe corpus, sanguinem, et animam quæ Christus in cruce obtulit, Christi hostiam et immolationem infirmitatis arguunt: quod est omnino satanicum et impium. Ideo Chrysostomus inquit, "Offerimus quidem, sed ad recordationem facientes mortis ejus." Et post pauca, "Id

[2 See Hebr. ch. ix. 7, and ch. x. 4, 11.]
[3 Chrysost. Hom. XVII. In Heb. Oper. Tom. IV. p. 523, l. 6. Τὸ μὲν οὖν προσφέρεσθαι ἔλεγχος ἁμαρτημάτων, κ.τ.λ. Eton. 1613.]

ipsum semper facimus; magis autem recordationem sacrificii operamur." Recordatio vero sacrificii Christi non est re ipsa id ipsum sacrificium, sed potius forma et exemplar sacrificii, et non ipsa veritas. Et hoc est quod D. Joannes dicit, "Lavit nos a peccatis nostris per sanguinem ipsius." Non dicit, ipse in cruce et sacrificulus in missa lavant nos a peccatis nostris per sanguinem ipsius: sed ipse (nimirum solus) per sanguinem suum peccata nostra expiat: ita ut omnium hominum peccata (sive laici, sive clerici sint) per solum Christum super crucem (et non alibi) sint expiata; et jam nullus alius restet qui hoc præstare posset, sive cruento sive incruento sacrificio, ut neoterici fingunt: nam absque sanguinis effusione non fit remissio peccatorum.

Per Christum solum expiata sunt omnium peccata.

Et quibus remittuntur peccata reges et sacerdotes facti sunt: reges autem in hoc, quod, cum ex natura sub tyrannide peccati et principatu Satanæ hactenus fuerint, jam per Christum manumissi sint a mortis servitute, peccati tyrannide, atque Satanæ imperio liberi. Vetus enim noster homo, velut occisus, est una cum Christo sublatus in crucem; et novus homo, qui e Christo cœlesti duxit originem, de peccato et morte triumphat. Sed Joannes dicit, quod hunc honorem et triumphum per Christi sanguinem omnes qui Christo vere fidunt sint assequuti, et non per Christum ab hominibus Deo oblatum. Et quemadmodum omnes ex æquo reges fecit, ita et omnes ex æquo sacerdotes fecit. Sacerdotes vero, quoad sacrificium et sacrificandi potestatem, pro devicta peccati et mortis tyrannide, æque omnes sunt, juxta sacras scripturas: non ut Christum denuo, cruento vel incruento sacrificio, Deo Patri pro peccatis immolaremus; sed ut, quemadmodum Christus se ipsum obtulit pro nobis, ita et ipsi nosmet illi vicissim immolaremus: quod equidem facimus, quoties judicii nostri vires, prudentiam, intellectum, rationem, et hujusmodi animi potentias, a solo Dei verbo pendere cogimus; ut si humana omnia, bonas intentiones, cultum, et religionem, humanitus introducta, ab animis nostris propulsemus, et a Dei voluntate ac sapientia in ejus verbo patefacta solum pendeamus. Et si neoterici tales essent sacerdotes, re vera victimas traditionum humanarum immolarent, ac Deo interficerent; et exurerent igne flammisque verbi divini omnes privatas missas, necnon hydromantiam panis, cinerum, frondium, luminum, execrationes, et divorum invocationes execrandas; et eucharistiam sanguinis

Jesu Christi, atque preces ab eo institutas, sedulo Deo offerrent: deinde sua ipsorum corpora (hoc est, vitiosos affectus, superbiam, iram effervescentem, ardentem libidinem, lascivas ac lubricas animi cogitationes, et odium erga innocentes) immolarent, jugularent, exurerent, ac sacrificarent. Hæc sunt sacrificia quæ sacerdotes Christi immolare debent; et non denuo Christum ipsum, cruento vel incruento sacrificio, offerre. Cum igitur omnes ex æquo Christus summus sacerdos reges fecerit ac sacerdotes, ut Joannes et S. Petrus testantur; unde *Apoc. i. 1 Pet. ii.* hic neotericorum sacerdotum ritus et privilegium, quod ipsis præ ceteris sacrificandi contigit potestas? Sane non ex Christo, sed antichristo. Nam quod ad regum et sacerdotum dignitatem, honorem, et officium pro expiatione peccatorum attinet, in Christo omnes pares sumus. Tantum in ecclesiis Christi hoc est discriminis, quod minister publicus docet verbum Dei, et sacramenta ministrat; populus vero verbum Dei audit, et sacramentis communicat. Sed tantum fructus habet qui pure verbum Dei audit, quantum ipse qui verbum Dei pure annunciat; et tantum Deo offert qui pure sacræ Domini cœnæ communicat, quantum ipse qui cœnam Domini pure distribuit. Gratias autem Deo pro morte Christi uterque agit: neuter tamen Christum Deo Patri pro expiatione peccatorum sacrificat. Hoc enim Christus semel pro utroque præstitit in cruce; et utrique tantum recordationem et memoriam hujus sacrificii per sacræ cœnæ actionem et administrationem commendavit. Ejusdemque sacrificii iteratam oblationem in remissionem peccatorum omnino prohibuit: nam unica oblatione perfectos fecit in perpetuum, ut D. Paulus *Heb. x.* testatur.

Sexta probatio nostræ assertionis, ex neotericorum concessis.

Dicunt se offerre ac Deo perlitare sacrificium propitiatorium, verum illud incruentum: hoc est, Christi sanguinem, quem in missis dicunt se offerre, non effundunt, nec corpus ejus morte afficiunt; sed vivum Deo Patri in remissionem peccatorum perlitant: nam de novo illum crucifigere videri nolunt. Ex his concessis concludemus, imo evincemus, veram cœnam Domini sacrificium propitiatorium non esse; nam pani illorum et vino in missis privatis sacramentorum corporis et sanguinis Christi nomina sine sacrilegio attribui non possunt: et ut hoc indubitato constet, primum definitionem sacrificii propitiatorii veram ponamus: tunc si illa sacrificio incruento in missis convenerit, oportet ut demus quod sit verum sacrificium propitiatorium, quamvis incruentum. Etsi vero non sit necesse Dei veritatem ad præcepta dialectica obstringere, tamen ut omnes intelligant neotericorum doctrinam non solum cum verbo Dei pugnare, verum etiam cum aliis scientiis, illam ad dialectica præcepta exigemus.

<small>Sacrificare Deo propitiatorie quid.</small>

<small>Sacrificium propitiatorium quid.</small>

Propitiatorie Deo sacrificare est Deum iratum propter peccata placare, clementemque ac propitium reddere. Qui hoc facit propitiator vocatur; quodque ille facit sacrificium propitiatorium appellamus. Sacrificium ergo propitiatorium est illud sacrificium quod Deum, iratum propter peccata, clementem et placatum reddit; peccatores vero a servitute peccatorum liberos facit, ac peccatorum redemptionis justum pretium persolvit. Jam illud quod Deum propitium ac placatum facit, oportet ut in se contineat non solum sufficientem peccatorum redemptionem a morte, inferno, peccato, et Satanæ tyrannide, verum etiam τὸ λύτρον, hoc est, justum et debitum pretium redemptionis a peccato, morte, inferno, et Satana. Si hæc omnia in sacrificio non conveniunt, sacrificium propitiatorium dici non debet. Nam Deus Pater, propter quod peccata remittit, propter illud idem peccatores a peccati servitute liberat: et propter quod Deus Pater peccata condonat, et peccatores a servitute peccati liberos fecit, propter illud etiam idem justum pretium redemptionis peccatorum illius iræ persolutum esse agnoscit.

<small>Hebr. ix.</small>

Jam Divus Paulus dicit, quod "absque sanguinis effusione non fiat remissio." Inde constat, cum non fiat peccatorum remissio absque sanguinis effusione, absque sanguinis effusione non fieri a peccatis et peccati servitute redemptionem. Nam prius, quamvis non prioritate temporis, verum prioritate ordinis, Deus remittit vere pœnitentibus peccata: deinde manumittit atque liberum facit peccatorem a servitute peccati. Si autem remissio peccatorum et redemptio a servitute peccati non fit absque sanguinis effusione; multo magis pretium redemptionis, quod est sacrificium propitiatorium, non fit absque sanguinis effusione: nam sacrificium propitiatorium omnia quæ diximus præstare debet. Jam Paulus testatur, ad Ephesios scribens, ista omnia per Christum fieri, ut Deus propitius reddatur; utque peccatores, vere pœnitentes, audacter illum tanquam benignum Patrem adeant. Sic enim scribit: "Nunc

<small>Ephes. ii.</small>

per Christum Jesum vos, qui quondam eratis longinqui, propinqui facti estis per sanguinem Christi." Et ne quis modum ignoraret quo Christus hoc pro nobis præstiterit, eum clare designat: "Per crucem," inquit; id est, per mortem in cruce peractam. Et idem multis ac præclarissimis docet ad Colos- Colos. i. senses: "Per eum placuit reconciliare cuncta erga se, pacificans per sanguinem crucis ejus, per eundem, sive quæ in terra sunt, sive quæ in cœlis." Ecce D. Paulus efficaciam ac virtutem mortis Christi clarissime depingit, atque ob oculos credentium ponit, propter quam Deus Pater mundo factus est propitius. Qui onere et servitute peccati premebantur, iis modo Christus facta est redemptio, modo vere præteritæ vitæ eos pœniteat. Qui repulsam a Deo hactenus propter peccata sunt passi, his (modo pie credant) ad Deum Patrem per mortem Filii sui factus est facilis aditus; et qui pretium redemptionis persolvere non valebant, his (si Christo indubitanter fidant) Christus factus est redemptio et redemptionis pretium. Et hoc Paulus significat cum ait, "Per sanguinem crucis ejus;" hoc est, per sanguinem, quem super crucem in immolatione et morte sui ipsius effudit.

Cum ergo neoterici fatentur suum sacrificium, quod fingunt esse in missis, esse incruentum, fieri non potest ut sit propitiatorium pro peccatis. Nam quemadmodum testamentum testatoris per mortem testatoris ad plenum absolvitur, et non nisi per mortem (nam vivente testatore testamentum non valet); ita peccatorum remissio non fit sine effusione sanguinis, et sola Christi sanguinis effusione: quemadmodum D. Paulus testatur, "Absque sanguinis effusione non fit remissio." Non satis est Hebr. ix. quod neoterici semper clamitant, se idem offerre in missis, et non aliud sacrificium quam Christus obtulit in cruce. Sed si idem illi in missis offerunt, oportet ut Christus idem etiam patiatur in missis quod olim passus est in cruce: alioqui Christus ipse eo modo oblatus non est sacrificium propitiatorium. Nam per mortem, et non per vitam, hoc sacrificium Deo Patri offerri debet; atque ita ipsemet obtulit: et jam vivens ejusdem sacrificii merita per Spiritum sanctum omnibus fidelibus benigne applicat et impertit. Fingant igitur quod velint neoterici: Christi certe catholica ecclesia nullum aliud sacrificium propitiatorium unquam novit præter cruentam mortem Christi. Sacrificia incruenta Omnia autem sacrificia incruenta sunt εὐχαριστικὰ et gratu- sunt εὐχα-ριστικά. latoria. Imo et hoc addam: cruenta mors martyrum, non Quale sit sacrificium propitiatorium, sed quo gratiæ aguntur, sacrificium semper tyrum.

fuit; quo Deus propter Christum honore quidem afficiebatur, sed non quo Deus erga peccata offerentis placabatur.

<small>Sacrificium missæ horrendum idolum.</small>

Quod si verum dicendum est, nec Christum nec sacrificium neoterici in missis suis offerunt, sed horrendum idolum. Nam ipsemet Christus in vera nostræ naturæ substantia et hypostasi semel in cruce Deo litavit: et jam, quemadmodum vivit, et

<small>tom. vi.</small>

amplius non moritur; ita non amplius vel per se vel per alium offertur in redemptionem peccatorum. Et si quis recte perpendat neotericorum doctrinam, facile animadvertet quod

<small>Neoterici in missis Christum ideam faciunt Platonicam.</small>

Christum Jesum verum Deum et verum hominem in missis suis tantum Platonicam ideam faciunt: nam illum omnibus naturæ humanæ conditionibus spoliant. Est verus homo, inquiunt, in missis, natus ex virgine Maria; sed qualitates et quantitates hominis exuit. Substantiam et hypostasim humanæ naturæ in missis suis verbis Christo tribuunt; sed nativas conditiones humanæ naturæ verbis factisque negant. Quid hoc est igitur nisi phantasma et ideam veri corporis tantum intellectu comprehendere? Nam extra intellectionem illud corpus Christi quod ipsi fingunt in missis nihil est. Oportet enim, dicunt, hoc corpus tantum intellectu et cogitatione concipere, citra omnes veri corporis humani proprietates et conditiones: quod est omnino impium et diabolicum. Nam, ut antea ostendimus, Christus (quoad veram humanæ naturæ substantiam et hypostasim) est similis fratribus per omnia, extra vitium et peccatum: hoc est, vere et positive humanum habet corpus atque substantiam humanam, non tantum intellectu, ut sit verus Deus et verus homo. Nam quod extra intellectionem non progreditur potest esse perpetuum in mente, etsi re ipsa substantia non exstet: ut in hieme, cum nullæ rosæ florent, notitia sive idea rosæ in mente existere potest: quemadmodum absentium notitia semper amicorum animis præsens indivulse hæret, cum absentium corpora non comparent. Horrendum autem est tales ac tantas injurias Christi corpori tribuere: vere enim ac positive pro nobis natus est, mortuus in cruce, resurrexit a mortuis, ascendit ad cœlos, sedet ad dextram Dei Patris omnipotentis; et vere ac positive veniet, ut judicet vivos et mortuos. Et usque ad illud tempus non aderit corporaliter nobiscum, nec realiter offerri potest pro redemptione peccatorum, dicant neoterici quicquid velint.

Septima probatio nostræ assertionis.

Credo sanctam ecclesiam catholicam.

Juxta plerosque historicos, qui computationem annorum a condito mundo ediderunt, præterita jam sunt ferme sex millia annorum: quatuor prope millia sub patriarchis et prophetis, et plus mille quingentis annis sub duce ac principe nostro Christo, qui per mortem suam illum destruxit qui mortis habebat imperium, hoc est, diabolum; et per gloriosam suam resurrectionem cœlestium, terrestrium, ac infernorum potitus est imperio. Per omnia istorum seculorum tempora cœlestis Pater unam semper servavit ecclesiam, sanctam, catholicam, et orthodoxam; quam una et immutabili fide a lapsu primo humani generis semper instruxit. Et quoad fidei integritatem, sufficientiam, et perpetuitatem, una et eadem est omnium temporum ac fidelium fides: ut D. Paulus testatur: "Unus (inquit) Dominus, una fides," etc. Et hanc unicam, absolutam, sufficientem, ac perpetuam fidem originem ac certitudinem suam ducere a Deo per prophetarum ac apostolorum prædicationem, scripta, et testimonia, ad Ephesios Paulus liquido testatur: "Non estis (inquit) jam hospites et incolæ, sed concives sanctorum, ac domestici Dei, superstructi super fundamentum apostolorum et prophetarum, summo angulari lapide ipso Jesu Christo," etc. Hæc fides, quemadmodum a Deo solo mundo innotuit, sic soli Deo innitebatur; per quam ea quæ Dei sunt, ac necessaria cognitu ad salutem æternam, cognoscimus et apprehendimus. Hanc tamen fidem, quæ apud omnes ætates una semper fuit et eadem, non uno modo Deus patefecit ac confirmavit: sed pro sua ineffabili dilectione et sapientia aliter sanctis patribus ante legem, aliter sub lege, aliter vero sub evangelio fecit. Sub lege quidem naturæ cœlitus sæpe emisit vocem suam, qua hanc fidem orthodoxam animis suorum imprimeret, atque cœlitus dimisso[1] ignis incendio, quo sacrificia suorum consumpsit, confirmavit. Sub lege vero Mosis prophetas sæpius Deus ipse est allocutus, quorum opera verbum suum propagavit, ut per fidem mundo innotesceret; atque eandem fidem multis sacramentis et sacrificiis in publica ecclesia obsignavit, ut circumcisio, agni victima, vaccæ rufæ holocaustum, et hujusmodi sacra testantur. Postremo

[1 Qu. demisso?]

sub finem seculi, ut hæc una et vera fides in Deum certior atque illustrior in ecclesiis suis fieret, eandem per Filium suum unigenitum mundo provulgavit, sacramentisque publicis, baptismo et cœna Domini, in ecclesiis obsignavit. Ita ut hæc una sancta et catholica fides, quæ eadem semper fuit ab exordio mundi, non eisdem rationibus fuerit semper patefacta et confirmata in ecclesiis: sed singula quæque tempora suum habuerint modum revelationis, suos ritus, cæremonias, et sacramenta; quæ omnibus ætatibus (ut Paulus testatur) significatione eadem erant. Nam inquit, "Omnes eundem cibum spiritualem manducabant, et eundem potum spiritualem biberunt," etc. Cui et Augustinus assentitur, Psalm. LXXVII. "Idem (inquit) in mysterio cibus et potus illorum qui noster; sed significatione idem, non specie[1]." Sacramenta patrum in signis diversa sunt, sed re significata paria sunt. Et adhuc clarius in libro suo De Utilitate Pœnitentiæ: "Eundem cibum spiritualem manducaverunt. Quid est eundem, nisi quia eum quem etiam et nos?" "Eundem non invenio quomodo intelligam, nisi eum quem manducamus et nos[2]." Externi ritus et sacramenta atque cæremoniæ diversæ fuere pro temporum et hominum conditione: sed fides semper eadem et una. Nam quemadmodum Deus ipse unus est et nunquam mutatur, ut Paulus dicit; ita fides qua illum apprehendimus una est, ut idem Paulus testatur (una fides), et nunquam mutatur; quamvis modus et ratio quibus fides[3] qua Deum apprehendimus, eadem semper non fuerint: sed (ut dixi) ætas ante Moysen alias rationes, sub Moyse alias, sub evangelio etiam alias obtinuit, uti Deo visum fuerat.

Ecclesia tamen Christi ab initio suis cæremoniis nunquam caruit, sed habuit sua sacramenta et sacrificia: sacramenta autem, quibus sacramentaliter per fidem rite illis utentibus Deus bona sua exhiberet, confirmaret, et obsignaret; sacrificia vero, quibus nos (qui in hoc mundo a Deo peregrinamur) Deo aliqua opera reddimus, ut illi pro collatis suis in nos beneficiis gratias agamus, et ut Deum largitorem omni honore, quo possumus, adficiamus. Sed hæc sacrificia nec sunt nec unquam fuerunt in ecclesiis unius atque ejusdem generis. Nam unum

[1 August. in Psal. lxxvii. Oper. Tom. VIII. col. 851. D. Basil. 1569.]
[2 Id. de Utilit. Pœnit. Op. Tom. IX. col. 1020. A. B.]
[3 Something is wanting here to complete the sense: supply *patefacta est et confirmata*.]

genus ἰλαστικὸν seu propitiatorium erat, cujus mors promeruit aliis remissionem peccatorum. Aliud vero genus εὐχαριστικὸν erat sive gratulatorium, quod non meretur remissionem peccatorum; sed cum fit a reconciliatis ut Deum afficiant honore, Deo placet. Primum autem genus sacrificii, quod ἰλαστικὸν vocatur, nomine et significatione tantum omnes ecclesiæ habuerunt et nunc habent; sed non re ipsa, nisi pro eo temporis spatio quo Christus in se ipso hoc obtulit Deo Patri super crucem in remissionem peccatorum. Et hoc genus sacrificii nec extra personam Christi, nec extra illud tempus quo semel Patri perlitavit, nec extra locum super crucem ubi Patri perlitavit, unquam migrare potuit, nec potest; ut luce clarius D. Paulus suis epistolis affirmat. Legalia sacrificia multa nomen sacrificii pro peccatis sortiebantur, non quia re ipsa peccata expiabant; sed quia Christum venturum significabant, qui solus peccata mundi tollit. Ita in nostris ecclesiis cœna Domini sortita est nomen sacrificii Christianorum, non re ipsa, sed memoria et recordatione, quod Christum semel in cruce immolatum repræsentet. *Ephes. i. ii. Colos. i. ii. Heb. vii. ix. x.*

Cum igitur sancta catholica ecclesia Christi aliud sacrificium ἰλαστικὸν ex verbo Dei non norit præter solam mortem Christi semel in cruce peractam; si nos quoque, qui Christum profitemur, aliud ignoramus, extra omnem culpam et peccatum sumus; nam illi ecclesiæ catholicæ credimus quæ vocem sponsi sui Christi audit. Tota autem sacrarum literarum series hujusmodi sacrificium non agnoscit: omnia sanctorum conciliorum ac patrum symbola quæ hodie exstant (quæ in fine hujus tractatus adjiciam) ne verbum quidem de tali Christo ac Christi sacrificio in missa quale neoterici impie fingunt mentionem fecerunt. Nonne satis igitur est ut omnia credamus quæ in sacris literis atque in symbolis sanctorum patrum et synodorum continentur? Illa certe ecclesias Christi satis contra omnes hæreses muniebant, et in vera fide instruebant, per quatuor fere millia annorum ante Christi incarnationem, et mille ducentos annos et ultra a Christi ascensione in cœlos, usque ad tempus Lotharii Levitæ, qui sedem occupavit episcopalem Romæ circa annum Domini 1215; qui et Innocentius tertius vocatur. Is quidem nova symbola, peregrinos, ignotos, atque impios articulos fidei excogitavit, cum antichristus ille Romanus non solum animas fidelium, verum etiam regum ac principum terras atque imperia, sub suam tyrannidem cogeret. *Lotharius Levita, qui et Innocentius tertius.*

Joannes Angliæ Rex.

Sit nobis testis illustrissimus rex hujus regni Angliæ Joannes, qui non solum mille marcas annue eidem Lothario Levitæ pontifici Romano pro tributo pendere coactus est, verum etiam his miserrimis conditionibus subscribere, ut nullus rex hoc florentissimo regno potiretur, quin easdem illi solveret[1]: quam tamen tyrannidem reges omnes hujus regni fortiter contempserunt. Atque iste quidem nebulo et verus antichristi vicarius, cum paucis suis præcessoribus, ab omnibus ecclesiis quod Deus illis contulerat abstulerat, nimirum veram verbi Dei prædicationem, et sacramentorum verum usum, atque apostolicam disciplinam. A regibus autem et principibus, quibus Deus terrarum imperium contulit, non solum auctoritatem et dominium, verum etiam ipsas terras, reditus, et patrimonia rapere non destitit. Sed ne nimis durus et crudelis videretur, voluit aliquo modo has injurias compensare. Quare ex con-

Circa annum Domini 1215.

cilio Lateranensi hos novos articulos fidei fictos atque ementitos, falsos et impios, de panis et vini transubstantiatione, de corporis Christi corporali præsentia, et de sacrificio propitiatorio in missis, ecclesiis, regnis, ac regibus (qui sub illius tyrannide egerunt) commendavit: ut in Decretalibus quisque videre potest, cap. "Firmiter[2]." Ante illius tempora in nullo symbolo vel transubstantiationis panis et vini, vel corporalis Christi præsentiæ in sacra cœna Domini, aut sacrificii propitiatorii in missa, fit mentio. Credimus ergo sacris literis, quæ abunde ac satis fidem veram et sanctam continent. Credimus præterea symbolis sanctorum patrum per mille ducentos annos: et hac fide, sacrorum librorum testimoniis atque sanctorum patrum symbolis comprehensa et suffulta, nos contenti sumus; novamque illam atque ementitam, quam neoterici impie populo Dei per vim et fraudes obtrudunt, ignoramus ac detestamur tanquam impiam et antichristianam, quæ penitus in subversionem sanctæ catholicæ ecclesiæ fidei tendit, ut infra pluribus dicam.

[1 See Annales Monasterii Burton. ap. Rerum Anglicanarum Scriptores Veteres. Tom. I. p. 270. Oxon. 1684.]

[2 Corp. Jur. Canon. Decret. Gregor. Lib. I. Tit. I. cap. 1. Innocentius III. in Conc. Gener. "Cujus corpus et sanguis in sacramento altaris sub speciebus panis et vini veraciter continentur, transubstantiatis pane in corpus, et vino in sanguinem potestate divina." Coll. 10, 11. Venet. 1604. See also Binii Conc. Lateran. cap. i. Tom. VII. Par. II. p. 806. col. 1. F. Lutet. Paris. 1636.]

Sed jam, ut simplici plebi egregie imponant, dicunt nos hunc sensum ex scripturis sacris per vim elicere, et violentiam sacris literis inferre, uti nostro proposito inserviant; verum sanctos patres illorum incruentum sacrificium agnoscere ac stabilire. Lubet igitur aliquot ex vetustioribus ac doctioribus patribus loca subscribere, ut pius lector intelligat sanctos patres nunquam tale sacrificium agnovisse quale neoterici praetendunt in missis suis habere; sed illud asserere ac credere quod nos affirmamus et credimus. Sint illorum libri judices.

Confirmatio nostræ assertionis ex sanctis patribus.

Irenæus, adversus Hæreses Valentini et similium, multa habet de sacrificiis et oblationibus quæ fiunt a Christianis, et inter cetera hæc habet verba: "Sacrificio non placatur Deus[3]." Quod omnino intelligi oportet de sacrificio per hominem oblato: nam Deus per sacrificium quod obtulit Christus fuit omnino placatus. Dixit enim, "Hic est Filius meus dilectus, in quo complacuit animæ meæ: ipsum audite." Sed quoniam Irenæus testatur Deum non placari sacrificio, non puto a re nostra esse alienum, si (priusquam hunc locum Irenæi ulterius discutiam) veterem et veram dialecticorum regulam paulisper sequar (quæ dicit, Qui bene distinguit bene docet), et sacrificandi vocabulum, quo omnes utuntur, per divisionem quid significet ostendam; ne, ambiguitate vocabuli decepti, sacrificia vel nimium deprimantur, vel extollantur: quod fieri non potest citra divinæ gloriæ jacturam, et nostrarum animarum salutem. *Irenæus, lib. iv. cap. 34.*

Sacrificare autem Deo est Deum iratum propter nostra peccata placatum facere, vel a Deo veniam peccatorum rogare, aut gratias Deo pro illius beneficiis reddere, vel nos ipsos totos in illius servitium consecrare. Primo modo nullus Deo sacrificare potest nisi solus Christus Deus et homo; ut propheta Esaias testatur: "Ipse vulneratus est propter iniquitates nostras; attritus est propter scelera nostra; disciplina pacis nostræ super eum; et livore ejus sanati sumus." Et paulo infra ostendit solum Christum propter nostras iniquitates vulneratum fuisse, et mortis atque inferni tyrannidem solum destruxisse: "Torcular (inquit) calcavi solus, et de gentibus non est quisquam mecum," etc. Et hoc est quod statim post Adæ lapsum Deus dixit serpenti: "Inimicitias ponam inter te et *Sacrificare Deo quid. Primum sacrificandi genus. Esai. liii. cap. lxiii. Gen. iii.*

[3 Iren. adv. Hæres. Lib. IV. cap. 34, p. 262. sect. 2. 1570.]

mulierem, et semen tuum et semen illius; et ipsum conteret caput tuum." Pollicitus est Deus Adamo remissionem peccatorum, destructionem mortis, diaboli, et inferni, et acceptationem illius in pristinum favorem et gratiam: sed hoc fieri oportebat per semen mulieris, quod est Christus, et non per multa semina, ut Paulus testatur. [Gal. iii.] De hac vero placatione iræ et indignationis Dei erga homines propter peccata per solum Christum, David sub persona Dei Patris Filium alloquitur in hunc modum: "Dominus dixit ad me, Filius meus es tu; ego hodie te genui: postula a me, et dabo tibi gentes hæreditatem tuam," etc. Psal. ii. Quibus docet quod Deus Pater erga nos placetur per Filium suum unigenitum; et quod nos hæredes simus per Christum solum, et nullo alio modo. De qua placanda Dei Patris ira per Christum erga mundum propter peccatum, ipsemet Christus mire testatur: "Pro eis (inquit) sanctifico me ipsum, ut sint et ipsi sanctificati per veritatem." Joan. xvii. Sanctificare autem se ipsum pro nobis est morti et cruci pro nobis sese offerre, ut nos Deo reconciliet, consociet, ac confœderet, destructis inimicitiis et odiis super crucem per sanguinem et immolationem sui ipsius, ut Paulus testatur. Ephes. i. ii. Colos. i. ii. Apoc. i. Et in hoc sanctificandi genere, quo Deus placatur, Christus nec socium præcessorem nec successorem admittit, sed omnia in se continet, et nihil extra se in alium quenquam effundit. Hoc sanctificandi genus in ecclesiis patriarcharum sub lege naturæ non fuit, nec in ecclesiis prophetarum sub Moyse, nec in ecclesiis nostris jam sub Christo; sed tantum cum hic Christus in terris viveret, et se ipsum in cruce Deo Patri pro peccatis nostris offerret ac sacrificaret: ita ut in hoc sacrificandi modo nihil commercii, participationis, communionis, conjunctionis, aut societatis habeat homo cum Christo; sed solus et semel Christus omnia perfecerit pro placanda Dei Patris ira erga homines propter peccata totius mundi: quamvis in electis hoc sacrificium tantum utile sit et efficax.

Secundum genus sacrificandi, quo impetrationem et veniam peccatorum a Deo postulamus, in ecclesiis semper inter vere pœnitentes exstitit, de quo passim in sacris literis legimus. Secundum sacrificandi genus in tres distinctum partes. 1. Et hoc sacrificandi genus tribus absolvitur modis: primo, ubi fides afflictam ac territam conscientiam per Spiritum sanctum consolatur et adjuvat certitudine et fiducia promissionum Dei: 2. secundo, ubi fides non solum interne per Spiritum sanctum mœstam et timidam conscientiam solatur, verum etiam corda et voces pœnitentis ad orationes et preces agitat atque impellit: tertio vero, ubi fides per Spiritum sanctum non solum interne afflictam mentem erigit, consolatur, atque in vocales preces perrumpere facit; sed etiam his duobus addit externam verbi Dei prædicationem et verum usum sacramentorum; ex quibus discit a Deo veniam petendam; quæque didicit, officiose ac diligenter a Deo exigit. Exempla omnium istorum sacrificandi generum ubique in sacris literis legimus. David veniam petiit: "Intellige, Deus, (inquit) הגיגי *Hagigi*, murmur meum," vel, tacitas cogitationes meas. Et in aliis psalmis conqueritur de tacita et interna animæ suæ tristi ac aspera conditione sacrificandi Deo pro impetranda peccatorum venia, inquiens, "Quare tristis es, anima mea? et quare conturbas me?" Ita Anna tacite et in præcordiis suis querelam suam Deo Patri cœlesti obtulit. Passim vero in sacris literis occurrunt hujus sacrificandi generis exempla, toties fere quoties vere pœnitentium nomina recitantur. In singulis igitur generibus satis erit unum aut alterum exemplum ad confirmationem eorum quæ dico adferre. Secundum genus sacrificandi, quo veniam peccatorum a Deo petimus, est, ubi non solum fides per Spiritum sanctum mentem conterritam et terrifactam solatur, verum etiam preces et invocationes adduntur, quibus veniam peccatorum rogitamus. Ubique hujus generis sacrificandi exempla in sacris literis inveniuntur: ut Moses mente et voce pro se ipso et populo sacrificabat: sic Elias: sic etiam David: "Verba mea (inquit) auribus percipe, Domine:" item et mulier Cananæa: "Jesu, fili David, miserere mei: filia mea male a dæmonio vexatur," etc. Tertium genus sacrificandi est pro venia peccatorum, quo non solum mentes, corda, et voces per fidem in Christum, operante Spiritu sancto, veniam peccatorum impetrant; verum etiam menti, cordi, et voci accedunt verbi Dei lectio vel prædicatio, et sacramentorum pius usus, quibus vere pœnitentes utuntur, ut organa et media quibus de condonatione peccatorum fiant certi. Hujus generis exempla passim in sacris scripturis occurrunt: ut sub patriarchis fidei, menti, cordi, ac precibus piorum concurrebat cœlestis ignis, qui illorum sacrificia consumebat: sub lege Mosis omnia sacrificia et sacramenta legis: sub Christo vero omnia sacramenta novi testamenti.

Tertium autem genus sacrificandi, quo gratias agimus pro impensis et oblatis nobis in Christo beneficiis, in totidem partes et genera dividitur. Primum, gratiam habemus Deo mente, cogitatione, fide illustrata per Spiritum Sanctum, absque vocis sonitu ac clamore. Secundo, mente, fide, et voce per Spiritum sanctum in Christo agimus. Tertio, mente, fide, voce, et verbo Dei ac sacramentis publice in medio ecclesiæ in Spiritu sancto per Christum gratias agimus. Hæc tam nota sunt omnibus piis, ut non opus sit exempla subjicere.

Quartum sacrificandi genus, duplici constans ratione.

Quartum vero sacrificandi genus, quo nosmet ipsos nostraque omnia Deo sacrificamus, omnia hæc etiam exigit: primum, ut mente per fidem in Spiritu sancto propter Christum agnoscamus quod nos ipsos atque nostra omnia Deo debeamus, a quo omnia suscepimus, per quem etiam omnibus fruimur, et in quo omnia servantur: secundo, ut non tantum per fidem in Spiritu sancto propter Christum nos hoc scire satis esse putemus; verum etiam ut nos ipsos nostraque omnia, tum vitam tum fortunas nostras, ad voluntatem ac mandatum Dei Patris componamus et exhibeamus, ad nominis sui gloriam, qui nos fecit, redemit, ac conservat ad vitam æternam. Hunc

Rom. xii.

vero sacrificandi modum exigit D. Paulus ad Romanos; ut quotquot Christo nomen dederunt sedulo ac perpetuo præstent quod nobis dare dignetur qui nos jubet, Jesus Christus; et ubi dederit quod jubet, jubeat (ut Augustinus dicit) quod vult.

Hanc equidem sacrificandi divisionem interponere licuit, non solum ut pii fratres intelligant nos nullum sacrificandi genus a Deo mandatum contemnere (quod procul sit ab omnibus qui Christo credunt); verum etiam quo admonerem ceteros, ne unum sacrificandi genus pro altero accipiant, et sic ex ambiguitate et amphibologia nominis sacrificandi deciperentur. Nam re vera tria posteriora sacrificandi genera in ecclesia habent a Christo mandata; hoc est, ut veniam peccatorum petant, ut gratias agant, et ut se ipsos et sua omnia Deo consecrent propter Christum. Sed primum genus sacrificandi, quo placatur Deus, nunquam ecclesiæ suæ commendavit, ut extra personam Christi usquam existeret; verum hoc munus, honorem, et dignitatem soli Filio suo Jesu Christo dedit; in cujus nomine omnia quæ nobis expediunt impetrare per fidem facile valemus. Quapropter sacrificium expiatorium extra Christum nullum ponimus; nec sacrificium propitiatorium per ullum alium offerri nisi per Christum solum, qui semel in cruce omnia peregit.

Irenæus.

Jam ad Irenæum: "Sacrificio non placatur Deus." De

sacrificio (ut dixi) per hominem oblato loquutus est hic Irenæus. Unde discrimen videmus inter sacrificium Christi, et sacrificia quæ nos Deo Patri per Christum offerimus. Christi autem sacrificium est tale, quo Deus Pater nos caros sibi habet, modo fide Christum apprehendimus, et erga nostram impietatem placatur. Nostra vero sacrificia tantum gratulatoria sunt, sive gratiarum actiones, quibus nos ipsos gratos erga Deum testamur pro nostra creatione, redemptione, et conservatione. Si autem Deus humano sacrificio non placatur, falsum est quod neoterici dicunt, in missis papisticis tale per ministros offerri sacrificium quo peccata nostra condonantur. Tale enim sacrificium solus Christus et semel Christum in cruce obtulit. Et ut res fiat dilucidior, paulo post in eodem capite Irenæus subjungit: "Igitur (inquit) non sacrificia sanctificant hominem; non enim indiget Deus sacrificio: sed conscientia ejus qui offert sanctificat sacrificium, pura existens, et præstat acceptare Deum quasi ab amico[1]." Sacrificia quæ per hominem fiunt non sanctificant hominem, inquit Irenæus. Profecto si sacrificia non sanctificant hominem, non sunt propitiatoria, quibus peccata remittuntur: peccata enim destruere ac tollere est hominem sanctificare et sanctum reddere. Neoterici ergo quod Irenæus sanctus pater negat affirmant. Nam Irenæus dicit, Sacrificia non sanctificant hominem: neoterici vero quod sanctificent hominem affirmant. Præterea Irenæus dicit, quod conscientia ejus qui offert sanctificet sacrificium, pura existens: neoterici autem illorum sacrificia conscientias sanctificare asserunt. Hic cuivis videre licet quam ex diametro neoterici cum veteribus pugnent. Quod isti negant illi affirmant. Hinc facile videmus quod omnia sacrificia quæ per hominem fiunt sint gratiarum actiones, quæ conscientiam non purificant; sed per puritatem fidei in conscientia pura ipsa sancta et grata sunt Deo. Sacrificium enim Christi super crucem solum conscientias nostras sanctificat ac purificat (ut inquit Paulus) a mortuariis operibus ad serviendum Deo viventi. Et de eucharistia ita apertis verbis loquitur Irenæus: "Offerimus autem ei non quasi indigenti, sed gratias agentes donationi ejus, et sanctificantes creaturam[2]." Ecce in sacra actione cœnæ Dominicæ gratias (inquit) offerimus, quod per mortem Filii ejus ab æterna damnatione liberamur. Non dicit quod in cœna Domini

Deus humano sacrificio non placatur.

Heb. ix.

[1 Iren. adv. Hæres. Lib. IV. cap. 34, p. 263. sect. 4. 1570.]
[2 Ibid. p. 264.]

Christum propitiatorie offeramus, cujus oblatione peccata vivorum ac mortuorum purgentur. Rogo igitur qui Latinam linguam callent, ut hoc caput Irenæi diligenter perlegant.

<small>Tertull. adversus Marcionem. lib. iii.</small>

"Hoc lignum et Hieremias tibi insinuat, prædicans Judæis, Venite, injiciamus lignum in panem ejus, utique in corpus. Sic enim Deus in evangelio quoque vestro revelavit, panem corpus suum appellans, ut et hinc jam eum intelligas corporis sui figuram panem dedisse; cujus retro corpus in pane prophetes figuravit, ipso Domino hoc sacramentum postea interpretaturo[1]." Tertullianus duo hic per sacramentum eucharistiæ animadvertit: primum, corpus Christi significari per panem; deinde, mortem ipsius corporis super crucem. Sed dicit panem eucharistiæ non re ipsa, sed figurative ac symbolice, esse corpus Christi ac mortem ejus. Et sic patres plerumque eucharistiam sacrificium vocant, quia est commemoratio sacrificii semel in cruce oblati. Sic etiam cœna Domini nomen sacrificii obtinuit, non re ipsa, sed nominis communicatione; ita ut signum rei signatæ nomine gauderet. Ideo est quod D. Cyprianus dicit, "Passio enim Domini est quod offerimus:" quod re ipsa fieri non potest; nam passio Domini non fit sine morte Christi, et sanguinis sui effusione. Sed quia eucharistia est memoria et commemoratio passionis Christi, communione et participatione nominis vocatur ipsa passio Christi. Tertullianus Libro IV contra Marcionem, pagina 291, multa docet de pane eucharistiæ, quomodo non sit re ipsa corpus Christi et sacrificium propitiatorium, sed figurative et symbolice[2].

<small>August. de Civitat. Dei. lib. x. cap. 5.</small>

"Sacrificium ergo visibile invisibilis sacrificii sacramentum, id est, sacrum signum est[3]." Et in eodem capite: quoniam "illud quod ab hominibus appellatur sacrificium signum est veri sacrificii," mirum est quod neoterici non permittunt, ut sancti patres sint suorum ipsorum interpretes. Omnes

[1 Tertull. adv. Marcion. Oper. pp. 493. D. 494. A. Paris. 1641.]

[2 Figuram sanguinis sui salutaris implere concupiscebat.—Acceptum panem et distributum discipulis, corpus illum suum fecit, Hoc est corpus meum, dicendo, id est, figura corporis mei. Figura autem non fuisset, nisi veritatis esset corpus.—Cur autem panem corpus suum appellat.— Ita et nunc sanguinem suum in vino consecravit, qui tunc vinum in sanguine figuravit.—Id. Lib. IV. Op. pp. 570. D. 571. A. B. D.]

[3 August. de Civit. Dei, Lib. X. cap. 5. pp. 109. C. 110. A. Paris. 1586.]

fere dederunt eucharistiæ nomen sacrificii: sed hoc fecerunt propter significationem, propterea quod eucharistia est (ut hic Augustinus dicit) invisibilis sacrificii sacrum signum. Et postea dicit, "Ideo ab hominibus appellatur sacrificium eo quod signum veri sacrificii sit." Qualis est hæc igitur audacia, seu potius impudentia et impietas, neotericorum, qui verba sanctorum patrum urgent ac stringunt, quo suam ipsi idololatriam et impietatem stabiliant; cum omnes veteres patres passim in suis scriptis quid velint per nomen sacrificii ipsimet interpretentur? Non, inquiunt, quia re ipsa eucharistia sit sacrificium; sed potius significatio, repræsentatio, figura, signum, et memoria veri sacrificii semel in cruce peracti. Si pius lector quid amplius ab Augustino desideret, rogo ut legat illius epistolam xxiii, ad Bonifacium: illic enim multa ac sanctissima contra hunc neotericorum errorem de sacrificio facile reperiet[4]. Docet autem ibidem eucharistiam non aliter esse sacrificium quam dies, in quo mortis Christi quotannis memoriam celebramus, sit dies ipse in quo Patri cœlesti super crucem pro peccatis totius mundi perlitavit; cum re vera non sit idem dies (nam is ante mille quingentos annos fuit elapsus) sed similis est illi, ac illius memoriam retinet. Sic de die Paschatis, quem ob venerationem ac religionem resurrectionis Christi diem resurrectionis appellamus; cum re vera non sit idem dies, sed nominis communicatione, significatione, ac revolutione anni vocatur idem dies. Idem etiam dicit de sacramento eucharistiæ: "Semel, inquit, Christus se ipsum obtulit; tamen in sacramento vel repræsentatione, non solum singulis festis paschatis, verum quotidie offertur populo, sic quod non mentitur qui dicit quod quotidie offertur[5]." Hæc et multa alia in illa epistola Augustini habentur; quæ annotarem, si

Sacrificii nomen quatenus eucharistiæ tribuitur a veteribus.

[4 Nempe sæpe ita loquimur, ut pascha propinquante dicamus crastinam vel perendinam Domini passionem, cum ille ante tam multos annos passus sit, nec omnino nisi semel illa passio facta sit. Nempe ipso die Dominico dicimus, Hodie Dominus resurrexit, cum ex quo resurrexit tot anni transierunt. Cur nemo tam ineptus est, ut nos ita loquentes arguat esse mentitos, nisi quia istos dies secundum illorum quibus hæc gesta sunt similitudinem nuncupamus; ut dicatur ipse dies qui non est ipse, sed revolutione temporis similis ejus; et dicatur illo die fieri propter sacramenti celebrationem quod non illo die, sed jam olim, factum est?—Id. Op. Tom. II. col. 93. B. C. Basil. 1569.]

[5 Nonne semel immolatus est Christus in se ipso? et tamen in sacramento, non solum per omnes Paschæ solemnitates, sed omni die

illius liber mihi præsto foret. Si quis autem illam e Latinis in nostram linguam transferre dignaretur, plurimum prodesset; quo pii Romanæ linguæ ignari a neotericorum impietate in hac causa eucharistiæ defenderentur.

<small>Joan. Chrysost. Homil. 17. in Epistolam ad Heb. cap. 10.</small>
"Quid ergo nos? nonne per singulos dies offerimus? Offerimus quidem, sed ad recordationem facientes mortis ejus." Et paulo post: "Hoc autem quod facimus in commemorationem quidem fit ejus quod factum est. Hoc enim facite, inquit, in meam commemorationem. Non aliud sacrificium, sicut pontifex, sed id ipsum semper facimus: magis autem recordationem sacrificii operamur[1]." Chrysostomus dicit quod in eucharistia recordationem mortis Christi offeramus, et non quod Christum ipsum in remissionem peccatorum offeramus. Propterea vocat eucharistiam sacrificium, scilicet propitiatorium; non quod re ipsa ita sit, sed quia memoria veri sacrificii est. Et ne quis verba sua in hunc sensum raperet, quasi eucharistiam sacrificium propitiatorium re ipsa constitueret, claudit homiliam hisce verbis: "Magis autem recordationem sacrificii operamur." Hæc vero satis clara ac perspicua sunt apud patres, quod eucharistiam sacrificium vocabant propter significationem et memoriam sacrificii semel in cruce peracti; et non quod re ipsa sacrificium propitiatorium esset. Hoc vidit etiam Lombardus.

<small>Lombardus lib. sentent. 4. Distinct. 12.</small>
"Quod offertur, inquit, et consecratur a sacerdote vocari sacrificium et oblatio potest, quia memoria est et repræsentatio veri sacrificii et sanctæ immolationis factæ in ara crucis. Et semel Christus mortuus in cruce est, ibique immolatus est in se ipso: quotidie autem immolatur in sacramento, quia in sacramento recordatio fit illius quod factum est semel[2]." Hic quamvis infelicissimo vixit tempore, quando papæ tyrannis omnes Christi ecclesias devastasset, quoad puram verbi Dei prædicationem et verum sacramentorum usum; eucharistiam tamen plus quam memoriam ac repræsentationem veri sacrificii semel in cruce peracti non fecit.

populis immolatur, nec utique mentitur, qui interrogatus eum responderit immolari.—Ibid.]

[1 Chrysost. Homil. xvii. In Hebr. x. Op. Tom. iv. p. 523. l. 20. Eton. 1613. Τί οὖν; ἡμεῖς καθ᾽ ἑκάστην ἡμέραν οὐ προσφέρομεν; κ.τ.λ. —l. 29. Τοῦτο εἰς ἀνάμνησιν γὰρ τοῦ τότε γενομένου, κ.τ.λ.]

[2 Pet. Lombard. Sentent. Lib. iv. Distinct. 12. c. "Si illud sit sacrificium." fol. 357. G. Colon. 1576.]

Epilogus hujus tertii capitis, in quo a neotericis dissentimus.

Cum sacraDomini cœna commemoratio sit sacrificii in cruce semel peracti, fit ut apud veteres pene omnes sacrificii nomen tribuatur cœnæ, et cœna Christianorum dicatur sacrificium, non re ipsa, sed communicatione nominis, quia sacramenta earum rerum sortiuntur nomina quarum sunt sacramenta; non solum propter sacramenti cum re sacramenti analogiam et proportionem, verum etiam quod per sacramenta res sacramenti ob oculos sacramentis rite utentium graphice depingantur: quemadmodum in cœna Domini panis et vinum non solum indicant quod, ut corpora nostra pane et vino communi aluntur, ita corpore ac sanguine Christi corpora et animæ nostræ pascuntur ad vitam æternam; sed etiam per prædicationem verbi Dei, fractionem panis, et hujusmodi sacras actiones in Dominica cœna, mors Christi et sanguinis illius effusio super crucem ob oculos fidelium contemplanda proponuntur. Panis autem et vinum in cœna communem usum amittunt, et fiunt sacramenta corporis et sanguinis Domini; sed veram naturam et substantiam panis et vini semper conservant. Corpus vero et sanguis (quod ad illorum substantiam attinet), quorum panis et vinum sunt sacramenta, substantialiter suis sacramentis nec insunt nec adsunt. Sed corpus et sanguis (quoad illorum corporalem præsentiam) a signis absunt, fidei tamen recte signis utentium præsunt; ita ut non solum res sacramenti in recte utentibus, Dei promissiones et gratia, repræsententur, confirmentur, et augeantur, verum etiam sacramentali modo exhibeantur. Pro quibus beneficiis per Christum in cruce nobis partis gratias agimus Deo per Christum; et Christum denuo Patri non offerimus. Nam solus Christus Christum offerre potuit; quod ipsemet semel tantum fecit super crucem; itá ut nec a se ipso nec ab alio quoquam iterum offerri possit. Et revera in sacra Domini cœna minister ecclesiæ non magis Christum offert quam populus qui cum illo communicant. Ipse autem ut minister sacra et veneranda Dei mysteria populo dispensat, et populus eadem religiose accipere debet. Eadem tamen sunt mysteria tum ministro tum populo, et sacramenta, testimonia, et recordationes corporis Christi immolati; pro quibus gratiæ sunt agendæ a toto cœtu, a ministris ceterisque communicantibus: sed nec ab uno nec ab altero

Panis et vinum usum priorem amittunt, non substantiam.

offerri Christus ut sacrificium pro peccatis potest. Christus enim non dixit ministris, Accipite et offerte; hoc est corpus meum: sed dixit, Accipite et manducate; hoc est corpus meum. Similiter D. Paulus non dixit ecclesiis Corinthiacis, Venite, accedite ad sacros conventus, procumbite in genua, videte, palmas erigite, et adorate Christum ex pane factum per ministros ecclesiæ; verum protulit universo cætui verba Christi, Accipite et manducate ex hoc omnes: ut tota ecclesia simul sacra Dei sacramenta acciperet; et non ut unus pro omnibus sacramentum sumeret, vel sacramentum pro remissione peccatorum offerret. Et quod sacramentum mortis Christi vocatur sacrificium, propterea est vel quod sit memoria sacrificii Christi semel peracti, vel quia in cœna Domini omnes fideles (qui rite sacramento utuntur) sint participes illius fructuosissimi sacrificii in cruce oblati; aut quod gratias agimus Deo et Christo cum Spiritu sancto, quod tam dira morte unigeniti Filii Dei humanum genus redimere dignatus sit. Et hæc est fides sanctæ catholicæ ecclesiæ, sponsæ Christi, quæ voces alienas non audit, sed semper voci sui mariti sese accommodat atque obtemperat. Fateor autem hanc non esse fidem catholicæ ecclesiæ, hoc est, Romanæ meretricis, quæ nimis catholica est et generalis. Deus illam pro sua inexhausta bonitate corrigat et emendet, vel suo justo judicio illam perdat, atque projiciat in lacum sulphure ac pice ardentem, ne populum suum nimis diu decipiat. Nam hæc catholica meretrix non audit Christum, nec voci illius sese accommodat nec obtemperat: sed, nomine tenus Christiana, totum Christianismum ferro igneque persequitur; et sacras literas et omnia sanctorum patrum testimonia ad scholasticorum interpretationes semper obstringit. Si autem quis Romanas catholicas ecclesias cum sancta catholica ecclesia Christi, patriarcharum, prophetarum, evangelistarum, martyrum, ac omnium sanctorum patrum conferat; facile videbit illam Romanam catholicam ecclesiam tantum commercii, societatis, conjunctionis, unitatis, et lucis cum sancta catholica Christi ecclesia habere, quantum habeat Belial cum Christo.

Sed ut clarius omnes pii id perspiciant, subjiciam omnia symbola et articulos fidei a primo nascentis ecclesiæ exordio post ascensionem Christi in cœlos: cujus fidei testimonium ac protestationem qui ex animo tenebant, ab omni schismatis et hæreseos suspicione, infamia, et periculo ab omnibus vere piis

Ecclesia Romana nimis catholica.

habebantur immunes. Quos tamen articulos firmiter, religiose, integre, ac purissime (eo quod ex verbo Dei originem et certitudinem ducant) confitemur: et tamen ab ista catholica et Babylonica ecclesia pro hæreticis habemur, ac proscindimur. Sacras etiam et authenticas scripturas omnes veneramur ac colimus; sacra et vetera concilia patrum nulla rejicimus; sanctorum patrum scripta religiose amplectimur, omniaque symbola, et ea omnia quæ in eisdem continentur, ad amussim tenemus atque confitemur: et tamen hæc impia ac catholica meretrix Romana ecclesia nos hæretici dogmatis infamia onerat.

Symbolum commune sive apostolorum.

Credo in Deum Patrem omnipotentem, creatorem cœli et terræ: et in Jesum Christum Filium ejus unicum, Dominum nostrum; qui conceptus est de Spiritu sancto; natus ex Maria virgine; passus sub Pontio Pilato; crucifixus, mortuus, et sepultus; descendit ad inferna; tertia die resurrexit a mortuis; ascendit ad cœlos; sedet ad dextram Dei Patris omnipotentis; inde venturus est judicare vivos et mortuos. Credo in Spiritum sanctum, sanctam ecclesiam catholicam, sanctorum communionem, remissionem peccatorum, carnis resurrectionem, et vitam æternam. Amen.

Symbolum Nicænum, ex Historia Ecclesiastica et Tripartita[1].

Credimus in unum Deum, Patrem omnipotentem, omnium visibilium et invisibilium factorem: et in unum Dominum Jesum Christum Filium Dei, de Patre natum unigenitum, id est, ex substantia Patris; Deum ex Deo; lumen ex lumine; Deum verum ex Deo vero; genitum, non factum; ὁμοούσιον, consubstantialem Patri; per quem omnia facta sunt quæ in cœlis et quæ in terra; qui propter nos homines et propter nostram salutem descendit, incarnatus, humanatus (homo factus est), passus est, et resurrexit tertia die; ascendit in cœlos, venturus judicare vivos et mortuos: et in Spiritum sanctum. Eos autem qui dicunt, Erat aliquando quando non erat, et antequam nasceretur non erat; et, quia ex non exstantibus (ex nihilo) factus est, aut ex altera substantia vel subsistentia dicentes esse, vel creatum, vel convertibilem, vel mutabilem, Filium Dei, hos anathematizat sancta et apostolica ecclesia.

[1 Hist. Trip. Lib. II. cap. ix., and Lib. VII. cap. iii. Cassiod. Op. Tom. I. pp. 228, 303. Rotomagi. 1679.]

Symbolum Constantinopolitanum, ex exemplari quodam Græco-latino[1].

Credo in unum Deum, Patrem omnipotentem, factorem cœli et terræ, visibilium omnium et invisibilium.

Et in unum Dominum Jesum Christum, Filium Dei unigenitum, ex Patre natum ante omnia secula, lumen ex lumine, Deum verum ex Deo vero, genitum, non factum, consubstantialem Patri; per quem omnia facta sunt.

Qui propter nos homines et propter nostram salutem descendit de cœlis, et incarnatus est ex Spiritu sancto et Maria virgine, et homo factus est: crucifixus etiam pro nobis sub Pontio Pilato, passus et sepultus est, et resurrexit tertia die, secundum scripturas, et ascendit in cœlos; sedet ad dextram Dei Patris, et iterum venturus est cum gloria judicare vivos et mortuos; cujus regni non erit finis.

Et in Spiritum sanctum, Dominum vivificatorem, ex Patre procedentem, et cum Patre et Filio coadorandum et glorificandum; qui loquutus est per prophetas. In unam catholicam et apostolicam ecclesiam. Confiteor unum baptisma in remissionem peccatorum. Expecto resurrectionem mortuorum, et vitam venturi seculi.

Brevis confessio fidei Ephesinæ synodi, selecta ex epistola xxviii. *Cyrilli, ad synodum missa, et ab eadem comprobata*[2].

Confitemur Dominum nostrum Jesum Christum, Filium Dei unigenitum, Deum esse perfectum, et hominem perfectum, ex anima rationali et corpore: ante secula quidem ex Patre secundum divinitatem; postremis vero diebus eundem ipsum propter nos et propter nostram salutem ex Maria virgine secundum humanitatem natum[3]. Duarum siquidem naturarum facta est unio: quapropter et unum Christum, unum Filium, et unum Dominum confitemur. Et secundum hunc inconfusæ unitatis intellectum, sanctam virginem Deiparam esse confi-

[[1] See Binii Conc. Tom. I. p. 663. Paris. 1636. where πιστεύομεν, ὁμολογοῦμεν, προσδοκῶμεν.]

[[2] See Concil. Ephes. Pars I. p. 163. and Pars II. Act. I. p. 241. Binii Tom. II.]

[[3] In Binius the following clause is inserted here: ὁμοούσιον τῷ Πατρὶ τὸν αὐτὸν κατὰ τὴν θεότητα, καὶ ὁμοούσιον ἡμῖν κατὰ τὴν ἀνθρωπότητα. This Confessio is given in a letter addressed by Cyril to John, Bishop of Antioch.—Concil. Chal. Act. I. Binii Tom. III. p. 89. E. F.]

temur, propterea quod Deus Verbum incarnatus et homo factus est, et ex ipsa conceptione acceptum ex ea templum sibi ipsi adunavit. Evangelicas vero et apostolicas de Domino voces scimus viros theologos, tanquam ad unam personam pertinentes, ratione duarum naturarum dividere; et alias quidem, utpote divinitati competentes, ad divinitatem Christi, alias vero humiles ad illius humanitatem referre.

Confessio fidei Chalcedonensis synodi, ex libro Isidori[4].

Consentientes itaque sanctis patribus, unum eundemque Filium confiteri Dominum nostrum Jesum Christum consona voce edocemus, pariter perfectum eundem in Deitate[5] unum, et hominem verum eundem ex anima rationali et corpore, secundum divinitatem unius cum Patre naturæ, secundum humanitatem eundem unius naturæ nobiscum, per omnia similis nobis absque peccato: ante secula quidem ex Patre natum secundum divinitatem; in novissimis vero diebus eundem propter nos et propter nostram salutem hominem factum[6]: hunc unum eundemque Christum, Filium, Dominum, unigenitum, in duas naturas inconfuse, immutabiliter, indivise, inseparabiliter cognoscendum, in nullo naturarum differentia[7] propter unitatem perimenda[7], magis autem salva utriusque naturæ, proprietate, et in una coeunte persona, unoque statu concurrente[8]; non in duabus personis partiendum vel dividendum, sed unum eundemque Filium unigenitum, Deum Verbum, Dominum Jesum Christum; sicut ab exordio prophetæ de eo et ipse nos erudivit, et nobis primum[9] tradidit symbolum. His ergo cum omni undique diligentia et sollicitudine a nobis ordinatis, statuit sancta et universalis synodus aliam fidem nulli licere profiteri, aut scribere, aut docere, aut dicere aliter.

[4 Binii Conc. Chal. Pars II. Act. v. Tom. III. p. 340.   See also Evagrius Scholast. Lib. II. c. 4.]

[5 Καὶ τέλειον τὸν αὐτὸν ἐν ἀνθρωπότητι, θεὸν ἀληθῶς, καὶ ἄνθρωπον ἀληθῶς τὸν αὐτὸν, κ. τ. λ.—Bin. in loc. cit.]

[6 Ἐκ Μαρίας τῆς παρθένου τῆς θεοτόκου κατὰ τὴν ἀνθρωπότητα.—Ibid.]

[7 Differentias perimendas, in Foxe.]

[8 Εἰς ἓν πρόσωπον, καὶ μίαν ὑπόστασιν συντρεχούσης.—Bin. in loc. cit.]

[9 Καὶ τὸ τῶν πατέρων ἡμῖν παραδέδωκε σύμβολον. Τούτων τοίνυν μετὰ πάσης πανταχόθεν ἀκριβείας τε καὶ ἐμμελείας παρ' ἡμῶν διατυπωθέντων, ὥρισεν ἡ ἁγία καὶ οἰκουμενικὴ σύνοδος ἑτέραν πίστιν μηδένι ἐξεῖναι προφέρειν, ἢ γοῦν συγγράφειν, ἢ συντιθέναι, ἢ φρονεῖν, ἢ διδάσκειν ἑτέρους.—Ibid.]

Symbolum Toletani concilii primi, ex libro Isidori[1].

Credimus in unum verum Deum Patrem omnipotentem, et Filium, et Spiritum sanctum, visibilium et invisibilium factorem, per quem omnia facta sunt in cœlo et in terra; unum Deum, et unam esse divinæ substantiæ Trinitatem.

Patrem autem non esse ipsum, sed habere Filium, qui Pater non sit: Filium non esse Patrem, sed Filium Dei Patris esse natura: Spiritum quoque esse Paracletum, qui nec Pater sit, nec Filius, sed a Patre Filioque procedens. Est ergo ingenitus Pater, genitus Filius, non genitus Paracletus, sed a Patre Filioque procedens. Pater est cujus vox hæc audita est de cœlis, "Hic est Filius meus dilectus, in quo mihi bene complacui: ipsum audite." Filius est qui ait, "Ego a Patre exivi, et a Deo veni in hunc mundum." Paracletus est Spiritus de quo Filius ait, "Nisi abiero ad Patrem, Paracletus non veniet." Hanc Trinitatem personis distinctam, substantia unicam, virtute et potestate et majestate indivisibilem, indifferentem: præter hanc nullam credimus divinam esse naturam, vel angeli, vel spiritus, vel virtutis alicujus, quæ Deus credatur.

Hunc ergo Filium Dei, Deum genitum a Patre ante omne omnino principium, sanctificasse uterum virginis Mariæ, atque ex ea verum hominem sine virili generatum semine suscepisse, duabus duntaxat naturis, id est, Deitatis et carnis, in unam convenientibus omnino personam, id est, Dominum nostrum Jesum Christum. Nec imaginarium corpus, aut phantasmatis alicujus, in eo fuisse, sed solidum atque verum: hunc et esurisse et sitisse et doluisse et flevisse et omnes corporis injurias pertulisse. Postremo a Judæis crucifixum, et sepultum, et tertia die resurrexisse: conversatum postmodum cum suis discipulis, et quadragesima post resurrectionem die ad cœlum ascendisse. Hunc Filium hominis, etiam Filium Dei, et Filium Dei et Filium hominis appellamus. Resurrectionem vero futuram humanæ credimus carnis: animam autem hominis non divinæ esse substantiæ, aut Dei Patris, sed creaturam voluntate Dei creatam.

Adjice huc symbolum Toletani concilii quarti, cujus exemplar ex eodem Isidori libro petas.

[1 Concil. I. Tolet. Binii Tom. I. p. 741. A. B. C. D. Paris. 1636.]

Ratio fidei, ex Irenæo martyre, libro I. *cap.* 2 *et* 3, *contra Valentinum*[2].

Ecclesia per universum orbem usque ad fines terræ dispersa ab apostolis et ipsorum discipulis eam accepit fidem quæ est in unum Deum Patrem omnipotentem, qui fecit cœlum et terram, mare, et omnia quæ in eis sunt: et in unum Jesum Christum Filium Dei, incarnatum pro nostra salute: et in Spiritum sanctum, qui per prophetas prædicavit dispensationis mysterium et adventum, et ex virgine nativitatem, et passionem, et resurrectionem ex mortuis, et in carne ad cœlos ascensionem dilecti Jesu Christi Domini nostri, et ipsius e cœlis in gloria Patris adventum ad instauranda omnia, et resuscitandam omnem humani generis carnem; ut Christo Jesu Domino nostro et Deo et Salvatori et Regi, juxta voluntatem Patris invisibilis, omne genu flectatur cœlestium et terrestrium ac infernorum, et omnis lingua confiteatur ipsi; et judicium justum in omnibus faciat, et spiritualia quidem nequitiei, et angelos transgressores ac desertores factos, et impios ac injustos et iniquos et blasphemos homines in æternum ignem mittat: justis vero et sanctis et qui mandata ejus servarunt et in dilectione ejus permanserunt, partim ab initio, partim ex pœnitentia, vitam largitus, incorruptibilitatem donet, et gloriam æternam tribuat.

Hanc prædicationem et hanc fidem ecclesia (velut dixi) adepta, quanquam per totum orbem dispersa, diligenter conservat, quasi unam domum inhabitans; et similiter his credit, velut unam animam et idem cor habens; et consone hæc prædicat et docet et tradit, velut uno ore prædita. Nam linguæ in mundo dissimiles sunt, verum virtus traditionis una et eadem est. Neque in Germania fundatæ ecclesiæ aliter credunt, aut aliter tradunt; neque in Hispaniis, neque in Celtis, neque in Oriente, neque in Ægypto, neque in Libya, neque hæ quæ in mundo constitutæ sunt: sed quemadmodum sol creatura Dei in toto mundo unus et idem est; sic etiam prædicatio veritatis ubique lucet, et illuminat omnes homines ad cognitionem veritatis venire volentes. Et neque qui valde potens est in dicendo ex ecclesiæ præfectis alia ab his dicet, (nemo enim est supra magistratum;) neque debilis in dicendo hanc traditionem minuet. Cum enim una et eadem fides sit, neque is qui multum de ipsa dicere potest plus quam oportet dicit, neque qui parum, ipsam imminuit.

[[2] Iren. Adv. Hæres. Lib. I. c. 2. pp. 34, 36. Nicol. Gallas. 1570.]

Regula fidei secundum Tertullianum, ex libro ejus de Præscriptoribus hæreticorum[1].

Regula est autem fidei, ut jam quid credamus profiteamur; illa scilicet, qua creditur unum omnino Deum esse, nec alium præter mundi creatorem; qui universa ex nihilo produxerit per verbum suum primo omnium emissum. Id verbum, Filium ejus appellatum, in nomine Dei varie visum patriarchis, in prophetis semper auditum, postremo, delatum ex Spiritu Patris Dei et virtute in virginem Mariam, carnem factum in utero ejus, et ex ea natum, egisse Jesum Christum: exinde prædicasse novam legem et novam promissionem regni cœlorum, virtutes fecisse, sedisse ad dextram Patris[2], fixum cruci, tertia die resurrexisse, in cœlos ereptum, sedere ad dextram Patris, misisse vicariam [vim][3] Spiritus sancti, qui credentes agat; venturum cum claritate ad sumendos sanctos in vitæ æternæ et promissionum cœlestium fructum, et ad profanos judicandos igni perpetuo, facta utriusque partis resuscitatione, cum carnis restitutione. Hæc regula a Christo, ut probabitur, instituta nullas habet apud nos quæstiones, nisi quas hæreses inferunt, et quæ hæreticos faciunt.

Symbolum beati Athanasii Alexandrini episcopi, ex libris ejus[4].

Quicunque vult salvus esse, ante omnia opus est ut teneat catholicam fidem; quam nisi quisque integram inviolatamque servaverit, absque dubio in æternum peribit: et cetera quæ in communi ecclesiæ usu sat nota et pervulgata habentur.

Symbolum beati Damasi Romani episcopi, ex secundo tomo S. Hieronymi[5].

Credimus in unum Deum Patrem omnipotentem, et in unum Dominum nostrum Jesum Christum Dei Filium, et in Spiritum sanctum: Deum, non tres Deos, sed Patrem, Filium, et Spiritum sanctum, unum Deum colimus et confitemur: non sic unum quasi solitarium; nec eundem, qui ipse sibi Pater sit, ipse et Filius: sed Patrem esse qui genuit, et Filium esse

---

[1 Tertull. De præscript. Hæreticor. Oper. p. 235. C. D. Lutet. 1641.]
[2 Sedisse ad dextram Patris, not in Tertull.]
[3 Vim, wanting in Foxe.]
[4 Athan. Op. Tom. II. pp. 31, 32, 33. Colon. 1686.]
[5 Hieron. Op. Tom. IV. fol. 44. D. E. F. Paris. 1533.]

qui genitus sit: Spiritum vero sanctum non genitum neque ingenitum, non creatum neque factum, sed de Patre Filioque procedentem, Patri et Filio coæternum et coæqualem et co-operatorem; quia scriptum est, "Verbo Domini cœli firmati sunt;" id est, a Filio Dei, "et spiritu oris ejus omnis virtus eorum." Et alibi: "Emitte Spiritum tuum, et creabuntur, et renovabis faciem terræ." Ideoque in nomine Patris et Filii et Spiritus sancti unum confitemur Deum; quod nomen est potestatis, non proprietatis. Proprium nomen est Patri Pater, et proprium nomen est Filio Filius, et proprium nomen Spiritui sancto Spiritus sanctus. In hac Trinitate unum Deum colimus, quia ex uno Patre quod est unius cum Patre naturæ est, unius substantiæ, et unius potestatis. Pater Filium genuit, non voluntate, nec necessitate, sed natura. Filius ultimo tempore ad nos salvandos et ad implendas scripturas descendit a Patre, qui nunquam desiit esse cum Patre; et conceptus est de Spiritu sancto, et natus ex virgine: carnem et animam et sensum, hoc est, perfectum suscepit hominem; nec amisit quod erat; sed cœpit esse quod non erat, ita tamen ut perfectus in suis sit, et verus in nostris. Nam qui Deus erat homo natus est; et qui homo natus est operatur ut Deus; et qui operatur ut Deus ut homo moritur; et qui ut homo moritur ut Deus resurgit: qui, devicto mortis imperio, cum ea carne qua natus et passus et mortuus fuerat et resurrexit, ascendit ad Patrem, sedetque ad dextram ejus in gloria, quam semper habuit et habet. In hujus morte et sanguine credimus emundatos nos, et ab eo resuscitandos die novissimo in hac carne qua nunc vivimus; et habemus spem nos consecuturos præmium boni meriti, aut pœnam pro peccatis æterni supplicii. Hæc lege, hæc crede, hæc retine, huic fidei animam tuam subjuga, et vitam consequeris et præmium a Christo.

In Tripartita Historia, libro VII. cap. 37, eandem fidem testatur S. Petrus, episcopus Alexandrinus: qui velit illam legat ex libro[6].

[[6] The reference seems to be to Lib. VIII. cap. xiv. where these words occur: Petro quippe revertente de Roma cum literis Damasi Romanæ urbis antistitis, confirmantis consubstantialitatis fidem, et Petri episcopi roborantis ordinationem.—Cassiod. Op. Tom. I. p. 329. Rotom. 1679.]

Decretum imperatorium de fide Catholica, ex Tripartitæ Historiæ libro IX. *cap.* 7[1].

Impp. Gratianus, Valentinianus, et Theodosius, Augusti, populo urbis Constantinopolitanæ. Cunctos populos, quos clementiæ nostræ regit imperium, in ea volumus religione versari, quam D. Petrum apostolum tradidisse Romanis religio usque nunc ab ipso insinuata declarat, quamque pontificem Damasum sequi claret, et Petrum Alexandriæ episcopum, virum apostolicæ sanctitatis; hoc est, ut secundum apostolicam disciplinam, evangelicamque doctrinam, Patris et Filii et Spiritus sancti unam Deitatem sub pari majestate et sub pia Trinitate credamus. Hanc legem sequentes Christianorum catholicorum nomen jubemus amplecti: reliquos vero dementes vesanosque judicantes, hæretici dogmatis infamiam sustinere divina primum vindicta, juxta etiam motus animi nostri, quem ex cœlesti arbitrio sumpserimus, ultione plectendos. Data 3 Calendas Martias Thessalonicæ, Gratiano 5, Valentiniano et Theodosio, Augustis, Coss.

Christiani.
Hæretici.

Fides sufficiens, et conveniens sacris literis ac sanctorum patrum testimoniis.

Omnia hæc symbola vera et sancta esse confitemur; quorum articulos singulos firmiter et indubitato tenemus, non solum tanquam sacris literis et sanctorum patrum testimoniis convenientes, verum etiam tanquam plenos, absolutos, et sufficientes; quibus credentes per Christum vitam assequi possimus æternam. Et quemadmodum post hanc vitam, qui hinc migraverint certitudine et fiducia hujus fidei ornati, in perpetuum florentes ac beati erunt; sic in hac vita commorantes a Christi vera et sancta ecclesia pro Christi discipulis, et non hæreticis, habebuntur. Nam Christus dicit, "Si vos manseritis in sermone meo, vere discipuli mei estis, et cognoscetis veritatem, et veritas liberos reddet vos." Satis igitur nos habere putamus, quod fides nostra Dei atque illius verbi certitudine et protectione contra hæreses et errores muniatur ac conservetur; et papistarum jactantiam, qui spreto Deo, et neglecto illius verbo, sua multitudine superbiunt, contemnimus. Ipsi enim (ut Augustinus *De Utilitate credendi* dicit) sunt hæretici, qui falsas et novas opiniones gignunt vel sequuntur alicujus temporalis com-

[1 Cassiod. Op. Tom. I. p. 334.]

modi, et maxime gloriæ principatusque sui, gratia². Quod autem neoterici docent de elementorum transubstantiatione in eucharistia, de corporali corporis præsentia in cœna Domini, vel ut id quod offertur in missa sit sacrificium expiatorium vel propitiatorium, sacræ scripturæ veterumque patrum testimonia haud meminerunt; imo omnia illa plane negant et abominantur, uti coram æquo atque competenti judice semper sumus probaturi: quem si Deus optimus maximus concedere dignetur, facile vincet illius verbi veritas atque auctoritas. Quod si iratus ob nostra peccata talem judicem in terris non sit nobis concessurus; tamen qualescunque (etsi illius verbi hostes infensissimos et Romano pontifici juratos) permiserit, quod illius Spiritus auxilio et verbi sui auctoritate præstare possumus, id omni consilio summaque opera et diligentia præstabimus. Quod vero præstare non valemus, judici Christo in novissimo die, cum universi mortales ad vitam revocabuntur, committemus; qui nostram ac adversariorum fidem ad rationem et regulam verbi sui reposcet, ubi ante tribunal ipsius impii omnes, qui fidem a verbo Dei alienam profitentur, seclusi a cœtu atque ecclesia fidelium, in perpetuas tenebras relegabuntur, ut ipsi in perpetuum a societate et communione piorum in vita futura excludantur, qui in hac vita fideles in Christo ferro, igne, carcere, atque exilio persequuntur. Nostrum igitur interim erit assiduis precibus Deum defatigare, ut fidem et gloriationem spei nostræ ad finem usque firmam teneamus, et non metuamus eos qui corpus tantum occidere valent et conantur; ut etiam illorum iras et tormenta patienter feramus. Ad Deum similiter supplices fundamus preces, quibus pro illis etiam oremus, ut tandem, ad meliorem mentem revocati, nos cum illis, atque illi nobiscum, requiescamus per Christum Jesum Dominum nostrum in pace, vitamque consequamur æternam. Amen.

[² Cap. I. Aug. Op. Tom. VI. col. 89. B. Basil. 1569.]

EPISTLE DEDICATORY

TO THE TREATISE ENTITLED

DE VERA RATIONE INVENIENDÆ

ET

FUGIENDÆ FALSÆ DOCTRINÆ BREVE SYNTAGMA.

[The following Dedicatory Epistle of the treatise entitled " Joannis Hoperi, Angli, nuper episcopi Vigorniensis et Glocestrensis, de vera ratione inveniendæ et fugiendæ falsæ doctrinæ breve syntagma," is reprinted from Strype's Ecclesiastical Memorials, Vol. III. Part II. No XXVI. Strype says (Vol. III. Part I. p. 283. Oxf. 1822): "The treatise (written in prison, and dated Dec. 1, 1554) was designed by the author for the press, and was in the hands of John Foxe when he was at Basil for that purpose: but whether printed or no, I cannot tell." See the preliminary notice to the Epistola ad Episcopos &c. p. 381.]

Joannis Hoperi, Angli, nuper episcopi Wigorniensis et Gloucestrensis, de vera ratione inveniendæ et fugiendæ falsæ doctrinæ breve syntagma.

Desiderantur quædam in initio.

.........ignarus vel idiota diligit. Sed dilectio nostra vera est amor in vera fide erga omnia præcepta divina, quibus humiliter obedimus cum quadam lætitia et animi exultatione; ut tum ad Deum propter se, tum proximum meum propter Deum, honore afficiamur. Et hanc dilectionem verbum Dei tantum docet; ut fidem, spem, caritatem, timorem, tolerantiam, ac ceteras virtutes omnes, quæ ab hoc Christiano necessario exiguntur. Qui ergo populum Dei ad carbonarios, vel ad quoscunque alios quibuscunque titulis et nomine inscriptos, et non ad verbum Dei relegant, impostores sunt, Deique et hominum hostes; de quibus etiam Deus gravissime per Hieremiam conqueritur, inquiens, "Duo mala," inquit, "fecit populus meus: me dereliquerunt fontem aquæ vivæ, et foderunt sibi cisternas, quæ aquas continere non valent." Idem et apud vos facere qui vestræ saluti præficiuntur conantur. Primum defectionem a verbo Dei docent, a quo uno omnis petenda est veritas in religione Christi; et per quod omnes spiritus, qui in ecclesiis docent, a populo probandi sunt, num sint ex Deo. Deinde certitudinem fidei nostræ ab ignaro, indocto, atque imperito carbonario[1] petendam esse docent, qui quid[2] sit fides plane ignorat. Quid hoc aliud est quam, juxta verbum Christi, "cæcum cæco præficere, ut ambo in foveam cadant?" Certe Christus longe alia tam a ministris ecclesiæ quam a populo exigit: nimirum ut minister verbum Dei duntaxat doceat, et populus id solum audiat, discat, et observet: et omnino Deus vetat, ne qui sapientissimi et sanctissimi inter homines habentur faciant ea quæ recta videantur in oculis ipsorum: multo magis non est credendum nec faciendum in causa fidei quod rectum videatur in oculis illiteratissimi et stupidissimi carbonarii.

Quare pro meo erga vos officio, munere, et amore, quo tenacius veritati verbi Dei adhæreatis, breve syntagma de

Hierem. v.
[Jer. ii. 13.]

Matt. xv.
Luc. vi.

[1 "He meant the collier's faith, 'to believe as the Church believes.'" Strype. Eccl. Mem. Vol. III. Pt. I. p. 283. Oxf. 1822.]

[2 In Strype *quicquid*, evidently a mistake.]

falsa religione dignoscenda et fugienda vestræ caritati dedicavi. Unde facile intelligetis quam horribiliter et impie quæ hodie in ecclesiis Anglicanis fiunt a veritate verbi Dei dissonent, et ex diametro pugnent. Quod vulgari ac nostro idiomate scripsissem, si typographum aliquem idoneum qui Anglice librum emitteret invenissem: sed, ut pii omnes probe norunt, hodie in Anglia vel prela in imprimendis fabulis sudant, aut penitus silent. Præterea nolui vestra causa hoc opus nostra lingua edere, ne episcopi, Dei ac hominum implacabiles hostes, severius et acrius in vos (quos in Christo Jesu unice diligo) animadverterent. Quam atrociter enim et inhumaniter pii hodie ubique in hoc regno tractentur, illorum lacrymæ et gemitus (quos Deus tandem dubio procul clementer in Christo aspiciet) testantur. Præterea Latine scribere volui (quanquam Latinæ orationis pompam, fucum, et calamistra assequi nec valeo nec affecto), ut quæ a me de rebus divinis inter vos olim dicta, et a vobis accepta, piis fratribus sparsim universum orbem incolentibus palam facerem; ut fidem meam atque vestram agnoscerent, judicarent, et approbarent verbi Dei calculo et auctoritate; et eandem apud Deum Patrem nostrum cœlestem suis precibus adjuvarent, ut constanter et intrepide in eadem ad finem usque, invitis etiam inferorum portis, perseveremus. Piis et religiosis viris ac sacrarum literarum amatoribus scribo, quibus Dei gloria et illius verbi veritas summopere est cordi; quamvis orationis fuco et pigmentis non illiniatur. Et quemadmodum perantiquus ille Lucilius poeta dicere solebat, se sua non Persio scribere, sed Siculis et Tarentinis; sic ego non solum quæcunque de vera religione scribo, verum quæcunque etiam cogito aut loquor, ea omnia piis tantum scripta, cogitata, aut dicta esse volo: quid livor virulentus carpat, non moror; nec plus papistarum flammas aut ferrum curo quam leæna latrantis catuli vocem. Corpus tantum occidere possunt: sed anima statim in Christo præsenti et sempiterno gaudio fruetur. Tantum igitur dum hic vivitur Deum supplici animo precemur, ut ipsi cor ac mentem nostram dedicemus; cujus tutela et gratia omnia pericula evitabimus. Interim hostes evangelii fortiter propter Christum contemnamus, omnesque in Christo comiter juvare studeamus.

Hæc assidue cum animis vestris cogitate, et meditatione ac studio legum divinarum vos ipsos oblectate, ut Deo et sanctæ suæ ecclesiæ cari habeamini. Cavete etiam ab iis qui vobis fodiunt (ut inquit David) foveas, quæ non sunt secundum legem Dei; et non per quem, sed quid dicatur, animadvertite. Nam quemadmodum inter bajulum et Alcibiadem supremo loco natum, si veram nobilitatem spectemus, nulla est differentia, modo absit virtus; ita nec inter idiotam Nota. et summum pontificem, sicut cathedram Petri occupantem, si veram religionem spectemus, nulla est differentia, modo absit verbi Dei auctoritas.

Imo qui aliud evangelium quam Christi docet anathemate Galat. i. (licet sanctissimus) est feriendus. Quare cum sanctissimo vate Davide dicite, " In æternum, Domine, verbum tuum permanet Psal. cxix. in cœlo et in terra;" illud non potest mutari, non potest antiquari, non potest augeri, nec potest diminui. Nam quicquid Deus ipse constituit ratum ac fixum esse oportet; hoc indicat et testatur cœlorum et terræ perennitas. Quicquid ergo reges, principes, episcopi, sacrificuli, vel is qui impie se ipsum pro summo capite ecclesiæ Christi militantis in terris jactitat, in causa religionis dixerint; vos ipsos ad scientiam legum divinarum recipite, et earum præsidio adversus omnis impietatis insidias et imposturas communite. In causa fidei nullam auctoritatem principum aut episcoporum agnoscite citra verbum Dei; nam ipsa universalis ecclesiæ auctoritas nulla est, nisi quatenus a verbo Dei pendeat: ementitam ac fictam Romani pontificis auctoritatem contemnite, et ex animis vestris omnino profligate. Deus enim omnes apostolos, quoad auctoritatem et dignitatem, pares fecit: omnibus dixit, " Accipite Spiritum Joan. xx. sanctum; quorum remiseritis peccata, sunt remissa; quorum retinueritis, sunt retenta." Omnes pares in docendo evangelio constituit; omnes pariter " lucem hujus mundi" et " salem Matt. v. terræ" appellavit; et omnes testes æternæ salutis pares assignavit. Quamobrem ex verbo Dei nullam prærogativam præ ceteris apostolis Christus Petro concessit: quod si concessisset, tamen nec cathedræ suæ nec suis successoribus eandem concedere Petrus a Christo potestatem habuit. Et si illi et aliis totius ecclesiæ curam Christus principaliter concessisset, nihil Romani antichristi partes adjuvaret. Nam an Petrus unquam An Petrus fuerit Romæ, adhuc sub judice lis est. Præterea an unquam lis est. Petrus supremam dignitatem et imperium ecclesiæ suis successoribus commendaverit, papa ostendere non valet. Et si etiam hæc omnia vera essent, quod Christus Petro, et Petrus suis successoribus, ut papicolæ fingunt, contulissent; tamen

[HOOPER, II.]

Romanis pontificibus nihil patrocinaretur. Hi enim qui Petri doctrinam promovent veri sunt Petri successores; et non qui illius sedem ac cathedram occupant.

Et quod suam auctoritatem conciliis et auctoritatibus patrum asserere conatur figmentum est. Nam cum in concilio Carthaginensi tertio nomen et dignitatem universalis episcopi patres obtulissent Romano pontifici, Pelagius Romanus episcopus omnibus modis eodem tempore illud nomen a se rejecit[1]. Et Gregorius Magnus quinque epistolis gravissime et maximo impetu orationis adversus Joannem Constantinopolitanum, quod tam insulsum nomen a Mauricio imperatore tentaverat, invehitur, illum vocans prædecessorem antichristi[2]. Affirmat præterea Gregorius Magnus, omnes qui in hoc scelesto vocabulo (generalis episcopi) consenserint fidem suam perdere[3]. Et quod auctoritatem suam ratam esse voluerit quasi a regibus et principibus concessam, certo scimus reges et principes, etsi vellent, non posse aliquam suæ dignitatis partem cuiquam conferre, nec a suo officio et honore deponere: nam quod Deus necessario alicui statui conjungit nemo in alium statum transferre valet. Reges autem sub se ministros, qui ecclesiæ et reipublicæ munia ministrent, habere possunt; sed pares vel superiores in ecclesiæ vel reipublicæ ministerio habere regibus non licet. Et si forte quispiam vel regis permissione, vel aliqua temporis præscriptione, vel tyrannide, in ecclesiis auctoritatem sibi vindicat, nemo tamen illius auctoritati obtemperare debet, nec episcopo, nec papæ, quatenus sunt episcopi; quandoquidem a Deo talem potestatem non habent; nec quia a regibus missi, propterea quod talem potestatem reges episcopo papali facere non possunt. Sed hanc potestatem papæ clare indicat Joannes originem suam habuisse nec a Deo nec ab homine, sed ex abysso: et in interitum procul dubio brevi ibit.

[1 See Expos. of Ps. xxiii. p. 234, and note. The words of Pelagius there referred to are contained in a letter addressed to the bishops, &c., unlawfully assembled by John, patriarch of Constantinople. See Binii Tom. IV. p. 477. col. 1. D. Lutet. Paris. 1636. Also Tom. I. p. 711. Conc. Carth. III. cap. 26.]

[2 Gregor. Magn. Mauricio Augusto. Ep. 32. Id. Constantiæ. Ep. 34. Id. Joanni Constantinop. Ep. 38. Lib. IV. Id. Mauric. Aug. Ep. 30. Lib. VI. Id. Eusebio Thessalon. Ep. 69. Lib. VII. Op. foll. 393, 395, 410, 424. Paris. 1533.]

[3 Id. Aniano Diac. Ep. 39. Lib. IV. In isto—scelesto vocabulo consentire nihil est aliud quam fidem perdere.—Op. fol. 395. M.]

Sed hanc violentiam et satanicam auctoritatem papæ non est præsentis instituti ulterius prosequi. Tantum admonere volui, quamvis contra omnia jura divina et humana nunc iterum (propter nostra peccata) inter Anglos caput ecclesiæ obtinuerit, non plus hic habere jurisdictionis quam infimus episcopus Angliæ habet Romæ; et tandem denuo Dominus interficiet illum spiritu oris sui, ut antehac fecit. Nihil tam perfectum tamque absolutum oculis nostris videmus inter ipsa opera Dei, cujus interitus videri non possit. At ipsa lex Dei nulla vi, nullave tyrannide, dolo, aut vetustate consumi aut obliterari potest, ut Christus testatur, " Cœlum et terra transibunt; verba autem mea non transibunt." Illud igitur amplectamini, ac omni studio et diligentia colite. In hoc omnes vires nervosque intendite, ut vita nostra sic instituatur et gubernetur a sancto Dei numine, ut nunquam ab illius legis observatione aberret. Tunc futurum erit, ut omnia vobis prospere succedant, ac felicissime cadant, si legem Dei ante oculos habueritis.

Præterea, si ad verbi Dei regulam quæ hodie a papistis in ecclesiis fiunt exigantur, tunc omnia impia et profana esse nullo negotio judicabitis. Quapropter ego hoc breve syntagma scripsi, ut pii et impii, veri et falsi cultus discrimen collatione quadam demonstrarem, quanta supplicia impiis cultoribus, quantaque piis præmia sint constituta. Deus apud Hieremiam judicio contendit cum Israelitis, et cum illorum filiis acerrime disceptat. "Transite, inquit, ad insulas Cethim, et videte, et [Jer. ii.] in Cedar mittite, et considerate vehementer, et diligentissime videte, si factum est hujusmodi, si mutavit gens deos suos; et certe ipsi non sunt dii: populus vero meus mutavit gloriam suam in idolum." An non de nobis etiam idem justissime ac merito conqueri potest Deus? Quæ enim gens usquam in toto terrarum orbe tam impia, fraudulenta, immanis, et truculenta est, quæ deos suos tantum ad præscriptum suæ legis non colit et veneratur? Nulla certe tam barbara natio reperitur sub sole. Nam si cultus Christianorum hodie in ecclesiis sub papæ tyrannide ad præscriptum verbi Dei conferatur, omnia ex diametro cum verbo Dei pugnare videbimus. Imo nec usus nec lectio evangelii in missa incognita lingua publicis ac sacris conventibus ad regulam verbi quadrat. Nam evangelium etiam iis a quibus non intelligitur nihil prodest. Christus igitur sæpe jubet: "Audite et intelligite." Et pulchre docet Chrysostomus in Matt. xv.

Chrysost.

1 Cor xiv. "Qui ignota, inquit, lingua loquitur quam non intelligit nec se ipsum necalium ædificat[1]." Quænam potest esse utilitas ex voce non intellecta? Nulla penitus. Ideo Deus ad vocem verbi sui non tantum hominum præsentiam, auditum, geniculationem, corporis erectionem, capitis denudationem, manuum expansionem, verum hoc exigit a singulis suis auditoribus, προσέχετε λαός μου τῷ νόμῳ μου, quod sonat, "Intendite et adhibete mentem, popule mi," vel, "adverte animum, ad legem meam:" κλίνατε οὖς ὑμῶν εἰς τὰ ῥήματα τοῦ στόματός μου, i. e. "Ita aures vestras ad verba oris mei applicate et accommodate," quasi nihil aliud cogitetis aut audiatis, quam quod de ore meo egreditur. Hanc attentionem et intelligentiam efficacius adhuc multo exprimit Ebræa veritas:

Psal. lxxviii.

האזינה עמי תרתי הטו אזנכם לאמרי־פי׃

Non solum istorum vocabulorum et thematum proprietas, verum etiam grammatica constructio, indicat mentis attentionem et aurium diligentissimam auscultationem lectioni verbi Dei adesse debere. Chaldæus explanator pulcherrime hæc verba explanat per duo verba, quasi Deus ad hunc modum fuisset locutus: "Popule mi, conservate et consecrate mentem vestram ad vocem meam, et aures vestras verbis oris mei relinquite; me concionantem solum audiant et observent." Hoc mandatum generale est ac universale; ut cum docti tum indocti non solum legem, verum etiam ænigmata et propositiones, nec non et singula verba, oris Dei audiant, intelligant, discant, et observent, exigit. Et quî id fieri potest, cum quid legatur, agatur, aut dicatur in ecclesiis populus non intelligit? Quare ex studio et observatione legum divinarum impia et falsa fugite, sanctaque et vera exosculamini; nisi a via veritatis aberrare volueritis, et tandem meritas ignorantiæ et ingratitudinis vestræ pœnas luere. Hæc pro meo erga vos amore ad vos scripsi: amanter igitur suscipite, quæso.

E carcere, 1 Decembris, 1554.

[[1] Chrysost. 1 Cor. xiv. 15. Εἶδες πῶς κατὰ μικρὸν τὸν λόγον ἀνάγων δείκνυσι ὅτι οὐκ ἄλλοις ἄχρηστος μόνον ὁ τοιοῦτος, ἀλλὰ καὶ ἑαυτῷ, εἴγε ὁ νοῦς αὐτοῦ ἄκαρπος; ἂν γάρ τις φθέγγηται μόνον τῇ Περσῶν γλώσσῃ ἢ ἑτέρᾳ τινὶ ἀλλοτρίᾳ, μὴ εἰδῇ δὲ ἃ λέγει, ἄρα καὶ ἑαυτῷ λοιπὸν ἔσται βάρβαρος, οὐχ ἑτέρῳ μόνον, διὰ τὸ μὴ εἰδέναι τὴν δύναμιν τῆς φωνῆς.—Op. Tom. III. pp. 476, 477. Eton. 1613.]

APOLOGY.

[The Apology is reprinted from the text of 1562: but it has been thought advisable, in order to preserve the series unbroken, to detach it from the letters (Nos. XLIV. XLV. and XLVI. of the following collection) with which it was connected in that edition, and to place it by itself.]

An apologye

made by the reverende fa-
ther and constante Martyr of
Christe John Hooper late Bishop of
Gloceter and Worceter againste the
untrue and sclaunderous report that
he should be a maintainer and enco-
rager of suche as cursed the Quenes
highnes that then was, Quene Ma-
rye. Wherein thou shalte see this
Godlye mannes innocency and
modest behaviour, and the
falshode and subtiltye of
the adversaries of
God's truth.

¶ Newelye set foorth and allowed accor-
dinge to the order appoynted in the
Quene's Maiestye's iniunc-
tions.

Anno. 1562.

¶ To the godly reader Henry Bull
wisheth grace and peace from God, with
unfeigned faith and a
good conscience, in
Christ Jesus our
Lord.

IT hath always been the practice of Satan, and his subtle soldiers the papists, even the sworn adversaries of God's truth, that when they cannot prevail against the same by tyranny and torments, they labour to deface it by most impudent slanders and lies (the chiefest defence and stay of their kingdom), as thou shalt see, good reader, in this treatise following. For when they could by no tyranny nor cruel handling discourage this man of God from the constant confession of the truth, they stirred up most shameful and cursed lies against him, that he should be a privy maintainer of such as cursed the queen; but to their own perpetual shame and ignominy.

For whilst they have sought by this means to bring God's eternal verity into contempt, and to make it more odious to the world; what else have they done but disclosed their own wickedness and malice, and given him occasion so to paint out their falsehood and lying spirit in their right colours, by this pithy, learned, and worthy little piece of work, that all men may hereby clearly perceive whose children they are, and they themselves shall need no other glass to see how like their father they look, the father of all falsehood and lies? And to the end that this their wicked dealing, which have thus proudly set themselves against God and against his Christ in his poor members, may be the better known and registered to the world and the posterity to come, to their shame and confusion, and to the advancing of God's glory in the innocent suffering of his saints, thus torn and rent by tyranny, torments, lies, and slanders for his name's sake; behold the providence of God, who hath now brought this work to light, which otherwise, by the negligence of some, was like to perish.

And here have I just occasion to discommend those men which do defraud the congregation of such worthy monuments. Great was the care of this blessed man and other for the church of God; and many fruitful works did they write in prison, in bands, in fetters; but few are come to light: and shall we, like careless and ungrateful people, suffer these godly labours, these painful travails, thus to perish? How desirous they were to have them published, to witness to the world that they taught and sealed with their blood, and to profit their brethren, it appeareth by this author's earnest request to the readers of this treatise; which is, that they will not keep it close to themselves, but, as soon as they have read it, set it abroad, and communicate it to other. And that request which he maketh concerning this treatise do I here generally make in his name and others, and in the behalf of the church of God, for the rest of their works, to them in whose hands they remain; that they will not suffer them to be suppressed any longer (for that is it which Satan and the enemies of the cross of Christ do most desire), but cause them to be set abroad in print to the commodity of many. And truly it might seem to be a labour no less commendable for the learned than profitable for the household of God, to be as diligent in searching and setting forth of such worthy works, as in penning and publishing of new. So full are they of heavenly doctrine, so full of power of God's Spirit, so full of comfort and consolation, being written as it were out of God's sanctuary, with the finger of God, by men even then out of the world and in heaven already, that indeed they are most worthy to be sought for as precious jewels and treasures. For God knoweth what lack we have of such trumpets to stir up our dull hearts in these dangerous days, wherein all states of men have turned this great blessing of God bestowed upon us (I mean these breathing days and time of rest from antichrist's tyranny) into a security, and are become like men rocked asleep; and many that seemed to be zealous, earnest, and constant in the Lord's quarrel so long as these captains were in the battle, and they themselves within the sound of the trumpet, are now well cooled. Pray we therefore that the Lord would warm them, heat them, inflame them again with the zeal of his house; that we may have many such valiant captains, such worthy prelates and shepherds, as

this was, over their lambs watchful and careful, in preaching
diligent and painful, in zeal fervent, hearty, and sincere, and
of like fortitude of spirit to help and maintain the travailing
faith of the gospel; that we may enjoy still this fatherly blessing
of our gracious God, and escape the wrath to come and plagues
at hand for our unworthy receiving again of this great
benefit of his word and liberty of conscience: which
plagues we may assuredly look for with double
woe, unless by speedy repentance we seek
to remove the cause thereof. God,
for his Christ's sake, grant
us heartily, earnestly,
and effectuously
so to do.
Amen.

⁋ An apology against the untrue and slanderous reports made against me John Hooper, late bishop of Worceter and Gloceter, that I should be a maintainer and encourager of such as cursed the Queen's Majesty's highness.

IT is the use and fashion of all wicked and evil disposed persons, gentle reader, that when one way will not serve to bring their wickedness to pass, they assay and prove (as Terence[1] saith) another. The whole congregation and company of godly and charitable people be not ignorant how falsely and uncharitably the papistical clergy hath, for this year and a half, openly and privily by all means laboured to persuade, not only the common sort of people, but also the magistrates, to judge and condemn me in their conscience for an heretic: by the which means they have much prevailed against me, but yet not as much as they desire and look for. Wherefore, seeing plain allegation of pretensed and falsely surmised heresy as yet sheddeth not my blood (without the which that whorish and unbridled false supremacy of Rome was never satisfied), now, because the princes and the magistrates may be their hangmen, although that wicked power of antichrist (as all chronicles and true historiographers do record) would have no power above it, equal with it, nor none under it, but such as hold their kingdoms and authorities in the world (as it were *in capite*) of that wicked and pestilent see and chair of Rome, which is indeed the very whore of Babylon that St John describeth in the Revelation of Jesus Christ, sitting upon a seven-headed beast, which St John himself interpreteth to be seven hills, and the children in the grammar-school do know that Rome is called *civitas septem montium*, the city of seven hills; this generation, I say, that always hath shed innocent blood, lest

Rev. xvii.

[1 Hac non successit, alia aggrediemur via.—Terent. Andr. Act. IV. Scen. I. 1. 47.]

the child should degenerate from the father's conditions (for he that gave the bishop of Rome his supremacy was a bloody murderer and traitor, one Phocas[2], that killed his master Mauricius the emperor, his mistress the empress, and six of their lawful children), would bear the world in hand that I were not only an heretic, but also a traitor. And, to affirm that assertion, they say I have written to comfort, encourage, and maintain such as cursed the queen. But if I may (as I ought) be heard indifferently, I shall try myself a true man, and prove mine accusers to be false in the face of all the world.

There be (as I hear say) now certain in the Counter in London that wished evil unto the queen's highness; unto whom mine adversaries say I wrote letters of encouragement, that they did well in so doing; and that, if they continued doing the same still, they should do better. First, I do require all good men to mark the tenor and contents of the letter which my friend sent unto me to advertise me of such men as were taken and imprisoned upon New Year's day at night last past: also, to mark the contents of mine answer unto his letter, wherewithal I did send this letter that the wicked calleth treason. I have set at the end of this Apology the true copy of all three letters[3]; and other letters than these I wrote not to them that were taken at that time.

Now mark how my letters will prove this twopenny treason that the wicked would charge me withal. First, I knew of nothing the congregation did but of prayer; which they used, as they be bound by God's laws, in the vulgar tongue (let the papists say to the contrary what they will); and there they gave God thanks for that they had received at his hands, and asked of him the things they lacked; and prayed also for the queen and the magistrates. Mark the information of the letter that advertised me wherefore they were taken. Now do the wicked papists feign matter, and change prayer, wherein I required them to persevere, for the queen into cursing of the queen. Mark again the place where prayer and serving of God, that I commended, was done: in a godly man's house (saith my friend) in Bow church-yard. The place where the queen, by report, was

[2 See Expos. of Psal. xxiii. p. 235.]
[3 See Letters, Nos. XLIV. XLV. XLVI.]

cursed was in the Counter by the stocks in London. Further, mark the time when the thing was done that I commended: before they were taken, as my letter to them doth testify. Mark also what the persons be that are accused of this cursing: such as yet until the tenth day of January I knew not nor have heard of: and to those that be accused of the crime my letters were not sent, nor never came. Yet doth the wickedness of the wicked papists say that I encouraged them in evil doings, my letters never coming unto them; nor, when I wrote, knew I of any such cursing. Further, such as be taken and imprisoned for that fault I never knew of, nor of any such thing to be done by them, until (as I said) the tenth day of January; which was (as I have learned) at the least six days after the fault was done, and three days also after my letter was written and delivered to them that were in another prison from such as did this crime. Wherefore, if the wicked were not past all shame, charity, love, and honesty, how could they of conscience blow and blast abroad such wicked lies and slanders, that neither agreeth with the matter of my letter, nor with the persons, nor with the place where the crime was committed, nor yet with the time when the curses were used?

There was never true subjects in such danger as we poor Englishmen be at these present days. The falsest men of the world, yea, the satanical papists, may say what they will, so that they speak against any that favoureth God, his word, and the holy catholic church of Christ; and his accusation (be it never so false), by that time it hath been in the consistory court and handling of the bishops one day or two, shall have some fair pretensed colour to make it appear true, and also to be done only for conscience' sake; as all their religion is hypocrisy, and coloured with holiness in name. I have been always a true man to all the estates of this realm: I will stand with the law in that point, and reprove mine accusers, whatsoever they be. As for my truth and loyalty to the queen's highness, the time of her most dangerous estate can testify with me, that when there was both commandments and commissions out against her, whereby she was, to the sight of the world, the more in danger, and less like to come to the crown; yet, when she was at the worst, I rode myself from place to place (as it is well known), to win and stay the people for her party: and whereas another was proclaimed, I preferred her, notwithstanding the proclamations. And to help her as much as I could when her highness was in trouble, I sent horses out of both shires, Gloucestershire and Worcestershire, to serve her in her great danger; as Sir John Talbot, knight, and William Ligon, esquire, can testify, the one dwelling in the one shire, and the other in the other. Seeing in adversity I was with her, and did her service then, I being at liberty, it is falsely and wickedly conspired by the papists that now, she being in real possession of the crown, and in prosperity, and I a prisoner in captivity, would be against her.

But whereas the pope will for a penny or twopence give remission of all sins *a pœna et culpa*[1], the wicked may say and do what they lust, and the innocent lambs of Christ suffer whatsoever God shall permit the members of antichrist's kingdom to lay upon them. Yet may the godly see the pretensed and false imagined treason of these antichrists against me. Doubtless it is not because they bear good will and loyalty to the queen's highness, that they would bring me into her displeasure. For all the world knoweth she hath no more nor no greater enemies than those that desire to leave no mouth open in this realm to speak and sound the name of Jesus Christ in faith and understanding. I take record hereof at the bishop of Winchester's book of True Obedience[2], of Bonner's epistle into the same book, of Culbert Tonstall's sermons, and doctor Sampson's oration, made only, advisedly, purposedly, and deliberately against the queen and the pope, and be openly in all men's hands, as well within the realm as without. But such be the inscrutable judgments of God, that her highness should punish her poor, true, and loving subjects, that never offended her, and also make false, traitorous bishops judges of truer men than they be themselves. Doubtless, if ever I had written or spoken the tenth part of treason that her own bishops' books do contain, I know their charity is so burning and fervent, that the crows and birds of the air should have eaten my flesh before this day. Yet I am not sorry, but doubtless (I speak and write from the bottom of my heart before God) very glad, to see mercy shewed unto

These are they which, without all shame and conscience, have condemned their own doings, and turned, like filthy swine, to their old puddle, and dogs to their vomit.

[1 From punishment and guilt.]
[2 See Exposition of Psal. lxii. p. 268.]

offenders: but I speak it to this end, that I verily suppose, as the queen doth forgive offenders, so would she not wittingly punish me and other true men, that always have done her good and no harm. For she is by the laws of God as much bound to be indifferent and favourable to true men, as true men be bound to give her obedience: and (be it spoken without all pride and malice) I defy him, whatsoever he be, (the magistrates being honoured,) that dare open his mouth to the contrary. But alas, saving I would not offend the law of my living God, that commandeth me to obey all magistrates and laws which disagree not from his holy word, it were for me a more easy death to be hanged like a traitor than burned like an heretic. But seeing death must ensue the true religion and faith of Jesus Christ, I will not appoint God by what death he shall take me out of this life. I am in Christ wholly and throughly at a point with the world. I pray daily, and will pray, for my persecutors even as for myself: but their tyranny and death that they will kill me withal I contemn and pass nothing of. I am no better than my master Christ was in his service. If I die therefore by his grace, whether it be by fire or sword or halter, it is all one to me; and the rather death cometh, the better shall it be welcome: for the sooner shall my soul rest with Abraham, Isaac, and Jacob in my heavenly Father's kingdom; whereof in Christ I am assured to be a right heir, ordained to the same of mercy by him before the world was made.

The Pharisees did not lay only heresy to Christ's charge; and indeed the manner of his death upon the cross was not appointed for heresy amongst the Jews, but rather stoning to death[1]. There was never a pair of stocks in the town that Jeremy the prophet scoured not; but still his accusers, the false priests, made their accusations in both states, as well in heresy as in treason, lest the king should not punish the poor preacher for preaching, but let him go. So Christ's accusers, the holy bishops and priests, when they perceived that Pilate favoured the innocent cause of Christ, and said he found nothing that they laid against him worthy of death, they made him (poor man!) eat that word (judge as he was), and told him, if he let Christ live, and would not proceed to condemn him,

[[1] See Levit. xxiv. 16, and Gal. iii. 13: also Pearson on the Creed, Art. IV.]

he was not the emperor's friend. This hath been always the pleading of the satanical clergy, sithence that wicked see of Rome falsely challenged supremacy, ever to put the princes and judges of the earth in the head, that all true preaching of God's word against their wickedness, superstition, and idolatry, was treason. But all kings, queens, and magistrates civil shall at the day of their death answer with eternal damnation of their souls for the shedding of all innocent blood within their realms and offices. God doth not bid the king and queen commit matters of religion to the bishops; neither doth he will them to give bishops power to condemn when they lust, and so afterwards commit such as they have condemned to the secular powers: but doth command all princes to be learned themselves, to hear them, and to judge themselves such doubtful and weighty causes by the word of God. It is both against God's laws and man's, that the bishops and clergy should be judges over any subject within this realm; for it is no part of their office. They can do no more but preach God's word, and minister God's sacraments, and excommunicate such as God's laws do pronounce worthy to be excommunicated. Who would give a sword into a madman's hand? There be not living more malicious, cruel, crafty, devilish, merciless, nor tyrannical tyrants than the bishops and clergy under that wicked bishop of Rome: as the chronicles and the histories of the bishops' lives do plainly record. And no marvel: for, as the bishop of Winchester saith in his book of True Obedience, wheresoever the pope hath supremacy, there Christ is dishonoured, and the kings suffer wrong. Yea, he saith more (let his book be judge), that there can be no truth where as the bishop of Rome is chief head. And therefore he saith that no prince can or may give the pope any such authority. For a king can no more give that part of his office that toucheth the governance of the one part of his people, which is the clergy, for matters of religion, to the bishops of Rome, than a wife may give the use of her body from her husband to another man. Yet, as St John saith, the princes of the earth shall be made so drunken with the cup of the whore of Babylon, that they will deliver their power to the beast: but yet St John saith plainly, although the kings do give to the beast against God's laws their kingdoms, yet be they none of the beast's.

But now the bishop of Winchester and the rest of his

fellows, against their oaths, their sermons, their preachings, their books, yea, their own knowledge and conscience, fall under that wicked and false pretensed power again; and make him the head of Christ's church, whom they all be not able to prove to be any member of Christ's church. Grant it were as true as it is false, that Christ had given such supremacy to St Peter (who, they say, was bishop of Rome, although I never knew man yet able to prove it) and his successors, yet no man should obey the things done by the pope. For the word of God is plain, that he is an excommunicate person, in that he teacheth doctrine besides and contrary to the word of God, as St Paul saith plainly. And how far both the doctrine and the use of the sacraments under the tyranny of the bishop of Rome be from the word of God, it shall appear plainly to all the estates of this realm, if my lord cardinal of his charity will accomplish the reasonable and gentle requests that I have made unto him[1]. I trust, as gently he received my letters, so he will grant me and my fellows that be in durance our lawful requests.

Gal. i.

But this I do write, good reader, not to make discourse of any matter, but only for the majesty and honour of God's word, to declare mine innocency of treason, or any evil will or malice that I bear to the queen's highness, or any superior power. Doubtless I thank our heavenly Father, I have read too many times the word of life, and marked it too well, to fight against or curse the magistrates. I pray God to give them understanding of his holy truth, with love to follow it: and the harm that I would to any man living happen to myself. For the commandment of God is, that we should not only love our friends, but also our enemies; and not only wish good and pray for our friends, as debtors unto God and them for the benefits we take at their hands, but also pray for our enemies, lamenting the tyranny and wickedness of sin, that causeth them to hate and persecute whom God requireth to love. Yet doth St John in his epistle command the readers thereof to beware they pray not for such as be subject to the sin which is to death. But I suppose that in these later days, wherein the spirit of judgment and discretion, or discerning of sins, is not so abundantly in men as it was in his time, no man should, without a special testimony of the Holy Ghost, particularly or

Matt. v.

1 John v.

[1 See the notice prefixed to the Epistola ad Episcopos, &c. p. 381.]

expressly judge that sin to be in any man: for the judgments of God, who shall turn from wickedness, or who shall fall from virtue, before this mortal life be ended, be not revealed nor known unto men. And yet in case I knew (as St John saith) a man that sinned unto death, for whom by the commandment of God I should not pray, it followeth not that I should curse him for whom I may not pray. And I rejoice that the inscrutable judgment of God suffereth the wicked to slander me with that evil that of all others I have been all my lifetime (I thank God) least troubled and in danger withal: for I never cursed man nor beast otherwise than the word of God willed me, for the time whilst I preached his word to rebuke sin. I do remember that St Augustine[2], in his book of Christ's sermon in the mount, hath many godly sentences and sayings in this matter. But I mind not to write a book of it, but only to speak the truth of myself against wicked slanderers, that care not, so they may hurt, how they hurt; nor, so they kill, by what means they kill.

In the psalms and in the prophets be marvellous execrations of the wicked, and specially against such as with the death of the godly go about to condemn the word of God, and to oppress it. Christ also and his apostles used marvellous execrations, when he said, "Woe be unto thee, Chorozaim; [Matt. xi.] woe be unto thee, Bethsaida," &c. St Paul wished them destroyed that troubled the church of the Galatians: also he [Gal. v.] called the high-priest 'painted wall' to his face: and Peter [Acts xxiii.] killed with a word Ananias and Sapphira his wife. St Paul [Acts v. Acts xiii.] strake blind Elymas the witch. Eliseus caused the wild bear [2 Kings ii.] to tear and kill the children that mocked him. Elias caused [2 Kings i.] fire from heaven to fall upon the messengers of Ochosias[3] the king. These things declare that there were at all times cursings used, and extreme punishment followed such as were by God's commandment cursed: and yet such as did curse remained still in the favour of God.

But these examples no private man may follow. For these men were public preachers of God's word, whose office was by all means so to rebuke and condemn sin as they were

[2 See Homil. VI. De eo quod Dominus dicit in Evangelio, Diligite inimicos vestros, benefacite his qui vos oderunt.—August. Op. Tom. x. col. 421, et seqq. Basil. 1569.]

[3 Ochosias: Ahaziah.]

instructed by the word of God. And he that marketh the condition of these persons shall perceive that in every one of them was two persons: the one, public, that could speak no more pleasant nor gently to the sinful world than God bade them; which was, to pronounce them cursed and damned for their sins and iniquity; yet, as private men, they wept and sorrowfully lamented the misery and loss of the same persons that they cursed as public ministers. Jeremy, as a public preacher, threatened the destruction of his own country, the captivity of his natural prince and king, and the servitude and bondage of all his countrymen; yet, as a private man, wept and cried out rather with floods of tears than with drops of weeping. So did Christ upon Jerusalem, David upon Saul and Absolon, and St Paul upon the Jews; and yet offended nothing at all. For although God require of public ministers to do that appertaineth to their public office in cursing and threatening of his ire and displeasure; yet he taketh not from them his natural affection to pity and bewail even such as they know most justly to be punished; but yet so in measure, that the affection of mercy and compassion murmur not against the will and just judgment of God. Wherefore, as it is forbidden a private man to revenge by force his own wrong, so it is forbidden him to curse or execrate any person, magistrate or other. Yea, the public person that preacheth in this point had need to be circumspect, and to beware he speak nothing of affection, but all for the correction of sin to the amendment of sinners; as the saints do ask vengeance in heaven, saying, "When wilt thou revenge our blood upon them of the earth?" where as it may not be thought that the saints pray uncharitably against their neighbours, that the world and the kingdom of sin might make an end in them. And so do all good men pray now upon the earth, that the kingdom of God may come, as it is in the Lord's prayer.

But what do these ungodly papists find fault with cursing, when not only all histories, chronicles, and records from time to time, ever sithence the pretensed and wicked authority of the Romish bishop, do testify, besides daily experience, that they have cursed kings and realms of malice, pride, and indignation; and for money have blessed them again; and so used kings and realms (as their wicked lusts have moved them) as slaves and beasts, contrary to God's express word? And daily it is seen in every consistory court, that, at the will and pleasure of a wicked man that is the bishop's officer, the innocents be cursed, and used worse than dogs, until such time as the officers' fury be pacified with gold or silver. If they knew God's laws (as they do not indeed), they should see and find, that no ordinary excommunication should be used by the bishop alone, but by the bishop and all the whole parish. So we read in the old law, that when such excommunications Deut. xxvii. were used, the whole congregation stood, the one party of the one hill, and the other party of the other hill. Also, when the incestuous man was excommunicated, St Paul alone did 1 Cor. v. not excommunicate him, but St Paul's consent and also the whole church with him.

Extraordinary excommunications that then the holy men used, which our bishops at this day neither have power to do nor know what they be, be not in use: as St Paul alone by Acts xiii. God's power made blind the witch Elymas; and Peter alone Acts v. by the same power killed Ananias and Sapphira his wife. The bishops can but strike and excommunicate with the word of God: if that serve not, they should commend the matter to God, and meddle no further. But now the bishops have learned God's word, and preach and teach fables and lies: and whoso will not believe them in such wickedness, they strike them with loss of goods, lands, liberties, friends, wife, and children; yea, with imprisonment, sword, fire, cord, and such like: and, to make all appear well, they strike true men with the false slander of treason. But such is God's just punishment for our sins most justly happened unto us: when we amend our lives, he will withdraw his scourge.

Thus mayest thou see, gentle reader, that such cursing as these ungodly papists slander me withal is both against my knowledge and my doings. And as I know I should not curse any man, even so I know I should pray for all men, and for mine enemies also, diligently and christianly; forgiving them, as much as lieth in me, here and before God, praying him to send them more grace and loving charity.

But here I would men should note and mark that, as they be forbid to curse the magistrates, so be they forbid to say, allow, or commend anything they shall do that is not agreeable with the word of God. For the scripture doth not only curse such as make wicked laws, but also holdeth them

36—2

accursed (whatsoever they be) that call good evil, and evil good. And although God doth require me to obey the magistrate, yet he forbiddeth me to flatter the magistrate, or stir him up to do evil, or to commend the evil when it is done; for we know not only evil-doers shall be damned, but also such as consent to evil-doing. And this old saying is true, 'The consenters and doers shall have like pain.'

Now these be the bees and stinging wasps that make the bishops so sore to rage and startle. They have taken the word of God from the people out of all churches in this realm, that nothing may be said in the vulgar tongue: which is clean contrary to the word of God, and expressly against the same, as St Paul saith. But they say St Paul there speaketh but of preaching alone, which should be in the vulgar tongue: but I say, and will justify it, that they say untruly in so saying; for the text plainly and expressly maketh as well mention of prayer said or sung as of preaching: "I will pray in my spirit and in mine understanding," saith St Paul, &c. And so do the old fathers altogether say as I say. Read John Chrysostom and St Ambrose[1] upon the same place.

Further, they have banished the holy supper of the Lord, and call the table where the communion was used an oyster-board, and the bread appointed to that use oyster-bread; and yet those things, both by name and effect, be contained and commanded us most plainly in the express word of God. And, for the supper of the Lord, they have brought in private masses of their own, or else of their wicked predecessors' invention; which is clean contrary to the word of God: let the book of the apostles and evangelists be judge. And whosoever will compare the mass (as they use it) with the supper of the Lord, shall see them as well agree as Christ and the wicked Pharisees agreed. Now because men cannot condescend unto these wicked things, and call that holy which is damnable, and that good which is evil; therefore be lies, slanders, and false matters picked and feigned against them. But if they will say good is evil, and evil good, the devil God, and God the devil, then shall men have peace with them, and not before.

[1 See Chrysost. Hom. xxxv. in 1 Cor. xiv. 15. Op. Tom. III. p. 477. Eton. 1613. Ambros. in 1 Cor. xiv. Op. Tom. III. col. 394, et seqq. Par. 1603.]

As I am sorry with all my heart that any man for troubles should curse his persecutors, except he have more special testimony of God's Spirit that he doth well than I have; so likewise I do lament that those men that be cursed (who they be, I know not) do not examine themselves, and search their own consciences, whether justly God stirreth the people to hate them or no; as David did, being a lawful king, and also a good king. When he heard Semei call him blood-sucker 2 Sam. xvi. and murderer, with many foul words, he entered in the judgment of his own conscience, and felt that the Lord had stirred the same wicked man up, being his own subject, to curse: whereby he learned (good king) to lament and beware of the sin that made him thus to be cursed. Alas! what man or woman living is there that, one ways or other, hath not deserved to be cursed both of God and man? But these carnal and fleshly bishops never consider that which is principally to be taken heed of in every plague that God sendeth; which is, the sin in the person plagued.

When the scourge of God so cometh, it were best for every man to say to himself, Good Lord! although I have not deserved thus to be spoken of one way, yet another way I have; for none is pure and innocent in thy sight. Let every man remove by grace the cause of cursings and other troubles, which be the very messengers of God and his scourges: and then God will remove the effects, which be the troubles themselves. If the party cursed by man be innocent, he may Matt. v. rejoice to be evil spoken of for justice' sake; and assure himself that God will bless that man cursed. If he be guilty, Mal. ii. the curse is as a preacher sent unto him from God to admonish him of his sins. And as for the person that curseth, if God's Spirit bear not record with his spirit that he did it for God's sake, and the hatred he did bear only to sin, and stirred thereunto by the Spirit of God, as the prophets and apostles were, he hath great cause to lament; for the curse that he would to others shall light upon himself. And such offenders had most need of comfort, to call them again to God and to the order of charity: for that we be bound to do, as the scripture of God doth teach; not to comfort them or aid them (as my false accusers say of me) as traitors in treason, but as creatures made unto the similitude of God, fallen into sin. The which similitude and dignity of God in man should not be abhorred nor detested for any crime that man committeth, but rather pitied and comforted; not left alone, as the manner of the world is at this present, but diligently sought and laboured for, as Christ did for the lost sheep; who did not only seek for it, but also carried it home upon his own shoulders, when he had found it.

Thus have I spoken and written, gentle reader, against the papists' proceedings, as it is my bounden duty, and all men's else that fear God. For I am sworn by the terrible, venerable, holy, and blessed name of God, as I trust to be saved by the riches, treasure, and merits of Christ's death, neither directly nor indirectly to agree unto the wicked and pretensed supremacy of the bishop of Rome; but with all my wit, learning, and other means, resist him. This oath (by God's help) I will not violate nor break, let the wicked perjured men, that be the wicked pope's adherents, say what they will, and do what God shall permit them. I fear not death, nor pass of their cruel imprisonment, which is more vile and cruel towards us true men than ever it was against murderers, traitors, and thieves. But that is no new thing: for there is no offence irremissible with the popish bishops but to believe truly in Christ, as his word teacheth. Cyprian, in a sermon *de Mortalitate*, hath these words: *Ejus est mortem timere, qui ad Christum nolit ire*[1]: he feareth death that would not go to Christ. But we desire and groan to be dissolved from this wicked life and world, if it please God. Howbeit, we will not gladly provoke enmity, nor yet suffer unprofitable persecution: but when the glory of God shall perish without the truth be testified, I defy all torments and tormentors. And let all good men and women rejoice also in Christ: for, doubtless, the church of Christ was first planted under the gospel by the death of Christ and his poor servants; and now it shall take no more harm by the persecution of the satanical papists than gold taketh by the goldsmith's furnace. There is no death can come to the creature without God's good leave and permission. Therefore let us rejoice that our time draweth so near to go from this ruinous and

[1 Quis hic anxietatis et sollicitudinis locus est? Quis inter hæc trepidus et mœstus est, nisi cui spes et fides deest? Ejus est enim mortem timere qui ad Christum nolit ire; ejus est ad Christum nolle ire, qui se non credat cum Christo incipere regnare.—Cyprian. Serm. IV. Op. Tom. I. p. 316. Antv. 1541.]

decayed city and tabernacle of our bodies: for there is an everlasting mansion in heaven prepared for us. And whiles we do live, let us pray to God for this our natural country. For whereas before it was cursed but by wicked man, the antichrist of Rome, now is it cursed of God; and whereas before it was interdicted but by a false wretch, that would be Christ's vicar in earth [2], now is it interdicted by the Maker and Creator of all the earth: as the word of God doth shew us, and all the old councils and doctors. Besides that, look upon the bishops' book, Winchester's oration, Doctor Sampson's oration, the bishop of Duresme's sermon, and the bishop of London's epistle.

I pray thee, gentle reader, as soon as thou readest this treatise, keep it not close, but make it open, and spare not. For it is not by sword and fire that the papists can fear [3] us from the truth of God's word.
Grace and peace
be with thee.
Amen.

[2 See Burnet's Hist. of the Reformation. Vol. I. Lib. III. Coll. Numb. 9.]

[3 Fear: frighten.]

LETTERS[1].

[1 Since the foregoing sheets were printed, it has been found necessary, in order to limit as much as possible the compass of the present volume, to withdraw from the following collection all such of bishop Hooper's letters as have already appeared in the Epistolæ Tigurinæ. To preserve, however, in some degree the completeness of the collection, the numbers of the letters so withdrawn have been printed in their order, together with the corresponding numbers of the above-named series.

As reference has been made in the preceding pages to several letters which will not now form a part of this work, the reader is requested to turn in all such cases to the corresponding portion of the Epistolæ Tigurinæ, or their English translation.

In the reprint of the rest of the letters, the text and, where the date is uncertain, the order of Coverdale's Letters of the Martyrs have been followed, with the exception of Nos. XLIV., XLV., and XLVI., which have been derived from another source, as indicated in the notice prefixed to No. XLIV.]

LETTERS.

Epistola I.   (See Epistólæ Tigurinæ, xxi. p. 21.)
        II.   (ibid. . . . . . xxii. p. 24.)
       III.   (ibid. . . . . . xxiii. p. 25.)
       IV.   (ibid. . . . . . xxiv. p. 27.)
        V.   (ibid. . . . . . xxv. p. 28.)
       VI.   (ibid. . . . . . xxvi. p. 31.)
      VII.   (ibid. . . . . . xxvii. p. 32.)
     VIII.   (ibid. . . . . . xxviii. p. 32.)
       IX.   (ibid. . . . . . xxix. p. 35.)
        X.   (ibid. . . . . . xxx. p. 36.)
       XI.   (ibid. . . . . . xxxi. p. 39.)
      XII.   (ibid. . . . . . xxxii. p. 41.)
     XIII.   (ibid. . . . . . xxxiii. p. 41.)
     XIV.   (ibid. . . . . . xxxiv. p. 43.)
      XV.   (ibid. . . . . . xxxv. p. 44.)
     XVI.   (ibid. . . . . . xxxvi. p. 45.)
    XVII.   (ibid. . . . . . xxxvii. p. 47.)
   XVIII.   (ibid. . . . . . xxxviii. p. 50.)
    XIX.   (ibid. . . . . . xxxix. p. 55.)
      XX.   (ibid. . . . . . xl. p. 58.)
     XXI.   (ibid. . . . . . xli. p. 61.)
    XXII.   (ibid. . . . . . xlii. p. 63.)
   XXIII.   (ibid. . . . . . xliii. p. 63.)
   XXIV.   (ibid. . . . . . xliv. p. 64.)

[In preparing the following letter for the press, the text of Coverdale has been collated with that of an edition printed at Rouen, 1553, and the variations of the latter, when the sense is in any way affected, are given in the notes, distinguished by the initial R. The title-page of the foreign edition is as follows:]

⁅ Whether Christian faith maye be kepte secret in the heart, without confession therof openly to the worlde as occasion shal serve. Also what hurt cōmeth by thē that hath received the Gospel, to be presēt at Masse unto the simple and unlearned.

III Regum XVIII.
Howe long halte ye on bothe the sides? If the Lord be God, the walk after him: but if Baal be he, thē follow him.

Matthew VI Chapter.
No man can serve two masters: for ether he shal hate the one, and love the other, or els he shal lean to the one, and dispise the other.

Luke XVI Chapi.
That which is high among men is an abhominatiō before god.

⁅ From Roane. Anno. M.D.Liii. the iii. of October.

2 Cor. VI. Chapi.

⁋ Bear not a straunge yoke with the unbelevers. For what feloship hath righteousnes with unrighteousnes? What company hath light with darknes? How agreeth Christ with Belial? Or what part hath the belever with the infidel? How accordeth the temple of God with images? Ye are the temple of the living God, as saith God: I wil dwel in them, and walke in them, and wyl be their God, and thei shal be my people. Wherefore come from amonge theim, and seperate youre selves (saith the Lorde) and touch no unclene thing: so will I receive you, and be your father, and ye shall be my sonnes and daughters, saith the almightie Lord. Deu. vii.
Matt. viii.
1 Cor. iii. vi.
Lev. xxvi.
Ezek. xxxvii.
Esai. lii.

LETTER XXV.

A Letter sent to the christian congregation, wherein he proveth that true faith cannot be kept secret in the heart without confession thereof openly to the world when occasion serveth.

ST PAUL, in the tenth chapter to the Romans, annexeth the faith of Christ in the heart with the[1] confession of the mouth; so that the one (it seemeth by him) can be no more without the other than fire can be without heat, saying these words: "With the heart man believeth unto righteousness, and with the mouth he confesseth unto salvation[2]." Wherein he declareth that, even as the cause of our acceptation[3] through Christ is the confidence and faith of the heart in the promises of God; so is the confession outwardly of the same faith by the[4] mouth the fruit that all christian faithful hearts bring forth through the same gift of God. And where as this effect of confession of faith[5] is not, there wanteth also the cause of confession, which is true faith: for as the tree is known by her fruits, so is faith by her effects. And as the want of fruit is a demonstration that the tree is unprofitable, so the want of true confession of faith is a token that the faith is dead. The end of the unprofitable tree is cut Matt. x.[6]

[1 'The,' omitted in R.]
[2 'The heart believeth to justice: the confession of the mouth is to salvation.' R.]
[3 'Acception,' R.]   [4 'The' omitted in R.]
[5 'Of faith,' omitted in R.]
[6 The text seems to refer rather to Luke xiii. 6. This reference is omitted in R.]

ting down and casting into the fire: the end of the fruitless faith is death and casting to eternal damnation.

Pet. iii. Wherefore St Peter requireth us to make answer to every man that demandeth of us of such hope as is in us with gentleness and reverence: which is a very testimony that we sanctify God in our hearts, as it is before expressed[1] in the same chapter. For the greatest honour that man can give to God is to confess[2] in the time of trouble truly and faithfully his holy word and faith. Wherefore it is the duty of every Christian to pray and study to have a thorough knowledge of his faith in Christ; and[3], as the glory of God shall require, and[4] the cause of his religion, to be ready to make answer for the same (howsoever the world, fear, displeasure, friendship, or other lets, shall move us to the contrary[5]) upon pain, saith Christ in the tenth of Matthew[6], *Matt. x.* that I will deny him before my Father which is in heaven. But how hard a thing it is to confess Christ in the days of trouble, not only the scripture, but also daily experience in good men and women, doth declare. True confession is warded[7] on every side with many dangers on the right hand and on the left hand, now with fair means, then with foul threatenings, fearful and dangerous; as it is said by Christ our Saviour[8], "They shall betray you to the judges; and of them ye shall be beaten and judged to death." Of[9] the other side shall pull us back the love of wife, children, brother, sister, kin, friends[10], and the love unto ourselves. But he that is overcome by any of these means hath his[11] judgment: he is not meet for me, saith Christ.

These things be impossible unto men; yet to christian men in Christ possible, and so necessary, that Christianity and true religion cannot be in him that is afeard to confess Christ and his gospel in the time of persecution. The wisdom of the world doth say, "Although I accomplish the desire of my friends, and to the sight of the world am present

[1 'Expressed,' omitted in R.]　　　[2 'And answer—to,' R.]
[3 'And that,' R.]　　　[4 'And his religion attempt,' R.]
[5 'Whatsoever—should say to the contrary,' R.]
[6 'In the tenth of Matth.' omitted in R. In margin Mark viii. Luke ix. xii.]
[7 'Environed,' R.]　　　[8 'Our Saviour,' omitted in R.]
[9 'On,' R.]　　　[10 'Lands and' &c. R.]
[11 'This,' R. In margin Matt. x. Luke xiii.]

at the mass, and with my body do as other men do, or as I may do; yet my heart is clean contrary to their belief, and I do detest such idolatry, and believe that the thing that I am present at is mere idolatry and abomination." Here be fair words for an evil purpose, and pretensed excuse for a just condemnation before God. For if it be true that[12] ye know the thing which[12] ye resort unto to be the dishonour of God, why do ye honour it with your presence? If ye know it to be evil, why refrain ye not from it? If your conscience say it is idolatry, why serveth your body such things as your faith abhorreth? If in your heart you know but one God, why with your exterior[13] presence serve ye the thing that ye know is not God? If your faith see idolatry, why doth your silence confess and allow[14] the same? Two men in one God loveth not. If the inward man know the truth, why doth the outward man confess a falsehood? If your spirit[15] be persuaded that the mass is idolatry, why do ye with your bodily presence use it as a God, and give godly honour to it[16]? Do ye not perceive that it is written[17], Esay xxix[18]. Matt. xv[18]., "These[19] people honour me with their[20] mouth, but their hearts be far from me?" The cause why God was offended with these[21] people was, that outwardly they confessed him and served him[22], but their hearts were far from him inwardly. Wherefore[23], ye may see what it is to bear two faces in one hood; outwardly to serve God, and inwardly to serve the devil. Now mark of this place, if it be so horrible and damnable a thing to be false in the heart, which none knoweth but God, and is worthy also of damnation; what is to be judged of the outward and manifest use of idolatry, which not only God, but also every good man, knoweth and abhorreth?

There is no colour[24] nor cloked hypocrisy that God can away with. If the heart think not as the tongue speaketh,

[12 'That,'—'which,' omitted in R.]
[13 'External,' R.]   [14 'Profess,' R.]   [15 'The spirit,' R.]
[16 'Why doth the corporal presence use it as God in doing godly honour, &c.' R.]
[17 'What is written,' R.]
[18 The references in margin, also Ezech. xxxiii. R.]
[19 'This,' R.]   [20 'The,' R.]   [21 'This,' R.]
[22 'And served him,' omitted in R.]   [23 'Whereof,' R.]
[24 'Coloured,' R.]

or else the tongue speak otherwise than the heart thinketh, both be abominable before God. Read ye[1] the third and the sixth chapters of the first Epistle of St Paul to the Corinthians, where as St Paul saith: "Know ye not that your body is the temple[2] of the Holy Ghost? If your body be the temple[2] of the Holy Ghost, what agreement hath it with idolatry?" Can one body at one time be the temple of the Holy Ghost, and be present at such idolatry as God abhorreth and detesteth? Can a man serve two masters? If he do, he loveth (as Christ saith) the one, and hateth the other. As God requireth of a faithful man a pure heart, even so requireth he that his external profession in all things be according thereunto[3]; for both body and soul be debtors unto God, and he redeemed them both. The word of God saith unto us, "Glorify and bear God in your bodies." If we be present at such idolatry as God forbiddeth, and our own knowledge in conscience is assured[4] to be evil, do we glorify God in our bodies? No[5], doubtless; we dishonour him, and make our bodies the servants of idolatry, not only to God's dishonour, but also to the great danger both of body and soul. For this is a true saying of St Augustine, "He that doth against his conscience buildeth to hell-fire[6]."

It is not enough for a christian man to say, I know the mass is naught; but to obey civil laws[7] and orders I will do outwardly as other men[8] do, yet in my heart abhor[9] it, and never think it to be good. Doubtless these two minds, the spirit to think well and the body to do evil, in this respect be both naught, and God will spue the whole man out of his mouth, as he did the minister of the congregation of Laodicea. Apoc. iii. The eighth chapter and the tenth of the first to the Corinthians[10] in this matter and in this time be

[1 'Ye,' omitted in R.]   [2 'Bodies be the temples,' R.]
[3 'The word of God saith unto us, Glorify and bear God in your bodies, even as God requireth that our external profession—be correspondent unto it' R.; omitting the quotation as it stands in the text.]
[4 'Assureth,' R.]   [5 'Nay,' R.]
[6 The editor has been unable to discover the exact saying here attributed to St Augustine; but for a similar sentiment see August. de Contrit. Cord. Op. Tom. IX. col. 840. B. Basil. 1569.]
[7 'Law,' R.]   [8 'Men,' omitted in R.]   [9 'I abhor,' R.]
[10 Look in the margin; for in this time the places be very much expedient, &c. R.]

places very much expedient to lead and govern the judgment of every christian man: where we may see that the Corinthians indeed had knowledge[11], and perceived right well that neither the idols amongst them, neither[12] the meat dedicated unto the idols, were anything, and passed as light of both[13] as of things of nothing; and upon that knowledge used to be present, and also to eat at the feast, and of the meats[14] dedicated unto idols. Wherewithal Paul was so sore offended, that he gave this sentence: "If[15] a man see thee, which hast knowledge, sit at table[16] in the idols' temple, shall not the conscience of him that[17] is weak be boldened to eat those things which are sacrificed[18] to idols? And[19] through thy knowledge shall the[20] weak brother perish, for whom Christ died. Now[21] when ye sin so against the brethren, and wound their weak conscience, ye sin against Christ." This judgment of Paul is more to be followed than all our own feigned and wretched[22] defences, which[23] would fain seem to do well when we halt on both sides, which God abhorreth. Paul hath a profound and deep consideration of that man's fault[24] that hath knowledge, and perceiveth his dissimulation to be dangerous and perilous to all persons which he dwelleth withal. 1 Cor. viii.

First, such[25] as be of a right and staid judgment, and will not prostrate their bodies to an idol[26], do condemn, and needs must, such dissimulation. The very idolaters themselves have a defence[27] of their abomination by the presence of him that the christian congregation knoweth to have knowledge. The weaker sort[28], that would gladly take the best way, by a dissembler's halting and playing of[29] both hands embraceth both in body and in soul the evil that he abhorreth in his

[11 'Where as the Corinthians indeed had,' &c. R.]
[12 'Nor,' R.]
[13 'Of both,' omitted in R.]
[14 'Meat dedicated to,' R.]
[15 'For if some man,' R.]
[16 'At meat,' R.]
[17 'Which,' R.]
[18 'Offered to the idols,' R.]
[19 'And so,' R.]
[20 'That,' R.]
[21 'Now,' omitted in R.]
[22 'Wrested,' R.]
[23 'That would seem,' R.]
[24 'Fact,' R.]
[25 'All such,' R.]
[26 'Doth he condemn. Secondly, by their such dissimulation the very,' R.]
[27 'Confirmation and defence,' R.]
[28 'Thirdly, the weak sort,' R.]
[29 'On,' R.]

heart; and[1] though he have knowledge, yet with his presence he esteemeth it as other do which have no knowledge. If St Paul said that the weak brother doth perish, for whom Christ died, by him[2] that abused knowledge in meats and drinks that of themselves be indifferent, how much more by[3] the knowledge of him that useth manifest idolatry forbidden of God as a thing not indifferent? Take heed[4] what St Paul meaneth, and what he would prove against this man which had knowledge that neither the idols[5], neither the meats dedicated to idols, were anything. Forsooth this would he prove: that a poor man that wanteth[6] knowledge, by the example of him that hath knowledge doth there[7] adventure to do evil, which he would not do in case he saw not those that he hath good opinion of[8] to go before him as authors[9] of the evil. And indeed[10] the ignorant people, or those that be half persuaded in a truth, yea, or else throughly persuaded what is evil, when[11] they have any notable men or women for an example to follow, they think in following of them they be excused, yea, although peradventure they do it against their consciences: as ye may see [12] how many good men[12] by the example of Peter began to dissemble, yea, Barnabas himself the apostle of the Gentiles.

Gal. ii.

But how great offence this is before God, so to make a doubtful[13] conscience, or striving against knowledge, to do any thing that is not godly, let the judgment of men pass, and measure it from[14] God's word. Christ saith, It were better a millstone were hanged about such an offender's neck, and cast into the sea. And doubtless the pain must be the greater, because we give offence willingly[15], and against our own consciences: and this before God is a wicked knowledge that causeth another to perish. Woe be unto him that is learned

Matt. xviii.

[1 'That hath knowledge, and yet with presence honoureth it as other do that, &c.' R.]
[2 'In him,' R.]   [3 'In,' R.]
[4 'Take heed therefore,' R.]   [5 'Idol nor,' R.]
[6 'Wanted,' R.]   [7 'There,' omitted in R.]
[8 'Of whom he hath good opinion, go,' R.]
[9 'Author,' R.]   [10 'When the ignorant,' R.]
[11 'Yet when,' R.]   [12 These clauses transposed in R.]
[13 'doubtful and relucting conscience to do, &c.' R.]
[14 'by,' R.]
[15 'And,' omitted in R. and wittingly for willingly.]

to bring his brother to destruction! Doth a christian man know the truth to bring his brother to a lie? For those weaklings that we make to stumble Christ died[16], as St Paul saith. God defend we should confirm any man's conscience in evil. Let every man of God weigh with himself the doctrine of St Paul, that commandeth us to fly[17] idolatry. 1 Cor. x.

And mark what St Paul in that place calleth idolatry. It is to be seen plainly, that he speaketh not of such idolatry as men that lack knowledge in their hearts what God is and what[18] God is not do commit. For in the eighth chapter before he saith, that men know that the idols were no gods, and that although by name the Gentiles had many gods, yet they knew that there was but one God. Therefore he meaneth nothing by this commandment, "flee idolatry," but to avoid such rites, ceremonies, and usages, as outwardly were used in the honour and reverence of the idols that were no gods[19]; and weighing the right use of the Lord's supper, and the dignity thereof, with the manner and use of the Gentiles towards their gods, he[20] would bring the church of the Corinthians to understand how that, as the divine and sacrate[21] rites, ceremonies, and use of the[22] sacrament of Christ's body and blood did sanctify[23] him, and declare him that used[24] it to be the servant and child of God; so did the rites and sacraments of the Gentiles defile[25] the users thereof, and declared them to be the servants and children of the idol, notwithstanding[26] that they knew in their hearts the idol was nothing. God by his sacrament[27] doth couple us unto him[28]: let us pray therefore[29] to him that we pollute not ourselves with any rites, ceremonies, or usages not instituted by God, and so divide ourselves from him[30].

In this cause, if a faithful man should be at the mass, it

[16 'Died for,' R.]   [17 'Fly from,' R.]
[18 'Is not God,' R. 'Do commit,' omitted.]
[19 'Not God,' R.]   [20 'He,' omitted in R.]
[21 'Sacred,' R.]   [22 'Blessed sacrament,' R.]
[23 'Sacrate, sanctify and,' &c., R.]   [24 'Useth,' R.]
[25 'Define and declare the users thereof to be,' &c. R.]
[26 'Notwithstanding in their heart they knew well enough,' &c., R.]
[27 'Sacraments,' R.]   [28 'To himself,' R.]
[29 'Therefore,' omitted in R.]
[30 This clause omitted in R.]

[HOOPER, II.]

is to be considered¹ with what mind those that he doth there accompany² himself withal do come³ thither, and what the end is of the work that the priest doth. The people come to honour the bread and wine for God; and the priest purposeth to consecrate both God and man, and so to offer Christ to the Father for remission of sin. Now do they⁴ that adjoin themselves unto those⁵ people profess and declare a society and fellowship of the same impiety as St Paul laid to the Corinthians' charge. St Paul was not offended with the Corinthians because they lacked knowledge of the true God, but because, contrary to their knowledge, they associated themselves with idolaters. For this is true, that in all rites, sacraments, and honourings, whether they be of God or of the devil, there is a profession of a⁶ communion: so that every⁷ man protesteth to be of the same religion that the rest be of that be partakers with him. I know there be many evasions made by men, that judge⁸ a man may with safeguard of conscience be at the mass. But forasmuch as M. Calvin, M. Bullinger, and other, have throughly answered them, such as be in doubt may read their books. This is my conscience after God's word⁹.

JOHN HOPER.

LETTER XXVI.

An exhortation to patience, sent to his godly wife ANNE HOOPER: *whereby all the true members of Christ may take comfort and courage to suffer trouble and affliction for the profession of his holy gospel.*

Matth. xviii.   Our Saviour Jesus Christ, dearly beloved and my godly wife, in St Matthew's gospel said to his disciples, that it was necessary slanders should come: and that they could not be avoided, he perceived as well by the condition of those that should perish and be lost for ever in the world to come, as

[¹ 'In this case a faithful man to be at the mass is to be considered,' &c., R.]
[² 'There he accompanieth,' R.]   [³ 'Cometh,' R.]
[⁴ 'Those,' R.]   [⁵ 'These,' R.]
[⁶ 'The,' R.]   [⁷ 'Any,' R.]
[⁸ 'Teach a man with safeguard of his conscience to be at mass,' R.]
[⁹ 'This is a true confession, and consonant to God's holy word,' R.]

also by their affliction that should be saved. For he saw the greatest part of the people would contemn and neglect whatsoever true doctrine or godly ways should be shewed unto them, or else receive it and use it as they thought good, to serve their pleasures, without any profit to their souls at all, not caring whether they lived as they were commanded by God's word or not; but would think it sufficient to be counted to have the name of a christian man, with such works and fruits of his profession and christianity as his fathers and elders, after their custom and manner, esteem and take to be good fruits and faithful works, and will not try them by the word of God at all. These men, by the just judgment of God, be delivered unto the craft and subtilty of the devil, that they may be kept by one slanderous stumbling-block or other, that they never come unto Christ, who came to save those that were lost: as ye may see how God delivereth wicked men up unto their own lusts, to do one mischief after another, careless until they come into a reprobate mind, that forgetteth itself, and cannot know what is expedient to be done, or to be left undone, because they close their eyes, and will not see the light of God's word offered unto them; and being thus blinded, they prefer their own vanities before the truth of God's word. Where as such corrupt minds be, there is also corrupt election and choice of God's honour: so that the mind of man taketh falsehood for truth, superstition for true religion, death for life, damnation for salvation, hell for heaven, and persecution of Christ's members for God's service and honour. Matth. xxiv. Rom. i. 1 Thess. ii.

And as these men wilfully and voluntarily reject the word of God, even so God most justly delivereth them into the blindness of mind and hardness of heart, that they cannot understand, nor yet consent to, anything that God would have preached and set forth to his glory, after his own will and word: wherefore they hate it mortally, and of all things most detest God's holy word. And as the devil hath entered into their hearts, that they themselves cannot nor will not come to Christ to be instructed by his holy word; even so can they not abide any other man to be a christian man, and to lead his life after the word of God; but hate him, persecute him, rob him, imprison him, yea, and kill him, whether he be man or woman, if God suffer it. And so much are those wicked John viii. ix.

men blinded, that they pass of no law, whether it be God's or man's, but persecute such as never offended; yea, do evil to those that daily have prayed for them, and wish them God's grace. In their Pharaonical and blind fury they have no respect to nature: for the brother persecuteth the brother, the father the son; and most dear friends, in devilish slander and offence, are become most mortal enemies. And no marvel; for when they have chosen sundry masters, the one the devil, the other God, the one shall agree with the other as God and the devil agree between themselves. For this cause, that the more part of the world doth choose to serve the devil under cloked hypocrisy of God's title, Christ said, "It is expedient and necessary that slanders should come;" and many means be devised to keep the little babes of Christ from the heavenly Father. But Christ saith, "Woe be unto him by whom the offence cometh." Yet is there no remedy, man being of such corruption and hatred towards God, but that the evil shall be deceived, and persecute the good; and the good shall understand the truth, and suffer persecution for it until the world's end. For as he that was born after the flesh persecuted in times past him that was born after the Spirit, even so it is now.

<small>Matth. xviii.</small>

<small>Gen. iv.
Gal. iv.</small>

Seeing therefore we live for this life amongst so many and great perils and dangers, we must be well assured by God's word how to bear them, and how patiently to take them, as they be sent to us from God. We must also assure ourselves that there is no other remedy for Christians in the time of trouble than Christ himself hath appointed us. In St Luke he giveth us this commandment: "Ye shall possess your lives in patience," saith he. In the which words he giveth us both commandment what to do, and also great comfort and consolation in all troubles. He sheweth also what is to be done, and what is to be hoped for, in troubles: and when troubles happen, he biddeth us be patient, and in no case violently nor seditiously to resist our persecutors, because God hath such cure and charge of us, that he will keep in the midst of all troubles the very hairs of our head, so that one of them shall not fall away without the will and pleasure of our heavenly Father. Whether the hair therefore tarry in the head, or fall from the head, it is the will of the Father. And seeing he hath such care for the hairs of our head, how much more doth he care for our life itself! Wherefore let God's adver-

<small>Luke xxi.</small>

<small>Matt. x.</small>

saries do what they lust, whether they take the life, or take it not, they can do us no hurt: for their cruelty hath no further power than God permitteth them; and that which cometh unto us by the will of our heavenly Father can be no harm, no loss, neither destruction unto us, but rather gain, wealth, and felicity. For all troubles and adversity that chance to such as be of God by the will of the heavenly Rom. viii. Father can be none other but gain and advantage.

That the spirit of man may feel these consolations, the Giver of them, the heavenly Father, must be prayed unto for the merits of Christ's passion; for it is not the nature James i. of man that can be contented, until it be regenerated and 1 Cor. i. possessed with God's Spirit, to bear patiently the troubles of the mind or of the body. When the mind and heart of a man seeth of every side sorrow and heaviness, and the worldly eye beholdeth nothing but such things as be troublous, and wholly bent to rob the poor man of that he hath, and also to take from him his life; except the man weigh these brittle and uncertain treasures that be taken from him with the riches of the life to come, and this life of the body with the life in Christ's precious blood, and so for the love and certainty of the heavenly joys contemn all things present; doubtless he shall never be able to bear the loss of goods, life, or any other things of this world. Therefore St Paul giveth a very godly and necessary lesson to all men in this short and transitory life, and therein sheweth how a man may best bear the iniquity and troubles of this world: "If Col. iii. ye be risen again with Christ (saith he), seek the things which are above, where Christ sitteth at the right hand of God the Father." Wherefore the christian man's faith must be always upon the resurrection of Christ, when he is in trouble; and in that glorious resurrection he shall not only see continual and perpetual joy and consolation, but also the victory and triumph of[1] all persecution, trouble, sin, death, hell, the devil, and all other persecutors and tyrants of Christ and of Christ's people, the tears and weepings of the faithful dried up, their wounds healed, their bodies made immortal in joy, their souls for ever praising the Lord, and conjunction and society everlasting with the blessed company of God's elects in perpetual joy. But the words of St Paul

[1 Of: over.]

in that place, if they be not marked, shall do little profit to the reader or hearer, and give him no patience at all in this impatient and cruel world.

In the first part St Paul commandeth us to think or set our affections on things that are above. When he biddeth us seek the things that are above, he requireth that our minds never cease from prayer and study in God's word, until we see, know, and understand the vanities of this world, the shortness and misery of this life, and the treasures of the world to come, the immortality thereof, and the joys of that life; and so never cease seeking, until such time as we know certainly and be persuaded, what a blessed man he is that seeketh the one and findeth it, and careth not for the other though he lose it: and in seeking to have right judgment between the life present and the life to come, we shall find how little the pains, imprisonment, slanders, lies, and death itself, is in this world, in respect of the pains everlasting, the prison infernal, and dungeon of hell, the sentence of God's just judgment, and everlasting death.

When a man hath, by seeking the word of God, found out what the things above be, then must he (as St Paul saith) set his affections upon them. And this commandment is more hard than the other. For man's knowledge many times seeth the best, and knoweth that there is a life to come better than this life present; as you may see how daily men and women can praise and commend, yea, and wish for heaven, and to be at rest there; yet they set not their affection upon it: they do more affect and love indeed a trifle of nothing in this world that pleaseth their affection than a treasure of all treasures in heaven, which their own judgment saith is better than all worldly things. Wherefore we must set our affections upon the things that be above; that is to say, when anything worse than heaven upon the earth offereth itself to be ours, if we will give our good wills to it, and love it in our hearts, then to see by the judgment of God's word whether we may have the world without offence of God, and such things as be for this worldly life without his displeasure. If we cannot, St Paul's commandment must take place, "Set your affection on things that are above." If the riches of this world may not be gotten nor kept with God's law, neither our lives be con-

tinued without the denial of his honour, we must set our
affection upon the riches and life that is above, and not upon
things that be on the earth. Therefore this second commandment of St Paul requireth that, as our minds judge
heavenly things to be better than things upon the earth, and
the life to come better than the life present; so we should
choose them before other, and prefer them, and have such
affection to the best, that in no case we set the worst before
it, as the most part of the world doth and hath done; for
they choose the best and approve it, and yet follow the worst.

But these things, my godly wife, require rather cogitation, meditation, and prayer, than words or talk. They
be easy to be spoken of, but not so easy to be used and
practised. Wherefore, seeing they be God's gifts, and none
of ours to have as our own when we would, we must seek
them at our heavenly Father's hand, who seeth and is privy
how poor and wretched we be, and how naked, how spoiled
and destitute of all his blessed gifts we be by reason of sin.
He did command therefore his disciples, when he shewed *Matth. xxiv. Luke xxi.*
them that they should take patiently the state of this present life full of troubles and persecution, to pray that they
might well escape those troubles that were to come, and to
be able to stand before the Son of man. When ye find
yourself too much oppressed (as every man shall be sometime
with the fear of God's judgment), use the 77th psalm that *Psal. lxxvii. Read also*
beginneth, "I will cry unto God with my voice, and he shall *his exposition upon*
hearken unto me:" in which psalm is both godly doctrine *this psalm, most com-*
and great consolation unto the man or woman that is in *fortable for all broken*
anguish of mind. Use also in such troubles the 88th psalm, *and afflicted hearts.*
wherein is contained the prayer of a man that was brought
into extreme anguish and misery, and, being vexed with adversaries and persecutions, saw nothing but death and hell.
And although he felt in himself that he had not only man,
but also God, angry towards him; yet he by prayer humbly
resorted unto God, as the only port of consolation, and in
the midst of his desperate state of trouble put the hope of
his salvation in him whom he felt his enemy. Howbeit, no
man of himself can do this; but the Spirit of God, that
striketh the man's heart with fear, prayeth for the man *Rom. viii.*
stricken and feared with unspeakable groanings. And when
you feel yourself, or know any other, oppressed after such

<small>Note this well to thy comfort that art afflicted, and read the 4th chap. of Eccles.</small>

sort, be glad; for after that God hath made you to know what you be of yourself, he will doubtless shew you comfort, and declare unto you what you be in Christ his only Son: and use prayer often; for that is the means whereby God will be sought unto for his gifts.

These psalms be for the purpose, when the mind can take no understanding, nor the heart any joy of God's promises: and therefore were these psalms also made, 6, 22, 30, 31, 38, 69; from the which you shall learn both patience and consolation. Remember, that although your life (as all christian men's be) be hid, and appeareth not what it is; yet "is it safe" (as St Paul saith) "with God in Christ; and when Christ shall appear, then shall our lives be made open in him with glory." <small>[Col. iii.]</small> But in the mean time, with seeking and setting our affections upon the things that be above, we must patiently suffer whatsoever God shall send unto us in this mortal life. Notwithstanding, it might fortune some would say, who is so perfect that can let all things pass as they come, and have no care of them; suffer all things, and feel nothing; be attempted of the devil, the world, and the flesh, and not be troubled? Verily, no man living. But this I say, that in the strength of Jesus Christ things that come may pass with care; for we be worldly: and yet are we not carried with them from Christ; for we be in him godly. We may suffer things, and feel them as mortal men; yet bear them, and overcome them as christian men. We may be attempted of the devil, the flesh, and the world; but yet although these things pinch, they do not pierce; and although they work sin in us, yet in Christ no damnation to those that be grafted in him. <small>[Rom. viii.]</small>

Hereof may the christian man learn both consolation and patience: consolation, in that he is compelled both in his body and goods to feel pain and loss, and in the soul heaviness and anguish of mind; howbeit none of them both shall separate him from the love that God beareth him in Christ. He may learn patience, forasmuch as his enemies both of the body and soul, and the pains also they vex us withal for the time, if they tarry with us as long as we live, yet when death cometh, they shall avoid, and give place to such joys as be prepared for us in Christ. For no pains of the world be perpetual; and whether they shall afflict us for all the time of our mortal life, we know not; for they be the servants of God to go and to come as he commandeth them. But we must take heed we meddle not forcibly nor seditiously to put away the persecution appointed unto us by God, but remember Christ's saying, "Possess you your lives by your patience." And in this commandment God requireth in every man and woman this patient obedience. He saith not, it is sufficient that other holy patriarchs, prophets, apostles, evangelists, and martyrs, continued their lives in patience and patient suffering the troubles of this world; but Christ saith to every one of his people, "By your own patience ye shall continue your life:" not that man hath patience of himself, but that he must have it for himself of God, the only giver of it, if he purpose to be a godly man. Now, therefore, as our profession and religion requireth patience outwardly, without resistance and force; so requireth it patience of the mind, and not to be angry with God, although he use us, that be his own creatures, as him listeth. We may not also murmur against God, but say always his judgments be right and just, and rejoice that it pleaseth him by troubles to use us as he used heretofore such as he most loved in this world; and have a singular care to this commandment, *Gaudete et exultate*, " Be glad and rejoice:" for he sheweth great cause why: " your reward (saith he), is great in heaven." _{Luke xxi.} _{Matt. v.}

These promises of him that is the truth itself shall (by God's grace) work both consolation and patience in the afflicted christian person. And when our Saviour Christ hath willed men in trouble to be content and patient, because God in the end of trouble in Christ hath ordained eternal consolation, he useth also to take from us all shame and rebuke, as though it were not an honour to suffer for Christ, because the wicked world doth curse and abhor such poor troubled Christians. Wherefore Christ placeth all his honourably, and saith, "Even so persecuted they the prophets that were before you." We may also see with whom the afflicted for Christ's sake be esteemed by St Paul to the Hebrews: whereas the number of the blessed and glorious company of saints appear now to our faith in heaven in joy; yet in the letter, for the time of this life, in such pains and contempt as was never more. Let us therefore consider both them and all other things of the world sithence the fall of man; and we shall perceive nothing to come to perfection, but with such confusion and disorder to the eye of the world, as though things were rather lost for ever than like to come to any perfection at all. For of godly men who ever came to heaven (no, not Christ himself) until such time as the world had thought verily that both he and all his had been clean destroyed and cast away? as the wise man saith of the wicked people, "We thought them to be fools, but they be in peace."

<small>Wisd. v.</small>

We may learn by things that nourish and maintain us, both meat and drink, to what loathsomeness and (in manner) abhorring they come unto, before they work their perfection in us. From life they be brought to the fire, and clean altered from that they were when they were alive; from the fire to the trencher and knife, and all-to hacked; from the trencher to the mouth, and as small ground as the teeth can grind them; and from the mouth into the stomach, and there so boiled and digested before they nourish, that whosoever saw the same would loath and abhor his own nourishment, before it come to his perfection. Is it then any marvel, if such Christians as God delighteth in be so mangled and defaced in this world, which is the kitchen and mill to boil and grind the flesh of God's people in, till they achieve their perfection in the world to come? And as man looketh for the nutriment of his meat when it is full digested, and not before; so must he look for his salvation when he hath passed this troublous world, and not before. Raw flesh is not meat wholesome for man: and unmortified men and women be no creatures meet for God. Therefore Christ saith that his people must be broken and all-to torn in the mill of this world, and so shall they be most fine meal unto the heavenly Father. And it shall be a christian man's part, and the duty of a mind replenished with the Spirit of God, to mark the order of God in all his things, how he dealeth with them, and how they suffer, and be content to let God do his will upon them; as St Paul saith, they 'weep until the number of the elects be fulfilled, and never be at rest, but look for the time when God's people shall appear in glery.'

<small>Matt. x.</small>

<small>Rom. viii.</small>

We must therefore patiently suffer, and willingly attend upon God's doings, although they seem clean contrary, after our judgment, to our wealth and salvation; as Abraham did when he was bid to offer his son Isaac, in whom God promised the blessing and multiplying of his seed. Joseph at the last came to that which God promised him, although in the mean time, after the judgment of the world, he was never like to be (as God said he should be) lord over his brethren. When Christ would make the blind man to see, he put clay upon his eyes, which, after the judgment of man, was means rather to make him double blind than to give him his sight; but he obeyed, and knew that God could work his desire, what means soever he used contrary to man's reasons: and as touching this world, he useth all his after the same sort. If any smart, his people be the first; if any suffer shame, they begin; if any be subject to slander, it is those that he loveth; so that he sheweth no face or favour, nor love almost, in this world outwardly to them, but layeth clay upon their sore eyes that be sorrowful: yet the patient man seeth (as St Paul saith) life hid under these miseries and adversities, and sight under foul clay; and in the mean time he hath the testimony of a good conscience, and believeth God's promises to be his consolation in the world to come, which is more worth unto him than all the world is worth besides: and blessed is that man in whom God's Spirit beareth record that he is the son of God, whatsoever troubles he suffer in this troublesome world.

John ix.
1 Pet. iv.
Col. iii.
Rom. viii.

And to judge things indifferently, my godly wife, the troubles be not yet generally as they were in our good fathers' times, soon after the death and resurrection of our Saviour Christ Jesu, whereof he spake in St Matthew; of the which place you and I have taken many times great consolation, and especially of the latter part of the chapter, wherein is contained the last day and end of all troubles (I doubt not) both for you and me, and for such as love the coming of our Saviour Christ to judgment. Remember, therefore, that place, and mark it again, and ye shall in this time see great consolation, and also learn much patience. Was there ever such troubles as Christ threatened upon Jerusalem? Was there sithence the beginning of the world such affliction? Who was then best at ease? The apostles, that suffered in body persecution, and gathered of it ease and quietness in the promises of God. And no marvel; for Christ saith, "Lift up your heads; for your redemption is at hand;" that is to say,

Matth. xxiv
Luke xxi.

your eternal rest approacheth and draweth near. The world is stark blind, and more foolish than foolishness itself; and so be the people of the world. For when God saith trouble shall come, they will have ease: and when God saith, "Be merry, and rejoice in trouble," we lament and mourn, as though we were cast-aways. But this the flesh (which is never merry with virtue, nor sorry with vice, never laugheth with grace, nor ever weepeth with sin) holdeth fast with the world, and letteth God slip.

But, my dearly beloved wife, you know how to perceive and to beware of the vanity and crafts of the devil well enough in Christ. And that ye may the better have patience in the Spirit of God, read again the 24th chapter of St Matthew, and mark what difference is between the destruction of Jerusalem, and the destruction of the whole world; and you shall see that then there were left alive many offenders to repent: but at the latter day there shall be absolute judgment and sentence, never to be revoked, of eternal life and eternal death upon all men; and yet towards the end of the world we have nothing so much extremity as they had then, but even as we be able to bear. So doth the merciful Father lay upon us now imprisonment (and, I suppose, for my part shortly death), now spoil of goods, loss of friends, and, the greatest loss of all, the knowledge of God's word. God's will be done! I wish in Christ Jesu, our only Mediator and Saviour, your constancy and consolation, that you may live for ever and ever; whereof in Christ I doubt not: to whom for his blessed and most painful passion I commit you. Amen.

<small>Matth. xxiv.</small>

Your brother in Christ,
13 October, 1553. JOHN HOPER.

LETTER XXVII.

A Letter which he wrote to certain godly persons, professors and lovers of the truth, instructing them how they should behave themselves at the beginning of the change of religion.

The grace, mercy, and peace of God the Father, through our Lord Jesus Christ, be with you, my dear brethren, and with all those that unfeignedly love and embrace his holy gospel. Amen.

It is told me that the wicked idol the mass is stablished again by a law, and passed in the parliament-house[1]. Learn the truth of it, I pray you, and what penalty is appointed in the act to such as speak against it: also, whether there be any compulsion to constrain men to be at it: the statute throughly known, such as be abroad and at liberty may provide for themselves, and avoid the danger the better. Doubtless there hath not been seen before our time such a parliament as this is, that as many as were suspected to be favourers of God's word should be banished out of both houses. But we must give God thanks for that truth he hath opened in the time of his blessed servant King Edward the Sixth, and pray unto him that we deny it not, nor dishonour it with idolatry; but that we may have strength and patience rather to die ten times than to deny him once. Blessed shall we be, if ever God make us worthy of that honour to shed our blood for his name's sake: and blessed then shall we think the parents which brought us into this world, that we should from this mortality be carried into immortality. If we follow the commandment of St Paul that saith, "If ye be risen again with Christ, seek the things that be above, where Christ sitteth at the right hand of God," we shall neither depart from the vain transitory goods of this world, nor from this wretched and mortal life, with so great pains as other do. Let us pray to our heavenly Father that we may know and love his blessed will, and the glorious joy prepared for us in time to come, and that we may know and hate all things contrary to his blessed will, and also the pain prepared for the wicked men in the world to come.

Col. iii.

There is no better way to be used in this troublesome time for your consolation than many times to have assemblies together of such men and women as be of your religion in Christ, and there to talk and renew among your-

[1 The bill "for repealing king Edward's laws about religion" was sent down from the House of Lords to the Commons on Oct. 31, 1553, and after being discussed six days in the Commons was carried, and sent back to the upper house. Burnet's Hist. of Reform. Vol. II. B. II. p. 255. Ed. 1683. See also Strype, Eccl. Mem. Vol. III. Part I. p. 83.]

selves the truth of your religion; to see what ye be by the word of God, and to remember what ye were before ye came to the knowledge thereof, to weigh and confer the dreams and false lies of the preachers that now preach, with the word of God that retaineth all truth: and by such talk and familiar resorting together, ye shall the better find out all their lies that now go about to deceive you, and also both know and love the truth that God hath opened to us. It is much requisite that the members of Christ comfort one another, make prayers together, confer one with another; so shall ye be the stronger, and God's Spirit shall not be absent from you, but in the midst of you, to teach you, to comfort you, to make you wise in all godly things, patient in adversity, and strong in persecution. Ye see how the congregation of the wicked, by helping one another, make their wicked religion and themselves strong against God's truth and his people. If ye may, have some learned man, that can out of the scriptures speak unto you of faith and true honouring of God; also that can shew you the descent of Christ's church from the beginning of it until this day, that ye may perceive by the life of your forefathers these two things: the one, that Christ's word, which said that all his must suffer persecution and trouble in the world, be true; the other, that none of all his, before our time, escaped trouble: then shall ye perceive that it is but a folly for one that professeth Christ truly to look for the love of the world. Thus shall ye learn to bear trouble, and to exercise your religion, and feel indeed that Christ's words be true, "In the world ye shall suffer persecution." And when ye feel your religion indeed, say, ye be no better than your forefathers; but be glad that ye may be counted worthy soldiers for this war: and pray to God when ye come together, that he will use and order you and your doings to these three ends, which ye must take heed of: the first, that ye glorify God; the next, that ye edify the church and congregation; the third, that ye profit your own souls.

John xvi.

In all your doings beware ye be not deceived. For although this time be not yet so bloody and tyrannous as the time of our forefathers, that could not bear the name of Christ without danger of life and goods; yet is our time more perilous both for body and soul. Therefore of us

Christ said, "Think ye, when the Son of man cometh, he Luke xviii. shall find any faith upon earth?" He said not, Think ye he shall find any man or woman christened, and in name a Christian? But he spake of the faith that saveth the Christian man in Christ: and doubtless the scarcity of faith is now more (and will, I fear, increase) than it was in the time of the greatest tyrants that ever were; and no marvel why. Read ye the sixth chapter of St John's Revelation, and ye shall perceive, among other things, that at the opening of the fourth seal came out a pale horse, and he that sat upon him was called Death, and Hell followed him. This horse is the time wherein hypocrites and dissemblers entered into the church under the pretence of true religion, as monkers, friars, nuns, massing-priests, with such other, that have killed more souls with heresies and superstition than all the tyrants that ever were killed bodies with fire, sword, or banishment, as it appeareth by his name that sitteth upon the horse, who is called Death: for all souls that leave Christ, and trust to these hypocrites, live to the devil in everlasting pain, as is declared by him that followeth the pale horse, which is Hell.

These pretensed and pale hypocrites have stirred the earthquakes, that is to wit, the princes of the world, against Christ's church, and have also darkened the sun, and made the moon bloody, and have caused the stars to fall from heaven; that is to say, have darkened with mists, and daily do darken (as ye hear by their sermons) the clear sun of God's most pure word: the moon, which be God's true preachers, which fetch only light at the sun of God's word, are turned into blood, prisons, and chains, that their light cannot shine unto the world as they would: whereupon it cometh to pass, that the stars, that is to say, christian people, fall from heaven, that is to wit, from God's most true word to hypocrisy, most devilish superstition and idolatry. Let some learned man shew you all the articles of your belief and monuments of christian faith, from the time of Christ hitherto; and ye shall perceive that there was never mention of such articles as these hypocrites teach. God bless you, and pray for me, as I do for you.

Out of the Fleet, by your brother in Christ,

JOHN HOPER.

LETTER XXVIII.

(See Epistolæ Tigurinæ, XLV. p. 65.)

LETTER XXIX.

To my beloved in the Lord, W. P.

The grace of God be with you. I have sent you letters for my wife, who is at Frankford in High Almayne[1]: I pray you, convey them trustily and speedily, and seal them close after the merchants' fashion, that they be not opened. William Downton, my servant, hath the first copy of that I wrote concerning master Hales' hurt. I would master Bradford did see it; and then the copy to be well kept, lest any man of malice should add anything to the matter more and worse than I have made it. I pass not of that may come of it, I thank God; and my conscience beareth me record, that I did it of zeal to the word of God, which the bishop of Winchester called the doctrine of desperation. Not only my heart, but also my mouth, my pen, and all my power, shall be against him even till death (by God's help) in this case, let God do with the matter as it pleaseth his high majesty; to whom I commend you. Yours,

29 April, 1554. JOHN HOPER.

LETTER XXX.

To master FERRAR, *Bishop of St* DAVID'S, *D.* TAYLOR, *master* BRADFORD, *and master* PHILPOT, *prisoners in the King's Bench in Southwark.*

The grace of God be with you, Amen. I am advertised by divers, as well such as love the truth as also by such as yet be not come unto it, that ye and I shall be carried shortly to Cambridge, there to dispute in the faith, and for the religion of Christ (which is most true) that we have and do profess. I am (as I doubt not ye be) in Christ ready, not only to go to Cambridge, but also to suffer, by God's help, death itself

[1 Upper Germany.]

in the maintenance thereof. Weston[2] and his complices have obtained forth the commission already, and speedily (most like) he will put it in execution. Wherefore, dear brethren, I do advertise you of the thing before for divers causes: the one, to comfort you in the Lord, that the time draweth nigh and is at hand that we shall testify before God's enemies God's truth: the next, that ye should prepare yourselves the better for it: the third, to shew you what ways I think were best to use ourselves in this matter, and also to hear of every one of you your better advice, if mine be not good. Ye know such as shall be censors and judges over us breathe and thirst our blood; and whether we by God's help overcome after the word of God, or by force and subtilty of our adversaries be overcome, this will be the conclusion: our adversaries will say they overcome, as you perceive how they report of those great learned men and godly personages at Oxford[3].

Wherefore I mind never to answer them, except I have the books present, because they use not only false allegation of the doctors, but also a piece of the doctors against the whole course of the doctors' mind. The next, that we may have sworn notaries, to take things spoken indifferently; which will be very hard to have; for the adversaries will have the oversight of all things, and then make theirs better than it was, and ours worse than it was. Then, if we see that two or three or more will speak together, or with scoffs and taunts illude and mock us, I suppose it were best to appeal to be heard before the queen and the whole council, and that would much set forth the glory of God. For many of them know already the truth; many of them err rather of zeal than malice; and the others that be indurate should be answered fully to their shame (I doubt not), although to our smart and bloodshedding. For of this I am assured, that the commissioners appointed to hear us and judge us mean nothing less than to

[[2] Weston, dean of Westminster, was prolocutor of the Lower House of Convocation.]

[[3] Cranmer, Ridley and Latimer. For an account of the pretended disputation at Oxford, see Foxe, Acts and Mon. B. x. p. 1428. Ed. 1583. Also Burnet's Hist. of Reform. Vol. II. B. II. p. 280. Ed. 1683. Hooper and his fellow-prisoners issued a "declaration concerning their disputation and doctrine of their religion," dated May 8, 1554, shewing on what terms they were prepared to dispute. Foxe, Acts and Mon. B. x. p. 1469.]

[HOOPER, II.]

hear the cause indifferently; for they be enemies unto us and unto our cause, and be at a point already to give sentence against us: so that if it were possible, with St Stephen, to speak so that they could not resist us, or to use such silence and patience as Christ did, they will proceed to revenging.

Wherefore, my dear brethren in the mercy of Jesus Christ, I would be glad to know your advice this day or to-morrow; for shortly we shall be gone, and I verily suppose that we shall not company together, but be kept abroad one from the other. They will deny our appeal: yet let us challenge the appeal, and take witness thereof of such as be present, and require, for indifferency of hearing and judgment, to be heard either before the queen and the council, or else before all the parliament, as they were used in king Edward's days.

Further, for my part, I will require both books and time to answer. We have been prisoners now three quarters of a year, and have lacked our books; and our memories, by close keeping and ingratitude of their parts, be not as present and quick as theirs be. I trust God will be with us, yea, I doubt not but he will, and teach us to do all things in his cause godly and constantly. If our adversaries, that shall be our judges, may have their purpose, we shall dispute one day, be condemned the next day, and suffer the third day. And yet is there no law to condemn us (as far as I know), and so one of the convocation-house said this week to D. Weston. To whom Weston made this answer; "It forceth not (quoth he) for a law: we have commission to proceed with them; when they be dispatched, let their friends sue the law."

Now how soon a man may have such a commission at my lord chancellor's hand, you know. It is as hard to be obtained as an indictment for Christ at Caiphas' hand. Besides that, the bishops, having the queen so upon their sides, may do all things both without the advice and also the knowledge of the rest of the lords of the temporalty; who at this present have found out the mark that the bishops shoot at, and doubtless be not pleased with their doings. I pray you, help that our brother Saunders and the rest in the Marshalsea may understand these things, and send me your answer betime. *Judas non dormit; nec scimus diem neque horam*[1]. *Dominus*

[1 Judas sleepeth not; neither know we the day nor the hour.]

Jesus Christus suo sancto numine nos omnes consoletur et adjuvet. The Lord Jesus Christ with his Holy Spirit comfort and strengthen us all. Amen. 6 May, 1554.

Yours, and with you unto death in Christ,

JOHN HOPER.

LETTER XXXI.

(See Epistolæ Tigurinæ, XLVI. p. 65.)

LETTER XXXII.

(See Epistolæ Tigurinæ, XLVII. p. 66.)

LETTER XXXIII.

Another letter to certain godly persons, written to the same effect[2].

The grace of God be with you. Amen. I do give our heavenly Father thanks, that moveth you to remember your afflicted brethren, and I do (as I am bound) pray for you, that, with your remembrance of me, ye provide help, and succour me with such goods as God doth endue you withal. Doubtless, if ever wretch and vile sinner was bound unto God, I am most specially bound. For these ten months almost, ever since my imprisonment, I have had no living nor goods to sustain myself withal, yet such hath been the favour of our heavenly Father, that I have had sufficient to eat and drink, and the same paid for. Seeing he is so merciful and careful for my sinful body, I doubt not but he hath more care of my wretched soul, so that in both I may serve his majesty, and be a lively and profitable member of his poor afflicted church. I do not care what extremity this world shall work or devise, praying you in the bowels of him that shed his precious blood for you, to remember and follow the knowledge ye have learned of his truth. Be not ashamed nor afraid to follow him; beware of this sentence,

[2 This letter stands after Letter XLVII. in Coverdale's work.]

that it take no place in you: "No man (saith Christ) that putteth his hand to the plough and looketh backward is meet for the kingdom of God." Remember, that Christ willed him that would build a tower to sit down first and look whether he were able to perform it, lest he should begin and leave off in the midst, and so be mocked of his neighbours, and lose therewithal as much as he bestowed. Christ told such as would build in him eternal life, what the price thereof was, even at the beginning of his doctrine, and said they should be persecuted: also they should sometime pay and bestow both goods and lands, before the tower of salvation would be builded.

<small>Luke ix.</small>

<small>Luke xiv.</small>

<small>Math. x</small>

Seeing the price of truth in religion hath been always the displeasure and persecution of the world, let us bear it, and Christ will recompense the charges abundantly. It is no loss to lack the love of the world, and to find the love of God; nor no harm to suffer the loss of worldly things, and find eternal life. If man hate and God love, man kill the body and God bring both body and soul to eternal life, the exchange is good and profitable. For the love of God use singleness towards him. Beware of this foolish and deceitful collusion, to think a man may serve God in spirit secretly to his conscience, although outwardly with his body and bodily presence he cleave, for civil order, to such rites and ceremonies as now be used contrary to God and his word. Be assured that whatsoever he be that giveth this counsel, shall be before God able to do you no more profit than the fig-leaves did unto Adam. "Glorify God both in your bodies and in your spirits, which are God's." Take heed of that commandment; no man is able to dispense with it. Such as be yet clear, and have not been present at the wicked mass and idolatrous service, let them pray to God to stand fast: such as for weakness and fear have been at it, repent and desire God of forgiveness, and doubtless he will have mercy upon you. It is a fearful thing, that many do not alonely thus dissemble with God, but also excuse and defend the dissimulation: beware of that, dear brethren; for it is a sore matter to delight in evil things. Let us acknowledge and bewail our evil; then God shall send grace to amend us, and strength better to bear his cross.

<small>1 Cor. vi.</small>

<small>Prov. ii.</small>

I doubt not but ye will judge of my writing as I mean

towards you in my heart, which is doubtless your eternal salvation in Christ Jesus; to whom I heartily commend you. 14 June, 1554.

LETTER XXXIV.

To my dearly beloved friend in Christ, master John Hall.

The grace of God be with you. Amen. It was much to my comfort, I assure you, when I understood by this bearer, my faithful servant, William Downton, that you and your wife were in health. Many times I had occasion to inquire for you, before the departure of my poor wife, to have holpen her out of the land from the hands of the cruel; but I could hear nothing where you were. It was told me you abode in the country with your wife, to whom make my hearty commendations, and to the rest of all your house that fear God: and my trust is you do not forget your duty towards God in this troublesome world. See that you tarry with him in one hour of trouble, and doubtless he will keep you for ever with him in the joys everlasting. I would write more, but this bearer can tell what need I have to make haste. Fare you well, as myself, and be strong in Christ; for I thank him, for my part, I am not ashamed of his gospel, neither afeard of the pope, the devil, nor the gates of hell. The Lord's will be done. Written the 4th day of August, Anno 1554.

Your poor friend,
JOHN HOPER.

LETTER XXXV.

To all my dear brethren, my relievers and helpers in the city of London.

The grace of God be with you. Amen. I have received from you, dearly beloved in our Saviour Jesus Christ, by the hands of my servant, William Downton, your liberality, for the which I do most heartily thank you; and I praise God highly in you and for you, who hath moved your hearts to shew this kindness towards me; praying him to preserve you from all famine, scarcity, and lack of the truth of his word, which is the lively food of your souls, as you preserve my body from hunger and other necessities which should happen unto me, were it not cared for by the benevolence and charity of godly people. Such as have taken all worldly goods and lands from me, and spoiled me of all that I had, have imprisoned my body, and appointed no one halfpenny to feed or to relieve me withal. But I do forgive them, and pray for them daily in my poor prayer unto God, and from my heart I wish their salvation, and quietly and patiently bear their injuries, wishing no farther extremity to be used towards us. Yet, if it seem contrary best unto our heavenly Father, I have made my reckoning, and fully resolve myself to suffer the uttermost that they are able to do against me, yea, death itself, by the aid of Christ Jesus, who died the most vile death of the cross for us wretches and miserable sinners. But of this I am assured, that the wicked world, with all his force and power, shall not touch one of the hairs of our heads without leave and licence of our heavenly Father, whose will be done in all things. If he will life, life be it; if he will death, death be it. Only we pray that our wills may be subject unto his will; and then, although both we and all the world see none other thing but death, yet if he think life best, we shall not die, no, although the sword be drawn out over our heads: as Abraham thought to kill his son Isaac; yet when God perceived that Abraham had surrendered his will to God's will, and was content to kill his son, God then saved his son.

Dearly beloved, if we be contented to obey God's will, and for his commandment's sake to surrender our goods and ourselves to be at his pleasure, it maketh no matter whether we keep goods and life, or lose them. Nothing can hurt us that is taken from us for God's cause, nor nothing can at length do us good that is preferred contrary unto God's commandment. Let us wholly suffer God to use us and ours after his holy wisdom, and beware we neither use nor govern ourselves contrary to his will by our own wisdom: for if we do, our wisdom will at length prove foolishness. It is kept to no good purpose that we keep contrary unto his commandments. It can by no means be taken from us that he would should tarry with us. He is no good Christian that ruleth himself and his as worldly means serveth: for he that so doth shall have as many changes as chance in the world. To-day with the world he shall like and praise the truth of God; to-morrow, as the world will, so will he like and praise the falsehood of man; to-day with Christ, and to-morrow with antichrist. Wherefore, dear brethren, as touching your behaviour towards God, use both your inward spirits and your outward bodies, your inward and your outward man (I say), not after the means of men, but after the infallible word of God. Refrain from evil in both, and glorify your heavenly Father in both. For if ye think ye can inwardly in the heart serve him, and yet outwardly serve with the world in external service the thing that is not God, ye deceive yourselves; for both the body and the soul must together concur in the honour of God, as St Paul plainly teacheth, 1 Cor. vi. For if an honest wife be bound to give both heart and body to faith and service in marriage, and if an honest wife's faith in the heart cannot stand with an whorish or defiled body outwardly; much less can the true faith of a Christian in the service of Christianity stand with the bodily service of external idolatry: for the mystery of marriage is not so honourable between man and wife, as it is between Christ and every christian man, as St Paul saith.

Therefore, dear brethren, pray to the heavenly Father, that, as he spared not the soul nor the body of his dearly beloved Son, but applied both of them with extreme pain to work our salvation both of body and soul; so he will give us all grace to apply our bodies and souls to be servants unto him: for doubtless he requireth as well the one as the other, and cannot be miscontented with one, and well pleased with the other. Either he hateth both, or loveth both; he divideth not his love to one, and his hatred to the other. Let not us therefore, good brethren, divide ourselves, and say our souls serve him, whatsoever our bodies do to the contrary for civil order and policy.

But, alas! I know by myself what troubleth you, that is, the great danger of the world, that will revenge (ye think) your service to God with sword and fire, with loss of goods and lands. But, dear brethren, weigh of the other side, that your enemies and God's enemies shall not do as much as they would, but as much as God shall suffer them, who can trap them in their own counsels, and destroy them in the midst of their furies. Remember, ye be the workmen of the Lord, and called into his vineyard, there to labour till evening-tide, that ye may receive your penny, which is more worth than all the kings of the earth. But he that calleth us into his vineyard hath not told us how sore or how fervently the sun shall trouble us in our labour; but hath bid us labour, and commit the bitterness thereof unto him, who can and will so moderate all afflictions, that no man shall have more laid upon him than in Christ he shall be able to bear: unto whose merciful tuition and defence I commend both your souls and your bodies. 2 September, 1554.

Matt. xx.

Yours with my poor prayer,
JOHN HOPER.

LETTER XXXVI.

To a merchant of London, by whose means he had received much comfort in his great necessities in the Fleet: where how cruelly he was handled, you shall see in the letter next following[1].

The grace of God be with you. Amen. I thank God and you for the great help and consolation I have received in the time of adversity by your charitable means, but most rejoice that you be not altered from truth, although falsehood cruelly seeketh to distain her. Judge not, my brother, truth by outward appearance; for truth now worse appeareth and more vilely is rejected than falsehood. Leave the outward shew, and see by the word of God what truth is, and accept truth, and dislike her not, though man call her falsehood. As it is now, so hath it been heretofore, the truth rejected, and falsehood received. Such as have professed truth for truth have smarted, and the friends of falsehood laughed them to scorn. The trial of both hath been by contrary success: the one having the commendation of truth by man, but the condemnation of falsehood by God, flourishing for a time, with endless destruction; the other afflicted a little season, with immortal joys.

Wherefore, dear brother, ask and demand of your book, the Testament of Jesus Christ, in these woeful and wretched

[1 See Letter XLVIII.]

days, what you should think, and what you should stay upon for a certain truth; and whatsoever you hear taught, try it by your book, whether it be true or false. The days be dangerous and full of peril, not only for the world and worldly things, but for heaven and heavenly things. It is a trouble to lose the treasures of this life, but yet a very pain if they be kept with the offence of God.

Cry, call, pray, and in Christ daily require help, succour, mercy, wisdom, grace, and defence, that the wickedness of this world prevail not against us. We began well; God preserve us until the end. I would write more often unto you, but I do perceive you be at so much charges with me, that I fear you would think when I write I crave. Send me nothing till I send to you for it; and so tell the good men your partners: and when I need, I will be bold of you. 3 December, 1554.

Yours with my prayer,
J. HOPER.

LETTER XXXVII.

(See Epistolæ Tigurinæ, XLVIII. p. 67.)

LETTER XXXVIII.

To mistress WILKINSON, *a woman hearty in God's cause, and comfortable to his afflicted members.*

The grace of God and the comfort of his Holy Spirit be with you. Amen.

I am very glad to hear of your health, and do thank you for your loving tokens. But I am a great deal more glad to hear how christianly you avoid idolatry, and prepare yourself to suffer the extremity of the world, rather than to endanger yourself to God. You do as you ought to do in this behalf; and in suffering of transitory pains you shall avoid permanent torments in the world to come. Use your life, and keep it with as much quietness as you can, so that you offend not God. The ease that cometh with his displeasure turneth at length to unspeakable pains; and the gains of the world, with the loss of his favour, is beggary and wretchedness. Reason is to be amended in this cause of religion: for it will choose and follow an error with the multitude, if it may be allowed, rather than turn to faith, and follow the truth with the people of God. Moses found the same fault in himself, and did amend it, choosing rather to be afflicted with the people of God than to use the liberty of the king's daughter, that accounted him as her son.

<small>Heb. xi.</small>

Pray for contentation and peace of the Spirit, and rejoice in such troubles as shall happen unto you for the truth's sake: for in that part Christ saith you be happy. Pray also for me, I pray you, that I may do in all things the will of our heavenly Father: to whose tuition and defence I commend you.

<small>Matt. v.</small>

LETTER XXXIX.

To my dearly beloved sister in the Lord, mistress A. W.[1]

The grace of God be with you. Amen. I thank you for your loving token. I pray you burden not yourself too much. It were meet for me rather to bear a pain than to be a hindrance to many. I did rejoice, at the coming of this bearer, to understand of your constancy, and how that you be fully resolved, by God's grace, rather to suffer extremity than to go from that truth in God which you have professed. He that gave you grace to begin in so infallible a truth will follow you in the same unto the end. But, my loving sister, as you be travelling this perilous journey, take this lesson with you, practised by wise men; whereof ye may read in the second of St Matthew's gospel. Such as travelled to find Christ followed only the star; and as long as they saw it, they were assured they were in the right way, and had great mirth in their journey. But when they entered into Jerusalem, whereas the star led them not thither, but unto Bethelem, and there asked the citizens the thing that the star shewed before; as long as they tarried in Jerusalem, and would be instructed where Christ was born, they were not only ignorant of Bethelem, but also lost the sight of the star that led them before.

[1 Ann Warcop.]

Whereof we learn, in any case whiles we be going in this life to seek Christ that is above, to beware we lose not the star of God's word, that only is the mark that sheweth us where Christ is, and which way we may come unto him. But as Jerusalem stood in the way, and was an impediment to these wise men; so doth the synagogue of antichrist, that beareth the name of Jerusalem, which by interpretation is called the vision of peace, and amongst the people now is called the catholic church, stand[2] in the way that pilgrims must go by through this world to Bethelem, the house of saturity and plentifulness, and is an impediment to all christian travellers; yea, and except the more grace of God be, will keep the pilgrims still in her, that they shall not come where Christ is at all. And to stay them indeed, they take away the star of light, which is God's word, that it cannot be seen: as ye may see how the celestial star was hid from the wise men, when they asked of the Pharisees at Jerusalem where Christ was born. Ye may see what great dangers happened unto these wise men, whiles they were a-learning of liars where Christ was. First, they were out of their way; and next, they lost their guide and conductor, the heavenly star. Christ is mounted from us into heaven, and there we seek him, as we say: let us therefore go thitherward by the star of his word, and beware we happen not to come into Jerusalem, the church of men, and ask for him. If we do, we go out of the way, and lose also our conductor and guide, that only leadeth us straight thither.

The poets write in fables, that Jason, when he fought with the dragon in the isle of Colchis, was preserved by the medicines of Medea, and so won the golden fleece. And they write also that Titan, whom they feign to be son and heir of the high god Jupiter, would needs upon a day have the conducting of the sun round about the world; but, as they feign, he missed of the accustomed course: whereupon when he went too high, he burned heaven; and when he went too low, he burned the earth and the water. These profane histories do shame us that be christian men. Jason against the poison of the dragon used only the medicine of Medea. What a shame is it for a christian man against the poison of the devil, heresy, and sin, to use any other remedy than Christ and his word! Titan for lack of knowledge was afeared of every sign of the

[2 Standeth, C.]

zodiac that the sun passeth by: wherefore he now went too low, and now too high, and at length fell down and drowned himself in the sea. Christian men for lack of knowledge, and for fear of such dangers as christian men must needs pass by, go clean out of order, and at length fall into the pit of hell.

Sister, take heed: you shall in your journey towards heaven meet with many a monstrous beast: have salve of God's word therefore ready. Ye shall meet husband, children, lovers and friends, that shall, if God be not with them (as, God be praised, he is; I would it were with all other alike), be very lets and impediments to your purpose. You shall meet with slander and contempt of the world, and be accounted ungracious and ungodly; you shall hear and meet with cruel tyranny to do you all extremities; you shall now and then see the troubles of your own conscience, and feel your own weakness; you shall hear that you be cursed by the sentence of the catholic church, with such like terrors: but pray to God, and follow the star of his word, and you shall arrive at the port of eternal salvation, by the merits only of Jesus Christ; to whom I commend you and all yours most heartily.

Yours in Christ,
JOHN HOPER.

LETTER XL.

To my dear friends in God, master JOHN HALL *and his wife.*

The grace of God be with you. Amen. I thank you for your loving and gentle friendship at all times, praying God to shew unto you such favour, that whatsoever trouble and adversity happen, ye go not back from him. These days be dangerous and full of peril: but yet let us comfort ourselves in calling to remembrance the days of our forefathers, upon whom the Lord sent such troubles, that many hundreds, yea, many thousands, died for the testimony of Jesus Christ, both men and women, suffering with patience and constancy as much cruelty as tyrants could devise, and so departed out of this miserable world to the bliss everlasting; where as now they remain for ever, looking always for the end of this sinful world, when they shall receive their bodies again in immortality, and see the number of the elects associated with them in full and consummate joys: and as virtuous men, suffering martyrdom, and tarrying a little while in this world with pains, by and by rested in joys everlasting; and as their pains ended their sorrows and began ease; so did their constancy and stedfastness animate and confirm all good people in the truth, and gave them encouragement and lust[1] to suffer the like, rather than to fall with the world to consent unto wickedness and idolatry. *Heb. xi.*

Wherefore, my dear friends, seeing God of his part hath illuminated you with the same gift and knowledge of true faith, wherein the apostles, the evangelists, and all martyrs suffered most cruel death, thank him for his grace in knowledge, and pray unto him for strength and perseverance, that through your own fault you be not ashamed nor afeared to confess it. Ye be in the truth, and the gates of hell shall never prevail against it, nor antichrist with all his imps prove it to be false. They may kill and prosecute, but never overcome. Be of good comfort, and fear more God than man. This life is short and miserable; happy be they that can spend it to the glory of God. Pray for me, as I do for you, and commend me to all good men and women. 22 December, 1554.

Your brother in Christ,

JOHN HOPER.

LETTER XLI.

To one that was fallen from the known truth of the gospel to antichrist and his damnable religion.

Grace, mercy, and peace of conscience, be multiplied in all penitent hearts. Amen.

Dear brother in Christ Jesus, it is not long since I was informed what love and fervent zeal ye have heretofore borne to God's true religion, appearing as well by your life and conversation, as by absenting yourself from the idolaters' temple, and congregation of false worshippers. But now,

[1 Lust: desire.]

(alas!) through the devilish persuasions and wicked counsel of worldly men, ye have declined from your former profession, building again that which before ye destroyed, and so are become a trespasser, bearing a stranger's yoke with the unbelievers. Of which thing ever since I was informed, I have been marvellously moved with inward affections, much lamenting so great and sudden a change, as to be turned from him that called you in the grace of Christ unto the dissimulation of wicked hypocrites; which (as St Paul saith) is nothing else, but that there be some which trouble you, intending to make you like as they are, even lovers of themselves, whose hearts are wedded to the perishing treasures of this world, wherein is the whole joy and felicity, contrary to St John, which saith, "See that ye love not the world, neither those things which are in the world." But they, as men without ears, and having hearts without understanding, do neither weigh the terrible threatenings of God against such offenders, and the most woeful punishment due for the same; nor yet consider the loving admonition and calling of God, who both teacheth how to avoid his wrath, and also by what means to attain to salvation.

Wherefore, dear brother, I humbly beseech you, even by the mercifulness of God, and as you tender your own salvation, to give ear no longer to their pestilent persuasions, but even now forthwith to repent, and have no longer fellowship with the unfruitful works of darkness; neither fashion you yourself again like unto the world: delight not in the friendship thereof; for all such be made the enemies of God. Grieve not any longer the Holy Spirit of God, by whom ye are sealed unto the day of redemption. Acknowledge your offence, and from whence ye are fallen: prostrate yourself before God, asking mercy for Christ's sake. Mourn with Mary Magdalen, lament with David, cry with Jonas, and weep with Peter;[1] and make no tarrying to turn to the Lord, whose pitiful eyes attend always to wipe away the tears from every troubled conscience. Such is his entire love toward all those that turn unto him, making them this sweet promise confirmed by a mighty and vehement kind of speaking: "Tell them, As truly as I live (saith he), I will not the death of a sinner, but much rather that he turn from his evil ways,

[1 The reference intended here is evidently Matth. xxvi. 75.]

and live. Turn you, turn you from your ungodly ways, O ye of the house of Israel. O wherefore will ye die?" Behold, ye are here forgiven, your sin is blotted out, and the most joyful countenance of God turned again towards you.

What now remaineth? Verily this, that you from henceforth keep circumspect watch, and become a follower of Christ, sustaining for his name's sake all such adversities as shall be measured unto you by the sufferance of God our heavenly Father, who so careth for us, that not one hair of our head shall perish without his will; who also, considering the tender and weak faith of his children, not able as yet to stand against the force of antichrist's tyranny, giveth them this loving liberty: "When ye be persecuted in one city, Matth. x. fly to another." O most tender compassion of Christ! how careful is he over his people! Who would not now, rather than to offend so merciful a God, fly this wicked realm, as your most christian brother and many other have done? or else with boldness of heart and patience of the spirit bear manfully the cross even unto the death, as divers of our brethren have done before us? as is declared at large in Paul's Epistle to the Hebrews, which I pass over, and Heb. xi. come to our Saviour Christ, whose example for our singular comfort St Paul encourageth us to follow, saying, "Let us Heb. xii. also, seeing that we are compassed with so great a multitude of witnesses, lay away all that presseth down, and the sin that hangeth on, and let us run with patience unto the battle that is set before us, looking unto Jesus, the author and finisher of our faith; who, for the joy that was set before him, abode the cross and despised the shame, and is set down on the right hand of the throne of God, &c." "From Rev. xxii. whence he shall come shortly," saith St John, "and his rewards with him, to give every man according as his deeds shall be. Blessed are they that do his commandments, that their power may be in the tree of life, and may enter in through the gates unto the city," where they (saith Esay) Isai. lviii. "shall have their pleasure in the Lord, who will carry them on high above the earth, and will feed them with the heritage of Jacob their father; for the Lord's own mouth hath so promised."

Thus I have been bold to write unto you for christian love's sake that I bear to you, whose salvation I wish as mine own, beseeching God that your whole spirit, soul, and body may be kept faultless unto the coming of our Lord Jesus Christ. Amen.

Your brother in Christ,
JOHN HOPER.

LETTER XLII.

To a certain godly woman, instructing her how she should behave herself in the time of her widowhood.

The grace of God and the comfort of his Holy Spirit be with you, and with all them that unfeignedly love his holy gospel. Amen.

I thank you, dear sister, for your most loving remembrance: and although I cannot recompense the same, yet do I wish with all my heart that God would do it; requiring you not to forget your duty towards God in these perilous days, in the which the Lord will try us. I trust you do increase by reading of the scriptures the knowledge you have of God, and that you diligently apply yourself to follow the same: for the knowledge helpeth not, except the life be according thereunto. Further, I do heartily pray you to consider the state of your widowhood; and if God shall put in your mind to change it, remember the saying of St Paul, 1 Corinthians vii. "It is lawful for the widow or maiden to marry to whom they list, so it be in the Lord," that is to say, to such a one as is of Christ's religion.

Dearly beloved in Christ, remember these words; for you shall find thereby great joy and comfort, if you change your state. Whereof I will, when I have better leisure (as now I have none at all), further advertise you. In the mean time I commend you to God, and the guiding of his good Spirit; who stablish and confirm you in all well doing, and keep you blameless to the day of the Lord. Watch and pray; for this day is at hand.

Yours assured in Christ,
JOHN HOPER.

LETTER XLIII.

An answer to a friend of his for a woman that was troubled with her husband in matters of religion, how she should behave herself towards him.

The grace and peace of God our dear Father through Jesus Christ our Lord. Amen.

As concerning the party whom you wrote unto me of, I have here sent you mine advice, and what I think is best in this case to be done. First, she shall remember the counsel of St Paul, 1 Cor. vii., where he speaketh to such as be coupled in matrimony, and be of two sundry and divers religions: if the unbelieving man will dwell with the faithful woman, the wife cannot forsake him; or in case the unbelieving woman will dwell with her believing husband, the husband cannot forsake her. But if the unbelieving party (whether it be husband or wife) will depart, the believing party is at liberty. Now in this time, to believe that the priest can make God, or to believe that which was not God yesterday can be both God and man to-day, and so to honour that which was but very bread yesterday for the true God, that made both heaven and earth and all that be in them, and for the body and soul of Christ, that suffered for our redemption, and took from us our sins upon the cross, is very idolatry, and to be committed of no christian man: for the pain of it, without repentance, is everlasting damnation.

In matrimony it is meet therefore, that which party soever be persuaded and knoweth the truth, be it the husband or the wife, the truth be spoken, taught, and opened unto the party that is not persuaded. For, as St Paul saith, " How knowest thou, O man, whether thou shalt save thy wife? or how knowest thou, O woman, whether thou shalt save thy husband?" Therefore let the best and more godly party be diligent in saving (by his or her labours) the party that is not instructed nor persuaded in the truth. If it prevail, then is the worse part amended, and the best part hath done his or her duty and office, as it is commanded. Ephes. iv. Coloss. iii. 1 Peter iii.

In case the worse part will not be amended, but tarry still in error, and so offend the Almighty God, the author of marriage, let the best part, that is persuaded and knoweth the truth, as in this case the woman, labour with her companion to be free and at liberty, and not to be compelled to honour any false god, or to serve God otherwise than she knoweth she may do with a good conscience, as she is taught by the word of God. And if she may thus obtain to be at liberty, and be not compelled to do things against her conscience, she may not in any wise depart from him that she is married unto. If this woman cannot win her husband to the truth, nor obtain to live freely and at liberty in the faith of Christ herself, let her cause some godly and grave men or women to persuade with her husband, as well for his own better knowledge as for the freedom and liberty of herself; and let her, and whosoever entreateth of the matter, use modesty, soberness, and charity, and pray unto God that their doings may take virtuous and godly success.

In case (which God forbid!) the husband will not reform himself of his error, nor suffer his wife to refrain the company and fellowship of such as be present at the mass, where as an idol is honoured for God, this wife must make answer soberly and christianly, that she is forbidden by God's laws to commit idolatry, and that God is more to be obeyed than man; and so in any case beware she offend not against the first commandment, which is, "Thou shalt have no other gods but me."

Acts v.

Exod. xx.

It may come to pass, that when the husband shall perceive the wife's love and reverence towards him, and also her constancy and strength in the truth and true religion of God, although he be not converted unto the truth by her, yet he will be contented to suffer her to use the liberty of her conscience, without compulsion to any religion that she doth by God's word detest and abhor. But if there be no remedy but either the wife must follow in idolatry her husband's commandment, or else suffer the extremity of the law; here must the wife remember and learn whether there be any law or not, that can compel her ordinarily to come to the mass, where as idolatry is committed. If there be no law or other means to compel her than her husband's foul words, which be nothing else but threatenings to put her in fear, she must, if she can, with wisdom and womanhood amend the same: if she cannot, then must she christianly and patiently bear them as a woman of God, that for his sake must suffer as much as his pleasure is to lay upon her.

In case there be a law to compel her and all other, if

otherwise she will not obey, to come to the mass, first, she must wisely and discreetly weigh her husband's nature, whether he is wont to be in deed, works, and offers, cruel as he is in words. If she can find that his nature is (as the most part of men's be) more churlish and cruel in words than in works, then howsoever he threateneth by dangerous words, he will not accuse his wife to harm her, but rather excuse her. In case, either for lack of love, or for fear of losing of his goods, she perceive verily that he mindeth to bring her in danger by a law, then must she pray to God, and use one of these two extreme remedies. First, if she find by prayer herself strong to abide the extremity of the law, yea, though she should die, let her in no case depart from her husband. In case she find herself too weak to suffer such extremity, then rather than to break company and marriage between God and her, conjoined by the precious blood of Christ, she must convey herself into some such place as idolatry may be avoided. For if the husband love the wife, or the wife the husband, more than Christ, he nor she be not meet for Christ. Matt. x. xvi. Luke xiv. ix. Yea, if a man love his own life more than Christ, he is not meet for Christ. And what doth it avail a man to win all the world, and to lose his soul? But here the woman must take heed, that in case, for the keeping of the marriage between God and her, she depart from her husband, that she be always in honest, virtuous, and godly company, that she may at all times have record for her godly behaviour, if anything should be laid to her charge; and let her live a sole, sober, and modest life, with prayer and soberness to God, that it may please him to banish such wicked laws and wicked religion as make debate between God and man, and husband and wife; and then God shall from time to time give counsel to every good man and woman what is best to be done in such pitiful cases, to his honour and to the salvation of our woeful and troubled consciences.

Out of the Fleet, by the prisoner of the Lord,

JOHN HOPER.

LETTER XLIV.

[The three following letters were annexed to the Exposition of Psalm XXIII. and the Apology, published by Henry Bull in 1562, and are reprinted from that edition, the variations of Coverdale, marked C, being given in the notes.]

¶ The copy of the letter wher-
by Maister Hooper was certifyed
of the takying of a godlye
company in bowe
churcheyarde at
prayer.

My duty humbly remembered, you hear (I know) of a godly company imprisoned, which were taken upon new-year's night: yet notwithstanding, forasmuch (perhaps) as you know not perfectly how nor wherefore, you shall understand that, being upon their knees in ending of prayer, (wherein they gave God thanks, prayed for the magistrates and estates of the realm, and required things necessary at his bountiful hands,) two of my lord chancellor's men (as I am informed) came first into the chamber where they were, in Bow church-yard; and immediately afterwards followed M. sheriff with others, who commanded them all to stay in the king and queen's majesties' name, whereunto they humbly obeyed: for they came not thither weaponed to conspire or make any tumult, but only, like Christians, christianly to pray, and to be instructed in the vulgar tongue by the reading and hearing of God's word, as their conscience did enforce them, without the displeasure of God, to do. For (as you well know) there is nothing so grievous to the patient in this world as the gnawing and biting worm of a troubled conscience, being accused by God's law for the wilful transgressing of the same: as by experience we know by Judge Hales[1], who, contrary to the knowledge of God's word, consented

[[1] Foxe speaks of him as "conscientiæ stimulis totus confusus confectusque." Rer. in Eccles. Gest. Commentarii. Basil. 1559. p. 264. See also Hooper's treatise respecting him, p. 374 of this volume; also Burnet's Hist. of Reform. Vol. II. B. I. p. 248.]

to the wicked traditions of the papists; which although in name they would be of the holy church, and preachers of the gospel of Christ, yet in fact and deed do they dissent from the same, and most detest that godly society: as by the cruel handling of the Christians by the prelates at this present it doth evidently appear. Therefore (I say), that they might, without the offence of God, quietly pray together, as they be taught by his word, there assembled a godly company together to the number of thirty, divided and sent to both the counters, where at commandment they yet remain. And with master Chambers, master Monger, and the rest in the counter at Bread-street, I was yesterday: who (God be thanked) be strong, and do rejoice that for well-doing they are imprisoned; not doubting but that, as God hath vouchsafed to accept them worthy to sustain imprisonment for his sake, so he will strengthen them rather to suffer death than to deny his truth: as the Lord knoweth; who assist you with his Holy Spirit, that unto the end you may persevere in his truth: unto whose tuition in my poor prayer I humbly commend you. 3 of January, 1554[5].

M. Chamber, M. Monger, M. Sh. and
the rest in the Counter do pray
for you, and in Christ
salute you most
heartily.

LETTER XLV.

⁋ The letter of Mayster Hooper's aunswer unto the
former letter.

The grace of God be with you. Amen. I perceive[2] by your letter how that, upon new-year's day at night, there were taken a godly company of Christians, whilst they were praying. I do rejoice in that men can be so well occupied in this perilous time, and fly unto God for remedy

[2 'Perceived,' C.]

by prayer, as well for their own lacks and necessities, as also charitably to pray for them that persecute them. So doth the word of God command all men to pray charitably for them that hate us[1], and not to revile any magistrate with words, or to mean him evil by force or violence. They also may rejoice that in well-doing they were taken to the prison. Wherefore I have thought it good to send them
this little writing of consolation, praying God to send
them patience, charity, and constancy in the truth
of his most holy word. Thus fare you well,
and pray to God to send his true word
into this realm again amongst us,
which the ungodly bishops
have now banished.
4. January.
1554[5].

LETTER XLVI.

¶ The copy of Mayster Hooper's Letter delyuered in the
Counter at breade
street.

To the godly and faithful company of prisoners in both the Counters, which were taken together at prayer in a house in Bow church-yard[2].

The grace, favour, consolation, and aid of the Holy Ghost be with you now and ever. So be it.

Dearly beloved in the Lord, ever sithence your imprisonment, I have been marvellously moved with great affections and passions, as well of mirth and gladness as of heaviness and sorrow. Of gladness in this, that I perceived how ye be bent and given to prayer, and invocation of God's help in these dark and wicked proceedings of men against God's glory. I have been sorry to perceive the malice and wickedness of

[1 'For those that hate them,' C.]   [2 Heading in C.]

men to be so cruel, devilish, and tyrannical, to persecute the people of God for serving[3], saying, and hearing of the holy psalms and the word of eternal life. These cruel doings do declare that the papists' church is more bloody and tyrannical than ever was the sword of the ethnics and gentiles. When I heard of your taking, and what ye were doing, wherefore, and by whom ye were taken, I remembered how the Christians in the primitive church were used by the cruelty of unchristened heathens in the time of Trajan the emperor[4], about seventy-seven years after Christ's ascension into heaven; and how[5] the Christians were persecuted very sore, as though they had been traitors and movers of sedition. Whereupon the gentile emperor Trajan required to know the true cause of christian men's trouble. A great learned man called Plinius[6] wrote unto him, and said it was because the Christians said certain psalms before day unto one called Christ, whom they worshipped for God. When Trajan the emperor understood it was for nothing but for conscience and religion, he caused by his commandments everywhere, that no man should be persecuted for serving of God. Lo! a gentile and heathen man would not have such as were of a contrary religion punished for serving of God: but the pope and his church hath[7] cast you into prison, being taken even doing[8] the work of God, and one of the excellentest[9] works that is required of christian men; that is to wit, whiles ye were in prayer, and not in such wicked and superstitious prayers[10] as the papists use, but in the same prayer that Christ hath taught you to pray: and in his name only ye gave God thanks for that ye have received, and for his sake ye asked for such things as ye want. O glad may ye be that ever ye were born, to be apprehended whilst ye were so virtuously occupied. Blessed be they that suffer for righteousness' sake. For if God had suffered them that took your bodies then to have taken your life also, now had

[Matth. v. C.]

[3 'Serving of God, for &c.,' C.]

[4 Plin. Epist. Lib. x. Epp. xcvii. xcviii. pp. 815-825. Amsterdam. 1734. The instructions of Trajan to Pliny were, that the Christians should not be *sought after;* but if they were brought before him and convicted of being Christians, they should be punished.]

[5 'And how,' omitted in C.]   [6 'Plinius secundus,' C.]
[7 'Have,' C.]   [8 'In doing,' C.]
[9 'Most excellent,' C.]   [10 'Prayer,' C.]

ye been following the Lamb in perpetual joys, away from the company and assembly of wicked men. But the Lord would not have you suddenly so to depart; but reserveth you gloriously to speak and maintain his truth to the world. Be ye not careful what ye shall say: for God will go out and in with you, and will be present in your hearts and in your mouths to speak his wisdom, although it seem foolishness to the world. He that hath begun this good work in you continue[1] you in the same unto the end: and pray unto him that ye may fear him only that hath power to kill both body and soul, and to cast them into hell-fire. Be of good comfort: all the hairs of your heads be numbered, and there is not one of them can perish, except your heavenly Father suffer it to perish. Now ye be even in the field, and placed in the forefront of Christ's battle. Doubtless it is a singular favour of God, and a special love of him towards you, to give you this fore-ward and pre-eminence, and a sign that he trusteth you before others of his people. Wherefore, dear brethren and sisters, continually fight this fight of the Lord. Your cause is most just and godly: ye stand for the true Christ (who is, after the flesh, in heaven) and for his true religion and honour, which is amply, fully, sufficiently, and abundantly contained in the holy testament sealed with Christ's own blood. How much be ye bound to God, to put you in trust with so holy and just a cause! Remember what lookers-upon ye have to see and behold you in your fight; God[2] and all his holy angels, who be ready alway to take you up into heaven, if ye be slain in this fight. Also ye have standing at your backs all the multitude of the faithful, who shall take courage, strength, and desire to follow such noble and valiant Christians as ye be. Be not afeard of your adversaries; for he that is in you is stronger than he that is in them. Shrink not, although it be pain to you. Your pains be not now so great as hereafter your joys shall be. Read the comfortable chapters to the Romans, viii. x. xv. Hebrews, xi. xii.; and upon your knees thank God that ever ye were accounted worthy to suffer anything for his name's sake. Read the second chapter of St Luke's gospel; and there ye shall see how the shepherds that watched upon their sheep all night, as soon as they heard that Christ was born at Bethelem, by and bye they went to see him. They did not reason nor

[Matth. x. C.]

[1 John iv. C.]

[1 'Confirm, strengthen, and continue,' C.]   [2 'Even God,' C.]

debate with themselves, who should keep the wolf from the sheep in the mean time, but did as they were commanded, and committed their sheep unto him whose pleasure they obeyed. So let us do now we[3] be called; commit[4] all other things unto him that called[5] us. He will take heed that all things shall be well: he will help the husband; he will comfort the wife; he will guide the servants; he will keep the house; he will preserve the goods; yea, rather than it should be undone, he will wash the dishes, and rock the cradle. Cast therefore all your [1 Pet. v. c.] care upon God; for he careth for you. Besides this, ye may perceive by your imprisonment that your adversaries' weapons against you be nothing but flesh, blood, and tyranny. For if they were able, they would maintain their wicked religion by God's word: but for lack of that, they would violently compel such as they cannot by the holy scripture persuade: because the holy word of God and all Christ's doings be clean contrary unto them. I pray you pray for me, and I will pray for you: and although we be asunder after the world, yet in Christ[6] (I trust) for ever joining in the spirit; and so shall meet in the palace of the heavenly joys, after this short and transitory life is ended. God's peace be with you. Amen.
4. of January.
1554[5].

LETTER XLVII.

To certain of his beloved friends in God, exhorting them to stick constantly to the professed truth of the gospel in those days of trial, and not to shrink for any trouble.

The grace of God be with you. Amen. I did write unto you of late, and told you what extremity the parliament had concluded upon concerning religion[7], suppressing the

[3 'When we,' C.]   [4 'And commit,' C.]
[5 'Calleth,' C.]   [6 'We are in,' C.]
[7 On new-year's day (says Strype, an. 1555) passed the act for restoring the supremacy to the see apostolic, and repealing a great

true, and setting forth the untrue; intending to cause all men by extremity to forswear themselves, and to take again for the head of the church him that is neither head nor member of it, but a very enemy, as the word of God and all ancient writers do record: and for lack of law and authority, they will use force and extremity, which have been the arguments to defend the pope and popery, sith this wicked authority began first in the world. But now is the time of trial, to see whether we fear more God or man. It was an easy thing to hold with Christ whiles the prince and world held with him: but now the world hateth him, is the true trial who be his. Wherefore in the name, and in the virtue, strength, and power of his holy Spirit, prepare yourselves in any case to adversity and constancy. Let us not run away when it is most time to fight: remember that none shall be crowned but such as fight manfully; and he that endureth unto the end shall be saved. Ye must now turn all your cogitations from the perils ye see, and mark by faith what followeth the peril, either victory in this world of your enemies, or else a surrender of this life to inherit the everlasting kingdom. Beware of beholding too much the felicity or the misery of this world; for the consideration and earnest love or fear of either of them draweth from God. Wherefore think with yourselves, as touching the felicity of the world, it is good; but yet none otherwise than it standeth with the favour of God. It is to be kept; but yet so far forth as by keeping of it we lose not God. It is good to abide and tarry still among our friends here; but yet so that we tarry not therewithal in God's displeasure, and hereafter to dwell in hell with the devils in fire everlasting. There is nothing under God but may be kept, so that God, being above all things we have, be not lost.

Of adversity judge the same. Imprisonment is painful; but yet liberty upon evil conditions is more painful. The prisons stink; but yet not so much as sweet houses where as the fear and true honour of God lacketh. I must be alone and solitary: it is better so to be, and have God with me, than to be in company with the wicked. Loss of goods is great; but loss of God's grace and favour is greater. I am a poor

many of king Henry's laws, that had been made to the prejudice of the see. Eccles. Mem. Vol. III. Pt. I. p. 328. Oxf. 1822. See also Burnet's Hist. of Reform. Vol. II. B. II. p. 293. Lond. 1683.]

simple creature, and cannot tell how to answer before such a great sort of noble, learned, and wise: it is better to make answer before the pomp and pride of wicked men than to stand naked in the sight of all heaven and earth before the just God at the latter day. I shall die then by the hands of the cruel man: he is blessed that loseth this life full of mortal miseries, and findeth the life full of eternal joys. It is a grief to depart[1] from goods and friends; but yet not so much as to depart from grace and heaven itself. Wherefore there is neither felicity nor adversity of this world that can appear to be great, if it be weighed with the joys or pains in the world to come.

I can do no more but pray for you; do the same for me for God's sake. For my part (I thank the heavenly Father), I have made my accounts, and appointed myself unto the will of the heavenly Father: as he will, so I will, by his grace. For God's sake, as soon as ye can, send my poor wife and children some letter from you, and my letter also which I sent of late to Downton. As it is told me, she had never letter from me sith the coming of master S. unto her: the more to blame the messengers; for I have written divers times. The Lord comfort them, and provide for them; for I am able to do nothing in worldly things. She is a godly and wise woman; and if my meanings had been accomplished, she should have had necessary things: but that I meant God can perform, to whom I commend both her and you all. I am a precious jewel now, and daintily kept, never so daintily: for neither mine own man, nor any of the servants of the house, may come at me, but my keeper alone, a simple rude man, God knoweth; but I am nothing careful thereof. 21 January, 1555.

Yours bounden,
JOHN HOPER.

LETTER XLVIII.

A report of his miserable imprisonment and most cruel handling by Babington, that enemy of God and of his truth, then warden of the Fleet.

The first of September, 1553, I was committed unto the Fleet from Richmond, to have the liberty of the prison; and

[1 Depart: part.]

within six days after I paid for my liberty five pounds sterling to the warden for fees: who, immediately upon the payment thereof, complained unto Stephen Gardiner, bishop of Winchester, and so was I committed to close prison one quarter of a year, in the tower-chamber of the Fleet, and used very extremely. Then by the means of a good gentlewoman I had liberty to come down to dinner and supper, and not to speak with any of my friends; but, as soon as dinner and supper was done, to repair to my chamber again. Notwithstanding, whiles I came down thus to dinner and supper, the warden and his wife picked quarrels with me, and complained untruly of me to their great friend the bishop of Winchester.

After one quarter of a year and somewhat more, the warden and his wife fell out with me for the wicked mass; and thereupon the warden resorted to the bishop of Winchester, and obtained to put me into the wards, where I have continued a long time, having nothing appointed to me for my bed but a little pad of straw, a rotten covering, with a tick and a few feathers therein, the chamber being vile and stinking, until by God's means good people sent me bedding to lie in. Of the one side of which prison is the sink and filth of all the house, and on the other side the town-ditch; so that the stench of the house hath infected me with sundry diseases. During which time I have been sick; and the doors, bars, hasps, and chains being all closed and made fast upon me, I have mourned, called, and cried for help. But the warden, when he hath known me many times ready to die, and when the poor men of the wards have called to help me, hath commanded the doors to be kept fast, and charged that none of his men should come at me, saying, "Let him alone; it were a good riddance of him." And among many other times he did thus the 18th of October, 1553, as many can witness.

I paid always like a baron to the said warden, as well in fees as for my board, which was twenty shillings a week, besides my man's table, until I was wrongfully deprived of my bishoprick. And sithence that time I have paid him as the best gentleman doth in his house: yet hath he used me worse and more vilely than the veriest slave that ever came to the hall-commons. The said warden hath also imprisoned my man, William Downton, and stripped him out of his clothes to search for letters, and could find none, but only a little remembrance of good people's names, that gave me their alms to relieve me in prison; and, to undo them also, the warden delivered the same bill unto the said Stephen Gardiner, God's enemy and mine.

I have suffered imprisonment almost eighteen months, my goods, living, friends, and comfort, taken from me; the queen owing me by just account fourscore pounds or more. She hath put me in prison, and giveth nothing to find me; neither is there suffered any to come at me, whereby I might have relief. I am with a wicked man and woman, so that I see no remedy (saving God's help) but I shall be cast away in prison, before I can come to judgment. But I commit my just cause to God, whose will be done, whether it be by life or death.

JOHN HOPER.

LETTER XLIX.

A letter concerning the vain and false reports which were spread abroad of him, that he had recanted and abjured that doctrine which he before had preached.

The grace and peace of God be with all them that unfeignedly look for the coming of our Saviour Christ. Amen.

Dear brethren and sisters in our Lord, and my fellow-prisoners for the cause of God's gospel, I do rejoice and give thanks unto God for your constancy and perseverance in affliction, wishing and praying unto him for your continuance therein to the end. And as I do rejoice in your faithful and constant affliction that be in prison, even so do I mourn and lament to hear of our dear brethren abroad, that yet have not suffered nor felt such dangers for God's truth as we have, and do feel, and are like daily to suffer more, yea, the very extreme death of the fire: yet such is the report abroad (as I am credibly informed), that I, John Hooper, a condemned man for the cause of Christ, now after sentence of death (being in Newgate prisoner, looking daily for execution) should recant and abjure that heretofore I have preached. And this talk riseth of this, that the bishop of London and his chaplains resort unto me. Doubtless, if our brethren were as godly as I could wish them to be, they would think that, in case I did refuse to talk with them, they might have just occasion to say that I were unlearned, and durst not speak with learned men; or else proud, and disdainful to speak with them[1]. Therefore, to avoid just suspicion of both, I have and do daily speak with them when they come, not doubting but they will report that I am neither proud nor unlearned. And I would wish all men to do as I do in this point. For I fear not their arguments, neither is death terrible unto me. Wherefore I pray you to make true report of the same, as occasion shall serve; and also that I am more confirmed in the truth that heretofore I have preached by their communication. And ye that may, send to the weak brethren abroad, praying them that they trouble me not with such reports of recantation as they do. For I have hitherto left all things of this world, and suffered great pains and long imprisonment; and I thank God I am ready even as gladly to suffer death for the truth I have preached as a mortal man may be. O Lord, how slippery the love of man, yea, man himself, is! It were better for them to pray for us, rather than to credit or raise rumours that be untrue, unless they were more certain thereof than ever they shall be able to prove. We have enemies enough of such as know not God. Truly this report of weak brethren is a double trouble and a triple cross. I do wish you eternal salvation in Christ Jesu, and also require your continual prayer, that he which hath begun in us may save us to the end. I have taught this truth with my tongue and pen heretofore, and hereafter shortly will confirm by God's grace the same with my blood. Pray for me, gentle brethren, and have no mistrust.

From Newgate, 2d February.

Your brother,
JOHN HOPER.

[[1] The reading in Coverdale's work is "that I were unlearned, and disdained to speak," &c. The words as they stand in the text are taken from Foxe, (Acts and Mon. p. 1507. Ed. 1583,) and are preferred as giving a more complete sense. Foxe's version, Ed. 1559, is, "me vel ob inscitiam non audere, vel ob insolentiam dedignari, secum manus conserere."]

INDEX.

A.

AARON, had his end with the law, 30.
Abecedarius, a learner of ABCD.? 487.
Abel, killed by Cain for the love that God did bear him, 268; meaning of the word in English is "vanity," 281.
Abraham, promise of God to, that in his seed all the nations of the earth shall be blessed, 6; Christ took his flesh, 12; his faith accounted unto him for justice, 89; with all his obedience was infirm and imperfect without Christ, *ib.*; with constancy of faith would have killed his son, 219; how preserved by God in the matter of his wife Sarah, 296; consolation promised to all his children, but none received the commodity thereof but such as in spirit followed his faith, 325.
Absalom, prevailed not against his father David, but died the death of a traitor, 105; his use of lies, 269.
Absolution, not to be given but by consent of the church, and that with prayer, 51.
Adam, promise of God to, that the seed of a woman should break the serpent's head, spoken of Christ, 5; called his best son Abel, that is to say, vanity, 281; caused his sons to hear of his own fall in paradise, and the redemption of his fall in the blood of Christ to come, 325.
Afflicted, God's providence most comfortable to all, 216; their comfort when God seemeth to have forsaken them, 220; by the commandment of God taketh audacity to approach his mercy, 257; no comfort to the, but God alone, 323.
Africa, council of, 236, 237.
"Agnus," not to be said before the communion, 128.
Ahab, not contented with his kingdom, would take Naboth's vineyard, 303.
Ahitophel, treason of, 105; lies of, 270.

Air, its corruption the cause of pestilence, 160.
Alasco, John, reformer of Poland, Hooper's intimacy with, and letter to, *Biog. Notice*, ix. and note 3; encourages Hooper in the matter of vestments, xiv.
Alexander, thought himself strong enough by natural strength to conquer his enemies, 85.
Alexander II., pope, history of, written by Cardinal Benno, 240.
Alexander III., pope, rested not to move men to sedition until King Henry the Second was content to be under him, 240.
All Souls' day, injunction respecting, 147.
Altars, or tables, to be abolished, 128.
Ambrose, St, calls the sacrament *significationem*, 405; says, we are not to seek Christ upon the earth, in the earth, or according to the flesh, 483; *referred to*, 48, 564.
Anabaptists, Hooper's "Lesson of the Incarnation of Christ," written against them, 2; their errors noted, 42, 54, 78; a great trouble and unquietness of many commonwealths in Europe, 76; they think they be able to save themselves of, and by themselves, *ib.*; their doctrine very pernicious and damnable, 121.
Anniversaries, injunction respecting, 146.
Antichrist, tyranny of, in forbidding the word of God to be read, 44; a true mark and note to know by, 56, 512.
'Ἀντίτυπα, a word used for the sacrament by Basil and Theodoret, 406.
Antoninus, *referred to*, 233, 234.
Archbishops and metropolitans, when instituted and why, 237; not heads generally of the church, *ib.*
Arian heresy condemned, 73, 74.
Aristophanes, quotation from, 86.
Aristotle, calleth the magistrate a keeper

of the law, 86; his opinion of felicity, 299; of substances, 473.

Armour, the first works of a christian man called by St Paul, and why, 115.

Articles concerning christian religion, given by bp. Hooper, 120; ministered by bp. Hooper, to which William Phelps, pastor of Cirencester, subscribed, 152.

Articles, the Six, not to be maintained, 129.

Arundel, sir Thomas, receives Hooper into his house as steward, and sends him to Gardiner, bishop of Winchester, *Biog. Notice*, viii.

Asaph, appointed by David to be a musician, till the building of the temple at Jerusalem, 324.

Ashes, not to be maintained, 129.

Askew, A., martyr, 376.

Astronomy, calculation by, a great evil, 294.

Athanasius, bishop of Alexandria, creed of, 538.

Augustine, how he understood, *This is my body*, 48; *referred to*, 73; what he saith of the sacraments, 124; not ashamed to acknowledge his error, 154; his use of the word *pope*, 236; calls the sacrament *signaculum* and *signum*, 405; shews in what the power of the *word* consists, 407; admits no miracle in the sacrament of the eucharist, 410; says, *Panis hominem alit, &c.*, 424; says, *the bread is consumed in receiving the sacrament*, 425; on the bread and wine, 426; on the unity of the church, *ib.*; *sacramentum constat ex re visibili, &c.*, 427; on the interpretation of *signs*, 428; on the figurative meaning of the sacrament, 429, 471; calls the sacrament a commemorative sacrifice, 429; how he understood the words of the holy supper, 462, 495; says, the body of Christ is in one place, 488; in heaven, 489; calls Christ visible, corporeal, and local, 491; on the method of reading the scriptures, 493; of interpreting the scriptures, 494; *Judas non manducabat panem Dominum*, 497; on eating by faith, *ib.*, 498; says, not the death, but the cause maketh a martyr, 504; says, that Christ only could offer for the remission of sins, and no other thing than his own body, 505; says, the sacraments of the fathers were the same in signification as ours, 520; shews in what way the sacrament is called a sacrifice, 528, 529; shews who are heretics, 540; hath many godly sayings of cursing, 561; his saying about conscience, 574.

B.

Babington, warden of the Fleet, his cruel treatment of bp. Hooper and his servant Wm. Downton, 620, sq.

Baldwin, compels the Greek church to agree to the supremacy of Rome, 238.

Baptism, the sign of the new league between God and us made by Jesus Christ, and the mark of Christians, 46; ought to be given to children as well as those that be great, and once for all, *ib.*; is the entry of the church, a washing into a new birth, and a renewing of the Holy Ghost, *ib.*; ought to be ministered only in clean water, and in the name of the Father, Son, and Holy Ghost, 47; not so necessary to salvation that one may not be saved without it in case of necessity, *ib.*; little children which die without, are saved in the faith of their parents, *ib.*; Hooper's judgment of, 88, 9.

Barnes, Robert, martyr, 376.

Bartram, calls the sacrament a figure, 405.

Basil, in his Liturgy calls the sacraments ἀντίτυπα, 406; on the taking of the eucharist, 433; on the authority of scripture, 435, sqq.

Bead-rolls, prohibited, 129, 135, 142.

Becket, Thomas, the pope's martyr, 240.

"Behold," meaning of the word in the prophecy of Isaiah concerning the Virgin Mary, 8.

Bells, injunction respecting the ringing of, 136; interrogatory respecting, 146.

Belshazzar, allusion to, 266.

Benedicere, poculo, quid, 408; various meanings of, 469.

Benedict IX., pope, history of, written by cardinal Benno, 240.

Benno, cardinal, his history of the popes he saw, referred to, 240.

Berengarius, his opinions concerning the eucharist condemned as heretical by the second Roman council, 48, note 2.
Beresh turaia, "on the tops of the mountains," misinterpretation of by a Romanist, 474.
Bethsaida, admonished by Christ, 209.
Bethulia, people of, their fall stayed by the hands of a woman, 296, 7.
Bible, one to be provided in every church, 139, 142.
Bishops, called high priests in the primitive church, 237; no part of the office of, to be judges, 559.
Board, the Lord's, to be set up in the form of a table, 128.
Boniface I., could not obtain to have causes deferred to the see of Rome, 236.
Boniface III., bishop of Rome, obtained from the emperor Phocas the title of universal head of the church, 235, 555.
Bonner, Edmund, bp. of London, suspected by Hen. VIII. to be a favourer of the pope, 267; set an epistle before Gardiner's book *de Vera Obedientia*, 268, 557, 567.
Bradford, John, martyr, letter to him and others, 592.
Bread, interrogatory respecting the breaking of the, 145.
Bridges, sir Edmund, order for Hooper's execution sent to, *Biog. Notice*, xxvi.
Brutus, the treason of, 105.
Bucer, Martin, Hooper corresponds with on the sacraments, *Biog. Notice*, ix. letter to, from Hooper, xiv.
Bull, Henry, editor of bp. Hooper's Exposition upon Psalm xxiii. Apology, &c. 182, note 1; his preface to the Apology, 551.
Bullinger, Henry, Hooper's intimacy with, and high regard for him, *Biog. Notice*, ix. his Lectures diligently attended by Hooper, *ib*.; expresses his fears that Hooper would forget his former friends, ix. Hooper's prophetic words to him on leaving Zurich, x.
Buying or selling in the church, etc. during divine service, not to be permitted, 129, 142.

C.

Cain, killed his brother Abel for the love that God did bear him, 268.
Caius, nephew of Augustus, his contemning of God, the cause, says Orosius, of the great dearth and famine which happened to the Romans, 166.
Canaan, the woman of, her constancy and the effect of it, 259.
Candles, articles respecting, 127, 129.
Capernaites, Christ's promise to, that the meat he would give them should work eternal salvation, 191; their folly rebuked by Christ, 450.
Carthage, Scipio's lamentation over, 79; council of, 546.
Cassius, treason of, 105.
Catechism, to be read and taught unto the children every Sunday and festival-day in the year, 126; interrogatories respecting, 140, 144, 149.
Catiline, treason of, 105.
Cecil, sir Wm., letters to, from Hooper, *Biog. Notice*, xviii, xix.
Ceremonies of the church may be altered according to the diversity of time, and manner of countries, 123, 520.
Chalcedon, council of, 74, 237; confession of faith of, 535.
Chaldees, amongst the, such as most commended the idol of fire, most esteemed, 271.
Chandos, Lord, order for Hooper's execution sent to, *Biog. Notice*, xxvi.
Charity, description of, 111.
Charles the Great, 238.
Chest, or box for the poor, interrogatory respecting, 149.
Chorazin, admonished by Christ, 299.
Christ, his humanity took its beginning in and of the holy virgin by the operation of the Holy Ghost, 9; is, touching his humanity, of the same nature that his mother was of, of the seed of David, 13; a seed and fruit without sin, *ib*., 124, 454; tempted that he might succour such as were tempted, 12; very God and very man, 17, 27, 73, 130, 427, 454, seqq.; the fulness, end, and accomplishment of the law, 26; must be spiritually conceived in heart, and brought forth in our mouths

and actions, 28; the very King, Prophet, and great Sacrificer, 29; the sacrifice of, not Levitical or carnal, but spiritual, *ib.*; what is meant by his descending into hell, 30; the body and blood of, not given to the mouth and belly, 49, 451, 486, seqq.; the very body of, in heaven, 36, 49, 90, 153, 444, seqq.; the humanity of, in one place always at one time, 36, 130, 445, seqq.; only, the means of our salvation, 73; to put on, what is, 116; the oblation of, once made on the cross a full satisfaction for all manner of sins, 123, 500, seqq.; the two natures of, not to be confounded, 130; to eat and drink, in the holy sacrament, what, 153; only, the remedy of all sins and sickness, 171; hated and troubled more than any man before or since his time, 214; feared death, 225; slandered before he was born, and persecuted as soon as he was born, 261; his own kinsfolk raised against him, *ib.*; slain, *ib.*; they that will live in him must suffer persecution, 263; none to be compared to, 414; to be in, what, 432; in what way a means of salvation to us, 477.

Christian man, duty of a, contained in two parts, 99; subject to two troubles, 230; men, not expedient that, be delivered from the troubles of the world, *ib.*

Christians, the office of, not only to remove false doctrine, but also to cut off springing evils, 3; by the anointing of Christ we bear the name of, 29; who only are, 56; may use punishments of death, and bear weapon, 127.

Chrysostom, how he understood, *This is my body*, 48; says, he that feareth more hell than Christ, is worthy of hell, 253; calls the sacrament *significationem*, 405; shews in what the virtue of the gospel lies, 407; says, that Christ drank wine, and not water, after his resurrection to root out a certain pernicious heresy, 438; speaks figuratively of the sacrament, 499; on Heb. x. 513; says, that in the eucharist we make a commemoration of Christ's sacrifice, 530; on the use of unknown tongues, 548, 564.

Church, one only catholic and universal, the assembly of all faithful believers, 40, 120; invisible to the eye of man, 41; wherefore called universal, *ib.*; the field of the Lord God, *ib.*; not limited within certain bounds, *ib.*; the visible, the congregation of the good and of the wicked, *ib.*; like unto the ark of Noah, 42; why called militant, 43; three principal marks by which it may be known, *ib.*; the keys of the, given of God to the whole, 51; the unity of the Spirit, a sign of the true catholic, 52; two swords or powers in the, 53; the catholic, preserved from errors by the operation of the Holy Ghost, 74; what, and where the true is, declared by two marks, 87; no, absolutely perfect, *ib.*; bound to no sort of people, or any ordinary succession of bishops, etc. 90, 121; the true, of Christ, cannot err from the faith, the visible may, *ib.*; Christ's inheritance, 229; the primitive, near unto Christ in time, and like unto him in doctrine, 237; always one holy catholic, 519; furnished with one faith, *ib.*; never without its sacraments and sacrifices, 520.

Churches, to be cleared of all inclosures and partitions, 135.

Churchwardens, the duties of, 129, 134; to make their account every year, 142.

Cicero, quotations from, 66; gave counsel that Cæsar should be chief ruler of the people, 83; his counsel after reason and experience to rule the commonwealth many times took not good effect for lack of the wisdom of God, 85; invented aids to memory, 461.

Circumcision, the seal of the justice that came by faith, and not by works, 89. God's infallible truth and promises confirmed to Abraham by, and not Abraham's obedience, *ib.*

Cistercian order, at Gloucester, Hooper a member of, *Biog. Notice*, vii.

Clergy, Hooper's Letter to his, 118; result of the examination of the, of Gloucester, 151.

Clinke, the, a prison in London, Hooper committed to, *Biog. Notice*, xxiv, 181.

Clodovius, king of France, named the

bishop of Rome, as other bishops, a bishop, 237.
Collections for the poor, to be made in every parish-church, 127.
Collier's faith, the, to believe as the church believes, 543, note 1.
Commandments, the law of the, wherefore given, 26.
Communicants, to rehearse the ten commandments, the articles of the faith, and the confession, 132.
Communion, of saints, definition of, 42; of the body and blood of Christ, no man ought to receive the, for another, but every man for himself, 125, 133; the holy, no market of to be made, 128; the people to be moved to the often and worthy receiving of, 129; whether used as masses at a funeral, 146.
Confession, auricular, whether required of communicants, 146; the general, whether said openly, *ib.*; of sin, without faith, nothing worth, 350.
Conscience, the, admonished of sin, bringeth the body into a trembling and fear, 313; what ensueth after the fear of, for sin, *ib.*; no trouble to be compared with the trouble of the, 315; a peaceable, a precious jewel, 327; Augustine's saying of, 574.
Consolation, hidden by God for a time to try us, 337.
Constantine, punished blasphemers, 87; presided over the disputation with the Arians, 385.
Constantinople, council of, 74; archbishops of, called universal patriarchs, 234; the church of, equal with the church of Rome, 237; the creed of the church of, 534.
Contracts for matrimony, all secret, forbidden, 137, 149.
Contraries to be holpen by contraries, 169.
Conversion of the soul, what degrees and orders the Lord uses in, 204.
Corporal presence of Christ in the eucharist, proofs against, 443, seqq.
Corporas, the cloth covering the sacrifice on the altar, interrogatory respecting, 145, 146.
Corpus Juris Canonici, Decr. I. Pars. dist. 99. c. *Nullus.* 234; dist. 22. c.

3—6, 235; dist. 99. c. 3, *ib.*; dist. 50. c. *De eo tamen, Absit,* 237; dist. 59. c. *Si officio. ib.*; Decr. Greg. Lib. I. *De elect.* Tit. VI. c. 34, 238; Extravag. comm. Lib. I. *De Majorit. et obed.* c. 1, 239; Decr. I. Pars. dist. 96. c. 9. &c., *ib.*; Decret. Greg. Lib. III. Tit. 44. c. I., 418; Decr. III. Pars. *De consecr.* dist. 2. c. 48, 427, 8; c. 35, 430; c. 23, gloss upon, 484; c. 44, 488; Decret. Greg. Lib. I. Tit. I. c. *Firmiter,* 522.
Cranmer, abp. accuses Hooper before the council, *Biog. Notice,* xii; dispensation granted to him by the king to depart from the usual forms of consecration in Hooper's case, *ib.*; writes to Bucer for his advice in the matter of garments, xiii; letter of Hooper to, xv, xvi.
Crantzius Albertus, *referred to,* 239.
Creed, division of, 21; part one, belief in God the Father, 22; part two, in Jesus Christ his only Son, 27; part three, in the Holy Ghost, 39; part four, in the holy Catholic Church and the communion of saints, 40; part five, in the forgiveness of sins, 58; the doctrine of the, to be taught, 120; taken out of the word of God, *ib.*
Creeping to the cross, superstition of, forbidden, 129.
Cross, whether any, put secretly upon the dead body, 147; the sure badge of God's children, 214.
Crotone, Pliny saith the pestilence was never at, 168.
"Cup," taken in the scriptures for any thing that may happen to us, 229; taken many times for adversity, 338.
Curates, injunctions respecting, 143, 4, 147, 149.
Cyprian, understood *This is my body* figuratively, 48; suffered martyrdom under Valerian, 109; *de Simplic. prælatorum,* 236; called *pope, ib.*; testifies that the sacred bread, being burnt, was reduced to ashes, 415; on the wine in the eucharist, 421, seqq. 500; says, that the body of Christ is in heaven, 482; shews that the wicked do not partake of the body of Christ, 497; says, he feareth death that would not go to Christ, 566.

40—2

D.

Damasus, bp. creed of, 538.

David, promise of God to, that Christ should be born of his seed, 6, 7; his reign full of miseries, 81; prays to God as the only remedy against pestilence, 164; in what sense he uses the words "rod, staff, table, oil, and cup," 229; how constantly his soul waited upon the Lord, 247; his sin ever before him, 320; his prayer after the murder of Uriah, 358.

Days, difference of, the devilish doctrine of antichrist, 56.

Death, punishment of, lawful in certain offences, 127.

Defence, two doctrines noted by the word, one touching God, the other touching man, 262, 3.

Despair, an hard matter to eschew, in great conflicts of the mind, 346.

Devil, the, unbound, when, 48; fell into ruin by pride, 70; who be the people of, 71.

Discipline, a mark of the church, 43, 51; very necessary, *ib.*; the ordinance of Christ, and practised by the apostles, *ib.*

Disobedience, evils of, 109.

Downton, Wm., servant to bp. Hooper, 592, 597; how used by Babington, warden of the Fleet, 621.

Dumb dogs, who called, by the prophet, 357.

E.

Ears and eyes, made by God to be instruments to hear and see his will and pleasure, 329.

Easter-day, new order about the keeping of, begun by Pius I., 233.

Edward VI., king, altered the oath of supremacy, *Biog. Notice,* xii; epistle to, by Hooper, 66, &c.

Egyptians, amongst the, such as most blasphemously could speak in defence of witchcraft and sorcery were taken for the best men, 271.

Election, vessels of, 25.

Elijah the prophet, contentment of, in his need, 302.

Elizabeth, her address to the virgin Mary, 13.

Englishmen, the disobedience of, in Hooper's time, 86.

Enim, the word, added by the papists, in the text *Hoc est corpus meum,* 470.

Ephesus, council of, 74; a short confession of faith of, 534.

Epicureans, 82.

Epistle, whether the people sit at the, and stand at the gospel, 146.

Erasmus, paraphrases of, upon the new testament to be provided in every church, 139, 143; says, the title of high bishop of the world not known to the old church, 237.

Esau, the deception of, 272.

Eusebius Emissenus on the change of the elements, 430.

Eutyches, heresy of, condemned, 74.

"Ever," has two meanings in the Hebrew, 335.

Excommunication not to be given at the pleasure of some, but by consent of all the church, and the same to be done with prayer, 51, 52; a sword, a key, and a rod, *ib.*; against what persons, and for what offences to be exercised, *ib.*, 126.

F.

Fabian, martyred at Rome under Decius, 109, note 1.

Faith, justifying, a mere and singular gift of God, the mother, spring, and root of all good works, 59, 262; once sealed in the heart, breaketh forth by confession, 218, 571; cannot be without the fruit of well-doing, *ib.*; the gift of, a treasure incomparable, 219; maketh the heart to feel the joys and mirth unspeakable, 220; in God only to appoint when and how it shall be given, *ib.*; at all times hath not like strength in man, 221, 222, 248; weakness of, no cause for despair, *ib.*; in Christ, bringeth tranquillity of conscience, 300; what it comprehends and applies to us of Christ, 477; of the church, the, one and the same in all ages, 519; made known by God in different ways at different periods, *ib.*

Faithful, the monuments and volumes of the, to be reverenced, 180; the sins of the, when they fall, not imputed unto them for Christ's sake, 274.

Fear, two sorts of, 107.

"Feed," used in scripture in many significations, 197.

Feet, in Psalm LXXIII, what is meant by the, 297.

Felicity, difference of opinion wherein it consisted, 299; consisteth in knowledge and working of God's will, 300; of this world, none otherwise good than it standeth with the favour of God, 618.

Ferrar, bp., letter of Hooper to, and others, 592.

Flagelliferi, sect of the, 76.

Flesh, no, can be tempted but man's, 12; and blood, men not to put their trust in, 278.

Forth-fares or knells, not to be rung for the death of any man, 137.

"Fruit of the belly," in scripture what taken for, 7.

Fryth, John, martyr, 376.

G.

Galen, on the causes of pestilence, 160, seqq.; saith, "To fly the air that is infected is best," 167; on contraries, 169.

Games, whether the ministers use any unlawful, 145.

Gaming in the church, &c. not to be permitted, 129.

Gardiner, bishop of Winchester, confers with Hooper, *Biog. Notice*, viii; challenged Hooper to dispute, xi; insulted Hooper before the council, xxii; examines, and condemns Hooper, *ib.*, seqq.; his book *De Vera Obedientia*, 268, 557, 559, 567; called the reformed religion a doctrine of desperation, 376, 377, 592; called God's enemy, 621.

Garments, difference of, a doctrine of antichrist, 56.

Gelasius, on the bread and wine in the sacrament, 425.

God, one in essence and substance, three in person, 22, 70, 71, 120; the author of life and salvation, 71; we must judge of, as we be taught in his word, *ib.*; how we may be delivered from his great ire, 99; we should call only upon, 100; the nature of, opened and disclosed by the name of a shepherd, 190, 191; the assurance of his defence and comfort must be learned out of his word, 193; a master and teacher, *ib.*; may be served in every kind of living, 194; what it is to be the sheep of, 195; his tuition of us here and in the life to come, compared, 196, 263, 264; how his voice and teaching doth heal the minds of the sheep, 196; why the preachers of, are contemned of the world, 202; he alone converteth man from evil, and keepeth him in goodness and virtue, 208; humility most acceptable to, 213; exerciseth his sheep in dangers and troubles, 214, 265, 587; the troubles of his sheep known and appointed by him, 215, 581; all troubles come by the providence of, 217; will not despise a troubled and broken heart, 218; he that hath his love and fear sealed in his heart liveth an angelical life, 219; nothing but the grace and presence of, able to defend his people, 224; help not to be asked or sought any where, saving of, *ib.*, 256, 349; punisheth his elect, 225; the friendship and familiarity of, towards his sheep, 227; will never permit his to be deadly and mortally wounded, 230; when doth the soul of man wait upon, or have silence towards, 247; able and willing to save, 255, 259; commandeth us to call unto him for help, 256; of himself is inclined to have mercy, *ib.*; the afflicted by his commandment taketh audacity to approach his mercy, 257; called by the psalmist his rock, 260; salvation to all that by faith believe in him, 262; his favour in this world annexed with troubles, 265, 587; leaveth desperation to his enemies, 265; the presence of his favour towards his, the destruction of the wicked, 266; laugheth the intent of the wicked to scorn, 269; no health but in, 275; wrong done unto, what, 280; although he scourge us, yet he loveth us, 292, 363; doth not punish without just cause, 292, 369; two impediments keep, from helping the troubled, 311; his nature and man's differ much, 315;

loveth and helpeth the poor afflicted, 316; hateth not the troubled man for his trouble, but for his sin, 317; nothing can quiet the comfortless spirit but, 323; the remembrance of his justice for sin greater pain than the death of the body, 335; hideth his consolation for a time to try us, 337; two manner of mercies of, 343; salvation only of, 348; none can pardon sin but, 351; the doer of wonders, 360; to whom he is merciful, and to whom severe, 362; worketh his will, and useth his creatures, as it seemeth to his wisdom most meet, 365; no creature disobeyeth, but the devil and man, 366; drieth up the seas of mistrust and heaviness out of the soul, 368; always preserveth penitent sinners, 369; careful of his afflicted faithful, 370; they that do things at his commandment can take no harm, 371; cannot away with any hypocrisy, 573; both body and soul be debtors unto, 574; delivereth wicked men up unto their own lusts, 579; the pains of the world be the servants of, 585; we may not murmur against, *ib.*

"God forbid that I should glory," &c., explanation of Paul's words, 279.

Gospel, the, preached by Jesus Christ in Judea and Galilee three years or thereabout, 30; the reading of the, ought not to be forbidden from any manner of persons, 44; cannot be too much opened unto the people, 80; only the, openeth unto us our salvation, 114.

Gratian, decree of, concerning the catholic faith, 540.

Greek church, why the, separated herself from the church of Rome, 232; compelled to acknowledge the supremacy of Rome, 238.

Gregory the Great, would not take the archbishop of Constantinople for the universal head of the church, 234; said that his arrogancy was a token that the time of antichrist drew nigh, *ib.*, 546; suffered great danger by the Lombards, 234; on the words, *Non est hic*, 492; what he says of those who concur in the expression of *universal bishop*, 546.

Gregory VI. his history written by cardinal Benno, 240.

Gregory VII. translated the empire into Germany, 236; took upon him to have authority to use two swords, 239; stirred up Radulphus, duke of Suevia, against the emperor, *ib.*; Benno the cardinal writeth horrible things of, 240.

Greis, to be taken away, 135.

H.

Hales, judge, wounded himself, 377, 378; conformed to the Romish faith, *ib.*; troubled in conscience, *ib.*, 612; strongly passed imprisonment, 379.

Hallowing of the fire or altar, forbidden by Hooper, 129.

Hall, John, Hooper's letter to, 597.

Harmogenes, fable of, 86.

Heaven, we must enter into, by many troubles, 337; the flesh of Christ in, 444, seqq.

Heavenly joys, description of, 264.

Hell, what is meant by Christ's descending into, 30.

Henry II., king, content to be under pope Alexander III., 240.

Henry IV., emperor, compelled by the bishop of Rome to make war 62 times in his life, 239.

Henry V., emperor, constrained to surrender his authority to pope Paschal II., 238.

Henry VII., emperor, poisoned by a monk that poisoned the idol of the mass, 240.

Heresies, should be punished, 87.

Hermes, induces Pius I. to alter the keeping of Easter-day, 233.

Hezekiah, king, prayed to God in his sickness, 164.

"Hidden of God," the godly and virtuous called in scripture the, 307.

Hippocrates, 164.

Historia Tripartita *Cassiodori*, 292, 533, 539, 540.

Holy bread, not to be maintained, 129.

Holy Ghost, a divine person, distinct from the Father and the Son, 39; no other vicar of Christ upon earth within the church than the, *ib.*; the pledge and earnest of our heavenly heritage, *ib.*; the finger of God, *ib.*; dwelling in us regenerates us, works in us all good works, *ib.*; the teacher of the ignorant, and comforter of the poor, 40; the spirit of life, which quickeneth all other spirits, *ib.*; the gifts and graces of, given to every member of the church, and to what end, 41; by his virtue, strength, and operation, the catholic church preserved from all errors, 74.

Homer saith that the gods appointeth their shields to defend princes, 85.

Homilies to be read every Sunday and holy-day, 128.

Hooper, bp., his birth, *Biog. Notice*, vii; graduated at Oxford, and embraced monastic life, *ib.*; his attention first drawn to religion by the perusal of writings of Zuinglius and Bullinger, *ib.*; returned to Oxford, *ib.*; compelled to retire on account of his attachment to the Reformation, viii; becomes steward to sir Thomas Arundel, *ib.*; his conference with Gardiner, *ib.*; escapes to Paris, *ib.*; escapes to Germany, *ib.*; his marriage, ix; his perilous journey to England, *ib.*; settles at Zurich, *ib.*; intimate with Bullinger and others, *ib.*; takes leave of his friends at Zurich, *ib.*; his prophetic words to Bullinger, x; returns to England, *ib.*; appointed chaplain to the duke of Somerset, *ib.*; his preaching and influence, *ib.*; severity of manners, *ib.*; becomes involved in controversy, xi; accuses Bonner, *ib.*; challenged by Gardiner to dispute, *ib.*; defended by Underhill, *ib.*; esteemed and employed by the king, xii; appointed to preach before the court, *ib.*; attacks the book of Ordination, *ib.*; refuses the bishoprick of Gloucester, *ib.*; favoured by the council, *ib.*; disputes with Ridley, xiii; preaches and speaks against the vestments, *ib.*; writes to Bucer and Peter Martyr, xiv; cautioned by Martyr against his bitter sermons, *ib.*; forbidden by the council to preach, xv; disobeying, is consigned to the archbishop's custody, *ib.*; committed to the Fleet, *ib.*; submits, *ib.*; his letter to the archbishop, *ib.*; is consecrated, and visits his diocese, xvi; attacked by the sweating sickness, xvii, 159; appointed bishop of Worcester, xvii;

visits his new diocese, *ib.*; his letters to sir William Cecil, xviii, xix; his controversy with Joliffe and Johnson, xix; his character by Foxe, xxi; his impartiality, *ib.*; his hospitality, *ib.*; supported the claims of queen Mary, xxii, 556, 7; summoned before the council, insulted by Gardiner, and committed to the Fleet, xxii; deprived of his bishoprick, *ib.*; wrote to Ferrar and others respecting the disputation, *ib.*, 592; his writings in prison, xxiii; brought before Gardiner, *ib.*; sent to the Counter, xxiv; condemned for heresy, and sent to Newgate, *ib.*; degraded by Bonner, *ib.*; his journey to Gloucester, *ib.*; his interviews with sir Anthony Kingston and others, xxv; his speech to the mayor, xxvi; the order for his execution, *ib.*; his prayer, xxviii; his execution, x, xix; his words at his death, *ib.*; lines written by him with a coal on the wall of the New Inn at Gloucester, xxx; why he wrote the confession and protestation of his faith, 67, 68; many false and erroneous opinions of, *ib.*, 74; his reasons for writing on Romans xiii, 96; his letter to his clergy, 118; his object in collecting the Articles, 119; his articles, 120; his injunctions, 130; his interrogatories of the people, 140; of the ministers, 143; examination of clergy, 150; his articles ministered to William Phelps, 152; his object in writing the homily for the time of pestilence, and order of writing, 160; abridgement of his life, 181; his object in writing upon Psalm xxiii, 186; why he wrote of judge Hales, 377; desired a better version of the Bible, 393; his reasons for writing his treatise on the Lord's Supper, 400; why he wrote the treatise *De Falsa Religione* in Latin, 544.

Hooper, Anne, wife of the bishop, escapes with her children to Frankfort, *Biog. Notice*, xxii; Hooper's letter to, 578.

Horace, quotation from, 84, 487.

I.

Idolatry, that which is done to the honouring of God contrary to his word

and commandment, 56; the invention of images the beginning of, 57.
Idols, number of, set up in queen Mary's time, 316.
Ignorance, much trouble and danger arising from, 78; a cause of evil, 173; horrible blasphemy is sprung of, 311; the remedy against, 312.
Images, the beginning of idolatry, snares and traps for the feet, 57; not to be honoured or worshipped, or suffered in churches, *ib.*, 58; article against, 121, 129; interrogatory of, 143.
Impatience, the, of the mind, many ways known, 249.
Imposition, of hands, not to be called a sacrament, 127.
Infidelity, the fountain and root of all wickedness, 59; ignorance or misunderstanding of God's word the cause of, 173; a cause of evil, *ib.*
Infidels, all the sins of, not pardoned, because of their infidelity, 60.
Iniquity, profane writers declare with the age of the world to increase, 83.
Injunctions given by bp. Hooper, 130, sqq.
Injuries, two ways of doing, to the souls of men, 67.
Innocent III., pope, introduced transubstantiation, &c., 48, 522; compelled king John to pay tribute to him, *ib.*
Intercessor, none other than Jesus Christ, 34.
Interpretis, officium, quid, 468.
Interrogatories of bp. Hooper, 140, 143.
Irenæus, 48; prevented Victor I. from excommunicating the Greek church, 233; on the bread and wine in the eucharist, 419, 420; on sacrifices, 523, 527; ratio fidei ex, 537.
Isidore, 535, 536.

J.

Jacob, promise of the seed made unto, 6.
Jason, fable of, 603.
Jehoiachin, taken prisoner by Nebuchadnezzar, 102.
Jenins, William, dean of Gloucester, Hooper's Epistle to, and others, 95.
Jerome, *Catal. Script. Eccles.*, 109; on the equality of bishops, 236; on the name *pope*, *ib.*; calls the sacrament *repræsentationem*, 405, 472; on the bread and wine, 431, 432, 439; on the flesh and blood of Christ, 486; says, that the wicked do not eat the flesh of Jesus, &c., 498; the creed of Damasus extracted from, 538.
Jesse, the virgin Mary a branch of the stock of, 8.
Jews, the, use their books of religion in their churches in the vulgar tongue, 207; adhere to the Talmud, 393.
Job, waited upon the Lord, 247.
John, bishop of Constantinople, created himself the universal head of the church, 234, 546; the forerunner of antichrist, *ib.*; king of England, compelled to pay tribute to Innocent III., 522.
Johnson, Robert, canon of Worcester, refused to subscribe Hooper's articles, *Biog. Notice*, xix.
Joliffe, Henry, canon of Worcester, refused to subscribe Hooper's articles, *Biog. Notice*, xix; published an account of his controversy, xx.
Jonah, the prophet, his being in the whale's belly a type of Christ's being laid in the sepulchre, 32.
Josias, king, defended by God in his tender age, 102; set forth the word of God to the people, 388.
Judas, with contemning Christ's admonitions, died in horrible despair, 324, 350.
Judgment, the, shall be general, 36; of great consolation to the good, 38.
Judith, her fall stayed by the Lord, 296.
Julian, emperor, caused the priests of the pagans to order their lives according to the example of the christian priests, 119; fought against the people of God, 231; saying of, when he received his death-wound, 292.
Justification, of man, comes only by the faith of Christ, 121.
Justin Martyr, on the conversion of the elements in the eucharist, 420.

K.

Keys of the church, the power to bind and loose, given of God to the whole church, 51.
King, the, is bound to be obedient unto the law, 101; of England, the only

and supreme magistrate of the church of England, 127.

Kings, cannot give any part of their dignity to any one, 546, 559; suffer wrong where the pope hath supremacy, *ib.*

Kingston, sir Anthony, cited by Hooper for immorality, and rebuked by him, *Biog. Notice*, xxi ; his interview with Hooper before his execution, xxv; order for Hooper's execution addressed to him and others, xxvi.

Kissing vestments, book, chalice, &c., interrogatory respecting, 145.

Knells, not to be rung for the death of any man, 137.

Knowledge, no burden, but to put it in experience body and soul shall find pain and trouble, 347.

Korah, consumed by fire whilst offering incense, 321.

L.

Lascelles, Jos., martyr, 376.
Lateran, council of, 48, 522.
Latimer, Hugh, treatment of, 401, 593.
Latin language, why used by the papists, 392.
Law, the, called a schoolmaster to come to Christ, 26; the offices of, *ib.*; Christ the fulness, end, and accomplishment of, *ib.*; accomplished through faith, and not through works, 27; buried with Christ, as touching the faithful, 33; the civil, must not repugn the law of God, 77; of God, the nature and property of, 205.
Laws, the form and manner of, not like in all places, 77; the very work of God, 81.
"Lead," word how used by David, 198.
Leo IX., 48, 240.
Lies, three manner of ways do harm, 270; use of amongst the faithless, 271.
Limbos of the fathers, &c., rejected as fables, 31.
Locris, Pliny saith pestilence was never at, 168.
Lombardus, Petrus, calls the eucharist a memory and representation of a true sacrifice, 530.
Love, christian, description of, 112.
Lucilius, poet, saying of, 544.

Lydia, the Lord opened the heart of, 201.

M.

"Made," hath in the scriptures two significations, 15.
Magistrate, the, an ordinance of God, 53, 85, 86, 103, 104; obedience to be paid not only to the faithful, but also to the infidel and wicked tyrant, 54, 80, 102, 104 ; it doth appertain to the, to have regard to ecclesiastical matters, 54 ; representeth the person of a great Lord, *ib.*; may minister an oath unto the faithful, *ib.*; God is in the, 85; called φύλαξ νόμου, 86 ; should use the law indifferently, *ib.*; should defend the two testaments as his own life, 87 ; the laws of a, be of two sorts, 102; God will revenge the abuse of his office in, 104; must not wax arrogant and proud, 106, 107 ; instituted and appointed by God for the wealth and commodity of the subject, *ib.*; his punishment is the very hand and will of God, 108; is a murderer if he kill any man that is not worthy by the law to die, *ib.*; the will of God sometimes made known by the aid of the, 388; appealed to, in support of God's word, *ib.*; not to be flattered, 564.
Magistrates, the keepers of discipline and peace, 81 ; not only ordained, but also preserved by God, 83; obedience due to, 101; we must not strive nor fight with the, 102, 104; damnable iniquity for any man to depose the, 104 ; the civil, every man ought to give obedience unto, 127.
Man, formed by the Lord, to what end, 24; the first, through the craft and subtlety of Satan did fall from his excellency, *ib.*, 71; nothing in, that might allure or provoke him to the help of his salvation, 72; the nature of, to go astray, 191; to feed on unwholesome and infected pastures, 192; what he is of himself, and how he is brought to feed in the pastures of God's word, shewn, 204, seqq.
Manichee, heresy of, of two gods, 74; against the magistrates, 76, 78.

Marcion, heresy of, 73, 74, 76, 78.
Mardocheus, made suit for the life of the Jews, 297.
Markets, injunction respecting, 136, 7; interrogatory of, 142.
Marriage, an honourable estate amongst all men, 55; the forbidding of, for certain persons the devilish doctrine of antichrist, *ib.*, 56; of priests, bishops, and other ministers not to be judged unlawful, 126.
Mary Magdalene, why persuaded to implore Christ's mercy, 259.
Mass, the popish, the invention and ordinance of man, a sacrifice of antichrist; and ought to be abolished, 32; is not, neither can be, the holy supper of the Lord, and why, 50, 51, 394, 413; a mere enemy against God's word, and Christ's institution, 126; not to be counterfeited in the communion, 127; defenders of, transgress the commandments of God for traditions of men, 390; the blindness of papists in celebrating, 392; contains an idol, 395, 518; not a sacrament of Christ, but an idol, 451; comparison between the, and Christ's institution of the Lord's supper, 465, seqq.; *contra sacrificium missæ*, 500; the Roman, sacrilegious, 508; difference between the sacrifice of Christ on the cross, and that of the priests in the, 509; the sacrifice of the, invalidates the sacrifice of Christ, 513; cannot be propitiatory, 517; the body of Christ in the ideal, 518; the wicked idol, the, stablished again, 589; at the, an idol honoured for God, 610.
Matrimony, banns of, to be three times openly proclaimed in the parish-church, 126; persons contracted in, to be compelled with all convenient speed to marry, 138.
Maurice, emperor, made the Lombards to besiege Rome, 234; murdered by Phocas, 235, 555; saying of, when his wife and children were killed before his face, 293.
Meats, the forbidding of certain, the devilish doctrine of antichrist, 56.
Mediator betwixt God and man, none other than Jesus Christ, 34.
Memory, natural, artificial, and spiritual, 461; all the kinds of, employed upon the substance of things absent, *ib.*
Mercies of God, two manner of, mentioned in the scripture, 343.
Metonomia, a figurative manner of speech common in the scriptures, 48.
Micronius, encouraged Hooper in his opposition to the vestments, *Biog. Notice*, xiv; wrote to Bullinger of Hooper's severity, xxi.
Midwives, interrogatory of, 141.
Ministers, no better than records and testimonies, and servants of God's word and sacraments, 91; should not be only reverenced of the people, but also honoured by the magistrates, *ib.*; the charge of, the greatest of all charges and vocations, 118; two ways of providing for the fitness of, *ib.*; must be lawfully called and sent, 123; the malice of, cannot hurt the doctrine, verity, and majesty of God's word and sacraments, 125; office of, especially in time of pestilence, 174; such as do nothing but as God commandeth, to be followed, 371.
Miracles, now no more need of new, 45; of antichrist, the false, wrought by the working of Satan, and why suffered, *ib.*; none in the sacrament of the eucharist, 410; what is a, 411.
Month-ends, not to be kept, 146.

N.

Nathan, the prophet, makes David afraid for the murder of Uriah, &c. 358.
Nativity, our, of itself altogether unclean and defiled with sin, purified and made holy by Christ's, 28.
Nature, corruption of, in all men generally, 24, 25; in man now consumed, effeminated, and worn out, 83.
Nebuchadnezzar, in wealth and riches envied the living God, and came to bestiality, 303.
Nero, St Paul submitted unto, 80, 102.
Nestorius, heresy of, condemned, 74.
Nice, council of, 74, 233, 234, 235, 236, 237; canon of, respecting the communion, 395.
Nicene creed, 120, 533.
Nicodemes, can speak of Christ in the night, but openly they will confess nothing, 357.

Nicodemus, dialogue between, and Christ, 171.
Night, in Romans, ch. xiii. called the time of false doctrine, 114.

O.

Oath, how to be used by the faithful, 55.
Oaths, the use of, the ordinance of the Lord, 54; the faithful may holily and justly use, in matters of controversy, *ib.*, 124; made contrary to God's word, may be broken, 55; all vain and unadvised, forbidden, 124; dispensed with by the pope, 240.
Oil, whether reverenced at the anointing of the sick, 147; what meant by, in the scriptures, 228, 9.
Opus operatum, inefficacy of, in the sacraments, 125.
Ordination, book of, attacked by Hooper, *Biog. Notice*, xii.
Origen, in the time of, the remains of the elements burned, 417; says, that the bread profits not, but the word spoken over it, 421; to be interpreted figuratively, 499.
Orosius, *referred to*, 79; says, the dearth and famine in the time of Augustus was because Caius refused to honour God, 166.

P.

Pallas defended Achilles, 85.
Palms, not to be maintained, 129.
Para, earth of, said to cure all wounds, 164.
Pardons, the doctrine of, against the commandments of God, 121; whether any, buried with the dead body, 147.
Participation, only of such things as is common between them that be partakers of one thing, 11.
Paschal, not to be maintained, 129.
Paschal II., pope, constrained the emperor, Henry V., to surrender his authority to him, 238.
Passur, the false prophet, advanced by the people, 269.
Pastor, what is the office of, when he understands the scriptures, 277.
Pasture, used for the word of God, 198.
Paulus Diaconus, *referred to*, 235.

Pelagian, the, worthily called "the enemy of grace," 73.
Pelagius II., bp. of Rome, would not have the name of general bishop, 234, 546.
Penitent sinners, God always preserveth, 369.
Pestilence, the causes of, 161, 165; nature and condition of, remarks on, 163; God the only remedy for, 165; an extraordinary magistrate to reform and punish sin, 166; sundry occasions of, *ib.*, 167; the scripture sheweth the only remedy against, 168; who may not flee from, *ib.*; the best preservative from, 169; Christ's medicine for, 170, 173.
Peter, bp. of Alexandria, 539, 40.
Peter, St., his denial of Christ, 348; doubtful whether he was ever at Rome, 545, 560; Christ gave no superiority to, over the other apostles, *ib.*; who are successors of, 546.
Pfaffus, a contemptuous term for priest, 413, note.
Pharisees, amongst the, he that could most speak for the maintenance of men's traditions was taken for the worthiest man, 271; felt not the consolation that the scripture did testify of Christ, 325; though they had the clearness of Christ's coming, yet did they put him to death, 331; saw the day of Messiah's birth, and were sad, 477.
Phelps, William, pastor of Cirencester, articles subscribed by, 152, seqq.
Phocas, murderer of his master Mauricius, judged Boniface III. to be head of the church, 235, 555.
Pius I., began a new order about the keeping of Easter-day, 233.
Platina, 233, 234, 235, 240.
Plato, quotation from, respecting order and policy, 84, 85.
Plinius Secundus, *referred to*, 164; saith, that pestilence was never at Locris and Crotone, 168; wrote to Trajan about the Christians, 615.
Policy, civil, see Magistrate.
Pope, a general name for all bishops, 236; the beginning and proceedings of the, of the devil, 238; to be killed with the staff of God's word, *ib.*, 240; the making of the, in the emperor's

authority, 238; saith that he can dispense and absolve from oaths, 240; the first-born of antichrist, 396, 465; John shews the power of, to be derived from the bottomless pit, 546; has no jurisdiction in England, 547; wheresoever the, hath supremacy, Christ is dishonoured, 559; an excommunicate person, 560.

Portesse, 86.

Power, the higher, every man should be obedient unto, 101; ecclesiastical laws cannot exempt any person from obedience to, *ib.*; not to be obeyed, if they command things contrary to the law of God, 102, 103, 109; not to be resisted, 103; many great and weighty causes wherefore they should be obeyed, *ib.*, seqq.; who should fear the, 108; tribute, a note of obedience, wherefore paid to, 109, 110.

Prayer, common, articles and injunctions respecting, 128, 130, 131, 136; continuance in, two things to be learnt of, 317; to be used, by God's laws, in the vulgar tongue, 555, 564; one of the excellentest works required of christian men, 615.

Prayers for the dead, against the commandments of God, 121.

Preachers of God, why contemned of the world, 202.

Preaching and prayers daily, utility of, 80; every Sunday and festival-day, article respecting, 129.

Primers, not to be maintained, 129.

Prodigal son, the parable of the, 253, 257; what caused the, to resort unto his father in the time of misery, 259.

Profession, wherein doth our, consist, 357.

Professors of the gospel, the cause why there be so few sincere and true, 217.

Psalms, the expositions of, written in the time of bishop Hooper's trouble, 182.

Ptolemy Lathure, the cruel treatment of the Jews by, 82.

Purgatory, a folly found out by man, 31; no other than the blood of Jesus Christ, 32; the doctrine of, against God's commandments, 121.

"Put on," what meant by in Romans, ch. xiii. 116.

R.

Radulphus, duke of Suevia, stirred up by Gregory VII. to war against his brother-in-law, 239.

Ravenna, the bishop of, began amongst the Latins to prepare the way to antichrist, 235.

Reason, at the beginning men obeyed and were ruled by, 82; how men descended from the regiment of, 83; until amended and removed from her natural blindness, can do none other than condemn God and his people, 307.

Relics, not to be maintained, 129; interrogatory of, 143.

Religion, exercise and diligence bringeth credit unto, 80; in matters of, manifest lies do take place, 271.

Remission of sins, exhibited and given in the holy church, 60.

Repentance, hath two parts, 60; is the return of the sinner from sin into a new life in Christ, 174; the medicine of, consisteth of five parts, *ib.*

Resurrection, the general, description of, 61; of the flesh, and not of the spirit, *ib.*; the second, what, *ib.*

Riches, why given unto man, 281.

Ridley, Nicholas, desired to discuss the matter of vestments with Hooper, *Biog. Notice*, xii; offers under certain conditions to admit Hooper as bishop, xiii; reconciled to Hooper in time of persecution, xvi; treatment of, by the Romanists, 401, 593.

Righteousness, what it is to believe unto, 218.

Rod, what is understood by, in the scripture, 225.

Rogers, John, degraded by Bonner together with Hooper, *Biog. Notice*, xxiv.

Rome, civil wars and contentions of, 78; the empire of, brought to nought by the Goths, Vandals, &c., *ib.*; the bishop of, hath not any manner of authority, power, or jurisdiction within this realm of England and Ireland, 127, 547; his authority the trouble of all christian souls, 232; oath against, *ib.*, 397, 566; why the Greek church separated herself from the church of, *ib.*; the bishop of, declared by Phocas

INDEX. 637

universal head of the church, 235; the bishops of, always subject to and made by the emperors, 236, 238; the Greek church subdued to the church of, 238; the bishop of, transferred the empire into France, 238; an idol exempt from all order and obedience, *ib.*; the bishops of, made themselves heads of emperors and kings, 239; and judges of God and his word, 442; the church of, neither a judge nor a witness of the word of God, 467, 468; too catholic, 532; doubtful whether St Peter was ever at, 545; the see of, the very whore of Babylon, 554; no truth where the bishop of, is chief head, 559; St Peter said to be bishop of, 560; England cursed by the antichrist of, 567.

Rubrics, not to be maintained, 129.

Rule, the great benefit of God, and to be taught to the people, 82.

S.

Sacrament, of the supper, by the, we are indeed made partakers of the body and blood of Jesus Christ, 47; ought to be given and ministered to all under both the kinds, *ib.*; the bread and wine not transubstantiated in the, 48, 122, 402, seqq.; consisteth in the use thereof, 48; containeth two things, 49; in the, no manner of corporal or local presence of Christ in, under, or with the bread and wine, 122, 153, 155, 443; how borne at the visitation of the sick, 147; in the, the very substance of bread and wine remain after the words of consecration, 152, 155, 402, seqq.; the use of the bread and wine in the, be changed, and not the substance, 152, 394, 408, 460, 469, 531; no miracle in the, 410; how far bread, and how far the body of Christ, 441; of the death of Christ, the, why called a sacrifice, 532.

Sacraments, the, signs and marks of God's church, 43, 88; definition of, 45; in number only two, *ib.*, 88, 127; not void and empty signs, but exhibit and give the thing that they signify, *ib.*; the fathers used the same in figure that we use in truth, 50, 88, 520; be called the confirmations or seals of God's promises, 88; visible signs of invisible grace, *ib.*; not confirmations of our obedience towards God hereafter, 89; in what way necessary, and in what way not necessary, 122; easy to be kept, and most august and excellent, 124; instituted of Christ to be used, and not to be gazed upon, *ib.*; certain impressions or prints of the grace or good will of God towards us, 125; not of any force by virtue of any outward work of the same, 125, 406; ought not to be kept nor worshipped, 125; no man ought to invent more, 127; called by various names by the fathers, 405, seqq.; how the, are sanctified, 406; not to be too much extolled, or too much depressed, 441; aids to the spiritual memory, 462; all, assume the names of those things of which they are sacraments, 495, 531.

Sacrifice, propitiatory, none other than that of Christ's body, 32, 123, 500, seqq.; *missæ, contra,* 500; of Christ, the, once offered, 501, seqq.; ἀπαράβατον, *ib.*; the fruit of, our salvation, 502; propitiatory, must not only be pure, but also be offered by one free from sin, 503, 506; none without shedding of blood, 508, 509, 516; no true, under the law of Moses, 511; definition of, 516; what kind of, is the death of martyrs, 517; different kinds of, 521, seqq.; God is not appeased by human, 527; in what sense the eucharist is called a, 528, 529.

Sacring bell, not to be rung, 128.

Saints, the blessed, to be had in honour, 35; communion of, what meant by the, 42; the invocation of, injurious to the honour of Christ, 121; the image or picture of, not to be painted in church-windows, 138.

Samosatenes, heresy of, condemned, 74.

Sarah, wife of Abraham, how preserved by God, 296.

Scipio, saying of, upon the burning of Carthage, 79.

Scriptures, the holy, to be diligently read and studied by the clergy, 129.

Sea, the creation and uses of the, 365.

Seage or seat, to be allowed in churches, 135.

Sedition, the preaching and teaching of God's word the chief remedy against, 79.
"Seed of a woman," what taken for in scripture, 5.
Selah, the use of the word by the Jews, 327.
Sennacherib, allusions to, 231, 266.
Sentlow, Mr, Hooper resides in the house of, *Biog. Notice*, viii.
Sepulch, not to be maintained, 129.
Servants, commanded by St Peter to obey their masters, though they be evil, 81.
Service, of God, in what the pure and true consists, 56; without God's word, &c., idolatry, *ib.*; interrogatories respecting the, 141, 142, 145.
Sidon, city of, allusion to, by Christ, 209.
Silvester III., pope, history of, written by cardinal Benno, 240.
Simony, in all kinds of ministers condemned, 123, 148.
Sin, original, how incurred, 24; the fountain and root of all other sins, 25; God hath wrapped all under, 58; whence cometh the knowledge of, and whence the forgiveness, *ib.*; none but God can forgive, 60; shall not be laid to the charge of the saints, *ib.*; one only irremissible, which is unbelief, 61; the devil and Adam's will wrought, 72; of believers, forgiven without the merits and deservings of Adam's posterity, *ib.*; doth remain in every man, although he be regenerate, 122; the oblation of Christ a full satisfaction for all manner of, 123; the cause of pestilence and all other diseases, 160, 165, 167, 172, 173; to feel and bewail, the work of God's Spirit, 217; how, should be felt, 218; what it bringeth a man unto, 230; fear and terror of, an intolerable burden, 313; the cause of all trouble, 323; the knowledge and confession of our, very necessary, 349; confession of, without faith, nothing worth, 350; unto death, the, not to be prayed for, 560.
Sleep, what St Paul calleth, and what to wake out of, 113.
Sleepers, the fond opinion of the, 63.
Smith, Dr, maligner of Hooper, bears testimony to his influence over the people, *Biog. Notice*, x.

Staff, in scripture, taken for strength power, and dominion, 226.
Strasburgh, Hooper sojourns at, *Biog. Notice*, viii.
Substance, not changed, without change of accidents, 409.
Sudary, explanation of the word, 128, note 1.
Supper of the Lord, not a sacrifice, but only a remembrance of Christ's sacrifice, 32, 47, 90, 394, 448, 460, 514, 515, 521, 528, seqq.; an holy and outward ceremony, instituted by Jesus Christ, 47; by it we are made partakers of the body and blood of Jesus Christ, *ib.*, 49, 50; ought to be ministered to all under both kinds, 47; the signs and badges not changed in the, 48, 402, seqq.; consisteth in the use thereof, 48; a sacrament of faith to the faithful only, 49; containeth two things, the one earthly, the other heavenly, *ib.*, 433; only the faithful ought to be admitted to, 50; the popish mass is not, nor can be the, but is contrary to the, 51, 394, 414, 467, 500; a seal and confirmation of Christ's body given unto death, 90; a visible word, *ib.*; ought not to be celebrated in any one church but once in the day, 126; Christ's holy, what is the chiefest and most principal commodity of, 218; Christ present in the, how, 394; called the sacrifice of Christians, why, *ib.*, 528, seqq.; no miracle in the, 412; no propitiatory sacrifice offered in the, 423; many profitable things learned from the true use of, 433; how Christ is present to the pious in his, 453; to perform the, what, 460; called by various names by the fathers, 463; how Christ used, and taught others to use, 464; compared with the mass, 465.
Supremacy, the king's, nothing to be taught against, 144; contentions of the Greek and Roman churches about, 234, seqq.; given to the see of Rome by Phocas, 236, 555; not of God's laws, but of man's, 237; the Greek church compelled to acknowledge the Roman, 238; the pope cannot establish his, 545, 6; Christ gave no, to St Peter, 545, 560; act for restoring the, to the see apostolic, 617, note 7.

Sweating sickness, Hooper and several of his family attacked by, *Biog. Notice*, xvii, 159, note.
Swords, two in the church, one ecclesiastical and spiritual, the other temporal, 53; both usurped by Gregory VII., 239.

T.

Table, for the communion, interrogatory respecting, 142; by the name of a, is set forth the love of God towards his sheep, 227; diversely taken in other parts of scripture, 228.
Tantalus, the pain of, 97.
Temptation, dangerous to be continually assaulted with, 305.
Terence, quotation from, 554.
Tertullian, how he understood, *This is my body*, 48, 472, 500; in Apolog., 376; calls the sacrament a figure, 405, 528; says that Christ represented his body by bread, 439; called his body bread, *ib.*, 528; his rule of faith, 538.
Theodoret, uses the word $\dot{\alpha}\nu\tau\acute{\iota}\tau\nu\pi\alpha$ for the sacrament, 406, note 1; says that the bread and wine do not lose their substance, 425.
Theodosius, decree of, concerning the catholic faith, 540.
Theophrastus, his opinion of felicity, 299.
Titan, fable of, 603.
Toledo, first council of, creed of, 536.
Trajan, emperor, commanded that no man should be persecuted for serving God, 615.
Transubstantiation, never heard of before the council of Lateran, 48, 522; the defence of, not to be allowed, 134; our conversion into Christ the very, that God delights in, 152; *contra*, 402, seqq.; contrary to the scriptures, and the testimonies of the fathers, 412, 440.
Trentals, of masses, the communion not to be used as, 146.
Tribute, a note and knowledge of our obedience, 109; why, ought to be paid to the higher powers, 110.
Trouble, how we should use ourselves in the time of, 313.
Troubles, of the world, not expedient that christian men be delivered from, and why, 230; patient expectation in,

declareth that we be bound unto God, 317.
Tserclas, Anne de, married to Hooper, *Biog. Notice*, ix.
Tunstall, Cuthbert, bishop of Durham, sermon of, against the bishop of Rome, 268, 557, 567.
Tyre, city of, allusion to, by Christ, 209.

U.

Underhill, Edward, answers the attacks against Hooper, and acquires the title of "Hooper's Champion," *Biog. Notice*, xi.
Urban I. gave the name of 'high priest' to all bishops, 237.

V.

Valentines, the doctrine of, monstrous, 74.
Valentinianus, decree of, concerning the catholic faith, 540.
Vestments, Hooper's objection to, *Biog. Notice*, xii; opinions of Bucer and Martyr respecting xiv.
Viaticum, why the Lord's supper called, 463.
Vicar, none other to Christ upon earth than the Holy Ghost, 39.
Victor I. hindered by Irenæus from condemning and excommunicating the Greek church, 233.
Vigils, the keeping of, interrogatory respecting, 147.
Virtue must be sealed in the conscience and loved, 217; and vice, knowledge and talk of, not sufficient, 219; soon spoken of to other men's instructions, but the putting thereof in practice and use very hard, 346.

W.

Warcop, Anne, bp. Hooper's letter to, 603.
Weston, obtained a commission for a disputation at Cambridge, 593.
Wilkinson, Mrs, bp. Hooper's letter to, 601.
Williams, Dr John, Hooper's epistle to, and others, 95.
Witchcraft, abominable evil of, 294.
Word, of God, office of such as teach the, 3; a sign and mark of God's church, 43; what it is, *ib.*; of far greater au-

thority than the church, *ib.*; the true pattern and perfect rule of life, *ib.*; the reading of, ought not to be forbidden to any, but common to all, and in a language which all do understand, 44, 391; the heavenly manna, 46; what it teacheth of God, 71; the preaching and teaching of, the chief remedy against sedition, 79; appealed to, as the end of all controversies, 82, 382, seqq.; nothing to be taught as necessary for salvation but what is contained in, 120, 130; the most holy treasure of, to be set forth to all the people, 131; the queen hath no authority to compel any man to believe anything contrary to, 186; the life of man consisteth in the food of, 198, 200, 201, 203; none giveth but God, *ib.*; none can eat of, but such as the Holy Ghost feedeth, 198, 201; the ignorance of, bringeth a murrain and rot of the soul, 200; whosoever do refuse or repugn, be unworthy of all mercy and forgiveness, 201; what every man shall have expressed and opened in, 203; general and provincial councils not the author of, 204; not enough for a man to hear, but he must be ruled by, 209; not only the man that abuseth, but he that will not learn, shall be damned, 210; the wicked will be always at discord and variance with, 214; the virtue and nature of, how sealed in the conscience, 218; he that would take the soul of man from, of all enemies the principal, 231, 543; the pope to be resisted by, 240; the taking away of, a just cause for lamentation, 252, 262; the abuse of, provoketh his vengeance, *ib.*; kings, &c. bound to have the, taught to others under their governance, 278; the reading, &c. of, the only remedy against ignorance, 312; two kinds of consolation in, 325; two manner of mercies in, 343; and works do nothing comfort the unfaithful, 353; how it must be used to profit us, 355, 357; the eyes of Christians, 396; all truth in religion to be sought from, 543; cannot be changed, 545; called the star of light, 603.

Works, good, not superfluous, &c. but necessary to salvation, 59; what they are, and why they ought to be done, *ib.*; grace the beginner of all, 73; in their greatest perfection wanteth grace to pardon their imperfection, *ib.*; do necessarily follow justification, 121; albeit they do not justify, yet do please God, *ib.*; God's, the consideration of, advisedly and by faith, and rashly and without faith, 353; comfort the faithful, but not the unfaithful, *ib.*; various ways of considering, 409.

Wynter, John, parson of Staunton, assertion and defence of the true use of the sacrament made by, 154, seqq.

Z.

Zuinglius, Hooper seriously impressed by the writings of, *Biog. Notice*, vii.

Zurich, arrival of Hooper at, and sojourn there, *Biog. Notice*, ix.

www.ingramcontent.com/pod-product-compliance
Lightning Source LLC
Chambersburg PA
CBHW052039290426
44111CB00011B/1558